Units, Measurements & Motion

Er. D.C. Gupta

Units, Measurements & Motion

for JEE Main & Advanced

(Study Package for Physics)

Fully Solved

Includes Past
JEE & KVPY Questions

Useful for Class 11,
KVPY & Olympiads

- **Head Office :** B-32, Shivalik Main Road, Malviya Nagar, New Delhi-110017

- **Sales Office :** B-48, Shivalik Main Road, Malviya Nagar, New Delhi-110017
  Tel. : 011-26691021 / 26691713

Page Layout : Prakash Chandra Sahoo

Typeset by Disha DTP Team

Printed at : **Repro Knowledgecast Limited, Thane**

DISHA PUBLICATION

For further information about the books from DISHA,
Log on to **www.dishapublication.com** or email to **info@dishapublication.com**

<table>
<tr><th colspan="4" align="center">STUDY PACKAGE IN PHYSICS FOR JEE MAIN & ADVANCED</th></tr>
<tr><th>Booklet No.</th><th>Title</th><th>Chapter Nos.</th><th>Page Nos.</th></tr>
<tr><td>1</td><td>Units, Measurements & Motion</td><td>Ch 0. Mathematics Used in Physics
Ch 1. Units and Measurements
Ch 2. Vectors
Ch 3. Motion in a Straight Line
Ch 4. Motion in a Plane</td><td>1-202</td></tr>
<tr><td>2</td><td>Laws of Motion and Circular Motion</td><td>Ch 5. Laws of Motion and Equilibrium
Ch 6. Circular Motion</td><td>203-318</td></tr>
<tr><td>3</td><td>Work Energy, Power & Gravitation</td><td>Ch 7. Work, Energy and Power
Ch 8. Collisions and Centre of Mass
Ch 9. Gravitation</td><td>319-480</td></tr>
<tr><td>4</td><td>Rotational Motion</td><td>Ch 1. Rotational Mechanics</td><td>1-120</td></tr>
<tr><td>5</td><td>Properties of Matter & SHM</td><td>Ch 2. Properties of Matter
Ch 3. Fluid Mechanics
Ch 4. Simple Harmonic Motion</td><td>121-364</td></tr>
<tr><td>6</td><td>Heat & Thermodynamics</td><td>Ch 5. Thermometry, Expansion & Calorimetry
Ch 6. Kinetic Theory of Gases
Ch 7. Laws of Thermodynamics
Ch 8. Heat Transfer</td><td>365-570</td></tr>
<tr><td>7</td><td>Waves</td><td>Ch 9. Wave – I
Ch 10. Wave –II</td><td>571-698</td></tr>
<tr><td>8</td><td>Electrostatics</td><td>Ch 0. Mathematics Used in Physics
Ch 1. Electrostatics
Ch 2. Capacitance & Capacitors</td><td>1-216</td></tr>
<tr><td>9</td><td>Current Electricity</td><td>Ch 3. DC and DC circuits
Ch 4. Thermal and Chemical effects of Current"</td><td>217-338</td></tr>
<tr><td>10</td><td>Magnetism, EMI & AC</td><td>Ch 5. Magnetic Force on Moving Charges & Conductor
Ch 6. Magnetic Effects of Current
Ch 7. Permanent Magnet & Magnetic Properties of Substance
Ch 8. Electromagnetic Induction
Ch 9. AC and EM Waves</td><td>339-618</td></tr>
<tr><td>11</td><td>Ray & Wave Optics</td><td>Ch 1. Reflection of Light
Ch 2. Refraction and Dispersion
Ch 3. Refraction at Spherical Surface, Lenses and Photometry
Ch 4. Wave optics</td><td>1-244</td></tr>
<tr><td>12</td><td>Modern Physics</td><td>Ch 5. Electron, Photon, Atoms, Photoelectric Effect and X-rays
Ch 6. Nuclear Physics
Ch 7. Electronics & Communication</td><td>245-384</td></tr>
</table>

Contents

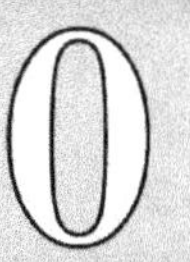

Mathematics Used in Physics

(1 - 16)

Chapter contents

ALGEBRA

Common Identities

(i) $(a+b)^2 = a^2 + b^2 + 2ab = (a-b)^2 + 4ab$

(ii) $(a-b)^2 = a^2 + b^2 - 2ab = (a+b)^2 - 4ab$

(iii) $a^2 - b^2 = (a+b)(a-b)$

(iv) $(a+b)^3 = a^3 + b^3 + 3ab(a+b)$
$$= a^3 + b^3 + 3a^2b + 3ab^2$$

(v) $(a-b)^3 = a^3 - b^3 - 3ab(a-b)$
$$= a^3 - b^3 - 3a^2b + 3ab^2$$

(vi) $a^3 + b^3 = (a+b)(a^2 - ab + b^2)$
$$= (a+b)^3 - 3ab(a+b)$$

(vii) $a^3 - b^3 = (a-b)(a^2 + ab + b^2)$
$$= (a-b)^3 + 3ab(a-b)$$

(viii) $(a+b)^2 + (a-b)^2 = 2(a^2 + b^2)$

(ix) $(a+b)^2 - (a-b)^2 = 4ab.$

QUADRATIC EQUATION

An algebraic equation of second order (highest power of variable is 2) is called a quadratic equation e.g.

$$ax^2 + bx + c = 0, \qquad a \neq 0$$

It has solution for two values of x which are given by

$$x = \frac{-b \pm \sqrt{b^2 - 4ac}}{2a}$$

The quantity $b^2 - 4ac$, is called discriminant of the equation.

BINOMIAL THEOREM

(i) The binomial theorem for any positive value of n

$$(x+a)^n = x^n + {}^nC_1 a x^{n-1} + {}^nC_2 a^2 x^{n-2} + \ldots\ldots + {}^nC_r a^r x^{n-r} + \ldots\ldots + a^n$$

where a is constant and $\quad {}^nC_r = \dfrac{n!}{r!(n-r)!}$

Here $\quad n! = n(n-1)(n-2)\ldots\ldots\ldots 3 \times 2 \times 1$

So $\quad 5! = 5 \times 4 \times 3 \times 2 \times 1 = 120$

(ii) $\quad (1+x)^n = 1 + nx + \dfrac{n(n-1)}{2!}x^2 + \dfrac{n(n-1)(n-2)}{3!}x^3 + \ldots\ldots$

For $|x| \ll 1$, we can neglect the higher power of x.

So $\quad (1+x)^n \simeq 1 + nx$

Similarly, $\quad (1-x)^n \simeq 1 - nx$

$$(1+x)^{-n} \simeq 1 - nx$$

$$(1-x)^{-n} \simeq 1 + nx$$

Here n may have any value.

Ex. 1 Evaluate $\sqrt{(1.01)}$

Sol.
$$(1.01)^{1/2} = (1+0.01)^{1/2}$$
$$\simeq 1+\frac{1}{2}\times 0.01$$
$$= 1.005$$

ARITHMETIC PROGRESSION (A.P.)

A sequence like $a, a+d, a+2d, \ldots\ldots\ldots$ is called arithmetic progression. Here d is the common difference.

(i) The nth term of an A.P. is given by
$$a_n = a+(n-1)d$$

(ii) The sum of first n term of an A.P. is given by
$$S_n = \frac{n}{2}\big[I \text{ term} + \text{last term}\big] = \frac{n}{2}(a_1 + a_n)$$

Here $a_1 = a$ and $a_n = a + (n-1)d$

$$\therefore \qquad S_n = \frac{n}{2}[2a+(n-1)d]$$

GEOMETRIC PROGRESSION (G.P.)

The progression like, $a, ar, ar^2, \ldots\ldots\ldots$ is called geometric progression, here r is called geometric ratio or common ratio.

(i) The nth term of G.P. is given by
$$a_n = ar^{n-1}$$

(ii) The sum of the first n terms of G.P. is given by
$$S_n = \frac{a(r^n-1)}{(r-1)} \text{ for } (r>0)$$

and $S_n = a\frac{(1-r^n)}{(1-r)}$ for $(r<0)$

(iii) The sum of infinite term of G.P. for $r<1$, is given by
$$S = \frac{I^{st} \text{ term}}{1-\text{Geometric ratio}}$$

or
$$S = \frac{a}{1-r}$$

Ex. 2 Find sum of the progression; $1, \dfrac{1}{2}, \dfrac{1}{4}, \dfrac{1}{8}, \ldots\ldots\ldots\infty$.

Sol. We have $S = \dfrac{a}{1-r}$

Here, $a=1, \ r=\dfrac{1}{2}$

$$\therefore \qquad S = \frac{1}{1-1/2} = 2$$

EXPONENTIAL SERIES

The value of e ;
$$e = \lim_{n\to\infty}\left(1+\frac{1}{n}\right)^n = 1+\frac{1}{1!}+\frac{1}{2!}+\frac{1}{3!}+\ldots\ldots\infty$$

$$= 1+1+\frac{1}{2}+\frac{1}{6}+\frac{1}{24}+\ldots\ldots\infty = 2.718$$

$\therefore$
$$e^x = 1+\frac{x}{1!}+\frac{x^2}{2!}+\frac{x^3}{3!}+\ldots\ldots\ldots\infty$$

and
$$e^{-x} = 1-\frac{x}{1!}+\frac{x^2}{2!}-\frac{x^3}{3!}+\ldots\ldots\ldots\infty$$

LOGARITHMIC SERIES

$$\log_e(1+x) = x-\frac{x^2}{2}+\frac{x^3}{3}-\frac{x^4}{4}+\ldots\ldots\ldots\ldots\infty$$

$$\log_e(2) = \log_e(1+1) = 1-\frac{1}{2}+\frac{1}{3}-\frac{1}{4}+\ldots\ldots\ldots\ldots\infty$$

$$\log(1-x) = -x-\frac{x^2}{2}-\frac{x^3}{3}-\frac{x^4}{4}-\ldots\ldots\ldots\ldots\infty$$

TRIGONOMETRIC SERIES

$$\sin x = x-\frac{x^3}{3!}+\frac{x^5}{5!}-\ldots\ldots\ldots$$

$$\cos x = 1-\frac{x^2}{2!}+\frac{x^4}{4!}-\ldots\ldots\ldots$$

LOGARITHMS

For a positive real number a and a rational number m, we have, $a^m = b$. The another way of expressing the same fact in that of logarithms of b to the base a is m

i.e., $\qquad \log_a b = m$

There are two bases of logarithms that are used these days. One is base e and the other base 10. The logarithms to base e are called natural logarithms. The logarithms to base 10 are called the common logarithms.

Thus we can write

(i)   1000 on the base of 10 as 10^3, and in logarithms it is; $\log_{10}1000 = 3$.

(ii)   Similarly $e^x = y$ can be written as
$$\log_e y = \ln y = x$$

Here $\log_e \to \ln$

$$\log_a 1 = 0 \ ; \ \log_{10}10 = 1; \ \log_{10}2 = 0.693; \ \log_e 10 = 2.303$$

LAWS OF LOGARITHMS

Ist Law $\qquad \log_a(mn) = \log_a m + \log_a n$

IInd Law $\qquad \log_a\left(\frac{m}{n}\right) = \log_a m - \log_a n$

IIIrd Law $\qquad \log_a(m)^n = n\log_a m$

ANGLES

(i) Degree measure

One sixtieth of a degree is called a minute, and written 1′,
and one sixtieth of a minute is called second, written as 1″.

Thus $\qquad 1° = 60'$

and $\qquad 1' = 60''$

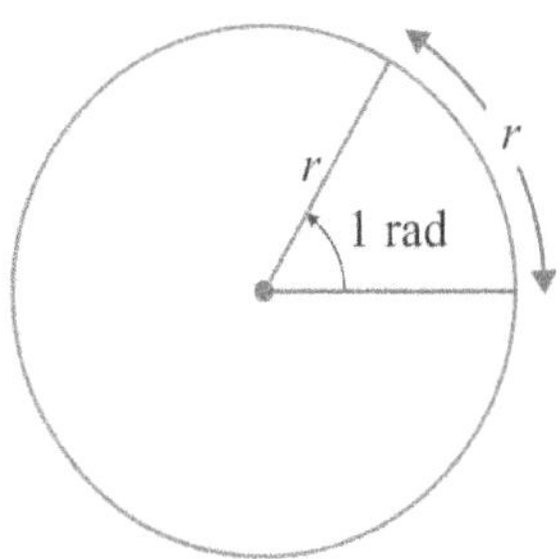

Figure. **0.1**

(ii) Radian measure

1 radian : An angle with its vertex at the centre of a circle which intercepts an arc equal in length
to the radius of the circle is said to have a measure of 1 radian.

The circumference, s, of a circle of radius r is $2\pi r$.

Thus one complete revolution subtends an angle

$$\theta = \frac{2\pi r}{r} = 2\pi \text{ rad}$$

Thus if a circle of radius r, an arc of length ℓ subtends an angle θ radian at the centre, we have

$$\theta = \frac{\ell}{r}$$

(iii) Relationship between degree and radian

$$2\pi \text{ radian} = 360°$$

or $\qquad \pi \text{ radian} = 180°$

or $\qquad 1 \text{ radian} = \dfrac{180°}{\pi} \simeq 57°16'$

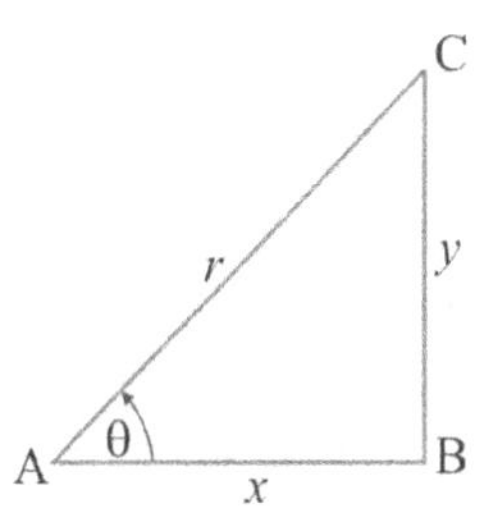

Figure. **0.2**

degree	30°	45°	60°	90°	180°	270°	360°
radian	$\dfrac{\pi}{6}$	$\dfrac{\pi}{4}$	$\dfrac{\pi}{3}$	$\dfrac{\pi}{2}$	π	$\dfrac{3\pi}{2}$	2π

TRIGONOMETRIC FUNCTION

In a right angled triangle ABC, we can define that

$$\sin\theta = \frac{y}{r}$$

$$\cos\theta = \frac{x}{r}$$

$$\tan\theta = \frac{y}{x}$$

$$\cot\theta = \frac{x}{y}$$

$$\operatorname{cosec}\theta = \frac{r}{y}$$

$$\sec\theta = \frac{r}{x}$$

Figure. **0.3**

From above ratios, we have

(i) $\qquad \operatorname{cosec}\theta = \dfrac{1}{\sin\theta}$

$$\sec\theta = \frac{1}{\cos\theta}$$

and $\qquad \tan\theta = \dfrac{1}{\cot\theta}$

(ii)   For small angle $(\theta \to 0)$, $r \to x$ and $y \to 0$

$$\therefore \qquad \sin\theta = \tan\theta$$

and $\cos\theta \to 1$

(iii)
$$\sin^2\theta + \cos^2\theta = 1$$
$$1 + \tan^2\theta = \sec^2\theta$$
$$1 + \cot^2\theta = \operatorname{cosec}^2\theta$$

TRIGONOMETRIC RATIO

Angle	0°	30°	45°	60°	90°	120°	135°	150°	180°
sin	0	$\dfrac{1}{2}$	$\dfrac{1}{\sqrt{2}}$	$\dfrac{\sqrt{3}}{2}$	1	$\dfrac{\sqrt{3}}{2}$	$\dfrac{1}{\sqrt{2}}$	$\dfrac{1}{2}$	0
cos	1	$\dfrac{\sqrt{3}}{2}$	$\dfrac{1}{\sqrt{2}}$	$\dfrac{1}{2}$	0	$-\dfrac{1}{2}$	$-\dfrac{1}{\sqrt{2}}$	$-\dfrac{\sqrt{3}}{2}$	-1
tan	0	$\dfrac{1}{\sqrt{3}}$	1	$\sqrt{3}$	∞	$-\sqrt{3}$	-1	$-\dfrac{1}{\sqrt{3}}$	0

THE VALUE OF TRIGONOMETRIC RATIO IN DIFFERENT QUADRANTS

Angle	$-\theta$	$90°-\theta$	$90°+\theta$	$180°-\theta$	$180°+\theta$	$270°-\theta$	$270°+\theta$	$360°-\theta$	$360°+\theta$
sin	$-\sin\theta$	$\cos\theta$	$\cos\theta$	$\sin\theta$	$-\sin\theta$	$-\cos\theta$	$-\cos\theta$	$-\sin\theta$	$\sin\theta$
cos	$\cos\theta$	$\sin\theta$	$-\sin\theta$	$-\cos\theta$	$-\cos\theta$	$-\sin\theta$	$\sin\theta$	$\cos\theta$	$\cos\theta$
tan	$-\tan\theta$	$\cot\theta$	$-\cot\theta$	$-\tan\theta$	$\tan\theta$	$\cot\theta$	$-\cot\theta$	$-\tan\theta$	$\tan\theta$

RATIO OF DIFFERENT TRIGONOMETRIC ANGLE

(i)   Consider an arc BC length l which subtends an angle θ radian at A. Draw a perpendicular on AC, we have

$$\theta = \frac{\widehat{BC}}{AB}$$

and
$$\sin\theta = \frac{BD}{AB}$$

$$\therefore \qquad \frac{\sin\theta}{\theta} = \frac{BD}{\widehat{BC}}$$

When $\theta \to 0$, $\widehat{BC} = BD$ $\qquad \lim\limits_{\theta \to 0} \dfrac{\sin\theta}{\theta} = 1$

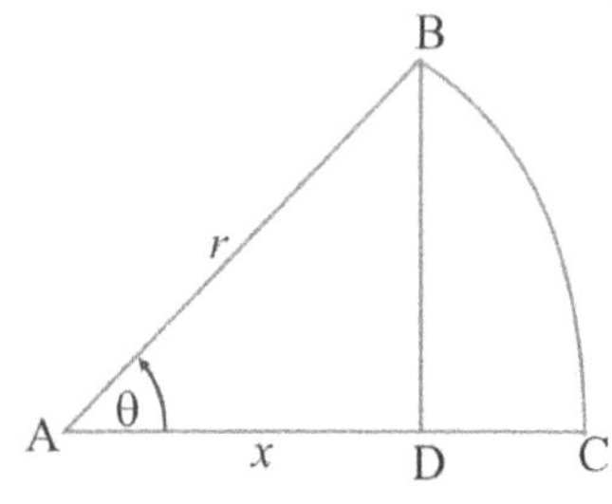

Figure. 0.4

(ii)   In a right triangle of sides 3, 4, 5, we have

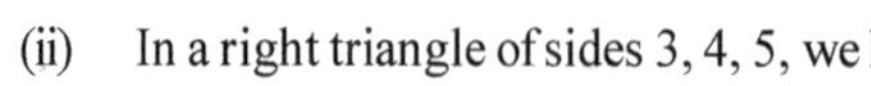

$$\sin 53° = \frac{4}{5} = 0.8 \,, \ \cos 37° = 0.8$$

and $\cos 53° = \dfrac{3}{5} = 0.6 \,, \ \sin 37° = 0.6.$

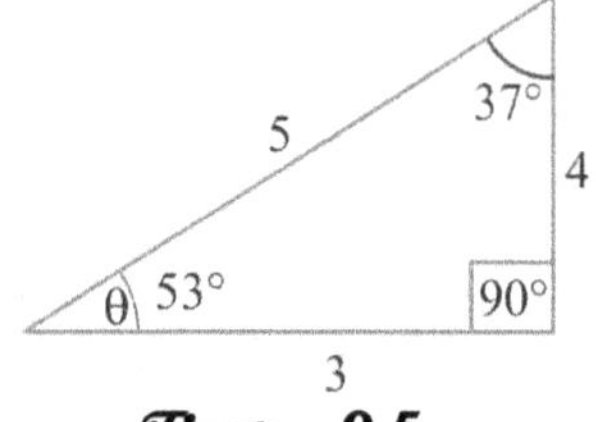

Figure. 0.5

IMPORTANT TRIGONOMETRIC FORMULAE

(i) $\sin(A+B) = \sin A \cos B + \cos A \sin B$

(ii) $\sin(A-B) = \sin A \cos B - \cos A \sin B$

(iii) $\cos(A+B) = \cos A \cos B - \sin A \sin B$

(iv) $\cos(A-B) = \cos A \cos B + \sin A \, \sin B$

(v) $\tan(A+B) = \dfrac{\tan A + \tan B}{1 - \tan A \tan B}$

(vi) $\tan(A-B) = \dfrac{\tan A - \tan B}{1 + \tan A \tan B}$

For $A = B$

(vii) $\sin 2A = 2\sin A \cos A$

(viii) $\cos 2A = \cos^2 A - \sin^2 A$

(ix) $\tan 2A = \dfrac{2\tan A}{1 - \tan^2 A}$

SUM AND DIFFERENCE FORMULAE

(i) $\sin A + \sin B = 2\sin\dfrac{A+B}{2}\cdot\cos\dfrac{A-B}{2}$

(ii) $\sin A - \sin B = 2\cos\dfrac{A+B}{2}\cdot\sin\dfrac{A-B}{2}$

(iii) $\cos A + \cos B = 2\cos\dfrac{A+B}{2}\cdot\cos\dfrac{A-B}{2}$

(iv) $\cos A - \cos B = 2\sin\dfrac{A+B}{2}\cdot\sin\dfrac{B-A}{2}$

PRODUCT FORMULAE

(i) $2\sin A \cos B = \sin(A+B) + \sin(A-B)$

(ii) $2\cos A \sin B = \sin(A+B) - \sin(A-B)$

(iii) $2\cos A \cos B = \cos(A+B) + \cos(A-B)$

(iv) $2\sin A \sin B = \cos(A-B) - \cos(A+B)$

PROPERTIES OF TRIANGLE

(i)   Laws of sines

The sides of a triangle are proportional to the sines of the opposite angle,

i.e., $\dfrac{a}{\sin A} = \dfrac{b}{\sin B} = \dfrac{c}{\sin C}$.

(ii)   Laws of cosines

In any triangle, the square of any side is equal to the sum of the squares of the other two sides minus twice the product of these two sides into the cosine of their included angle,

i.e., $a^2 = b^2 + c^2 - 2bc \cos A$

$b^2 = a^2 + c^2 - 2ac \cos B$

and $c^2 = a^2 + b^2 - 2ab \cos C$

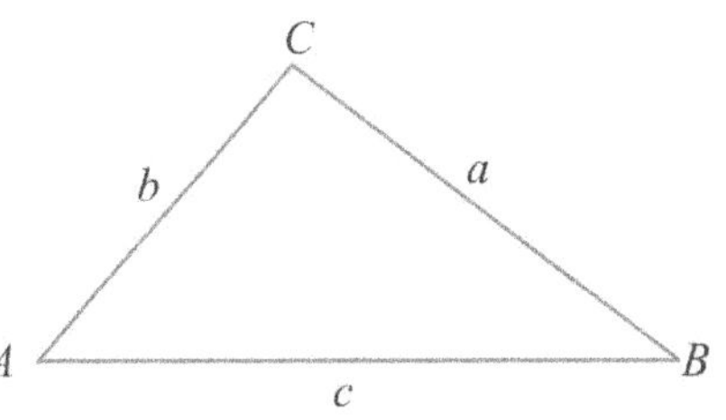

Figure **0.6**

$$
\begin{aligned}
1 \text{ foot} &= 12 \text{ inch} \\
1 \text{ yard} &= 3 \text{ feet} = 91.44 \text{ cm} \\
1 \text{ mile} &= 1609 \text{ m} \\
1 \text{ ton} &= 1000 \text{ kg} \\
1 \text{ hectare} &= 10000 \text{ m}^2 \\
1 \text{ m}^3 &= 1000 \text{ litre}
\end{aligned}
$$

AREA AND VOLUME

(i) Area of triangle of height h and base b;

$$A = \frac{1}{2}bh$$

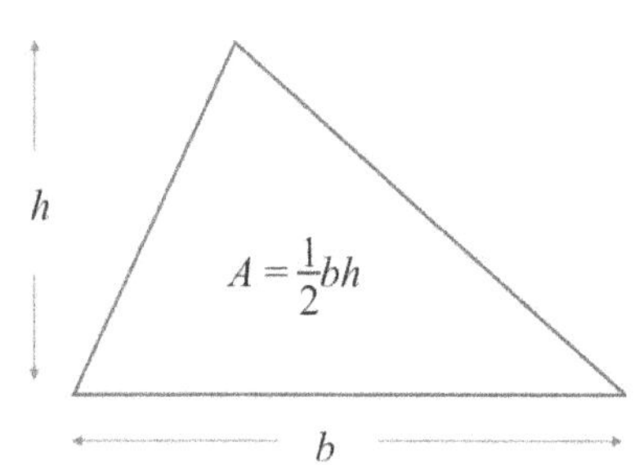

Figure. **0.7**

(ii) Area of trapezium

$$A = \frac{1}{2}(a+b)h$$

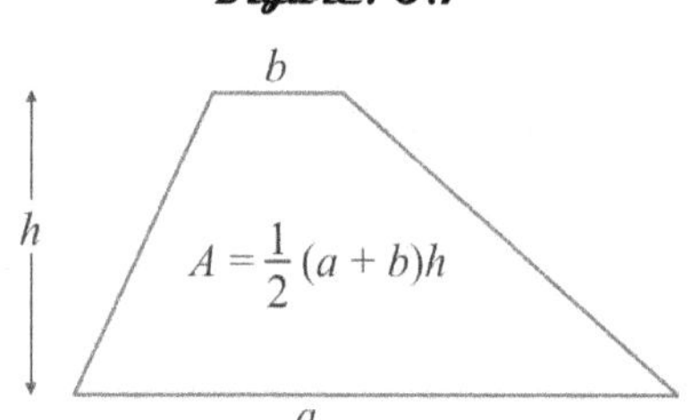

Figure. **0.8**

(iii) Area of circle

$$A = \pi R^2$$

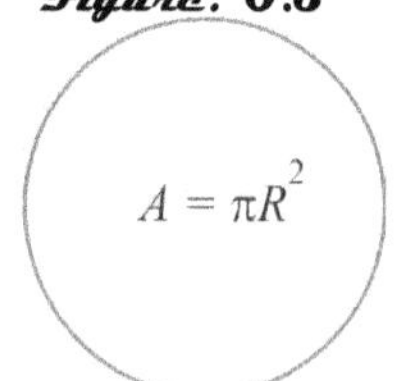

Figure. **0.9**

(iv) Surface area of cone, $A = \pi R \ell$

Volume of cone, $V = \dfrac{\pi R^2 h}{3}$

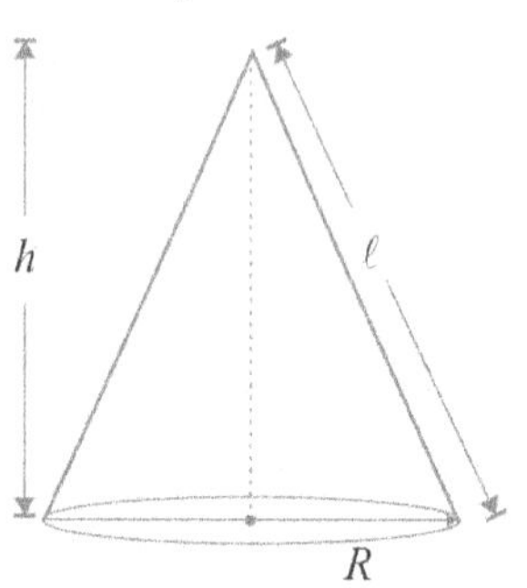

Figure. **0.10**

(v) Surface area of sphere, $A = 4\pi R^2$

Volume of sphere, $V = \dfrac{4}{3}\pi R^3$

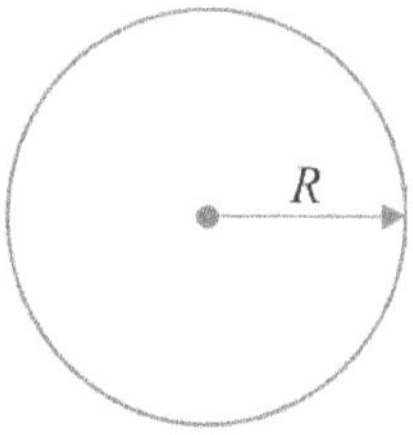

DIFFERENTIATION

If y is the function of x, then we can write

$$y = f(x)$$

Figure. **0.11**

Here x is the independent variable and y is the dependent variable. If x varies from x to $x + \Delta x$, then

$$y + \Delta y = f(x + \Delta x)$$

$$\therefore \quad \Delta y = (y + \Delta y) - y$$

$$= f(x + \Delta x) - f(x)$$

And the ratio

$$\frac{\Delta y}{\Delta x} = \frac{f(x + \Delta x) - f(x)}{\Delta x}$$

Taking limits on both sides of above expression, we have

$$\lim_{\Delta x \to 0} \left(\frac{\Delta y}{\Delta x} \right) = \lim_{\Delta x \to 0} \frac{f(x + \Delta x) - f(x)}{\Delta x}$$

The quantity $\lim_{\Delta x \to 0} \left(\frac{\Delta y}{\Delta x} \right)$ is called differentiation of y w.r.t. x and we can written as $\left(\frac{dy}{dx} \right)$.

Thus we write,

$$\frac{dy}{dx} = \lim_{\Delta x \to 0} \frac{f(x + \Delta x) - f(x)}{\Delta x}$$

Ex. 3   Given $y = 3x^2 + 5$, differentiate y w.r.t. x.

Sol. **Step - I**   Substitute $(x + \Delta x)$ in place of x in the given function, so we have

$$y + \Delta y = 3(x + \Delta x)^2 + 5$$

Step -II $\Delta y = (y + \Delta y) - y$

$$= [3(x + \Delta x)^2 + 5] - [3x^2 + 5]$$

or $\Delta y = [3(x^2 + \Delta x^2 + 2x\Delta x) + 5] - [3x^2 + 5]$

$$= 3(\Delta x^2 + 2x\Delta x)$$

Step -III $\dfrac{\Delta y}{\Delta x} = \dfrac{3(\Delta x^2 + 2x\Delta x)}{\Delta x}$

$$= 3(\Delta x + 2x)$$

Step - IV $\lim\limits_{\Delta x \to 0} \left(\dfrac{\Delta y}{\Delta x} \right) = 3(0 + 2x)$

$$= 3 \times 2x$$

$$= 6x$$

That is $\dfrac{dy}{dx} = \dfrac{d[3x^2 + 5]}{dx} = 3 \times 2x^{2-1} + 0 = 6x$

Similarly, we can get

(i) $\dfrac{d}{dx}(ax^n + b) = anx^{n-1}$

     Where n may have any value.

(ii)   Differentiation of sum or difference of two or more function:

     Suppose $y = u \pm v$, u and v are function of x.

     Then $\dfrac{dy}{dx} = \dfrac{d}{dx}(u \pm v) = \dfrac{du}{dx} \pm \dfrac{dv}{dx}$

(iii)   Differentiation of the product of two functions :

     Suppose $y = uv$

     Then $\dfrac{dy}{dx} = \dfrac{d(uv)}{dx} = u\dfrac{dv}{dx} + v\dfrac{du}{dx}$

(iv)   Differentiation of quotient of two functions :

     Suppose $y = \dfrac{u}{v}$

$$\frac{dy}{dx} = \frac{d\left(\dfrac{u}{v}\right)}{dx} = \frac{\left[v\dfrac{du}{dx} - u\dfrac{dv}{dx} \right]}{v^2}$$

(v)   Differentiation of a function of a function :

     We can write $\dfrac{dy}{dx} = \left(\dfrac{dy}{du} \right) \times \left(\dfrac{du}{dx} \right)$

Ex. 4   Given, $y = (ax + b)^2$, evaluate $\dfrac{dy}{dx}$.

Sol. **Method -I**

Substituting $(ax + b) = u$

Then $\dfrac{du}{dx} = \dfrac{d(ax + b)}{dx} = a$

and $\dfrac{dy}{du} = \dfrac{d(ax + b)^2}{du} = \dfrac{d(u)^2}{du} = 2u$

$\therefore$ $\dfrac{dy}{dx} = \dfrac{dy}{du} \times \dfrac{du}{dx} = 2u \times a = 2(ax + b)a$

$$= 2a(ax + b)$$

Method - II $y = (ax + b)^2$

$$= a^2 x^2 + b^2 + 2abx$$

Then $\dfrac{dy}{dx} = \dfrac{d}{dx}\left[a^2 x^2 + b^2 + 2abx \right]$

$$= \frac{d}{dx}(a^2 x^2) + \frac{d}{dx}(b^2) + \frac{d}{dx}(2abx)$$

$$= a^2 \frac{d(x)^2}{dx} + 0 + 2ab\frac{dx}{dx}$$

$$= a^2 \times 2x + 2ab \times 1$$

$$= 2a(ax + b)$$

DIFFERENTIATION OF TRIGONOMETRIC FUNCTION

Let $y = \sin x$, then find $\dfrac{dy}{dx}$.

Step-I Substitute $x + \Delta x$ in place of x in the function, we have

$$y + \Delta y = \sin(x + \Delta x)$$

Step-II

$$\Delta y = (y + \Delta y) - y$$

$$= \sin(x + \Delta x) - \sin x$$

$$= 2\cos\left(\frac{x + \Delta x + x}{2}\right)\sin\left(\frac{x + \Delta x - x}{2}\right)$$

$$= 2\cos\left(\frac{2x + \Delta x}{2}\right)\sin\left(\frac{\Delta x}{2}\right)$$

Step-III

$$\frac{\Delta y}{\Delta x} = \frac{2\cos\left(\dfrac{2x + \Delta x}{2}\right)\sin\left(\dfrac{\Delta x}{2}\right)}{\Delta x}$$

$$= \cos\left(\frac{2x + \Delta x}{2}\right)\frac{\sin\left(\dfrac{\Delta x}{2}\right)}{\dfrac{\Delta x}{2}}$$

Step-IV

$$\lim_{\Delta x \to 0}\frac{\Delta y}{\Delta x} = \left\{\lim_{\Delta x \to 0}\cos\left(\frac{2x + \Delta x}{2}\right)\right\} \times \left\{\lim_{\Delta x \to 0}\frac{\sin\left(\dfrac{\Delta x}{2}\right)}{\left(\dfrac{\Delta x}{2}\right)}\right\}$$

$$= \cos\left(\frac{2x + 0}{2}\right) \times 1$$

$$= \cos x$$

(i) Thus $\dfrac{dy}{dx} = \dfrac{d}{dx}(\sin x) = \cos x$ (ii) $\dfrac{d\cos x}{dx} = -\sin x$

Similarly, we can get

(iii) $\dfrac{d}{dx}(\tan x) = \sec^2 x$ (iv) $\dfrac{d}{dx}(\cot x) = -\text{cosec}^2 x$

(v) $\dfrac{d}{dx}(\text{cosec}\, x) = -\cot x\, \text{cosec}\, x$ (vi) $\dfrac{d}{dx}(\sec x) = \tan x\, \sec x$

(vii) $\dfrac{d}{dx}(\sin^{-1} x) = \dfrac{1}{\sqrt{1 - x^2}}$ (viii) $\dfrac{d}{dx}(\cos^{-1} x) = -\dfrac{1}{\sqrt{1 - x^2}}$

DIFFERENTIATION OF LOGARITHMIC AND EXPONENTIAL FUNCTIONS

(i) Let $\quad y = \ln x$ (ii) $\qquad \dfrac{d(e^x)}{dx} = e^x$

Then $\dfrac{dy}{dx} = \dfrac{d(\ln x)}{dx} = \dfrac{1}{x}$

Ex. 5 Given $y = \sin 2x$, then find $\dfrac{dy}{dx}$.

Sol.
$$\frac{dy}{dx} = \frac{d}{dx}(\sin 2x)$$

$$= \frac{d(\sin u)}{du} \times \frac{du}{dx}$$

Here $u = 2x$

$$\therefore \frac{du}{dx} = \frac{d(2x)}{dx} = 2 \quad \text{and} \quad \frac{d(\sin u)}{du} = \cos u$$

$$\therefore \qquad \frac{dy}{dx} = \cos u \times 2$$

$$= 2\cos 2x$$

OR

$$\frac{dy}{dx} = \frac{d}{dx}(\sin 2x)$$

$$= \frac{d}{d(2x)}\sin(2x) \times \frac{d(2x)}{dx}$$

$$= \cos 2x \times 2 = 2\cos 2x$$

Ex. 6 Given $y = \ln(ax + b)$, then find $\dfrac{dy}{dx}$.

Sol.
$$\frac{dy}{dx} = \frac{d}{dx}\ln(ax + b)$$

$$= \frac{d\ln(ax + b)}{d(ax + b)} \times \frac{d(ax + b)}{dx}$$

$$= \frac{a}{ax + b}$$

SUCCESSIVE DIFFERENTIATION

$\dfrac{dy}{dx}$ is called differentiation of y w.r.t. x or first derivative of y.

$\dfrac{d^2 y}{dx^2} = \dfrac{d}{dx}\left(\dfrac{dy}{dx}\right)$ is called second derivative of y and so on.

Ex. 7 $y = x^3 - 4x^2 + 5$, find $\dfrac{dy}{dx}$, $\dfrac{d^2 y}{dx^2}$ and $\dfrac{d^3 y}{dx^3}$.

Sol.
$$\frac{dy}{dx} = \frac{d}{dx}(x^3 - 4x^2 + 5)$$

$$= \frac{d(x^3)}{dx} - \frac{d}{dx}(4x^2) + \frac{d}{dx}(5)$$

$$= 3x^2 - 4 \times 2x + 0$$

$$= 3x^2 - 8x$$

and
$$\frac{d^2 y}{dx^2} = \frac{d}{dx}(3x^2 - 8x)$$

$$= \frac{d}{dx}(3x^2) - \frac{d}{dx}(8x)$$

$$= 3 \times 2x - 8$$

$$= 6x - 8$$

Also
$$\frac{d^3 y}{dx^3} = \frac{d}{dx}(6x - 8)$$

$$= \frac{d}{dx}(6x) - \frac{d}{dx}(8)$$

$$= 6$$

GEOMETRICAL MEANING OF DIFFERENTIATION

Figure represents the graph of y versus x. Choose two points P(x, y) and Q($x + \Delta x, y + \Delta y$) on the curve. The slope of line PQ is given by

$$\frac{\Delta y}{\Delta x} = \tan\theta$$

If point Q approaches P, the slope $\tan\theta$ of the line PQ approaches the slope of the tangent at P. Thus we have

$$\lim_{\Delta x \to 0}\left(\frac{\Delta y}{\Delta x}\right) = \frac{dy}{dx}$$

$$= \tan\theta$$

i.e., $\left(\dfrac{dy}{dx}\right)$ at any point of the curve gives slope of the tangent at that point.

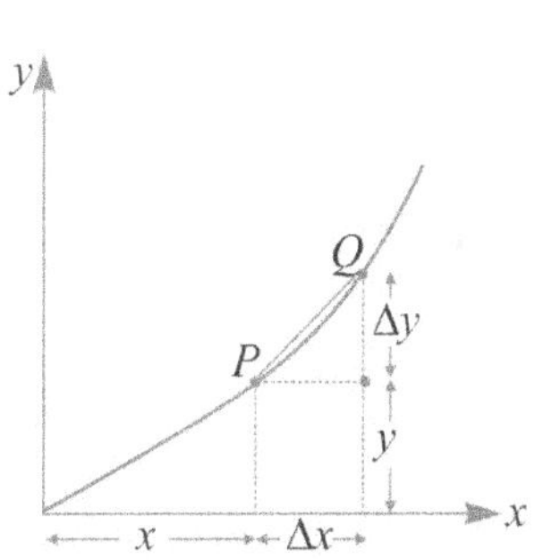

Figure 0.12

INTEGRATION

The integration is the inverse operation of differentiation. Thus if the differentiation of a function $f(x)$ w.r.t. x is $f'(x)$, then the integration of $f'(x)$ w.r.t. x will be $f(x)$. That is

$$\frac{d}{dx} f(x) = f'(x)$$

Then

$$\int f'(x)\, dx = f(x)$$

Constant of integration : The differentiation of a constant is zero, therefore in integration there may involve constant of integration, let C. Thus we can write $\int f'(x)\,dx = f(x) + c$

(i) $\quad \int dx = x + c$

(vii) $\int \sin x\, dx = -\cos x + c$

(ii) $\quad \int c\, dx = c \int dx = cx$

(viii) $\int \cos x\, dx = \sin x + c$

(iii) $\quad \int x^n dx = \frac{x^{n+1}}{(n+1)} + c \quad (n \neq -1)$

(ix) $\int \sec^2 x\, dx = \tan x + c$

(iv) $\quad \int x^{-1}\, dx = \ln x + c$

(x) $\int \mathrm{cosec}^2 x\, dx = -\cot x + c$

(v) $\quad \int (u+v)\, dx = \int (u)\, dx + \int (v)\, dx + c$

(xi) $\int \mathrm{cosec}\, x \cot x\, dx = -\mathrm{cosec}\, x + c$

where u and v are function of x.

(vi) $\quad \int e^x\, dx = e^x + c$

(xii) $\int \sec x \tan x\, dx = \sec x + c$

INTEGRATION BY SUBSTITUTION

Ex. 8 **Find value of** $\int (ax+b)^{3/2}\, dx$.

Sol. Substitute $(ax + b) = z$ in the given function.

Also, $\quad \dfrac{d}{dx}(ax+b) = \dfrac{dz}{dx}$

or $\quad\quad\quad a = \dfrac{dz}{dx}$

$\therefore \quad\quad\quad dx = \dfrac{dz}{a}$

and $\quad \int (ax+b)^{3/2} dx = \int z^{3/2} \times \dfrac{dz}{a}$

$$= \frac{1}{a} \int z^{3/2} dz$$

$$= \frac{1}{a} \frac{z^{\left(\frac{3}{2}+1\right)}}{\left(\frac{3}{2}+1\right)} + c$$

$$= \frac{1}{a} \frac{z^{5/2}}{5/2} + c$$

Substitute back for z, we get

$$\int (ax+b)^{3/2} dx = \frac{2}{5a}(ax+b)^{5/2} + c$$

Ex. 9 **Find value of** $\int \dfrac{dx}{(ax+b)}$.

Sol. Substitute $(ax + b) = z$ in the given function.

Also $\quad \dfrac{d}{dx}(ax+b) = \dfrac{dz}{dx}$

or $\quad\quad\quad a = \dfrac{dz}{dx}$

$\therefore \quad\quad\quad dx = \dfrac{dz}{a}$

and $\quad \int \dfrac{dx}{(ax+b)} = \int \dfrac{(dz/a)}{z}$

$$= \frac{1}{a} \int \frac{dz}{z}$$

$$= \frac{1}{a} \ln z + c$$

Substitute back for z, we get

$$\int \frac{dx}{(ax+b)} = \frac{1}{a}\ln(ax+b) + c$$

Ex. 10 **Find value of** $\int \sin 2x\, dx$.

Sol. Substitute $2x = z$ in the given function.

Also $\quad \dfrac{d}{dx}(2x) = \dfrac{dz}{dx}$

or $\quad\quad\quad 2 = \dfrac{dz}{dx}$

$$\therefore \qquad dx = \frac{dz}{2}$$

$$\text{and} \qquad \int \sin 2x \, dx = \int \sin z \left(\frac{dz}{2}\right)$$

$$= \frac{1}{2} \int \sin z \, dz$$

$$= \frac{1}{2}(-\cos z) + c$$

Substitute back for z, we get

$$\int \sin 2x \, dx = \frac{1}{2}(-\cos 2x) + c$$

DEFINITE INTEGRAL

When a function is integrated between lower and upper limit, it is called definite integral.
If a and b are the lower and upper limits of variable x, then

$$\int_a^b f'(x)\,dx = \left[f(x)+c\right]_a^b$$

$$= \{f(b)+c\}-\{f(a)+c\}$$
$$= f(b)-f(a)$$

Here constant of integration c get cancelled so there is no need to place it in definite integration.

Ex. 11 Given, $\varepsilon - L\dfrac{di}{dt} = iR$, find the value of i at any time t in terms of constant ε, L and R. At $t = 0$, $i = 0$.

Sol. We have, $\varepsilon - L\dfrac{di}{dt} = iR$

or $\qquad (\varepsilon - iR) = L\dfrac{di}{dt}$

or $\qquad \dfrac{di}{(\varepsilon - iR)} = \dfrac{dt}{L} \qquad \text{....(i)}$

Integrating both sides of the equation (i), we get

$$\int \frac{di}{(\varepsilon - iR)} = \int \frac{dt}{L}$$

Here limit of time varies from 0 to t and corresponding limits of i varies from 0 to i.

$$\therefore \qquad \int_0^i \frac{di}{(\varepsilon - iR)} = \int_0^t \frac{dt}{L}$$

For integration of LHS, substitute $\varepsilon - iR = z$.

Also $\qquad \dfrac{d}{di}(\varepsilon - iR) = \dfrac{dz}{di}$

or $\qquad (0 - R) = \dfrac{dz}{di} \qquad \therefore \ di = \dfrac{dz}{(-R)}$

and $\qquad \displaystyle\int_0^i \frac{di}{(\varepsilon - iR)} = \int_0^i \frac{dz/(-R)}{z} = \left(\frac{1}{-R}\right)\int_0^i \frac{dz}{z}$

$$= \left(-\frac{1}{R}\right)\left|\ln z\right|_0^i$$

$$= \left(-\frac{1}{R}\right)\left|\ln(\varepsilon - iR)\right|_0^i$$

$$= \left(-\frac{1}{R}\right)\{\ln(\varepsilon - iR) - \ln(\varepsilon - 0)\}$$

$$= \left(-\frac{1}{R}\right)\ln\frac{(\varepsilon - iR)}{\varepsilon} \qquad \text{....(ii)}$$

and RHS $\qquad \displaystyle\int_0^t \frac{dt}{L} = \left(\frac{1}{L}\right)|t|_0^t = \frac{1}{L}(t - 0) = \frac{t}{L}$

From equations (i) and (ii), we have

$$\left(-\frac{1}{R}\right)\ln\left(\frac{\varepsilon - iR}{\varepsilon}\right) = \frac{t}{L}$$

or $\qquad \ln\left(\dfrac{\varepsilon - iR}{\varepsilon}\right) = -\dfrac{R}{L}t$

or $\qquad \left(\dfrac{\varepsilon - iR}{\varepsilon}\right) = e^{-\frac{Rt}{L}}$

or $\qquad i = \dfrac{\varepsilon}{R}(1 - e^{-\frac{tR}{L}})$

PARTIAL DIFFERENTIATION

In physics, we often come across quantities which depend on two or more variables. For example electric potential V depends on x, y coordinates as : $V = xy$. For given pair of value of x and y, V has a definite value. If we differentiate quantity V w.r.t. x keeping y constant, then it is known as partial differentiation and represented by $\dfrac{\partial V}{\partial x}$. Similarly differentiation of V w.r.t. y keeping x is constant is represented by $\dfrac{\partial V}{\partial y}$.

Thus
$$\frac{\partial V}{\partial x} = \frac{\partial (xy)}{\partial x} = y$$

and
$$\frac{\partial V}{\partial y} = \frac{\partial (xy)}{\partial y} = x$$

In general if f is a function of n variables $x_1, x_2, \ldots x_n$, then partial differential coefficient of f with respect to x_1, keeping all the variables except x_1 as constant can be written as $\frac{\partial f}{\partial x_1}$.

Ex. 12 Given $\phi = a\left(x^2 + y^2\right) + bz^2$, where a and b are constants. Find partial differentiation of ϕ w.r.t. x, y and z.

Sol.
$$\frac{\partial \phi}{\partial x} = \frac{\partial}{\partial x}\left[a\left(x^2 + y^2\right) + bz^2\right]$$
$$= a \times 2x = 2\,ax,$$

$$\frac{\partial \phi}{\partial y} = \frac{\partial}{\partial y}\left[a\left(x^2 + y^2\right) + bz^2\right]$$
$$= a \times 2y = 2ay,$$

and
$$\frac{\partial \phi}{\partial z} = \frac{\partial}{\partial z}\left[a\left(x^2 + y^2\right) + bz^2\right]$$
$$= b \times 2z = 2bz$$

SOME USEFUL PHYSICAL CONSTANTS

(i)   Acceleration due to gravity, $g = 9.8 \text{ m/s}^2$

(ii)   Speed of light, $c = 3 \times 10^8 \text{ m/s}$

(iii)   Universal gravitation constant, $G = 6.67 \times 10^{-11}\, \dfrac{\text{N} - \text{m}^2}{\text{kg}^2}$

TERRESTRIAL CONSTANTS

(i)   Mean radius of Earth, $R = 6.37 \times 10^6 \text{ m} \simeq 6.4 \times 10^6 \text{ m}$

(ii)   Mass of the Earth, $M = 6 \times 10^{24} \text{ kg}$

(iii)   Mass of the Sun, $M_s = 1.99 \times 10^{30} \text{ kg}$

(iv)   Mass of the Moon, $M_m = 7.34 \times 10^{22} \text{ kg}$

(v)   Earth – Moon distance $= 3.84 \times 10^8 \text{ m}$

(vi)   Earth – Sun distance $= 1.49 \times 10^{11} \text{ m}.$

Nature of curve

The nature of curve along which the particle move can be understood by making the relationship between x, y coordinates of the curve. Some of the common curves are;

1.   **Straight line :** $y = mx + c$

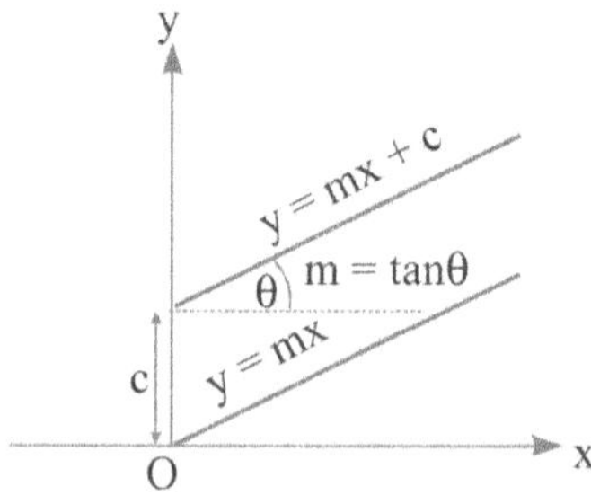

Figure **0.13**

2.   **Circle :** $x^2 + y^2 = R^2$

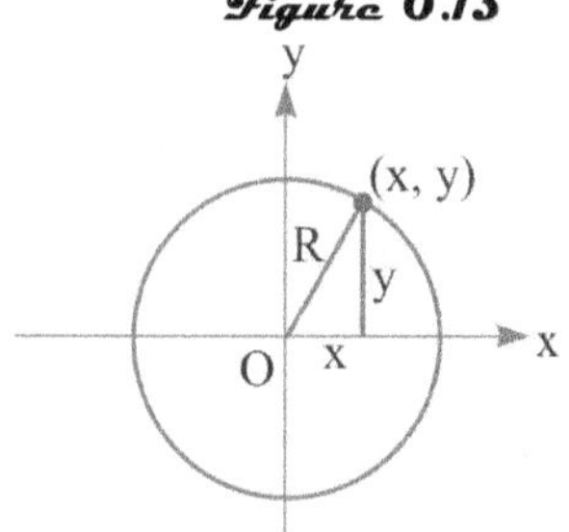

Figure. **0.14**

3. **Parabola :** The following may be the equations of a parabola.

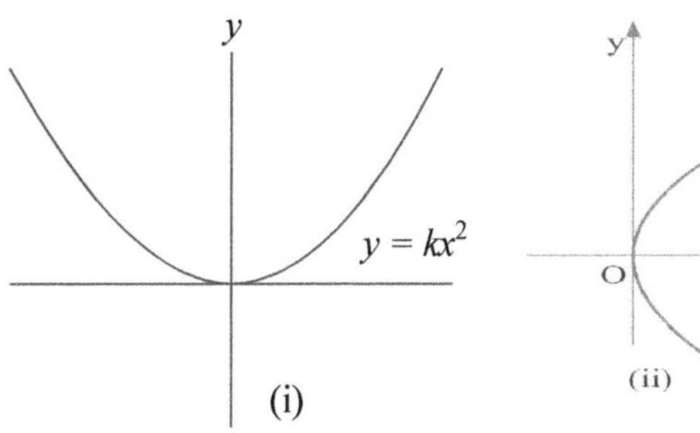

Figure **0.15**

4. **Ellipse :** $\dfrac{x^2}{a^2}+\dfrac{y^2}{b^2}=1$

Also eccentricity, $e=\sqrt{1-\dfrac{b^2}{a^2}}$

Latus rectum, $AB=\dfrac{2b^2}{a}$

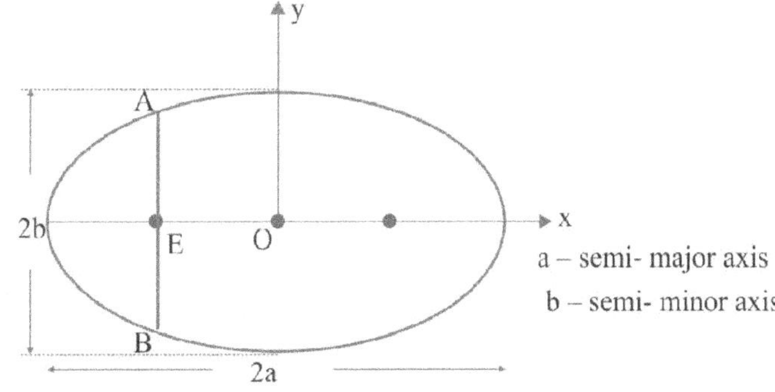

Figure **0.16**

5. **Rectangular hyperbola :** $xy=$ constant

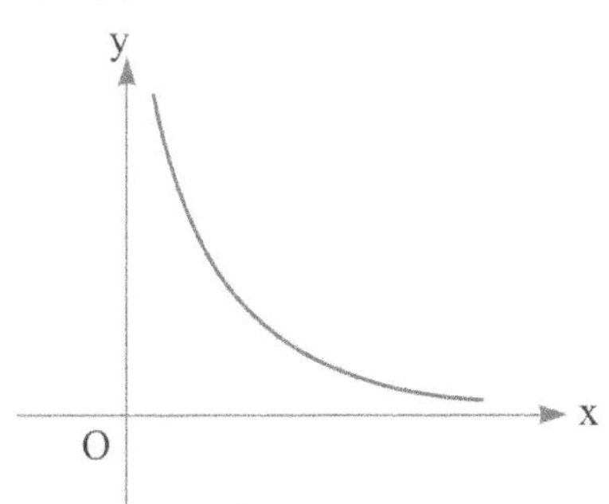

Figure **0.17**

6. **Sinusoidal curve :**

(a) $y = A\sin x$

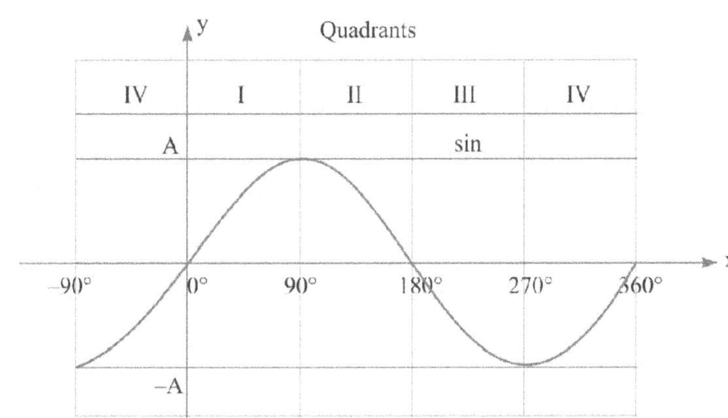

Figure **0.18**

(b) $y = A \cos x$

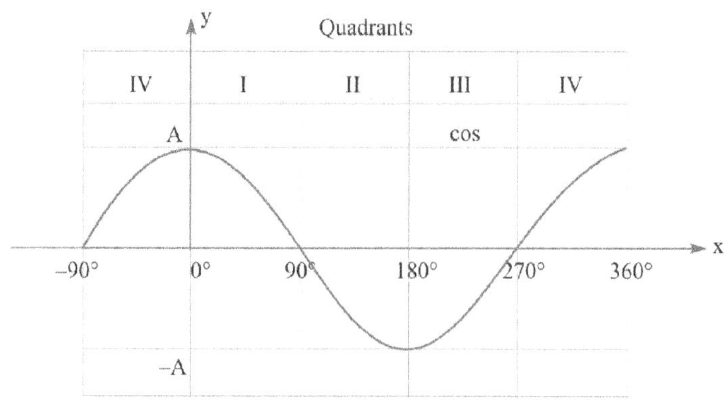

Figure **0.19**

Some Important Constants

Name	Symbol	Value
Speed of light in vacuum	c	2.9979×10^8 ms^{-1}
Charge of electron	e	1.602×10^{-19} C
Gravitational constant	G	6.673×10^{-11} N m^2 kg^{-2}
Planck constant	h	6.626×10^{-34} J s
Boltzmann constant	k	1.381×10^{-23} J K^{-1}
Avogadro number	N_A	$6..022 \times 10^{23}$ mol^{-1}
Universal gas constant	R	8.314 J mol^{-1} K^{-1}
Mass of electron	m_e	9.110×10^{-31} kg
Mass of neutron	m_n	1.675×10^{-27} kg
Mass of proton	m_p	1.673×10^{-27} kg
Electron-charge to mass ratio	e/m_r	1.759×10^{11} C/kg
Faraday constant	F	9.648×10^4 C/mol
Rydberg constant	R	1.097×10^7 m^{-1}
Bohr radius	a_0	5.292×10^{-11} m
Stefan-Boltzmann constant	σ	5.670×10^{-8} W m^{-2} K^{-4}
Wien's Constant	b	2.898×10^{-3} m K
Permittivity of free space	ε_0	8.854×10^{-12} C^2 N^{-1} m^{-2}
	$1/4\pi\,\varepsilon_0$	8.987×10^9 N m^2 C^2
Permeability of free space	μ_0	$4\pi \times 10^{-7}$ T m A^{-1} $\cong 1.257 \times 10^{-6}$ Wb A^{-1} m^{-1}

Other useful Constants

Name	Symbol	Value
Mechanical equivalent of heat	J	4.186 J cal^{-1}
Standard atmospheric pressure	1 atm	1.013×10^5 Pa
Absolute zero	0 K	$-273.15°$ C
Electron volt	1 eV	1.602×10^{-19} J
Unified Atomic mass unit	1 u	1.661×10^{-27} kg
Electron rest energy	mc^2	0.511 MeV
Energy equivalent of 1 u	1 uc^2	931.5 MeV
Volume of ideal gas(0° C and 1 atm)	V	22.4 L mol^{-1}
Acceleration due to gravity (sea level, at equator)	g	9.78049 ms^{-2}

Units and Measurements

(17 - 60)

Chapter contents

Rebort Boyle

Rebort Boyle (1627-1691) was a chemist who did many practical experiments. He showed that for a gas which is kept at a constant temperature, then the pressure that the gas is under is proportional to its volume. So squash a gas into half its volume, and its pressure doubles. This is Boyle's law. ....

Definitions Explanations and Derivations

1.1 FUNDAMENTAL QUANTITIES

The physical quantities which are independent of other quantities are called fundamental quantities.
Example : mass, length, time etc.

1.2 DERIVED QUANTITIES

The physical quantities which are derived from fundamental quantities are known as derived quantities.
Example : area, velocity, force etc.

1.3 THE SI SYSTEM OF UNITS

In 1971, General Conference of Weights and Measures introduced a logical and rationalised system of units known as International System of Units, abbreviated as SI in all language. In this system, there are seven fundamental quantities and two supplementary quantities.

Fundamental quantities and their units

S.No.	Physical quantity	Unit	Symbol
1	Length	metre	m
2	Mass	kilogram	kg
3	Time	second	s
4	Temperature	kelvin	K
5	Electric current	ampere	A
6	Luminous intensity	candela	cd
7	Amount of substance	mole	mol

Supplementary quantities and their units

S.No.	Physical quantity	Unit	Symbol
1	Plane angle	radian	rad
2	Solid angle	steradian	sr

Rules of writing unit

1. In writing the unit of any quantity, small letters must be used for symbol of unit. Example : m, m/s etc.
2. Symbol are not followed by a full stop.
3. If any unit is named after a scientist, its initial letter of a symbol is to be capital. Example N (Newton), W (Watt), K (Kelvin) etc.
4. The full name of a unit always begins with a small letter even if it is named after a scientist. Example : 5 N or 5 newton.
5. Symbols do not take plural form.

Some practical units

There are some practical units which are simultaneously used with SI units.

(i)	1 fermi $= 10^{-15}$m	(ii)	1 angstrom (Å) $= 10^{-10}$m
(iii)	1 nanometer (nm) $= 10^{-9}$m	(iv)	1 micron (μm) $= 10^{-6}$m
(v)	1 light year $= 9.46 \times 10^{15}$ m	(vi)	1 astronomical unit (AU)
(vii)	1 parsec $= 3.03 \times 10^{18}$m		$= 1.496 \times 10^{11}$m
(viii)	1 amu $= 1.66 \times 10^{-27}$kg	(x)	1 tonne $= 1000$ kg
(xi)	1 lunar month $= 27.3$ days	(xii)	1 solar day $= 365.25$ average solar days
(xiii)	1 shake $= 10^{-8}$s		$= 366.25$ sidereal days

1.4 DEFINITIONS OF SI UNITS

(i) **Metre (m)** : One metre defined as the length of the path travelled by light in vacuum in 1/(299, 792,458) of a second. (1983)

(ii) **Kilogram (kg)** : One kilogram is the mass of prototype [a certain platinum-iridium cylinder] preserved at the International Bureau of Weights and Measures, at Severs, near Paris. (1889)

(iii) **Second (s)** : One second is the duration of 9,192,631,770 periods of the radiation corresponding to the transition between the two hyperfine levels of the ground state of the cesium-133 atom. (1967)

(iv) **Ampere (A)** : One ampere is that constant current which , if maintained in two straight parallel conductors of infinite length, of neglegible circular cross-section, and placed 1 metre apart in vacuum would produce between these conductors a force equal to 2×10^{-7} newton per metre of length. (1946)

(v) **Kelvin (K)** : One Kelvin is the fraction 1/(273.16) of the thermodynamic temperature of the triple point of water. (1967)

(vi) **Candela (Cd)** : One candela is the luminous intensity, in a given direction, of a source that emits monochromatic radiation of frequency 540×10^{12} hertz and that has a radiant intensity of 1/683 watt per steradian in that direction.

(vii) **Mole (mol)** : One mole is that amount of substance which contains as many elementary entities as there are atoms in 0.012 kg of carbon-12 isotope. The entities may be atoms, molecules, ions etc.

The two supplementary SI units are defined as follows

(i) **Radian (rad)** : 1 radian is the angle subtended at the centre of a circle by an arc equal in length to the radius of the circle.

Thus
$$\theta = \frac{\text{Arc}}{\text{Radius}} = \frac{r}{r} = 1\,\text{rad}$$

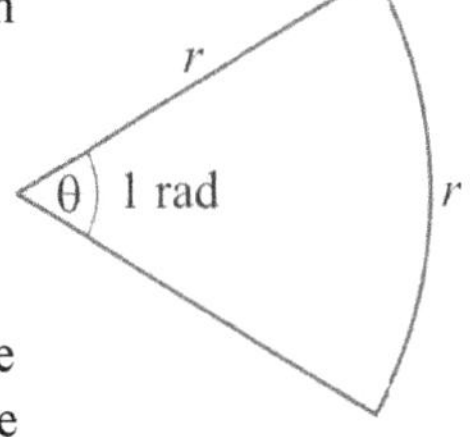

Figure. 1.1

(ii) **Steradian (sr)** : 1 steradian is the solid angle subtended at the centre of a sphere by a surface of the sphere equal in area to that of a square, having each side equal to the radius of the sphere.

Thus
$$\omega = \frac{\text{Surface area}}{\text{Radius}^2}$$

$$= \frac{r^2}{r^2} = 1\,\text{sr}$$

Figure. 1.2

Definition of some practical units

(i) **Light year** : It is the distance travelled by light in vacuum in one year. Thus

$$\text{1 light year} = \text{Speed of light in Vacuum} \times \text{1 year}$$
$$= 3 \times 10^8 \times (365.25 \times 24 \times 60 \times 60)$$

or $\quad$ 1 ly $\quad = \quad 9.46 \times 10^{15}\,\text{m}$

(ii) **Astronomical unit** : It is the average distance of earth from the sum (centre to centre).

$$\text{1 astronomical unit} = 1\,\text{AU} = 1.496 \times 10^{11}\,\text{m}$$

(iii) **Parsec (parallactic second)** : It is defined as the distance at which an arch of length 1 AU subtends an angle of 1 second of arc. If r is the distance, then

$$\theta = \frac{\ell}{r} \quad \text{or} \quad r = \frac{\ell}{\theta}$$

Thus $\quad$ 1 parsec $= \dfrac{1\,\text{AU}}{1''}$

$$= \frac{1.496 \times 10^{11}}{\left(\dfrac{\pi}{180} \times \dfrac{1}{60} \times \dfrac{1}{60}\right)} = 3.08 \times 10^{16}\,\text{m}$$

Also $\quad$ 1 parsec $= 3.26$ ly.

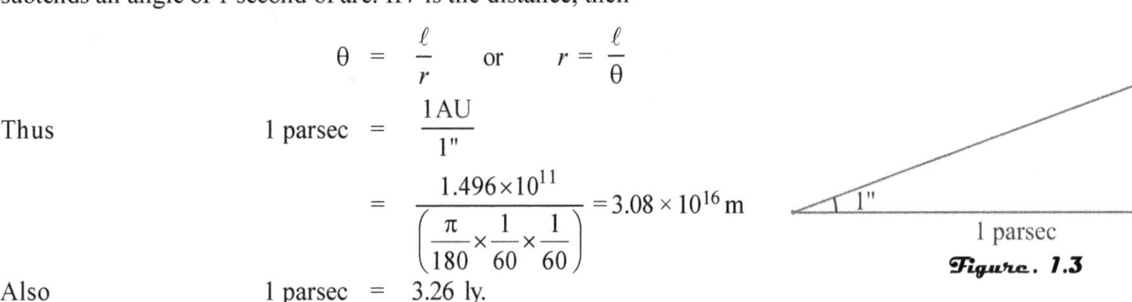

Figure. 1.3

1.5 ADVANTAGES OF SI SYSTEM

(i)   **SI is a coherent system of units.** All derived units can be obtained by simple multiplication or devision of fundamental units without introducing any numerical factor.

(ii) **SI is a rational system of units.** It uses only one unit for a given physical quantity. For example all forms of energy are measured in joule, heat energy in calories and electrical energy in watt hour.

(iii) **SI is a metric system.** The mulitples and subsultiples of SI units can be expressed as powers of 10.

(iv) **SI is an absolute system of units.** It does not used gravitational units. The use of 'g' is not required.

(v)   **SI is an internationally accepted system of units.**

1.6 DIMENSIONS OF A PHYSICAL QUANTITY

The dimensions of a physical quantity are the powers to which the unit of fundamental quantities are raised to represent that quantity.

Dimensions of fundamental quantities

S.No.	Physical quantity	Dimension
1	Length	[L]
2	Mass	[M]
3	Time	[T]
4	Temperature	[K]
5	Electric current	[A]
6	Luminous intensity	[Cd]
7	Amount of substance	[Mol]

Note: Two supplementary fundamental quantities that is plane angle and solid angle have no dimensions.

Dimensional equation : The equation obtained by equating a physical quantity with its dimensions formula is called dimensional equation of the given physical quantity. Example : The dimensional equation of momentum is

$$[\text{Momentum}] = [MLT^{-1}]$$

Dimensions of some physical quantities

S.No.	Physical Quantity	Relation with Other Quantities	Unit	Dimensional Formulae
1.	Force	Mass × Acceleration	N	$[MLT^{-2}]$
2.	Work	Force × Displacement	J	$[ML^2T^{-2}]$
3.	Pressure	$\dfrac{\text{Force}}{\text{Area}}$	N/m²	$[ML^{-1}T^{-2}]$
4.	Force constant	$\dfrac{\text{Force}}{\text{Distance}}$	N/m	$[ML^0T^{-2}]$
5.	Gravitational constant G	$\dfrac{\text{Force} \times \text{distance}^2}{\text{Mass}^2}$	Nm²/kg²	$[M^{-1}L^3T^{-2}]$
6.	Impulse of force	Force × Time	Ns	$[MLT^{-1}]$
7.	Stress	$\dfrac{\text{Force}}{\text{Area}}$	N/m²	$[ML^{-1}T^{-2}]$

8.	Strain	$\dfrac{\text{Change in dimension}}{\text{Original dimension}}$	—	$[M^0L^0T^0]$
9.	Modulus of elasticity	$\dfrac{\text{Stress}}{\text{Strain}}$	N/m^2	$[ML^{-1}T^{-2}]$
10.	Surface tension	$\dfrac{\text{Force}}{\text{Length}}$	N/m	$[ML^0T^{-2}]$
11.	Coefficient of viscosity	$\dfrac{\text{Force}\times\text{distance}}{\text{Area}\times\text{velocity}}$	$N\text{-}s/m^2$	$[ML^{-1}T^{-1}]$
12.	Latent heat	$\dfrac{\text{Heat}}{\text{Mass}}$	J/kg	$[M^0L^2T^{-2}]$
13.	Electric charge	Current $\times$ time	C	$[M^0L^0TA]$
14.	Electric potential	$\dfrac{\text{Work}}{\text{Charge}}$	J/C or V	$[ML^2T^{-3}A^{-1}]$
15.	Resistance R	$\dfrac{\text{Potential}}{\text{Current}}$	ohm (Ω)	$[ML^2T^{-3}A^{-2}]$
16.	Capacitance C	$\dfrac{\text{Charge}}{\text{Potential}}$	farad (F)	$[M^{-1}L^{-2}T^4A^2]$
17.	Inductance L	$\dfrac{\text{Potential}}{\text{Current/time}}$	henry (H)	$[ML^2T^{-2}A^{-2}]$
18.	Magnetic field B	$\dfrac{\text{Force}}{\text{Charge}\times\text{velocity}}$	tesla (T)	$[ML^0T^{-2}A^{-1}]$
19.	Plank's constant h	$\dfrac{\text{Energy}}{\text{Frequency}}$	J-s	$[ML^2T^{-1}]$
20.	Permittivity, ε	$\varepsilon=\dfrac{q_1q_2}{Fr^2}$	$A^2C^2N^{-1}m^{-2}$	$[M^{-1}L^{-3}T^4A^2]$
21.	Permeability, μ	$\mu=\dfrac{4\pi.F}{I_1I_2l}$	$N/A^2\text{-}m$	$[MLT^{-2}A^{-2}]$

Note :

1. Some of physical quantities have no dimensions (dimensionless). Example : plane angle, solid angle, specific gravity, strain, refractive index.
2. Quantities having same dimensions
   (a) Momentum and impulse
   (b) Work, energy, torque
   (c) Pressure, stress and modulus of elasticity.
3. Dimensionless physical parameters : Reynolds number, Mack number, refractive index.
4. CR, $\dfrac{L}{R}$ and $\sqrt{LC}$ have dimensions of time.

Principle of homogeneity of dimensions

According to this principle, the dimensions of all the terms occuring on both sides of the equation must be same.

Uses of dimensions

1. **Conversion of unit of one system to another :** It is based on the fact that product of numerical value contained in and the unit of physical quantity remains constant, that is, larger unit has smaller magnitude or $n[u]$ = constant.

If a physical quantity has dimensional formula $[M^a L^b T^c]$ and units of that quantity in two systems are $[M_1{}^a L_1{}^b T_1{}^c]$ and $[M_2{}^a L_2{}^b T_2{}^c]$ respectively, then

$$n_1 [u_1] = n_2 [u_2]$$

$$\therefore \qquad n_2 = n_1 \frac{[u_1]}{[u_2]}$$

or

$$n_2 = n_1 \left[\frac{M_1}{M_2}\right]^a \left[\frac{L_1}{L_2}\right]^b \left[\frac{T_1}{T_2}\right]^c$$

where n_1 and n_2 are numerical values in first and second system of units.

2. **To check the correctness of a physical relations :** This is based on the principle of homogeneity of dimensions.

3. **Deriving the relation among the physical quantities** : By using the principle of homogeneity of dimensions, we can derive an expression of a physical quantity if we know the various factors on which it depends.

Let physical quantity X depends on other quantities P, Q and R, then we can write

$$X = k\, P^a\, Q^b\, R^c$$

where k is a dimensionless constant, whose value can be determined by experiment or otherwise, but not by dimensions. By equating dimensions of both sides of equation, we can get required relation between the quantities.

4. **Finding the dimensions of constants** : It is based on homogeneity of dimensions.

Limitations of dimensional analysis

1. The method of dimensional analysis does not give any information about the constant k.
2. It fails to derive the relation if any quantity depends on more than fundamental quantities (in mechanics three fundamental quantities). *Example :* Capillary rise $h = \dfrac{2T \cos\theta}{r\rho g}$, here h depends on four quantities of mechanics. We have only three equations.

3. It fails to derive the relation like $s = ut + \dfrac{1}{2} at^2$.

4. The method fails to derive relationship which involves trigonometric, logarithmic or exponential functions.

1.7 ORDER OF MAGNITUDE

The order of magnitude of a physical quantity is that power of 10 which is closest to its magnitude. It gives an idea about how big magnitude. It gives an idea about how big and how small a given physical quantity is?

A number N can be expressed as $\qquad N = n \times 10^x$.

If $0.5 < n \le 5$, then x will be the order of magnitude of N.

1.8 RULES OF SIGNIFICANT FIGURES

Significant figures

In any measurement, the reliable digits plus the first uncertain digit are known as significant figures. e.g., The length of an object measured to be 475.2 cm. Here the digits 4, 7, 5 are reliable while the digit 2 is uncertain. The significant figures in above measured values are four.

All the non-zero digits are significant. All zeros between non-zero digits are significant e.g., 2.005 has four significant figures.

The zeros on the right of decimal point but left of the first non-zero digit are not significant. Trailing zeros in a number with a decimal are significant e.g., 0.0002500 have four significant figures.

The trailing zeros in a number without a decimal point are not significant e.g., 2500 have two significant figures. In addition or subtraction, the final result should have as many decimal places as are there in the number with the least decimal places, e.g., in the sum of 2.50 cm and 4.275cm. Their arithmetic sum is 6.775 cm but the least precise measurement is 2.50 cm. So, the final result should be 6.78 cm.

In multiplication or division, the final result should have as many as significant figures as are the figures least significant in any number taking part in the operation.

e.g. $1.25 \times 2.0 = 2.50$, should be 2.5.

Note: The number of significant figures do not change with the change in system of units e.g. The observed length 5.208 cm has four significant figures.

In different units, it can be written as 52.08 mm, 0.05208 m or 52080 μm. All these numbers have the same number of significant figures i.e., four.

FORMULAE USED

1. $n_1 u_1 = n_2 u_2$

2. $n_1[M_1^a L_1^b T_1^c] = n_2[M_2^a L_2^b T_2^c]$

3. $n_2 = n_1 \left[\dfrac{M_1}{M_2}\right]^a \left[\dfrac{L_1}{L_2}\right]^b \left[\dfrac{T_1}{T_2}\right]^c$

EXAMPLES BASED ON UNITS DIMENSIONS AND SIGNIFICANT FIGURES

Example 1. Express 1 parsec in terms of metre. Write its order of magnitude.

Sol.   1 parsec $= 3.08 \times 10^{16}$ m

Here $0.5 < 3.08 < 5$

$\therefore$ Order of magnitude $= 16$ *Ans.*

Example 2. Write the order of magnitude of the following measurements :   (i) 45,710,000 m   (ii) 0.00000 532 kg

Sol.

(i) $45,710,000 = 4.571 \times 10^7$ m

Here $0.5 < 4.571 < 5$,

$\therefore$ Order of magnitude is $= 7$ *Ans.*

(ii) $0.00000532 = 0.532 \times 10^{-5}$ kg

Here $0.5 < 0.532 < 5$,

$\therefore$ Order of magnitude is $= -5$ *Ans.*

Example 3. A calorie is a unit of heat or energy and it equals about 4.2J, where $1J = 1$ kgm^{2}s^{-2}. Suppose, we employ a system of units in which the unit of mass equals α kg, the unit of length equals βm and the unit of time is γs. Show that a calorie has a magnitude of $4.2 \, \alpha^{-1}\beta^{-2}\gamma^2$ in terms of new units.

                           [NCERT]

Sol. 1 calorie $= 4.2J = 4.2$ kg m^2 s^{-2}

If α kg $=$ new unit of mass

Then, $1\text{kg} = \dfrac{1}{\alpha}$ new unit of mass

         $= \alpha^{-1}$ new unit of mass

Similarly, $1\text{m} = \beta^{-1}$ new unit of length

         $1\text{s} = \gamma^{-1}$ new unit of time

Now, 1 calorie $= 4.2 \, (\alpha^{-1}$ new unit of mass)

                 $(\beta^{-1}$ new unit of length$)^2$

                 $(\gamma^{-1}$ new unit of time$)^{-2}$

         $= 4.2 \, \alpha^{-1} \beta^{-2}\gamma^2$ unit of energy.

Example 4. A new unit of length is chosen such that the speed of light in vacuum is unity. What is the distance between the Sun and the Earth in terms of the new unit, if light takes 8 min and 20 sec to cover this distance?   **[NCERT]**

Sol. Velocity of light $= c$

             $= 1$ new unit of length s^{-1}

Time taken by light of Sun to reach the Earth $= t = 8$ min 20 s $= 8 \times 60 + 20 = 500$ s

$\therefore$ Distance between the Sun and Earth,

     $x = c \times t = 1$ new unit of length s$^{-1} \times 500$ s

             $= 500$ new units of length.

Example 5. The density of a material in CGS system is 8 g/cm^3. In a system of units in which unit of length is 5 cm and unit of mass is 20 g, what is the density of material ?

Sol. The dimensions of density are $[ML^{-3}]$.

We know that $n_1 \, [u_1] = n_2 \, [u_2]$

$\therefore$ $n_2 = n_1 \dfrac{[u_1]}{[u_2]}$

         $= n_1 \left[\dfrac{M_1}{M_2}\right]^1 \left[\dfrac{L_2}{L_1}\right]^3$

         $= 8 \left(\dfrac{1g}{20g}\right)\left(\dfrac{5cm}{1cm}\right)^3$

         $= 50$

i.e., the density of material in new system is 50 unit.

Example 6. State the number of significant figures in the following:

   (i)   0.007 m^2 (ii) 2.64×10^{24} kg

   (iii)   0.2370 g/cm^3 (iv)   6.320 J

   (v)   6.032 N/m^2 (vi)   0.0006032 m^2

   (vii)   2.000 m   (viii)   5100 kg

                              (ix)   0.050 cm

Sol.

(i)　One : 7

(ii)　three : 2, 6, 4

(iii)　Four : 2, 3, 7, 0

(iv)　Four : 6, 3, 2, 0

(v)　Four : 6, 0, 3, 2

(vi)　Four : 6, 0, 3, 2

(vii)　Four : 2, 0, 0, 0

(viii)　Four : 5, 1, 0, 0

(ix)　Two : 5, 0

> **Note :**　5100 kg is the measured value, and so it has four significant figures. If it simply a numerical value 5100, then significant number in it will be two.

Example 7. Solve the following and express the result to an appropriate number of significant figure :

(i)　Add 6.2 g, 4.33 g and 17.456 g.

(ii)　Subtract 63.54 kg from 187.2 kg

(iii)　$75.5 \times 125.2 \times 0.51$

(iv)　$\dfrac{2.13 \times 24.78}{458.2}$

(v)　$\dfrac{2.51 \times 10^{-4} \times 1.81 \times 10^{7}}{0.4463}$

Sol.

(i)　$6.2\,g + 4.33\,g + 17.456\,g = 27.986\,g$

The result should be rounded off to first decimal place.

$\therefore \qquad = 28.0\,g$

(ii)　$187.2\,kg - 63.54\,kg = 123.66\,kg$

The result should be rounded off to first decimal place.

$\therefore \qquad = 123.7\,kg$

(iii)　$75.5 \times 125.2 \times 0.51 = 4820.826$

The result should be rounded off to two significant figures, because of (0.51).

$\therefore \qquad = 4800$

(iv)　$\dfrac{2.13 \times 24.78}{458.2} = 0.115193$

The result should be rounded off to three significant figure because of (2.13).

$\therefore \qquad = 0.115$

(v)　$\dfrac{2.51 \times 10^{-4} \times 1.81 \times 10^{7}}{0.4463} = 10.1795 \times 10^{3}$

The result should be rounded off to three significant figure because of 1.81

$\therefore \qquad = 10.2 \times 10^{3}$

Example 8. A book with many printing errors contains four different formulas for the displacement y of a particle undergoing a certain periodic motion:　　　　[NCERT]

(a)　$y = a \sin \dfrac{2\pi t}{T}$

(b)　$y = a \sin vt$

(c)　$y = \left(\dfrac{a}{T}\right) \sin \dfrac{t}{a}$

(d)　$y = \left(a\sqrt{2}\right)\left(\sin \dfrac{2\pi t}{T} + \cos \dfrac{2\pi t}{T}\right)$

(a = maximum displacement of the particle, v = speed of the particle, T = time-period of motion).

Rule out the wrong formulas on dimensional grounds.

Sol. According to dimensional analysis an equation must be dimensionally homogeneous.

(a)　$y = a \sin \dfrac{2\pi t}{T}$

Here, $[\text{L.H.S.}] = [y] = [L]$

and　$[\text{R.H.S.}] = \left[a \sin \dfrac{2\pi t}{T} \right]$

$= \left[L \sin \dfrac{T}{T} \right] = [L]$

So, it is correct.

(b)　$y = a \sin vt$

Here, $[y] = [L]$

and $[a \sin vt] = [L \sin (LT^{-1}.T)]$

$= [L \sin L]$

So, the equation is wrong.

(c)　$y = \left(\dfrac{a}{T}\right) \sin \dfrac{t}{a}$

Here, $[y] = [L]$

and　$\left[\left(\dfrac{a}{T}\right) \sin \dfrac{t}{a} \right] = \left[\dfrac{L}{T} \sin \dfrac{T}{L} \right]$

$= \left[LT^{-1} \sin TL^{-1} \right]$

So, the equation is wrong.

(d)　$y = \left(a\sqrt{2}\right)\left(\sin \dfrac{2\pi t}{T} + \cos \dfrac{2\pi t}{T}\right)$

Here, $[y] = [L]$, $\left[a\sqrt{2} \right] = [L]$

and $\left[\sin \dfrac{2\pi t}{T} + \cos \dfrac{2\pi t}{T} \right] = \left[\sin \dfrac{T}{T} + \cos \dfrac{T}{T} \right]$

$\therefore\ [\text{LHS}] = [\text{RHS}]$

$= $ dimensionless

So, the equation is correct.

Example 9. When the planet Jupiter is at a distance of 824.7 million km from Earth, its angular diameter is measured to be 35.72" of arc. Calculate the diameter of Jupiter?　　[NCERT]

Sol.　$r = 824.7 \times 10^{6}\ km$

$\theta = 35.72" = \dfrac{35.72}{60 \times 60} \times \dfrac{\pi}{180}$ radian

$\therefore\ l = r\,\theta = 824.7 \times 10^{6} \times \dfrac{35.72}{60 \times 60} \times \dfrac{\pi}{180}$ km

$= 1.429 \times 10^{5}$ km.

Example 10. A great physicist of this century (P.A.M. Dirac) loved playing with numerical values of Fundamental constants of nature. This led him to an interesting observation. Dirac found that from the basic constants of atomic physics (c, e, mass of electron, mass of proton) and the gravitational constant G, he could arrive at a number with the dimension of time. Further, it was a very large number, its magnitude being close to the present estimate on the age of the universe (~15 /billion years). From the table of fundamental constants in this book, try to see if you too can construct this number (or any other interesting number you can think of). If its coincidence with the age of the universe were significant, what would this imply for the constancy of fundamental constants? [NCERT]

Sol. Using basic constants such as speed of light (c), charge on electron (e), mass of electron (m_e), mass of proton (m_v) and gravitational constant (G), we can construct the quantity,

$$\tau = \left(\frac{e^2}{4\pi\varepsilon_0}\right)^2 \times \frac{1}{m_p m_e^2 c^3 G}$$

Now $\left[\dfrac{e^2}{4\pi\varepsilon_0}\right] = \left[\dfrac{1}{4\pi\varepsilon_0}\dfrac{e^2}{r^2}r^2\right] = \left[Fr^2\right]$

$$= [MLT^{-2} \cdot L^2] = [ML^3T^{-2}]$$

$$\therefore \quad [\tau] = \frac{\left[ML^3T^{-2}\right]^2}{[M][M]^2\left[LT^{-1}\right]^3\left[M^{-1}L^3T^{-2}\right]} = [T]$$

Clearly, the quantity τ has the dimensions of time.
Put $G = 6.67 \times 10^{-11}$ Nm^2 kg^{-2},
$c = 3 \times 10^8$ m/s
$e = 1.6 \times 10^{-19}$ C, $m_e = 9.1 \times 10^{-31}$ kg,
$m = 1.67 \times 10^{-27}$ kg

and $\dfrac{1}{4\pi\varepsilon_0} = 9 \times 10^9$ Nm^{2}C^2

$$\therefore \tau = \frac{\left[9\times10^9 \times \left(1.6\times10^{-19}\right)^2\right]^2}{1.67\times10^{-27}\times\left(9.1\times10^{-31}\right)^2\times\left(3\times10^8\right)^3\times6.67\times10^{-11}}$$

$$= 2.13 \times 10^{16} \text{ s}$$

$$= \frac{2.13\times10^{16}}{3.156\times10^7}\text{ years} = 0.667\times10^9 \text{ years.}$$

$$= 0.667 \text{ billion years.}$$

This time is slightly less than the age of the universe ($\approx$ 15 billion years). It implies that the values of the basic constants of physics should change with time because the age of the universe increases with time.

Example 11. Find the dimensions of $a \times b$ in the relation

$P = \dfrac{b - x^2}{at}$; where P is power, x is distance and t is time.

Sol. Dimensions of b = dimensions of x^2
$$= L^2$$

Dimensions of $\dfrac{x^2}{at}$ = dimensions of P

$\therefore$ Dimensions of a = dimensions of $\left[\dfrac{x^2}{Pt}\right]$

$$= \frac{L^2}{ML^2T^{-3}T} = M^{-1}T^2$$

Hence dimensions of $a \times b$ = $L^2 \times M^{-1}$ T^2
$$= M^{-1}L^2T^2 \qquad \textit{Ans.}$$

Example 12. Check by dimensions whether the equation

$\tan\theta = \dfrac{rg}{v^2}$ is correct, where r is the radius of the path, g acceleration due to gravity and v speed of the vehicle θ is the banking angle.
Sol.
The dimensions of LHS = $[M^0L^0T^0]$

The dimensions of RHS = $\dfrac{rg}{v^2}$

$$= \left[\frac{L.LT^{-2}}{(LT^{-1})^2}\right]$$

$$= [M^0L^0T^0]$$

Since both sides of equation has same dimensions, therefore given equation is dimensionally correct.

1. The equation $\tan\theta = \dfrac{rg}{v^2}$ is not physically correct. The correct

   equation is $\tan\theta = \dfrac{v^2}{rg}$.

2. The dimensionally correct equation need not be physically correct.

Example 13. The velocity (v) of water waves may depend upon their wavelength λ, the density of water ρ and the acceleration due to gravity g. Find the relation between these quantities by method of dimensions.

Sol. Suppose, $\quad v = k\,\lambda^a\rho^b g^c$

Substituting dimensions of all quantities in a above equation, we get
$$[M^0LT^{-1}] = [L]^a \,[ML^{-3}]^b\,[LT^{-2}]^c$$
or $\quad [M^0LT^{-1}] = [M^b L^{a-3b+c} T^{-2c}]$

Equating dimensions of both sides, we get
$$b = 0$$
$$a - 3b + c = 1$$
and $\quad -2c = -1$

After solving we get, $\quad a = \dfrac{1}{2}, b = 0$ and $c = \dfrac{1}{2}$

The required relation is $v = k\lambda^{1/2}g^{1/2}$ $\qquad\textit{Ans.}$

In Chapter Exercise 1.1

1. Why length, mass and time are choosen as base quantities in mechanics? **[NCERT Exemplar]**
2. Given an example of the following : **[NCERT Exemplar]**
   (a) A physical quantity which has a unit but no dimensions.
   (b) A physical quantity which has neither unit nor dimensions.
   (c) A constant which has a unit.
   (d) A constant which has no unit.
3. If the unit of force is 100 N, unit of length is 10 m and unit of time is 100 s, what is the unit of mass in this system of units? **[NCERT Exemplar]**
   Ans. 10^5 **kg**
4. In the expression $P = El^2m^{-5}G^{-2}$ where E, m, l and G denote energy, mass, angular momentum and gravitational constant, respectively. Show that P is a dimensionless quantity. **[NCERT Exemplar]**
   Ans. $[\mathbf{M^0L^0T^0}]$
5. If velocity of light c, Planck's constant h and gravitational constant G are taken as fundamental quantities, then express mass, length and time in terms of dimensions of three quantities. **[NCERT Exemplar]**

   Ans. $m = k\sqrt{\dfrac{ch}{G}}$, $L = k\sqrt{\dfrac{hG}{c^3}}$, $T = k\sqrt{\dfrac{hG}{c^5}}$

6. A new system of units is proposed in which unit of mass is α kg, unit of length is β m and unit of time is γ s. How much will 5 J measure in this new system?

   [NCERT Exemplar] *Ans.* $\dfrac{5\gamma^2}{\alpha\beta^2}$

7. An artificial satellite is revolving around a planet of mass M and radius R, in a circular orbit of radius r. From kepler's third law about the period of a satellite around a common central body, square of the period of revolution T is proportional tothe cube of the radius of the orbit r. Show using dimensional analysis, that $T = \dfrac{k}{R}\sqrt{\dfrac{r^3}{g}}$, where k is a dimensionless constant and g is acceleration due to gravity. **[NCERT Exemplar]**
8. The number of particles crossing a unit area perpendicular to x-axis in unit time is given by

   $$n = -D\,\frac{n_2 - n_1}{x_2 - x_1}$$

   where n_1 and n_2 are number of particles per unit volume for the values of x meant to x_1 and x_2. Find the dimensions of the diffusion constant D. *Ans.* $[\mathbf{D}] = [\mathbf{L^2T^{-1}}]$
9. A body of mass m is moving in a circle of radius r with angular velocity ω . Find the expression for centripetal force acting on it by the method of dimensions.

   Ans. $\mathbf{F = Km\omega^2 r}$.

10. Find the dimensions of $\dfrac{a}{b}$ in the equation; $F = a\sqrt{x} + bt^2$,

    where F is force, x is distance and t is time.

    Ans. $\mathbf{L^{-1/2}T^2}$

1.9 ERRORS IN MEASUREMENT

Every measurement is limited by the reliability of the measuring instrument and skill of the person making the measurement. If we repeat a particular measurement, we usually do not get the same result every time. This imperfection in measurement can be expressed in two ways :

Accuracy and precision

Accuracy refers to the closeness of observed values to its true value of the quantity while precision refers to closeness between the different observed values of the same quantity. High precision does not mean high accuracy. The difference between accuracy and precision can be understand by the following example : Suppose three students are asked to find the length of a rod whose length is known to be 2.250 cm. The observations are given in the table.

Student	Measurement-1	Measurement-2	Measurement-3	Average length
A.	2.25 cm	2.27 cm	2.26 cm	2.26 cm
B.	2.252 cm	2.250 cm	2.251 cm	2.251 cm
C.	2.250 cm	2.250 cm	2.251 cm	2.250 cm

It is clear from the above table, that the observations taken by student A are neither precise nor accurate. The observations of student B are more precise. The observations of student C are precise as well as accurate.

Error : Each instrument has its limitation of measurement. While taking the observation, some uncertainty gets introduced in the observation. As a result, the observed value is somewhat different from true value. Therefore,

$$\text{Error} = \text{True value} - \text{Observed value}$$

Systematic errors : The errors which tend to occur of one sign, either positive or negative, are called systematic errors. Systematic errors are due to some known cause which follow some specified rule. We can eliminate such errors if we know their causes. Systematic errors may occur due to zero error of an instrument, imperfection in experimental techniques, change in weather conditions like temperature, pressure etc.

Random errors : The errors which occur randomly and irregularly in magnitude and sign are called random errors. The cause of random errors are not known. If a person repeat the observations number of times, he may get different readings every time. Random errors have almost equal chances for positive and negative sign. Hence the arithmetic mean of large number of observations can be taken to minimize the random error.

Mean value of a quantity : Since the probability of occurrence of positive and negative errors are same, so the arithmetic mean of all observations can be taken as the true value of a observed quantity.

If $a_1, a_2, ...a_n$ are the observed values of a quantity, then its true value $\overline{a}$ can be given by

$$\overline{a} \quad = \quad a_{\text{mean}} = \frac{a_1 + a_2 + ...+ a_n}{n}$$

$$= \quad \frac{1}{n}\sum_{i=1}^{n} a_i$$

The absolute errors in individual observations are:

$$\Delta a_1 = \overline{a} - a_1$$
$$\Delta a_2 = \overline{a} - a_2$$
$$......................$$
$$\Delta a_n = \overline{a} - a_n$$

The mean absolute error is defined as

$$\Delta\overline{a} \quad = \quad \frac{|\Delta a_1| + |\Delta a_2| +................+|\Delta a_n|}{n}$$

$$= \quad \frac{1}{n}\sum_{i=1}^{n} |\Delta a_i|$$

Thus the final result of the observed quantity can be expressed as $a = \overline{a} \pm \Delta\overline{a}$.

It is clear from above that any observed value can by $(\overline{a} - \Delta\overline{a}) \le a \le (\overline{a} + \Delta\overline{a})$.

Relative or fractional error : The ratio of the mean absolute error to the true value of the quantity is called relative error.

$$\text{Thus relative error} = \frac{\Delta\overline{a}}{a}$$

Percentage error : If relative error is expressed in percentage is called percentage error.

$$\text{Thus percentage error} = \frac{\Delta\overline{a}}{a} \times 100$$

Note : Absolute error has the unit of quantity. But relative error has no unit.

Combination of errors

Let we want to get the volume of sphere, $V = \frac{4}{3}\pi r^3$. There involves multiplication of radius three times.

The measurement of radius has some error, then what will be error in calculating the volume of sphere? The error in final result depends on the individual measurement as well as the mathematical operations involved in calculating the result. Following rules are used to evaluate maximum possible error in any computed quantity.

1. **Error in addition**

   Let $Z = X + Y$. Suppose $\pm \Delta x$ be absolute errors in X and $\pm \Delta y$ be the absolute error in Y, then we have

   $$\begin{aligned} Z + \Delta z &= (X \pm \Delta x) + (Y \pm \Delta y) \\ &= (X + Y) \pm (\Delta x + \Delta y) \\ \therefore \quad \Delta z &= (Z + \Delta z) - Z \\ &= \pm (\Delta x + \Delta y) \end{aligned}$$

> **Note :** The maximum value of Δx or Δy can be least count of the instrument used.
> Example : $x = 2.20$ cm, Δx will be 0.01 cm.

RULE : The maximum possible error in the addition of quantities is equal to the sum of their absolute error.

% error in Z, $$\frac{\Delta z}{Z} \times 100 = \pm \left[\frac{\Delta x + \Delta y}{X + Y} \right] \times 100$$

2. **Error in subtraction**

   Let

   $$\begin{aligned} Z &= X - Y \\ Z + \Delta z &= (X \pm \Delta x) - (Y \pm \Delta y) \\ &= (X - Y) \pm (\Delta x \mp \Delta y) \\ \therefore \quad \Delta z &= (Z + \Delta z) - Z \\ &= \pm \Delta x \mp \Delta y \end{aligned}$$

   For maximum possible error Δx and Δy must be of same sign.

   $$\therefore \quad \Delta z = \pm (\Delta x + \Delta y)$$

   RULE : The maximum possible error in subtraction of quantities is equal to the sum of their absolute errors.

   % error in Z, $\dfrac{\Delta z}{Z} \times 100 = \pm \left[\dfrac{\Delta x + \Delta y}{X - Y} \right]$.

3. **Error in product**

   Let

   $$\begin{aligned} Z &= XY \\ Z + \Delta z &= (X \pm \Delta x)(Y \pm \Delta y) \\ &= XY \pm \Delta x Y \pm X \Delta y \pm \Delta x \Delta y \\ \therefore \quad \Delta z &= (Z + \Delta z) - Z \\ &= \pm (\Delta x Y + X \Delta y) \pm \Delta x \Delta y \end{aligned}$$

   If Δx and Δy are both small, their product be very small, therefore we can neglect it.

   $$\therefore \quad \Delta z = \pm (\Delta x Y + X \Delta y)$$

   The maximum fractional error in Z,

   $$\frac{\Delta z}{Z} = \pm \left[\frac{\Delta x}{X} + \frac{\Delta y}{Y} \right]$$

   and maximum percentage error in Z,

   $$\frac{\Delta z}{Z} \times 100 = \pm \left[\frac{\Delta x}{X} + \frac{\Delta y}{Y} \right] \times 100$$

   RULE : The maximum fractional error in the product is equal to the sum of the fractional errors in the individual quantities.

> **Note :** The product $\Delta x\, \Delta y$ can not be neglected if the errors in x and y are order of 10% or more. The product can be neglected, if the error in x and y are 1% or little more than this (say 2 to 3%).

4. Error in quotient or division

Let
$$Z = \frac{X}{Y}$$

Then
$$Z + \Delta z = \frac{X \pm \Delta x}{Y \pm \Delta y}$$

$$= \frac{X\left(1 \pm \dfrac{\Delta x}{X}\right)}{Y\left(1 \pm \dfrac{\Delta y}{Y}\right)}$$

$$= \frac{X}{Y}\left(1 \pm \frac{\Delta x}{X}\right)\left(1 \pm \frac{\Delta y}{Y}\right)^{-1}$$

$$= \frac{X}{Y}\left(1 \pm \frac{\Delta x}{X}\right)\left(1 \mp \frac{\Delta y}{Y}\right)$$

or
$$Z + \Delta z = Z\left(1 \pm \frac{\Delta x}{X}\right)\left(1 \mp \frac{\Delta y}{Y}\right)$$

$$1 + \frac{\Delta z}{Z} = \left(1 \pm \frac{\Delta x}{X}\right)\left(1 \mp \frac{\Delta y}{Y}\right)$$

$$= 1 \pm \frac{\Delta x}{X} \mp \frac{\Delta y}{Y} \pm \frac{\Delta x}{X} \cdot \frac{\Delta y}{Y}$$

As the term $\dfrac{\Delta x}{X}$ and $\dfrac{\Delta y}{Y}$ are small, so their product can be neglected. The maximum fractional error is given by

$$\frac{\Delta z}{Z} = \pm \left(\frac{\Delta x}{X} + \frac{\Delta y}{Y}\right)$$

And maximum possible percentage error in Z,

$$\therefore \qquad \frac{\Delta z}{Z} \times 100 = \pm \left(\frac{\Delta x}{X} + \frac{\Delta y}{Y}\right) \times 100$$

RULE : The maximum fractional error in the quotient is equal to the sum of their individual fractional errors.

5. Error in the power of a quantity

Let
$$Z = X^n$$
$$Z + \Delta z = (X \pm \Delta x)^n$$

$$= X^n\left(1 \pm \frac{\Delta x}{X}\right)^n$$

$$\simeq Z\left(1 \pm n\frac{\Delta x}{X}\right)$$

or
$$\frac{Z + \Delta z}{Z} = \left(1 \pm n\frac{\Delta x}{X}\right)$$

or
$$1 + \frac{\Delta z}{Z} = 1 \pm n\frac{\Delta x}{X}$$

$$\therefore \qquad \frac{\Delta z}{Z} = \pm n \frac{\Delta x}{X}$$

Maximum percentage error in Z

$$\frac{\Delta z}{Z} \times 100 = \pm n \left(\frac{\Delta x}{X} \times 100 \right)$$

RULE : The fractional error in the quantity with n powers is n times the fractional error in that quantity.

Note : Here n may have any value. It may be a whole number, fraction, positive or negative.

General case : If $Z = \dfrac{X^a Y^b}{W^c}$, the maximum possible fractional error in Z,

$$\frac{\Delta z}{Z} = \pm \left[a \frac{\Delta x}{X} + b \frac{\Delta y}{Y} + c \frac{\Delta w}{W} \right]$$

The maximum possible percentage error

$$\frac{\Delta z}{Z} \times 100 = \pm \left[a \frac{\Delta x}{X} + b \frac{\Delta y}{Y} + c \frac{\Delta w}{W} \right] \times 100$$

The above used algebraic method in many operations become difficult to operate. In such situations we can used differential method to find the error.

Differential method of calculation of errors

1.   Let
$$Z = k \frac{X^a Y^b}{W^c}$$

where k is a constant.
Taking logarithms of both sides of equation, we get
$$\ln Z = \ln k + a \ln X + b \ln Y - c \ln W$$
Now differentiating partially the above expression, we have

$$\frac{\delta z}{Z} = a \frac{\delta x}{X} + b \frac{\delta y}{Y} - c \frac{\delta w}{W}$$

We can write above equation by writing Δ in place of δ;

$$\frac{\Delta z}{Z} = a \frac{\Delta x}{X} + b \frac{\Delta y}{Y} - c \frac{\Delta w}{W}$$

Errors calculated by above equation, is known as mathematical error. But our interest is in finding the maximum possible error.

$$\therefore \qquad \frac{\Delta z}{Z} \times 100 = \pm \left[a \frac{\Delta x}{X} + b \frac{\Delta y}{Y} + c \frac{\Delta w}{W} \right] \times 100$$

2.   Let
$$Z = \frac{W}{(X + Y)}$$

Taking logarithms of both sides of above equation, we have
$$\ln Z = \ln W - \ln (X + Y)$$
Differentiating partially, we get

$$\frac{\delta z}{Z} = \frac{\delta w}{W} - \frac{\delta (x + y)}{(X + Y)} = \frac{\delta w}{W} - \frac{(\delta x + \delta y)}{X + Y}$$

(a)   The maximum possible error in Z

$$\frac{\Delta z}{Z} = \pm\left[\frac{\Delta w}{W} + \frac{\Delta x + \Delta y}{(X+Y)}\right]$$

(b)   For

$$Z = \frac{W}{X-Y}$$

$$\frac{\Delta z}{Z} = \pm\left[\frac{\Delta w}{W} + \frac{\Delta x + \Delta y}{X-Y}\right]$$

3.   Let

$$Z = \frac{XY}{U+V}$$

Taking logarithms of both sides of above equation, we have

$$\ell n\, Z = \ell n\, X + \ell n\, Y - \ell n\,(U+V)$$

Differentiating partially, we get

$$\frac{\delta z}{Z} = \frac{\delta x}{X} + \frac{\delta y}{Y} - \frac{\delta(u+v)}{U+V}$$

$$= \frac{\delta x}{X} + \frac{\delta y}{Y} - \frac{(\delta u + \delta v)}{U+V}$$

The maximum possible error in Z

(a)

$$\frac{\Delta z}{Z} = \pm\left[\frac{\Delta x}{X} + \frac{\Delta y}{Y} + \frac{(\Delta u + \Delta v)}{U+V}\right]$$

(b)   For

$$Z = \frac{XY}{U-V}, \quad \frac{\Delta z}{Z} = \pm\left[\frac{\Delta x}{X} + \frac{\Delta y}{Y} + \frac{\Delta u + \Delta v}{U-V}\right]$$

4.   Let

$$Z = \sin x$$

Differentiating partially, we get

$$\delta z = \cos x\, \delta x$$

or

$$\Delta z = \cos x\, \Delta x$$

and

$$\frac{\Delta z}{Z} = \frac{\cos x}{\sin x}\Delta x = \frac{\sqrt{1-\sin^2 x}}{\sin x}\Delta x$$

or

$$\frac{\Delta z}{Z} = \frac{\sqrt{1-z^2}}{Z}\Delta x$$

1.10 INDIRECT METHODS OF MEASURING LARGE DISTANCES

Triangulation method

It is based on the relationship between sides and angles of a triangle.

(i)   Height of an accessible object :

Let h be the height of the tree or tower to be measured. Place a sextant at a distance x from the foot and measure the angle of elevation. If θ is the angle of elevation of the top, then

$$\tan \theta = \frac{h}{x}$$

or $h = x\tan\theta$

knowing the distance x, the height h can be determined.

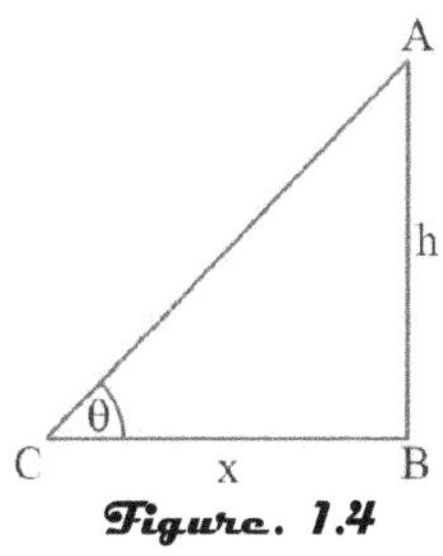

Figure. 1.4

(ii)   **Height of an inaccessible object :**

Let h is the height of the mountain to be measured. Measure angles of elevation of the top of the mountain by using a sextant. If θ_1 and θ_2 are the angles taken from C and D respectively, then in $\triangle ABC$,

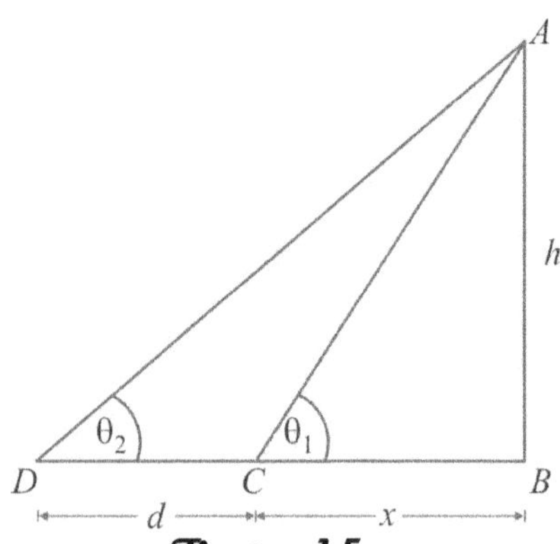

Figure. 1.5

$$\cot\theta_1 = \frac{x}{h}$$

and in $\triangle ABD$,

$$\cot\theta_2 = \frac{d+x}{h}$$

$$\therefore \quad \cot\theta_2 - \cot\theta_1 = \frac{d}{h}$$

or

$$h = \left[\frac{d}{\cot\theta_2 - \cot\theta_1}\right]$$

Parallax method

Parallax : It is the apparent shift in the position of an object with respect to another when we shift our eye sidewise.

To understand it, hold a pencil P at a distance s from eyes. Look towards the pencil first by left eye L (closing right eye) and then by the right eye R(closing left eye). The position of the pencil appears to change with respect to the background. This shift in position of the object is called **parallax**. The distance between the two points of observation is called **basis.** In the figure the distance LR between the eyes is the basis, and angle θ is called parallax angle or parallactic angle.

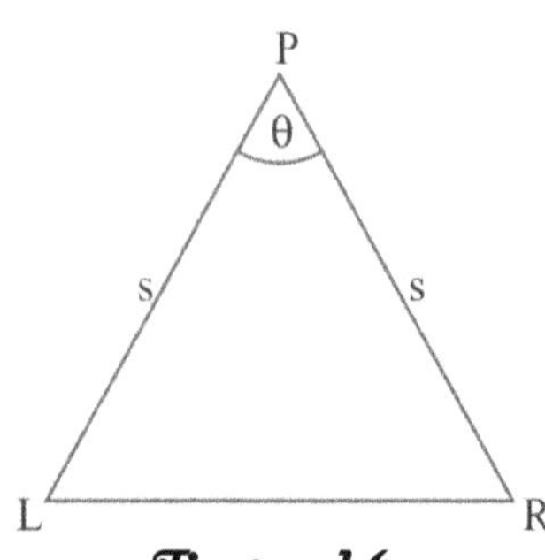

Figure. 1.6

(i)   **Distance of moon or near by heavenly body**

To measure the distance s of the moon, we observe it simultaneously from two different positions on the earth, separated by a large distance. We select a distant star (for reference) whose positon can be taken approximately same during the observations. In figure θ_1 and θ_2 are the angular positions (from reference star) of the moon taken simultaneously from A and B respectively.

The parallactic angle

$$\theta = \theta_1 + \theta_2$$

$$= \frac{\text{arc}}{\text{radius}} = \frac{b}{s}$$

$$\therefore \quad s = \frac{b}{\theta}$$

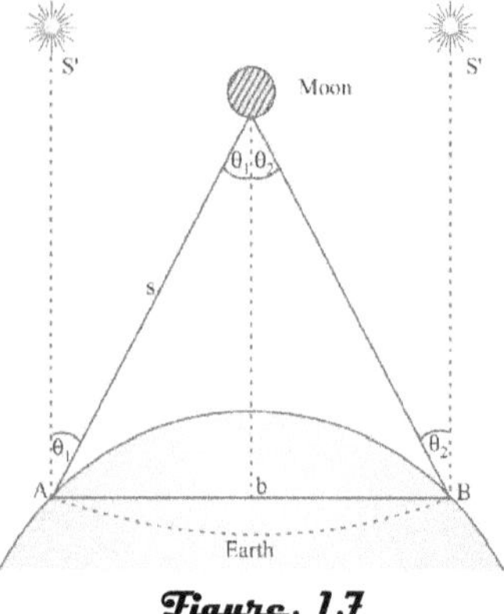

Figure. 1.7

(ii)   **Distance of a nearly star**

If figure N is the near by star whose distance s is to be found. Taking a distance star F(fixed star) whose position remains fix for all positions of the earth in its orbital motion. When the earth is at positon A, let θ_1 is the angle subtended by star from reference AF and θ_2 when earth is at the position B.

The parallactic angle $\quad \theta = \theta_1 + \theta_2$

$$= \frac{\text{Arc}}{\text{Radius}} = \frac{AB}{s}$$

$$\therefore \quad s = \frac{AB}{\theta}.$$

The distance AB is the diameter of the orbital plane of earth around sun. This method is useful for the determination of distances which are less than 100 light years away from the earth.

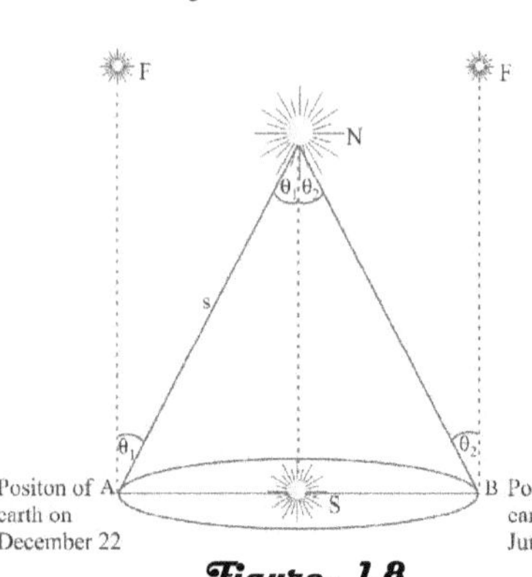

Figure. 1.8

Note: For a star more than 100 light years away, the parallax angle is so small that it cannot be measured accurately.

Reflection method

In this method waves are to be send towards the obstruction and time of reflected waves is to be noted. If t is the time the waves taken and v is the speed, then

$$s = \frac{vt}{2}.$$

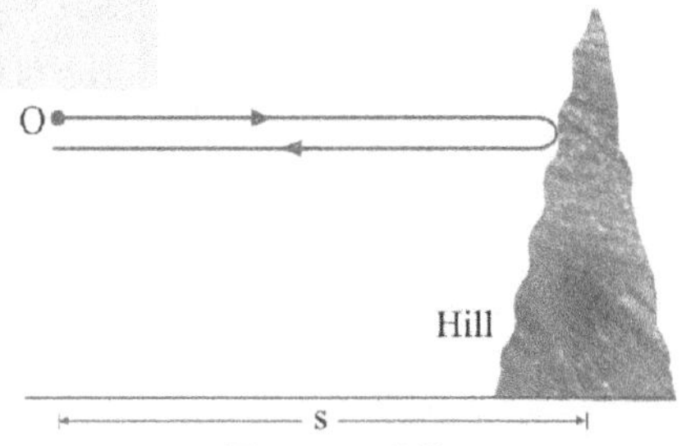

Figure. 1.9

(i) **LASER method :** The word LASER stands for Light Amplification by Stimulated Emission of Radiation. The Laser light can travel long distances without fading its intensity. A laser beam is sent towards the object (moon etc) whose distance is to be measured and its reflected pulse is received. If t is the time elapsed between the instants the laser beam is sent and return back, then the distance of the moon from the earth is given by

$$s = \frac{ct}{2}, \text{ where } c \text{ is the speed of light, which is } 3 \times 10^8 \text{ m/s.}$$

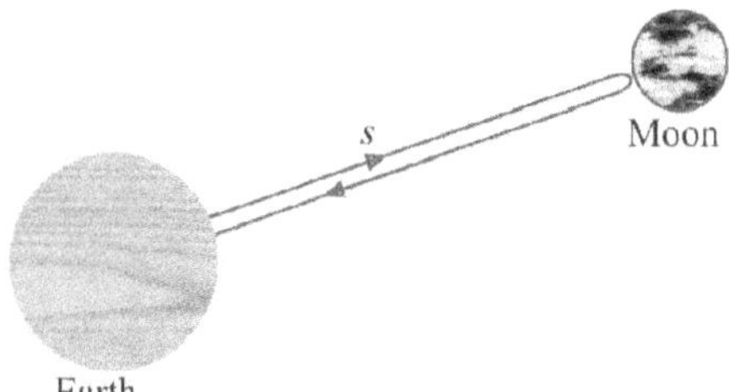

Figure. 1.10

(ii) **RADAR method :** The word RADAR stands for Radio Detection and Ranging. A radar can be used to measure accurately the distance of an aeroplane etc. Radiowaves are sent from a transmitter which after reflection from the aeroplane are detected by the receiver. If t is the time between the instants the radiowaves are sent and received, then the distance of the aeroplane is given by

$$s = \frac{ct}{2}, \text{ where } c = 3 \times 10^8 \text{ m/s is the speed radio waves.}$$

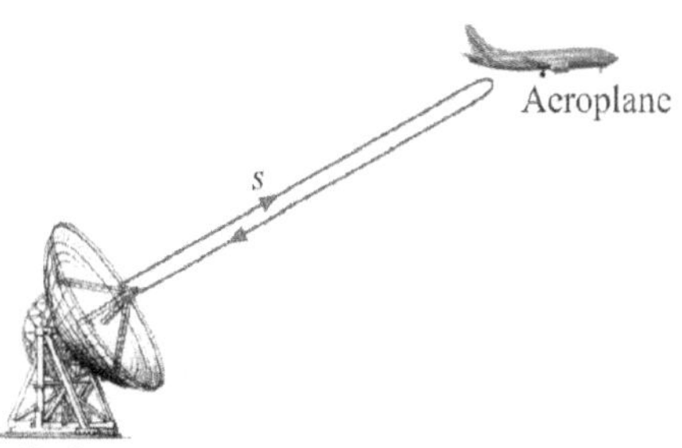

Figure. 1.11

(iii) **SONAR method :** The word SONAR stands for Sound Navigation And Ranging. This method is used to detect the submarines or to find the depth of sea. Ultrasonic waves (waves of frequency greater than 20000 Hz) are sent into the sea; they are reflected by the bottom of sea and received by the receiver. Transmitter and receiver are set into the ship. If t is the time taken by the ultrasonic waves from the instant of transmission to receiving, then depth of sea is given by

$$s = \frac{vt}{2}$$

where v is the speed of sound waves in water, which is nearly 1498 m/s.

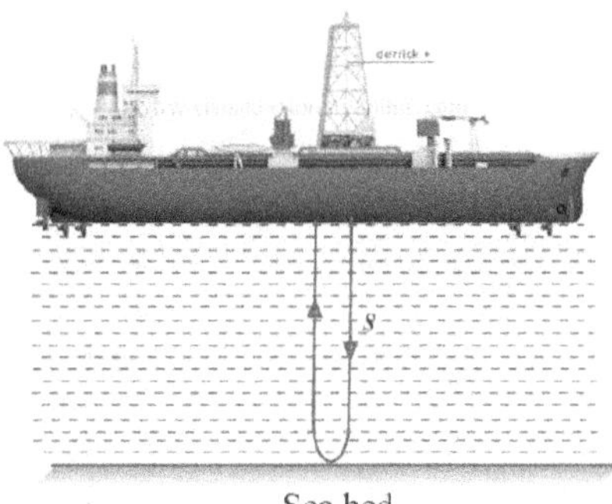

Figure. 1.12

1.11 INDIRECT METHOD OF MEASURING SMALL DISTANCES

Atomic radius by Avogadro's hypothesis

When large number of atoms are packed together, some empty spaces are left between them. According to Avogadro's hypothesis, the actual volume occupied by the atoms is two third of the volume of the substance.

If M be the molecular mass of a substance, then number of atoms in it is N (Avogadro number). Consider m gm of the substance.

$$\text{The number of moles in the substance} = \frac{m}{M},$$

$$\text{and the number of atoms in it} = \frac{mN}{M}$$

If r is the radius of the each atom, then volume of the atoms in the substance

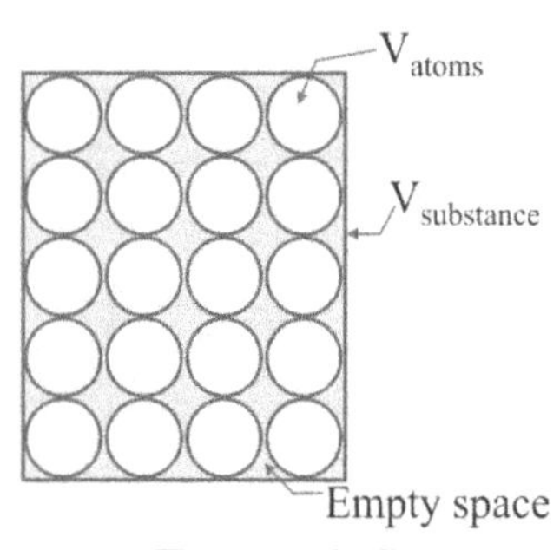

Figure. 1.13

$$V_{atoms} = \left(\frac{mN}{M}\right) \times \frac{4}{3}\pi r^3 \qquad \ldots (i)$$

If ρ is the density of the substance, then its volume

$$V_{substance} = \frac{m}{\rho} \qquad \ldots(ii)$$

According to Avogadro's hypothesis

$$V_{atoms} = \frac{2}{3}V_{substance}$$

or

$$\left(\frac{mN}{M}\right) \times \frac{4}{3}\pi r^3 = \frac{2}{3}\frac{m}{\rho}$$

or

$$r = \left[\frac{M}{2\pi N\rho}\right]^{1/3}$$

1.12 VERNIER CALLIPERS AND CCREW GAUGE

Introduction : The metre scale which commonly used in practice is the simplest instrument for measuring length. By metre scale we can measure upto 1 mm because the length of the smallest division made on the scale is 1 mm. In order to measure still smaller lengths accurately upto $\left(\frac{1}{10}\right)$th or $\left(\frac{1}{100}\right)$th of a millimeter, the instruments commonly used in laboratory are :

1. Vernier callipers
2. Screw gauge

Vernier callipers

It was invented by French Mathematician Pierre Vernier and hence the instrument is named Vernier. It is used to measure accurately upto $\left(\frac{1}{10}\right)$th of millimeter.

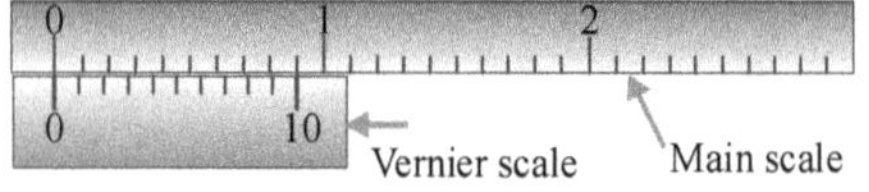

Figure. 1.14

Vernier callipers comprises of two scales, viz., main scale S and vernier scale V which is called auxiliary scale. The main scale is fixed but the vernier scale is movable. The divisions of vernier scale are usually a little smaller in size than the smallest division on the main scale. It also has two jaws, one attached with the main scale and other with the vernier scale. The purpose of jaws are to grip the object between them. Vernier has a strip, which slide along with vernier scale, over the main scale. This strip is used to measure the depth of hollow object.

Construction : The main parts of Vernier callipers are :

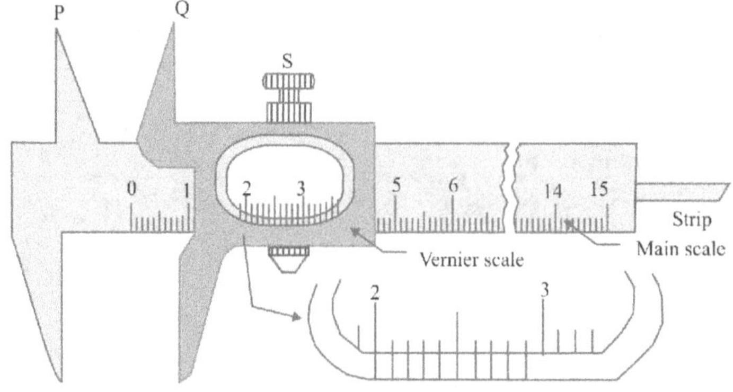

Figure. 1.15

Vernier constant (*VC*) : Suppose the size of one main scale division is S and that of one vernier scale division is V units. Also suppose that length of n vernier division is equal to the length of $(n-1)$ division of main scale. Thus we have

$$(n-1)\,S = n\,V$$

or
$$nS - S = n\,V$$

or
$$S - V = \frac{S}{n}$$

The quantity $(S-V)$ is called vernier constant (VC).

Least count : The smallest value of a physical quantity which can be measured accurately with an instrument is called the least count (LC) of the instrument. For vernier callipers, its least count is equal to its vernier constant. Thus

$$\text{Least count} = S - V = \frac{S}{n}$$

or $LC =$ [length of one division of main scale – length of one division of vernier scale]

$$= \frac{\text{length of one division of main scale}}{\text{number of divisions on vernier scale}}$$

Reading a vernier : Suppose that while measuring the length of an object, the positions of the main scale and vernier scale are shown in figure. First of all we read the position of the zero of the vernier on the main scale. As it is clear that the zero position of the vernier lies between 4.2 cm and 4.3 cm. In fact the objective of the instrument is to measure accurately small length 'x' which lies between zero mark of the vernier scale and 4.2 cm mark on the main scale. We can see that x can not be read directly on the main scale, as this scale is smaller than the smallest division on the main scale.

Next find out which division on the vernier scale exactly coincides with some division of the main scale. In figure it is quite clear that 3rd division of vernier scale coincide with some division of the main scale. Therefore, the value of length x will be given by the relation :

4.2 cm $+ x + 3$ vernier scale division $= 4.2$ cm $+ 3$ main scale division

$\Rightarrow$
$$\begin{aligned}
x &= 3 \text{ main scale division} - 3 \text{ vernier scale division} \\
&= 3\,(1 \text{ main scale division} - 1 \text{ vernier scale division}) \\
&= 3\,(0.10 - 0.09) \\
&= 3 \times 0.01 \\
&= 0.03
\end{aligned}$$

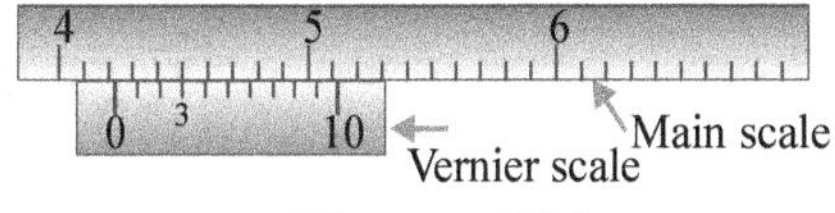

Figure. 1.16

$\therefore$ The required length is given by
$$\begin{aligned}
L &= 4.2 + 0.03 \\
&= 4.23 \text{ cm}
\end{aligned}$$

Thus,   Length of the object = Main scale reading $+ n\,(LC)$

Where n, vernier division exactly coinciding with some main scale division.

Determination of zero error : When jaws of the vernier are made touch each other and the zero mark of the vernier scale coincide with the zero mark of the main scale, there will no zero error in the instrument. However, in practice it is never so. Due to wear and tear of the jaws and due to some manufacturing defect, the zero mark of the main scale and vernier scale may not coincide, it give rise to an error, is called zero error. It may be positive or negative zero error.

Positive and negative zero error : When the zero mark of the vernier scale lies towards the right side of the zero of main scale when jaws are in contact, the measured length will be greater than the actual length. Because of this fact the zero error is called positive zero error. On the other hand, when zero mark of the vernier scale lies towards the left side of the zero of the main scale when jaws in contact with each other, the length of the object measured by the instrument will be less than the actual length of the object. Because of this reason is called negative zero error.

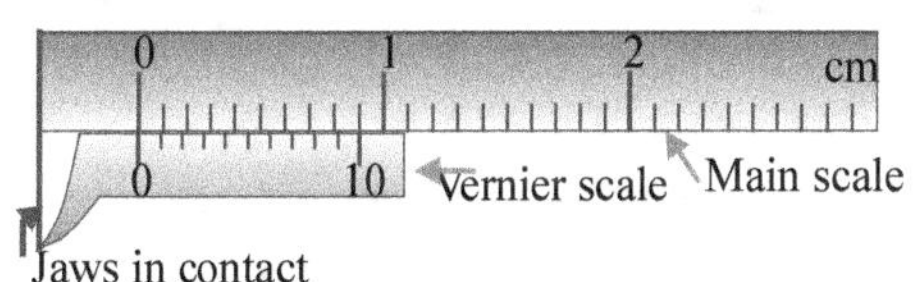

No zero error of the vernier calliper
Figure. 1.17

True reading = Observed reading – Zero error with proper sign

Correction for positive zero error : Let us see the vernier callipers, shown in figure. When its jaws are in contact with each other, suppose 3rd vernier division coincides with the any of the division of main scale. Thus we have

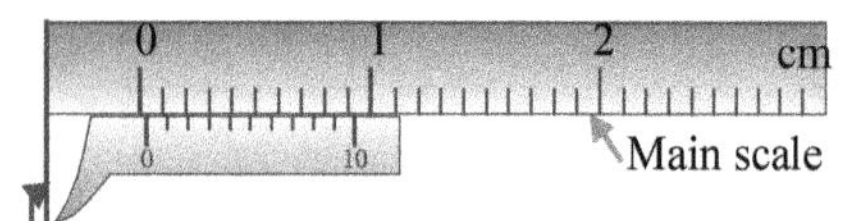

Jaws in contact   **Third division coinciding**

Figure. 1.18

$$\text{Zero error} = + [0.00 \text{ cm} + 3\,(LC)]$$
$$= + [0.00 + 3 \times 0.01 \text{ cm}]$$
$$= + 0.03 \text{ cm}$$
$$\text{Correct reading} = \text{observed reading} - (0.03 \text{ cm})$$
$$= \text{observed reading} - 0.03 \text{ cm}$$

Correction for negative error : Let us see the vernier callipers shown in figure when jaws are in contact with each other, suppose sixth division of vernier coincides with any of the division of main scale. Thus we have

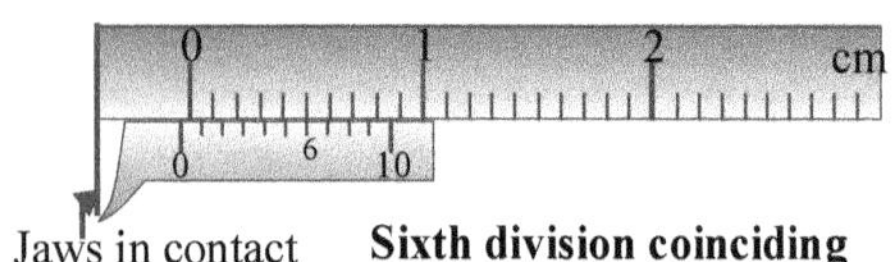

Jaws in contact   **Sixth division coinciding**

Figure. 1.19

$$\text{Zero error} = [0.00 - (10 - 6)\,LC]$$
$$= [0.00 - 4 \times 0.01]$$
$$= -0.04 \text{ cm}$$
$$\therefore \quad \text{Correct reading} = \text{observed reading} - (-0.04 \text{cm})$$
$$= \text{observed reading} + 0.04 \text{ cm}$$

Screw gauge

It is used to measure small lengths like diameter of wire or thickness of sheet etc. It consists of a U-shaped metal frame.

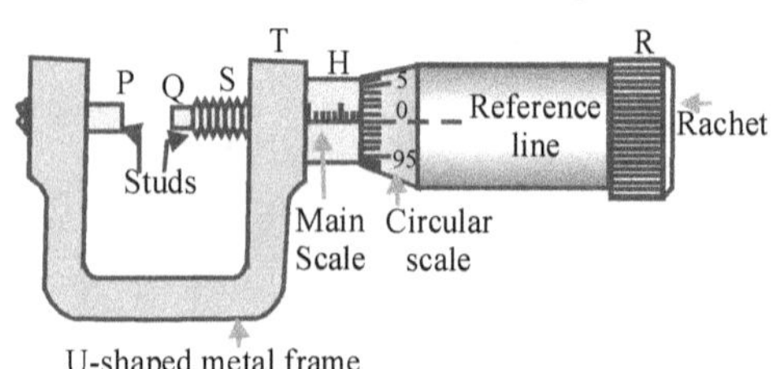

U-shaped metal frame

Figure. 1.20

A main scale which graduate in millimeter or half a millimeter. The main scale also called pitch scale. A cap fits on to the screw and carries on its inner edge H, 50 to 100 equal divisions, is called circular or head scale. The object whose length to be measured is gripped between the studs P and Q by moving the rachet R.

Pitch : It is defined as the linear distance moved by the screw forward or backward when one complete rotation is given to the circular cap.

$$\text{Least count } (LC) = \text{Pitch / [Total number of divisions on the circular scale]}$$

Zero error : When the studs P and Q of the screw gauge are brought in contact without apply induce pressure and if the zero of the circular scale coincides with the reference line, then there is no zero error, otherwise there will be zero error.

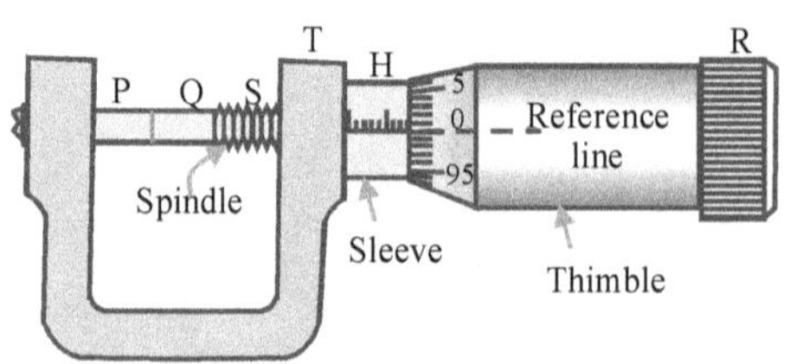

Screw gauge with no zero error

Figure. 1.21

Positive zero error : In this case, the zero of the circular scale lies below the reference line as the gap between studs P and Q reduces to zero.

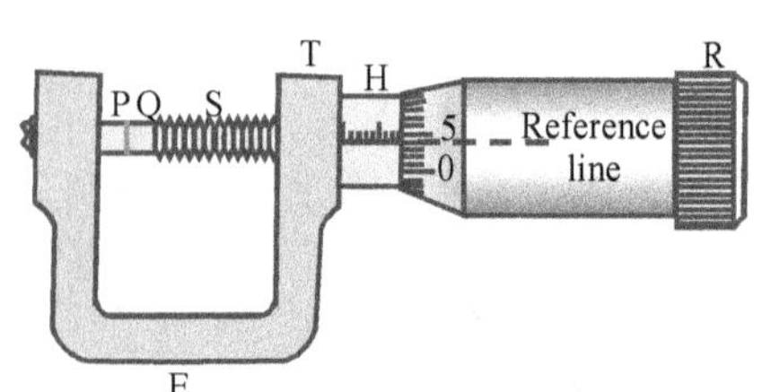

Positive zero error (4 division error) i.e., + 0.004 cm

Figure. 1.22

Let us determine the magnitude of positive error by taking an example. Suppose in a screw gauge, (when the gap between P and Q is reduced to zero) the zero line of the circular scale is 4 division below the reference line. In other words, the 4th division of the head scale is in line with the line of graduation. Thus,

$$\text{zero error} = + 4 \times (LC)$$
$$= + 4 \times (0.01 \text{ mm})$$
$$= + 0.04 \text{ mm}$$
$$\text{Zero correction} = - \text{ Zero error}$$

It must be remembered that the zero correction whether positive or negative should always be added algebraically to the observed reading to get the correct reading.

Negative zero error : In this case, the zero of the circular scale lies above the reference line when the gap between the studs P and Q become zero. Under this condition, the edge of the circular scale lies to the left hand side of the zero of the main scale. That is why it called negative zero error.

Let us determine the magnitude of the negative error with the help of an example. Suppose on reducing the gap between studs P and Q to zero, the zero line of the circular scale is 3 divisions above the reference line, i.e., 97th division of the circular scale is in line with the reference line.

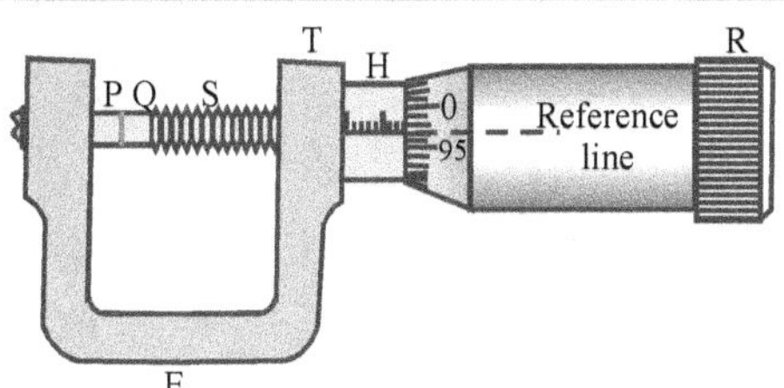

Negative zero error (3 division error) i.e., $- 0.003$ cm

Figure. 1.23

Thus　　　　　　　zero error $= (97 - 100) \times (LC)$
　　　　　　　　　　　　$= - 3 \times 0.01$ mm
　　　　　　　　　　　　$= - 0.03$ mm

Thus　　　　　　　zero error $= - 0.03$ mm
and　　　　　　　zero correction $= + 0.03$ mm.

Backlash error : Sometimes, in a screw gauge, there may be loose fitting between the screw and the nut. It is either because of wear and tear of the nut as well as that of the screw or due to some manufacturing defect. In such an instrument, if the screw is adjusted by turning it in one direction and then in opposite direction, the linear movement of the screw is not proportional to the circular motion. This implies that for no change in the gap length between the stud and the screw, the circular scale reading undergoes some appreciable change resulting in an error, is called backlash error.

FORMULAE USED

1. **The true value :** If $a_1, a_2, \dots\dots\dots, a_n$ are the observed value of a quantity, then its true value is given by

$$\bar{a} = \frac{a_1 + a_2 + \dots\dots + a_n}{n} = \sum_{i=1}^{n} a_i$$

2. Absolute error = true value – obseved value

   or　　　$\Delta a_i = \bar{a} - a_i$

3. Mean absolute error

$$\Delta\bar{a} = \frac{|\Delta a_1| + |\Delta a_2| + \dots\dots + |\Delta a_n|}{n} = \frac{1}{n}\sum_{i=1}^{n} |\Delta a_i|$$

4. Relative error $= \dfrac{\Delta\bar{a}}{\bar{a}}$, and percentage error

$$= \frac{\Delta\bar{a}}{a} \times 100$$

5. **Error in computed quantity**

   (i) If $\pm\Delta x$ and $\pm\Delta y$ be the absolute errors in X and Y respectively and

   if $Z = X + Y$, then maximum possible error in Z; $\Delta z = \pm(\Delta x + \Delta y)$

   (ii) If $Z = X - Y$, then $\Delta z = \pm(\Delta x + \Delta y)$

   (iii) If $Z = XY$, then $\dfrac{\Delta z}{Z} = \pm\left[\dfrac{\Delta x}{X} + \dfrac{\Delta y}{Y}\right]$

   (iv) If $Z = \dfrac{X}{Y}$, then $\dfrac{\Delta z}{Z} = \pm\left[\dfrac{\Delta x}{X} + \dfrac{\Delta y}{Y}\right]$

(v)　If $Z = X^n$, then $\dfrac{\Delta z}{Z} = \pm n\left[\dfrac{\Delta x}{X}\right]$

(vi)　If $Z = \dfrac{KX^a Y^b}{W^c}$, then　$\dfrac{\Delta z}{Z} = \pm\left[a\dfrac{\Delta x}{X} + b\dfrac{\Delta y}{Y} + c\dfrac{\Delta w}{W}\right]$

The absolute error has the same unit as the quantity itself, but fractional error has no unit.

6.　If $Z = \dfrac{XY}{X+Y}$, then $\dfrac{\Delta z}{Z} = \pm\left[\dfrac{\Delta x}{X} + \dfrac{\Delta y}{Y} + \dfrac{(\Delta x + \Delta y)}{X+Y}\right]$

7.　**Least count of vernier callipers**

L.C. = Length of one division of main scale – length of one division of vernier scale

or　L.C. = $\dfrac{\text{Length of one division of main scale}}{\text{number of divisions on Vernier scale}}$

8.　**Least count of a screw gauge**

L.C. = $\dfrac{\text{Pitch}}{[\text{total number of divisions on the circular scale}]}$

EXAMPLES BASED ON INSTRUMENTS AND ERRORS

Example 14. It is claimed that two cesium clocks, if allowed to run for 100 years, free from any disturbance, may differ by only about 0.025 s. What does this imply for the accuracy of the standard cesium clock in measuring a time interval of 1 s?

[NCERT]

Sol. Error in 100 years = 0.02 s

∴　Error in 1 sec

$\dfrac{\Delta t}{t} = \dfrac{0.02}{100 \times 365 \times 2.5 \times 24 \times 60 \times 60}$

$= \dfrac{0.02}{3.5576 \times 10^9}$

$= 0.0063 \times 10^{-9} = 0.63 \times 10^{-11}$

So, there is an accuracy of 1s is 10^{-11}s.

Example 15. A physical quantity P is related to four observations a, b, c and d as follows : $P = \dfrac{a^3 b^2}{\sqrt{c}\, d}$.

The percentage errors of measurement in a, b, c and d are 1%, 3%, 4% and 2% respectively. What is the percentage error in the quantity P? If the value of P calculated using the above relation turns out to be 3.763, to what value should you round off the result?

Sol. Given　$P = \dfrac{a^3 b^2}{\sqrt{c}\, d}$

The maximum possible percentage error in P is given by

$\dfrac{\Delta P}{P} \times 100 = \pm\left[3\dfrac{\Delta a}{a} + 2\dfrac{\Delta b}{b} + \dfrac{1}{2}\dfrac{\Delta c}{c} + \dfrac{\Delta d}{d}\right] \times 100$

$= \pm[3 \times 1\% + 2 \times 3\% + \dfrac{1}{2} \times 4\% + 2\%]$

$= \pm 13\%$

or　$\Delta P = \pm 0.13$

There are two significant figures in 0.13. Hence P should also be rounded off to 2 significant figures

∴　P = 3.763 = 3.8　*Ans.*

Example 16. Which of the following is the most precise device for measuring length?

(a)　a Vernier callipers with 20 divisions on the sliding scale coinciding with 19 main scale division

(b)　a screw gauge of pitch 1 mm and 100 divisions on the circular scale

(c)　an optical instrument that can measure length within a wavelength of light ?　[NCERT]

Sol.

(a)　Least count of Vernier callipers = 1 SD – 1 VD

$= 1\ \text{SD} - \dfrac{19}{20}\,\text{SD} = \dfrac{1}{20}\,\text{SD} = \dfrac{1}{20}\ \text{mm}$

$= 0.005\ \text{cm}$

(b)　Least count of screw gauge

$= \dfrac{\text{pitch}}{\text{no. of division on circular scale}}$

$= \dfrac{1}{100}\ \text{mm} = 0.001\ \text{cm}$

(c)　Wavelength of light, $\lambda = 10^{-5}$ cm = 0.00001 cm

Since most precise device should have minimum least count, optical instrument is the most precise one.

Example 17.　Answer the following :

(a)　**You are given a thread and a metre scale. How will you estimate the diameter of the thread?**

(b) A screw gauge has a pitch of 1.0 mm and 200 divisions on the circular scale. Do you think it is possible to increase the accuracy of the screw gauge arbitrarily by increasing the number of divisions on the circular scale?

(c) The mean diameter of a thin brass rod is to be measured by Vernier callipers. Why is a set of 100 measurements of the diameter expected to yield a more reliable estimate than a set of 5 measurements only?   **[NCERT]**

Sol.(a) Meter scale can not measure small diameter of thread. No. of turns of the thread to be wound to get turns closely one another.

Let l– measured length of windings on the scale which contains n no. of turns.

$\therefore$ Diameter of thread $= \dfrac{l}{n}$.

(b) Least count

$$= \dfrac{\text{pitch}}{\text{no. of division in circular scale}}$$

i.e. least count decreases when no. of division on the circular scale increases. Thereby accuracy would increase. but practically, it is impossible to take precise reading due to low resolution of human eye.

(c) Large no. of observations (say 100) gives more reliable result, because probability of making random error in positive side of a physical quantity would be same that of in negative side. Therefore, when no. of observations is large random errors would cancel each other and hence result would be reliable.

Example 18. One mole of an ideal gas at standard temperature and pressure occupies 22.4 L (molar volume). What is the ratio of molar volume to the atomic volume of a mole of hydrogen? (Take the size of hydrogen molecule to be about 1 Å). Why is this ratio so large?   **[NCERT]**

Sol. Volume of one mole of ideal gas, V_g

$$= 22.4 \text{ litre} = 22.4 \times 10^{-3} \text{m}^3$$

Radius of hydrogen molecule $= \dfrac{1\text{Å}}{2}$

$$= 0.5 \text{ Å} = 0.5 \times 10^{-10} \text{ m}$$

Volume of hydrogen molecule $= \dfrac{4}{3}\pi r^3$

$$= \dfrac{4}{3} \times \dfrac{22}{7} \left(0.5 \times 10^{-10}\right)^3 \text{m}^3$$

$$= 0.5238 \times 10^{-30} \text{ m}^3$$

One mole contains 6.023×10^{23} molecules.

$\therefore$ Volume of one mole of hydrogen,

$$V_H = 0.5238 \times 10^{-30} \times 6.023 \times 10^{23} \text{ m}^3$$

$$= 3.1548 \times 10^{-7} \text{ m}^3$$

Now, $\dfrac{V_g}{V_H} = \dfrac{22.4 \times 10^{-3}}{3.1548 \times 10^{-7}} = 7.1 \times 10^4$

The ratio is very large. This is because the interatomic separation in the gas is very large compared to the size of a hydrogen molecule.

Example 19. The shadow of a tower standing on a level plane is found to be 100 m longer when sun's altitude is 30° than when it is 60°. Find the height of the tower.

Sol. If h is the height of tower, then

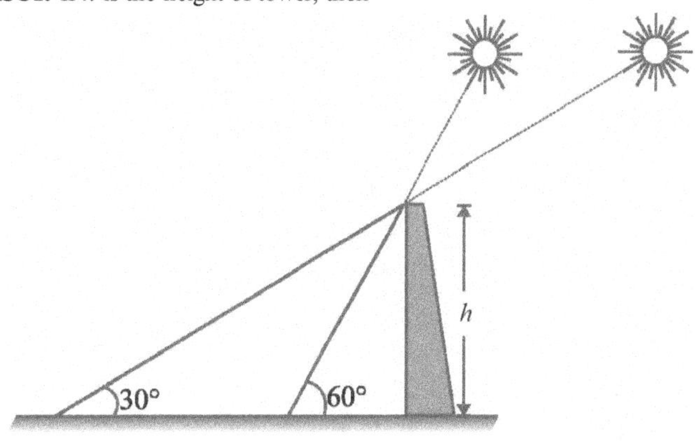

Figure. 1.24

$$h = \dfrac{d}{\cot\theta_2 - \cot\theta_1}$$

$$= \dfrac{100}{\cot 30° - \cot 60°}$$

$$= 50\sqrt{3} \qquad\qquad Ans$$

Example 20. When the planet Jupiter is at a distance of 824.7 million kilometers from the earth, its angular diameter is measured to be 35.72 s of arc. Calculate the diameter of Jupiter.

Sol. The distance of Jupiter from the earth

$$s = 824.7 \times 10^6 \text{ km}$$

Angular diameter $\quad \theta = 35.72''$

$$= \left(\dfrac{35.72}{60 \times 60}\right) \times \dfrac{\pi}{180} \text{ rad}$$

Figure. 1.25

Diameter of Jupiter $\quad D = s\,\theta$

$$= 824.7 \times 10^6 \times \left(\dfrac{35.72}{60 \times 60}\right) \times \dfrac{\pi}{180}$$

$$= 148217.8 \text{ km}$$

Example 21. In a submarine equipped with a SONAR, the time delay between generation of a probe wave and the reception of its echo after reflection from an enemy submarine is found to be 77s. What is the distance of the enemy submarine? (speed of sound in water = 1450 m/s)

Sol. The distance of enemy submarine is given by

$$s = \dfrac{vt}{2}$$

$$= \dfrac{1450 \times 77}{2} = 55825 \text{ m} \qquad Ans.$$

Example 22. One mole of an ideal gas at STP occupies 22.4 L. What is the ratio of molar volume to the atomic volume of a mole of hydrogen? Why is this ratio so large ? Take the radius of hydrogen molecule to be 1 Å.

Sol. Radius of a hydrogen molecule

$$r = 1 \text{ Å} = 10^{-10} \text{ m}$$

Atomic volume of 1 mole of hydrogen

$$= N \times \frac{4}{3}\pi r^3 = 6.023 \times 10^{23} \times \frac{4}{3}\pi \times (10^{-10})^3$$

$$= 25.2 \times 10^{-7} \text{ m}^3$$

Molar volume $= 22.4 \text{ L} = 22.4 \times 10^{-3} \text{ m}^3$

$$\therefore \quad \frac{\text{Molar volume}}{\text{atomic volume}} = \frac{22.4 \times 10^{-3}}{25.2 \times 10^{-7}} = 0.89 \times 10^4 \simeq 10^4$$

This ratio is so large because the actual size of the gas molecules is negligible small in comparision to the intermolecular separation.

Example 23. The unit of length convenient on the unclear scale is a fermi: 1f $= 10^{-15}$ m. Nuclear sizes obey roughly the following empirical relation $r = r_0 A^{1/3}$; where r is the radius of the nucleus, A its mass number and r_0 is a constant equal to about 1.2 f. Show that the rule implies that nuclear mass density is nearly constant for different nuclei. Estimate the mass density of sodium nucleus.

Sol. Given radius of nucleus,

$$r = r_0 A^{1/3}$$

Mass of the nucleus $= \dfrac{\text{Mass number}}{\text{Avogadro's number}}$

$$= \frac{A}{N}$$

Nuclear mass density $= \dfrac{\text{Mass of nucleus}}{\text{volume of nucleus}}$

or $\qquad \rho = \dfrac{A/N}{\dfrac{4}{3}\pi r^3}$

or $\qquad \rho = \dfrac{A}{N\dfrac{4}{3}\pi (r_0 A^{1/3})^3}$

$$= \frac{3}{4\pi N r_0^3}$$

$$= \frac{3}{4\pi \times 6.02 \times 10^{23} \times (1.2 \times 10^{-15})^3}$$

$$= 2.3 \times 10^{17} \text{ kg /m}^3$$

Example 24. In four complete revolution of the cap, the distance travelled on the pitch scale is 2 mm. If there are 50 divisions on the circular scale, then calculate the least count of the screw gauge.

Sol. $\qquad$ Pitch $= \dfrac{\text{distance travelled on pitch scale}}{\text{number of rotations}}$

$$= \frac{2\text{mm}}{4} = 0.5 \text{ mm}$$

Least count $= \dfrac{\text{pitch}}{\text{number of divisions on circular scale}}$

$$= \frac{0.5\text{mm}}{50} = 0.01 \text{ mm}$$

In Chapter Exercise 1.2

1. Times for 20 oscillations of a pendulum is measured as t_1 = 39.6 s; t_2 = 39.9 s; t_3 = 39.5 s. What is the precision in the measurement? What is the accuracy of the measurement?

    Ans. ± 0.2 s $\qquad$ **[NCERT Exemplar]**

2. A physical quantity x is related to four measurable quantities a, b, c and d as follows

    $$x = a^2 b^3 c^{5/2} d^{-2}$$

    The percentage error in the measurement of a, b, c and d are 1%, 2%, 3% and 4% respectively. What is the percentage error in quantity x? If the value of x calculated on the basis of the above relation is 2.763, to what value should you round-off the result? *Ans.* $x = 2.8$ **[NCERT Exemplar]**

3. Each side of a cube is measured to be 7.203 m. What are the total surface area and the volume of the cube to appropriate significant figures ? *Ans.* 311.3m^2, 373.7 m^3.

4. The farthest objects in our universe discovered by modern astronomers are so distant that light emitted by them takes billions of years to reach the earth. These objects (known as quasars) have many puzzling features which have not yet been satisfactorily explained. What is the distance in km of a quasar from which light takes 3.0 billion years to reach us? **[NCERT]**

    Ans. **284 × 10²² km**

5. In an experiment, refractive index of glass was observed to be 1.45, 1.56, 1.54, 1.44, 1.54 and 1.53. Calculate (i) mean value of refractive index (ii) mean absolute error (iii) fractional effort (iv) percentage error. Express the result in terms of absolute error and percentage error.

    Ans. (i) 1.51 (ii) $\simeq$ 0.04 (iii) 0.03 (iv) 3%

    $\mu = 1.51 \pm 0.04,\ 1.51 \pm 3\%$.

EXAMPLES FOR JEE-(MAIN AND ADVANCED)

Example 1. The speed of light c, gravitational constant G and Plank's constant h are taken as the fundamental units in a system. Find the dimensions of length and time in this new system of unit.

Sol. Dimension of

$$c = [LT^{-1}] \qquad ....(i)$$
$$G = [M^{-1}L^3T^{-2}] \qquad ....(ii)$$
$$\text{and} \quad h = [ML^2T^{-1}] \qquad ....(iii)$$

From equation (i),

$$c^3 = [L^3T^{-3}]$$

And from equations (ii) & (iii), we have

$$Gh = [L^5T^{-3}]$$

$$\therefore \quad \frac{Gh}{c^3} = L^2$$

which gives $\quad L = G^{1/2}h^{1/2}c^{-3/2}$

Again from equation (i),

$$T = \frac{\text{length}}{\text{speed}}$$

$$= \frac{G^{1/2}h^{1/2}c^{-3/2}}{c}$$

$$= G^{1/2}h^{1/2}c^{-5/2} \qquad \textbf{\textit{Ans.}}$$

Example 2. By the method of dimension test the accuracy of the equation $\delta = \dfrac{mg\,\ell^3}{4bd^3Y}$, where δ is the depression produced in the middle of a bar of length ℓ, breath b and depth d, when it is loaded in the middle with mass m. Y is the Young's modulus of the material of the bar.

Sol. The dimensions of left hand side of the equation

$$\text{LHS} \qquad \delta = [L]$$

and

$$\text{RHS} = \frac{mg\,\ell^3}{4bd^3Y}$$

$$= \left[\frac{M.LT^{-2}.L^3}{L.L^3.ML^{-1}.T^{-2}}\right] = L$$

Dimensions of LHS = dimensions of RHS, therefore the above equation is dimensionally correct.

Example 3. Given that the period T of oscillation of a gas bubble from an explosion under water depends upon p, d and E, where p is the static pressure, d is the density of water and E is the total energy of explosion, find dimensionally a relation of T.

Sol. Suppose, $\qquad T = k\, p^a\, d^b\, E^c$

Substituting dimensions of all quantities in above equation,

$$[M^0L^0T^1] = [ML^{-1}T^{-2}]^a [ML^{-3}]^b [ML^2T^{-2}]^c$$

$$\text{or} \quad [M^0L^0T^1] = [M^{a+b+c}L^{-a-3b+2c}T^{-2a-2c}]$$

Equating the powers of M, L and T, we have

$$a + b + c = 0$$
$$-a - 3b + 2c = 0$$
$$\text{and} \quad -2a - 2c = 1$$

After solving above equations, we get

$$a = -\frac{5}{6},\, b = \frac{1}{2} \text{ and } c = \frac{1}{3}$$

Therefore required relation is

$$T = k\frac{d^{1/2}E^{1/3}}{p^{5/6}} \qquad \textbf{\textit{Ans.}}$$

Example 4. In the gas equation $\left(p + \dfrac{a}{V^2}\right)(V-b) = R\theta$, where θ is absolute temperature, p is pressure and V is volume, what are dimensions of constants a?

Sol. According to principle of homogeneity of dimensions;

$$\text{Dimensions of } b = \text{Dimensions of } V$$
$$= [L^3]$$

$$\text{Dimensions of } \frac{a}{V^2} = \text{Dimensions of } p$$

Hence, dimensions of $a = $ (Dimensions of p) $\times$ (Dimensions of V^2)

$$= [ML^{-1}T^{-2}]\,[L^3]^2$$
$$= ML^5T^{-2} \qquad \textbf{\textit{Ans.}}$$

Example 5. Pressure P varies as $P = \dfrac{\alpha}{\beta}\exp\left(-\dfrac{\alpha Z}{k_\beta\theta}\right)$, where Z denotes the distance, k_β is Boltzmann's constant, θ is absolute temperature and α, β are constant. Find dimensions of β.

Sol. We know that power of exponent is a dimensionless number

$$\therefore \quad \frac{\alpha Z}{k_\beta\theta} = M^0L^0T^0$$

$$\text{or} \quad \alpha = [M^0L^0T^0]\left[\frac{k_\beta\theta}{Z}\right]$$

$$= [M^0L^0T^0]\left[\frac{ML^2T^{-2}}{L}\right]$$

$$= [MLT^{-2}]$$

$$\text{Dimensions of } \frac{\alpha}{\beta} = \text{Dimensions of } P.$$

$$\therefore \quad \text{Dimensions of } \beta = \frac{\text{dimensions of } \alpha}{\text{dimensions of } P}$$

$\therefore$ Dimensions of β $= \dfrac{[MLT^{-2}]}{[ML^{-1}T^{-2}]} = [M^0 L^2 T^0]$

Example 6. If two resistors of resistances $R_1 = (4 \pm 0.5)\ \Omega$ and $R_2 = (16 \pm 0.5)\ \Omega$ are connected (i) in series and (ii) in parallel; find the equivalent resistance in each case with limits of percentage error.

Sol. (i)   In series, the equivalent resistance
$$R = R_1 + R_2 = 4 + 16 = 20\ \Omega$$

$\therefore$ $\dfrac{\Delta R}{R} \times 100 = \pm \left[\dfrac{\Delta R_1 + \Delta R_2}{R_1 + R_2} \right] \times 100$

$$= \pm \left[\dfrac{0.5 + 0.5}{4 + 16} \right] \times 100 = \pm 5\%$$

$\therefore$ Equivalent resistance in series $R = (20 \pm 5\%)\Omega$

(ii)   In parallel, the equivalent resistance

$$R = \dfrac{R_1 R_2}{R_1 + R_2} = \dfrac{4 \times 16}{4 + 16} = 3.2\ \Omega$$

$\therefore$ $\dfrac{\Delta R}{R} \times 100 = \pm \left[\dfrac{\Delta R_1}{R_1} + \dfrac{\Delta R_2}{R_2} + \dfrac{\Delta R_1 + \Delta R_2}{R_1 + R_2} \right] \times 100$

$$= \pm \left[\dfrac{0.5}{4} + \dfrac{0.5}{16} + \dfrac{0.5 + 0.5}{4 + 16} \right] \times 100 = 20.625\ \%$$

$\therefore$ Equivalent resistance in parallel $= (3.2 \pm 20.625\%)\ \Omega$

Example 7. Graph of position of image vs position of point object from a convex lens is shown. Find, focal length of the lens with possible error.   **[IIT-JEE 2006]**

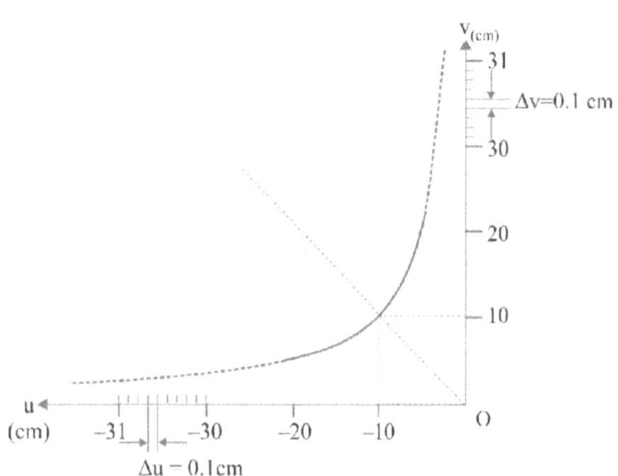

Figure. 1.26

Sol. We know that

$$\dfrac{1}{f} = \dfrac{1}{v} - \dfrac{1}{u} = \dfrac{1}{10} - \dfrac{1}{-10}$$

$\therefore$ $f = 5$ cm

Also, $\dfrac{1}{f} = \dfrac{1}{v} - \dfrac{1}{-u}$

or $f = \dfrac{uv}{u + v}$

$\therefore$ $\dfrac{\Delta f}{f} = \pm \left[\dfrac{\Delta u}{u} + \dfrac{\Delta v}{v} + \dfrac{\Delta u + \Delta v}{u + v} \right]$

where $\Delta u = 0.1$ cm and $\Delta v = 0.1$ cm

$\therefore$ $\dfrac{\Delta f}{f} = \pm \left[\dfrac{0.1}{10} + \dfrac{0.1}{10} + \dfrac{0.1 + 0.1}{10 + 10} \right]$

$$= \pm 0.03$$

and $\Delta f = \pm 0.03\ f$

$$= \pm 0.03 \times 5 = \pm 0.15\ cm$$

Thus the focal length of lens $f = (5.00 \pm 0.15)$cm   *Ans.*

Example 8. While measuring the length of the rod by vernier callipers the reading on main scale is 6.4 cm and the eight division on vernier is in line with marking on main scale division. If the least count of callipers is 0.01 and zero error –0.04 cm, find the length of the rod.

Sol.   Lenght of the rod = observed reading – zero error

= (Main scale division + Vernier scale division $\times LC$) – Zero error

$$= (6.4 + 8 \times 0.01) - (-0.04)$$
$$= 6.4 + 0.08 + 0.04 = 6.52\ \text{cm} \quad \textit{Ans.}$$

Example 9. The length of a cube is measured with the help of a vernier callipers. The observations are shown in figure. Find length of the cube with these observations.

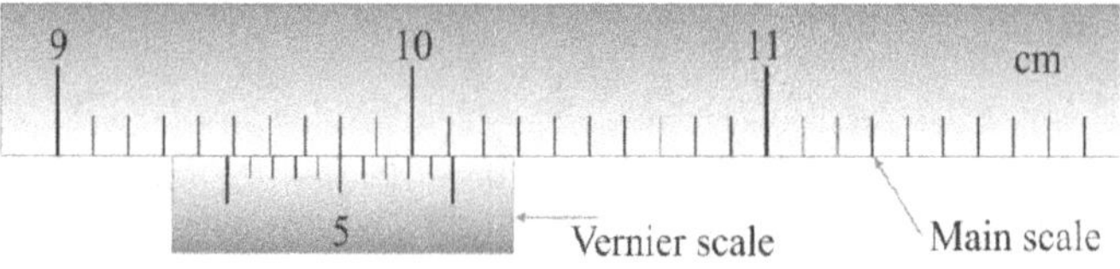

Figure. 1.27

Sol. LC of the vernier callipers = 1 cm / 10 = 0.1 cm

Main scale reading = 9.4 cm

Vernier scale reading coinciding with main scale = 5

Length of the cube = Main scale divisions + Vernier scale divisions $\times LC$

$$= 9.4 + 5 \times 0.01 = 9.45\ \text{cm} \quad \textit{Ans.}$$

Example 10. The circular head of a screw gauge is divided into 200 divisions and move 1 mm ahead in one revolution. Find the pitch and least count of the screw gauge. If the same instrument has a zero error of –0.05 mm and the reading on the main scale in measuring diameter of a wire is 6 mm and that on circular scale is 45, find the diameter of the wire.

Sol.   Pitch $= 1$ mm

Number of divisions on circular scale = 200

$$LC = \dfrac{\text{pitch}}{\text{number of divisions on circular scale}}$$

$$= \dfrac{1\ \text{mm}}{200} = 0.005\ \text{mm} = 0.0005\ \text{cm} \quad \textit{Ans.}$$

Diameter of the wire

= (Main scale reading + Circular scale reading $\times LC$) – Zero error

$$= 6\ \text{mm} + 45 \times 0.005 - (-0.05)$$
$$= 6\ \text{mm} + 0.225\ \text{mm} + 0.05\ \text{mm}$$
$$= 6.275\ \text{mm} \quad \textit{Ans.}$$

| Mechanics | MCQ Type 1 | Exercise 1.1 |

Units and Dimensions

1. Which of the following statements is correct about a scalar quantity:
(i)   it remain conserved in a process
(ii) can never take negative sign
(iii) does not vary from one place to another in space
(iv) has same value for observers with different orientation of axis
(a) (i) (b) (ii)
(c) (iii) (d) (iv)

2. Which of the following is not the unit of time
(a) Micro second (b) Leap year
(c) Lunar month (d) Parallactic second

3. Temperature can be expressed as a derived quantity in terms of any of the following
(a) length and mass (b) mass and time
(c) length, mass and time (d) none of these

4. With the usual notations, the following equation
$$S_1 = u + \frac{1}{2}a(2t-1) \text{ is}$$
(a) only numerically correct
(b) only dimensionally correct
(c) both numerically and dimensionally correct
(d) neither numerically nor dimensionally correct

5. Which of the following readings is the most accurate
(i)   4000 m (ii) 40×10^2 m
(iii) 4×10^3 m (iv) 0.4×10^4 m
(a) (i) (b) (ii)
(c) (iii) (d) (iv)

6. If unit of length and force are increased 4 times. The unit of energy:
(a) is increased by 4 times
(b) is increased by 16 times
(c) is increased by 8 times
(d) remain unchanged

7. Which one of the following is a set of dimensionless physical quantities :
(a) strain, specific gravity, angle
(b) strain, work, couple
(c) work, angle, specific gravity
(d) work, energy, frequency

8. Which one of the following does not have the same dimensions
(a) work and energy
(b) angle and strain
(c) relative density and refractive index
(d) plank constant and energy

9. The density of a material in CGS system is 8 g / cm^3. In a system of a unit in which unit of length is 5 cm and unit of mass is 20 g. The density of material is :
(a) 8 (b) 20
(c) 50 (d) 80

10. In a new system the unit of mass is α kg, unit of length is β m and unit of time is γ s. The value of 1 J in this new system is **[AMU B.Tech. 2012]**
(a) $\gamma^2/\alpha\beta^2$ (b) $\gamma\alpha/\beta^2$
(c) $\alpha\beta\gamma$ (d) $\alpha\gamma^2/\beta^2$

11. A boy recalls the relation almost correctly but forgets where to put the constant c (speed of light). He writes;
$$m = \frac{m_0}{\sqrt{1-v^2}},$$ where m and m_0 stand for masses and v for speed. Right place of c is
(a) $m = \dfrac{cm_0}{\sqrt{1-v^2}}$ (b) $m = \dfrac{m_0}{c\sqrt{1-v^2}}$
(c) $m = \dfrac{m_0}{\sqrt{c^2-v^2}}$ (d) $m = \dfrac{m_0}{\sqrt{1-\dfrac{v^2}{c^2}}}$

12. The equation of state of some gases can be expressed as $\left(P+\dfrac{a}{V^2}\right)(V-b) = RT$. Here P is the pressure, V is the volume, T is the absolute temperature and a, b, R are constants. The dimensions of a are :
(a) $ML^5 T^{-2}$ (b) $ML^{-1}T^2$
(c) $M^0L^3T^0$ (d) $M^0L^6T^{-2}$

Answer	1	(d)	2	(d)	3	(d)	4	(a)	5	(a)	6	(b)
Key	7	(a)	8	(d)	9	(c)	10	(a)	11	(d)	12	(a)

13. A spherical body of mass m and radius r is allowed to fall in a medium of viscosity η. The time in which the velocity of the body increases from zero to 0.63 times the terminal velocity (v) is called time constant (τ). Dimensionally τ can be represented by

(a) $\dfrac{mr^2}{6\pi\eta}$

(b) $\sqrt{\left(\dfrac{6\pi mr\eta}{g^2}\right)}$

(c) $\dfrac{m}{6\pi\eta rv}$

(d) none of the above

14. The dimensions of universal gravitational constant are

(a) $M^{-2}L^2T^{-2}$

(b) $M^{-1}L^3T^{-2}$

(c) $ML^{-1}T^{-2}$

(d) ML^2T^{-2}

15. The frequency of vibration of string is given by $f = \dfrac{p}{2\ell}\sqrt{\dfrac{F}{\mu}}$

Here p is number of segments in the string and ℓ is the length. The dimension formula for μ will be :

(a) $[M^0LT^{-1}]$

(b) $[M^1L^2T^1]$

(c) $[ML^{-1}T^0]$

(d) $[M^0L^2T^{-1}]$

16. Dimensions of coefficient of viscosity are

(a) $M\,L^2\,T^{-2}$

(b) $M\,L^2\,T^{-1}$

(c) $M\,L^{-1}\,T^{-1}$

(d) $M\,L\,T$

17. In the formula $X = 3\,YZ^2$, X and Z have dimensions of capacitance and magnetic induction respectively. The dimensions of Y in MKSA system are :

(a) $[M^{-3}L^{-2}T^{-2}A^{-4}]$

(b) $[ML^{-2}]$

(c) $[M^{-3}L^{-2}A^4T^8]$

(d) $[M^{-3}L^2A^4T^4]$

18. The physical quantities not having same dimensions are

(a) speed and $(\mu_0\varepsilon_0)^{-1/2}$

(b) torque and work

(c) momentum and Planck's constant

(d) stress and Young's modulus

19. Inductance L can be dimensionally represented as

(a) $M\,L^2\,T^{-2}A^{-2}$

(b) $M\,L^2\,T^{-4}A^{-3}$

(c) $M\,L^{-2}\,T^{-2}A^{-2}$

(d) $M\,L^2\,T^4A^3$

20. If the time period (T) of vibration of a liquid drop depends on surface tension (S), radius (r) of the drop and density (ρ) of liquid, then the expression of T is

(a) $T = k\sqrt{\rho r^3/S}$

(b) $T = k\sqrt{\rho^{1/2}r^3/S}$

(c) $T = k\sqrt{\rho r^3/S^{1/2}}$

(d) none of these

21. If energy E, velocity v and time T are chosen as fundamental units, the dimensions of surface tension will be :

(a) $[Ev^{-2}T^{-2}]$

(b) $[Ev^{-1}T^{-2}]$

(c) $[Ev^2T^{-1}]$

(d) $[E^2v^{-1}T^{-1}]$

22. A physical quantity x depends on quantities y and z as follows : $x = Ay + B\tan Cz$, where A, B and C are constants. Which of the following do not have the same dimensions :

(a) x and B

(b) C and z^{-1}

(c) y and B/A

(d) x and A

23. The time dependence of a physical quantity P is given by $P = P_0 \exp(\alpha t^2)$ where α is a constant and t is time. The constant α :

(a) is dimensionless

(b) has dimensions of T^{-2}

(c) has dimensions as that of P

(d) has dimensions equal to the dimensions of PT^{-2}

24. If L and R denote inductance and resistance respectively, then the dimensions of L/R is :

(a) $M^0L^0T^0$

(b) $M^0L^0T^1$

(c) $M^2L^0T^2$

(d) MLT^2

25. The dimensions of the quantity $\vec{E} \times \vec{B}$ where $\vec{E}$ represents the electric field and $\vec{B}$ the magnetic field may be given as:

(a) MT^{-3}

(b) $M^2LT^{-5}A^{-2}$

(c) $M^2LT^{-3}A^{-1}$

(d) $MLT^{-2}A^{-2}$

26. The electric field is given by $\vec{E} = \dfrac{A}{x^3}\hat{i} + By\hat{j} + Cz^2\hat{k}$. The SI units of A, B and C are respectively:

[AMU B.Tech. 2013]

(a) $\dfrac{N - m^3}{C}$, V/m^2, N/m^2-C

(b) V-m^2, V/m, N/m^2-C

(c) V/m^2, V/m, N-C/m^2

(d) V/m, N-m^3/C, N-C/m

27. What are the dimensions of A/B in the relation $F = A\sqrt{x} + Bt^2$, where F is the force, x is the distance and t is time?

[AMU B.Tech. 2013]

(a) ML^2T^{-2}

(b) $L^{-1/2}T^2$

(c) $L^{-1/2}T^{-1}$

(d) LT^{-2}

28. The potential energy of a particle is given by the expression $U(x) = -\alpha x + \beta \sin\dfrac{x}{\gamma}$. A dimensionless combination of the constants α, β and γ is :

[KVPY - 2012]

(a) $\dfrac{\alpha}{\beta\gamma}$

(b) $\dfrac{\alpha^2}{\beta\alpha}$

(c) $\dfrac{\gamma}{\alpha\beta}$

(d) $\dfrac{\alpha\gamma}{\beta}$

Answer	13	(d)	14	(b)	15	(c)	16	(c)	17	(c)	18	(c)	19	(a)	20	(a)
Key	21	(a)	22	(d)	23	(b)	24	(b)	25	(b)	26	(a)	27	(b)	28	(d)

29. The value of resistance is 10.845 Ω and the value of current is 3.23 A. The potential difference is 35.02935 volt. Its value in significant number would be :

(a) 35 V   (b) 35.0 V

(c) 35.03 V   (d) 35.029 V

Instruments and Errors

30. The least count of a stop watch is $\dfrac{1}{5}$ s. The time of 20 oscillations of a pendulum is measured to be 25 s. What is the maximum percentage error in this measurement ?

(a) 8 %   (b) 1 %

(c) 0.8 %   (d) 16 %

31. The refractive index of water measured by the relation $\mu = \dfrac{\text{real depth}}{\text{apparent depth}}$ is found to have values of 1.34, 1.38, 1.32 and 1.36; the mean value of refractive index with percentage error :

(a) $1.35 \pm 1.48\ \%$ (b) $1.35 \pm 0\ \%$

(c) $1.36 \pm 6\ \%$ (d) $1.36 \pm 0\ \%$

32. A wire has a mass 0.3 ± 0.003 g, radius 0.5 ± 0.005 mm and length 6 ± 0.06 cm. The maximum percentage error in the measurement of its density is :

(a) 1   (b) 2

(c) 3   (d) 4

33. A physical quantity X is given by $X = \dfrac{a^3 b^2 d}{c^{1/2}}$, the percentage error in the measurement a, b, c and d are 1 %, 3 %, 2 % and 4 % respectively. The maximum percentage error in X is :

(a) 11 %   (b) 14 %

(c) 10 %   (d) 19 %

34. In a vernier callipers N division of vernier coincide with ($N - 1$) divisions of main scale in which length of a division in 1 mm. The least count of the instrument in cm is:

(a) N (b) $N - 1$

(c) $\dfrac{1}{10N}$ (d) $(1/N) - 1$

35. The resistance of a metal is given by $R = V/I$, where V is potential difference and I is the current. In a circuit the potential difference across resistance is $V = (10 \pm 0.5)$ V and current in resistance, $I = (2 \pm 0.2)$ A. The value of resistance in Ω with percentage error is:

(a) $5 \pm 10\ \%$ (b) $5 \pm 15\ \%$

(c) $5 \pm 20\ \%$ (d) $5 \pm 25\ \%$

36. One centimetre on the main scale of a vernier callipers is divided into 10 equal parts. If 10 divisions of vernier coincide with 8 small divisions of the main scale, the least count of callipers is :

(a) 0.01 cm   (b) 0.02 cm

(c) 0.05 cm   (d) 0.005 cm

37. While measuring the length of the rod by vernier callipers the reading on main scale is 6.4 cm and the eight division on vernier is in line with marking on main scale division. If the least count of callipers is 0.01 and zero error –0.04 cm, the length of the rod is

(a) 6.50 cm   (b) 6.48 cm

(c) 6.52 cm   (d) 6.60 cm

Answer	29	(b)	30	(c)	31	(a)	32	(d)	33	(b)
Key	34	(c)	35	(b)	36	(b)	37	(c)		

LEVEL – 2 (ONLY ONE OPTION CORRECT)

Units and Dimensions

1. Dimensional formula of magnetic flux is

(a) $ML^2T^{-2}A^{-1}$ (b) $ML^0T^{-2}A^{-2}$

(c) $M^0L^{-2}T^{-2}A^{-3}$ (d) $ML^2T^{-2}A^3$

2. E, M, J and G denote energy, mass, angular momentum and gravitational constant respectively. The dimensions of $\dfrac{EJ^2}{M^5G^2}$ are that of :

(a) angle   (b) length

(c) mass   (d) time

3. Using mass [M], length (L), time (T) and current [A] as fundamental quantities, the dimensions of permitivity is :

(a) $ML^{-2}T^2A$ (b) $M^{-1}L^{-3}T^4A^2$

(c) $MLT^{-2}A$ (d) $ML^2T^{-1}A^2$

4. Which of the following units denotes the dimensions $\dfrac{ML^2}{Q^2}$, where Q denotes the electric charge :

(a) weber (Wb)   (b) $\dfrac{Wb}{m^2}$

(c) henry (H)   (d) $\dfrac{H}{m^2}$

5. If the constant of gravitational constant (G) and Plank's constant (h) and the velocity of light (c) be chosen as fundamental units. The dimensions of the radius of gyration is :

(a) $h^{1/2}\,c^{-3/2}G^{1/2}$ (b) $h^{1/2}c^{3/2}G^{1/2}$

(c) $h^{1/2}\,c^{-3/2}G^{-1/2}$ (d) $h^{-1/2}\,c^{-3/2}G^{1/2}$

6. The dimensions of $\dfrac{1}{\sqrt{\varepsilon_0\mu_0}}$ is that of

   (a) velocity   (b) time

   (c) capacitance   (d) distance

Instruments and Errors

7. Two full turns of the circular scale of a screw gauge cover a distance of 1 mm on its main scale. The total number of divisions on the circular scale is 50. Further, it is found that the screw gauge has a zero error of -0.03 mm. While measuring the diameter of a thin wire, a student notes the main scale reading of 3 mm and the number of circular scale divisions in line with the main scale as 35. The diameter of the wire is

   (a) 3.73 mm   (b) 3.67 mm

   (c) 3.38 mm   (d) 3.32 mm

8. The period of oscillation of a simple pendulum is given by $T = 2\pi\sqrt{\dfrac{\ell}{g}}$, where l is about 100 cm and is known to have 1 mm accuracy. The period is about 2 s. The time of 100 oscillations is measured by a stop watch of least count 0.1 s. The percentage error in g is :

   (a) 0.1%   (b) 1%

   (c) 0.2%   (d) 0.8%

Answer	1	(d)	2	(a)	3	(b)	4	(c)
Key	5	(a)	6	(a)	7	(c)	8	(c)

| Mechanics | **MCQ Type 2** | Exercise 1.2 |

MULTIPLE CORRECT OPTIONS

1. Which of the following are dimensionless?
   (a) acceleration due to gravity
   (b) strain
   (c) mach number
   (d) refractive index

2. Which of the following are dimensionless constant?
   (a) Gravitational constant
   (b) Reynold's number
   (c) Mach number
   (d) permeability

3. Select the correct statement(s) :
   (a) a dimensionally correct equation may be correct
   (b) a dimensionally correct equation may be incorrect
   (c) a dimensionally incorrect equation may be correct
   (d) a dimensionally incorrect equation may be incorrect

4. Which of the following pairs have same dimensions :
   (a) torque and work
   (b) angular momentum and work
   (c) energy and Young's modulus
   (d) light year and wavelength

5. The pair(s) of physical quantities that have the same dimensions, is (are)
   (a) Reynolds number and coefficient of friction
   (b) Latent heat and gravitational potential
   (c) Curie and frequency of a light wave
   (d) Planck's constant and torque

6. The expression $\dfrac{dx}{\sqrt{a^2 - x^2}} = \dfrac{1}{a}\sin^{-1}\dfrac{a}{x}$; where x and a stand for distance :
   (a) mathematically correct   (b) mathematically incorrect
   (c) dimensionally correct   (d) dimensionally incorrect

7. The dimensions $ML^{-1}T^{-2}$ are corresponding to
   (a) modulus of elasticity
   (b) pressure
   (c) energy density
   (d) angular momentum

8. Which of the following group have different dimensions ?
   (a) potential difference, EMF, voltage
   (b) pressure, stress, Young's modulus
   (c) heat, energy, work done
   (d) dipole moment, electric flux, magnetic field

9. Which of the following pairs have the same dimension?
   (a) electric flux and q/ϵ_0 (b) electric flux and $\mu_0 i$
   (c) $\dfrac{h}{e}$ and electric flux   (d) $\dfrac{h}{e}$ and magnetic flux

10. If L, C and R represent inductance, capacitance and resistance respectively, then which of the following have dimensions of time?
    (a) L/R   (b) CR
    (c) $\sqrt{LC}$ (d) LC/R

11. A book with many printing errors contains different formulas for the displacement of a particle undergoing periodic motion :
    (i) $y = a \sin \dfrac{2\pi t}{T}$
    (ii) $y = a \sin vt$
    (iii) $y = \dfrac{a}{t}\sin\dfrac{t}{a}$
    (iv) $y = (a\sqrt{2})(\sin\dfrac{2\pi t}{T} + \cos\dfrac{2\pi t}{T})$
    where a = maximum displacement of the particle, v = speed of the particle, T = time period of motion. Rule out the wrong formulas on dimensional ground.
    (a) i   (b) ii   (c) iii   (d) iv

12. If the dimensions of length are expressed as $G^x c^y h^z$; where G, c and h are the universal gravitational constant, speed of light and Planck's constant respectively, then

(a) $x = \dfrac{1}{2}, y = \dfrac{1}{2}$

(b) $x = \dfrac{1}{2}, z = \dfrac{1}{2}$

(c) $y = \dfrac{1}{2}, z = \dfrac{3}{2}$

(d) $y = -\dfrac{3}{2}, z = \dfrac{1}{2}$

Answer	1	(b, c, d)	2	(b, c)	3	(a, b, c, d)	4	(a, d)	5	(a, b, c)	6	(b, d)
Key	7	(a, b, c)	8	(a, b, c)	9	(a, d)	10	(a, b, c)	11	(b, c)	12	(b, d)

Mechanics

Reasoning Type Questions

Exercise 1.3

Read the two statements carefully to mark the correct option out of the options given below:

(a) **Statement - 1** is true, **Statement - 2** is true; **Statement - 2** is correct explanation for **Statement - 1**.

(b) **Statement -1** is true, **Statement - 2** is true; **Statement - 2** is not correct explanation for **Statement - 1**.

(c) **Statement - 1** is true, **Statement - 2** is false.

(d) **Statement - 1** is false, **Statement - 2** is true

1. Statement - 1

Dimensional constants are the quantities whose values are constant.

Statement - 2

Dimensional constants are dimensionless.

2. Statement - 1

Number of significant figures in 0.005 is one and that in 0.500 is three.

Statement - 2

This is because zeros are not significant.

3. Statement - 1

L / R and CR both have same dimensions.

Statement - 2

L / R and CR both have dimensions of time.

4. Statement - 1

Angle and strain are dimensionless.

Statement - 2

Angle and strain have no unit.

5. Statement - 1

The dimensional formula for relative velocity is same as that of the change in velocity.

Statement - 2

| Relative velocity | = | change in velocity |

6. Statement - 1

In the equation momentum, $P = \dfrac{\text{mass}}{\text{area}} x$, the dimensional formula of x is LT^{-2}.

Statement - 2

Quantities with different dimensions can be multiplied.

7. Statement - 1

If $y = A \sin(\omega t + \phi)$, then dimensions of A are equal to dimensions of y.

Statement - 2

$\sin(\omega t + \phi)$ is dimensionless.

8. Statement - 1

Units of Rydberg constant R is m^{-1}.

Statement - 2

It follows from Bohr's formula $\dfrac{1}{\lambda} = R\left(\dfrac{1}{n_1^2} - \dfrac{1}{n_2^2}\right)$,

where the symbols have their usual meaning.

9. Statement - 1

Now a days a standard *metre* is defined in terms of the wavelength of light.

Statement - 2

Light has no relation with length.

10. Statement - 1

In $y = A\sin(\omega t - kx)$, $(\omega t - kx)$ is dimensionless.

Statement - 2

Because dimensions of $\omega = [M^0 L^0 T]$

Answer	1	(c)	2	(c)	3	(a)	4	(c)	5	(a)
Key	6	(d)	7	(a)	8	(a)	9	(c)	10	(c)

PASSAGES

Passage for Questions. 1 & 2 :

Resistor is used in electric circuit, which opposes the flow of charge. When two resistors are put in series in the circuit, they offer total resistance $R = R_1 + R_2$, and when they placed in parallel, they offer the resistance $R = R_1 R_2 / R_1 + R_2$. In any experiment the value of resistances are found as ; $R_1 = 100 \pm 3 \ \Omega$ and $R_2 = 200 \pm 4 \ \Omega$.

1. The equivalent resistance when resistors are connected in series :

   (a) $300 \ \Omega$ (b) $300 \pm 7 \ \Omega$

   (c) $300 \pm 3 \ \Omega$ (d) $300 \pm 4 \ \Omega$

2. The equivalent resistance when resistors are connected in parallel

   (a) $66.7 \pm 12 \ \Omega$ (b) $66.7 \pm 7 \ \Omega$

   (c) $66.7 \pm 1.8 \ \Omega$ (d) none of these

Passage for Questions. 3 & 4 :

A dense collection of equal number of electrons and positive ions is called neutral plasma. Certain solids containing fixed positive ions surrounded by free electrons can be treated as neutral plasma. Let 'N' be the number density of free electrons, each of mass 'm'. When the electrons are subjected to an electric field, they are displaced relatively away from the heavy positive ions. If the electric field becomes zero, the electrons begin to oscillate about the positive ions with a natural angular frequency 'ω_p' which is

called the plasma frequency. To sustain the oscillations, a time varying electric field needs to be applied that has an angular frequency ω, where a part of the energy is absorbed and a part of it is reflected. As ω approaches ω_p all the free electrons are set to resonance together and all the energy is reflected. This is the explanation of high reflectivity of metals.   **[IIT-JEE 2011]**

3. Taking the electronic charge as 'e' and the permittivity as 'ε_0'. Use dimensional analysis to determine the correct expression for ω_p.

   (a) $\sqrt{\dfrac{Ne}{m\varepsilon_0}}$ (b) $\sqrt{\dfrac{m\varepsilon_0}{Ne}}$

   (c) $\sqrt{\dfrac{Ne^2}{m\varepsilon_0}}$ (d) $\sqrt{\dfrac{Ne^2}{m\varepsilon_0}}$

4. Estimate the wavelength at which plasma reflection will occur for a metal having the density of electrons $N \approx 4 \times 10^{27} \ \mathrm{m}^{-3}$. Taking $\varepsilon_0 = 10^{-11}$ and mass $m \approx 10^{-30}$, where these quantities are in proper SI units.

   (a) 800 nm   (b) 600 nm

   (c) 300 nm   (d) 200 nm

MATRIX MATCHING

5.

	Column I		Column II
A.	Curie	(p)	MLT^{-2}
B.	Light year	(q)	M
C.	Dielectric constant	(r)	Dimensionless
D.	Atomic weight	(s)	T
E.	Decibel	(t)	ML^2T^2
		(u)	MT^{-3}
		(v)	T^{-1}
		(w)	L

6.

	Column - I		Column - II
A.	Force	(p)	T^{-1}
B.	Angular velocity	(q)	MLT^{-2}
C.	Work	(r)	$ML^{-1}T^{-2}$
D.	Surface tension	(s)	$ML^{-1}T^{-1}$
		(t)	MT^{-2}

7.

	Column - I		Column - II
A.	Angular momentum	(p)	$ML^{-1}T^{-1}$
B.	Torque	(q)	MT^{-2}
C.	Surface tension	(r)	ML^2T^{-1}
D.	Coefficient of viscosity	(s)	ML^2T^{-2}

Answer	1	(a)	2	(d)	3	(c)	4	(b)	5	A → p, q ; B → r, s ; C → r, s ; D → r, s
Key	7	A → q ; B → p ; C → t ; D → r		7	A → r ; B → s ; C → q ; D → p					

8.

	Column - I		Column - II
A.	Energy	(p)	$M^1L^2T^{-1}$
B.	Moment of inertia	(q)	$M^1L^2T^0$
C.	Angular acceleration	(r)	$M^1L^2T^{-2}$
D.	Angular momentum	(s)	$M^0L^0T^{-2}$

9.

	Column - I		Column - II
A.	Spring constant	(p)	$M^1L^2T^{-2}$
B.	Pascal	(q)	$M^0L^0T^{-1}$
C.	Hertz	(r)	$M^1L^0T^{-2}$
D.	Joule	(s)	$M^1L^{-1}T^{-2}$

10.

	Column - I		Column - II
A.	Capacitance	(p)	ohm - second
B.	Inductance	(q)	$coul^2\ Joule^{-1}$
C.	Magnetic induction	(r)	coulomb - $volt^{-1}$
		(s)	newton (ampere - $metre)^{-1}$
		(t)	volt - second $(ampere)^{-1}$

11.

	Column I		Column II
A.	Magnetic field intensity	(p)	Wbm^{-1}
B.	Magnetic flux	(q)	Wb/m^2
C.	Magnetic potential	(r)	Wb
D.	Magnetic induction	(s)	Am^{-1}

12.

	Column I		Column II
(A)	Capacitance	(p)	volt $(ampere)^{-1}$
(B)	Magnetic induction	(q)	volt-sec $(ampere)^{-1}$
(C)	Inductance	(r)	$newton(ampere)^{-1}\ (metre)^{-1}$
(D)	Resistance	(s)	$coulomb^2\ (joule)^{-1}$

13.

	Column I		Column II
(A)	Distance between earth & stars	(p)	micron
(B)	Inter-atomic distance in a solid	(q)	angstrom
(C)	Size of the nucleus	(r)	light year
(D)	Wavelength of infrared laser	(s)	fermi
		(t)	kilometre

14.   Column - I   Column - II   [IIT 2007]

A. GM_eM_s
G - universal gravitation constant
M_e - mass of the earth
M_s - mass of the sun

    (p)   (volt)(coulomb) (metre)

B. $\dfrac{3RT}{M}$

R - universal gas constant
T - absolute temperature
M - molar mass

    (q)   (kilogram) $(metre)^3\ (second)^{-2}$

C. $\dfrac{F^2}{q^2B^2}$

F - force
q - charge
B - magnetic field

    (r) $(metre)^2\ (second)^{-2}$

D. $\dfrac{GM_e}{R_e}$

G - universal gravitational constant
M_e - mass of the earth
R_e - radius of earth

    (s) $(farad)(volt)^2(kg)^{-1}$

15. Match List I with List II and select the correct answer using the codes given below the lists: [JEE Adv. 2013]

	Column - I		Column - II
A.	Boltzmann constant	(p).	$[ML^2T^{-1}]$
B.	Coefficient of viscosity	(q)	$[ML^{-1}T^{-1}]$
C.	Planck constant	(r)	$[MLT^{-3}K^{-1}]$
D.	Thermal conductivity	(s)	$[ML^2T^{-2}K^{-1}]$

Answer Key	8	A→r ; B→q ; C→s ; D→p	9	A→r ; B→s ; C→q ; D→p	10	A→q,r ; B→p,t ; C→s
	11	A→s ; B→r ; C→p ; D→q	12	A→s ; B→r ; C→q ; D→p	13	A→r ; B→q ; C→s ; D→p
	14	A→p,q ; B→r,s ; C→r,s ; D→r,s	15	A→s ; B→q ; C→p ; D→r		

Mechanics   Best of JEE (Main & Advanced)   Exercise 1.5

JEE- (Main)

1. The physical quantities not having same dimensions are
    (a) stress and Young's modulus   **[AIEEE 2003]**
    (b) speed and $(\mu_0 \varepsilon_0)^{-1/2}$
    (c) torque and work
    (d) momentum and Planck's constant.

2. Out of the following pairs, which one does NOT have identical dimensions?   **[AIEEE 2005]**
    (a) moment of inertia and moment of a force
    (b) work and torque
    (c) angular momentum and Planck's constant
    (d) impulse and momentum.

3. A body of mass $m = 3.513$ kg is moving along the x-axis with a speed of 5.00 ms^{-1}. The magnitude of its momentum is recorded as   **[AIEEE 2008]**
    (a) 17.6 kg m s^{-1} (b) 17.565 kg m s^{-1}
    (c) 17.56 kg m s^{-1} (d) 17.57 kg m s^{-1}

4. Two full turns of the circular scale of a screw gauge cover a distance of 1 mm on its main scale. The total number of divisions on the circular scale is 50. Further, it is found that the screw gauge has a zero error of -0.03 mm. While measuring the diameter of a thin wire, a student notes the main scale reading of 3 mm and the number of circular scale divisions in line with the main scale as 35. The diameter of the wire is   **[AIEEE 2008]**
    (a) 3.32 mm   (b) 3.73 mm
    (c) 3.67 mm   (d) 3.38 mm

5. In an experiment, the angles are required to be measured using and instrument. 29 divisions of the main scale exactly coincide with the 30 divisions of the vernier scale. If the smallest division of the main scale is half-a-degree $(=0.5°)$, then the least count of the instrument is :   **[AIEEE 2009]**
    (a) one degree   (b) half degree
    (c) one minute   (d) half minute

6. A screw gauge gives the following reading when used to measure the diameter of a wire.   **[AIEEE 2011]**
    Main scale reading   :   0 mm
    Circular scale reading   :   52 divisions
    Given that 1 mm on main scale corresponds to 100 divisions of the circular scale.
    The diameter of wire from the above data is :
    (a) 0.52 cm   (b) 0.052 cm
    (c) 0.026 cm   (d) 0.005 cm

7. A spectrometer gives the following reading when use to measure the angle of a prism.
Main scale reading :58.5 degree
Vernier scale reading : 09 divisions
Given that 1 division on main scale corresponds to 0.5 degree. Total divisions on the vernier scale is 30 and match with 29 divisions of the main scale. The angle of the prism from the above data is: **[AIEEE 2012]**
    (a) 58.77 degree   (b) 58.65 degree
    (c) 59 degree   (d) 58.59 degree.

8. Resistance of a given wire is obtained by measuring the current flowing in it and the voltage difference applied across it. If the percentage errors in the measurement of the current and the voltage difference are 3% each, then error in the value of resistance of the wire is :   **[AIEEE 2012]**
    (a) zero   (b) 1%
    (c) 3%   (d) 6%

9. The dimensions of $(\mu_0 \varepsilon_0)^{-1/2}$ are: **[AIEEE 2012, 2011]**
    (a) $[L^{1/2}T^{-1/2}]$ (b) $[L^{-1}T]$
    (c) $[LT^{-1}]$ (d) $[L^{1/2}T^{1/2}]$

10. A student measured the length of a rod and wrote it as 3.50 cm. Which instrument did he use to measure it?   **[JEE -Main 2014]**
    (a) A screw gauge having 50 divisions in the circular scale and pitch as 1 mm.
    (b) A meter scale
    (c) A vernier calliper where the 10 divisions in vernier scale matches with 9 divisions in main scale and main scale has 10 division in 1 cm.
    (d) A screw gauge having 100 divisions in the circular scale and pitch as 1 mm.

11. The current voltage relation of diode is given by $I = (e^{1000V/T} - 1)$ mA, where the applied voltage V is in volt and temperature T is in kelvin. If a student makes an error measuring ± 0.01 V while measuring the current of 5 mA at 300 K, what will be the error in the value of current in mA?   **[JEE-Main 2014]**
    (a) 0.05 mA   (b) 0.2 mA
    (c) 0.02 mA   (d) 0.5 mA

12. The period of oscillation of a simple pendulum is $T = \sqrt{\dfrac{L}{g}}$.
Measured value of L is 20.0 cm known to 1 mm accuracy and time for 100 oscillations of the pendulum is found to be 90 s using wrist watch of 1 s resolution. The accuracy in the determination of g is   **[JEE Main 2015]**
    (a) 3%   (b) 1%
    (c) 5%   (d) 2%

Answer	1	(d)	2	(a)	3	(a)	4	(d)	5	(c)	6	(b)	7	(b)
Key	8	(d)	9	(c)	10	(c)	11	(b)	12	(a)				

JEE- (Advanced)

13. A cube has a side of length 1.2×10^{-2}m. Calculate its volume. **[IIT-JEE 2003]**

(a) $1.7 \times 10^{-6}\,\text{m}^3$ (b) $1.73 \times 10^{-6}\,\text{m}^3$

(c) $1.70 \times 10^{-6}\,\text{m}^3$ (d) $1.732 \times 10^{-6}\,\text{m}^3$

14. In the relation $P = \dfrac{\alpha}{\beta} e^{-\frac{\alpha z}{k\theta}}$

P is pressure, Z is distance, k is Boltzmann constants and θ is the temperature. The dimensional formula of β will be

[IIT-JEE 2004]

(a) $[M^0L^2T^0]$ (b) $[M^1L^2T^1]$

(c) $[M^1L^0T^{-1}]$ (d) $[M^0L^2T^{-1}]$

15. A wire has a mass 0.3 ± 0.003g, radius 0.5 ± 0.005 mm and length 6 ± 0.006 cm. The maximum percentage error in the measurement of its density is **[IIT-JEE 2004]**

(a) 1   (b) 2

(c) 3   (d) 4.

16. Screw gauge shown in the figure has 50 divisions on its circular scale and in one complete rotation of circular scale the main scale moves by 0.5 mm. The diameter of a sphere is measured using this screw gauge. Two positions of screw gauge are shown in the figure. The diameter of sphere is

[IIT-JEE 2006]

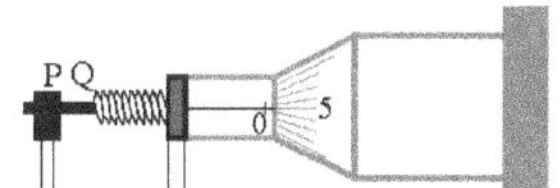 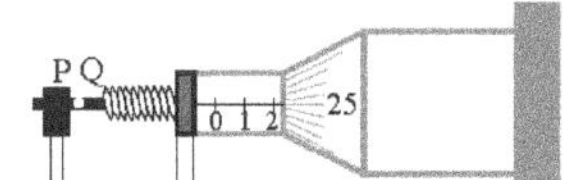

(a) 1.25 mm   (b) 1.20 mm

(c) 2.25 mm   (d) 2.20 mm

17. A student performs an experiment for determination of $g\left(=\dfrac{4\pi^2 l}{T^2}\right), l \approx 1m$, and he commits an error of Δl. For T, he takes the time of n oscillations with the stop watch of least count ΔT and he commits a human error of 0.1s. For which of the following data, the measurement of g will be most accurate ? **[IIT-JEE 2006]**

	Δl	ΔT	n	Amplitude of oscillation
(a)	5 mm	0.2 s	10	5 mm
(b)	5 mm	0.2 s	20	5 mm
(c)	5 mm	0.1 s	20	1 mm
(d)	1 mm	0.1 s	50	1 mm

18. A student performs on experiment to determine the Young's modulus of a wire, exactly 2 m long, by Searle's method. In a particular reading, the student measures the extension in the length of the wire to be 0.8 mm with on uncertainty of ± 0.05 mm at a load of exactly 1.0 kg. The student also measures the diameter of the wire to be 0.4 mm with an uncertainty of ± 0.01 mm. Take $g = 9.8$ m s^{-2}(exact). The Young's modulus obtained from the reading is close to

(a) $(2.0 \pm 0.3) \times 10^{11}$ Nm^{-2} **[IIT-JEE 2007]**

(b) $(2.0 \pm 0.2) \times 10^{11}$ Nm^{-2}

(c) $(2.0 \pm 0.1) \times 10^{11}$ Nm^{-2}

(d) $(2.0 \pm 0.05) \times 10^{11}$ Nm^{-2}

19. Students I, II and III perform an experiment for measuring the acceleration due to gravity (g) using a simple pendulum. They use different lengths of the pendulum and / or record time for different number of oscillations.

The observations are shown in the table.

Least count for length = 0.1 cm

least count for time = 0.1 s   **[IIT-JEE 2008]**

Student	Length of the pendulum(cm)	Number of oscillations (n)	Total time for (n) oscillations (s)	Time period (s)
I	64.0	8	128.0	16.0
II	64.0	4	64.0	16.0
III	20.0	4	36.0	9.0

If E_I, E_{II} and E_{III} are the percentage errors in g, i.e., $\left(\dfrac{\Delta g}{g} \times 100\right)$ for students I, II and III, respectively, then

(a) $E_I = 0$ (b) E_I is minimum

(c) $E_I = E_{II}$ (d) E_{II} is minimum

20. A Vernier callipers has 1 mm marks on the main scale. It's 20 equal divisions on the Vernier scale which match with 16 main scale divisions, For this Vernier callipers, the least count is **[IIT-JEE 2010]**

(a) 0.02 mm   (b) 0.05 mm

(c) 0.1 mm   (d) 0.2 mm

21. A student uses a simple pendulum of exactly 1 m length to determine g, the acceleration due to gravity. He uses a stop watch with the least count of 1 second for this and records 40 second for 20 oscillations. For this observation, which of the following statements (s) is (are) true?**[IIT-JEE 2010]**

(a) Error ΔT in measuring T, the time period, is 0.05 second

(b) Error ΔT in measuring T, the time period, is 1 second.

(c) Percentage error in the determination of g is 5%

(d) Percentage error in the determination of g is 2.5%

22. The density of a solid ball is to be determined in an experiment. The diameter of the ball is measured with a screw gauge, whose pitch is 0.5 mm and there are 50 divisions on the circular scale. The reading on the main scale is 2.5 mm and that on the circular scale is 20 divisions. If the measured mass of the ball has a relative error of 2% the relative percentage error in the density is **[IIT-JEE 2011]**

(a) 0.9%   (b) 2.4%

(c) 3.1%   (d) 4.2%

Answer	13	(a)	14	(a)	15	(d)	16	(b)	17	(d)
Key	18	(b)	19	(b)	20	(d)	21	(a, c)	22	(c)

23. In the determination of Young's modulus $\left(Y = \dfrac{4MLg}{\pi l d^2}\right)$ by using Searle's method, a wire of length $L = 2$ m and diameter $d = 0.5$ mm is used. For a load M = 2.5 kg, an extension $l = 0.25$ mm in the length of the wire is observed. Quantities d and l are measured using a screw gauge and a micrometer, respectively. They have the same pitch of 0.5 mm. The number of divisions on their circular scale is 100. The contributions to the maximum probable error of the Y measurement **[IIT-JEE 2012]**

(a) due to the errors in the measurements of d and l are the same.

(b) due to the error in the measurement of d is twice that due to the error in the measurement of l.

(c) due to the error in the measurement of l is twice that due to the error in the measurement of d.

(d) due to the error in the measurement of d is four times that due to the error in the measurement of l.

24. The dimensional formula of magnetic flux is **[IIT-JEE 2012]**

(a) $[ML^2T^{-2}A^{-1}]$ (b) $[ML^2T^{-2}A^{-2}]$

(c) $[MLT^{-3}A^{-1}]$ (d) $[ML^0T^{-2}A^{-1}]$

Answer Key	23	(a)	24	(a)							

Hints & Solutions

In Chapter Exercise -1.1

1. Length, mass and time are chosen as base quantities in mechanics because
   (i) Nothing is simpler than length, mass and time.
   (ii) All other quantities in mechanics can be expressed in terms of length, mass and time
   (iii) Length, mass and time cannot be derived from one another.

2. (a) Plane angle has unit as radian but has no dimensions.
   (b) Strain has neither unit nor dimensions
   (c) Gravitational constant $(G) = 6.67 \times 10^{-11}$ N-m^2/kg^2
   (d) Reynold number is a constant which has no unit.

3. Here, force (F) = $[MLT^{-2}] = 100$ N ... (i)
   Length (L) = $[L] = 10$ m ... (ii)
   Time (t) = $[T] = 100$ s ... (iii)
   Substituting values of L and T from Eqs (ii) and (iii) in Eq. (i) we get
   $$M \times 10 \times (100)^2 = 100$$
   or
   $$\frac{M \times 10}{100 \times 100} = 100$$
   or
   $$M = 100 \times 1000 \text{ kg}$$

4. The given expression is $P = EL^2m^{-5}G^{-2}$
   Dimension of (E) = $[ML^2T^{-2}]$
   (L) = $[ML^2T^{-1}]$
   (m) = $[M]$
   (G) = $[M^{-1}L^3T^{-2}]$
   Substitution dimensions of each term in the given expression,
   $$(P) = [ML^2T^{-2}] \times [ML^2T^{-1}]^2 \times [M]^{-5} \times [M^{-1}L^3T^{-2}]^{-2}$$
   $$= [M^{1+2-5+2} L^{2+4-6} T^{2-2+4}]$$
   $$= [M^0L^0T^0]$$
   Therefore, P is a dimensionless quantity.

5. Dimensions of (c) = $[LT^{-1}]$
   Dimension of Planck;s constant (h) = $[ML^2T^{-1}]$
   Dimension of gravitational constant (G) = $[M^{-1}L^3T^{-2}]$
   (a) Let $m \propto c^x h^y G^z$
   or $m = kc^x h^y G^z$ ... (i)
   where, k is a dimensionless constant of proportionality.
   Substituting dimensions of each term in Eq. (i), we get
   $$[ML^0T^0] = [LT^{-1}]^x \times [ML^2T^{-1}]^y \times [M^{-1}L^3T^{-2}]^z$$
   $$= [M^{y-z} L^{x+2y+3z} T^{-x-y-2z}]$$
   Comparing powers of same terms on both sides, we get
   $$y - z = 1$$
   $$x + 2y + 3z = 0$$
   $$-x - y - 2z = 0$$
   After solving above equation, we get

$$x = \frac{1}{2}, y = \frac{1}{2}, z = -\frac{1}{2}$$

Putting values of x, y and z in Eq. (i), we get
$$m = kc^{1/2}h^{1/2}G^{-1/2}$$
or
$$m = k\sqrt{\frac{ch}{G}}$$

(b) Let $L \propto c^x h^y G^z$
   or $L = kc^x h^y G^z$
   where, k is a dimensionless constant.
   Substituting dimensions of each term, we get
   $$[M^0LT^0] = [MT^{-1}]^x \times [ML^2T^{-1}]^y \times [M^{-1}L^3T^{-2}]^z$$
   $$= [M^{y-z}L^{x+2y+3z}T^{-x-y-2z}]$$
   On comparing powers of same terms, we get
   $$y - z = 0$$
   $$x + 2y + 3z = 1$$
   $$-x - y - 2z = 0$$
   After solving above equation, we get
   $$x = -\frac{3}{2}, y = \frac{1}{2}, z = \frac{1}{2}$$
   Putting values of x, y and z, we get
   $$L = kc^{-3/2}h^{1/2}G^{1/2}$$
   $$= k\sqrt{\frac{hG}{c^3}}$$

(c) Let $T \propto c^x h^y G^z$
   or $T = kc^x h^y G^z$
   where, k is a dimensionless constant
   Substituting dimensions of each term in Eq. (ix), we get
   $$[M^0L^0T] = [LT^{-1}]^x \times [ML^2T^{-1}]^y \times [M^{-1}L^3T^{-2}]^z$$
   $$= [M^{y-z}L^{x+2y+3z}T^{-x-y-2z}]$$
   On comparing powers of same terms, we get
   $$y - z = 0$$
   $$x + 2y + 3z = 0$$
   $$-x - y - 2z = 1$$
   After solving above equation, we get
   $$x = -\frac{5}{2}, y = \frac{1}{2}, z = \frac{1}{2}$$
   Putting values of x, y and z in Eq., we get
   $$T = kc^{-3/2}h^{1/2}G^{1/2}$$
   $$T = k\sqrt{\frac{hG}{c^5}}$$

6. Dimensions of energy = $[ML^2T^{-2}]$
   Let M_1, L_1, T_1 and M_2, L_2, T_2 are units of mass, length and time in given two systems.
   $\therefore$ $m_1 = 1$ kg, $L_1 = 1$ m, $T_1 = 1$s
   $m_2 = \alpha$ kg, $L_2 = \beta$ m, $T_2 = \gamma$ s
   Using,

$$n_2 = n_1 \frac{[M_1 L_1^2 T_1^2]}{[M_2 L_2^2 T_2^2]}$$

$$= 5\left[\frac{M_1}{M_2}\right] \times \left[\frac{L_1}{L_2}\right]^2 \times \left[\frac{T_1}{T_2}\right]^{-2}$$

$$= 5\left[\frac{1}{\alpha} kg\right] \times \left[\frac{1}{\beta} m\right]^2 \times \left[\frac{1}{\gamma} s\right]^{-2}$$

$$= 5 \times \frac{1}{\alpha} \times \frac{1}{\beta^2} \times \frac{1}{\gamma^{-2}}$$

$$n_2 = \frac{5\gamma^2}{\alpha\beta^2} \text{ new unit of energy}$$

7. From Kelper's third law
$$T^2 \propto r^3 \text{ or } T \propto r^{3/2}$$
and T is a function of R and g

Let $\quad\quad\quad T \propto r^{3/2} R^a g^b$

or $\quad\quad\quad T = k r^{3/2} R^a g^b \quad\quad$ ..... (i)

where, k is a dimensionless constant of proportionality.
Substituting the dimensions of each term in Eq. (i), we get
$$[M^0 L^0 T] = k[L]^{3/2}[L]^a[LT^{-2}]^n$$
$$= k[L^{a+b+3/2}T^{-2b}]$$

On comparing the powers of same terms, we get
$$a + b + 3/2 = 0 \quad\quad ..... \text{(ii)}$$
$$-2b = 1 \Rightarrow b = -1/2$$

From Eq. (ii), we get
$$a - 1/2 + 3/2 = 0 \Rightarrow a = -1$$

Substituting the values of a and b in Eq. (i), we get
$$T = k r^{3/2} R^{-1} g^{-1/2}$$

or $\quad\quad\quad T = \dfrac{k}{R}\sqrt{\dfrac{r^3}{g}}$

8. Given $\quad\quad n = -D\dfrac{n_2 - n_1}{x_2 - x_1}$

$\therefore \quad\quad D = -\dfrac{n(x_2 - x_1)}{(n_2 - n_1)}$

Dimensions of $\quad D = \dfrac{\text{dimensions of } n \times \text{dimensions of } x}{\text{dimensions of } n_2 \text{ or } n_1}$

$$= \frac{T^{-1}L^{-2} \times L}{L^{-3}} = L^2 T^{-1} \quad\quad \textbf{\textit{Ans.}}$$

9. We can write, $\quad F = k \, m^a \omega^b r^c$

or $\quad [M][L][T]^{-2} = [M]^a [T^{-1}]^b [L]^c$

On comparing the dimensions on both sides, we get
$$a = 1, b = 2 \text{ and } c = 1$$

Thus $\quad\quad F = km\omega^2 r. \quad\quad \textbf{\textit{Ans.}}$

10. Given, $\quad\quad F = a\sqrt{x} + bt^2$

The dimensions of $a\sqrt{x} = $ dimensions of bt^2
$$= \text{dimensions of } F = MLT^{-2}$$

$\therefore \quad$ dimensions of $\quad a = \dfrac{MLT^{-2}}{L^{1/2}} = ML^{1/2}T^{-2}$

$$b = \frac{MLT^{-2}}{T^2} = MLT^{-4}$$

Thus dimensions of $\dfrac{a}{b} = L^{-1/2} T^2 \quad\quad \textbf{\textit{Ans.}}$

In Chapter Exercise -1.2

1. Given, $\quad\quad t_1 = 39.6$ s
$$t_2 = 39.9 \text{ s}$$
$$t_3 = 39.5 \text{ s}$$

Least count of measuring instrument = 0.1s
[As measurement have only one decimal place]
precision in the measurement
$\quad\quad$ = Least count of the measuring instrument = 0.1 s

Mean value of time for 20 oscillations
$$t = \frac{t_1 + t_2 + t_3}{3} = \frac{39.6 + 39.9 + 39.5}{3} = 39.7s$$

Absolute errors in the measurements
$$\Delta t_1 = t - t_1 = 39.7 - 39.6 = 0.1s$$
$$\Delta t_2 = t - t_2 = 39.7 - 39.9 = -0.2s$$
$$\Delta t_3 = t - t_3 = 39.7 - 39.5 = 0.2s$$

Mean absolute error $= \dfrac{|\Delta t_1| + |\Delta t_2| + |\Delta t_3|}{3}$

$$= \frac{0.1 + 0.2 + 0.2}{3} = \frac{0.5}{3} = 0.17 \approx 0.2$$

(rounding-off upto one decimal place)

$\therefore$ Accuracy of measurement $= \pm 0.2$ s

2. The given physical quantity
$$x = a^2 b^3 c^{5/2} d^{-2}$$

Maximum percentage error in x.

$$\frac{\Delta x}{x} \times 100$$

$$= \pm\left[2\left(\frac{\Delta a}{a} \times 100\right) + 3\left(\frac{\Delta b}{b} \times 100\right) + \frac{5}{2}\left(\frac{\Delta c}{c} \times 100\right) + 2\left(\frac{\Delta d}{d} \times 100\right)\right]$$

$$= \pm\left[2(1) + 3(2) + \frac{5}{2}(3) + 2(4)\right]\%$$

$$= \pm\left[2 + 6 + \frac{15}{2} + 8\right]$$

$$= \pm 23.5\%$$

$\therefore$ percentage error in quantity $x = \pm 23.5\%$

Mean absolute error in $x = \pm 0.235$
$$= \pm 0.24 \text{ (round-off upto two significant digits)}$$

The calculate value of x should be round-off upto two significant digits.

$\therefore \quad x = 2.8$

3. Total surface area $= 6 \times (7.203)^2$
$$= 311.299254 \text{ m}^2$$

The result should be rounded off to four significant figures, so it becomes 311.3 m^2

Volume of the cube $= (7.203)^3 = 373.714754$ m^3
$$= 373.7 \text{ m}^3 \quad\quad \textbf{\textit{Ans.}}$$

4. Here $t = 3.0$ billion years
$$= 3.0 \times 10^9 \times 365.25 \times 24 \times 60 \times 60 \text{ s}$$

Speed of light, c $= 3 \times 10^5$ kms^{-1}

Distance of quasar
$$= ct = 3 \times 10^5 \times 3.0 \times 10^9 \times 365.25 \times 24 \times 60 \times 60$$
$$= 2.84 \times 10^{22} \text{ km.}$$

5. (i) Mean value of refractive index
$$\mu = \frac{1.45 + 1.56 + 1.54 + 1.44 + 1.54 + 1.53}{6}$$
$$= 1.51.$$

(ii) Absolute errors in measurements are :

$$\Delta\mu_1 \quad = 1.51 - 1.45 = 0.06$$
$$\Delta\mu_2 \quad = 1.51 - 1.56 = -0.05$$
$$\Delta\mu_3 \quad = 1.51 - 1.54 = -0.03$$
$$\Delta\mu_4 \quad = 1.51 - 1.44 = 0.07$$
$$\Delta\mu_5 \quad = 1.51 - 1.54 = -0.03$$
$$\Delta\mu_6 \quad = 1.51 - 1.53 = -0.02$$

Mean absolute error

$$\Delta\bar{\mu} = \left[\frac{|\Delta\mu_1| + |\Delta\mu_2| + |\Delta\mu_3| + |\Delta\mu_4| + |\Delta\mu_5| + |\Delta\mu_6|}{6}\right]$$

$$= 0.0433 = 0.04.$$

(iii) Fractional error $= \dfrac{\Delta\bar{\mu}}{\bar{\mu}} = \dfrac{0.04}{1.51} = 0.02649$

$$= \quad 0.03$$

(iv) Percentage error $= \dfrac{\Delta\bar{\mu}}{\bar{\mu}} \times 100 = 3\%$

Thus, $\quad \mu = 1.51 \pm 0.04$

or $\quad \mu = 1.51 \pm 3\%$ ***Ans.***

1. (d) Scalar quantity can be negative and may have any value in the process.

2. (d) Parallactic second is the unit of distance.

3. (d) Temperature is a fundamental quantity, so it can not be expressed in terms of other quantities.

4. (a) On *LHS*, S_t is the distance while on *RHS*, u is the speed, so it is not dimensionally correct. It is numerically correct only.

5. (a) Reading 4000 has for significant figures, which are largest in the given values.

6. (b) The work done = force × displacement

$$\therefore \text{ unit, } \quad u_1 = Fs$$
$$\text{and} \quad u_2 = 4F \times 4s = 16u.$$

7. (a) Strain $= \dfrac{\Delta\ell}{\ell}$; sp. gravity $= \dfrac{\text{density of substance}}{\text{density of water}}$;

angle $= \dfrac{\text{arc distance}}{\text{radius}}$

8. (d) The dimensions of Plank constant $= ML^2T^{-1}$

Energy $= ML^2T^{-2}$.

9. (c) $n_1 u_1 = n_2 u_2$

$$\therefore \ n_2 = n_1 \frac{u_1}{u_2} = 8\left[\frac{M_1}{M_2}\right]\left[\frac{L_2}{L_1}\right]^3$$

$$= 8\left[\frac{1}{20}\right]\left[\frac{5}{1}\right]^3 = 50.$$

10. (a) $n_2 = n_1 \dfrac{\left[M_1 L_1^2 T_1^{-2}\right]}{\left[M_2 L_2^2 T_2^{-2}\right]} = 1\dfrac{1}{\alpha} \times \left(\dfrac{1}{\beta}\right)^2 \times \left(\dfrac{1}{\gamma}\right)^{-2}$

$$= \ \gamma^2 / \alpha\beta^2$$

11. (d) In, $1 - v^2$, v^2 should be dimensionless, so it should be

$$1 - \frac{v^2}{c^2}.$$

12. (a) The dimensions of $\dfrac{a}{V^2}$ = dimensions of P

$$\therefore \quad \text{dimensions of } a = ML^{-1}T^{-2} \times L^6$$
$$= ML^5 T^{-2}.$$

13. (d) Time constant has the dimensions of time.

14. (b) $F = G\dfrac{m_1 m_2}{r^2}$; $\qquad \therefore G = \dfrac{Fr^2}{m_1 m_2} = M^{-1}L^3T^{-2}$

15. (c) The dimension of $m = \dfrac{F}{f^2\ell^2} = \dfrac{MLT^{-2}}{T^{-2}L^2} = ML^{-1}$

16. (c) $F = \eta\, A\dfrac{dv}{dy}$; $\qquad \therefore \eta = \dfrac{F}{A\left(\dfrac{dv}{dy}\right)} = ML^2 T^{-2}$

17. (c) Dimensions of $Y = \dfrac{\text{dimensions of X}}{\text{dimensions of Z}^2}$

$$= \frac{M^{-1}L^{-2}T^4 A^2}{(MT^{-2}A^{-1})^2}$$

$$= M^{-3}L^{-2}T^8 A^4.$$

18. (c) The dimensions of momentum $= MLT^{-1}$

The dimensions of plank's constant $= ML^2 T^{-1}$.

19. (a) Inductance $= \dfrac{\text{potential}}{\text{charge}} = ML^2 T^{-2} A^{-2}$.

20. (a) Time period, $T = k\, S^a\, r^b\, \rho^c$

$$M^0 L^0 T^1 = [MT^{-2}]^a\,[L]^b\,[ML^{-3}]^c$$
$$= [M]^{a+c}\,[L]^{b-3c}\,[T]^{-2a}$$

$$\therefore \qquad -2a = 1 \qquad \text{or} \qquad a = -1/2$$
$$\text{Also} \qquad a + c = 0 \qquad \text{or} \qquad c = 1/2$$
$$\text{and} \qquad b - 3c = 0 \qquad \text{or} \qquad b = 3c = 3/2$$

Thus $\quad T = k\sqrt{\dfrac{\rho r^3}{S}}$.

21. (a) Surface tension $= \dfrac{\text{force}}{\text{length}}$

$$= \frac{\text{energy}}{\text{length} \times \text{length}} = \frac{\text{energy}}{(\text{speed/time})^2}$$

$$= EV^{-2}T^{-2}.$$

22. (d) The dimensions of Ay = dimensions of x.

$$\therefore \text{dimension of A} = \frac{x}{y}$$

23. (b) $P = P_0 e^{\alpha t^2}; \quad \alpha t^2 = 1$

$\therefore$ dimensions of $\alpha = \dfrac{1}{t^2} = T^{-2}$.

24. (b) $\dfrac{L}{R} = \dfrac{ML^2T^{-2}A^{-2}}{ML^2T^{-3}A^{-2}} = T$

25. (b) $\vec{E} \times \vec{B} \rightarrow (MLT^{-3}A^{-1}) \times (MT^{-2}A^{-1}) = M^2LT^{-5}A^{-2}$.

26. (a)　　　　　27. (b)　　　　　28. (d)

29. (b) The significant number in the potential, $V = iR$; should be the minimum of either i or R. So corresponding to $i = 3.23\ A$, we have only three significant numbers in $V = 35.02935\ V$. Thus the result is $V = 35.0\ V$.

Error and Instrument

30. (c) The percentage error $= \dfrac{1}{5} \times \dfrac{100}{25} = 0.8\%$

31. (a) The mean value of refractive index,

$\mu = \dfrac{1.34 + 1.38 + 1.32 + 1.36}{4} = 1.35$

and

$\Delta\mu = \dfrac{|(1.35-1.34)| + |(1.35-1.38)| + |(1.35-1.32)| + |(1.35-1.36)|}{4}$

$= 0.02$

Thus $\dfrac{\Delta\mu}{\mu} \times 100 = \dfrac{0.02}{1.35} \times 100 = 1.48$

32. (d) Density, $\rho = \dfrac{M}{V} = \dfrac{M}{\pi r^2 \ell}$

$\therefore \quad \dfrac{\Delta\rho}{\rho} \times 100 = \left[\dfrac{\Delta M}{M} + \dfrac{2\Delta r}{r} + \dfrac{\Delta\ell}{\ell}\right] \times 100$

$= \left[\dfrac{0.003}{0.3} + 2\dfrac{0.005}{0.5} + \dfrac{0.06}{6}\right] \times 100 = 4$

33. (b) $\dfrac{\Delta x}{x} \times 100 = 3\dfrac{\Delta a}{a} \times 100 + 2\dfrac{\Delta b}{b} \times 100 + \dfrac{\Delta d}{d} \times 100 + \dfrac{1}{2}\dfrac{\Delta c}{c} \times 100$

$= 3 \times 1\% + 2 \times 3\% + 4\% + \dfrac{1}{2} \times 2\%$

$= 14\%$

34. (c) $L.C. = \dfrac{\text{value of 1 division of main scale}}{\text{number of division on main scale}} = \dfrac{1}{N}\ mm = \dfrac{1}{10N}\ cm.$

35. (b) $R = \dfrac{V}{I} = \dfrac{10}{2} = 5\Omega$

Also, $\dfrac{\Delta R}{R} \times 100 = \dfrac{\Delta V}{V} \times 100 + \dfrac{\Delta I}{I} \times 100$

$= \dfrac{0.5}{10} \times 100 + \dfrac{0.2}{2} \times 100 = 15\%$

Thus, $R = 5 \pm 15\%\ \Omega$.

36. (b) The value of 1 division of main scale $= \dfrac{1}{10} = 0.1$ cm

The value of 1 division of vernier scale $= \dfrac{8 \times 0.1}{10}$

$= 0.08$ cm

Thus $L.C. = 0.1 - 0.08$

$= 0.02$ cm

37. (c) Length of the rod $=$ observed reading $-$ zero error

$=$ (Main scale division $+$ Vernier scale division $\times LC$)

$-$ Zero error

$= (6.4 + 8 \times 0.01) - (-0.04)$

$= 6.4 + 0.08 + 0.04$

$= 6.52$ cm

1. (a) Magnetic flux, $\phi = BA$

$= MT^{-2}A^{-1} \times L^2$

$= ML^2T^{-2}A^{-1}$.

2. (a) The dimensions of

$\dfrac{EJ^2}{M^5 G^2} = \dfrac{(ML^2T^{-2})(ML^2T^{-1})^2}{(M^5)(M^{-1}L^3T^{-2})^2} = 1$

So it represents dimensions quantity like angle.

3. (b) We know that,

$F = \dfrac{1}{4\pi\epsilon_0}\dfrac{q_1 q_2}{r^2}$

$\therefore \quad \epsilon_0 = \dfrac{1}{4\pi\epsilon_0}\dfrac{q_1 q_2}{r^2}$

$= \dfrac{1}{MLT^{-2}} \times \dfrac{(AT)^2}{L^2}$

$= M^{-1}L^{-3}T^4A^2$.

4. (c) We have $e = L\left(\dfrac{\Delta i}{\Delta t}\right), \quad L \rightarrow$ inductance

$\therefore \quad L = \dfrac{e}{\left(\dfrac{\Delta i}{\Delta t}\right)} = \dfrac{ML^2T^{-3}A^{-1}}{(A/T)} = \dfrac{ML^2}{(AT)^2} = \dfrac{ML^2}{Q^2}$

5. (a) The dimensions of radius of gyration

$=$ dimensions of L

$= G^{1/2}\,h^{1/2}\,c^{-3/2}$.

6. (a) $\dfrac{1}{\sqrt{\epsilon_0\,\mu_0}} = \dfrac{1}{\sqrt{(M^{-1}L^{-3}A^2T^4) \times MLT^{-2}A^{-2}}}$

$= \sqrt{L^2T^{-2}} = LT^{-1}$

$\Rightarrow$ velocity

7. (c) $L.C. = \dfrac{0.5}{50} = 0.01$ mm

The diameter of the wire

$$= 3 + 35 \times 0.01 - (-0.03)$$
$$= 3.38 \text{ mm.}$$

8. (c)
$$T = 2\pi\sqrt{\frac{\ell}{g}}$$

$$\therefore \quad g = \frac{4\pi^2\ell}{T^2}$$

and
$$\frac{\Delta g}{g} \times 100 = \left[\frac{\Delta\ell}{\ell} + 2\frac{\Delta T}{T}\right] \times 100$$

$$= \left[\frac{0.1}{100} + 2\frac{0.1}{2 \times 100}\right] \times 100$$

$$= 0.2\%$$

---

1. (b,c,d) Strain,
$$e = \frac{\Delta\ell}{\ell} = \frac{L}{L} = 1$$

Mach number $= \dfrac{v_0}{v} = \dfrac{LT^{-1}}{LT^{-1}} = 1$

Refractive index $= \dfrac{c}{v} = \dfrac{LT^{-1}}{LT^{-1}} = 1$

2. (b,c) Similar to question 10.

3. (a,b,c,d)

    (a) Any physical relation.

    (b) $\tan\theta = \dfrac{rg}{v^2}$, is dimensionally correct. but it is

physically wrong equation.

    (c) $s^n = u + \dfrac{a}{2}(2n-1)$ is dimensionally incorrect, but

it is correct equation.

    (d) Obvious.

4. (a,d) The dimensions of torque and work, are
$$= ML^2T^{-2}.$$
The dimensions of light year and wavelength both are
$= L.$

5. (a,b,c)

    (a) Reynolds number and coefficient of friction are dimensionless.

    (b) Latent heat and gravitational potential both have same unit. i.e., Joul/kg.

    (c) Curie and frequency both are per second.

6. (b,d) LHS is dimensionless and so RHS must be. But

dimensions of RHS are $\dfrac{1}{L} = L^{-1}$.

7. (a,b,c) Modulus of elasticity,
$$E = \frac{f}{e} = MLT^{-2}/L^2 = ML^{-1}T^{-2}$$

Pressure,
$$P = \frac{F}{A} = \frac{MLT^{-2}}{L^2} = ML^{-1}T^{-2}$$

Energy density
$$U = \frac{\text{Energy}}{\text{Vol}} = \frac{ML^2T^{-2}}{L^3} = ML^{-1}T^{-2}$$

8. (a,b,c) Heat, energy and work done have same dimensions.

9. (a,d) The dimension of electric flux
$$\phi = EA = \frac{F}{q}A = \frac{MLT^{-2}}{AT}\cdot L^2 = ML^3T^{-3}A^{-1}$$

and
$$\frac{q}{\epsilon_0} = \frac{AT}{M^{-1}L^{-3}A^2T^4} = ML^3T^{-3}A^{-1}.$$

10. (a,b,c) $\dfrac{L}{R} = \dfrac{ML^2T^{-2}A^{-2}}{ML^2T^{-3}A^{-2}} = T$

$$CR = (M^{-1}L^{-2}T^4A^2) \times (ML^2T^{-3}A^{-2}) = T$$

$$\sqrt{LC} = \left[(ML^2T^{-2}A^{-2}) \times (M^{-1}L^{-2}T^4A^2)\right]^{1/2} = T$$

11. (b,c) In $\sin vt$, vt must be dimensionless. Similarly $\dfrac{t}{a}$ is not dimensionless.

12. (b,d) lenght $\quad \ell = G^x c^y h^z$

or $\quad M^0LT^0 = [M^{-1}L^3T^{-2}]^x [LT^{-1}]^y [ML^2T^{-1}]^z$

After comparing, we get

$$x = 1/2, \; y = -3/2, \; z = 1/2.$$

---

1. (c) Dimensional constants are not dimensionless.

2. (c) Zeros after a digit are significant.

3. (a) Statement-2 is the explanation of statement-1.

4. (c) Angle is dimensionless, but it has unit radian.

5. (a) Statement-2 is the explanation of statement-1.

6. (d) $P = \dfrac{\text{mass}}{\text{area}} x$

$$\therefore \quad x = \frac{P \times \text{area}}{\text{mass}} = \frac{MLT^{-1}}{M} \times L^2 = L^3T^{-1}$$

Quantities with different dimensions can be multiplied.

7. (a) $\sin(\omega t + \phi)$ is the ratio of sides of a triangle, so it is dimensionless.

8. (a) In LHS, $\dfrac{1}{\lambda}$ has unit $\dfrac{1}{m} = m^{-1}$.

9. (c) Light has well defined relation with length.

10. (c) Angle has no dimensions, but ω has dimensions T^{-1}.

Passage (Questions 1 & 2)

1. (b)   The equivalent resistor
$$R = R_1 + R_2$$
$$= 100 + 200 = 300\ \Omega$$
Also, $\Delta R = \Delta R_1 + \Delta R_2 = \pm (3 + 4) = \pm 7\ \Omega$
Thus $R = 300 \pm 7\ \Omega$.

2. (d) $R = \dfrac{R_1 R_2}{R_1 + R_2} = \dfrac{100 \times 200}{100 + 200} = 66.7\ \Omega$

Also, $\dfrac{\Delta R}{R} = \dfrac{\Delta R_1}{R_1} + \dfrac{\Delta R_2}{R_2} + \dfrac{\Delta R_1 + \Delta R_2}{R_1 + R_2}$

$$= \dfrac{3}{100} + \dfrac{4}{200} + \dfrac{3 + 4}{(100 + 200)} = 0.073$$

$\therefore$ $\Delta R = 0.073 \times 66.7 = 4.9\ \Omega$
Thus, $R = 66.7 \pm 4.9\ \Omega$

Passage (Questions 3 & 4)

3. (c) $e = [AT]$, $\omega = [T^{-1}]$
$N = [L^{-3}]$, $\epsilon_o = [M^{-1}\, L^{-3}\, A^2\, T^4]$
We do not want Ampere [A] in the expression. This is only possible when ϵ_0 occurs as square. Therefore options a and b are incorrect.

$$\sqrt{\dfrac{Ne^2}{m\,\epsilon_o}} = \sqrt{\dfrac{L^{-3}A^2T^2}{M\,M^{-1}L^{-3}A^2T^4}} = \sqrt{T^{-2}} = T^{-1}$$

4. (b) $\omega_p = \sqrt{\dfrac{Ne^2}{m\,\epsilon_o}} = 2\pi v = 2\pi\dfrac{c}{\lambda}$

$$\lambda = 2\pi c\sqrt{\dfrac{m\,\epsilon_o}{Ne^2}}$$

$$= 2 \times \dfrac{22}{7} \times 3 \times 10^8 \sqrt{\dfrac{10^{-30} \times 10^{-11}}{4 \times 10^{27} \times (1.6 \times 10^{-19})^2}} = 600\ \text{nm}$$

Passage (Q5 – 11) Are given in the theory of the chapter.

12. **A $\to$ s ; B$\to$ r ; C$\to$ q ; D$\to$ p**
(b) (A) Energy, $E = \dfrac{Q^2}{2C}$

$\therefore$ $C = Q^2/2E = (\text{Joule})^{-1}$ coulomb^2
(B) Force, $F = Bil$

$\therefore$ $B = \dfrac{F}{i\ell}$ = newton (ampere)$^{-1}$ (metre)$^{-1}$

(C) Induced emf, $e = L\,\Delta i/\Delta t$

$$\therefore\ \ L = \dfrac{e\,\Delta t}{\Delta i} = \text{volt– sec (ampere)}^{-1}$$

(D) Resistance, $R = \dfrac{V}{I}$ = volt (ampere)$^{-1}$

13. **A $\to$ r ; B$\to$ q ; C$\to$ s ; D$\to$ p**
Given in the theory of the chapter.
Error and Instrument

14. **A $\to$ p, q ; B$\to$ r, s ; C $\to$ r, s ; D$\to$ r, s**
(A) (p,q)   The unit of $GM_e M_s = Fr^2 = Nm^2$
$$= kg\,m^3 s^{-2}$$
Also volt $\times$ coulomb $\times$ metre = joule $\times$ metre
$$= Nm^2 = kg\ m^3\ s^{-2}$$

(B) (r,s)   The unit of $\dfrac{3RT}{M} = v_{ms}^2$
$$= m^2 s^{-2}.$$
Also (farad) (volt)^2 $(kg)^{-1}$ = (joule) kg^{-1}
$$= kg \times ms^{-1} \times mkg^{-1} = m^2 s^{-2}.$$

(C) (r, s) $F = qvB \Rightarrow v^2 = \dfrac{F^2}{q^2 B^2} = m^2 s^{-2}.$

(D) (r,s) $v_e = \sqrt{\dfrac{2GM}{R}}$

$$\Rightarrow \qquad v_e^2 = \dfrac{2GM}{R} = m^2 s^{-2}\,.$$

15. **A $\to$ s ; B$\to$ q ; C$\to$ p ; D$\to$ r**

Boltzmannn constant $= \dfrac{R}{N} = \dfrac{PV}{nTN} = \dfrac{ML^{-1}T^{-2} \times L^3}{K}$

$$= ML^2 T^{-2} K^{-1}$$

Coefficient of viscosity $= \dfrac{F}{6\pi r v} = \dfrac{MLT^{-2}}{L \times LT^{-1}} = ML^{-1}T^{-1}$

Planck constant $= \dfrac{E}{v} = \dfrac{ML^2 T^{-2}}{T^{-1}} = ML^2 T^{-1}$

Thermal conductivity $= \dfrac{H\ell}{tA\Delta T} = \dfrac{ML^2 T^{-2} \times L}{T \times L^2 \times K}$

$$= MLT^{-3}K^{-1}$$

(c) is the correct option.

1. (d)
2. (a)
3. (a) Momentum, $p = m \times v$
$= (3.513) \times (5.00) = 17.565$ kg m/s
$= 17.6$ (Rounding off to get three significant figures)

4. (d) Least count of screw gauge $= \dfrac{0.5}{50}$ mm $= 0.01$ mm

Reading = [Main scale reading + circular scale reading $\times$ L.C] – (zero error)
$= [3 + 35 \times 0.01] – (-0.03) = 3.38$ mm

5. (c) 30 Divisions of vernier scale coincide with 29 divisions of main scales

Therefore 1 V.S.D $= \dfrac{29}{30}$ MSD

Least count = 1 MSD – 1VSD = 1 MSD– $\dfrac{29}{30}$ MSD

$$= \dfrac{1}{30}\text{MSD} = \dfrac{1}{30} \times 0.5° = 1\ \text{minute}.$$

6. **(b)** L.C. = $\dfrac{1}{100}$ mm

Diameter of wire = MSR + CSR × L.C.

$$= 0 + \dfrac{1}{100} \times 52$$

$$= 0.52 \text{ mm} = 0.052 \text{ cm}$$

7. **(c)** Reading of Vernier = Main scale reading
+ Vernier scale reading × least count.

Main scale reading = 58.5

Vernier scale reading = 09 division

least count of Vernier = 0.5°/30

Thus $\qquad R = 58.5° + 9 \times \dfrac{0.5°}{30}$

$$R = 58.65$$

8. **(d)** $R = \dfrac{V}{I} \Rightarrow R \pm \Delta R = \dfrac{V \pm \Delta V}{I \pm \Delta I}$

$$R\left(1 \pm \dfrac{\Delta R}{R}\right) = \dfrac{V}{I}\left(\dfrac{1 \pm \Delta V / V}{1 \pm \dfrac{\Delta I}{I}}\right)$$

$$\left(\dfrac{\Delta R}{R}\right) = \left(\dfrac{\Delta V}{V}\right) + \left(\dfrac{\Delta I}{I}\right) = (3 + 3)\% = 6\%$$

9. **(c)**   10. **(c)**

11. **(b)** At $\qquad I = 5mA$

$\qquad 5 = (e^{1000V/T} - 1) \Rightarrow e^{1000V/T} = 6$

Now $\dfrac{dI}{dV} = \dfrac{d}{dV}[e^{1000V/T} - 1] = \dfrac{1000}{T}\left(e^{1000V/T}\right)$

or $\qquad dI = \left[\dfrac{1000}{T}e^{1000V/T}\right] \times (dV)$

$$= \dfrac{1000}{300} \times 6 \times 0.01 = 0.2 mA$$

12. **(a)** $g = \dfrac{4\pi^2 L}{T^2}$

$$\dfrac{\Delta g}{g} = \dfrac{\Delta L}{L} = 2\left(\dfrac{\Delta T}{T}\right)$$

$$\dfrac{\Delta L}{L} = \dfrac{0.1}{20}, \quad \dfrac{\Delta T}{T} = \dfrac{0.01}{0.9}$$

$$100\left(\dfrac{\Delta g}{g}\right) = 100\left(\dfrac{\Delta L}{L}\right) + 2 \times 100 \times \left(\dfrac{\Delta T}{T}\right) = 3\%$$

13. **(a)** $V = \ell^3 = (1.2 \times 10^{-2} \text{ m})^3 = 1.728 \times 10^{-6} \text{ m}^3$

$\Rightarrow V = 1.7 \times 10^{-6} \text{ m}^3$.

Note : ℓ has two significant figures. Hence V will also have two significant figures.

14. **(a)** Unit of k is joules per kelvin or dimensional formula of k is $[ML^2T^{-2}\theta^{-1}]$

Note : The power of an exponent is a number.

Therefore, dimensionally $\dfrac{\alpha z}{k\theta} = M°L°T°$

$\therefore \alpha = \dfrac{k\theta}{z} \times$ a dimension less quantity

$\therefore$ Dimensional formula of

$$\alpha = \dfrac{[ML^2T^{-2}\theta^{-1}][\theta]}{[L]} = \left[MLT^{-2}\right]$$

Also, dimensional formula of P = $[ML^{-1}T^{-2}]$

and dimensionally P = $\dfrac{\alpha}{\beta}$ $\beta = \dfrac{\alpha}{P}$

$\therefore \qquad [\beta] = \dfrac{MLT^{-2}}{ML^{-1}T^{-2}} = M^0L^2T^0$

15. **(d)** $\rho = \dfrac{m}{\ell \pi r^2}$

$$\dfrac{\Delta\rho}{\rho} = \dfrac{\Delta m}{m} + \dfrac{2\Delta r}{r} + \dfrac{\Delta\ell}{\ell}$$

Putting the values

$\Delta\ell = 0.06$ cm, $\ell = 6$cm $\Delta r = 0.005$ cm; $r = 0.5$ cm, $m = 0.3$ gm; $\Delta m = 0.003$ gm

we get $\dfrac{\Delta\rho}{\rho} = \dfrac{4}{100}$

$\therefore \dfrac{\Delta\rho}{\rho} \times 100 = 4\%.$

16. **(d)** $d = 2 + 25 \times 0.01 - 0.05$

$$= 2.20 \text{ mm}$$

17. **(d)** $\dfrac{\Delta g}{g} = \dfrac{\Delta\ell}{\ell} + 2\dfrac{\Delta T}{T}$

$\Delta\ell$ and ΔT are least and number of readings are maximum in option (d), therefore the measurement of g is most accurate with data used in this option.

18. **(b)** We know that $Y = \dfrac{mg}{\pi\dfrac{D^2}{4}} \times \dfrac{L}{\ell}$

$\Rightarrow Y = \dfrac{4mgL}{\pi D^2 \ell} = \dfrac{4 \times 1 \times 9.8 \times 2}{\pi\left(0.4 \times 10^{-3}\right)^2 \times \left(0.8 \times 10^{-3}\right)}$

$$= 2.0 \times 10^{11} \text{ N/m}^2$$

Now $\dfrac{\Delta Y}{Y} = \dfrac{2\Delta D}{D} + \dfrac{\Delta\ell}{\ell}$

[$\because$ the value of m, g and L are exact]

$= 2 \times \dfrac{0.01}{0.4} + \dfrac{0.05}{0.8} = 2 \times 0.025 + 0.0625$

$= 0.05 + 0.0625 = 0.1125$

$\Rightarrow \Delta Y = 2 \times 10^{11} \times 0.1125 = 0.225 \times 10^{11}$

$$= 2.0 \times 10^{11} \text{ N/m}^2$$

Note : we can also take the value of Y from options given without calculating it as it is same in all options.

$\therefore \qquad Y = (2 \pm 0.2) \times 10^{11} \text{ N/m}^2$

19. **(b)** The time period of a simple pendulum is given by

$$T = 2\pi\sqrt{\dfrac{\ell}{g}} \therefore T^2 = 4\pi^2\dfrac{\ell}{g} \Rightarrow g = 4\pi^2\dfrac{\ell}{T^2}$$

$$\Rightarrow \frac{\Delta g}{g}\times 100 = \frac{\Delta \ell}{\ell}\times 100 + 2\frac{\Delta T}{T}\times 100$$

Case (i)

$\Delta \ell = 0.1$ cm, $\ell = 64$cm, $\Delta T = 0.1$s, $T = 128$s

$$\therefore \frac{\Delta g}{g}\times 100 = 0.3125$$

Case (ii)

$\Delta \ell = 0.1$ cm, $\ell = 64$cm, $\Delta T = 0.1$s, $T = 64$s

$$\therefore \frac{\Delta g}{g}\times 100 = 0.46875$$

Case (iii)

$\Delta \ell = 0.1$ cm, $\ell = 20$cm, $\Delta T = 0.1$s, $T = 36$s

$$\therefore \frac{\Delta g}{g}\times 100 = 1.055$$

Clearly, the value of $\dfrac{\Delta g}{g}\times 100$ will be least in case (i).

20. **(d)** 20 divisions on the vernier scale

$\qquad\qquad\qquad$ = 16 divisions of main scale

$\therefore$ 1 division on the vernier scale

$= \dfrac{16}{20}$ divisions of main scale $= \dfrac{16}{20}\times 1\text{mm} = 0.8$ mm

We know that least count = 1MSD – 1VSD

$\qquad\qquad\qquad$ = 1 mm – 0.8 mm = 0.2 mm

21. **(a,c)** As the length of the string of simple pendulum is exactly 1 m (given), therefore the error in length $\Delta l = 0$.

Further the possibility of error in measuring time is 1s in 40s.

$$\therefore \frac{\Delta t}{t} = \frac{\Delta T}{T} = \frac{1}{40}$$

The time period $T = \dfrac{40}{20} = 2$ seconds

$$\therefore \frac{\Delta T}{T} = \frac{1}{40} \Rightarrow \frac{\Delta T}{2} = \frac{1}{40} \Rightarrow \Delta T = 0.05\sec$$

We know that $T = 2\pi\sqrt{\dfrac{l}{g}} \Rightarrow T^2 = 4\pi^2\dfrac{l}{g}$

$$\therefore g = 4\pi^2\frac{l}{T^2}$$

$$\therefore \frac{\Delta g}{g}\times 100 = \frac{\Delta l}{l}\times 100 + 2\frac{\Delta T}{T}\times 100$$

$$\therefore \frac{\Delta g}{g}\times 100 = 0 + 2\left(\frac{1}{40}\right)\times 100 = 5$$

22. **(c)** Diameter D = M.S.R. + (C.S.R) × L.C.

$$D = 2.5 + 20\times\frac{0.5}{50}$$

D = 2.70 mm

The uncertainty in the measurement of diameter $\Delta D = 0.01$ mm.

We know that

$$\rho = \frac{\text{Mass}}{\text{Volume}} = \frac{M}{V} = \frac{M}{\dfrac{4}{3}\eth\left(\dfrac{D}{2}\right)^3}$$

$$\therefore \frac{\Delta \rho}{\rho}\times 100 = \frac{\Delta M}{M}\times 100 + 3\frac{\Delta D}{\Delta}\times 100$$

$$= 2 + 3\times\frac{0.01}{2.70}\times 100 = 3.1\%$$

23. **(a)** The maximum possible error in Y due to l and d are

$$\frac{\Delta Y}{Y} = \frac{\Delta l}{l} + \frac{2\Delta d}{d}$$

The least count

$$= \frac{\text{Pitch}}{\text{Number of divisions on circular scale}}$$

$$= \frac{0.5}{100}\text{mm} = 0.005 \text{ mm}$$

Error contribution of $l = \dfrac{\Delta l}{l} = \dfrac{0.005 \text{ mm}}{0.25 \text{ mm}} = \dfrac{1}{50}$

Error contribution of $d = \dfrac{2\Delta d}{d} = \dfrac{2\times 0.005 \text{ mm}}{0.5 \text{ mm}} = \dfrac{1}{50}$

24. **(a)**

Chapter

2

Vectors

(61 - 92)

Chapter contents

Amedio Avogadro

Amedio Avogadro (1776-1856) worked as a lower before taking up science and becoming professor of physics. In about 1811, he imagined a row of the same-sized containers. Each held a different gas, but at the same temperature and pressure. Avogadro said that there would be exactly the same numbers of atoms of molecules in each container. This now known as Avogadro's law - equal volumes of all gases, when at the same temperature and pressure, have the same numbers of atoms of molecules. ....

Definitions Explanations and Derivations

2.1 SCALAR QUANTITY OR SCALAR

A physical quantity which has magnitude only is called scalar quantity. Example : speed, distance, mass, pressure, electric current, surface tension etc.

2.2 VECTOR QUANTITY OR VECTOR

A physical quantity which has magnitude and direction and must obey law of vector addition is called vector quantity. Example : displacement, velocity, angular velocity, force, torque, angular momentum, momentum, impulse etc.

Surface tension is a scalar quantity

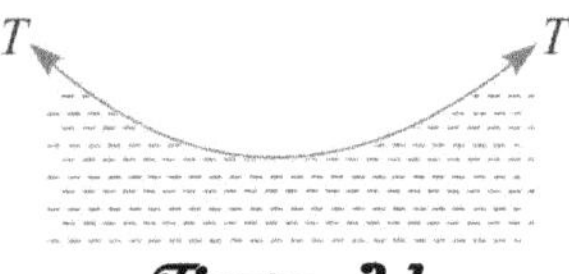

Figure. 2.1

Surface tension is represented by direction, but it is not a vector quantity. Any quantity which has unified direction is treated as scalar. Surface tension always directs along the tangent of the surface of the liquid, therefore it is a scalar quantity.

Note:

1. Scalar quantity may be negative. e.g. charge, electric current, potential energy, work etc.
2. Scalar quantity may have direction. e.g., pressure, electric current, surface tension etc.
3. Small element of length $\vec{d\ell}$, small element of surface $d\vec{A}$ and small angular displacement are treated as vectors.

Electric current is a scalar quantity

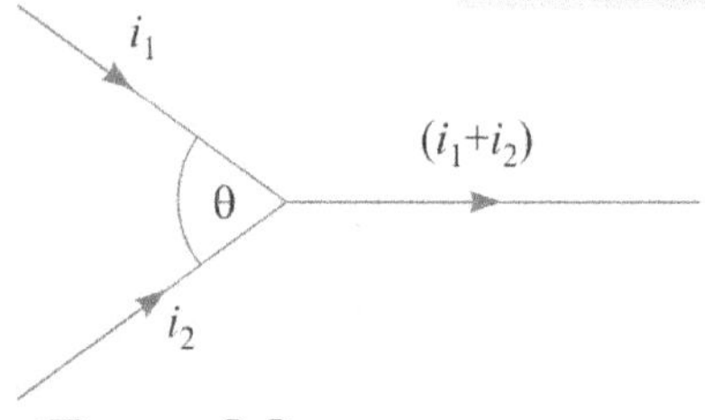

Figure. 2.2

Electric current is always associated with direction, but it is not a vector quantity. It does not obey the law of vector addition for its addition.

The resultant of i_1 and i_2 is $(i_1 + i_2)$ by Kirchhoff's law. The result does not depend on angle between currents i_1 and i_2.

Polar vector

A vector which has translational effect, that is its tail and head lie on a line, is called polar vector. *Example :* velocity, force, momentum etc.

Axial vector

A vector which has rotational effect and act along axis of rotation is called axial vector. *Example :* angular velocity, torque, angular momentum, angular acceleration etc. Direction of axial vector is given by right hand screw rule.

Tensor

A physical quantity which can neither be treated as scalar nor as vector is called a **tensor**. *Example : **moment of inertia**.* It has different values about different axes, but never negative.

An important note on angular displacement

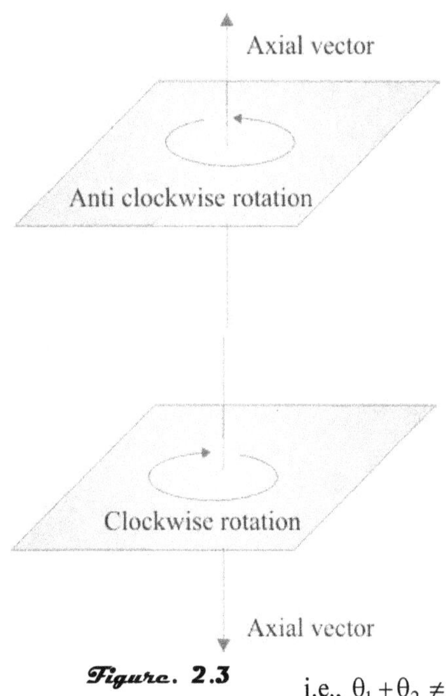

Figure. 2.3

A vector quantity must be commutative in addition. If it is not commutative, then it can not in general be represented by a parallelogram operation and is thus not a vector. With this mind, consider the angle of rotation of a body about some axis. We can associate a magnitude (degrees or radians) and a direction (the axis and a sense of clockwise or anticlockwise) with this quantity. However, the angle of rotation can not be considered a vector because it does not obey commutative law of vector addition i.e., $\theta_1 + \theta_2 \neq \theta_2 + \theta_1$. To understand this, place a book on the floor as in figure (a). Now give the two successive 90° angular displacements, first about the x-axis and then about y-axis (see figure), it gives us $\theta_1 + \theta_2$.

Now, with the book in the same initial position as in figure (b), give two 90° angular displacements in the reverse order (that is, first about y-axis and then about x-axis), it gives us $\theta_2 + \theta_1$. It can be seen from the figure that $(\theta_1 + \theta_2)$ is not same as $(\theta_2 + \theta_1)$. Thus we can say that large anuglar displacement is not a vector quantity.

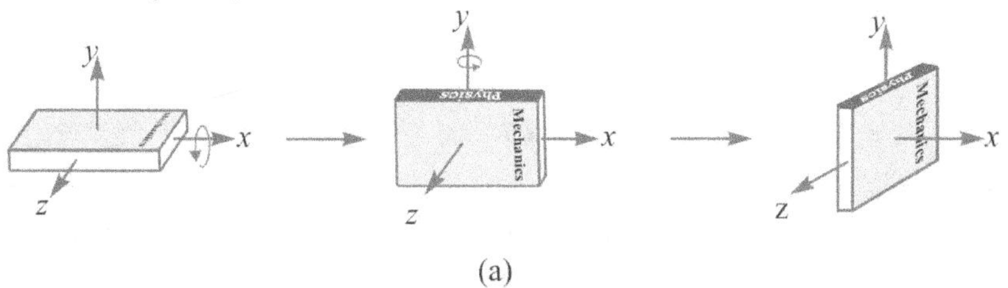

(a)

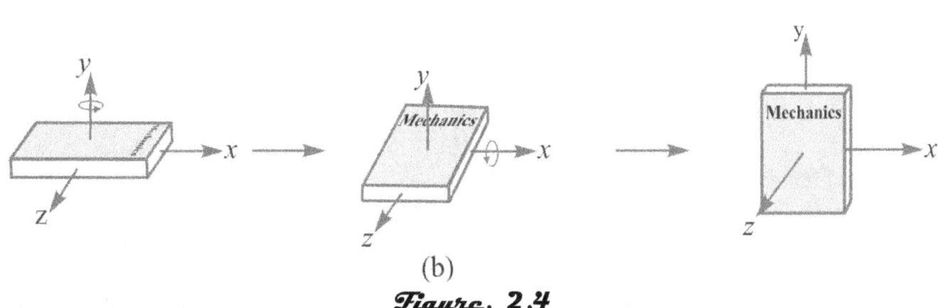

(b)

Figure. **2.4**

Position vector and displacement vector

A vector which gives the position of an object with reference to some specified point in a system is called position vector. Displacement vector refers to the change of position vectors. Thus

displacement vector = final position vector – initial position vector

or

$$\vec{\Delta r} = \vec{r_2} - \vec{r_1}$$

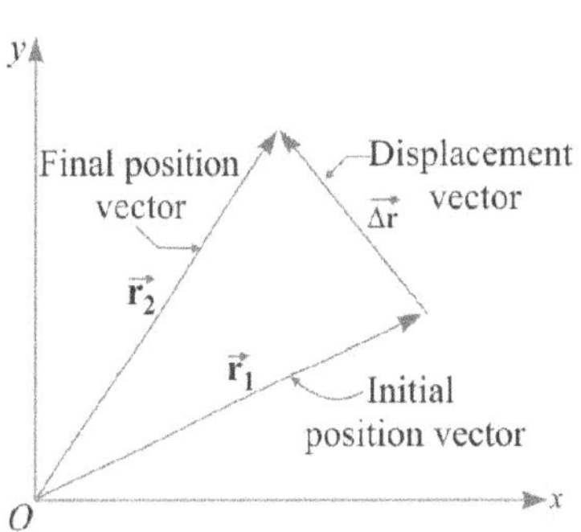

Fixed and free vectors

The vector whose initial point is fixed, is called fixed or localised vector. Example : position vector of a particle; because its initial point lies on the origin. A vector whose initial point is not fixed, is called a free or a non-localised vector. *Example :* displacement vector, velocity vector etc.

Modulus of a vector

The modulus of a vector means the length of the vector. It therefore has no sign and no direction.

Modulus of vector $\vec{A}$ is represented as $|\vec{A}|$ or A.

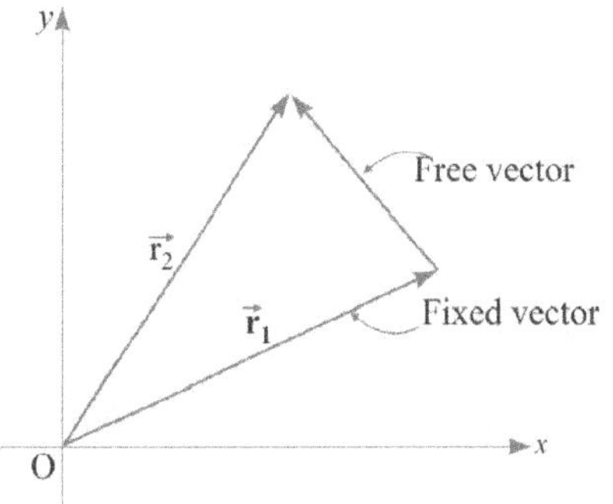

Zero vector or null vector

A vector whose magnitude is zero and has any arbitrary direction is called zero vector. It is represented by $\vec{0}$. The need of a zero arises in the situations :

(i) If $\vec{A} = \vec{B}$, then $\vec{A} - \vec{B} = \vec{0}$

(ii) If $\mu = -\lambda$, then $(\lambda + \mu) \vec{A} = \vec{0}$.

Properties of zero vector : $\vec{A} + \vec{0} = \vec{A}$; $\lambda \vec{0} = \vec{0}$; $0\vec{A} = \vec{0}$

Unit vector

A vector whose magnitude is one unit, is called unit vector. A unit vector in the direction of vector $\vec{A}$ is represented by $\hat{A}$, and is given by $\dfrac{\vec{A}}{A}$.

∴ Any vector can be expressed as $\vec{A} = A\hat{A}$

$\hat{i}$, $\hat{j}$ and $\hat{k}$ are unit vectors along x, y and z-axes.

Figure. **2.5**

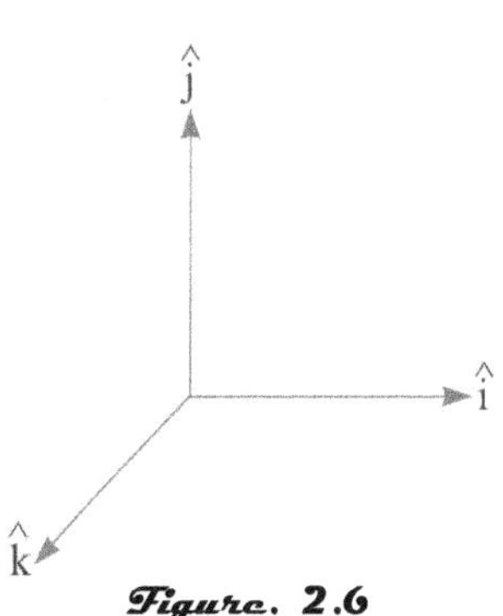

Figure. **2.6**

Equal vectors

Two vectors are said to be equal if they have same magnitude and same direction.

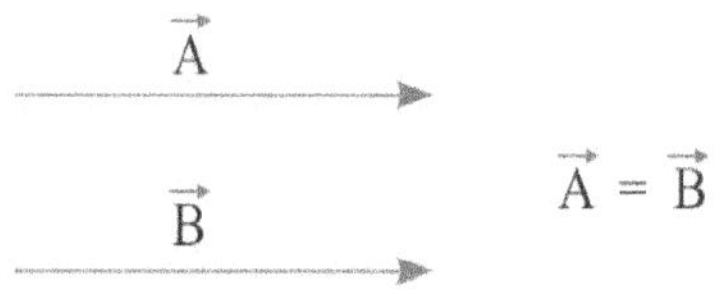

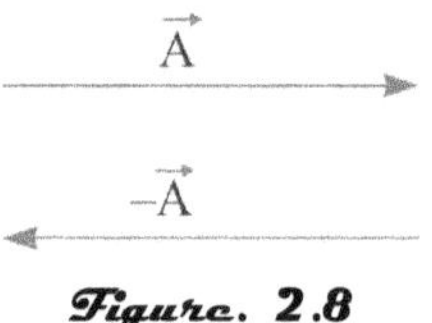

Figure. 2.7

Negative of a vector

The negative of a vector is defined as vector having same magnitude but an opposite direction.

Figure. 2.8

Multiplication of a vector by a scalar

When a vector is multiplied by a scalar λ, we get a new vector which is λ times the vector $\vec{A}$ i.e $\lambda\vec{A}$. The direction of resulting vector is that of $\vec{A}$. If λ has negative value then vector becomes $-\lambda\vec{A}$, whose direction is opposite of $\vec{A}$. The unit of resulting vector is the multiplied units of λ and $\vec{A}$. For example when mass is multiplied with velocity, we get momentum. The unit of momentum is obtained by multiplying unit of mass and velocity.

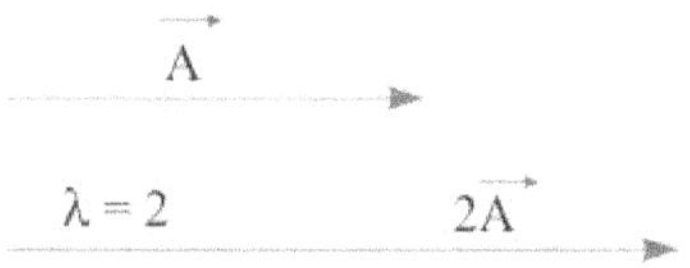

Figure. 2.9

Similarly, we can have vector $\vec{A}$ divided by a scalar λ. The resulting vector becomes $\dfrac{\vec{A}}{\lambda}$. The magnitude of $\vec{A}$ decreases by λ and direction is as that of $\vec{A}$. Or $\lambda = -2$, the resulting vector becomes twice in magnitude and opposite in direction, with as follows:

Figure. 2.10

Collinear or parallel vectors

The vectors which act along the same line or along parallel lines are called collinear vectors.

Figure. 2.11

(a)   Like or parallel vectors.

Figure. 2.12

(b)   Unlike or antiparallel vectors.

If $\vec{A}$ and $\vec{B}$ be two collinear vectors, then there exists a scalar k such the $\vec{B} = k\vec{A}$; the absolute value of k being the ratio of the length of the two collinear vectors.

Coplanar and concurrent vectors

$\vec{A}$, $\vec{B}$ and $\vec{C}$ are coplanar and concurrent vectors

Figure. **2.13**

Vectors started from same point are known as concurrent vectors. In *fig.* 2.13 $\vec{\mathbf{A}}$, $\vec{\mathbf{B}}$ and $\vec{\mathbf{C}}$ are coplanar and concurent vectors.

2.3 Vectors operations

The possible vectors operations are :

(i) Addition or subtraction of vectors.

(ii) Multiplication of vectors.

Note: Division of a vector by a vector is not possible.

The addition or subtraction of vectors can be done by following two methods :

(i) *Analytical method.*

(ii) *Geometrical method.*

Geometrical method is more suitable for addition of more number of vectors while analytical method is suitable for addition of less number of vectors.

2.4 Addition or subtraction of two vectors

Geometrical method

(a) Triangle law of vector addition : If two non-zero vectors can be represented by the two sides of a triangle taken in same order, then their resultant is represented by third side of the triangle taken in the opposite order. Consider two vectors $\vec{\mathbf{A}}$ and $\vec{\mathbf{B}}$ at an angle θ between them.

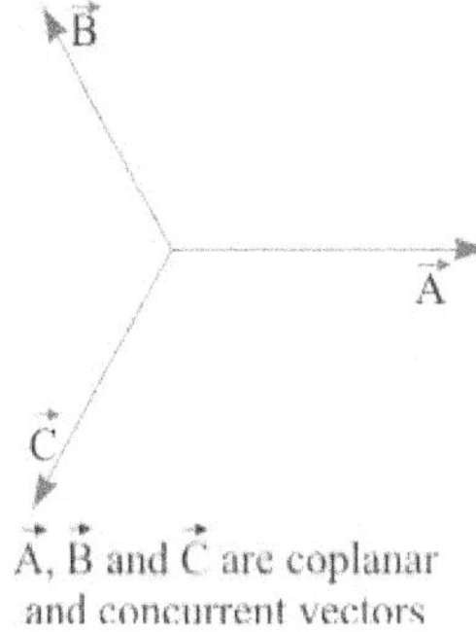

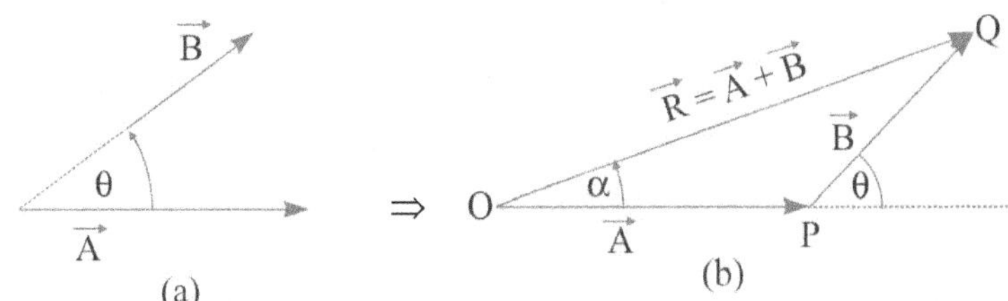

Figure. **2.14**

(i) **Finding $\vec{\mathbf{A}}+\vec{\mathbf{B}}$:** First draw vector $\vec{\mathbf{A}}$ ($\overrightarrow{\mathbf{OP}}$) in the given direction. Then draw vector $\vec{\mathbf{B}}$ ($\overrightarrow{\mathbf{PQ}}$); starting from the head of the vector $\vec{\mathbf{A}}$. Then close the triangle. $\vec{\mathbf{R}}$ ($\overrightarrow{\mathbf{OQ}}$) will be their resultant (*fig.* 2.15).

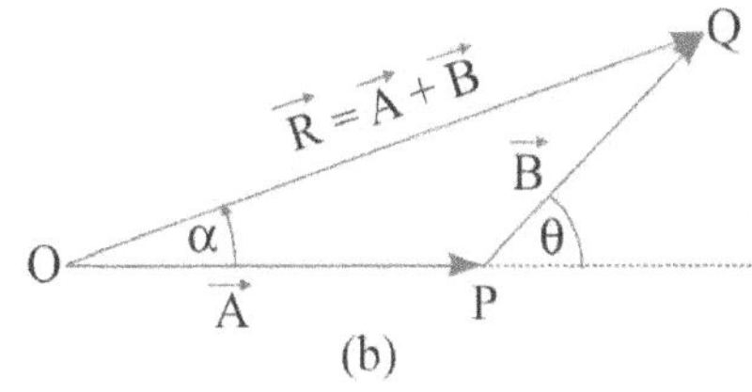

Figure. **2.15**

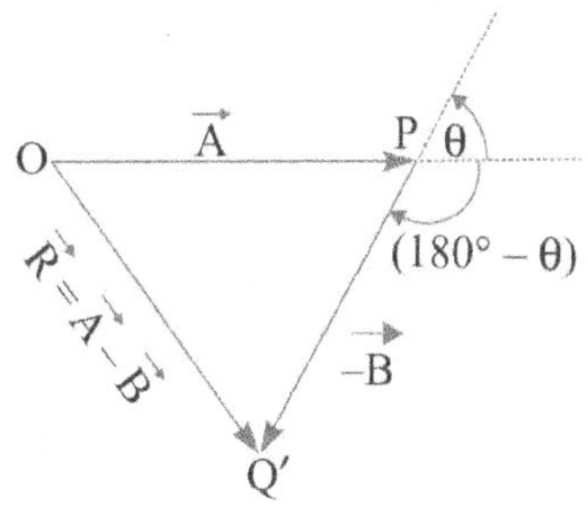

Figure. **2.16**

(ii) **Finding $\vec{\mathbf{A}}-\vec{\mathbf{B}}$:** First draw vector $\vec{\mathbf{A}}$ ($\overrightarrow{\mathbf{OP}}$) in the given direction. Then draw vector $-\vec{\mathbf{B}}$ ($\overrightarrow{\mathbf{PQ}}$). starting from head of the vector $\vec{\mathbf{A}}$. Then close the triangle, $\vec{\mathbf{R}}$ ($\overrightarrow{\mathbf{OQ'}}$) be their resultant (see *fig.* 2.16)

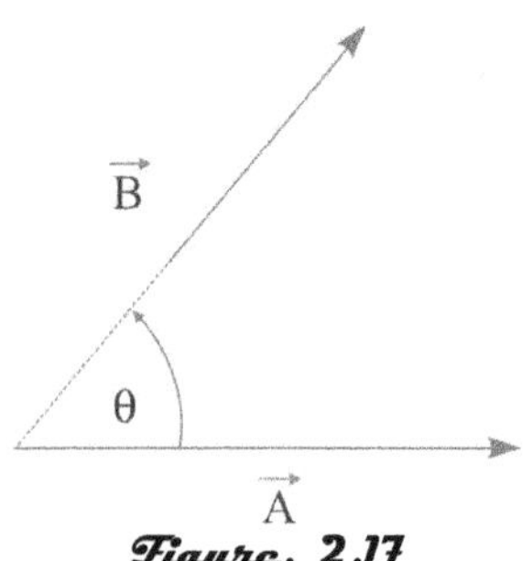

Figure. 2.17

(b) **Parallelogram law of vector addition :** If two non-zero vectors can be represented by the two adjacent sides of a parallelogram, then their resultant is represented by the diagonal of the parallelogram passing through the point of intersection of the vectors. Suppose two vectors $\vec{A}$ and $\vec{B}$ as shown in *fig.* 2.17.

(i) **Finding $\vec{A} + \vec{B}$:** Draw vectors $\vec{A}$ ($\overrightarrow{OP}$) and $\vec{B}$ ($\overrightarrow{OQ}$) starting from a common point O in the given directions. Then complete parallelogram. The diagonal $\overrightarrow{OS}$ will represent their resultant.

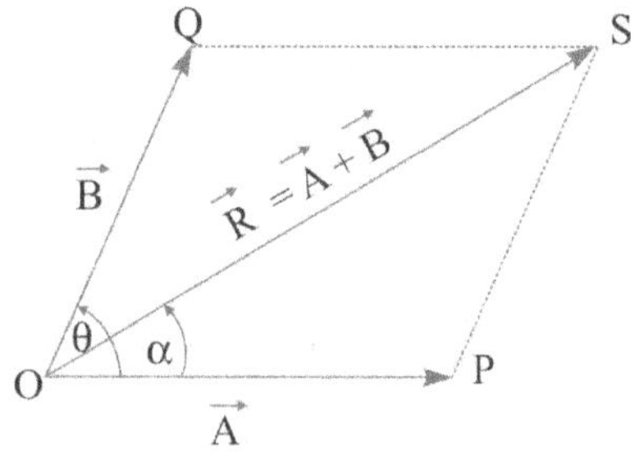

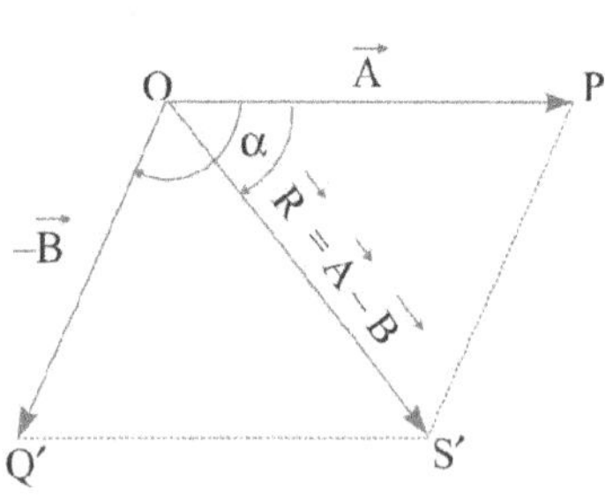

Figure. 2.18

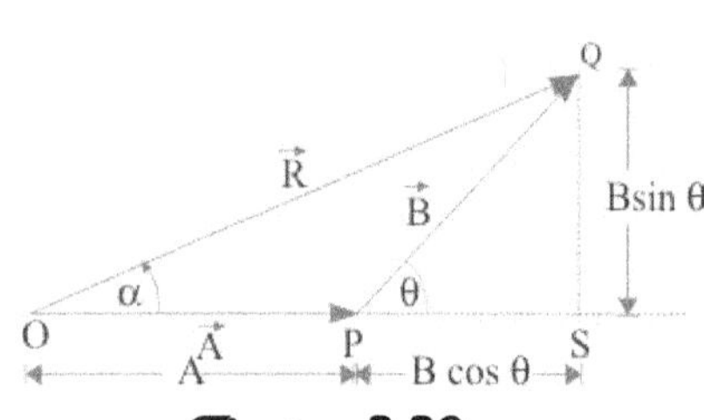

Figure. 2.19

(ii) **Finding $\vec{A} - \vec{B}$:** Draw vectors $\vec{A}$ ($\overrightarrow{OP}$) and $-\vec{B}$ ($\overrightarrow{OQ'}$) starting from a common point O. Then complete the parallelogram. The diagonal $\overrightarrow{OS'}$ will represent their resultant.

Analytical method:

Finding $\vec{A} + \vec{B}$:

It is clear from the geometry of the figure that resultant of $\vec{A}$ and $\vec{B}$ is equal to the resultant of $(\vec{A} + \vec{B}\cos\theta)$ and $\vec{B}\sin\theta$. By Pythagorous theorem, we have

$$\therefore \quad R^2 = (A + B\cos\theta)^2 + (B\sin\theta)^2 = A^2 + B^2\cos^2\theta + 2AB\cos\theta + B^2\sin^2\theta$$

or

$$R = \sqrt{A^2 + B^2 + 2AB\cos\theta}$$

If α is the angle which resultant $\vec{R}$ makes with $\vec{A}$, then

$$\tan\alpha = \frac{B\sin\theta}{A + B\cos\theta}$$

Special cases :

(i)   For $\theta = 0°$; $R_{max} = \sqrt{A^2 + B^2 + 2AB} = A + B$

(ii)   For $\theta = 180°$, $R_{min} = \sqrt{A^2 + B^2 - 2AB} = A - B$

Thus resultant of two vectors R can be; $(A - B) \leq R \leq (A + B)$

(iii)   If $A = B$, $R = \sqrt{A^2 + A^2 + 2AA\cos\theta}$

$$= \sqrt{2A^2(1 + \cos\theta)}$$

$$= \sqrt{2A^2 \times 2\cos^2\theta/2}$$

$$= 2A\cos\theta/2$$

and $\quad \alpha = \dfrac{\theta}{2}$

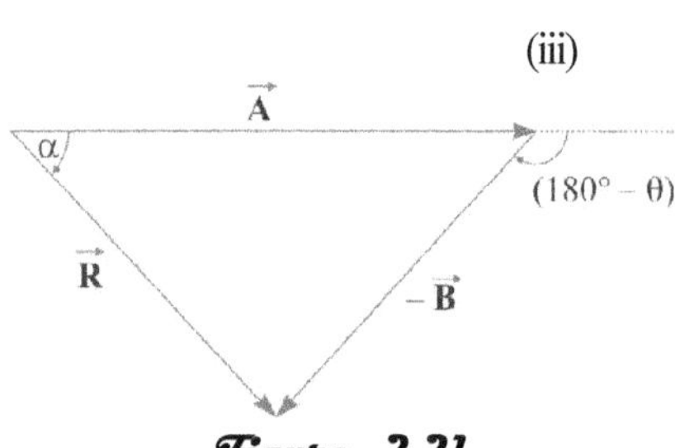

Figure. 2.20

Figure. 2.21

(iv) $\vec{R} = \vec{A} - \vec{B}$

$$= \vec{A} + (-\vec{B})$$

The subtraction of $\vec{B}$ from $\vec{A}$ means addition of $\vec{B}$ to $\vec{A}$ with an angle $(180° - \theta)$.

$$\therefore\ R = \sqrt{A^2 + B^2 + 2AB\cos(180° - \theta)}$$

$$= \sqrt{A^2 + B^2 - 2AB\cos\theta}$$

and $\tan\alpha = \dfrac{B\sin(180° - \theta)}{A + B\cos(180° - \theta)} = \dfrac{B\sin\theta}{A - B\cos\theta}$.

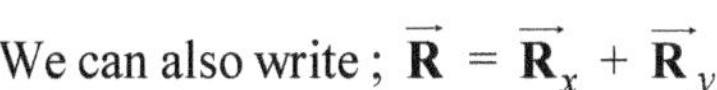

Note: For $\theta = 90°$, $|\vec{A} + \vec{B}| = |\vec{A} - \vec{B}|$.

Resolution of a vector into two perpendicular components

Consider a vector $\vec{R}$ in xy- plane which makes an angle θ with $+x$-axis. Let $\vec{R}_x$ and $\vec{R}_y$ are the components along x and y-axes respectively, then

$$\frac{R_x}{R} = \cos\theta$$

$$\Rightarrow \quad R_x = R\cos\theta$$

and

$$\frac{R_y}{R} = \sin\theta$$

$$\Rightarrow \quad R_y = R\sin\theta$$

We can also write ; $\vec{R} = \vec{R}_x + \vec{R}_y$

or $\qquad \vec{R} = R_x\hat{i} + R_y\hat{j} \qquad$ (2D – Vector)

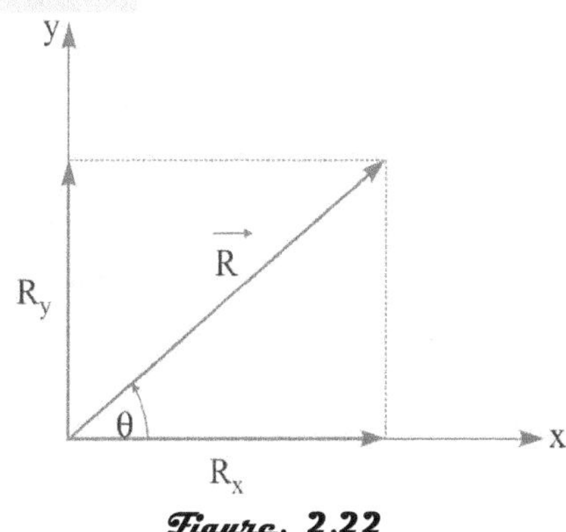

Figure. **2.22**

Rectangular components of 3D-vector

If $\vec{R}$ makes an angle α with x-axis, β with y-axis and γ with z-axis, then

$$\cos\alpha = \frac{R_x}{R} = \ell,$$

$$\cos\beta = \frac{R_y}{R} = m,$$

and $\qquad \cos\gamma = \dfrac{R_z}{R} = n$

where ℓ, m, n are called direction cosines of the vector $\vec{R}$
Squaring and adding, we get

$$\cos^2\alpha + \cos^2\beta + \cos^2\gamma = \frac{R_x^2 + R_y^2 + R_z^2}{R^2}$$

As $\qquad R_x^2 + R_y^2 + R_z^2 = R^2,$

$$\therefore \quad \cos^2\alpha + \cos^2\beta + \cos^2\gamma = 1$$

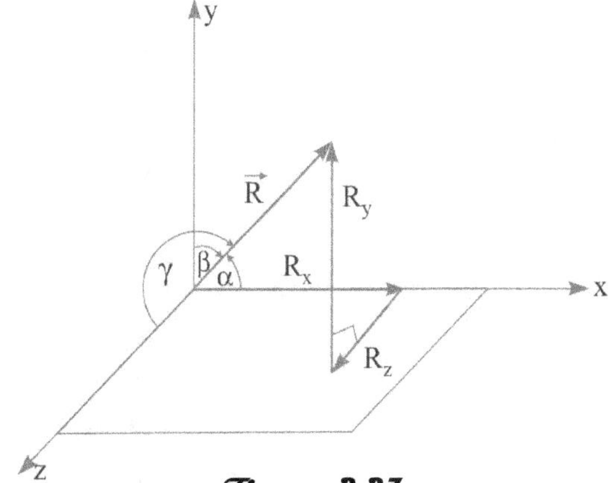

Figure. **2.23**

Writing the position vector

The position of a point from any reference point, such as the origin O of the cartesian coordinate system, is uniquely specified by the vector $\overrightarrow{OP} = \vec{r}$, called the position vector of point P relative to O. The coordinates of point P being (x, y, z). We can write $\vec{r} = x\hat{i} + y\hat{j} + z\hat{k}$ and $r = \sqrt{x^2 + y^2 + z^2}$.

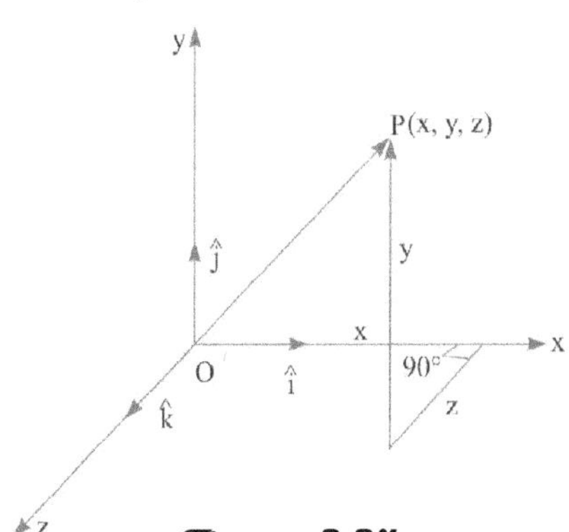

Figure. **2.24**

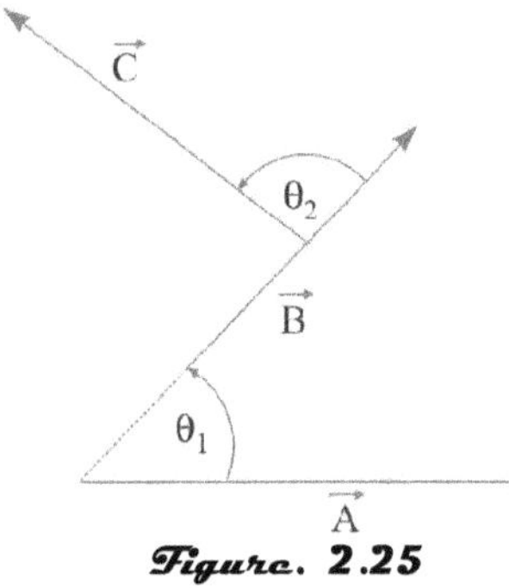

Figure. **2.25**

2.5   ADDITION OR SUBTRACTION OF MORE THAN TWO VECTORS

Consider three vectors $\vec{A}$, $\vec{B}$ and $\vec{C}$ as shown in *fig.* 2.27.

Finding $\vec{R} = \vec{A} + \vec{B} + \vec{C}$:

Geometrical method

Polygon law of vector addition : If a number of vectors are represented by the sides of an open polygon taken in the same order, then their resultant is represented by the closing side of the polygon taken in opposite order.

Here in the *fig.* 2.26 $\vec{R}$ (closing side of polygon) represents the resultant. of vectors $\vec{A}$, $\vec{B}$ and $\vec{C}$.

Analytical method

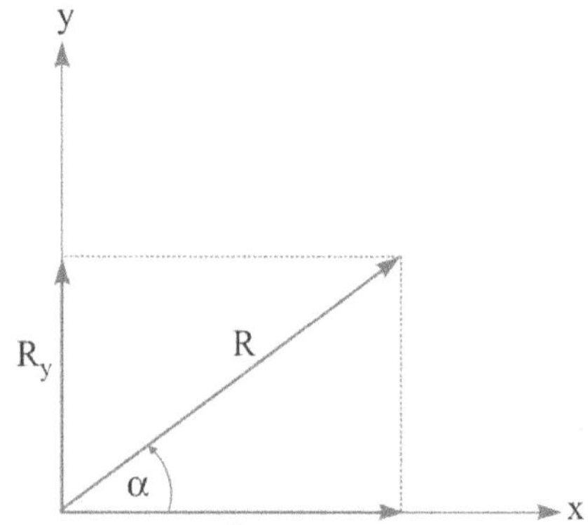

In this method first we have to resolve all the vectors into two **perpendicular axes.** Then by using Pythagorous theorem, their resultant can be obtained. Let R_x and R_y be the sum of the components along x-axis and y-axis, then their resultant,

$$R = \sqrt{R_x^2 + R_y^2}$$

and $\qquad \tan \alpha = \dfrac{R_y}{R_x}$

where $R_x = A \cos 0° + B \cos \theta_1 + C \cos (\theta_1 + \theta_2)$,

and $\quad R_y = A \sin 0° + B \sin \theta_1 + C \sin (\theta_1 + \theta_2)$.

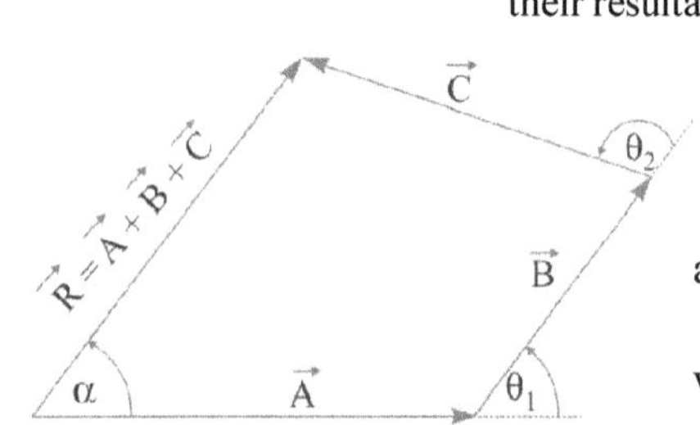

Figure. **2.26**

Figure. **2.27**

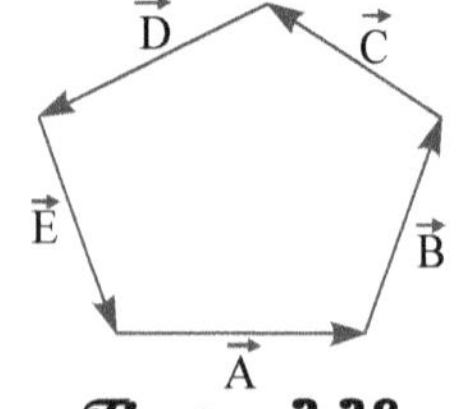

Figure. **2.28**

Note :

If a number of vectors makes a closed polygon, their resultant will be zero. Here vectors $\vec{A}$, $\vec{B}$, $\vec{C}$, $\vec{D}$ and $\vec{E}$ make closed polygon.

$$\therefore \quad \vec{A} + \vec{B} + \vec{C} + \vec{D} + \vec{E} = \vec{0}$$

Condition of collinearity of vectors $\vec{A}$ and $\vec{B}$

Let $\vec{A} = A_1 \hat{i} + A_2 \hat{j} + A_3 \hat{k}$ and $\vec{B} = B_1 \hat{i} + B_2 \hat{j} + B_3 \hat{k}$

Obviously, to be collinear (or parallel), the direction cosines of vector $\vec{A}$ must be equal to the respective direction cosines of vector $\vec{B}$, i.e., we should have

$$\frac{A_1}{A} = \frac{B_1}{B}, \; \frac{A_2}{A} = \frac{B_2}{B} \; \text{and} \; \frac{A_3}{A} = \frac{B_3}{B}$$

which gives $\dfrac{A_1}{B_1} = \dfrac{A_2}{B_2} = \dfrac{A_3}{B_3} = \dfrac{A}{B}$.

FORMULAE USED

1. The resultant of two vectors with angle θ between them is given by;

$$R = \sqrt{A^2 + B^2 + 2AB\cos\theta}$$

$$R_{min} = A - B, \quad R_{max} = A + B,$$

and

$$\tan\alpha = \left[\frac{B\sin\theta}{A + B\cos\theta}\right].$$

For $A = B$, $R = 2A\cos\theta/2$ and $\alpha = \theta/2$.

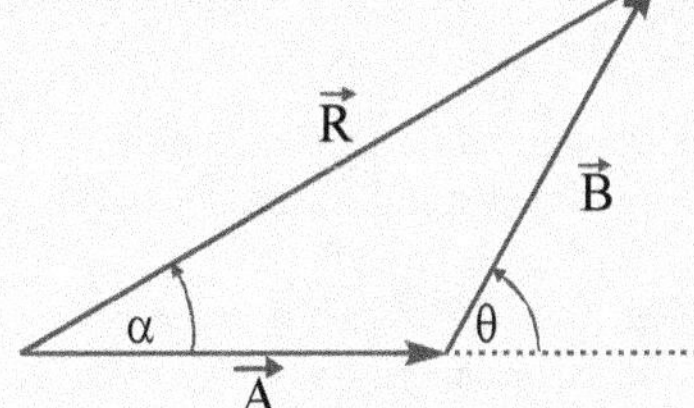

2. If A_x, A_y and A_z are the rectangular components of $\vec{A}$ and $\hat{i}, \hat{j}$ and $\hat{k}$ are the unit vectors along x-, y- and z-axis respectively, then

$$\vec{A} = A_x\hat{i} + A_y\hat{j} + A_z\hat{k}$$

and

$$A = |\vec{A}| = \sqrt{A_x^2 + A_y^2 + A_z^2}$$

$$\hat{A} = \frac{\vec{A}}{|\vec{A}|} = \frac{A_x\hat{i} + A_y\hat{j} + A_z\hat{k}}{\sqrt{A_x^2 + A_y^2 + A_z^2}}$$

3. **Resolution of a vector :** If a vector $\vec{R}$ makes angle θ with the positive x-axis, then components of $\vec{R}$:

$$R_x = R\cos\theta$$

and

$$R_y = R\sin\theta$$

Also

$$\vec{R} = R_x\hat{i} + R_y\hat{j} = R\cos\theta\hat{i} + R\sin\theta\hat{j}$$

and

$$R = \sqrt{R_x^2 + R_y^2}.$$

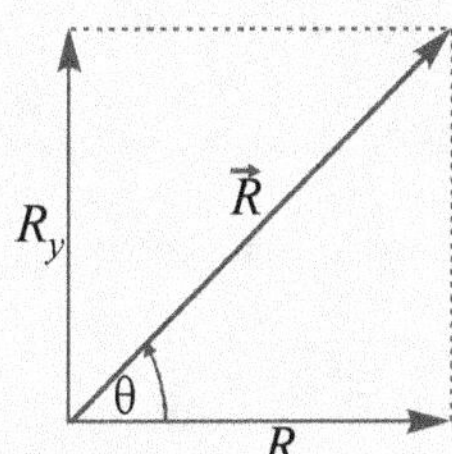

EXAMPLES BASED ON ADDITION OR SUBTRACTION OF VECTORS

Example 1. Read each statement below carefully and state with reasons, if it is true or false : [NCERT]

(a) The magnitude of a vector is always a scalar.

(b) Each component of a vector is always a scalar.

(c) The total path length is always equal to the magnitude of the displacement vector of a particle.

(d) The average speed of a particle (defined as total path length divided by the time taken to cover the path) is either greater or equal to the magnitude of average velocity of the particle over the same interval of time.

(e) Three vectors not lying in a plane can never add up to give a null vector.

Sol. (a) True : The magnitude of a vector is a pure number, and so is a scalar.

(b) False : Component of a vector is also a vector.

(c) False : They are equal only along a straight line without changing the direction, otherwise total path length will be greater than magnitude of acceleration.

(d) True : $\left|\dfrac{\text{Average velocity}}{\text{average speed}}\right| \leq 1.$

(e) True : This is because the resultant of the two vectors will not lie in the plane of the third vector and so cannot be cancel out to give zero resultant.

Example 2. Which of the following quantities are independent of the choice of orientation of the coordinate axes : $\vec{a} + \vec{b}, 3a_x + 2a_y, |\vec{a} + \vec{b} - \vec{c}|$, the angle between $\vec{b}$ and $\vec{c}$, $\lambda\vec{a}$, where λ is a scalar ?

Sol. A vector and its magnitude do not depend on the choice of the orientation of the axes, but component of a vector depends on the orientation of the axes. Thus $\vec{a} + \vec{b}, |\vec{a} + \vec{b} - \vec{c}|$, the angle between the vector, $\lambda\vec{a}$ are independent of orientation of axis, while $3a_x + 2a_y$ depends on the orientation of the axes.

Example 3. State with reasons, whether the following algebraic operations with scalar and vector physical quantities are meaningful. [NCERT]

(a) adding any two scalars,

(b) adding a scalar to a vector of the same dimensions,

(c) multiplying any vector by any scalar,

(d) multiplying any two scalars,

(e) adding any two vectors,

(f) adding a component of a vector to the same vector.

Sol.

(a) No, because only the scalars of same dimensions can be added.

(b) No, because a scalar cannot be added to a vector.

(c) Yes, multiplying a vector with a scalar gives the scalar (number) times the vector quantity which makes sense and one gets a bigger vector. For example, when acceleration $\vec{A}$ is multiplied by mass m, we get a force $\vec{F} = m\,\vec{A}$.

(d) Yes, two scalars multiplied yield a meaningful result, for example multiplication of rise in temperature of water and its mass gives the amount of heat absorbed by that mass of water.

(e) No, because the two vectors of same dimensions can be added.

(f) Yes, because both are vectors of the same dimensions.

Example 4. **Establish the following vector inequalities geometrically or otherwise:** [NCERT]

(a) $\left|\vec{A} + \vec{B}\right| \le \left|\vec{A}\right| + \left|\vec{B}\right|$

(b) $\left|\vec{A} + \vec{B}\right| \ge \left|\vec{A}\right| - \left|\vec{B}\right|$

(c) $\left|\vec{A} - \vec{B}\right| \le \left|\vec{A}\right| + \left|\vec{B}\right|$

(d) $\left|\vec{A} - \vec{B}\right| \ge \left|\vec{A}\right| - \left|\vec{B}\right|$

When does the equality sign above apply?

Sol. Consider two vectors $\vec{A}$ and $\vec{B}$ be represented by the sides $\overrightarrow{OP}$ and $\overrightarrow{OQ}$ of a parallelogram $OPSQ$. According to parallelogram law of vector addition, $(\vec{A} + \vec{B})$ will be represented by $\overrightarrow{OS}$ as shown in the adjoining **figure**. Thus, $OP = |\vec{A}|$, $OQ = PS = |\vec{B}|$ and $OS = |\vec{A} + \vec{B}|$.

(a) to prove $|\vec{A} + \vec{B}| \le |\vec{A}| + |\vec{B}|$

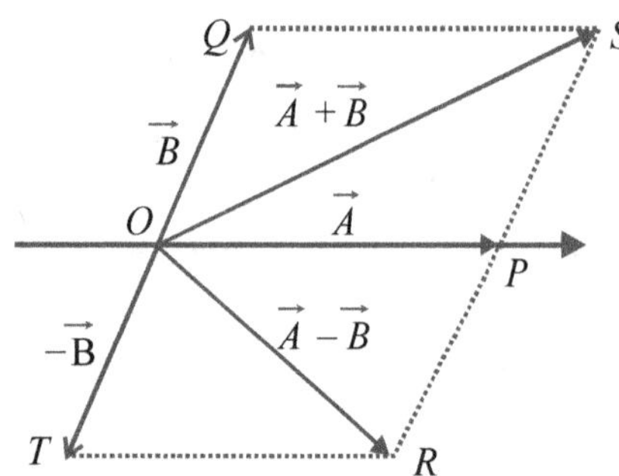

We know that the length of one side of triangle is always less than the sum of the lengths of the other two sides. Hence from $\triangle OPS$, we have

$OS < OP + PS$ or, $OS < OP + OQ$ or,

$|\vec{A} + \vec{B}| \le |\vec{A}| + |\vec{B}|$ ...... (1)

If the two vectors $\vec{A}$ and $\vec{B}$ are acting along the same straight line and in the same direction then,

$|\vec{A} + \vec{B}| = |\vec{A}| + |\vec{B}|$ ...... (2)

(b) $|\vec{A} + \vec{B}| \ge ||\vec{A}| - |\vec{B}||$
From $\triangle OPS$, we have,
$OS + PS > OP$ or, $OS > |OP - PS|$ or,
$OS > |OP - OQ|$ ...... (3)
(Since $PS = OQ$)

The modulus of $(\overrightarrow{OS} - \overrightarrow{PS})$ has been taken because the LHS is always positive but the RHS may be negative if $OP < PS$. Thus from (3) we have,

$|\vec{A} + \vec{B}| > ||\vec{A}| - |\vec{B}||$ ...... (4)

If the two vectors $\vec{A}$ and $\vec{B}$ are acting along a straight line in opposite directions, then

$|\vec{A} + \vec{B}| = ||\vec{A}| - |\vec{B}||$ ...... (5)

Considering (4) and (5) together, we get,

$|\vec{A} + \vec{B}| \ge ||\vec{A}| - |\vec{B}||$

(c) $|\vec{A} - \vec{B}| \le |\vec{A}| + |\vec{B}|$

In Fig, $|\vec{A}| = OP$ and $|-\vec{B}| = OT = PR$ and $|(\vec{A} - \vec{B})| = OR$

From $\triangle OPS$ we note that $OR < OP + PR$.

or $|\vec{A} - \vec{B}| < ||\vec{A}| + |-\vec{B}||$

or, $|\vec{A} - \vec{B}| < ||\vec{A}| + |\vec{B}||$ ...... (6)

If the two vectors are acting along the straight line but in opposite direction, then,

$|\vec{A} - \vec{B}| = ||\vec{A}| + |\vec{B}||$ ...... (7)

Considering (6) and (7) together, we get,

$|\vec{A} - \vec{B}| \le |\vec{A}| + |\vec{B}|$

(d) $|\vec{A} - \vec{B}| \ge ||\vec{A}| - |\vec{B}||$
In Fig, from $\triangle OPS$ we have,
$OR + PR > OP$ or, $OR > |OP - PR|$
or, $OR > |OP - OT|$ ...... (8)
(Since $OT = PR$)

The modulus of $(\overrightarrow{OP} - \overrightarrow{OT})$ has been taken because LHS is positive and RHS may be negative if $OP < OT$.
From (8),

$|\vec{A} - \vec{B}| > |\vec{A}| - |\vec{B}|$ ...... (9)

If the two vectors $\vec{A}$ and $\vec{B}$ are along the same straight line in the same direction then,

$|\vec{A} - \vec{B}| = |\vec{A}| - |\vec{B}|$ ...... (10)

Considering (9) and (10) together, we get,

$|\vec{A} - \vec{B}| \ge ||\vec{A}| - |\vec{B}||$

Example 5. **Given $\vec{a} + \vec{b} + \vec{c} + \vec{d} = 0$, which of the following statements are correct ?** [NCERT]

(a) **$\vec{a}, \vec{b}, \vec{c}$ and $\vec{d}$ must each be a null vector.**

(b) **The magnitude of $(\vec{a} + \vec{c})$ equals the magnitude of $(\vec{b} + \vec{d})$.**

(c) **The magnitude of $\vec{a}$ can never be greater than the sum of the magnitudes of $\vec{b}, \vec{c},$ and $\vec{d}$.**

(d) **$\vec{b} + \vec{c}$ must lie in the plane of $\vec{a}$ and $\vec{d}$ if $\vec{a}$ and $\vec{d}$ are not collinear, and in the line of $\vec{a}$ and $\vec{d}$, if they are collinear ?**

Sol. (a) $\vec{a}, \vec{b}, \vec{c}$ and $\vec{d}$ need not each be a null vector. The resultant of four non-zero vectors even in different planes can be zero resultant.

(b) $\vec{a} + \vec{b} + \vec{c} + \vec{d} = 0$,

$\therefore (\vec{a} + \vec{c}) = -(\vec{b} + \vec{d})$ or $\left|(\vec{a} + \vec{c})\right| = \left|(\vec{b} + \vec{d})\right|$,   hence given statement is correct.

(c) As $\vec{a} + \vec{b} + \vec{c} + \vec{d} = 0$, $\therefore \vec{a} = -(\vec{b} + \vec{c} + \vec{d})$.

Thus magnitude of $\vec{a}$ is equal to the magnitude of $(\vec{b} + \vec{c} + \vec{d})$. The given statement is correct.

(d) As $\vec{a} + \vec{b} + \vec{c} + \vec{d} = 0$, $\therefore (\vec{b} + \vec{c}) = -(\vec{a} + \vec{d})$ and hence plane of $(\vec{b} + \vec{c})$ and $(\vec{a} + \vec{d})$ must be same.

Example 6. A person moves 30 m north, then 20 m east and finally $30\sqrt{2}$ m south-west. What is his displacement from the initial position ?

Sol. If $\hat{i}, \hat{j}$ are the unit vectors along east and north respectively, then

$\vec{s}_1 = 30\,\hat{j}$,

$\vec{s}_2 = 20\,\hat{i}$,

and $\vec{s}_3 = 30\sqrt{2}\left(\cos 45° \,\hat{i} + \sin 45° \,\hat{j}\right)$

$= -30\hat{i} - 30\hat{j}$

The total displacement

$\vec{s} = \vec{s}_1 + \vec{s}_2 + \vec{s}_3$

$= 30\hat{j} + 20\hat{i} - 30\hat{i} - 30\hat{j} = -10\hat{i}$.

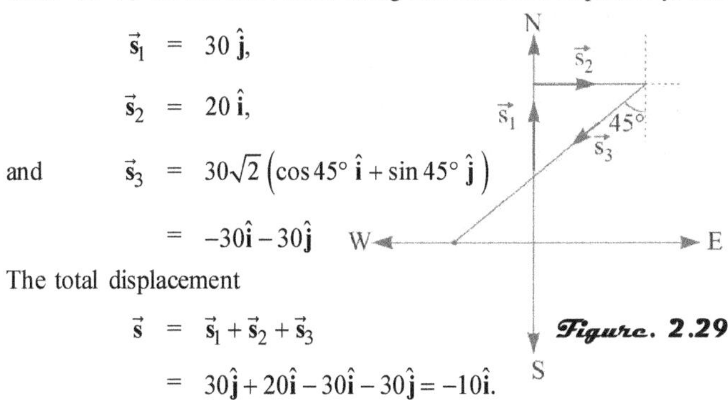

Figure. 2.29

i.e., the resultant displacement is 10 m along west. *Ans.*

Example 7. A motorboat is racing towards north at 25 km/h and the water current in that region is 10 km/h in the direction of 60° east of south. Find the resultant velocity of the boat.

Sol. The velocity of motorboat, $v_b = 25$ km/h, due north velocity of water current, $v_c = 10$ km/h, 60° east of south.

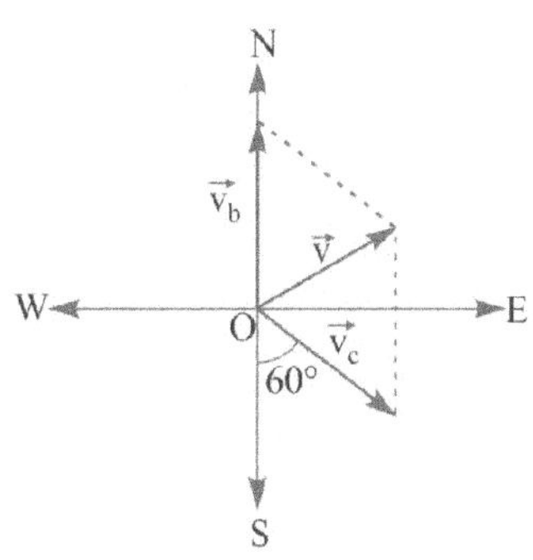

Figure. 2.30

Let motorboat starts moving from O, as shown in *fig.* 2.25. From the figure, the angle between $\vec{v}_b$ and $\vec{v}_c$ is 120°. The resultant velocity of boat is the resultant of $\vec{v}_b$ and $\vec{v}_c$. Thus

$\vec{v} = \sqrt{v_b^2 + v_c^2 + 2v_b v_c \cos 120°}$

$= \sqrt{25^2 + 10^2 + 2 \times 25 \times 10 \times \left(-\dfrac{1}{2}\right)}$

$= 21.8$ km/h *Ans.*

Let the resultant velocity $\vec{v}$ makes an angle α with the direction of $\vec{v}_b$, then

$\tan \alpha = \dfrac{v_c \sin 120°}{v_b + v_c \cos 120°} = \dfrac{10\left(\sqrt{3}/2\right)}{25 + 10 \times (-1/2)}$

$= \dfrac{\sqrt{3}}{4}$

or $\alpha = \tan^{-1}\left(\dfrac{\sqrt{3}}{4}\right)$. *Ans.*

Example 8. Two billiard balls are rolling on a flat table. One has the velocity components $v_x = 1$ m/s, $v_y = \sqrt{3}$ m/s and the other has components $v'_x = 2$ m/s and $v'_y = 2$ m/s. If both the balls start moving from the same point, what is the angle between their paths ?

Sol. If θ and θ' are the angles made by resultant velocities of first and second ball respectively from the x-axis, then

$\tan \theta = \dfrac{v_y}{v_x} = \dfrac{\sqrt{3}}{1} = \sqrt{3}$

or $\theta = 60°$

and $\tan \theta' = \dfrac{v'_y}{v'_x} = \dfrac{2}{2} = 1$

or $\theta' = 45°$

Angle between the paths of the balls

$= \theta - \theta' = 60° - 45° = 15°$ *Ans.*

Example 9. Two vectors, both equal in magnitude, have their resultant equal in magnitude of the either vector. Find the angle between the vectors.

Sol. Let θ is the angle between the vectors

$\therefore \qquad A^2 = A^2 + A^2 + 2AA \cos \theta$

which gives $\cos \theta = -\dfrac{1}{2}$

or $\theta = 120°$. *Ans.*

Example 10. On an open ground, a motorist follows a track that turns to his left by an angle of 60° after every 500 m. Starting from a given turn, specify the displacement of the motorist at the third, sixth and eighth turn. Compare the magnitude of the displacement with the total path length covered by the motorist in each case. [NCERT]

Sol. In this question, the path is a regular hexagon $ABCDEF$ of side length 500 m. In Fig,

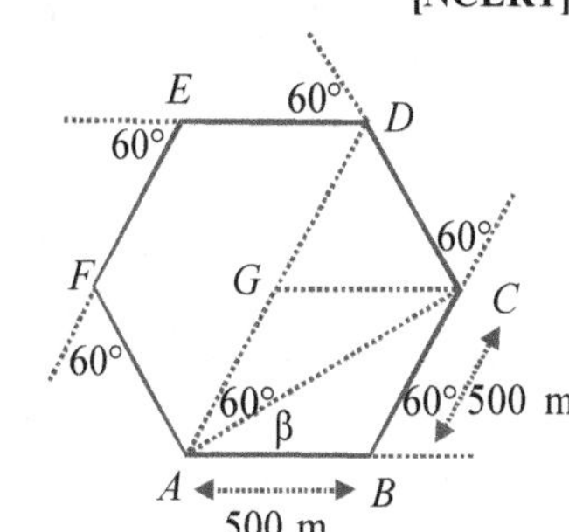

Let the motorist start from A.

Third Turn

The motorcyclist will take the 3rd turn at D. Displacement vector at D
$= AD$

Magnitude of this displacement
$$= 500 + 500 = 1000 \text{ m}$$

Total path length from A to $D = AB + BC + CD$
$$= 500 + 500 + 500 = 1500 \text{ m}$$

Sixth Turn

The motorcyclist will take the 6th turn at A.

$\therefore$ Displacement vector is null vector.

Total path length $= AB + BC + CD + DE + EF$
$$= 500 + 500 + 500 + 500 + 500 + 500 = 3000 \text{ m}$$

Eighth Turn

The motorcyclist takes the 8th turn at C.

$\therefore$ Displacement vector $= AC$, which is represented by the diagonal of the parallelogram $ABCG$.

$$\therefore \quad \sqrt{[(500)^2 + (500)^2 + 2 \times (500) \times (500)\cos 60°]}$$

$$= \sqrt{[(500)^2 + (500)^2 + 250000]} = 866.03 \text{m}$$

$$\tan \beta = 500 \sin 60°/\{500 + 500 \cos 60°]$$

$$= (500\sqrt{3}/2)/\{500(1+1/2)\} = 1/\sqrt{3}$$

$$= \tan 30° \text{ or, } \beta = 30°$$

Example 11. The sum of the magnitudes of two forces acting at a point is 18 N and the magnitude of their resultant is 12 N. If the resultant makes an angle of 90° with the force of smaller magnitude, what are the magnitude of the two forces ?

Sol. It is clear from geometry of the figure that the resultant of $\vec{P}$ and $\vec{R}$ is equal to $\vec{Q}$.

$\therefore$ $P^2 + R^2 = Q^2$

or $Q^2 - P^2 = R^2$

         $= 12^2 = 144$

or $(Q + P)\,(Q - P) = 144$ ...(i)

Given $P + Q = 18$ ...(ii)

$\therefore$ $18\,(Q - P) = 144$

or $Q - P = 8$ ...(iii)

Now from equation (ii) and (iii), we get
$$P = 5\text{N}$$

and $Q = 13\text{N}$ *Ans.*

Example 12. A bird moves with velocity 20 m/s in a direction making an angle of 60° with the eastern line and 60° with vertical upward. Represent the velocity vector in rectangular form.

Sol. Let eastern line be taken as x-axis, northern as y-axis and vertical upward as z-axis. Let the velocity v makes angle α, β and γ with x, y and z-axis respectively, then $\alpha = 60°$, $\gamma = 60°$.

We have $\cos^2\alpha + \cos^2\beta + \cos^2\gamma = 1$

or $\cos^2 60 + \cos^2 \beta + \cos^2 60 = 1$ or $\cos\beta = \dfrac{1}{\sqrt{2}}$

$$\therefore \quad \vec{v} = v\cos\alpha\,\hat{i} + v\cos\beta\,\hat{j} + v\cos\gamma\,\hat{k}$$

$$= 20\left[\frac{1}{2}\hat{i} + \frac{1}{\sqrt{2}}\hat{j} + \frac{1}{2}\hat{k}\right]$$

$$= 10\hat{i} + 10\sqrt{2}\,\hat{j} + 10\hat{k} \qquad\qquad \textit{Ans.}$$

Example 13. Check whether three vectors of magnitude 1, 2 and 4 can give zero resultant.

Sol. Choose any two of them, let $A = 1$ and $B = 4$, then
$A \sim B = 3$ and $A + B = 5$.

The third vector $C = 2$ does not lie between $(A - B)$ and $(A + B)$, therefore they can not give zero resultant.

Example 14. Check whether three vectors of magnitude 2, 3 and 5 be in equilibrium?

Sol. Choose any two of them, let $A = 2$ and $B = 3$ then
$A \sim B = 1$ and $A + B = 5$.

The third vector $C = 5$, lies between $(A - B)$ and $(A + B)$. Therefore the given vectors can give zero resultant.

Example 15. Four forces $\vec{P}, 2\vec{P}, 3\vec{P}$ and $4\vec{P}$ act along sides of a square taken in order. Find their resultant.

Sol. The forces are drawn along the sides of a square as shown in the *fig.* 2.31. It is clear from the figure that :

$$R = \sqrt{(2P)^2 + (2P)^2} = 2\sqrt{2}\,P$$

and it makes angle

$$\alpha = 180° + 45°$$

$$= 225° \text{ with } x\text{-axis.}$$

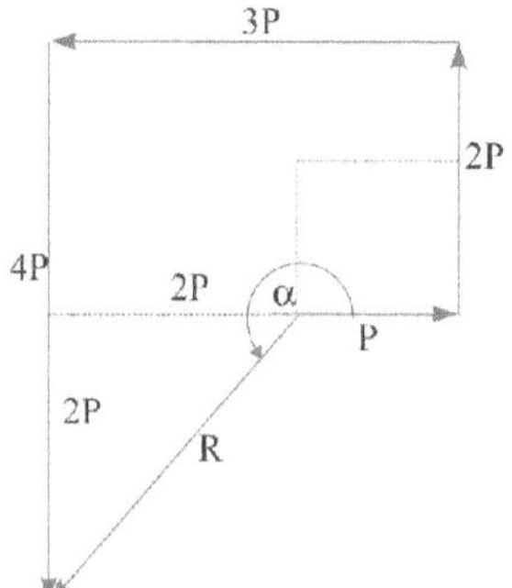

Example 16. If $\vec{A} + \vec{B} = \vec{C}$ and $A^2 + B^2 = C^2$, then prove that $\vec{A}$ and $\vec{B}$ are perpendicular to each other.

Sol. We have, $\vec{A} + \vec{B} = \vec{C}$

$\therefore$ $|\vec{A} + \vec{B}| = |\vec{C}|$

or $A^2 + B^2 + 2AB\cos\theta = C^2$

given $A^2 + B^2 = C^2$

$\therefore$ $C^2 + 2AB\cos\theta = C^2 \Rightarrow AB\cos\theta = 0$

or $\cos\theta = 0$

$\therefore$ $\theta = 90°$.

In Chapter Exercise 2.1

1. If $\vec{A} = \vec{B} - \vec{C}$, then, determine the angle between $\vec{A}$ and $\vec{B}$.

$$Ans.\ \theta = \cos^{-1}\left[\frac{A^2 + B^2 - C^2}{2AB}\right]$$

2. In a regular hexagon $ABCDEF$,

   prove that $\overrightarrow{AB} + \overrightarrow{AC} + \overrightarrow{AD} + \overrightarrow{AE} + \overrightarrow{AF} = 6\overrightarrow{AO}$.

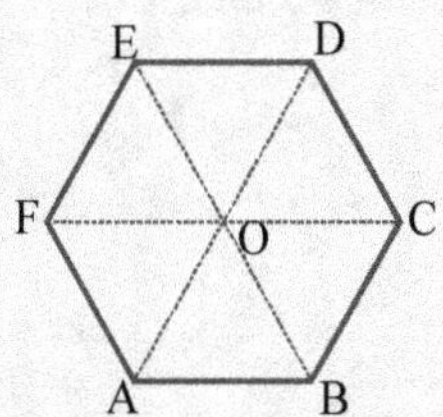

3. When $t = 0$, a particle at $(1, 0, 0)$ moves towards $(4, 4, 12)$ with a constant speed of 65 m/s. The position of the particle is measured in metre and time in second. Assume constant velocity, find the position of the particle for $t = 2$ s.

   $Ans.\ (31\hat{i} + 40\hat{j} + 120\hat{k})$ metre

4. The resultant vector $\vec{P}$ and $\vec{Q}$ is $\vec{R}$. On reversing the direction of $\vec{Q}$, the resultant vector becomes $\vec{S}$. Show that : $R^2 + S^2 = 2\left(P^2 + Q^2\right)$.

5. If the resultant of the vectors $3\hat{i} + 4\hat{j} + 5\hat{k}$ and $5\hat{i} + 3\hat{j} + 4\hat{k}$ makes an angle θ with x-axis, then find $\cos\theta$.   *Ans.* **0.574**

6. At what angle do the two forces $(P + Q)$ and $(P - Q)$ act so that the resultant is $\sqrt{3P^2 + Q^2}$.   *Ans.* **60°.**

7. Two forces equal to $2P$ and P, respectively act on a particle; if the first is doubled and the second increased by 12 N the direction of the resultant is unaltered. Find the value of P.

   Ans. **12 N.**

8. The angle of inclination between two vectors $\vec{P}$ and $\vec{Q}$ is θ. If $\vec{P}$ and $\vec{Q}$ are interchanged in position, show that the resultant will be turn through an angle ϕ, where

   $$\tan\frac{\phi}{2} = \left[\frac{P-Q}{P+Q}\right]\tan\frac{\theta}{2}.$$

9. Two forces $(P + Q)$ and $(P - Q)$ make an angle 2α with one another and their resultant makes an angle θ with the bisector of the angle between them. Show that $P\tan\theta = Q\tan\alpha$.

2.6 Product of Two Vectors

The way in which two vectors enter into combination in physics, we come across are two distinct kinds of vector products :

(1) Scalar or dot product :

The scalar product of two vectors $\vec{A}$ and $\vec{B}$ is defined as the product of the magnitudes

of $\vec{A}$ and $\vec{B}$ and cosine of the angle between them. Thus

$$\vec{A} \cdot \vec{B} = AB \cos\theta.$$

As A, B and $\cos\theta$ all are scalars, so their product is a scalar quantity.

Geometrical interpretation of scalar product

We have, $\quad \vec{A} \cdot \vec{B} \quad = AB \cos\theta$

$\qquad\qquad\qquad = A\,(B \cos\theta)$

or $\qquad\qquad\quad = (A \cos\theta)\,B$

(a) $\qquad \vec{A} \cdot \vec{B} \quad = A \times B \cos\theta$

$\qquad\qquad\qquad = AB \cos\theta$

(b) $\qquad \vec{A} \cdot \vec{B} \quad = A \cos\theta \times B$

$\qquad\qquad\qquad = AB \cos\theta$

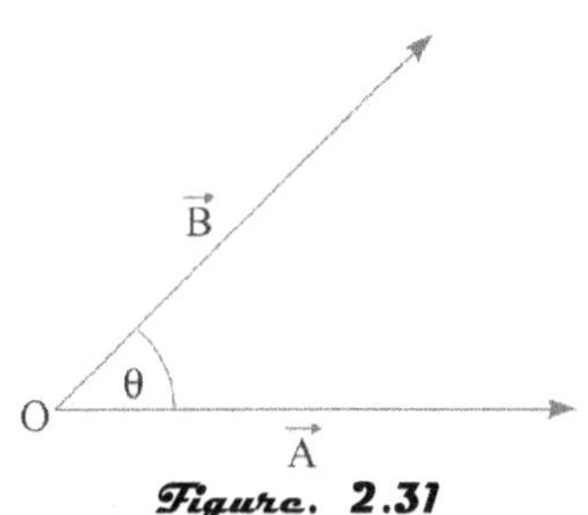

Figure. **2.31**

Properties of scalar product

(i) The scalar product is commutative i.e., $\vec{A} \cdot \vec{B} = \vec{B} \cdot \vec{A}$.

(ii) The scalar product is distributive over addition i.e., $\vec{A} \cdot (\vec{B} + \vec{C}) = \vec{A} \cdot \vec{B} + \vec{A} \cdot \vec{C}$.

(iii) If $\vec{A}$ and $\vec{B}$ are perpendicular to each other, then $\vec{A}.\vec{B} = AB \cos 90° = 0$.

(iv) If $\vec{A}$ and $\vec{B}$ are parallel having same direction, then

$$\vec{A}.\vec{B} = A B \cos 0° = AB.$$

(v) If $\vec{A}$ and $\vec{B}$ are antiparallel, then $\vec{A}.\vec{B} = A B \cos 180° = -AB$.

(vi) The scalar product of two identical vectors $\vec{A}.\vec{A} = A A \cos 0° = A^2$.

(vii) If $\hat{i}$, $\hat{j}$ and $\hat{k}$ are mutually perpendicular unit vectors, then

$$\hat{i}.\hat{i} = (1)(1) \cos 0° = 1$$
$$\therefore \quad \hat{i}.\hat{i} = \hat{j}.\hat{j} = \hat{k}.\hat{k} = 1$$
$$\hat{i}.\hat{j} = (1)(1) \cos 90° = 0$$
$$\therefore \quad \hat{i}.\hat{j} = \hat{j}.\hat{k} = \hat{k}.\hat{i} = 0$$

(viii) If $\vec{A} = A_1\hat{i} + A_2\hat{j} + A_3\hat{k}$ and $\vec{B} = B_1\hat{i} + B_2\hat{j} + B_3\hat{k}$, then

$$\vec{A}.\vec{B} = A_1B_1 + A_2B_2 + A_3B_3.$$

Applications of scalar product

(i) **Work done :** If a force $\vec{F}$ causes displacement $\vec{s}$, then work done

$$W = \vec{F}.\vec{s} = Fs \cos \theta.$$

(ii) **Angle between the vectors :** For two vectors $\vec{A}$ and $\vec{B}$, we have

$$\vec{A}.\vec{B} = AB \cos \theta$$

$$\therefore \quad \cos \theta = \frac{\vec{A}.\vec{B}}{AB}$$

or

$$\cos \theta = \frac{A_1B_1 + A_2B_2 + A_3B_3}{\sqrt{A_1^2 + A_2^2 + A_3^2}\ \sqrt{B_1^2 + B_2^2 + B_3^2}}.$$

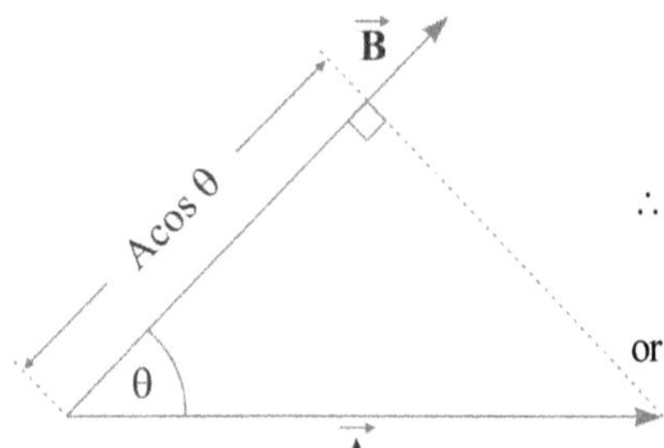

Figure. **2.33**

(iii) **Component or projection of one vector along other vector :**

(a) Component of vector $\vec{A}$ along vector $\vec{B}$ is given by

$$A \cos \theta\ \hat{B} = \frac{AB\cos\theta}{B}\hat{B}$$

$$= \left(\frac{\vec{A}.\vec{B}}{B}\right)\hat{B}$$

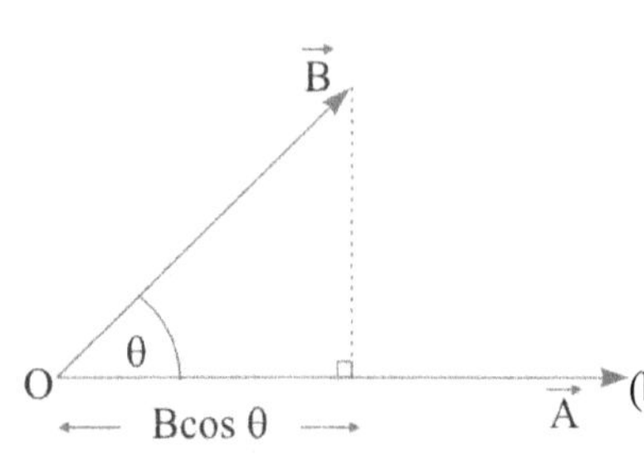

Figure. **2.34**

(b) Component of vector $\vec{B}$ along vector $\vec{A}$; is given by

$$B \cos \theta\ \hat{A} = \frac{AB\cos\theta}{A}\hat{A}$$

$$= \left(\frac{\vec{A}.\vec{B}}{A}\right)\hat{A}.$$

(2) Vector or cross product

The vector product of two vectors is defined as the vector whose magnitude is equal to the product of the magnitudes of two vectors and sine of angle between them and whose direction is perpendicular to the plane of the two vectors and is given by right hand rule. Mathematically, if θ is the angle between $\vec{A}$ and $\vec{B}$, then

$$\vec{A} \times \vec{B} = AB \sin \theta\, \hat{n}.$$

where $\hat{n}$ is a unit vector perpendicular to the plane of vectors $\vec{A}$ and $\vec{B}$.

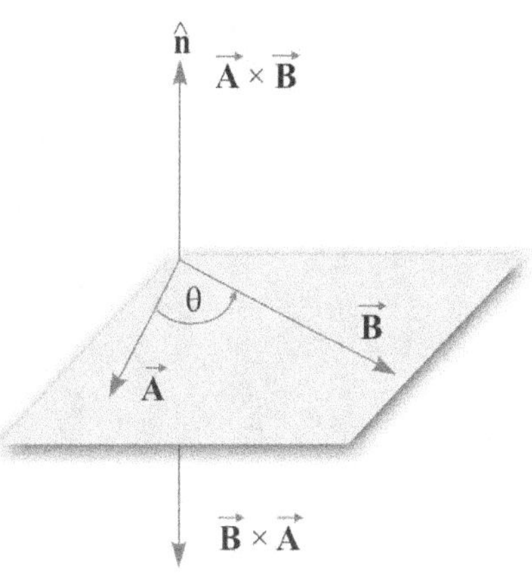

Figure. **2.35**

Geometrical interpretation of vector product

Suppose two vectors $\vec{A}$ and $\vec{B}$ are represented by the sides OP and OQ of a parallelogram, as shown in *fig.* 2.37. The magnitude of vector product $\vec{A} \times \vec{B}$ is

$$
\begin{aligned}
|\vec{A} \times \vec{B}| &= AB \sin\theta \\
&= A\,(B \sin\theta) \\
&= \text{area of rectangle } OPTS \\
&= \text{area of parallelogram } OPRQ
\end{aligned}
$$

Thus the magnitude of the vector product of two vectors is equal to the area of the parallelogram formed by the two vectors as its adjacent sides.

Moreover, the area of parallelogram $OPRQ$

$$= 2 \times \text{area of triangle } OPQ.$$

$\therefore$ Area of triangle $OPQ = \dfrac{1}{2}$ (area of parallelogram $OPRQ$).

or $\qquad\qquad\qquad = \dfrac{1}{2}|\vec{A} \times \vec{B}|.$

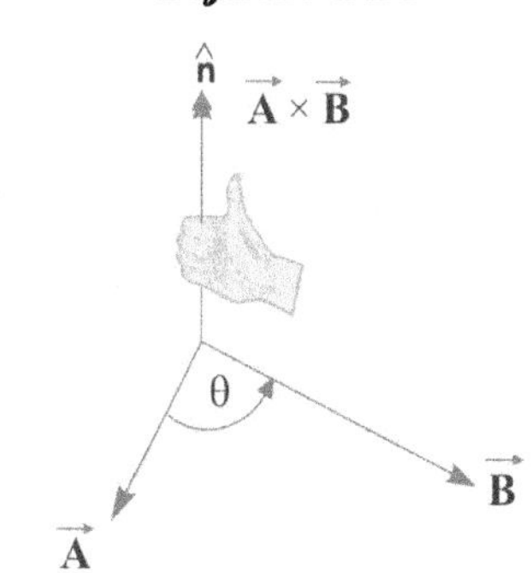

Figure. **2.36**

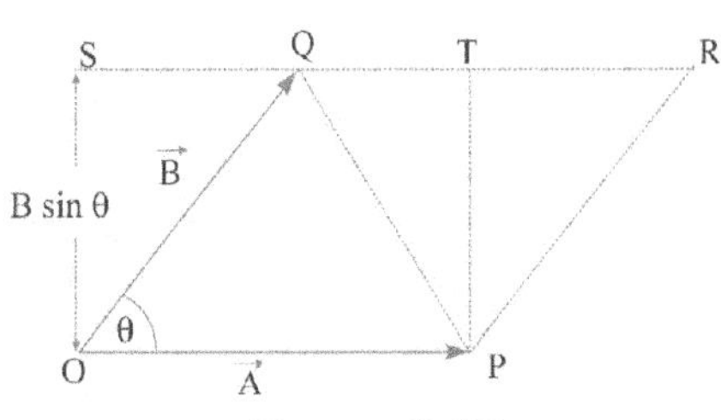

Figure. **2.37**

Properties of vector product

(i) Vector product is not commutative. It is anticommutative i.e.,

$$\vec{A} \times \vec{B} = -(\vec{B} \times \vec{A}).$$

(ii) Vector product is distributive i.e.,

$$\vec{A} \times (\vec{B} + \vec{C}) = \vec{A} \times \vec{B} + \vec{A} \times \vec{C}.$$

(iii) Vector product of two parallel vectors

$$\vec{A} \times \vec{B} = AB \sin(0° \text{ or } 180°)\hat{n} = 0.$$

(iv) Vector product of two identical vectors

$$\vec{A} \times \vec{A} = AA \sin 0°\, \hat{n} = 0.$$

(v) The vector product of two mutually perpendicular vectors

$$
\begin{aligned}
|\vec{A} \times \vec{B}| &= AB \sin 90° \\
&= AB.
\end{aligned}
$$

(vi) For unit vectors $\hat{i}$, $\hat{j}$ and $\hat{k}$

$$\hat{i} \times \hat{i} = (1)(1)\sin 0°\,\hat{n} = 0$$

$$\therefore \quad \hat{i} \times \hat{i} = \hat{j} \times \hat{j} = \hat{k} \times \hat{k} = 0$$

and $\hat{i} \times \hat{j} = (1)(1)\sin 90°\,\hat{k}$

$$= \hat{k}$$

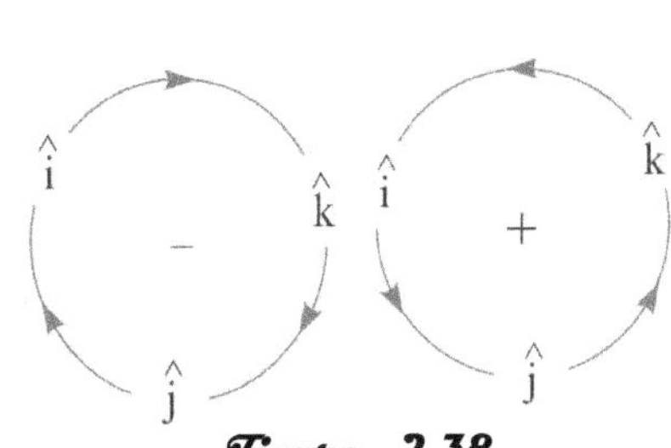

Figure. **2.38**

Similarly $\hat{j} \times \hat{k} = \hat{i}$ and $\hat{k} \times \hat{i} = \hat{j}$

$\therefore$ $\hat{j} \times \hat{i} = -\hat{k},\ \hat{k} \times \hat{j} = -\hat{i},\ \hat{i} \times \hat{k} = -\hat{j}$

Vector product of consecutive two gives next and positive in anticlockwise sense.

Application of vector product

1. **Moment of force or torque :** Let a force $\vec{F}$ is acting on a body which is free to rotate about

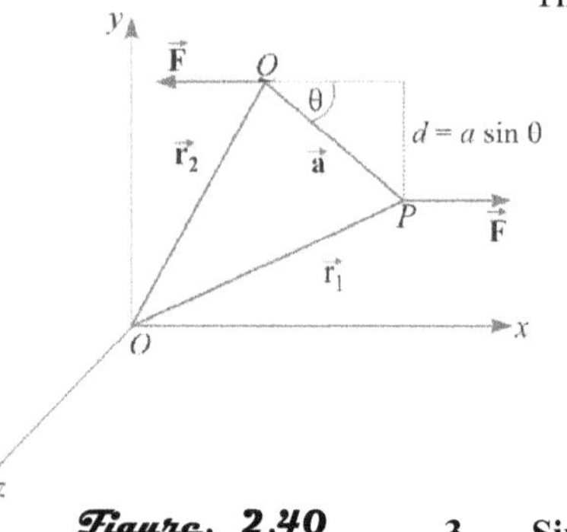

Figure. 2.39

O, and let $\vec{r}$ is the position vector of any point P on the line of action of the force. Since, torque = force × perpendicular distance of its line of action from O, so

$$\tau = F(r \sin \theta)$$

or
$$\tau = Fr \sin \theta$$

Its direction is perpendicular to the plane containing $\vec{F}$ and $\vec{r}$, and given by right hand screw rule.

We know that $F r \sin \theta$ is the magnitude of the cross product $\vec{r} \times \vec{F}$. So in vector notation, we can write

$$\vec{\tau} = \vec{r} \times \vec{F}$$

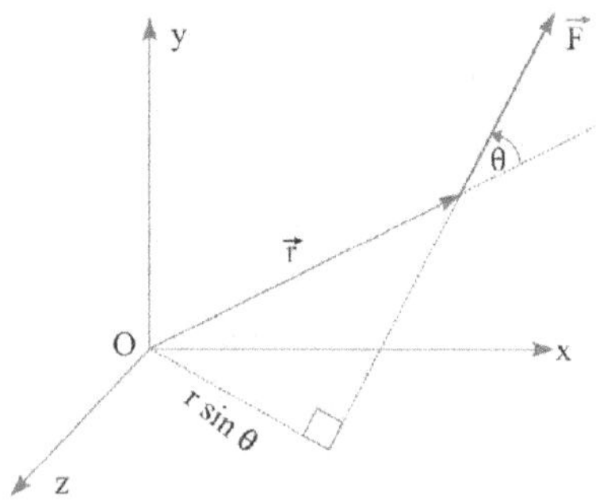

If we draw a set of three coordinate axes through O, as shown in figure 2.39, we will have

$$\vec{r} = x\hat{i} + y\hat{j} + z\hat{k},$$

where $x\hat{i}$, $y\hat{j}$ and $z\hat{k}$ are the rectangular components of $\vec{r}$ along the three axes respectively.

Similarly, $\vec{F} = F_x\hat{i} + F_y\hat{j} + F_z\hat{k}$.

$$\therefore \quad \vec{\tau} = \vec{r} \times \vec{F} = \begin{vmatrix} \hat{i} & \hat{j} & \hat{k} \\ x & y & z \\ F_x & F_y & F_z \end{vmatrix}$$

or $\quad \vec{\tau} = \hat{i}(F_z y - F_y z) + \hat{j}(F_x z - F_z x) + \hat{k}(F_y x - F_x y).$

2. **Couple :** We know that couple is a combination of two equal and opposite forces whose line of actions are different. Let $\vec{F}$ and $-\vec{F}$ be two forces acting at points P and Q and let the position vectors of P and Q with respect to O be $\vec{r}_1$ and $\vec{r}_2$ respectively.

The moment of couple with respect to O = Vector sum of moment of forces $\vec{F}$ and $-\vec{F}$. i.e.,

$$\vec{\tau} = -\vec{r}_1 \times \vec{F} + \vec{r}_2 \times \vec{F}$$

$\therefore$
$$\vec{\tau} = (\vec{r}_2 - \vec{r}_1) \times \vec{F}$$

From the figure $\vec{r}_2 - \vec{r}_1 = \vec{a}$

$\therefore$
$$\vec{\tau} = \vec{a} \times \vec{F}$$

$$= F a \sin \theta\, \hat{n} \quad (\text{Here} \quad \hat{n} = \hat{k})$$

and
$$|\vec{\tau}| = F a \sin\theta$$

or
$$\tau = Fd \quad (a \sin \theta = d)$$

Figure. 2.40

3. **Sine of angle between the vectors :** If θ is the angle between vectors $\vec{A}$ and $\vec{B}$, then we have

$$|\vec{A} \times \vec{B}| = A B \sin\theta$$

$\therefore$
$$\sin \theta = \frac{|\vec{A} \times \vec{B}|}{AB}.$$

4. **Unit vector along the direction perpendicular to plane of $\vec{A}$ and $\vec{B}$**

$$\vec{n} = \frac{\vec{A} \times \vec{B}}{|\vec{A} \times \vec{B}|}.$$

2.7 Geometrical Interpretation of Scalar Triple Product

Let us take three vectors $\vec{A}$, $\vec{B}$ and $\vec{C}$ which form a parallelopiped as shown in *fig.* 2.41.

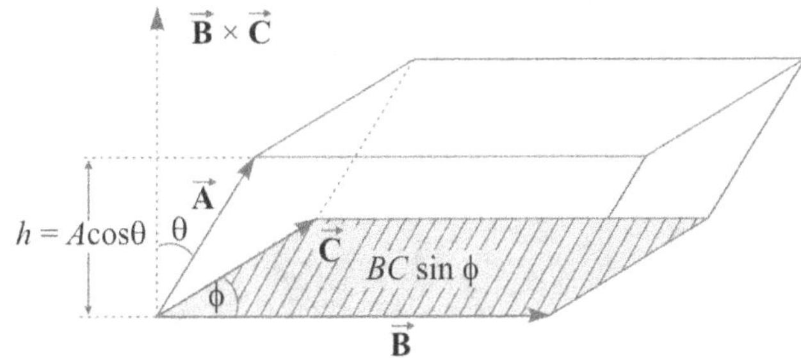

Figure. **2.41**

It is clear from the *fig.* 2.45 that the area of base of parallelopiped $= BC \sin \phi$. If θ is the angle made by the vector $\vec{B} \times \vec{C}$ with $\vec{A}$, then height of parallelopiped h = Acos θ. Therefore volume of parallelopiped

$$V = (BC \sin \phi)(A \cos \theta) = |\vec{B} \times \vec{C}| A \cos \theta$$

or we can write $\quad V = \vec{A}.(\vec{B} \times \vec{C})$.

Thus, we see that scalar triple product $\vec{A}.(\vec{B} \times \vec{C})$ represents the volume of parallelopiped, with the three vectors forming its three edges.

Note:

1. It can be easily proved that $\vec{A}.(\vec{B} \times \vec{C}) = \vec{A}.(\vec{C} \times \vec{B}) = \vec{B}.(\vec{A} \times \vec{C}) = \vec{C}.(\vec{A} \times \vec{B})$

2. The order of vectors in scalar triple product is immaterial. Therefore we can simply write it as $[\vec{ABC}]$.

   The scalar triple product $[\vec{ABC}]$ can directly calculated by using a determinant. For vectors $\vec{A} = A_1\hat{i} + A_2\hat{j} + A_3\hat{j}$, $\vec{B} = B_1\hat{i} + B_2\hat{j} + B_3\hat{k}$ and $\vec{C} = C_1\hat{i} + C_2\hat{j} + C_3\hat{k}$, we have

$$[\vec{ABC}] = \begin{vmatrix} A_1 & A_2 & A_3 \\ B_1 & B_2 & B_3 \\ C_1 & C_2 & C_3 \end{vmatrix}$$
$$= A_1(B_2C_3 - C_2B_3) + A_2(B_3C_1 - B_1C_3) + A_3(B_1C_2 - C_1B_2).$$

More about scalar triple product

1. In case the three vectors are coplanar, their scalar triple product is zero. i.e., $[\vec{ABC}] = 0$.

2. If two of the vectors be equal, the scalar triple product is zero i.e., $[\vec{AAB}] = [\vec{A} \times \vec{A}].\vec{B} = 0$.

3. If two vectors are parallel, the scalar triple product is zero. Let $\vec{A}$ and $\vec{B}$ are parallel, we can have $\vec{B} = k\vec{A}$, where k is a scalar. Then $[\vec{ABC}] = (k\vec{A} \times \vec{A})\vec{B} = 0$.

4. The scalar triple product of the orthogonal vector triad is unity i.e. $[\hat{i}\hat{j}\hat{k}] = (\hat{i} \times \hat{j}).\hat{k} = 1$.

Vector triple product : If $\vec{A}$, $\vec{B}$ and $\vec{C}$ are three vectors, then $\vec{A} \times (\vec{B} \times \vec{C})$, $\vec{B} \times (\vec{C} \times \vec{A})$ and $\vec{C} \times (\vec{A} \times \vec{B})$ are the examples of vector triple product. You can prove the following relations by previous knowledge

$$\vec{A} \times (\vec{B} \times \vec{C}) = (\vec{A}.\vec{C})\vec{B} - (\vec{A}.\vec{B})\vec{C}$$

$$\vec{B} \times (\vec{C} \times \vec{A}) = (\vec{B}.\vec{A})\vec{C} - (\vec{B}.\vec{C})\vec{A}$$

and $\quad \vec{C} \times (\vec{A} \times \vec{B}) = (\vec{C}.\vec{B})\vec{A} - (\vec{C}.\vec{A})\vec{B}$.

FORMULAE USED

1. **Scalar product :** $\vec{A}.\vec{B} = AB\cos\theta.$

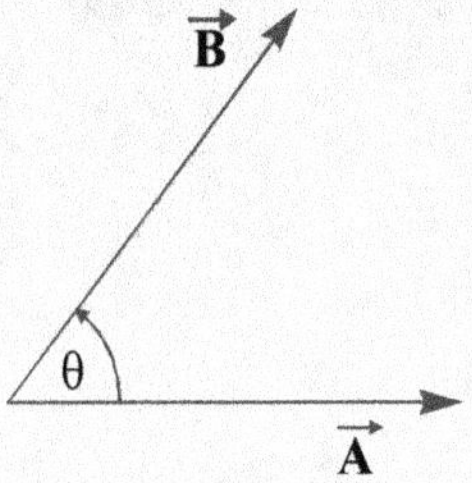

   (i)   If $\theta = 90°$, $\vec{A}.\vec{B} = 0.$

   (ii) Angle between $\vec{A}$ and $\vec{B}$ is given by
   $$\cos\theta = \frac{\vec{A}.\vec{B}}{AB}.$$

   (iii) If $\vec{A} = A_1\hat{i} + A_2\hat{j} + A_3\hat{k}$ and $\vec{B} = B_1\hat{i} + B_2\hat{j} + B_3\hat{k}$, then
   $$\vec{A}.\vec{B} = A_1B_1 + A_2B_2 + A_3B_3.$$

   (iv) $\vec{A}.\vec{B} = \vec{B}.\vec{A}.$

   (v) $\hat{i}.\hat{i} = \hat{j}.\hat{j} = \hat{k}.\hat{k} = 1.$

   (vi) Work done, $W = \vec{F}.\vec{s}$

2. **Vector product :**

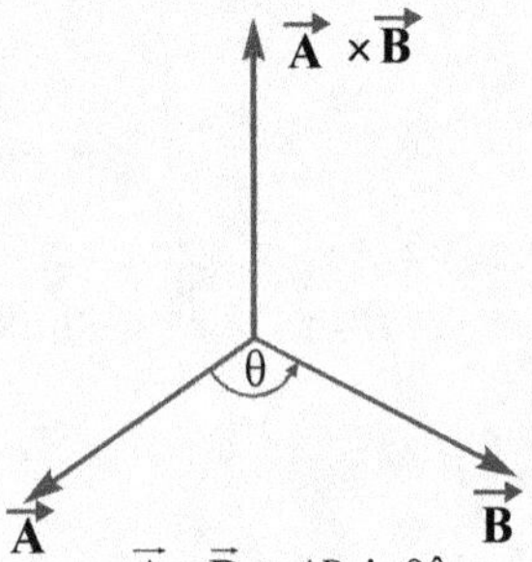

   (i) $\hat{\eta} = \dfrac{\vec{A} \times \vec{B}}{|\vec{A} \times \vec{B}|}$

   (ii) Angle between $\vec{A}$ and $\vec{B}$, $\sin\theta = \dfrac{|\vec{A} \times \vec{B}|}{AB}.$

   (iii) If $\vec{A} = A_1\hat{i} + A_2\hat{j} + A_3\hat{k}$ and $\vec{B} = B_1\hat{i} + B_2\hat{j} + B_3\hat{k}$, then
   $$\vec{A} \times \vec{B} = \begin{vmatrix} \hat{i} & \hat{j} & \hat{k} \\ A_1 & A_2 & A_3 \\ B_1 & B_2 & B_3 \end{vmatrix}$$
   $$= \hat{i}(A_2B_3 - A_3B_2) + \hat{j}(B_1A_3 - B_3A_1) + \hat{k}(A_1B_2 - A_2B_1).$$

   (iv) For parallel vectors $\vec{A} \times \vec{B} = AB\sin 0\,\hat{\eta} = \vec{0}$

   (v) $\vec{A} \times \vec{B} = -\vec{B} \times \vec{A}.$

   (vi) $\hat{i} \times \hat{j} = \hat{k},\ \hat{j} \times \hat{k} = \hat{i},\ \hat{k} \times \hat{i} = \hat{j}.$

   (vii) Moment of force or torque, $\vec{\tau} = \vec{r} \times \vec{F}.$

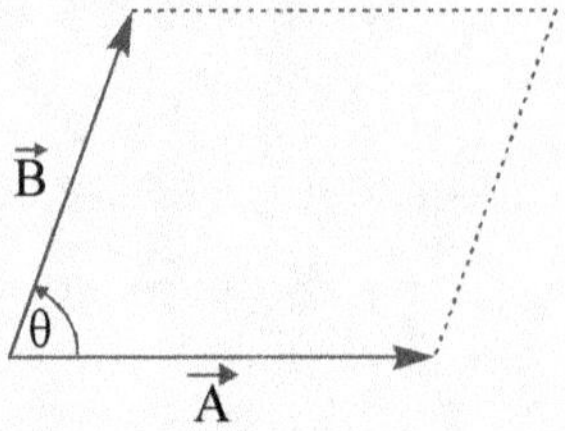

   (viii) Area of a parallelogram which has adjacent sides $\vec{A}$ and $\vec{B}$;
   $$A = |\vec{A} \times \vec{B}|$$

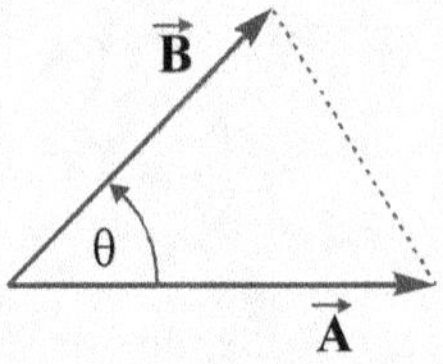

   (ix) Area of triangle $\quad A = \dfrac{1}{2}|\vec{A} \times \vec{B}|$

   (x)   Condition of **collinearity** of two vectors $\vec{A}$ and $\vec{B}$;
   $$(A_1\hat{i} + A_2\hat{j} + A_3\hat{k}) \times (B_1\hat{i} + B_2\hat{j} + B_3\hat{k}) = 0$$
   which gives, $\quad \dfrac{A_1}{B_1} = \dfrac{A_2}{B_2} = \dfrac{A_3}{B_3} = \dfrac{A}{B}.$

   (xi) Condition of coplanarity of three vectors $\vec{A}$, $\vec{B}$ and $\vec{C}$
   $$\vec{A}.(\vec{B} \times \vec{C}) = \begin{vmatrix} A_1 & A_2 & A_3 \\ B_1 & B_2 & B_3 \\ C_1 & C_2 & C_3 \end{vmatrix} = 0$$
   Or $A_1(B_2C_3 - C_2B_3) + A_2(B_3C_1 - B_1C_3) + A_3(B_1C_2 - C_1B_2) = 0.$

EXAMPLES BASED ON DOT PRODUCT AND CROSS PRODUCT

Example 17. A point P lies in the x-y plane. Its position can be specified by its x, y coordinates or by a radially directed vector $\vec{r} = (x\,\hat{i} + y\,\hat{j})$, making an angle θ with the x-axis. Find a vector $\hat{i}_r$ of unit magnitude in the direction of vector $\vec{r}$ and a vector $\hat{i}_\theta$ of unit magnitude normal to the vector $\hat{i}_r$ and lying in the x-y plane.

Sol. The unit vector in the direction of vector $\vec{r}$ is given by

$$\hat{i}_r = \frac{\vec{r}}{r} = \frac{x\hat{i} + y\hat{j}}{r} = \frac{x}{r}\hat{i} + \frac{y}{r}\hat{j}$$

From the geometry of figure, we have

$$x = r\cos\theta \quad \text{and} \quad y = r\sin\theta$$

$$\therefore \quad \hat{i}_r = \cos\theta\,\hat{i} + \sin\theta\,\hat{j}.$$

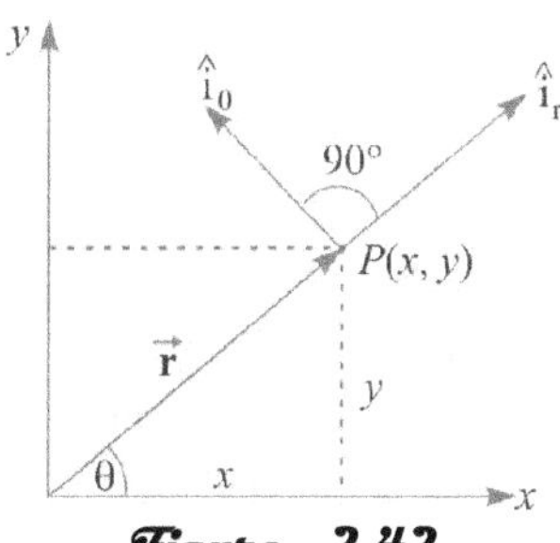

Figure. 2.42

Let the unit vector normal to the unit vector $\hat{i}_r$ be given by

$$\hat{i}_\theta = x'\hat{i} + y'\hat{j}$$

where x' and y' are to be determined by using the fact that $\hat{i}_\theta$ is perpendicular to $\hat{i}_r$, so

$$\hat{i}_r . \hat{i}_\theta = 0,$$

or $\quad (\cos\theta\,\hat{i} + \sin\theta\,\hat{j}) . (x'\hat{i} + y'\hat{j}) = 0,$

or $\quad x'\cos\theta + y'\sin\theta = 0$

$$\therefore \quad x' = -y'\frac{\sin\theta}{\cos\theta}. \qquad \text{...(i)}$$

Since $\hat{i}_\theta$ is a unit vector, so

$$x'^2 + y'^2 = 1$$

From equation (i),

$$y'^2\frac{\sin^2\theta}{\cos^2\theta} + y'^2 = 1$$

$$\therefore \quad y'^2(\sin^2\theta + \cos^2\theta) = \cos^2\theta$$

or $\quad y' = \cos\theta$

and $\quad x' = -\sin\theta$

Hence $\quad \hat{i}_\theta = -\sin\theta\,\hat{i} + \cos\theta\,\hat{j}.$

Example 18. Given two vectors $\vec{A} = \hat{i} + \hat{j} + \hat{k}$ and $\vec{B} = \hat{i} + \hat{j} - \hat{k}$. Find angle between vectors $\vec{A}$ and $\vec{B}$.

Sol. We know that $\cos\theta = \left(\dfrac{\vec{A}.\vec{B}}{AB}\right)$.

Here $\quad \vec{A}.\vec{B} = (\hat{i} + \hat{j} + \hat{k}).(\hat{i} + \hat{j} - \hat{k})$
$$= 1 \times 1 + 1 \times 1 + 1 \times (-1) = 1$$

and $\quad A = \sqrt{1^2 + 1^2 + 1^2} = \sqrt{3},$

$$B = \sqrt{1^2 + 1^2 + (-1)^2} = \sqrt{3}$$

Now $\quad \cos\theta = \dfrac{1}{\sqrt{3}\sqrt{3}} = \dfrac{1}{3}$

or $\quad \theta = \cos^{-1}\left(\dfrac{1}{3}\right)$ *Ans.*

Example 19. Find the components of $\vec{a} = 2\hat{i} + 3\hat{j}$ along the directions of vectors $(\hat{i} + \hat{j})$ and $(\hat{i} - \hat{j})$. **[NCERT]**

Sol. Let $\vec{b} = (\hat{i} + \hat{j})$ and $\vec{c} = (\hat{i} - \hat{j})$

The component of $\vec{a}$ along $\vec{b}$

$$a\cos\theta\,\hat{b} = \left(\frac{\vec{a}.\vec{b}}{b}\right)\hat{b}$$

$$\frac{(2\hat{i} + 3\hat{j}).(\hat{i} + \hat{j})}{\sqrt{1^2 + 1^2}}\frac{(\hat{i} + \hat{j})}{\sqrt{1^2 + 1^2}}$$

$$= \frac{2 \times 1 + 3 \times 1}{\sqrt{2}}\frac{(\hat{i} + \hat{j})}{\sqrt{2}}$$

$$= \frac{5}{2}(\hat{i} + \hat{j}) \qquad \text{*Ans.*}$$

The component of $\vec{a}$ along $\vec{c}$ is given by

$$a\cos\theta\,\hat{c} = \left(\frac{\vec{a}.\vec{c}}{c}\right)\hat{c}$$

$$= \frac{(2\hat{i} + 3\hat{j}).(\hat{i} - \hat{j})}{\sqrt{1^2 + 1^2}}\frac{(\hat{i} - \hat{j})}{\sqrt{1^2 + 1^2}}$$

$$= -\frac{1}{2}(\hat{i} - \hat{j}). \qquad \text{*Ans.*}$$

Example 20. Find the area of the triangle formed by the tips of the vectors $\vec{a} = \hat{i} - \hat{j} - 3\hat{k}$, $\vec{b} = 4\hat{i} - 3\hat{j} + \hat{k}$ and $\vec{c} = 3\hat{i} - \hat{j} + 2\hat{k}$.

Sol. Let ABC is the triangle formed by the tips of the given vectors, then

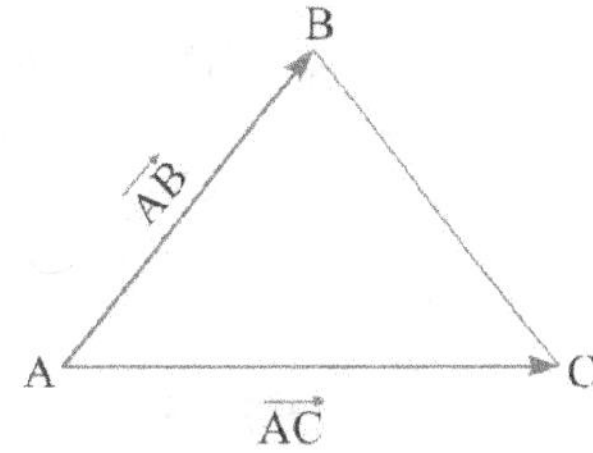

Figure. 2.43

$$\overrightarrow{AB} = \vec{b} - \vec{a}$$

$$= (4\hat{i} - 3\hat{j} + \hat{k}) - (\hat{i} - \hat{j} - 3\hat{k})$$

$$= 3\hat{i} - 2\hat{j} + 4\hat{k}$$

and $\quad \overrightarrow{AC} = \vec{c} - \vec{a}$

$$= (3\hat{i} - \hat{j} + 2\hat{k}) - (\hat{i} - \hat{j} - 3\hat{k})$$

$$= 2\hat{i} + 5\hat{k}$$

Now $\quad \overrightarrow{AB} \times \overrightarrow{AC} = (3\hat{i} - 2\hat{j} + 4\hat{k}) \times (2\hat{i} + 5\hat{k})$

$$= \begin{vmatrix} \hat{i} & \hat{j} & \hat{k} \\ 3 & -2 & 4 \\ 2 & 0 & 5 \end{vmatrix}$$

$$= \hat{i}(-10 - 0) + \hat{j}(8 - 15) + \hat{k}(0 + 4)$$

$$= -10\hat{i} - 7\hat{j} + 4\hat{k}$$

and $\quad |\overrightarrow{AB} \times \overrightarrow{AC}| = \sqrt{(-10)^2 + (-7)^2 + (4)^2}$

$$= \sqrt{165} = 12.8$$

$\therefore \quad$ Area of $\Delta ABC = \dfrac{1}{2} |\overrightarrow{AB} \times \overrightarrow{AC}|$

$$= \dfrac{1}{2} \times 12.8 = 6.4 \text{ sq unit.} \quad \textit{Ans.}$$

Example 21. **The diagonals of a parallelogram are given by the vectors $3\hat{i}+\hat{j}+2\hat{k}$ and $\hat{i}-3\hat{j}+4\hat{k}$. Find the area of the parallelogram.**

Sol. If $\vec{A}$ and $\vec{B}$ represent the adjacent sides of the parallelogram, then diagonals

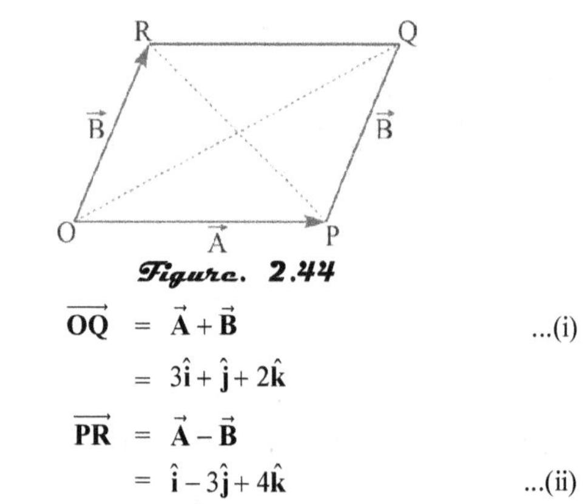

Figure. 2.44

$\overrightarrow{OQ} = \vec{A} + \vec{B}$ $\qquad$ ...(i)

$$= 3\hat{i} + \hat{j} + 2\hat{k}$$

and $\quad \overrightarrow{PR} = \vec{A} - \vec{B}$

$$= \hat{i} - 3\hat{j} + 4\hat{k} \qquad \text{...(ii)}$$

From equations (i) and (ii), we have

$$\vec{A} = \frac{\overrightarrow{OQ} + \overrightarrow{PR}}{2}$$

$$= 2\hat{i} - \hat{j} + 3\hat{k}$$

and $\qquad \vec{B} = \dfrac{\overrightarrow{OQ} - \overrightarrow{PR}}{2}$

$$= \hat{i} + 2\hat{j} - \hat{k}$$

Area of parallelogram is given by

$$= \left| \vec{A} \times \vec{B} \right|$$

$$= \begin{vmatrix} \hat{i} & \hat{j} & \hat{k} \\ 2 & -1 & 3 \\ 1 & 2 & -1 \end{vmatrix}$$

$$= \left| \hat{i}(1-6) + \hat{j}(3+2) + \hat{k}(4+1) \right|$$

$$= \left| -5\hat{i} + 5\hat{j} + 5\hat{k} \right|$$

$$= \sqrt{(-5)^2 + 5^2 + 5^2} = 5\sqrt{3} \; \textit{sq. unit Ans.}$$

Example 22. **Prove that the four points $(4\hat{i}+5\hat{j}+\hat{k})$, $-(\hat{j}+\hat{k})$, $(3\hat{i}+9\hat{j}+4\hat{k})$ and $4(-\hat{i}+\hat{j}+\hat{k})$ are coplanar.**

Sol. Let given vectors be the position vectors of four points A, B, C and D with reference to an origin O. It is clear that the given points will be coplanar if the vectors $\overrightarrow{BA}, \overrightarrow{BC}$ and $\overrightarrow{CD}$ are coplanar.

$$\overrightarrow{BA} = \overrightarrow{OA} - \overrightarrow{OB} = (4\hat{i}+5\hat{j}+\hat{k}) - [-(\hat{j}+\hat{k})] = 4\hat{i}+6\hat{j}+2\hat{k}$$

and $\overrightarrow{BC} = \overrightarrow{OC} - \overrightarrow{OB} = (3\hat{i}+9\hat{j}+4\hat{k}) - [-(\hat{j}+\hat{k})] = (3\hat{i}+10\hat{j}+5\hat{k})$

and $\overrightarrow{CD} = \overrightarrow{OD} - \overrightarrow{OC} = -4\hat{i}+4\hat{j}+4\hat{k} - (3\hat{i}+9\hat{j}+4\hat{k}) = -7\hat{i}-5\hat{j}$

Now $[\overrightarrow{BA} \; \overrightarrow{BC} \; \overrightarrow{CD}] = \begin{vmatrix} 4 & 6 & 2 \\ 3 & 10 & 5 \\ -7 & -5 & 0 \end{vmatrix}$

$$= 4(0 + 25) + 6(-35 - 0) + 2(-15 + 70) = 0$$

Since scalar triple product $[\overrightarrow{BA} \; \overrightarrow{BC} \, \overrightarrow{CD}]$ is zero, therefore given points are coplanar.

In Chapter Exercise 2.2

1. Calculate the values of
   (i) $\hat{j}.\left(2\hat{i}-3\hat{j}+\hat{k}\right)$ and (ii) $\left(2\hat{i}-\hat{j}\right).\left(3\hat{i}+\hat{k}\right)$.

   $\qquad\qquad\qquad\qquad$ *Ans.* (i) –3 (ii) 6.

2. Find the value of a for which the vectors $3\hat{i}+3\hat{j}+9\hat{k}$ and $\hat{i}+a\hat{j}+3\hat{k}$ are parallel. $\qquad$ *Ans.* $a = 1.$

3. Find the value of m so that the vector $3\hat{i}-2\hat{j}+\hat{k}$ is perpendicular to the vector $2\hat{i}+6\hat{j}+m\hat{k}$. $\qquad$ *Ans.* 6.

4. Find a vector of magnitude 18 which is perpendicular to both the vectors $4\hat{i}-\hat{j}+3\hat{k}$ and $2\hat{i}+\hat{j}-2\hat{k}$.

   $\qquad\qquad\qquad\qquad$ *Ans.* $-6\hat{i}+12\hat{j}+12\hat{k}.$

5. Show that the vectors $\vec{A} = 3\hat{i}-2\hat{j}+\hat{k}$, $\vec{B} = \hat{i}-3\hat{j}+5\hat{k}$ and $\vec{C} = 2\hat{i}+\hat{j}-4\hat{k}$ form a right angle triangle.

6. Find the cosine of the angle between the vectors $\vec{A} = 3\hat{i}+\hat{j}+2\hat{k}$ and $\vec{B} = 2\hat{i}-2\hat{j}+4\hat{k}$. Find also the unit vector perpendicular to both $\vec{A}$ and $\vec{B}$.

   $\qquad\qquad\qquad$ *Ans.* $\dfrac{3}{\sqrt{21}} \; ; \; \dfrac{1}{\sqrt{3}}(\hat{i}-\hat{j}-\hat{k})$

7. Write down the values of (i) $[\hat{i}\hat{j}\hat{k}]$ (ii) $\vec{a}\times(\vec{b}\times\vec{c})$.

   $\qquad\qquad\qquad$ *Ans.* (i) 1 ; (ii) $(\vec{a}.\vec{c})\vec{b} - (\vec{a}.\vec{b})\vec{c}$

8. Show that $\vec{a}\times(\vec{b}\times\vec{c}) + \vec{b}\times(\vec{c}\times\vec{a}) + \vec{c}\times(\vec{a}\times\vec{b}) = 0$.

MISCELLANEOUS EXAMPLES FOR JEE-(MAIN AND ADVANCE)

Example 23. The position vectors of four points A, B, C and D are $\vec{a} = 2\hat{i} + 3\hat{j} + 4\hat{k}$, $\vec{b} = 3\hat{i} + 5\hat{j} + 7\hat{k}$, $\vec{c} = \hat{i} + 2\hat{j} + 3\hat{k}$ and $\vec{d} = 3\hat{i} + 6\hat{j} + 9\hat{k}$ respectively. Examine whether vectors $\overrightarrow{AB}$ and $\overrightarrow{CD}$ are collinear.

Sol.

Vector $\overrightarrow{AB} = \vec{b} - \vec{a}$

$$= (3\hat{i} + 5\hat{j} + 7\hat{k}) - (2\hat{i} + 3\hat{j} + 4\hat{k}) = \hat{i} + 2\hat{j} + 3\hat{k}$$

and $\overrightarrow{CD} = \vec{d} - \vec{c}$

$$= (3\hat{i} + 6\hat{j} + 9\hat{k}) - (\hat{i} + 2\hat{j} + 3\hat{k}) = 2\hat{i} + 4\hat{j} + 6\hat{k}$$

For collinearity of vectors, we have the condition

$$\frac{a_1}{b_1} = \frac{a_2}{b_2} = \frac{a_3}{b_3}.$$

Here $\dfrac{a_1}{b_1} = \dfrac{1}{2}$, $\dfrac{a_2}{b_2} = \dfrac{1}{2}$ and $\dfrac{a_3}{b_3} = \dfrac{3}{6} = \dfrac{1}{2}$; i.e., condition of collinearity is satisfied. The two vectors are thus collinear. **Ans.**

Example 24. If $\overrightarrow{A} = 3\hat{i} + 4\hat{j}$ and $\overrightarrow{B} = 7\hat{i} + 24\hat{j}$, find a vector having the same magnitude as $\overrightarrow{B}$ and parallel to $\overrightarrow{A}$.

Sol. The required vector is $= B\hat{A}$

$$B = \sqrt{7^2 + 24^2} = 25$$

and $\hat{A} = \dfrac{\overrightarrow{A}}{A} = \dfrac{3\hat{i} + 4\hat{j}}{\sqrt{3^2 + 4^2}}$

$$= \frac{1}{5}(3\hat{i} + 4\hat{j})$$

$\therefore \quad B\hat{A} = 25 \times \dfrac{1}{5}(3\hat{i} + 4\hat{j})$

$$= 15\hat{i} + 20\hat{j} \qquad \textit{Ans.}$$

Example 25. A bird is at a point P whose coordinates are (4m, –1m, 5m). The bird observes two points P_1 and P_2 having coordinates (–1m, 2m, 0m) and (1m, 1m, 4m) respectively. At time $t = 0$, it starts flying in a plane of three positions, with a constant speed of 5 m/s in a direction perpendicular to the straight line $P_1 P_2$ till it sees P_1 and P_2 collinear at time t. Calculate t.

Sol. The situation is shown in the *fig.* 2.44. The bird flies in a direction perpendicular to line $P_1 P_2$. Let it reaches the point P_2 in time t.

$$t = \frac{d}{v} \qquad \ldots(i)$$

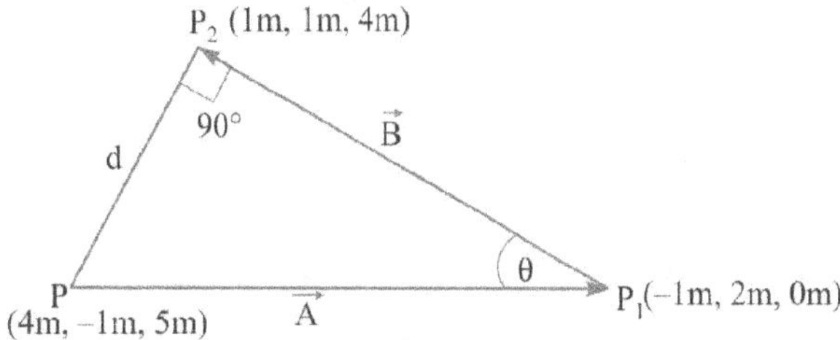

Figure. 2.45

where $d = A\sin\theta$

$$= \frac{|\overrightarrow{A} \times \overrightarrow{B}|}{B}$$

$\therefore \quad t = \dfrac{|\overrightarrow{A} \times \overrightarrow{B}|}{vB} \quad \ldots(ii)$

$\overrightarrow{A} = (-1-4)\hat{i} + (2+1)\hat{j} + (0-5)\hat{k}$

$$= -5\hat{i} + 3\hat{j} - 5\hat{k}$$

and $\overrightarrow{B} = (1+1)\hat{i} + (1-2)\hat{j} + (4-0)\hat{k}$

$$= 2\hat{i} - \hat{j} + 4\hat{k},$$

$$B = \sqrt{2^2 + (-1)^2 + 4^2} = \sqrt{21} = 4.58$$

$$\overrightarrow{A} \times \overrightarrow{B} = \begin{vmatrix} \hat{i} & \hat{j} & \hat{k} \\ -5 & 3 & -5 \\ 2 & -1 & 4 \end{vmatrix}$$

$$= \hat{i}(12 - 5) + \hat{j}(-10 + 20) + \hat{k}(5 - 6)$$

$$= 7\hat{i} + 10\hat{j} - \hat{k}$$

and $|\overrightarrow{A} \times \overrightarrow{B}| = \sqrt{7^2 + 10^2 + (-1)^2}$

$$= 12.25 \text{ m}^2$$

Now from equation (ii), we get

$$t = \frac{|\overrightarrow{A} \times \overrightarrow{B}|}{vB} = \frac{12.25}{5 \times 4.58} = 0.54 \text{ s.} \qquad \textit{Ans.}$$

MCQ Type 1

LEVEL - I (ONLY ONE OPTION CORRECT)

Addition or Subtraction of Vectors

1. A vector $\vec{A}$ makes an angle $240°$ with the positive x-axis, its components along x-axis and y-axis are :
   (a) A and $\sqrt{3}\dfrac{A}{2}$
   (b) $-\dfrac{A}{2}$ and $\sqrt{3}\dfrac{A}{2}$
   (c) $-\dfrac{A}{2}$ and $-\sqrt{3}\dfrac{A}{2}$
   (d) $-\dfrac{A}{2}$ and $\sqrt{3}A$

2. Two billiard balls are rolling on a flat table. One has the velocity components $v_x = 1\text{ m/s}, v_y = \sqrt{3}\text{ m/s}$ and the other has components $v'_x = 2\text{ m/s}$ and $v'_y = 2\text{ m/s}$. If both the balls start moving from the same point, The angle between their paths is
   (a) $30°$
   (b) $45°$
   (c) $60°$
   (d) $15°$

3. Two vectors, both equal in magnitude, have their resultant equal in magnitude of the either vector. The angle between the vectors is
   (a) $90°$
   (b) $120°$
   (c) $180°$
   (d) zero

4. The resultant of two unit vectors equal in magnitude is equal to either of them, then their difference is
   (a) 1
   (b) $\sqrt{3}$
   (c) 3
   (d) $\sqrt{2}$

5. Given vector $\vec{R} = 2\hat{i} + 3\hat{j}$. The angle between $\vec{R}$ and y-axis is:
   (a) $\tan^{-1}\dfrac{3}{2}$
   (b) $\tan^{-1}\dfrac{2}{3}$
   (c) $\sin^{-1}\dfrac{2}{3}$
   (d) $\cos^{-1}\dfrac{2}{3}$

6. The length of a second's hand in a watch is 1cm. The change in velocity in 15 sec is :
   (a) zero
   (b) $\dfrac{\pi}{30\sqrt{2}}$ cm/s
   (c) $\dfrac{\pi}{30}$ cm/s
   (d) $\dfrac{\pi}{30}\sqrt{2}$ cm/s

7. The angle between two vectors $\vec{A}$ and $\vec{B}$ is θ. Resultant of these vectors $\vec{R}$ makes an angle $\dfrac{\theta}{2}$ with $\vec{A}$ which of the following is true :
   (a) $\vec{A} = 2\vec{B}$
   (b) $\vec{A} = \dfrac{\vec{B}}{2}$
   (c) $|\vec{A}| = |\vec{B}|$
   (d) $AB = 1$

8. How many minimum number of coplanar vectors having different magnitudes can be added to give zero resultant:
   (a) 2
   (b) 3
   (c) 4
   (d) 5

9. How many minimum number of vectors in different planes can be added to give zero resultant :
   (a) 2
   (b) 3
   (c) 4
   (d) 5

10. Given $\vec{A} + \vec{B} + \vec{C} = 0$. Which of the following statements is not correct:
    (a) $\vec{A}$, $\vec{B}$ and $\vec{C}$ each must be a null vector
    (b) the magnitude of $\vec{A}$ equals the magnitude of $\vec{B} + \vec{C}$
    (c) the magnitude of $\vec{A}$ can never be greater than the sum of the magnitudes of $\vec{B}$ and $\vec{C}$
    (d) $\vec{A}$, $\vec{B}$ and $\vec{C}$ must lie in the same plane

11. Can the resultant of 2 vectors be zero:
    (a) yes, when the 2 vectors are same in magnitude and direction
    (b) no
    (c) yes, when the 2 vectors are same in magnitude but opposite in sense.
    (d) yes, when the 2 vectors are same in magnitude making an angle of $\dfrac{2\pi}{3}$ with each other

12. Two vectors $\vec{A}$ and $\vec{B}$ are such that $\vec{A} + \vec{B} = \vec{C}$ and $\left|\vec{A}\right| + \left|\vec{B}\right| = \left|\vec{C}\right|$. Then the vectors $\vec{A}$ and $\vec{B}$ are
    [AMU B.Tech. 2014]
    (a) parallel
    (b) perpendicular
    (c) anti-parallel
    (d) null vectors

13 Four forces $\vec{P}, 2\vec{P}, 3\vec{P}$ and $4\vec{P}$ act along sides of a square taken in order. Their resultant is
   (a) $2\sqrt{2}P$
   (b) $2P$
   (c) $P/\sqrt{2}$
   (d) Zero

14. The value of $(\vec{A} + \vec{B}) \times (\vec{A} - \vec{B})$ is :
    (a) 0
    (b) $A^2 - B^2$
    (c) $\vec{A} \times \vec{B}$
    (d) $-2(\vec{A} \times \vec{B})$

Answer	1	(c)	2	(d)	3	(b)	4	(b)	5	(b)	6	(d)	7	(c)
Key	8	(b)	9	(c)	10	(a)	11	(c)	12	(a)	13	(a)	14	(d)

15. If $|\vec{V}_1 + \vec{V}_2| = |\vec{V}_1 - \vec{V}_2|$ and $\vec{V}_1$ and $\vec{V}_2$ are finite, then:

(a) $\vec{V}_1$ is parallel to $\vec{V}_2$

(b) $\vec{V}_1 = \vec{V}_2$

(c) $|\vec{V}_1| = |\vec{V}_2|$

(d) $\vec{V}_1$ and $\vec{V}_2$ are mutually perpendicular

16. The vector that is added to $\left(\hat{i} - 5\hat{j} + 2\hat{k}\right)$ and $\left(3\hat{i} + 6\hat{j} - 7\hat{k}\right)$ to give a unit vector along the *x*-axis is :

(a) $3\hat{i} + \hat{j} + 5\hat{k}$

(b) $\hat{i} + 3\hat{j} + 5\hat{k}$

(c) $-3\hat{i} - \hat{j} + 5\hat{k}$

(d) $3\hat{i} + \hat{j} - 5\hat{k}$

17. The two vectors $\vec{A}$ and $\vec{B}$ that are parallel to each other are :

(a) $\vec{A} = 3\hat{i} + 6\hat{j} + 9\hat{k}$ $\qquad$ $\vec{B} = \hat{i} + 2\hat{j} + 3\hat{k}$

(b) $\vec{A} = 3\hat{i} - 6\hat{j} + 9\hat{k}$ $\qquad$ $\vec{B} = \hat{i} + 2\hat{j} + 3\hat{k}$

(c) $\vec{A} = 2\hat{i} + 3\hat{j} + 3\hat{k}$ $\qquad$ $\vec{B} = \hat{i} + 2\hat{j} - 3\hat{k}$

(d) $\vec{A} = 2\hat{i} + 6\hat{j} - 9\hat{k}$ $\qquad$ $\vec{B} = \hat{i} - 2\hat{j} - 3\hat{k}$

18. The condition for $\vec{A} + \vec{B} = \vec{A} - \vec{B}$ is that

(a) $A = B$

(b) $\vec{B} = 0$

(c) $A = 0$

(d) B is unit vector

Dot and Cross Product

19. If $\vec{A} = 5\hat{i} + 7\hat{j} - 3\hat{k}$ and $\vec{B} = 2\hat{i} + 2\hat{j} - a\hat{k}$ are perpendicular vectors, the value of a is:

(a) -2

(b) 8

(c) -7

(d) -8

20. Three vector $\vec{A}$, $\vec{B}$ and $\vec{C}$ satisfy the relation $\vec{A} \cdot \vec{B} = 0$ and $\vec{A} \cdot \vec{C} = 0$. The vector $\vec{A}$ is parallel to :

(a) $\vec{B}$

(b) $\vec{C}$

(c) $\vec{B} \cdot \vec{C}$

(d) $\vec{B} \times \vec{C}$

21. The condition for $\vec{A} + \vec{B}$ to be perpendicular to $\vec{A} - \vec{B}$ is that

(a) $|\vec{A}| = |\vec{B}|$

(b) $\vec{A} = \vec{B}$

(c) $\vec{B} = 0$

(d) $|\vec{A} + \vec{B}| = |\vec{A} - \vec{B}|$

22. The angle between $(\vec{A} \times \vec{B})$ and $(\vec{A} + \vec{B})$ is :

(a) 0

(b) $\dfrac{\pi}{4}$

(c) $\dfrac{\pi}{2}$

(d) π

23. Find the component of vector $\vec{A} = (2\hat{i} + 3\hat{j})$ along the direction $(\hat{i} - \hat{j})$

(a) $-\dfrac{1}{2}(\hat{i} - \hat{j})$

(b) $-\dfrac{1}{2}(\hat{i} + \hat{j})$

(c) $\dfrac{1}{2}(\hat{i} - \hat{j})$

(d) $\dfrac{1}{2}(\hat{i} + \hat{j})$

24. If $\vec{A} = \hat{i}A\cos\theta + \hat{j}A\sin\theta$, then another vector $\vec{B}$ which is perpendicular to $\vec{A}$ can be expressed as :

(a) $\hat{i}B\cos\theta - \hat{j}B\sin\theta$

(b) $\hat{i}B\sin\theta - \hat{j}B\cos\theta$

(c) $iB\cos\theta + jB\cos\theta$

(d) $\hat{i}B\cos\theta + \hat{j}B\sin\theta$

25. If $\vec{P} \cdot \vec{Q} = 0$ and $\vec{P} \times \vec{R} = 0$, what is the angle between $\vec{Q}$ and $\vec{R}$:

(a) $0°$

(b) $90°$

(c) $120°$

(d) $180°$

26. The condition that $\left(\vec{a} \cdot \vec{b}\right)^2 = \left(\vec{a}^2 \cdot \vec{b}^2\right)$ is satisfied when

(a) $\vec{a} \parallel \vec{b}$

(b) $\vec{a} \neq \vec{b}$

(c) $\vec{a} \cdot \vec{b} = 1$

(d) $\vec{a} \perp \vec{b}$

Answer	15	(d)	16	(c)	17	(d)	18	(b)	19	(d)	20	(d)	21	(a)
Key	22	(c)	23	(a)	24	(b)	25	(b)	26	(a)				

Addition or Subtraction of Vectors

1. If the magnitudes of vectors $\vec{A}$, $\vec{B}$ and $\vec{C}$ are 12, 5 and 13 units respectively and $\vec{A} + \vec{B} = \vec{C}$, the angle between vectors A and B is :

(a) 0

(b) π

(c) $\dfrac{\pi}{2}$

(d) $\dfrac{\pi}{4}$

2. If $\vec{A} = 3\hat{i} + 4\hat{j}$ and $\vec{B} = 7\hat{i} + 24\hat{j}$, the vector having the same magnitude as $\vec{B}$ and parallel to $\vec{A}$ is

(a) $15i + 20j$

(b) $3i + 4j$

(c) $7i + 24j$

(d) none of these

3. From figure, the correct relation is :

(a) $\vec{A} + \vec{B} + \vec{E} = \vec{0}$

(b) $\vec{C} - \vec{D} = -\vec{A}$

(c) $\vec{B} + \vec{E} - \vec{C} = -\vec{D}$

(d) all of these

4. A bird moves with velocity 20 m/s in a direction making an angle of 60° with the eastern line and 60° with vertical upward. The velocity vector in rectangular form.

(a) $10\hat{i} + 10\hat{j} + 10\hat{k}$

(b) $10\hat{i} + 10\sqrt{2}\,\hat{j} + 10\hat{k}$

(c) $-20\hat{i} + 10\sqrt{2}\,\hat{j} + 20\hat{k}$

(d) $10\sqrt{2}\,\hat{i} + 10\hat{j} + \hat{k}$

5. The x and y components of $\vec{A}$ are 4 m and 6 m, respectively. The x and y components of $\left(\vec{A}+\vec{B}\right)$ are 10 m and 9 m respectively. The magnitude of vector $\vec{B}$ is :

(a) 19 m   (b) $\sqrt{27}$ m

(c) $\sqrt{45}$ m   (d) $\sqrt{50}$ m

Dot and Cross Product

6. Three particles A, B and C start from the origin at the same time, A with velocity a along x-axis, B with velocity b along y-axis and C with velocity c in xy- plane along a line $x = y$. The magnitude of c, so that they always remain collinear is

(a) $\dfrac{a+b}{2}$ (b) $\sqrt{ab}$

(c) $\dfrac{ab}{a+b}$ (d) $\dfrac{\sqrt{2}\,ab}{a+b}$

7. The vector having magnitude equal to 3 and perpendicular to the two vectors $\vec{A} = 2\hat{i}+2\hat{j}+\hat{k}$ and $\vec{B} = 2\hat{i}-2\hat{j}+3\hat{k}$ is:

(a) $\pm\left(2\hat{i}-\hat{j}-2\hat{k}\right)$ (b) $\pm\left(3\hat{i}+\hat{j}-2\hat{k}\right)$

(c) $-\left(3\hat{i}+\hat{j}-3\hat{k}\right)$ (d) $\left(3\hat{i}-\hat{j}-3\hat{k}\right)$

8. The area of a triangle bounded by vectors **a**, **b** and **c** is :

(a) $\dfrac{1}{6}|\vec{a}+\vec{b}+\vec{c}|$

(b) $\dfrac{1}{6}|\vec{a}\cdot\vec{b}+\vec{b}\cdot\vec{c}+\vec{c}\cdot\vec{a}|$

(c) $\dfrac{1}{6}\left[|\vec{b}\times\vec{c}|+|\vec{c}\times\vec{a}|+|\vec{a}\times\vec{b}|\right]$

(d) $\dfrac{1}{6}\left[\left(\vec{a}\cdot\vec{b}\right)+\left(\vec{b}\cdot\vec{c}\right)+\left(\vec{c}\cdot\vec{a}\right)\right]$

9. Given $|\vec{A}_1|= 2$, $|\vec{A}_2|=3$ and $|\vec{A}_1+\vec{A}_2|=3$. Find the value of $\left|\left(\vec{A}_1+2\vec{A}_2\right)\cdot\left(3\vec{A}_1-4\vec{A}_2\right)\right|$:

(a) 64   (b) 60

(c) 62   (d) 61

10. The area of the triangle having vertices at $P(1, 3, 2)$, $Q(2, -1, 1)$ and $R(-1, 2, 3)$ is :

(a) $\dfrac{1}{2}\sqrt{107}$ (b) $\dfrac{1}{2}\sqrt{105}$

(c) $\sqrt{110}$ (d) None

11. If the vectors $(\hat{i} + \hat{j} + \hat{k})$ and $3\hat{i}$ form two sides of a triangle, the area of the triangle is :

(a) $\sqrt{3}$ (b) $2\sqrt{3}$

(c) $\dfrac{3}{\sqrt{2}}$ (d) $3\sqrt{2}$

12. The components of $\vec{a} = 2\hat{i} + 3\hat{j}$ along the direction of vector $(\hat{i} + \hat{j})$ is

(a) $\hat{i}+\hat{j}$ (b) $\dfrac{1}{2}(\hat{i}+\hat{j})$

(c) $\dfrac{5}{2}(\hat{i}+j)$ (d) $\dfrac{5}{2}(\hat{i}-\hat{j})$

Answer	1	(c)	2	(a)	3	(d)	4	(b)	5	(c)	6	(d)	7	(a)
Key	8	(c)	9	(a)	10	(a)	11	(c)	12	(c)				

Mechanics   **MCQ Type 2**   **Exercise 2.2**

MULTIPLE CORRECT OPTIONS

1. The resultant of $\vec{A}$ and $\vec{B}$ makes an angle α with $\vec{A}$ and β with $\vec{B}$ then :

(a) $\alpha < \beta$ (b) $\alpha < \beta$ if $A < B$

(c) $\alpha < \beta$ if $A > B$ (d) $\alpha = \beta$ if $A = B$

2. The magnitude of resultant of three unit vectors can be :

(a) zero   (b) 1

(c) 3   (d) $3\sqrt{2}$

3. The magnitude of the vector product of two vectors $\vec{A}$ and $\vec{B}$ may be :

(a) greater than AB (b) equal to AB

(c) less than AB (d) equal to zero

4. The following sets of three vectors act on a body, whose resultant can be zero. These are :

(a) 10, 10, 10   (b) 10, 10, 20

(c) 10, 20, 20   (d) 10, 20, 40

5. The x-component of the resultant of several vectors :

(a) is equal to the sum of the x-components of the vectors

(b) may be smaller than the sum of the magnitudes of the vectors

(c) may be greater than the sum of the magnitudes of the vectors

(d) may be equal to the sum of the magnitudes of the vectors

6. Which of the following vectors is/are perpendicular to the vector $5\hat{k}$?

(a) $4\hat{i}+3\hat{j}$
(b) $6\hat{i}$

(c) $7\hat{k}$
(d) $3\hat{i}+4\hat{j}$

7. For two vectors $\vec{A}$ and $\vec{B}$, identify the correct relation :

(a) $\vec{A}+\vec{B}=\vec{B}+\vec{A}$

(b) $\vec{A}\cdot\vec{B}=\vec{B}\cdot\vec{A}$

(c) $\vec{A}\times\vec{B}=\vec{B}\times\vec{A}$

(d) $(\vec{A}-\vec{B})\times(\vec{B}-\vec{A})=0$

8. If $\vec{A}=\vec{B}$, the angle between the vectors is 0°. Now if $A=B$, the angle between vectors may be :

(a) 0°
(b) 90°
(c) 180°
(d) 30°

9. Which of the following is/are correct :

(a) $|\vec{a}+\vec{b}|\le|\vec{a}|+|\vec{b}|$

(b) $|\vec{a}+\vec{b}|\ge|\vec{a}|+|\vec{b}|$

(c) $|\vec{a}-\vec{b}|\le|\vec{a}|+|\vec{b}|$

(d) $|\vec{a}-\vec{b}|\ge|\vec{a}|-|\vec{b}|$

10. Given $\vec{a}+\vec{b}+\vec{c}+\vec{d}=0$, which of the following statements are correct :

(a) $\vec{a},\vec{b},\vec{c}$ and $\vec{d}=0$ must each be a null vector

(b) The magnitude of $(\ +\vec{c})$ equals the magnitude of $(\vec{b}+\vec{d})$

(c) The magnitude of $\vec{a}$ can never be greater than the sum of the magnitude of $\vec{b},\vec{c}$ and $\vec{d}$

(d) $\vec{b}+\vec{c}$ must lie in the plane of $\vec{a}$ and $\vec{d}$ if $\vec{a}$ and $\vec{d}$ are not collinear, and in the line of $\vec{a}$ and $\vec{d}$, if they are collinear

11. The incorrect expression(s) in the following is/are

(a) $\vec{A}\times(\vec{B}\times\vec{C})+\vec{B}\times(\vec{C}\times\vec{A})+\vec{C}\times(\vec{A}\times\vec{B})=0$

(b) $\vec{A}\cdot(\vec{B}\cdot\vec{C})+\vec{B}\cdot(\vec{C}\cdot\vec{A})+\vec{C}\cdot(\vec{A}\cdot\vec{B})=0$

(c) $\vec{A}\cdot(\vec{B}\times\vec{C})+\vec{B}\cdot(\vec{C}\times\vec{A})+\vec{C}\cdot(\vec{A}\times\vec{B})=0$

(d) $\vec{A}\cdot(\vec{B}+\vec{C})+\vec{B}\cdot(\vec{C}+\vec{A})+\vec{C}\cdot(\vec{A}+\vec{B})=0$

Answer	1	(c, d)	2	(a, b, c)	3	(b,c,d)	4	(a, b, c)	5	(b, d)	6	(a, b, d)
Key	7	(a, b, d)	8	(a, b, c, d)	9	(a, c, d)	10	(b, c, d)	11	(b, c, d)		

Reasoning Type Questions — Exercise 2.3

Mechanics

Read the following questions and give your answer using the following options (a, b, c and d) :

(a) **Statement - 1** is true, **Statement - 2** is true; **Statement - 2** is correct explanation for **Statement - 1**.

(b) **Statement - 1** is true; **Statement - 2** is true; **Statement - 2** is not correct explanation for **Statement - 1**.

(c) **Statement - 1** is true, **Statement - 2** is false.

(d) **Statement - 1** is false, **Statement - 2** is true.

1. Statement - 1

Two vector are said to be like vectors if they have same direction but different magnitude.

Statement - 2

Vector quantities always have a fixed direction.

2. Statement - 1

Vector product of two vectors is an axial vector.

Statement - 2

$\vec{\omega}=\vec{v}\times\vec{r}$.

3. Statement - 1

$\vec{A}\times\vec{B}$ is perpendicular to $\vec{A}+\vec{B}$.

Statement - 2

$\vec{A}+\vec{B}$ lies in the plane containing $\vec{A}$ and $\vec{B}$, but $\vec{A}\times\vec{B}$ lies perpendicular to plane containing $\vec{A}$ and $\vec{B}$.

4. Statement - 1

If $\vec{A}\cdot\vec{B}=\vec{B}\cdot\vec{C}$, then $\vec{A}$ may not equal to $\vec{C}$.

Statement - 2

The dot product of two vectors involves cosine of the angle between two vectors.

5. Statement - 1

If $\hat{A}=\hat{B}$, then $\hat{A}\times\hat{B}=0$.

Statement - 2

If angle between $\hat{A}$ and $\hat{B}$ is 0°, then their cross product is a null vector.

6. Statement - 1

$\vec{A}\times\vec{B}$ is perpendicular to both $\vec{A}+\vec{B}$ as well as $\vec{A}-\vec{B}$

Statement - 2

$\vec{A}+\vec{B}$ as well as $\vec{A}-\vec{B}$ lie in the plane containing $\vec{A}$ and $\vec{B}$, but $\vec{A}\times\vec{B}$ lies perpendicular to the plane containing $\vec{A}$ and $\vec{B}$.

7. **Statement - 1**

The sum of two vectors can never be zero.

Statement - 2

Sum of two equal and opposite vectors is zero.

8. **Statement - 1**

The scalar product of two vectors can be zero.

Statement - 2

If two vectors are perpendicular to each other, their scalar product will be zero.

Answer	1	(c)	2	(c)	3	(a)	4	(a)
Key	5	(b)	6	(a)	7	(d)	8	(a)

Mechanics　　　　　# Passage & Matrix　　　　Exercise 2.3

PASSAGES

Passage for Questions. 1 - 3 :

Given two vectors $\vec{\mathbf{A}} = 2\hat{\mathbf{i}} + 6\hat{\mathbf{j}} + 4\hat{\mathbf{k}}$ and $\vec{\mathbf{B}} = \hat{\mathbf{i}} - 2\hat{\mathbf{j}} + 8\hat{\mathbf{k}}$

1. The magnitude of their resultant is
  (a)　5　　　　　　　(b)　8
  (c)　9　　　　　　　(d)　13

2. The value of $\vec{\mathbf{A}} \cdot \vec{\mathbf{A}} \times \vec{\mathbf{B}}$ is
  (a)　5　　　　　　　(b)　13
  (c)　3　　　　　　　(d)　zero

3. The unit vector perpendicular to the plane of $\vec{\mathbf{A}}$ and $\vec{\mathbf{B}}$ is

  (a)　$\dfrac{1}{13\sqrt{5}}\left(28\hat{\mathbf{i}} - 6\hat{\mathbf{j}} - 5\hat{\mathbf{k}}\right)$　(b)　$\dfrac{1}{5\sqrt{13}}\left(6\hat{\mathbf{i}} - 28\hat{\mathbf{j}} - 5\hat{\mathbf{k}}\right)$

  (c)　$\dfrac{1}{\sqrt{5}}\left(28\hat{\mathbf{i}} - 6\hat{\mathbf{j}} - 5\hat{\mathbf{k}}\right)$　　(d)　none of these

MATRIX MATCHING

4. If $|\vec{A}| = 2$ and $|\vec{B}| = 4$, then match the relations in column I with the angle θ between $\vec{A}$ and $\vec{B}$ in column II.

Column - I	Column - II
A.　$\vec{A} \cdot \vec{B} = 0$	(p)　$\theta = 0°$
B.　$\vec{A} \cdot \vec{B} = +8$	(q)　$\theta = 90°$
C.　$\vec{A} \cdot \vec{B} = 4$	(r)　$\theta = 180°$
D.　$\vec{A} \cdot \vec{B} = -8$	(s)　$\theta = 60°$

5. If $|\vec{A}| = 2$ and $|\vec{B}| = 4$, then match the relations in column I with the angle θ between $\vec{A}$ and $\vec{B}$ in column II.

Column - I	Column - II
A.　$|\vec{A} \times \vec{B}| = 0$	(p)　$\theta = 30°$
B.　$|\vec{A} \cdot \vec{B}| = +8$	(q)　$\theta = 45°$
C.　$|\vec{A} \times \vec{B}| = 4$	(r)　$\theta = 90°$
D.　$|\vec{A} \cdot \vec{B}| = 4\sqrt{2}$	(s)　$\theta = 0°$

Answer	1	(d)	2	(d)	3	(a)	4	$A \to q, B \to p, C \to s, D \to r,$
Key	5	$A \to s, B \to r, C \to p, D \to q,$						

Hints & Solutions

In Chapter Exercise -2.1

1. Given, $\quad \vec{A} = \vec{B} - \vec{C}$

$\therefore \quad \vec{C} = \vec{B} - \vec{A}$

If θ is the angle between $\vec{A}$ and $\vec{B}$, then

$$C^2 = B^2 + A^2 - 2AB\cos\theta$$

$\therefore \quad \cos\theta = \dfrac{B^2 + A^2 - C^2}{2AB} \quad$ ***Ans.***

2. $\vec{R} = \overrightarrow{AB} + \overrightarrow{AC} + \overrightarrow{AD} + \overrightarrow{AE} + \overrightarrow{AF}$

$= \overrightarrow{AB} + \left(\overrightarrow{AB} + \overrightarrow{BC}\right) + \left(\overrightarrow{AB} + \overrightarrow{BC} + \overrightarrow{CD}\right)$

$+ \left(\overrightarrow{AB} + \overrightarrow{BC} + \overrightarrow{CD} + \overrightarrow{DE}\right) + \left(\overrightarrow{CD}\right)$

As $\quad \overrightarrow{DE} = -\overrightarrow{AB}$

$\therefore \quad \vec{R} = 3\left(\overrightarrow{AB} + \overrightarrow{BC} + \overrightarrow{CD}\right)$

$= 3 \times \overrightarrow{AD} = 3 \times 2\overrightarrow{AO}$

$= 6\,\overrightarrow{AO} \quad$ ***Ans.***

3. The distance travelled in 2 second $= 65 \times 2 = 130$ m

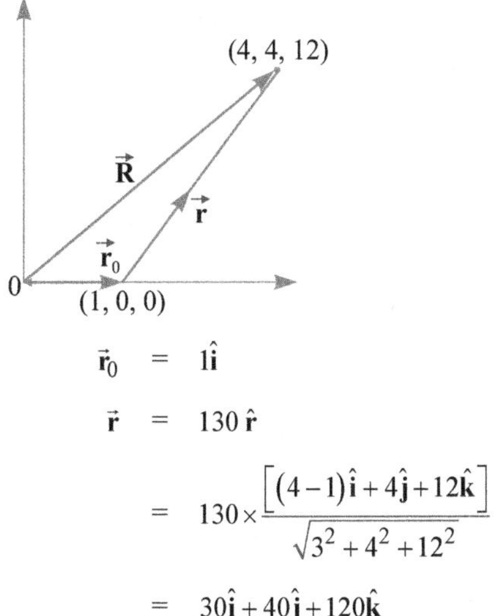

$\vec{r}_0 = 1\hat{i}$

$\vec{r} = 130\,\hat{r}$

$= 130 \times \dfrac{\left[(4-1)\hat{i} + 4\hat{j} + 12\hat{k}\right]}{\sqrt{3^2 + 4^2 + 12^2}}$

$= 30\hat{i} + 40\hat{j} + 120\hat{k}$

$\therefore \quad \vec{R} = \vec{r}_0 + \vec{r} = 31\hat{i} + 40\hat{j} + 120\hat{k} \quad$ ***Ans.***

4. We have $\quad R^2 = P^2 + Q^2 + 2PQ\cos\theta$ ...(i)

and $\quad S^2 = P^2 + Q^2 - 2PQ\cos\theta$ ...(ii)

Adding equations (i) and (ii), we get

$$R^2 + S^2 = 2\left(P^2 + Q^2\right).$$

5. The resultant vector $= \left(3\hat{i} + 4\hat{j} + 5\hat{k}\right) + \left(5\hat{i} + 3\hat{j} + 4\hat{k}\right)$

$= 8\hat{i} + 7\hat{j} + 9\hat{k}$

$\cos\theta = \dfrac{8}{\sqrt{8^2 + 7^2 + 9^2}} = 0.574$ ***Ans.***

6. We know that $\quad R^2 = A^2 + B^2 + 2AB\cos\theta$

or $\left(3P^2 + Q^2\right) = (P+Q)^2 + (P-Q)^2 + 2(P+Q)(P-Q)\cos\theta$

7.

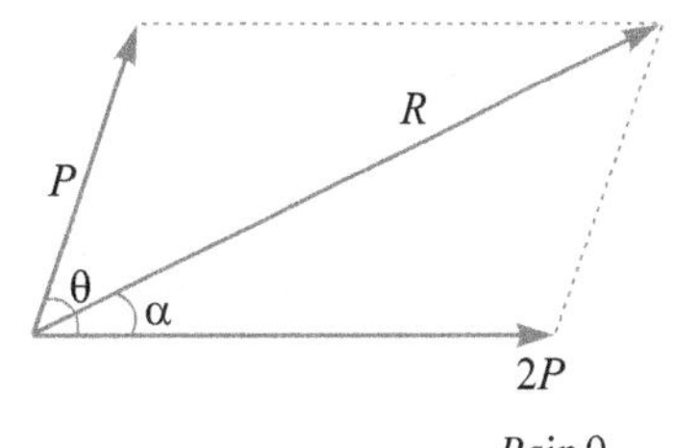

$\tan\alpha = \dfrac{P\sin\theta}{2P + P\cos\theta}$

$= \dfrac{(P+12)\sin\theta}{4P + (P+12)\cos\theta}$

After simplifying, we get

$$P = 12\,\text{N} \quad \text{***Ans.***}$$

8. If α is the angle which resultant $\vec{R}$ makes with $\vec{P}$, then

$2\alpha + \phi = \theta$

$\therefore \quad \phi = (\theta - 2\alpha)$

or $\quad \dfrac{\phi}{2} = \left(\dfrac{\theta}{2} - \alpha\right)$

or $\quad \tan\dfrac{\phi}{2} = \tan\left(\dfrac{\theta}{2} - \alpha\right)$ ...(i)

where $\quad \tan\alpha = \dfrac{Q\sin\theta}{P + Q\sin\theta}$ ...(ii)

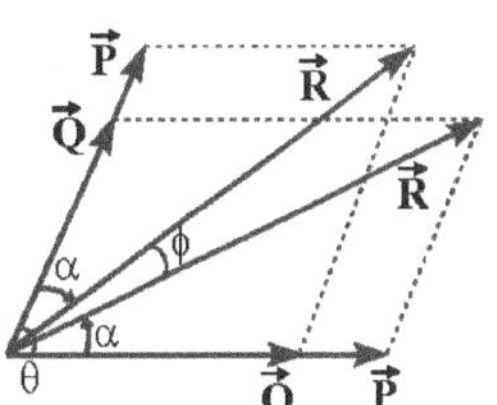

After solving equations (i) and (ii), we get

$$\tan\dfrac{\phi}{2} = \left[\dfrac{P-Q}{P+Q}\right]\tan\dfrac{\theta}{2}.$$

9. The angle which the resultant makes with $P + Q$ will be $(\alpha - \theta)$.

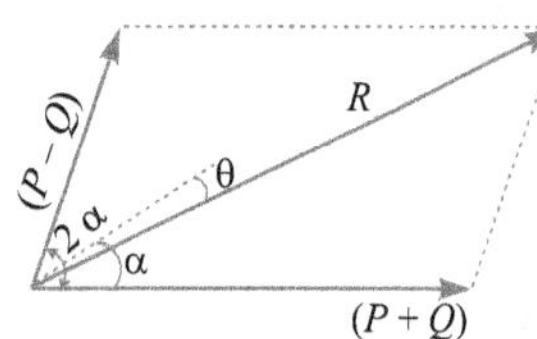

Thus
$$\tan(\alpha - \theta) = \frac{(P-Q)\sin 2\alpha}{(P+Q)+(P-Q)\cos 2\alpha}$$

or
$$\frac{\sin(\alpha - \theta)}{\cos(\alpha - \theta)} = \frac{(P-Q)\sin 2\alpha}{(P+Q)+(P-Q)\cos 2\alpha}$$

or $\quad (P+Q)\sin(\alpha - \theta) = (P-Q)\sin(\alpha + \theta)$

or $\quad P\big[\sin(\alpha + \theta) - \sin(\alpha - \theta)\big] = Q\big[\sin(\alpha + \theta) + \sin(\alpha - \theta)\big]$

or $\quad P \times 2\cos\alpha\sin\theta = Q \times 2\sin\alpha\cos\theta$

$\therefore \quad P\tan\theta = Q\tan\alpha$

In Chapter Exercise -2.2

1. (i) $\hat{j}\cdot\big(2\hat{i} - 3\hat{j} + \hat{k}\big) = 1 \times (-3) = -3$

    (ii) $\big(2\hat{i} - \hat{j}\big)\cdot\big(3\hat{i} + \hat{k}\big) = 2 \times 3 + (-1) \times 0 + 0 \times 1$
    $$= 6 \qquad \textbf{\textit{Ans.}}$$

2. For vectors to be parallel, the angle between them should be $0°$ or $180°$. Thus
    $$\vec{A} \times \vec{B} = AB\sin 0°\,\hat{n} = 0$$

    or $\quad \big(3\hat{i} + 3\hat{j} + 9\hat{k}\big) \times \big(\hat{i} + 9\hat{j} + 3\hat{k}\big) = 0$

    After solving, we get $a = 1$ $\qquad$ **_Ans._**

3. $\big(3\hat{i} - 2\hat{j} + \hat{k}\big)\cdot\big(2\hat{i} + 6\hat{j} + m\hat{k}\big) = 0$

    or $\quad 3 \times 2 - 2 \times 6 + 1 \times m = 0$
    $$m = 6 \qquad \textbf{\textit{Ans}}$$

4. A vector perpendicular to $\vec{A}$ and $\vec{B}$ is given by
    $$\hat{n} = \frac{\vec{A} \times \vec{B}}{\big|\vec{A} \times \vec{B}\big|}$$
    $$= \frac{\big(4\hat{i} - \hat{j} + 3\hat{k}\big) \times \big(-2\hat{i} + \hat{j} - 2\hat{k}\big)}{\big|\big(4\hat{i} - \hat{j} + 3\hat{k}\big) \times \big(-2\hat{i} + \hat{j} - 2\hat{k}\big)\big|}$$

$$= \frac{-\hat{i} + 2\hat{j} + 2\hat{k}}{3}$$

Thus, required vector will be $= 18\hat{n}$
$$= 18\left[\frac{-\hat{i} + 2\hat{j} + 2\hat{k}}{3}\right]$$
$$= -6\hat{i} + 12\hat{j} + 12\hat{k} \qquad \textbf{\textit{Ans..}}$$

5. $(\vec{A} \times \vec{B}) = \big|\vec{A} \times \vec{B}\big|^2 = (AB\sin\theta)^2$
    $$= A^2 B^2 \big(1 - \cos^2\theta\big)$$
    $$= A^2 B^2 - A^2 B^2\cos^2\theta$$
    $$= A^2 B^2 - \big(\vec{A} \cdot \vec{B}\big)^2$$

6. Angle between $\vec{A}$ and $\vec{B}$ is given by
    $$\cos\theta = \frac{\vec{A} \cdot \vec{B}}{AB}$$
    $$= \frac{3 \times 2 + 1 \times (-2) + 2 \times 4}{\sqrt{3^2 + 1^2 + 2^2}\,\sqrt{2^2 + (-2)^2 + 4^2}}$$
    $$= \frac{3}{\sqrt{21}} \qquad \textbf{\textit{Ans.}}$$

The unit vector perpendicular to $\vec{A}$ and $\vec{B}$ is given by
$$\hat{n} = \frac{\vec{A} \times \vec{B}}{\big|\vec{A} \times \vec{B}\big|} = \frac{\big(3\hat{i} + \hat{j} + 2\hat{k}\big) \times \big(2\hat{i} - 2\hat{j} + 4\hat{k}\big)}{\big|\big(3\hat{i} + \hat{j} + 2\hat{k}\big) \times \big(2\hat{i} - 2\hat{j} + 4\hat{k}\big)\big|}$$
$$= \frac{8\hat{i} - 8\hat{j} - 8\hat{k}}{\sqrt{8^2 + (-8)^2 + (-8)^2}} = \frac{\hat{i} - \hat{j} - \hat{k}}{\sqrt{3}} \qquad \textbf{\textit{Ans.}}$$

7. (i) $\big[\hat{i}\,\hat{j}\,\hat{k}\big] = \hat{i}\cdot\big(\hat{j} \times \hat{k}\big) = \hat{i}\cdot\hat{i} = 1$

    (ii) $\vec{a} \times \big(\vec{b} \times \vec{c}\big) = \big(\vec{a} \cdot \vec{c}\big)\vec{b} - \big(\vec{a} \cdot \vec{b}\big)\vec{c} \qquad \textbf{\textit{Ans.}}$

8. $\vec{a} \times \big(\vec{b} \times \vec{c}\big) + \vec{b} \times \big(\vec{c} \times \vec{a}\big) + \vec{c} \times \big(\vec{a} \times \vec{b}\big)$
    $$= \big(\vec{a} \cdot \vec{c}\big)\vec{b} - \big(\vec{a} \cdot \vec{b}\big)\vec{c} + \big(\vec{b} \cdot \vec{a}\big)\vec{c} - \big(\vec{b} \cdot \vec{c}\big)\vec{a}$$
    $$+ \big(\vec{c} \cdot \vec{b}\big)\vec{a} - \big(\vec{c} \cdot \vec{a}\big)\vec{b} = 0 \quad \textbf{\textit{Ans.}}$$

1. (c) $A_x = A\cos 240° = -\dfrac{A}{2}$

    and $A_y = A\sin 240° = -\sqrt{3}\dfrac{A}{2}$

2. (d) If θ and θ' are the angles made by resultant velocities of first and second ball respectively from the x-axis, then
    $$\tan\theta = \frac{v_y}{v_x} = \frac{\sqrt{3}}{1} = \sqrt{3}$$

    or $\qquad \theta = 60°$

and $\quad \tan \theta' = \dfrac{v'_y}{v'_x} = \dfrac{2}{2} = 1$

or $\quad \theta' = 45°$

Angle between the paths of the balls

$$= \theta - \theta' = 60° - 45° = 15° \quad \textbf{\textit{Ans.}}$$

3. (b) Let θ is the angle between the vectors

$\therefore \quad A^2 = A^2 + A^2 + 2AA \cos \theta$

which gives $\cos \theta = -\dfrac{1}{2}$

or $\quad \theta = 120°.$ **Ans.**

4. (b) $1^2 = 1^2 + 1^2 + 2 \times 1 \times 1 \times \cos \theta$

$\therefore \cos \theta = -\dfrac{1}{2}.$

Now $R = \sqrt{1^2 + 1^2 - 2 \times 1 \times 1 \cos \theta}$

$= \sqrt{1^2 + 1^2 - 2 \times 1 \times 1 \times \left(-\dfrac{1}{2}\right)} = \sqrt{3}$

5. (b) From the figure as shown, $\tan \theta = 2/3$.

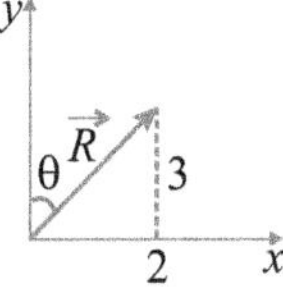

6. (d) The second's needle gets rotated by 90° in 15 seconds,

so $\Delta v = \sqrt{v^2 + v^2 - 2vv \cos 90°}$

$= \sqrt{2}\, v = \sqrt{2}\, \omega r = \sqrt{2} \times \dfrac{2\pi}{60} \times 1 = \dfrac{\pi\sqrt{2}}{30}$ cm/s.

7. (c) $\tan \theta/2 = \dfrac{B \sin \theta}{A + B \cos \theta}$

$\therefore \quad A = B.$

8. (b) For three vectors in a plane

$\vec{A} + \vec{B} + \vec{C} = 0$

9. (c) The resultant of any three vectors will be cancel out by fourth vector.

10. (a) As $\vec{A} + \vec{B} + \vec{C} = 0$, so $\vec{A} = -(\vec{B} + \vec{C})$. They must be in a plane. Also $|\vec{A}| = |\vec{B} + \vec{C}|$

11. (c) Two equal and opposite vectors will cancel each other.

12. (a)

13. (b) The forces are drawn along the sides of a square as shown in the *fig.* 2.31. It is clear from the figure that:

$$R = \sqrt{(2P)^2 + (2P)^2} = 2\sqrt{2}\, P$$

and it makes angle

$\alpha = 180° + 45°$

$= 225°$ with x-axis.

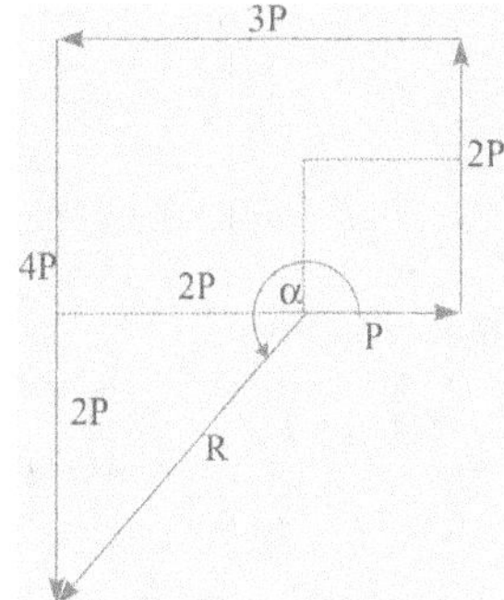

14. (d) $(\vec{A} + \vec{B}) \times (\vec{A} - \vec{B}) = \vec{A} \times \vec{A} + \vec{B} \times \vec{A} - \vec{A} \times \vec{B} - \vec{B} \times \vec{B}$

$= -\vec{A} \times \vec{B} - \vec{A} \times \vec{B} = -2(\vec{A} \times \vec{B}).$

15. (d) $|\vec{V_1}| + |\vec{V_2}| = |\vec{V_1} - \vec{V_2}|$

or $V_1^2 + V_2^2 + 2V_1 V_2 \cos \theta = V_1^2 + V_2^2 - 2V_1 V_2 \cos \theta$

or $\cos \theta = 0$

$\therefore \quad \theta = 90°$

16. (c) If $\vec{A}$ is the required vector, then

$\vec{A} + (\hat{i} - 5\hat{j} + 2\hat{k}) + (3\hat{i} + 6\hat{j} - 7\hat{k}) = \hat{i}$ or $\hat{j}$ or $\hat{k}$

$\therefore \vec{A} = -3\hat{i} - \hat{j} + 5\hat{k}$

17. (d) For parallel vectors

$\dfrac{A_1}{B_1} = \dfrac{A_2}{B_2} = \dfrac{A_3}{B_3}$

18. (b) If $\vec{A} + \vec{B} = \vec{A} - \vec{B}$

or $\vec{B} = 0.$

19. (d) $\vec{A}.\vec{B} = 0$

or $(5\hat{i} + 7\hat{j} - 3\hat{k}).(2\hat{i} + 2\hat{j} - a\hat{k}) = 0$

$\therefore \quad 5 \times 2 + 7 \times 2 + 3a = 0$

or $\quad a = -8$

20. (d) As $\vec{A}.\vec{B} = 0$, so $\vec{A}$ and $\vec{B}$ are perpendicular,

also $\vec{A}.\vec{C} = 0$, so $\vec{A}$ and $\vec{C}$ are perpendicular. i.e., $\vec{A}$ is perpendicular to the plane of $\vec{B}$ and $\vec{C}$. So $\vec{}$ will be parallel to $\vec{B} \times \vec{C}$.

21. (a) $\qquad (\vec{A}+\vec{B}).(\vec{A}-\vec{B}) = 0$

or $\vec{A}.\vec{A} + \vec{B}.\vec{A} - \vec{A}.\vec{B} - \vec{B}.\vec{B} = 0$

$\therefore \qquad A = B.$

22. (c) $(\vec{A} \times \vec{B})$ will be perpendicular to the plane of $\vec{A}$ and $\vec{B}$

23. (a) The required result is ,

$$\frac{(\vec{A}.\vec{B})\vec{B}}{B^2} = \frac{[(2\hat{i}+3\hat{j}).(\hat{i}-\hat{j})]}{(\sqrt{2})^2}(i-j)$$

$$= \frac{-(\hat{i}-\hat{j})}{2} .$$

24. (b) For perpendicular, $\vec{A}.\vec{B} = 0$,

$\therefore \vec{B} = \hat{i}B\sin\theta - \hat{j}B\cos\theta.$

25. (b) If $\vec{P}.\vec{Q} = 0$, then $\vec{Q}$ is perpendicular to $\vec{P}$

and $\vec{P} \times \vec{R} = 0$.

So $\vec{R}$ is parallel to $\vec{P}$. Thus $\vec{Q}$ and $\vec{R}$ must be perpendicular.

26. (a) $(\vec{a}.\vec{b})^2 = (\vec{a}^2 \vec{b}^2)$

or $(ab\cos\theta)^2 = a^2 b^2$

or $\cos\theta = 1$

$\therefore \qquad \theta = 0°,$

1. (c) $13^2 = 12^2 + 5^2 + 2 \times 12 \times 5 \cos\theta$

$\therefore \quad \theta = 90°$

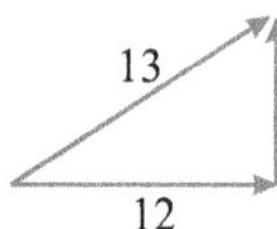

2. (a) The required vector is $= B\,\hat{A} = \dfrac{B\,\vec{A}}{A}$

$$= \sqrt{7^2 + 24^2} \times \frac{(3\hat{i}+4\hat{j})}{\sqrt{3^2+4^2}}$$

$$= 15\hat{i} + 20\hat{j} .$$

3. (d) Use law of vector addition.

4. (b) Let eastern line be taken as x-axis, northern as y-axis and vertical upward as z-axis. Let the velocity v makes angle α, β and γ with x, y and z-axis respectively, then $\alpha = 60°$, $\gamma = 60°$.

We have $\cos^2\alpha + \cos^2\beta + \cos^2\gamma = 1$

or $\cos^2 60 + \cos^2\beta + \cos^2 60 = 1$ or $\cos\beta = \dfrac{1}{\sqrt{2}}$

$\therefore \quad \vec{v} = v\cos\alpha\,\hat{i} + v\cos\beta\,\hat{j} + v\cos\gamma\,\hat{k}$

$$= 20\left[\frac{1}{2}\hat{i} + \frac{1}{\sqrt{2}}\hat{j} + \frac{1}{2}\hat{k}\right]$$

$$= 10\hat{i} + 10\sqrt{2}\,\hat{j} + 10\hat{k}$$

5. (c) $\vec{A} = 4\hat{i} + 6\hat{j}$. If B_x and B_y are the components of vector along x and y axes, then

$4 + B_x = 10$, $\therefore B_x = 6$.

Also $6 + B_y = 9$, $\therefore \qquad B_y = 3$.

Thus, $B = \sqrt{B_x^2 + B_y^2} = \sqrt{6^2 + 3^2} = \sqrt{45}$.

6. (d) The situation is shown in figure.

$$\frac{bt - ct\sin 45°}{ct\cos 45°} = \frac{ct\sin 45°}{at - ct\cos 45°}$$

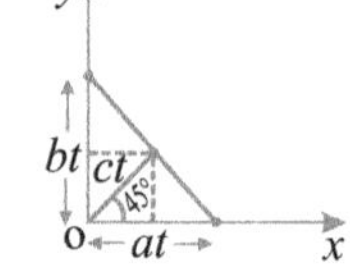

$\therefore \quad c = \dfrac{\sqrt{2}\,ab}{a+b} .$

7. (a) The required vector is,

$$= 3\frac{(\vec{A}\times\vec{B})}{|\vec{A}\times\vec{B}|} = 3\frac{[(2\hat{i}+2\hat{j}+\hat{k})\times(2\hat{i}-2\hat{j}+3\hat{k})]}{|\vec{A}\times\vec{B}|}$$

$$= 3\frac{(8\hat{i}-4\hat{j}-8\hat{k})}{\sqrt{8^2+4^2+8^2}} = 2\hat{i}-\hat{j}-2\hat{k} .$$

8. (c) The area of the triangle of sides $\vec{a}, \vec{b}$ and $\vec{c}$ can be written as;

$$A = \frac{|\vec{a}\times\vec{b}|}{2} = \frac{|\vec{b}\times\vec{c}|}{2} = \frac{|\vec{c}\times\vec{a}|}{2}$$

$$\therefore 3A = \frac{|\vec{a}\times\vec{b}|}{2} + \frac{|\vec{b}\times\vec{c}|}{2} + \frac{|\vec{c}\times\vec{a}|}{2}$$

or $A = \dfrac{1}{6}\left[\,|\vec{a}\times\vec{b}| + |\vec{b}\times\vec{c}| + |\vec{c}\times\vec{a}|\,\right].$

9. (a) If θ is the angle between $\vec{A_1}$ and $\vec{A_2}$, then

$$A^2 = A_1^2 + A_2^2 + 2A_1 A_2 \cos\theta$$

or $3^2 = 2^2 + 3^2 + 2 \times 2 \times 3 \cos\theta$

$\therefore \cos\theta = -1/3$.

Now, $(\vec{A_1} + 2\vec{A_2}) \cdot (3\vec{A_1} - 4\vec{A_2})$

$$= 3\vec{A_1}.\vec{A_1} + 6\vec{A_2}.\vec{A_1} - 4\vec{A_1}.\vec{A_2} - 8\vec{A_2}.\vec{A_2}$$

$$= 3A_1^2 + 2\vec{A_1}.\vec{A_2} - 8A_2^2$$

$$= 3 \times 2^2 + 2 \times 2 \times 3 \times (-1/3) - 8 \times 3^2 = -64$$

10. (a) Two sides of a triangle are;

$$\vec{PQ} = (2\hat{i} - \hat{j} + \hat{k}) - (\hat{i} + 3\hat{j} + 2\hat{k}) = \hat{i} - 4\hat{j} - \hat{k}$$

and $\vec{PR} = (-\hat{i} + 2\hat{j} + 3\hat{k}) - (\hat{i} + 3\hat{j} + 2\hat{k}) = -2\hat{i} - \hat{j} + \hat{k}$

Thus area of the triangle

$$A = \frac{1}{2} | \vec{PQ} \times \vec{PR} |$$

$$= \frac{1}{2} | (\hat{i} - 4\hat{j} - \hat{k}) \times (-2\hat{i} - \hat{j} + \hat{k}) | = \frac{1}{2}\sqrt{107}.$$

11. (c) The area of the triangle

$$A = \frac{1}{2} | (\hat{i} + \hat{j} + \hat{k}) \times (3\hat{i}) | = \frac{3}{\sqrt{2}}.$$

12. (c) Let $\vec{b} = (\hat{ } + \hat{j})$ and $\vec{c} = (\hat{i} - \hat{j})$

The component of $\vec{a}$ along $\vec{b}$

$$a \cos\theta \, \hat{b} = \left(\frac{\mathbf{a}.\mathbf{b}}{\mathbf{b}} \right) \hat{b}$$

$$= \frac{(2\hat{i} + 3\hat{j}) \cdot (\hat{i} + \hat{j})}{\sqrt{1^2 + 1^2}} \frac{(\hat{i} + \hat{j})}{\sqrt{1^2 + 1^2}}$$

$$= \frac{2 \times 1 + 3 \times 1}{\sqrt{2}} \frac{(\hat{i} + \hat{j})}{\sqrt{2}}$$

$$= \frac{5}{2} (\hat{i} + \hat{j})$$

1. (c,d) From the figure, it is clear that if $A > B$, $\alpha < \beta$. And if

$A = B$, $\alpha = \beta$.

2. (a,b,c) If unit vectors are along the same direction, then resultant be zero. The resultant may be zero when each one has angle $120°$ from other.

3. (b,c,d) $|\vec{A} \times \vec{B}| = A B \sin\theta$. As $\sin\theta \le 1$, so $|\vec{A} \times \vec{B}|$ can not be greater than $A B$.

4. (a,b,c) If A, B and C are the magnitudes of three vectors, then for their resultant to be zero,

$$(A - B) \le C \le (A + B).$$

5. (b,d) If all the vectors are in the same direction, then (d) will be correct, otherwise (b) will be correct.

6. (a,b,d) The dot product of $5\hat{k}$ with $4\hat{i} + 3\hat{j}, 6\hat{i}$ and $3\hat{i} + 4\hat{j}$ is zero, so these are perpendicular vectors to $5\hat{k}$.

7. (a,b,c) $\vec{A} \times \vec{B} = -\vec{B} \times \vec{A}$, so option (c) is not correct.

8. (a,b,c,d) The angle between $\vec{A}$ and $\vec{B}$ may have any value.

9. (a,c,d) The resultant $\vec{R}$ of $\vec{a}$ and $\vec{b}$ is such that

$$| \vec{A} - \vec{B} | \le \vec{R} \le | \vec{A} + \vec{B} |,$$ so options (a, c, d) are correct.

10. (b,c,d) $\vec{a} + \vec{b} + \vec{c} + \vec{d} = 0$

or $\vec{a} + \vec{c} = -(\vec{b} + \vec{d})$, so $|\vec{a} + \vec{c}| = -|\vec{b} + \vec{d}|$

Also $\vec{a} = -(\vec{b} + \vec{c} + \vec{d})$, so $\vec{a} = |\vec{b} + \vec{c} + \vec{d}|$

11. (b,c,d)

$$\vec{A} \times (\vec{B} \times \vec{C}) + \vec{B} \times (\vec{C} \times \vec{A}) + \vec{C} \times (\vec{A} \times \vec{B})$$

$$= (\vec{A}.\vec{C})\vec{B} - (\vec{A}.\vec{B})\vec{C} + (\vec{B}.\vec{A})\vec{C} - (\vec{B}.\vec{C})\vec{A}$$
$$+ (\vec{C}.\vec{B})\vec{A} - (\vec{C}.\vec{A})\vec{B} = 0.$$

The options (b, c, d) are incorrect.

EXERCISE 2.3

1. (c) Vector quantity may have any direction, so statement-2 is not correct.

2. (c) The vector product of two vectors is perpendicular to the plane of given vectors, so it is axial vector.

    Also $\vec{V} = \vec{\omega} \times \vec{r}$, so statement-2 is incorrect.

3. (a) Statement-2 is the explanation of statement-1

4. (a) $AB \cos \theta_1 = BC \cos \theta_2$, so $A \cos \theta_1 = C \cos \theta_2$.

    $A = C$, only if $\theta_1 = \theta_2$, otherwise $A \neq C$.

5. (b) $\hat{A} \times \hat{B} = AB \sin 0° = 0$.

6. (a) $\vec{A} + \vec{B}$ and $\vec{A} - \vec{B}$ are in the plane of $\vec{A}$ and $\vec{B}$. But $\vec{A} \times \vec{B}$ is perpendicular to the plane of $\vec{A}$ and $\vec{B}$.

7. (d) The sum of two equal and opposite vectors is equal to zero.

8. (a) If $\theta = 90°$, then $AB \cos \theta = 0$.

EXERCISE 2.4

Passage (Questions 1 to 3)

1. (d) $\vec{A} + \vec{B} = (2\hat{i} + 6\hat{j} + 4\hat{k}) + (\hat{i} - 2\hat{j} + 8\hat{k})$

    $= 3\hat{i} + 4\hat{j} + 12\hat{k}$

    $\therefore \quad |\vec{A} + \vec{B}| = \sqrt{3^2 + 4^2 + 12^2} = 13$

2. (d) $\vec{A}.(\vec{A} \times \vec{B}) = \vec{A}.(AB \sin \theta \, \hat{\eta}) = A(AB \sin \theta) \cos 90° = 0.$

3. (a) $\hat{\eta} = \dfrac{\vec{A} \times \vec{B}}{|\vec{A} \times \vec{B}|} = \dfrac{56\hat{i} - 12\hat{j} - 10\hat{k}}{\sqrt{56^2 + 12^2 + 10^2}} = \dfrac{1}{13\sqrt{5}}(28\hat{i} - 6\hat{j} - 5\hat{k})$

Matching (Q 4 &5)

4. A $\rightarrow$ q, B $\rightarrow$ p, C $\rightarrow$ s, D $\rightarrow$ r,

5. A $\rightarrow$ s, B $\rightarrow$ r, C $\rightarrow$ p, D $\rightarrow$ q,

Chapter 3

Motion in a Straight Line (93 - 146)

Chapter contents

Galileo Galilei

Galileo Galilei (1564-1642) was one of the greatest scientists who ever lived. He made many discoveries about gravity and acceleration. But he is especially famous because he was the first to use a telescope to scan the heavens and make many important discoveries, described in his book. The Story Messenger (1610). He was the first to see mountains on the Moon the moons of Jupiter and sunspots - through looking of the Sun badly damaged his eyesight. ...

Definitions, Explanations and Derivations

3.1 CONCEPT OF A POINT OBJECT

If the position of an object changes by distances much greater than its size in a considerable interval of time, then the object can be regarded as a point object.

Example : A car under a journey of several kilometers can be regarded as a point object. Moon can be regarded as a point object for studying its motion around the earth.

3.2 REST AND MOTION ARE RELATIVE TERMS

A person in a car is at rest with respect to the driver of the car but he is in motion with respect to the observer outside the car. Thus an object may be at rest w.r.t. one object and the same time it may be in motion relative to another object. Hence rest and motion are relative terms. No object in the universe is in a state of absolute rest or motion.

3.3 MOTION

One dimensional motion (1D) : The motion of an object whose position changes with time along a straight line, may be any one of the coordinate axes is known as one dimensional motion or rectilinear motion.

Example : Motion of a car, a train along a straight track, motion of a freely falling body etc.

Two dimensional motion (2D) : If an object moves in such a way that it covers two directions simultaneously, its motion is known as two dimensional motion.

Example : All motions on curved path in a plane are two dimensional. (see fig. 3.1)

Three dimensional motion (3D) : The motion of an object is said to be three dimensional if all the three coordinates specifying its position change with time.

Example : Motion of a kite, motion of a fly etc. (see fig 3.2)

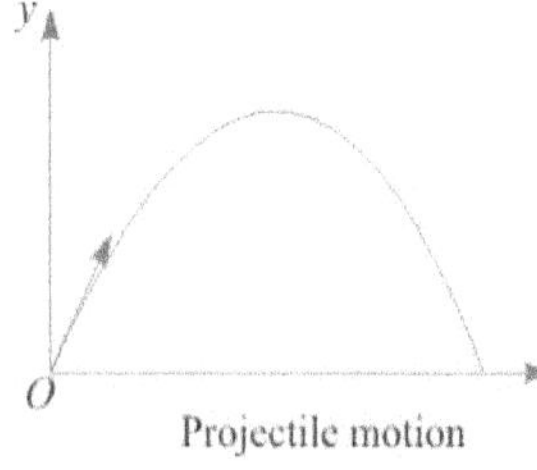

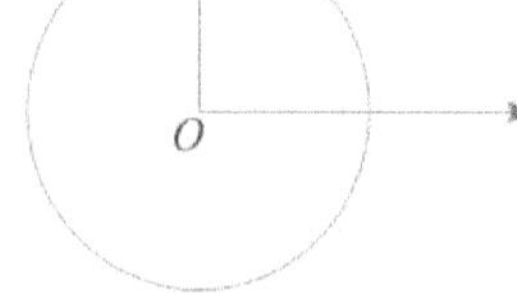

Figure. 3.1 Motion in 2D

3.4 MOTION PARAMETERS

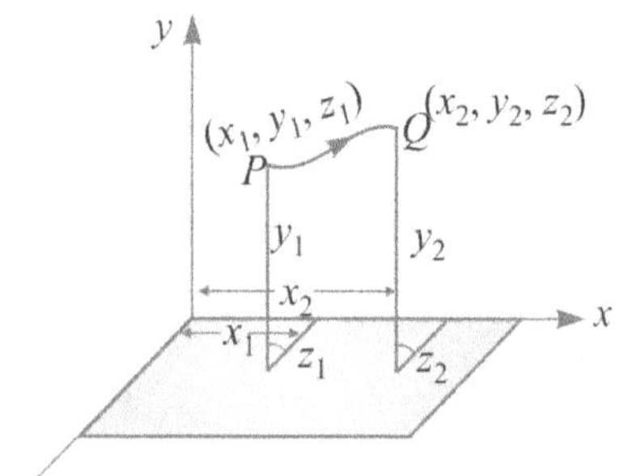

Figure. 3.2 Motion in 3D

Distance

It is the actual length of path traversed by a moving particle. It is a scalar quantity. Its SI unit is metre (m).

Displacement

It is the shortest distance between the initial and final position of the particle. It is a vector quantity. Its SI unit is metre (m). If $\vec{r_1}$ and $\vec{r_2}$ are the position vectors of a particle at time t_1 and t_2 respectively, then its displacement in this interval $\Delta t = t_2 - t_1$ is $\vec{s} = \vec{r_{21}} = \vec{r_2} - \vec{r_1}$ (see fig. 3.3)

More about distance and displacement

1. Distance can never be negative and can not decrease with time. Displacement may be zero or negative.
2. Until particle changes the direction of motion, displacement is equal to distance. Otherwise displacement will be less than distance. Thus

$$\left| \frac{\text{displacement}}{\text{distance}} \right| \leq 1$$

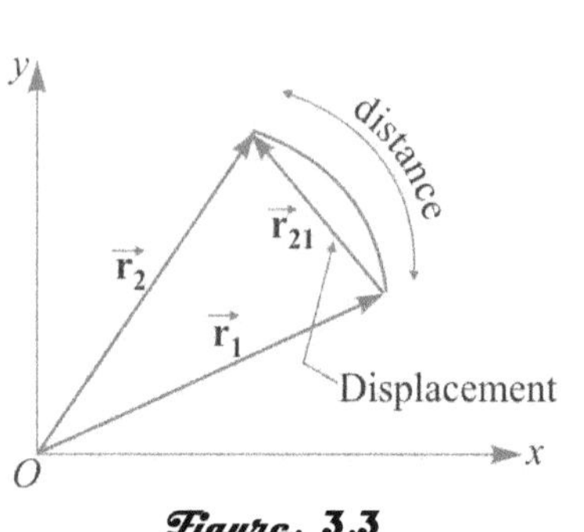

Figure. 3.3

Speed

It is the distance travelled by object in unit time. It is a scalar quantity. Its SI unit is m/s.

Average speed

The average speed is the total distance travelled by the object in any time interval divided by that time interval.

$$\text{Average speed} = \frac{\text{total distance travelled}}{\text{time interval}}$$

Suppose an object travels a distance Δs, in time Δt, then its average speed

$$v_{av} = <v> = \frac{\Delta s}{\Delta t}.$$

Instantaneous speed

The speed of object at a particular instant is called instantaneous speed. The limiting value of average speed when time interval Δt approaches to zero, gives the instantaneous speed at any instant t. Thus

$$v_{\text{inst}} = \lim_{\Delta t \to 0} \frac{\Delta s}{\Delta t} = \frac{ds}{dt}.$$

Velocity

It is the displacement covered by the object per unit time. It is a vector quantity. Its unit is m/s.

Average velocity

The average velocity is the displacement covered by object in any time interval divided by that time interval.

$$\therefore \quad \text{Average velocity} = \frac{\text{displacement}}{\text{time interval}}$$

Suppose an object travels a displacement $\Delta \vec{s}$ in time interval Δt, then its average velocity is

$$\vec{v}_{av} = <\vec{v}> = \frac{\Delta \vec{s}}{\Delta t}.$$

The direction of average velocity is that of the direction of displacement.

Instantaneous velocity

The velocity of an object at a particular instant of time is called instantaneous velocity. It is equal to the limiting value of average velocity of the object when the time interval approaches zero. Thus

$$\text{Instantaneous velocity } \vec{v} = \lim_{\Delta t \to 0} \frac{\Delta \vec{s}}{\Delta t} = \frac{d\vec{s}}{dt}.$$

More about speed and velocity

1. The instantaneous velocity in magnitude is equal to instantaneous speed.
2. A particle may have constant speed but variable velocity. In uniform circular motion speed remains constant while velocity changes because of change in direction of motion.
3. If particle is moving along a straight line without changing the direction, its average velocity will be equal to its average speed. Otherwise average velocity will be less than average speed. Thus

$$\left| \frac{\text{average velocity}}{\text{average speed}} \right| \leq 1$$

Uniform motion and non-uniform motion

If an object covers equal distance in equal time interval or object moves with constant speed then it is said to be in *uniform motion*. For uniform motion

$$\text{distance} = \text{speed} \times \text{time}$$

$$s = vt$$

In uniform circular motion

$$2\pi R = vt$$

where R is the radius of path and t is the time to complete the circle.

A body is said to be in *non-uniform motion* if its speed changes with time. Ex. Motion under gravity, car starts from rest etc.

Note :

1. In uniform motion average speed is equal to the instantaneous speed.
2. In a uniform motion along a straight line without change in direction, the average velocity is equal to instantaneous velocity.
3. In uniform motion along a straight line without change in direction of motion,

$$\frac{d\,|\,\vec{\mathbf{v}}\,|}{dt} = 0 \ \text{ and } \ \left|\frac{d\vec{\mathbf{v}}}{dt}\right| = 0$$

4. If body moves uniformly but its direction of motion changes, then $\dfrac{d\,|\,\vec{\mathbf{v}}\,|}{dt} = 0$, but $\left|\dfrac{d\vec{\mathbf{v}}}{dt}\right| \neq 0$.

Calculating average speed and average velocity

1. **A body covering different distances with different speeds :** Suppose a body covers distances s_1, s_2,....., s_n with speed v_1, v_2,....., v_n respectively, then

$$\text{Average speed} = \frac{\text{Total distance travelled}}{\text{total time taken}} = \frac{s}{t}$$

$$= \frac{(s_1 + s_2 + ... + s_n)}{(t_1 + t_2 + ... + t_n)}$$

$$v_{av} = \frac{(s_1 + s_2 + ... + s_n)}{\dfrac{s_1}{v_1} + \dfrac{s_2}{v_2} + ... + \dfrac{s_n}{v_n}}$$

Special case : If $s_1 = s_2 = s$

$$v_{av} = \frac{2s}{\dfrac{s}{v_1} + \dfrac{s}{v_2}} = \frac{2v_1 v_2}{v_1 + v_2}$$

It is the harmonic mean of the individual speeds.

Figure. 3.4

2. **A body moving with different speeds in different time interval :** Suppose a body travels with speeds v_1, v_2, ..., v_n in time intervals t_1, t_2, ..., t_n respectively, then

$$\text{Average speed} = \frac{\text{total distance travelled}}{\text{total time taken}} = \frac{s}{t}$$

$$= \frac{s_1 + s_2 + ... + s_n}{t_1 + t_2 ..... + t_n}$$

$$= \frac{(v_1 t_1 + v_2 t_2 + ... + v_n t_n)}{(t_1 + t_2 + ... + t_n)}$$

Special case : If $t_1 = t_2 = ... = t_n = t$, then

$$v_{av} = \frac{v_1 + v_2 .... + v_n}{n}$$

It is the arithmetic mean of the individual speeds.

3. For continuously changing speed with time, the average speed is defined as

$$v_{av} = \frac{s}{t} = \frac{\displaystyle\int_{t_1}^{t_2} v\,dt}{\displaystyle\int_{t_1}^{t_2} dt}.$$

Acceleration

The rate of change of velocity of an object with time is called *acceleration*. It is a vector quantity. It can be negative. Negative acceleration is called *retardation or deceleration*. Its SI unit is m/s^2.

Average acceleration

For an object moving with variable velocity, the average acceleration is defined as the ratio of the change of velocity of the object to the time of change of velocity. Suppose $\vec{v}_1$ and $\vec{v}_2$ are the velocities of an object at time t_1 and t_2 respectively, then its average acceleration ;

$$\vec{a}_{av} = \frac{\vec{v}_2 - \vec{v}_1}{t_2 - t_1} = \frac{\Delta \vec{v}}{\Delta t}.$$

Acceleration occurs due to change of velocity of the object. The velocity of the object may change due to change in its magnitude or may due to change in direction of motion or due to change in both magnitude and direction.

Instantaneous acceleration

The acceleration of any object at any instant is called its instantaneous acceleration. It is equal to the limiting value of the average acceleration of the object when time interval approaches to zero . Thus

$$\vec{a} = \lim_{\Delta t \to 0} \frac{\Delta \vec{v}}{\Delta t} = \frac{d\vec{v}}{dt}$$

As $\quad \vec{v} = \dfrac{d\vec{s}}{dt},$

$$\therefore \qquad \vec{a} = \frac{d}{dt}\left(\frac{d\vec{s}}{dt}\right) = \frac{d^2\vec{s}}{dt^2}.$$

Acceleration can also we written as

$$a = \frac{dv}{dt} = \frac{dv}{dt}.\frac{ds}{ds} = v\frac{dv}{ds}$$

In vector form, $\qquad \vec{a} = \vec{v}.\dfrac{d\vec{v}}{ds}.$

3.5 EQUATIONS OF MOTION

Consider a body moving along a straight line with constant acceleration a. Let its initial velocity be u, after covering a displacement s its velocity becomes v.

Figure. 3.5

(i) **First equation of motion**

By the definition, the acceleration

$$a \quad = \quad \frac{dv}{dt}$$

[Here we can drop the vector sign with displacement, velocity and acceleration, because motion is along the straight line]

Above equation can be written as;

$$dv \quad = \quad adt \qquad\qquad \text{...(i)}$$

Integrating equation (i), we get

$$\int_u^v dv \quad = \quad \int_0^t adt$$

$$\left|v\right|_u^v \quad = \quad a\left|t\right|_0^t$$

or $\qquad\qquad (v - u) \quad = \quad a(t - 0)$

or $\qquad\qquad\qquad v \quad = \quad u + at \qquad\qquad \text{...(1)}$

(ii)   **Second equation of motion**

By the definition, the instantaneous velocity v is given by

$$v = \frac{ds}{dt} \quad \text{or} \quad ds = v\,dt$$

From equation (i), we have $v = u + at$

$$\therefore \qquad ds = (u + at)\,dt \qquad\qquad \text{...(ii)}$$

Integrating equation (ii), we get

$$\int_0^s ds = \int_0^t (u + at)\,dt$$

$$\left| s \right|_0^s = \left| ut + \frac{1}{2}at^2 \right|_0^t$$

or

$$s = ut + \frac{1}{2}at^2. \qquad\qquad \text{...(2)}$$

(iii)   **Third equation of motion**

By the definition, acceleration a is given by

$$a = \frac{dv}{dt} = \frac{dv}{dt} \times \frac{ds}{ds} = v\frac{dv}{ds}$$

or

$$v\,dv = a\,ds \qquad\qquad \text{...(iii)}$$

Integrating equation (iii), we have

$$\int_u^v v\,dv = \int_0^s a\,ds \quad \text{or} \quad \left| \frac{v^2}{2} \right|_u^v = a\,|\,s\,|_0^s$$

$$\therefore \qquad (v^2 - u^2) = 2a(s - 0)$$

or

$$v^2 = u^2 + 2as. \qquad\qquad \text{...(3)}$$

(iv)   **Fourth equation of motion**

By the definition of velocity, we have

$$v = \frac{ds}{dt} \quad \text{or} \quad ds = v\,dt$$

or

$$ds = (u + at)\,dt \qquad\qquad \text{...(iv)}$$

Let at $t = n - 1$, displacement travelled $= s_{n-1}$ and at $t = n$, displacement travelled $= s_n$.
Thus the displacement travelled in n^{th} second $s_n^{\text{th}} = s_n - s_{n-1}$
Integrating equation (iv), we have

$$\int_{s_{n-1}}^{s_n} ds = \int_{(n-1)}^{n} (u + at)\,dt$$

$$|\,s\,|_{s_{n-1}}^{s_n} = \left| ut + \frac{1}{2}at^2 \right|_{n-1}^{n}$$

or

$$s_n - s_{n-1} = \left[un + \frac{1}{2}an^2 \right] - \left[u(n-1) + \frac{1}{2}a(n-1)^2 \right]$$

or

$$s_n^{\text{th}} = u + \frac{a}{2}(2n - 1). \qquad\qquad \text{...(4)}$$

Calculating distance from $s = ut + \dfrac{1}{2}at^2$

Case 1. When acceleration and velocity are along same direction.
In such cases the displacement calculated by second equation of motion is equal to the distance travelled.

Case 2. When acceleration and velocity are opposite to each other.

In this case, if t_0 is the time at which the velocity becomes zero, then

$$\therefore \quad 0 = u - at_0 \Rightarrow t_0 = \left(\frac{u}{a}\right).$$

$$t = 0 \quad \overset{u}{\underset{A}{\bullet}} \xrightarrow{\hspace{4cm}} \overset{v}{\underset{B}{\bullet}} \; t = t_0$$

Figure. 3.6

(a) For the motion $t \le t_0$, the displacement calculated by second equation of motion is equal to distance travelled. Thus we have

$$s = ut_0 - \frac{1}{2}at_0^2 = u \times \frac{u}{a} - \frac{1}{2}a\left(\frac{u}{a}\right)^2$$

or

$$AB = \frac{u^2}{2a}.$$

(b) For the motion $t > t_0$: Let $t = 1.5\, t_0 = 1.5\dfrac{u}{a}$

Displacement

$$s = ut - \frac{1}{2}at^2$$

$$= u\left(1.5\frac{u}{a}\right) - \frac{1}{2}a\left(1.5\frac{u}{a}\right)^2$$

or

$$AC = 0.375\left(\frac{u^2}{a}\right)$$

Distance,

$$s = AB + BC$$

AB is the distance travelled in the duration t_0. BC is the distance travelled in the duration $t - t_0$.

Here $AB = \dfrac{u^2}{2a}$ calculated previously and $BC = v_B(t - t_0) + \dfrac{1}{2}a(t - t_0)^2$

As $v_B = 0$,

$$\therefore \quad BC = \frac{1}{2}a(1.5t_0 - t_0)^2 = \frac{1}{2}a \times (0.5t_0)^2$$

$$= \frac{1}{2}a \times 0.5^2 \times \left(\frac{u}{a}\right)^2 = 0.125\frac{u^2}{a}$$

Thus total distance $s = AB + BC$

$$= \frac{u^2}{2a} + 0.125\frac{u^2}{a} = 0.625\frac{u^2}{a}.$$

Thus if body travels for time t and it changes the direction of motion after t_0, where $t > t_0$, then

displacement is given by

$$s = ut - \frac{1}{2}at^2$$

and distance is given by

$$s = \left|ut_0 - \frac{1}{2}at_0^2\right| + \left|\frac{1}{2}a(t - t_0)^2\right|$$

In case when acceleration is not constant

Let the time of motion be t and body changes direction of motion after time t_0 $(t_0 < t)$.

The displacement is given by,

$$s = \int_0^t v\, dt$$

The distance travelled is given by

$$s = \left|\int_0^{t_0} v\, dt\right| + \left|\int_{t_0}^{(t-t_0)} v\, dt\right|$$

Motion in presence of air resistance

Suppose a body is thrown vertically upward with initial velocity u. Let it experiences a constant retardation 'a' due to air. In upward journey, its retardation is $(g + a)$ and in downward journey its acceleration becomes $(g - a)$. Let t_1 be the time of upward journey and t_2 be the time of downward journey, then:

Upward journey : From first equation

$$v = u - (g + a)t_1$$

As $\quad v = 0$

$$\therefore \qquad t_1 = \frac{u}{(g + a)}. \qquad \qquad ...(i)$$

Height attained by the body;

$$v^2 = u^2 - 2(g + a)h$$
$$h = u^2 - 2(g + a)h$$

or

$$h = \frac{u^2}{2(g + a)}. \qquad \qquad ...(ii)$$

Downward journey: $u = 0$

$$\therefore \qquad h = 0 + \frac{1}{2}(g - a)t_2^2$$

or

$$\frac{u^2}{2(g + a)} = \frac{1}{2}(g - a)t_2^2$$

or

$$t_2 = \frac{u}{\sqrt{g^2 - a^2}}. \qquad \qquad ...(iii)$$

To understand simply, let $g = 10$ m/s^2 and $a = 1$ m/s^2

$$\therefore \qquad t_1 = \frac{u}{10 + 1} = \frac{u}{11} s$$

and

$$t_2 = \frac{u}{\sqrt{10^2 - 1^2}} = \frac{u}{\sqrt{99}} s.$$

Now it is clear that $t_2 > t_1$ i.e., time of descend will be greater than time of ascend.

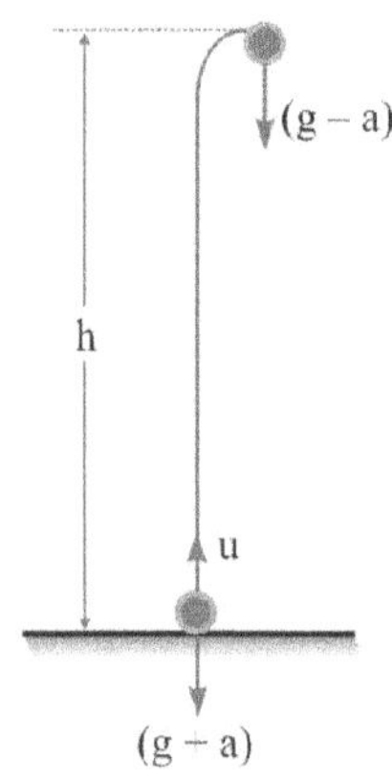

Figure. **3.8**

Stopping distance :

The distance travels before stopping when breaks are applied is called stopping distance.

It depends on the initial velocity of the vehicle and the braking capacity or deceleration $(-a)$ that is caused by braking.

If u is the initial velocity of the vehicle, then using third equation of motion,

$$v^2 = u^2 + 2as, \text{ we have}$$
$$0 = u^2 + 2(-a)s$$

$$\therefore \qquad s = \left(\frac{u^2}{2a}\right)$$

Clearly, if speed of which is doubled, its stopping distance will be four times.

Reaction time : Reaction time is the time a person takes to observe, think and act. For example, if a person is driving and suddenly a boy appears on the road, then time elapsed before he applied the brakes of the car is the reaction time. The reaction time roughly is about 0.2s.

1.   (i)   Av. speed $= \dfrac{\text{total distance}}{\text{total time}} = \dfrac{s}{t} = \dfrac{s_1 + s_2 + ... + s_n}{t_1 + t_2 + ... + t_n}$

       For body cover different distances with different speeds,

$$v_{av} = \frac{s_1 + s_2 + ... + s_n}{\left(\dfrac{s_1}{v_1} + \dfrac{s_2}{v_2} + ... + \dfrac{s_n}{v_n}\right)}$$

(ii) For a body having different speeds in different time

$$v_{av} = \frac{v_1 t_1 + v_2 t_2 + ... + v_n t_n}{t_1 + t_2 + ... + t_n}$$

$$v_{av} = \frac{\int_{t_1}^{t_2} v\, dt}{(t_2 - t_1)}$$

2. Equations of motion

   (i) $v = u + at$ (ii) $s = ut + \dfrac{1}{2}at^2$

   (iii) $v^2 = u^2 + 2as$ (iv) $s_n^{th} = u + \dfrac{a}{2}(2n - 1)$

3. Motion under gravity

   (i) $v = u + gt$ (ii) $h = ut + \dfrac{1}{2}gt^2$

   (iii) $v^2 = u^2 + 2gh$ (iii) $h_n^{th} = u + \dfrac{g}{2}(2n - 1)$

4. For a freely falling particle under gravity, g is taken as positive and for body thrown upward, g is taken negative.
5. For a particle just drop, $u = 0$.
6. Rising of balloon is not motion under gravity, in such a case its acceleration is positive in upward direction.

PROBLEM SOLVING STRATEGY

Average velocity

1. If particle is going in a straight line without change in direction of motion, then
   Average velocity = average speed
2. If body changes direction of motion, then find displacement and distance separately. In this case
   $$\text{average velocity} < \text{average speed}$$

Motion with constant acceleration

Identify the relevant concepts : In majority of problems, you can use the constant acceleration equations. Occasionally, however, you will encounter a situation in which the acceleration is not constant. In such a case you need a different approach, which you will encounter is next section.

Setup the problem using the following steps :

Step I   First decide which direction of motion is positive. It is often easiest to place the particle at the origin at $t = 0$; then $x = 0$.

Step II   (i)   Remember that your choice of positive axis direction automatically determines the positive direction for x-velocity and x-acceleration, if x is positive to the right of the origin, then v_x and a_x are also positive towards the right.

          (ii)   You may choose cartesion coordinates system for the motion parameters. Students always confused in putting the signs in case of motion in vertical direction. According to this system, if particle is moving up then, displacement = $+y$, velocity = $+v$, acceleration = $-g$.

             When particle moves down, displacement = $-y$, velocity = $-v$ and acceleration = $-g$.

Step III   Make a list of all the known quantities, such as x, u, a and t. Look out the informations given; as car starts with constant acceleration, here $u = 0$. A particle starts falling, $u = 0$. A particle thrown vertically up $v = 0$.

Execute the solution

Choose an equation of motion that contains only one unknown. Then substitute the known values and compute the unknown quantity. Sometimes you will have to solve two simultaneous equations for two unknown quantities.

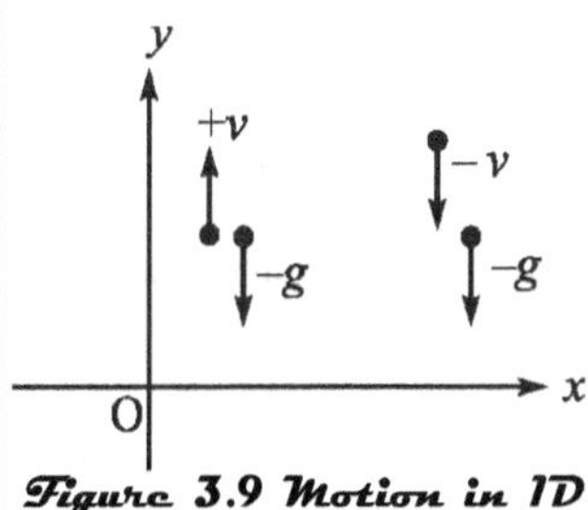

Figure 3.9 Motion in 1D

EXAMPLES BASED ON AVERAGE VELOCITY AND CONSTANT ACCELERATION

Example 1. A cyclist travels from centre O of a circular park of radius 1 km and reaches point P. After cycling 1/4 th of the circumference along PQ, he returns to the centre of the park QO. If the total time taken is 10 minute, calculate   [NCERT]

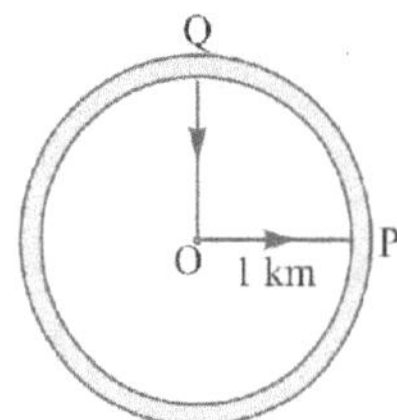

Figure. **3.10**

(i)   net displacement
(ii)   average velocity and
(iii)   average speed of the cyclist.

Sol. (i)   The net displacement becomes zero.

(ii)   As net displacement is zero, so average velocity

$$v_{av} = \frac{\text{Net displacement}}{\text{time taken}} = 0.$$

(iii)   Total distance covered $= OP + \text{Arc } PQ + OQ$

$$= r + \frac{2\pi r}{4} + r$$

$$= 1 + \frac{2 \times 22 \times 1}{7 \times 4} + 1 = \frac{25}{7} \, km$$

Time taken $= 10$ min $= 1/6$ h.

$$\text{Average speed} = \frac{\text{total distance covered}}{\text{time taken}}$$

$$= \frac{\left(\dfrac{25}{7}\right)}{\left(\dfrac{1}{6}\right)} = 21.43 \, \text{km} / \text{h} \qquad \textit{Ans.}$$

Example 2. If a point moves in a straight line with uniform acceleration and covers successive equal distances in times t_1, t_2, t_3, then show that

$$\frac{1}{t_1} - \frac{1}{t_2} + \frac{1}{t_3} = \frac{3}{t_1 + t_2 + t_3}.$$

Sol. Let s be the successive equal distances and v_1, v_2, v_3 the initial velocities for the successive distances and v_4, the final velocity in the third distance. Since the acceleration is constant, so velocities in the three intervals and in the total time are

$$\frac{v_1 + v_2}{2}, \frac{v_2 + v_3}{2}, \frac{v_3 + v_4}{2} \text{ and } \frac{v_1 + v_4}{2}.$$

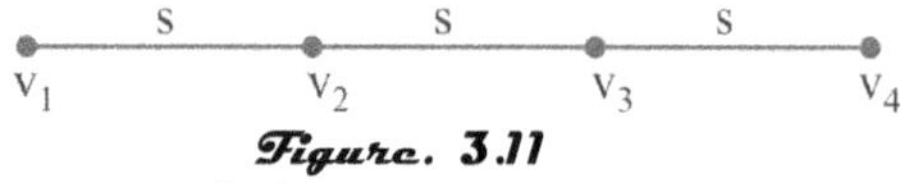

Figure. **3.11**

We know that average velocity

$$v_{av} = \frac{\text{distance}}{\text{time}},$$

$$\therefore \qquad \frac{v_1 + v_2}{2} = \frac{s}{t_1}, \qquad\qquad ...(i)$$

$$\frac{v_2 + v_3}{2} = \frac{s}{t_2}, \qquad\qquad ...(ii)$$

$$\frac{v_3 + v_4}{2} = \frac{s}{t_3}, \qquad\qquad ...(iii)$$

$$\text{and} \quad \frac{v_1 + v_4}{2} = \frac{3s}{t_1 + t_2 + t_3} \qquad\qquad ...(iv)$$

Doing (i) – (ii) + (iii), we get

$$\frac{v_1 + v_4}{2} = s\left[\frac{1}{t_1} - \frac{1}{t_2} + \frac{1}{t_3}\right] \qquad\qquad ...(v)$$

Now from equations (iv) and (v), we get

$$\frac{1}{t_1} - \frac{1}{t_2} + \frac{1}{t_3} = \frac{3}{t_1 + t_2 + t_3}.$$

Example 3. A point traversed half the distance with a velocity v_0. The remaining part of the distance was covered with velocity v_1 for half the time, and with velocity v_2 for the other half of the time. Find the mean velocity of the point averaged over the whole time of motion.

Sol. Since direction of motion is not changing

$$\therefore \quad \text{average or mean velocity} = \frac{\text{total distance}}{\text{total time}}.$$

Let t_0 and t be the time of motion of first half of distance and rest half of the distance respectively, then

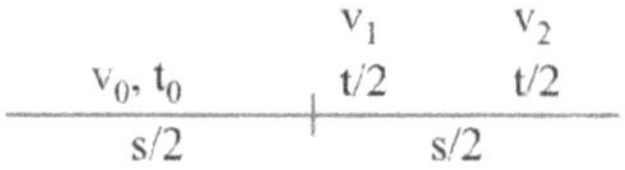

Figure. **3.12**

$$v_{av} = \frac{s/2 + s/2}{t_0 + t}$$

where $t_0 = \dfrac{s/2}{v_0}$, and $\dfrac{v_1 t}{2} + \dfrac{v_2 t}{2} = \dfrac{s}{2}$

$$\text{or} \qquad t = \frac{s}{v_1 + v_2}$$

$$\therefore \qquad v_{av} = \frac{s}{\dfrac{s/2}{v_0} + \dfrac{s}{(v_1 + v_2)}}$$

$$= \frac{2v_0(v_1 + v_2)}{2v_0 + v_1 + v_2}. \qquad \textit{Ans.}$$

Example 4. A man walks on a straight road from his home to a market 2.5 km away with a speed of 5 km / h. Finding market closed, he instantly turns and walks back home with a speed of 7.5 km/h. What is the   [NCERT]

(a)   magnitude of average velocity,
(b)   average speed of the man over the interval of time
     (i)   0 to 30 min   (ii)   0 to 50 min   (iii)   0 to 40 min ?

Sol. The time taken in ongoing journey from A to B is

$$= \frac{2.5}{5} = \frac{1}{2} \text{ hr} = 30 \text{ min}$$

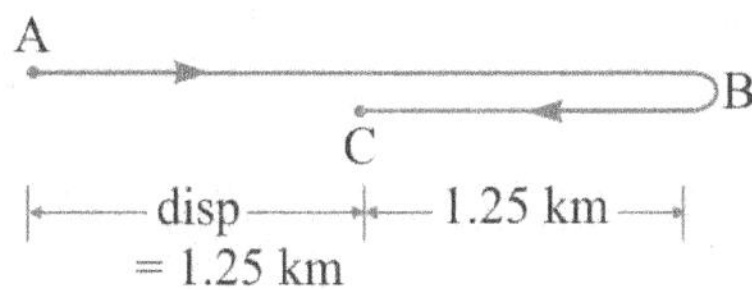

Figure. **3.13**

Time taken in returning journey from B to A

$$= \frac{2.5}{7.5} = \frac{1}{3} \text{ hr} = 20 \text{ min}$$

(i)   In the interval 0 to 30 min;

$$\text{Average velocity} = \frac{\text{displacement}}{\text{time}}$$

$$= \frac{2.5}{1/2} = 5 \text{ km/h}$$

(ii)   In the interval 0 to 50 min;
The distance travelled in 20 min. in return journey is 2.5 km.

$$\text{Average velocity} = \frac{\text{displacement}}{\text{time}} = \frac{0}{\dfrac{1}{2} + \dfrac{1}{3}} = 0$$

$$\text{Average speed} = \frac{\text{distance}}{\text{time}} = \frac{2.5 + 2.5}{\dfrac{1}{2} + \dfrac{1}{3}} = 6 \text{ km/h}$$

(iii)   In the interval 0 to 40 min;
The distance travelled in 10 min in return journey

$$= \frac{10}{60} \times 7.5 = 1.25 \text{ km}$$

Figure. **3.14**

$$\text{Average velocity} = \frac{\text{net displacement}}{\text{time}}$$

$$= \frac{2.50 - 1.25}{\dfrac{1}{2} + \dfrac{1}{6}} = 1.875 \text{ km/h}$$

$$\text{Average speed} = \frac{\text{total distance}}{\text{total time}}$$

$$= \frac{2.50 + 1.25}{\dfrac{1}{2} + \dfrac{1}{6}} = 5.625 \text{ km/h}.$$

Example 5. **A particle starts moving along x axis, with constant velocity of 4 m/s. After 2 s from the start of motion of the first particle, another particle starts in the same direction, with the same position with constant velocity of 6 m/s. Calculate the time at which second particle will catch the first particle.**

Sol. If t is the time, the first particle takes, till meeting, then for the second particle the time will be $(t-2)$. For the meeting, the displacement of both the particles must be same. Thus

$$4t = 6(t-2)$$

or $$t = 6 \text{ s}$$ ***Ans.***

Example 6. **A particle is moving at a speed of 5 m/s along east. After 10 s its velocity changes and becomes 5 m/s along north. What is the average acceleration during this interval?**

Sol.

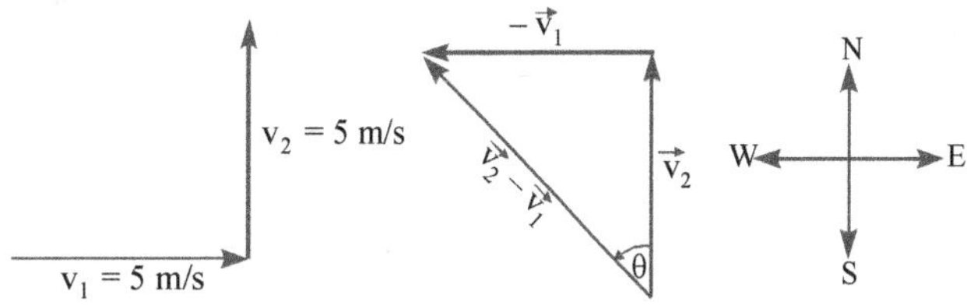

Figure. **3.15**

Average acceleration is given by

$$\vec{a} = \frac{\vec{v}_2 - \vec{v}_1}{\Delta t}$$

$\therefore$ $$a = \frac{\sqrt{5^2 + 5^2}}{10} = \frac{1}{\sqrt{2}} \text{ m/s}^2$$

The direction of acceleration is the direction of change of velocity, $\vec{v}_2 - \vec{v}_1$. Thus

$$\tan\theta = \frac{v_1}{v_2} = \frac{5}{5} = 1$$

or $$\theta = 45° \text{ North-West.}$$ ***Ans.***

Example 7. **Let a body falls from height h. After collision with the ground it rises to height h'. Suppose Δt is the time of collision, then find the average acceleration during contact.**

Sol.

Figure. **3.16**

Velocity before collision $v_1 = \sqrt{2gh}$.

Velocity after collision $v_2 = -\sqrt{2gh'}$.

The change in velocity $\Delta v = -\sqrt{2gh'} - \sqrt{2gh}$.

Thus acceleration $a = \dfrac{\Delta v}{\Delta t} = \dfrac{-\sqrt{2g}(\sqrt{h'} + \sqrt{h})}{\Delta t}$.

Example 8. **An athlete runs a distance of 1500 m in the following manner. (i) Starting from rest, he accelerates himself uniformly at 2 m/s^2 till he covers a distance of 900 m. (ii) He, then runs the remaining distance of 600 m at the uniform speed developed. Calculate the time taken by the athlete to cover the two parts of the distance covered. Also find the time, when he is at the centre of the track.**

Sol. The situation is shown in figure.

Figure. **3.17**

For the motion between $t = 0$ to t_1; $s = 750$ m. We know that

$$s = ut + \frac{1}{2}at^2$$

$$750 = 0 + \frac{1}{2} \times 2 \times t_1^2$$

$\therefore$ $$t_1 = 27.4 \text{ s.} \textit{ns.}$$

(i)   For the motion from $t = 0$ to $t = t_2$; $s = 900$ m

$$900 = 0 + \frac{1}{2} \times 2 \times t_2^2$$

$\therefore$ $t_2 = 30$ s. *Ans.*

(ii) Let v is the velocity of the athlete at $t = t_2$, then

$$v = 0 + 2 \times 30$$
$$= 60 \text{ m/s.}$$

For the motion between t_2 and t_3; $s = 600$ m.
If t is the time of motion, then

$$t = \frac{\text{distance}}{\text{speed}}$$

$$= \frac{600}{60} = 10 \text{ s.}$$ *Ans.*

Example 9. A driver takes 0.20 s to apply the brakes after he sees a need for it. This is called the reaction time of the driver. If he is driving car at a speed of 54 km/h and the brakes cause a deceleration of 6.0 m/s^2, find the distance travelled by the car after he sees the need to put the brakes.

Sol. During the reaction time car continues to move with constant speed of 54 km/h or 15 m/s.

$\therefore$ Distance travelled during this time
$$s_1 = 15 \times 0.20 = 30 \text{ m}$$

There after brakes start decelerating the car, the distance travelled till stop is s_2, then

$$v^2 = u^2 - 2as$$

or $$0 = 15^2 - 2 \times 6 \times s_2$$

$\therefore$ $$s_2 = \frac{15^2}{12} = 18.75 \, m.$$

Total distance travelled $= s_1 + s_2 = 3.0 + 18.75 = 21.75$ m. *Ans.*

Example 10. A body covers 12 m in 2nd and 20 m in 4th second. How much distance will it cover in 4 second after the 5th second ?

Sol. Given : $s_{2nd} = 12$ m, $s_{4th} = 20$ m.

We known that $s_n = u + \dfrac{a}{2}(2n - 1)$

$\therefore$ $$12 = u + \frac{a}{2}(2 \times 2 - 1) = u + \frac{3a}{2} \qquad \dots(i)$$

and $$20 = u + \frac{a}{2}(2 \times 4 - 1) = u + \frac{7a}{2} \qquad \dots(ii)$$

Solving equations (i) and (ii), we get
$$a = 4 \text{m/s}^2 \text{and } u = 6 \text{ m/s.}$$

Now distance covered in 4 second after 5th second $= s_9 - s_5$

$$= \left(6 \times 9 + \frac{1}{2} \times 4 \times 9^2\right) - \left(6 \times 5 + \frac{1}{2} \times 4 \times 5^2\right)$$

$$= 136 \text{ m.}$$ *Ans.*

Example 11. A man is $s = 9$ m behind the door of a train when it starts moving with acceleration $a = 2$m/s^2. The man runs at full speed. How far does he have to run and after what time does he get into the train ? What is his full speed ?

Sol.

Figure. **3.18**

Let the full speed of man is v, and he takes time t to pick the train. In this time his distance from bus becomes $\left(9 + \dfrac{1}{2}at^2\right)$. He covers this distance with constant speed v, then we have

$$vt = 9 + \frac{1}{2}at^2$$

or $$\frac{1}{2} \times 2 \times t^2 - vt + 9 = 0$$

or $$t^2 - vt + 9 = 0$$

$\therefore$ $$t = \frac{v \pm \sqrt{v^2 - 4 \times 1 \times 9}}{2} = \frac{v \pm \sqrt{v^2 - 36}}{2}$$

t will have real solution, if
$$v^2 - 36 \geq 0$$
or $$v \geq 6 \text{ m/s.}$$

Thus, $v = 6$ m/s is enough to pick the train

The time $t = \dfrac{v}{2} + 0 = \dfrac{6}{2} = 3$ s. *Ans.*

The distance travelled by man $= vt = 6 \times 3 = 18$ m. *Ans.*

Example 12. Two balls are thrown simultaneously, A vertically upwards with a speed of 20 m/s from the ground, and B vertically downwards from height of 40 m with the same speed along the same line of motion. At what point do the two balls collide ? Take $g = 9.8$ m/s^2.

Sol. Suppose the balls collide at a height y from the ground after time t from the start.

For downward motion of ball B

$$40 - y = 20\, t + \frac{1}{2}gt^2 \qquad \dots\dots(i)$$

For upward motion of ball A

$$y = 20t - \frac{1}{2}gt^2 \qquad \dots\dots(ii)$$

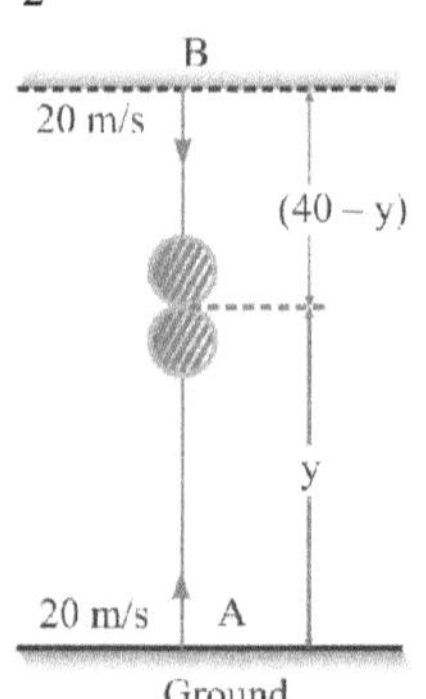

Figure. **3.19**

Adding equations (i) and (ii), we get
$$40 = 40t \qquad \text{or} \qquad t = 1 \text{ s}$$

Now from equation (ii), we get

$$y = 20 \times 1 - \frac{1}{2}9.8 \times 1^2 = 15.1 \text{ m}$$ *Ans.*

(In Chapter Exercise 3.1)

1. A proton moves along the x-axis according to the equation
$$t = \sqrt{\frac{x - 50t}{10}},$$
where x is in metres and t is in seconds. Calculate the average velocity of the proton during the first 3.0 s of its motion. *Ans.* **80 m/s.**

2. A body travels, with uniform acceleration for time t_1 and with uniform acceleration a_2 for time t_2. What is the average acceleration ?
$$Ans. \ \frac{a_1 t_1 + a_2 t_2}{t_1 + t_2}$$

3. A body travels 200 cm in the first 2 second and 220 cm in the next 4 second. What will be the velocity at the end of the 7th second of the start ? *Ans.* **10 cm/s**

4. A train moving with a velocity of 30 km/h has to slow down to 15 km/h due to repairs along the road. If the distance covered during retardation be 1 km and that covered during acceleration be 0.5 km, find the time lost in the journey. *Ans.* **1 minute**

5. A body falling freely under gravity passes two points 30 m apart in 1s. Find, from what point above the upper point it began to fall ? Take $g = 9.8$ m/s^2. *Ans.* **32.1 m**

6. A car moving with constant acceleration covered the distance between two points 60.0 m apart in 6.00 s. Its speed as it passes the second point was 15.0 m/s.

   (a) What was the speed at the first point ?

   (b) What was the acceleration ?

   (c) At what prior distance from the first point was the car at rest ? *Ans.* (a) 5.00 m/s (b) 1.67 m/s^2 (c) 7.50 m.

7. Two bodies are projected vertically upwards from one point with the same initial velocities v_0, the second τ sec after the first. How long after will the bodies meet ?
$$Ans. \ t = \frac{v_0}{g} + \frac{\tau}{2}.$$

3.6 STUDY OF MOTION BY GRAPHS

Our previous knowledge reveals that, the motion of uniformly accelerated body can be studied by $v = u + at$ and $s = ut + \frac{1}{2}at^2$. The equation $v = u + at$ is an inclined straight line between v and t and $s = ut + \frac{1}{2}at^2$ is a parabola between s and t.

From the above discussion it is clear that the curve of a uniformly accelerated body be either a straight line between $\vec{v}$ and t and parabola between $\vec{s}$ and t, no circle no ellipse.

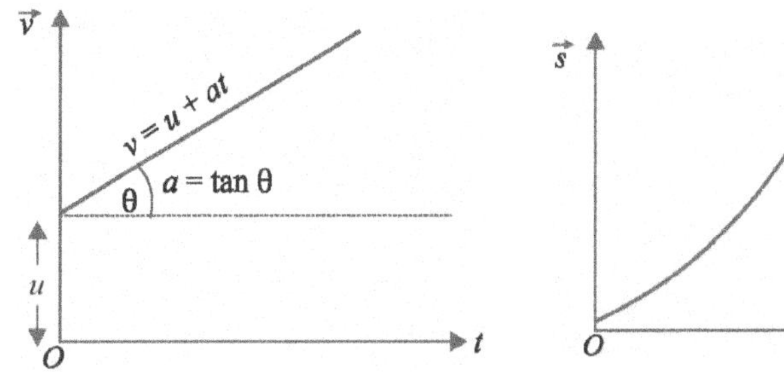

Figure. **3.20**

The following points must be remembered regarding with graphs :

1. Usually independent variable is taken on the x-axis and dependent variable is taken on the y-axis.

2. Usually the previous direction of motion is taken as positive. A body thrown up; its upward journey is taken as positive and return journey negative. If a body thrown down; its downward journey is taken as positive and return journey is taken as negative. Sometimes the graph may be drawn according to cartesian coordinate system.

3. When body moves along a straight line without change in direction its distance-time and displacement time graphs remain identical. Similarly its speed-time and velocity-time-graphs remain identical.

4. As distance and speed can never be negative, so no part of their graphs can be below time axis.

5. Any line perpendicular to time axis indicates, that quantity under consideration is changing without spending the time, which is not possible. During collision a very large change in velocity occurs in very short time. Also no proper informations about motion during collision are available. Therefore in such cases time of collision is neglected.

About slope

The slope of the curve at any point is defined by tan θ, where θ is the angle made from x-axis. In terms of differentiation, tan θ = dy/dx. The following points should be remembered regarding with the slope:

1. A straight line graph has a **single slope**. If line makes angle θ < 90°, the slope tan θ = +ve, and if line makes an angle θ > 90°, the slope tan θ = –ve. For line parallel to x-axis, θ = 0, tan θ = 0 (see figure).

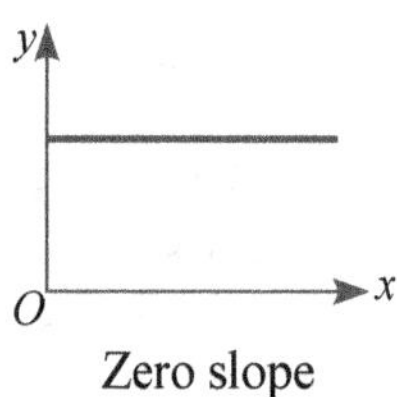

Zero slope

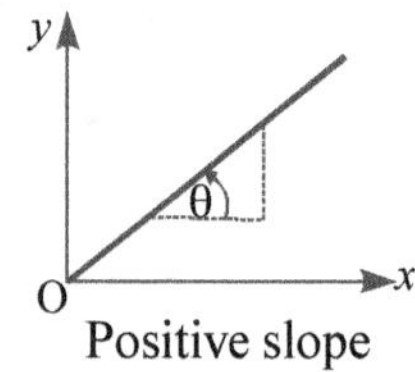

Positive slope

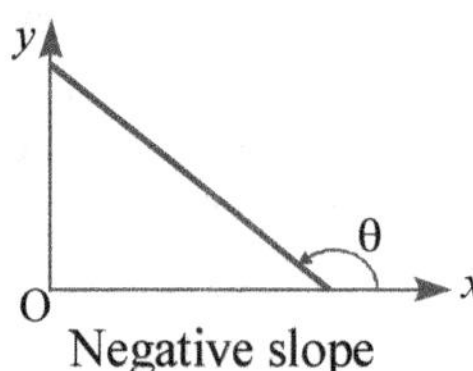

Negative slope

2. A curved graph has variable slopes. In a curve with a trough, the slope increases with increasing value of x. In a curve with crest upward, slope decreases with increasing value of x (see figure).

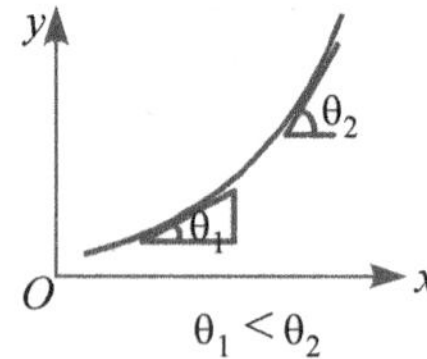

$\theta_1 < \theta_2$

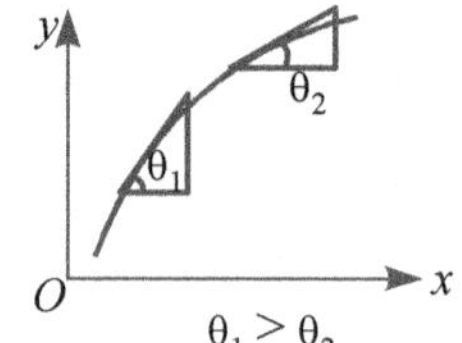

$\theta_1 > \theta_2$

Graphs showing rest :

For a particle is at rest, its position will not change with time and so $\vec{s}_1 = \vec{s}_2$. Also $\vec{v} = 0$ and $\vec{a} = 0$.

The following graphs represents rest on $\vec{s} - t$, $\vec{v} - t$ and $\vec{a} - t$:

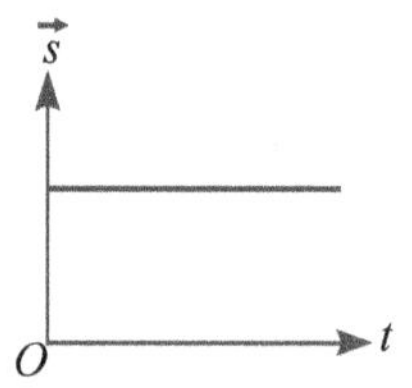

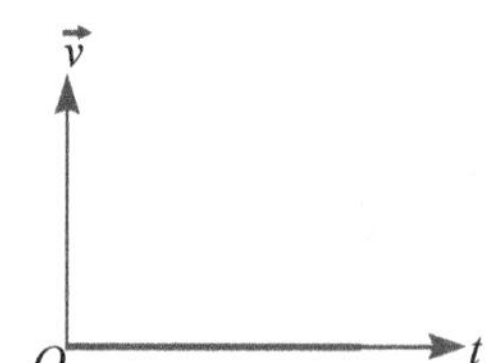

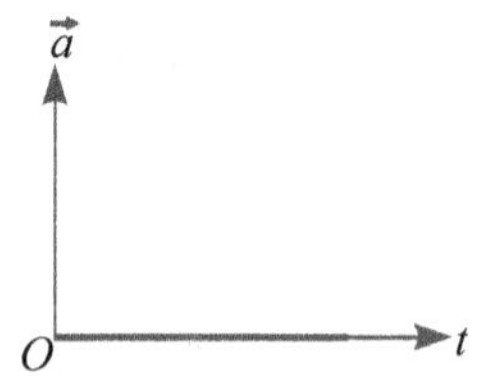

Graphs showing constant velocity :

The slope of displacement-time curve gives velocity, so for constant velocity, it must be a straight line. For $\vec{v}$ = constant, $\vec{a} = 0$. The following graphs represents constant velocity on $\vec{s} - t$, $\vec{v} - t$ and $\vec{a} - t$:

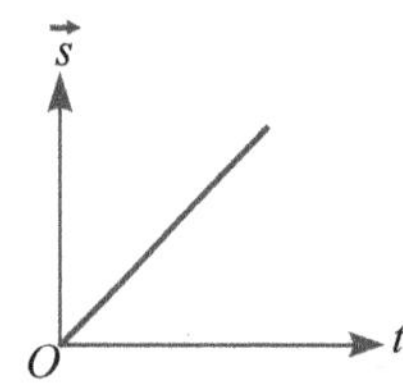

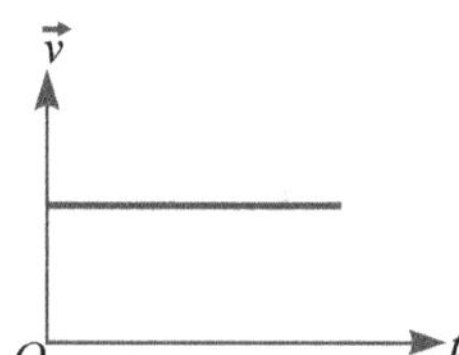

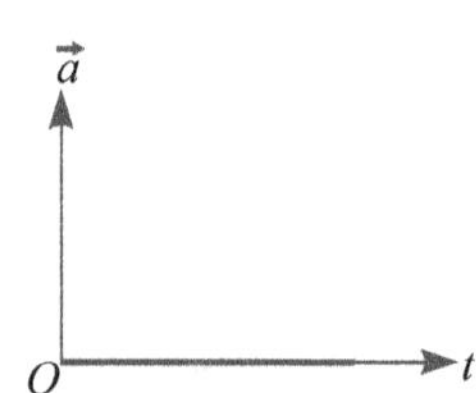

Graphs showing constant acceleration :

For constant acceleration motion of a particle, the **dis-time** curve must be of increasing slope (increasing velocity), so it is a parabolic curve with trough upward.

As acceleration is constant, so $\dfrac{d\vec{v}}{dt} = \vec{a}$ (constant). It must be a straight line between velocity-time. The following graphs represents constant acceleration on $\vec{s} - t$, $\vec{v} - t$ and $\vec{a} - t$:

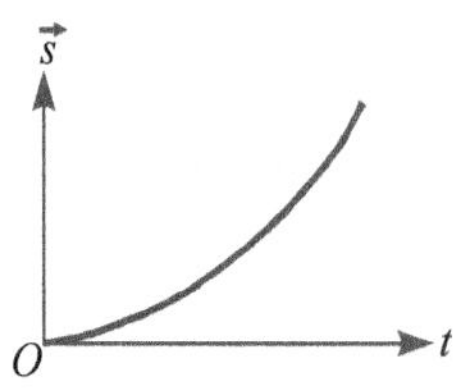

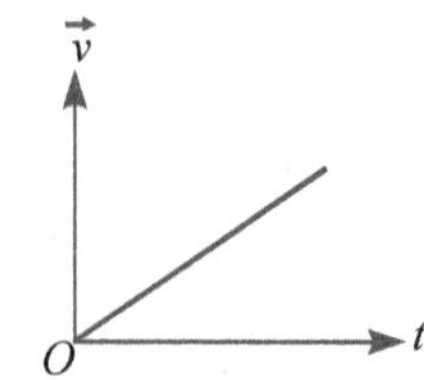

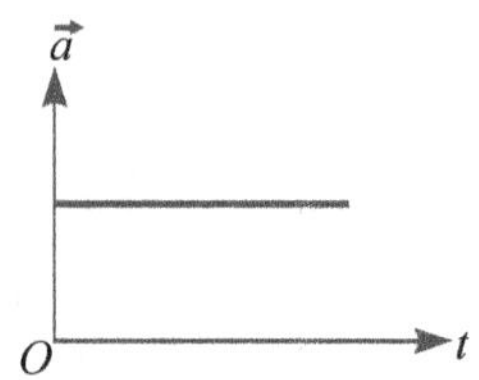

Graphs showing constant retardation :

For constant retardation motion of a particle, the **disp-time** curve must be of decreasing slope (decreasing velocity), so it is a parabolic curve with crest upward.

As acceleration is negative and so it must be a straight line with negative slope between velocity-time. The following graphs represents constants retardation on $\vec{s} - t$, $\vec{v} - t$ and $\vec{a} - t$:

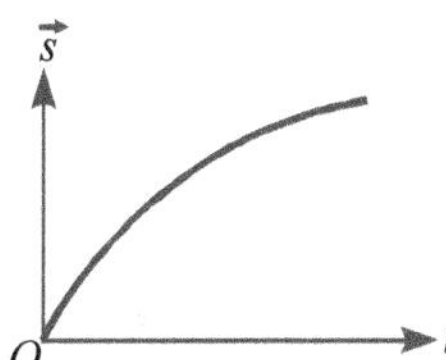 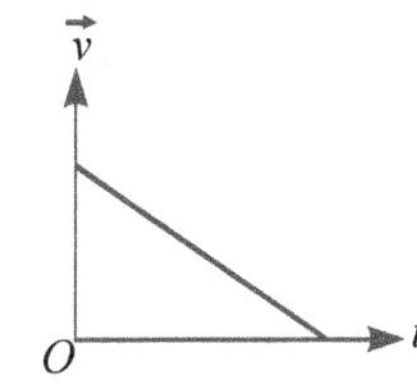 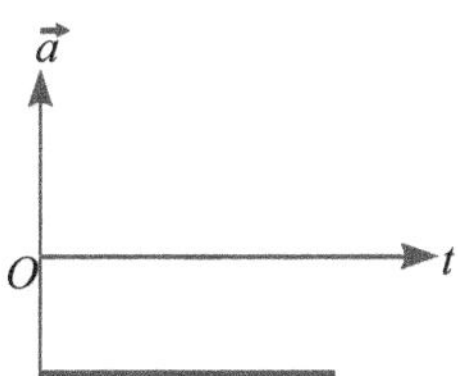

Following graphs cannot exist in practice :

- Distance travelled by a particle cannot decrease with time. Also it never negative.
- Speed also can never be negative.
- A quantity cannot change without spending time.

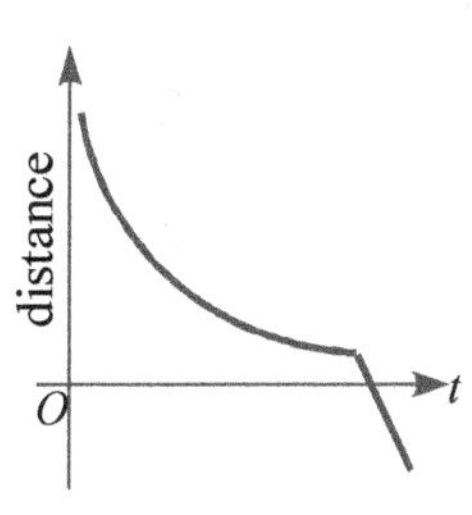 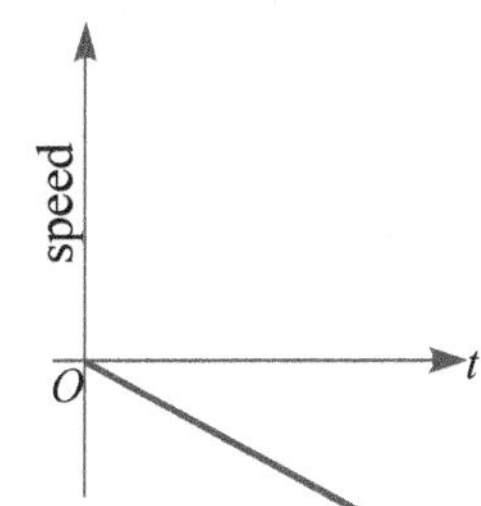

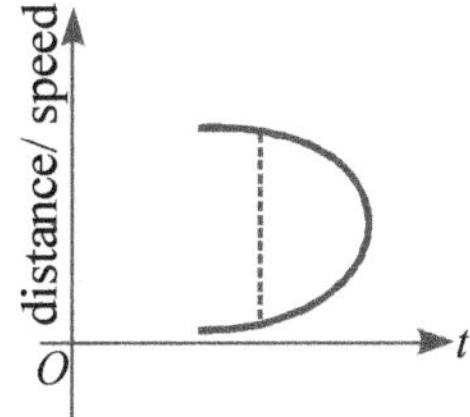 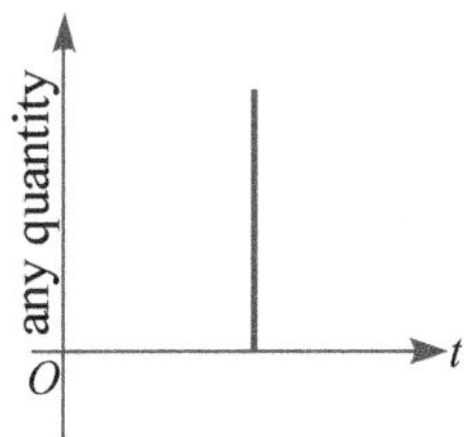

Quantities calculated from different types of graphs :

1. Slope of displacement-time graph gives the velocity at the point. i.e., $\vec{v} = \dfrac{d\vec{s}}{dt}$.

2. Slope of velocity-time graph gives the acceleration at the point. i.e., $\vec{a} = \dfrac{d\vec{v}}{dt}$.

3. The area under the speed-time or velocity-time graph gives the displacement/ distance. In the following $\vec{v} - t$ graph, the displacement and distance may be calculated as follows :

   displacement = area A – area B,
   distance = area A + area B.

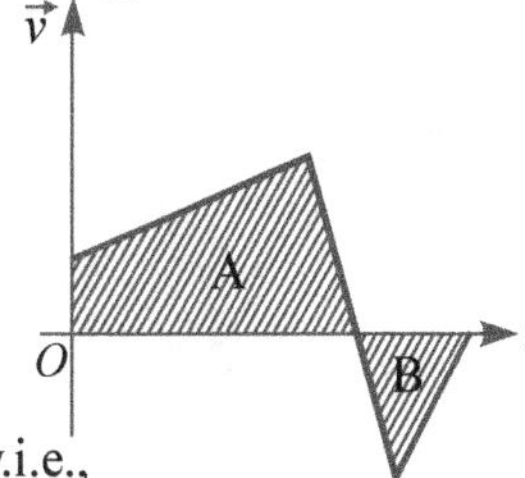

4. The area under acceleration-time graph gives the change in velocity. i.e.,

$$\vec{a} = \frac{\Delta \vec{v}}{\Delta t}$$

or $\quad \Delta \vec{v} = \vec{a} \times \Delta t$

$\qquad$ = area of $\vec{a} - t$ graph

$\qquad$ = area A – area B

If $\vec{v}_i = 0$, $\vec{v}_f$ = area of $\vec{a} - t$ graph.

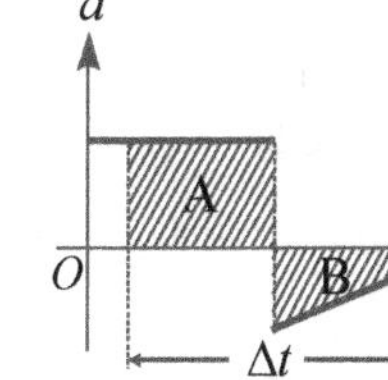

EXAMPLES BASED ON GRAPHS

Example 13. The position-time (x-t) graphs for two children A and B returning from their school O to their homes P and Q respectively are shown in figure. Choose the correct entries in the brackets below: **[NCERT]**
(a) (A/B) lives closer to school than (B/A)
(b) (A/B) starts from the school earlier than (B/A)
(c) (A/B) walks faster than (B/A)
(d) A and B reach home at the (same/different) time.
(e) (A/B) overtakes on the road (once/twice)

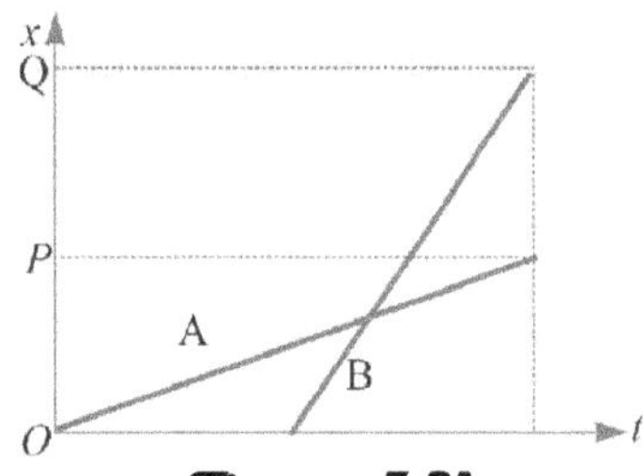

Figure. 3.21

Sol. (a) It is clear from the graph that $OP < OQ$, $\therefore$ A lives closer to the school than B.

(b) As A starts from $t = 0$ while B starts little later. So A starts the school earlier than B.

(c) The slope of $x - t$ graph for motion of $B >$ slope of $x - t$ graph of A. Hence B walks faster than A.

(d) The value of t corresponding to positions P and Q of there homes is same, so A and B reach home at the same time.

(e) It is clear from the graph that B overtake A once on the road.

Example 14. A train moves from one station to another in two hours time. Its speed time-graph during the motion is shown in figure.
(i) **Determine the maximum acceleration during the journey**
(ii) **Also calculate the distance covered during the time interval from 0.75 hour to 1 hour.**

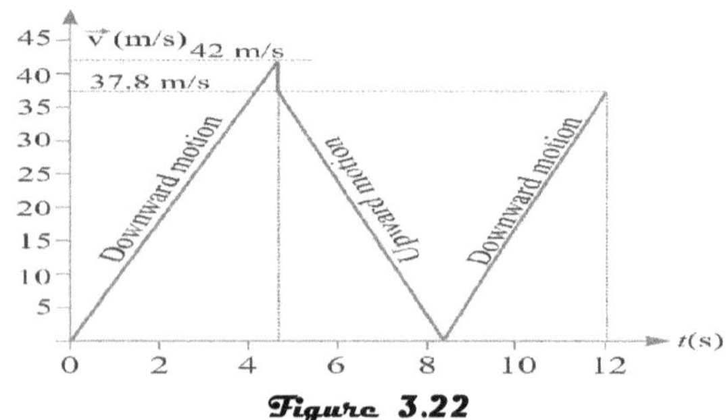

Figure 3.22

Sol.
(i) As the part BC of the graph has maximum slope, so acceleration is maximum in this duration.

$\therefore$ Maximum acceleration $a =$ slope of line BC

$$= \frac{v_2 - v_1}{t_2 - t_1} = \frac{(50 - 20)}{1.00 - 0.75}$$

$$= 120 \text{ km/h}^2. \qquad \textbf{\textit{Ans.}}$$

(ii) Distance travelled in the duration 0.75 to 1 hour.

$$= \text{Area of trapezium } BCEF$$

$$= \frac{1}{2}[20 + 50] \times (1.00 - 0.75)$$

$$= 8.75 \text{ km.} \qquad \textbf{\textit{Ans.}}$$

Example 15. A ball is dropped and its displacement versus time graph is as shown in given figure. (Displacement x is from ground and all quantities are +ve upwards). **[NCERT Exemplar]**

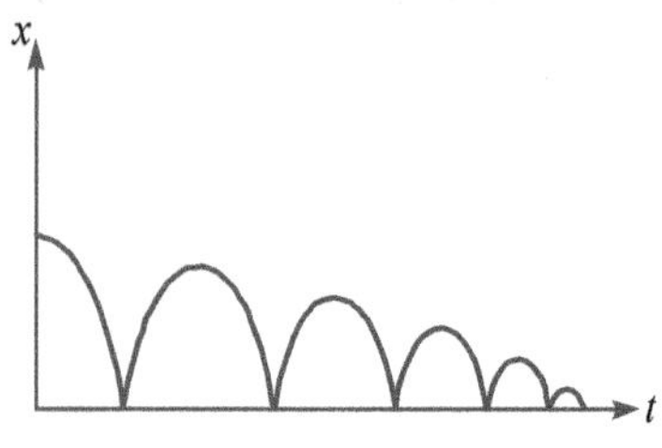

Figure. 3.23

(a) Plot qualitatively velocity versus time graph.
(b) Plot qualitatively acceleration versus time graph.

Sol. From the given graph x is positive upwards. Ball is dropped from a height and its velocity increases in downward direction due to gravity pull. In this condition v is negative but acceleration of the ball is equal to acceleration due to gravity i.e., a = –g.

When ball rebounds in upward direction its velocity is positive but acceleration is a = –g

(a) The velocity-time graph of the ball is shown in fig (i).

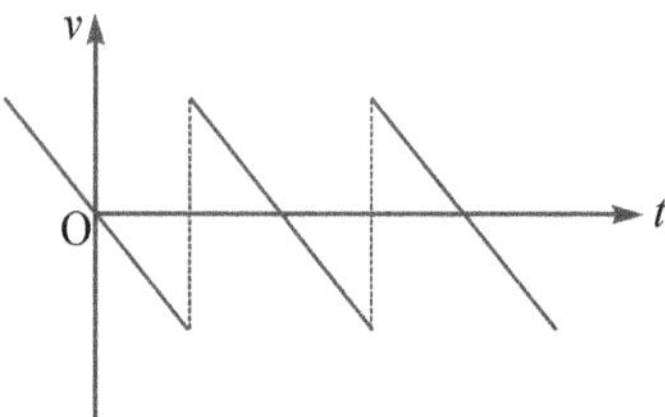

Figure (i)

(b) The acceleration-time graph of the ball is shown in fig (ii).

Figure (ii)

Example 16. Suggest a suitable physical situation for each of the following graphs? **[NCERT]**

Sol. **Figure (a):** The x-t graph shows that initially x is zero i.e. at rest, then it increases with time, attains a constant value and again reduces to zero with time, then it increases in opposite direction till it again attains a constant value i.e. comes to rest. The similar physical situation arises when a ball resting on a smooth floor is kicked which rebounds from a wall with reduced speed. It then moves to the opposite wall, which stops it.

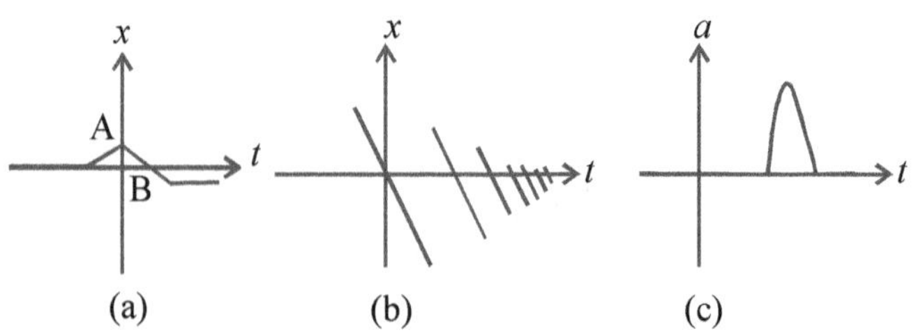

(a)   (b)   (c)

Figure (b): The velocity changes sign again and again with passage of time and every time some speed is lost. The similar physical situation arises when a ball is thrown up with some velocity, returns back and falls freely. On striking the floor, it rebounds with reduced speed each time it strikes against the floor.

Figure (c): Initially body moves with uniform velocity. Its acceleration increases for a short duration and then falls to zero and thereafter the body moves with a constant velocity. The similar physical situation arises when a cricket ball moving with a uniform speed is hit with a bat for very short interval of time.

Example 17. **A woman starts from her home at 9.00 am, walks with a speed 5km/h on straight road up to her office 2.5 km away, stays at the office up to 5.00 pm and returns home by an auto with a speed of 25 km/h. Choose suitable scales and plot the *x-t* graph of her motion.** **[NCERT]**

Sol. Time taken in reaching office = distance/ speed = 2.5/5 = 0.5 hr. Time taken in returning from office = 2.5/25 = 0.1 hr. = 6 minutes It means the woman reaches the office at 9.30 am and returns home at 5.06 pm. The *x-t* graph of this motion will be as shown below:

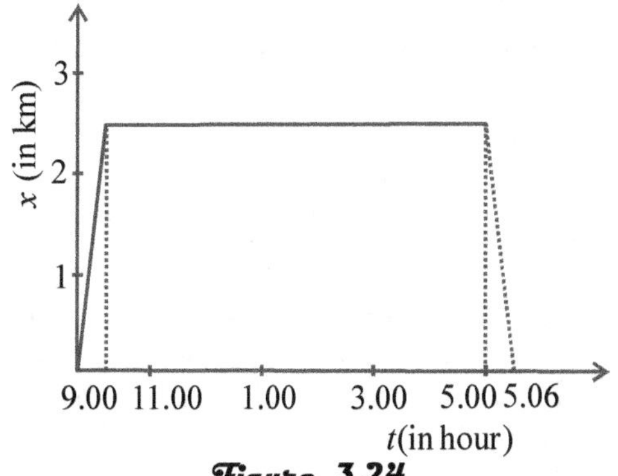

Figure 3.24

Example 18. As soon as a car just starts from rest in a certain direction, a scooter moving with a uniform speed overtakes the car. Their velocity-time graphs are shown in figure. Calculate

(i) The difference between the distances travelled by the car and the scooter in 15 s.

(ii) The distance of car and scooter from the starting point at that instant.

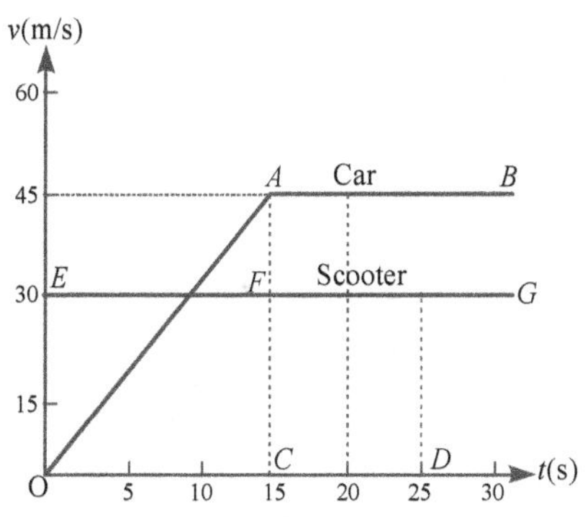

Figure 3.25

Sol.

(i) The distance travelled by car in 15 s

$$= \text{area of } \Delta OAC$$

$$= \frac{1}{2} \times 15 \times 45 = 337.5 \text{ m}$$

Distance travelled by scooter in 15 s

$$= \text{area of rectangle } OCFE$$

$$= 15 \times 30 = 450 \text{ m}.$$

Thus difference between distance travelled by them

$$= 450 \text{ m} - 337.5 \text{ m}$$

$$= 112.5 \text{ m}. \qquad \textit{Ans.}$$

(ii) Let after time t from start car will catch up the scooter. In time t the distance travelled by them are equal.

Distance travelled by car $= \frac{1}{2} \times 15 \times 45 + 45 \, (t - 15).$

Distance travelled by scooter $= 30 \, t$

$$\therefore \quad \frac{1}{2} \times 15 \times 45 + 45 \, (t - 15) = 30t$$

which gives $t = 22.5$ s. $\qquad \textit{Ans.}$

Distance travelled by car or scooter in 22.5 s

$$= 30 \times 22.5$$

$$= 675 \text{ m} \qquad \textit{Ans.}$$

So the car catches the scooter when both are at 675 m from the starting point.

Example 19. **A body falls from some height and returns back to initial position. Draw displacement ($\vec{s}$) – time (*t*), distance (*s*) – time (*t*), velocity ($\vec{v}$) – time, speed-time and acceleration ($\vec{a}$) – time (*t*) graphs for the motion of the body.**

Sol. Let body falls from height h. It takes time $\sqrt{\dfrac{2h}{g}}$ to strike the ground, its velocity just before strike is $\sqrt{2gh}$. Neglecting time of collision, we have following graphs:

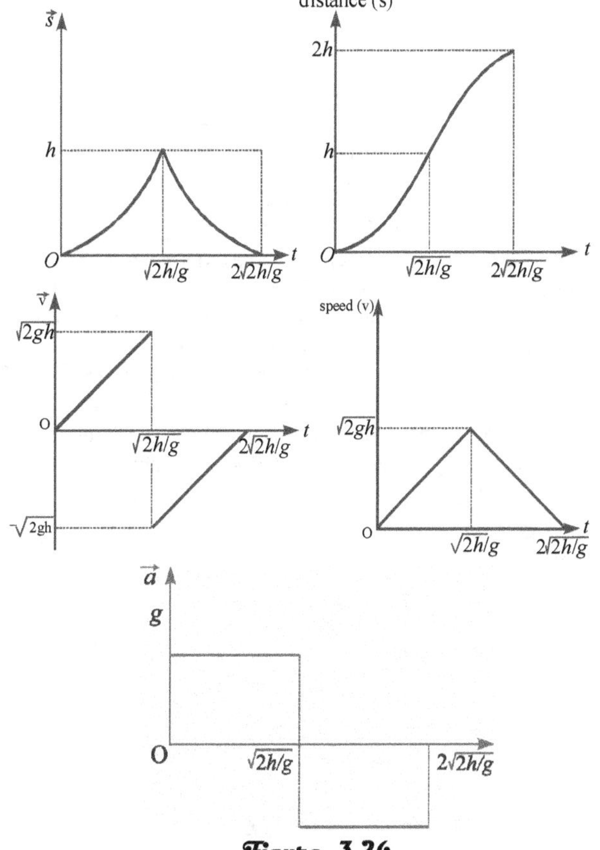

Figure 3.26

Example 20. **A body is thrown up and returns back to its initial position. Draw displacement ($\vec{s}$) – time (t), distance (s) – time (t), velocity ($\vec{v}$) – time (t) and speed (s) – time (t) graphs for the motion of the body.**

Sol. Let the body be thrown with initial velocity u, it takes time $\dfrac{u}{g}$ to

reach the highest position. It goes to a height $h = \dfrac{u^2}{2g}$. Neglecting air resistance we have following graphs:

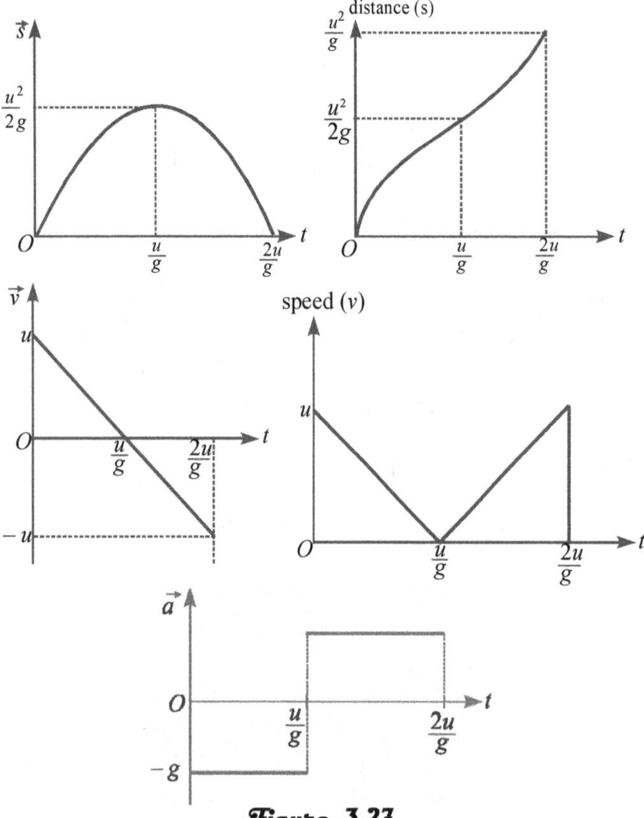

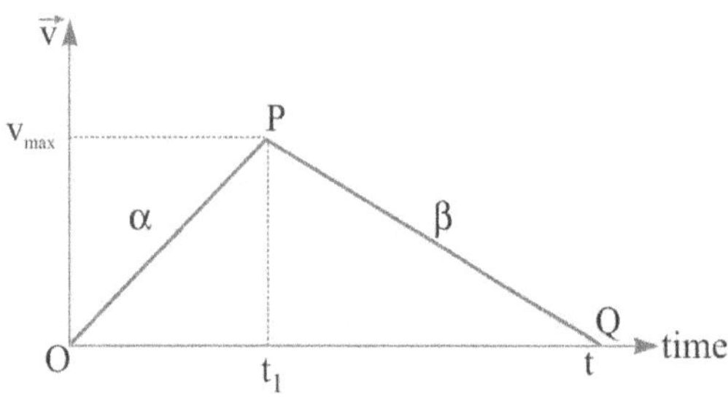

Figure 3.27

Example 21. A car accelerates from rest at a constant rate α for some time, after which it decelerates at a constant rate of β to come to rest. If the total time elapsed is t second, then calculate;
(i)   the maximum velocity attained by the car, and
(ii)   the total displacement travelled by the car in terms of α, β and t.

Sol. Let $v_{\max}$ be the maximum velocity attained and t_1 be the time at which maximum velocity will occur. The velocity vs time graph can be drawn as follows:

Figure 3.28

The slope of line OP,

$$\alpha = \frac{v_{\max}}{t_1}$$

$$\Rightarrow \qquad v_{\max} = \alpha t_1 \qquad\qquad …(i)$$

The slope of line PQ,

$$\beta = \frac{v_{\max}}{t - t_1}$$

$$\Rightarrow \qquad v_{\max} = \beta\,(t - t_1). \qquad\qquad …(ii)$$

From equations (i) and (ii), we get

$$\alpha t_1 = \beta\,(t - t_1)$$

which gives

$$t_1 = \frac{\beta t}{\alpha + \beta} . \qquad\qquad …(iii)$$

Substituting value of t_1 in equation (i), we get

(i) $$v_{\max} = \frac{\alpha \beta t}{\alpha + \beta} . \qquad\qquad \textit{Ans.}$$

(ii)   Total displacement $\vec{s}$ = area of $\vec{v} - t$ graph

$$= \frac{1}{2} \times v_{\max} \times t$$

$$= \frac{1}{2} \times \frac{\alpha \beta t}{\alpha + \beta} \times t = \frac{\alpha \beta t^2}{2(\alpha + \beta)} . \quad \textit{Ans.}$$

Example 22. **The distance (s) between two stations is to be covered in minimum time. The maximum value of acceleration or retardation of a car can not exceed α and β respectively. Find the time of motion.**

Sol. To cover the distance in minimum time the car must get the maximum possible acceleration α and then retard to maximum possible value β. Let t_1 is the time up to which car accelerates and t is the required time of motion. The velocity-time graph of motion of car can be drawn as in figure 3.29.

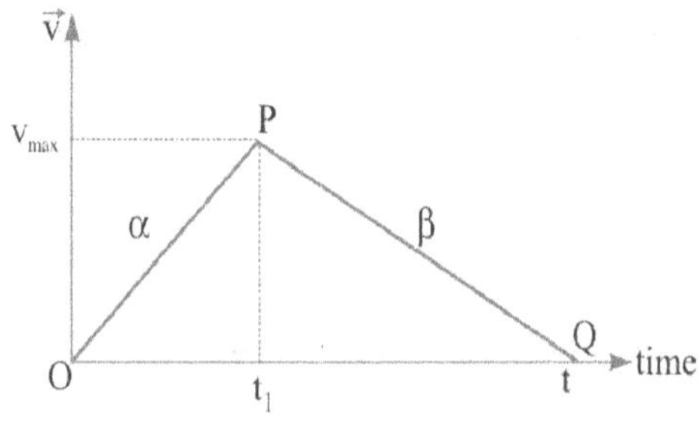

Figure 3.29

We have already calculated that $s = \dfrac{\alpha \beta t^2}{2(\alpha + \beta)}$.

Solve above equation for t, we have

$$t = \sqrt{\frac{2s(\alpha + \beta)}{\alpha \beta}} = \sqrt{2s\left(\frac{1}{\alpha} + \frac{1}{\beta}\right)} . \quad \textit{Ans.}$$

Example 23. **A particle of mass m moves on x-axis as follows: It starts from rest at $t = 0$ from the point $x = 0$ and comes to rest at $t = 1$ and the point $x = 1$. No other information is available about its motion at intermediate times ($0 \leq t \leq 1$). Discuss about the acceleration of the particle.**

Sol. Let α and β are the acceleration and retardation of the particle during the motion.

The velocity-time graph of motion of a particle is shown in figure 3.30.

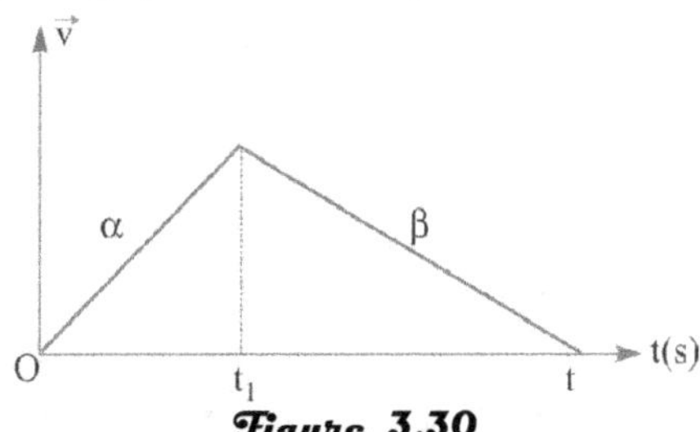

Figure 3.30

We have, from the graph (already calculated)

$$s = x = \frac{\alpha\beta t^2}{2(\alpha+\beta)}$$

Given $x = 1$m, $t = 1s$

let $|\alpha| = |\beta|$, then $\quad 1 = \dfrac{\alpha^2(1)^2}{2(\alpha+\alpha)}$

which gives $\alpha = 4$

When $|\alpha| > |\beta|$ then $|\alpha|$ will be greater than 4, and $|\beta|$ will be less than 4.

Example 24. **A car starts moving rectilinearly, first with acceleration $\alpha = 5$ m/s^2 (the initial velocity is equal to zero), then uniformly, and finally, decelerating at the same rate α comes to a stop. The total time of motion equals $\tau = 25$ s. The average velocity during that time is equal to <v> = 72 km/h. How long does the car move uniformly?**

Sol. Let t be the time upto which car accelerates or decelerates. The maximum velocity attained in this duration is $5\,t$. The time upto which car move uniformly $= 25 - 2t$. The velocity – time graph of the motion of car is drawn as in figure 3.31.

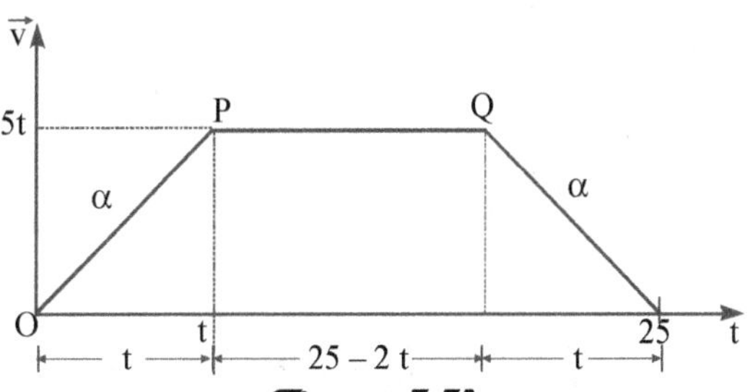

Figure 3.31

Given the average velocity in whole time of motion

$$v_{av} = \frac{72 \times 5}{18} = 20 \text{ m/s.}$$

The average velocity from the graph can be obtained as

$$v_{av} = \frac{\text{total displacement}}{\text{total time}}$$

$$= \frac{\text{area of } \vec{v} - t \text{ graph}}{\text{total time}}$$

$$\therefore \quad 20 = \frac{\frac{1}{2} \times [25 + (25 - 2t)] \times 5t}{25}$$

$$= \frac{\frac{1}{2} \times [50 - 2t)] \times 5t}{25}$$

or $\quad\quad\quad 200 = 50t - 2t^2$

or $\quad\quad t^2 - 25t + 100 = 0$

$$(t - 20)(t - 5) = 0$$

$$t = 5 \text{ s} \quad \text{or} \quad 20 \text{ s}$$

But $t = 20$ is not possible

$\therefore \quad\quad\quad t = 5\ s.$

The time upto which car moves uniformly

$$= 25 - 2t = 25 - 2 \times 5$$

$$= 15 \text{ s.} \quad\quad\quad\quad Ans.$$

In Chapter Exercise 3.2

1. Figure shows the velocity-time graph for the motion of a certain body. Determine the nature of this motion. Find acceleration and write the variation of displacement with time.

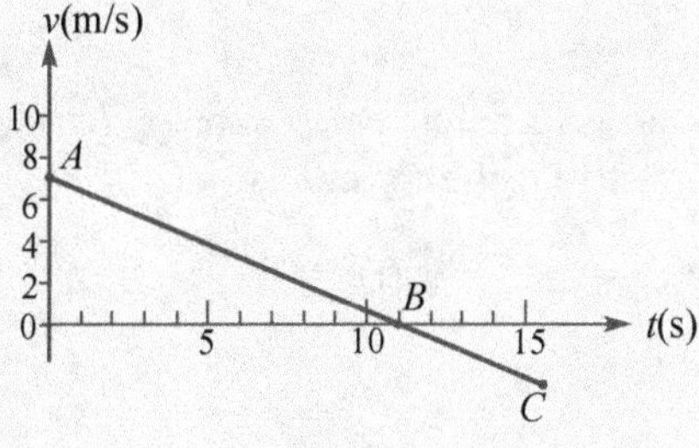

Ans. a = 0.64 m/s^2, s = 7t – 0.32 t^2.

2. The velocity - time graph of an object moving along straight line is shown in the figure. Find the net distance covered by the object in time interval between $t = 0$ to $t = 10$ s. Also find the displacement in time 0 to 10 s.

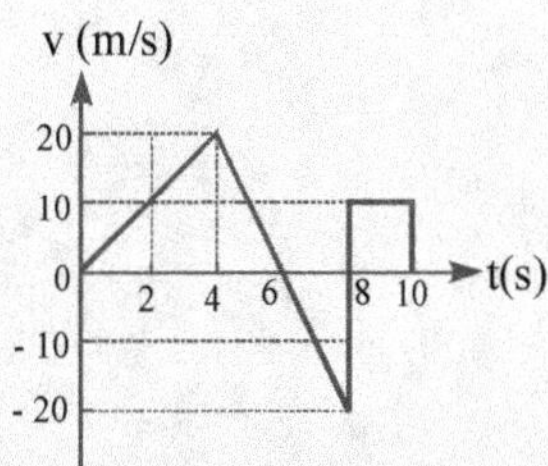

Ans: **100 m , 60 m**

3. The speed-time graph of a particle moving along a fixed direction is shown in figure.

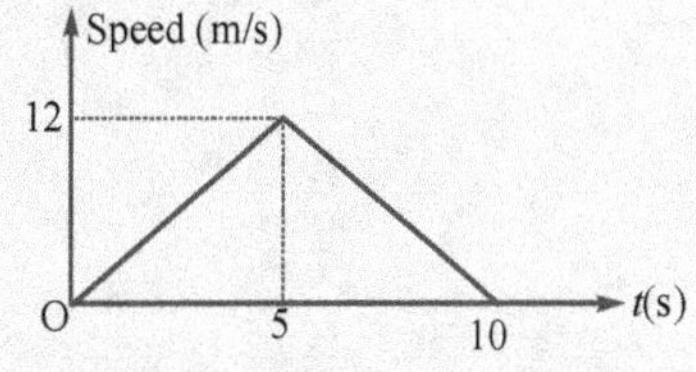

Find :

(i) distance travelled by the particle between 0s to 10s,

(ii) average speed between this interval,

(iii) the time when the speed was minimum.

(iv) the time when speed was maximum.

Ans. **(i) 60 m (ii) 6 m/s (iii) 0s and 10 s. (iv) 5s.**

4. Figure shows the position - time graphs of three cars A, B and C. On the basis of the graphs, answer the following questions :

(i) Which car has the highest speed and which the lowest?

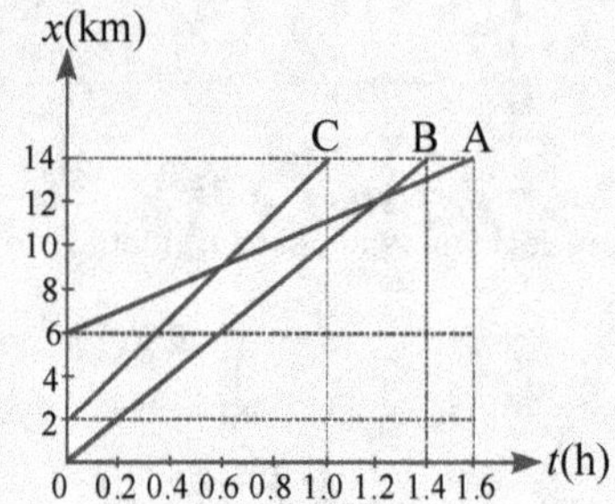

(ii) Are the three cars ever at the same point on the road?

(iii) When A passes C, where B is ?

(iv) How far did car A travel between the time it passed cars B and C ?

(v) What is the relative velocity of car C with respect to car A ?

(vi) What is the relative velocity of car B with respect to car C ?

***Ans :* (i) C has the highest speed and A has the lowest speed**

(ii) No (iii) 6 km from the origin (iv) 6 km

(v) 7 km/h (vi) - 2 km/h

3.7 RELATIVE VELOCITY

Consider the motion of the car moving towards right and two observers O_1 and O_2 are coming from opposite directions as shown in *figure 3.32*.

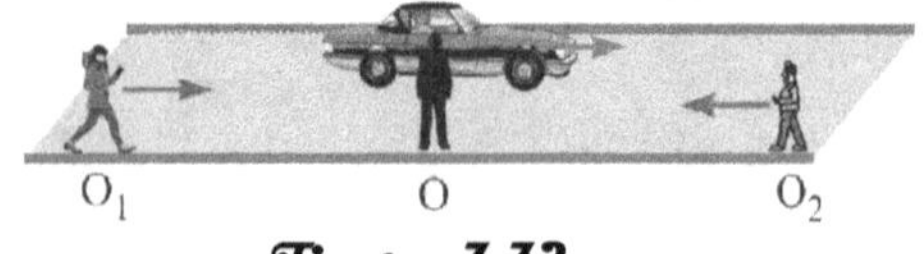

Figure 3.32

Observer O_1 finds that car is moving slower while observer O_2 finds that car is moving faster in comparison to when observer is at rest. The motion of same object looks different for two different observers. To understand such observations, there is a need of the concept of relative velocity.

Consider two objects A and B moving with constant velocities $\vec{v}_A$ and $\vec{v}_B$ in one dimension, say along x-axis. Let objects start from origin, their positions x_A and x_B at time t are given by :

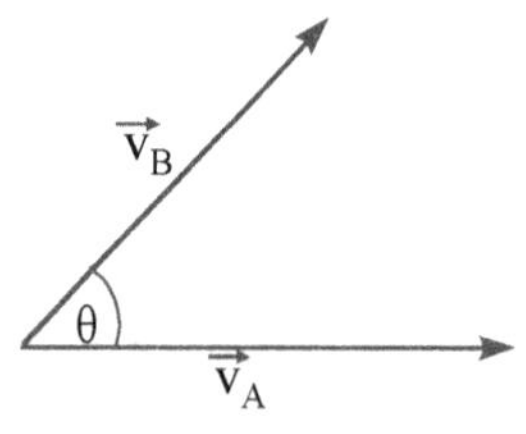

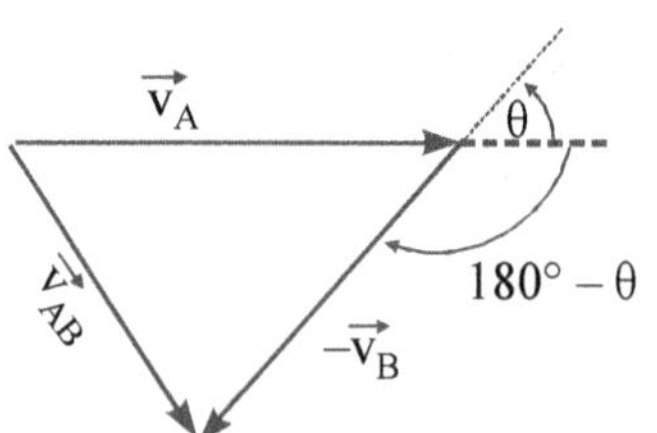

Figure 3.33

$$x_A = v_A t \qquad \text{...(i)}$$

and
$$x_B = v_B t \qquad \text{...(ii)}$$

Then, the displacement from object A to object B is given by

$$x_{BA} = x_B - x_A$$
$$= (v_B - v_A) t. \qquad \text{...(iii)}$$

Equation (iii) can easily be understood. It tells us that as seen from object A, object B has a velocity $v_B - v_A$. We can say that the velocity of the object B relative to the object A is;

$$\vec{v}_{BA} = \vec{v}_B - \vec{v}_A . \qquad \text{...(1)}$$

Similarly, velocity of the object A relative to object B is:

$$\vec{v}_{AB} = \vec{v}_A - \vec{v}_B . \qquad \text{...(2)}$$

The result of $\vec{v}_{BA}$ or $\vec{v}_{AB}$ depends on the angle between their directions of motion.

Now consider two objects A and B moving with velocities $\vec{v}_A$ and $\vec{v}_B$ respectively, having an angle θ between their directions of motion as shown in *fig. 3.33*.

The relative velocity of object A with respect to object B is given by

$$\vec{v}_{AB} = \vec{v}_A - \vec{v}_B$$

or

$$v_{AB} = \sqrt{v_A^2 + v_B^2 + 2v_A v_B \cos(180° - \theta)}$$

$$= \sqrt{v_A^2 + v_B^2 - 2v_A v_B \cos\theta} \; .$$

Suppose the relative velocity $\vec{v}_{AB}$ makes an angle α with $\vec{v}_A$, then

$$\tan\alpha = \frac{v_B \sin(180° - \theta)}{v_A + v_B \cos(180° - \theta)}$$

or

$$\tan\alpha = \frac{v_B \sin\theta}{v_A - v_B \cos\theta} \; .$$

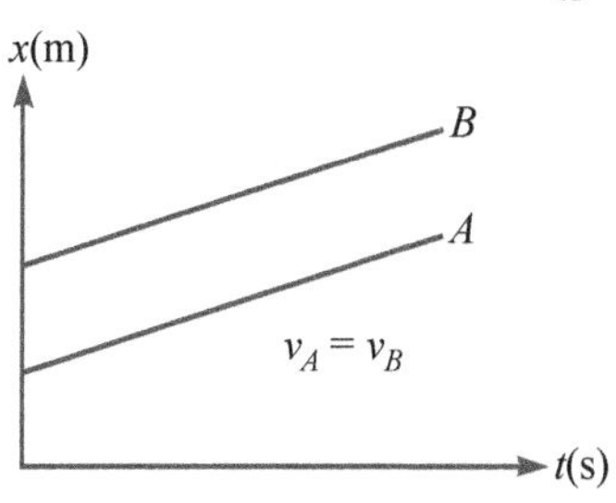

Position-time graph of two objects with equal velocities.

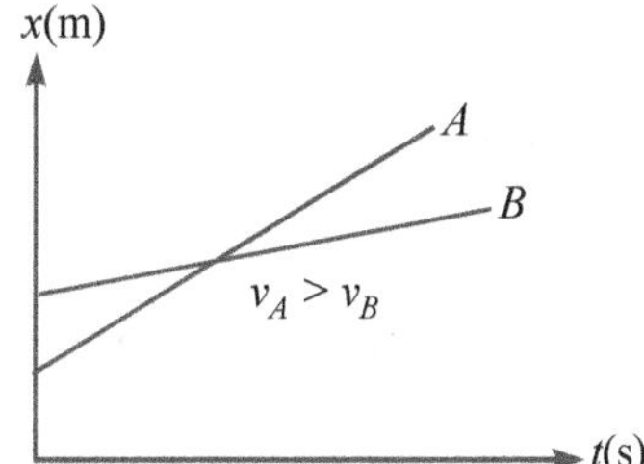

Position- time graph of two objects with unequal velocities.

Figure 3.34

Special cases :

1. When both the objects are moving along same direction, we have $\theta = 0°$

$$\therefore \quad v_{AB} = \sqrt{v_A^2 + v_B^2 - 2v_A v_B \cos\theta}$$

$$= v_A - v_B.$$

Thus the relative velocity of object A with respect to object B is equal to the difference between magnitudes of their velocities.

If $v_A = v_B$, $v_A - v_B = 0$. The relative velocity v_{AB} or v_{BA} becomes zero.

2. When the objects are moving in opposite directions, we have $\theta = 180°$.

$$\therefore \quad v_{AB} = \sqrt{v_A^2 + v_B^2 - 2v_A v_B \cos\theta}$$

$$= v_A + v_B.$$

Thus relative velocity of object A with respect to B is equal to the sum of magnitudes of their velocities.

Position time graph of two objects with velocities in opposite directions.

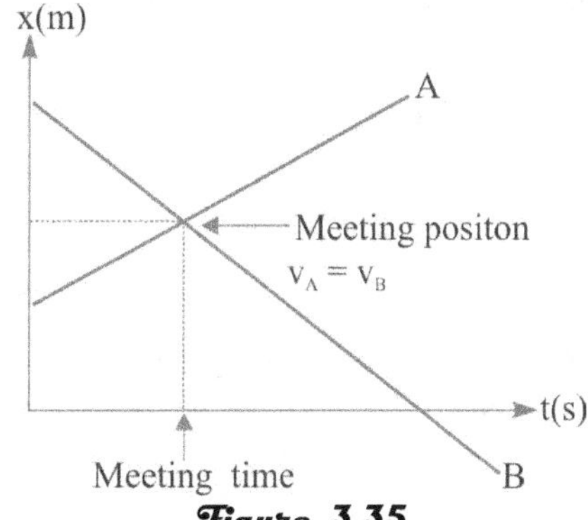

Figure 3.35

Relative acceleration

The treatment that we have done for relative velocity, can be done for relative acceleration also. Thus relative acceleration of the object A with respect to B is given by :

$$\vec{a}_{AB} = \vec{a}_A - \vec{a}_B, \qquad \ldots(1)$$

and relative acceleration of object B with respect to A is given by :

$$\vec{a}_{BA} = \vec{a}_B - \vec{a}_A. \qquad \ldots(2)$$

FORMULAE USED

1. Relative velocity of particle A w.r.t. particle B

$$\vec{v}_{AB} = \vec{v}_A - \vec{v}_B$$

2. Relative velocity of particle B w.r.t. particle A

$$\vec{v}_{BA} = \vec{v}_B - \vec{v}_A$$

3. When particles move in the same direction, the velocity of approach/ separation

$$v_{AB} = v_A - v_B$$

4. When the particle B moves in opposite of A, velocity of approach

$$v_{AB} = v_A + v_B$$

5. Relative distance, x = relative velocity × time

6. If two trains of lengths ℓ_1 and ℓ_2 with initial separation x_0, coming from opposite directions, the time to cross them

$$t = \frac{(x_0 + \ell_1 + \ell_2)}{(v_1 + v_2)}$$

7. If first train is to be over taken by second train, then time to cross them

$$t = \frac{(x_0 + \ell_1 + \ell_2)}{(v_2 - v_1)}$$

PROBLEM SOLVING STRATEGY

Relative velocity

Identify the concepts : Whenever you see the phrase like velocity relative to, velocity with respect to, velocity of approach, velocity of separation, its likely that the concepts of relative velocity will be helpful.

In many problems you asked the time to cross the objects going in the same direction or coming from opposite directions, the concepts of relative velocity will be used.

Setup the problem : To get the relative velocity $(\vec{v}_A - \vec{v}_B)$, the velocity of both the particles must be in the same frame of reference, otherwise they have to be converted into same frame of reference.

Execute the solution : Solve the problem by using equations of relative velocity. If the velocities are not along the same direction, you will need to use the vector form of the equation. In case if objects velocity makes some angle with line of relative motion, then

$$(\vec{v}_{AB})_x = \vec{v}_{Ax} - \vec{v}_{Bx}$$

or $\quad (v_{AB})_x = v_A \cos\theta_A + v_B \cos\theta_B.$

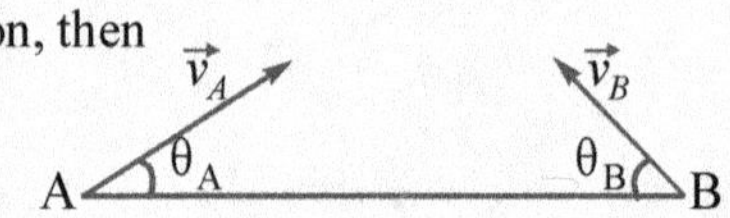

Figure **3.36**

EXAMPLES BASED ON RELATIVE VELOCITY

Example 25. A police van moving on a highway with a speed of 30 km/h fires a bullet at a thief's car speeding away in the same direction with a speed of 192 km/h. If the muzzle speed of the bullet is 150 m/s, with what speed does the bullet hit the thief's car? [NCERT]

Sol. Speed of police van = $30 \times \dfrac{5}{18} = \dfrac{25}{3}$ m/s.

The muzzle velocity, that is velocity of bullet with respect to van

Figure 3.37

$$[v_{\text{bullet}}]_{\text{van}} = [v_{\text{bullet}}]_{\text{ground}} - [v_{\text{van}}]_{\text{ground}}$$

or

$$[v_{\text{bullet}}]_{\text{ground}} = [v_{\text{bullet}}]_{\text{van}} + [v_{\text{van}}]_{\text{ground}}$$

$$= 150 + \frac{25}{3}$$

$$= \frac{475}{3} \text{ m/s}$$

Speed of thief's car = $192 \times \dfrac{5}{18} = \dfrac{160}{3}$ m/s

Now velocity of bullet with respect to the thief's car

$$[v_{\text{bullet}}]_{\text{car}} = [v_{\text{bullet}}]_{\text{ground}} - [v_{\text{van}}]_{\text{ground}}$$

$$= \frac{475}{3} - \frac{160}{3}$$

$$= 105 \text{ m/s}.$$

Hence the speed of the bullet with which it hits the thief's car = 105 m/s.

Example 26. A bird is tossing (flying to and fro) between two cars moving towards each other on a straight road. One car has a speed of 18 km/h while the other has the speed of 27 km/h. The bird starts moving from first car towards the other and is moving with the speed of 36 km/h and when the two cars were separated by 36 km. What is the total distance covered by the bird? [NCERT Exemplar]

Sol. Speed of first car = 18 km/h

Speed of second car = 27 km/h

∴ Relative speed of each car w.r.t. each other

$$= 18 + 27 = 45 \text{ km/h}$$

Distance between the cars = 36 km

∴ Time of meeting the cars (t) = $\dfrac{\text{Distance between the cars}}{\text{Relative speed of car}} = \dfrac{36}{45}$

$$= \frac{4}{5}\text{h} = 0.8 \text{ h.}$$

Speed of the bird (v_b) = 36 km/h

∴ Distance covered by the bird = $v_b \times t$

$$= 36 \times 0.8$$

$$= 28.8 \text{ km} \qquad Ans.$$

Example 27. The engineer of a train moving at a speed v_1 sights a freight train a distance d ahead of him on the same track moving in the same direction with a slower speed v_2. He puts on the brakes and gives his train a constant deceleration α. Find the minimum value of d at which brakes are applied so as to avoid collision.

Sol. Collision will be avoided if speed of the train v_1 becomes equal to v_2 in travelling a relative distance d. Therefore final relative speed of trains becomes zero. The initial relative speed $v_{12} = v_1 - v_2$. By third equation of motion, we have

$$v_{12}^2 = u_{12}^2 - 2\, a_{12}s$$
$$0 = (v_1 - v_2)^2 - 2\,(\alpha - 0)\, d$$

or

$$d = \frac{(v_1 - v_2)^2}{2\alpha}.$$

The collision can be avoided if $d \geq \dfrac{(v_1 - v_2)^2}{2\alpha}$.

Example 28. A car travelling at 60 km/h overtakes another car travelling at 42 km/h. Assuming each car to be 5.0 m long, find the time taken during the overtake and the total road distance used for the overtake.

Sol. The velocity of car which is overtaking

$$v_1 = 60 \times \frac{5}{18} = \frac{50}{3} \text{ m/s}$$

and the velocity of car to be overtaken, $v_2 = 42 \times \dfrac{5}{18} = \dfrac{35}{3}$ m/s.

The relative velocity between them $v_{12} = v_1 - v_2$

$$= \frac{50}{3} - \frac{35}{3}$$

$$= 5 \text{ m/s}$$

The distance travelled by car 1 in overtaking car 2 = 10 m

∴ Time taken in overtaking this distance = $\dfrac{10}{5} = 2\ s$.

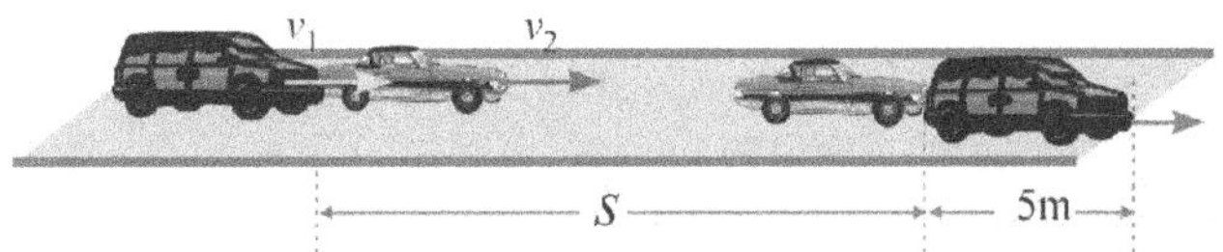

Figure. 3.38

The distance travelled by car 1 in this duration

$$s = \frac{50}{3} \times 2 = 33.3 \text{ m.}$$

The total road distance used for overtaking

$$= s + 5 = 33.3 + 5 = 38.5 \text{ m.} \quad Ans.$$

Example 29. On a two lane road, car A is travelling with a speed of 36 km/h. Two cars B and C approach car A in opposite directions with a speed of 54 km/h each. At a certain instant, when the distance AB is equal to AC, both 1 km B decided to overtake A before C does. What minimum acceleration of car B is required to avoid an accident? [NCERT]

Sol. At the instant when car B decides to overtake car A, the velocities of cars are ;

$$v_A = 36 \times \frac{5}{18} = 10 \text{ m/s}$$

$$v_B = 54 \times \frac{5}{18} = 15 \text{ m/s}$$

and $$v_C = -54 \times \frac{5}{18} = -15 \text{ m/s}$$

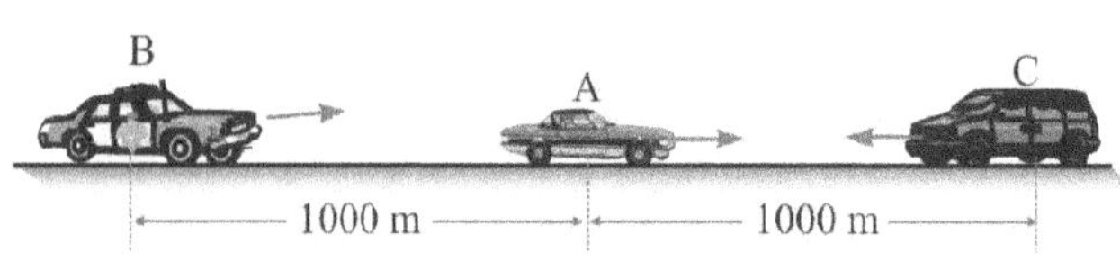

Figure. **3.39**

Velocity of car B relative to A, $v_{BA} = v_B - v_A = 15 - 10 = 5$ m/s
Velocity of car C relative to A, $v_{CA} = v_C - v_A = -15 - 10 = -25$ m/s
Time the car C requires to just cross A

$$= \frac{1000}{v_{CA}} = \frac{1000}{25} = 40 \ s.$$

In order to avoid accident, car B must overtake A in this time, so

$$1000 = u_{BA}\, t + \frac{1}{2}\, a_{BA}\, t^2$$

or $$1000 = 5 \times 40 + \frac{1}{2}\, a_{BA} \times 40^2$$

$\therefore$ $$a_{BA} = 1 \text{ m/s}^2$$

Thus the minimum acceleration that car B requires to avoid an accident is 1 m/s^2.

Example 30. *Two towns A and B are connected by a regular bus service with a bus leaving in either direction every T min. A man cycling with a speed of 20 km/h in the direction A to B notices that a bus goes past him every 18 min in the direction of his motion, and every 6 min in the opposite direction. What is the period T of the bus service and with what speed (assumed constant) do the buses ply on the road?* **[NCERT]**

Sol. Let speed of each bus = v km/h.
The distance between the nearest buses plying on either side
$$= vT \text{ km.} \qquad \qquad \ldots(i)$$

For buses going from town A to B :
Relative speed of bus in the direction of motion of man, $= (v - 20)$.
Buses plying in this direction go past the cyclist after every 18 min.

Therefore separation between the buses $= (v - 20) \times \dfrac{18}{60}$.

From equation (i),

$$(v - 20) \times \frac{18}{60} = vT. \qquad \qquad \ldots(ii)$$

For buses coming from B to A :
The relative velocity of bus with respect to man $= (v + 20)$
Buses coming from town B past the cyclist after every 6 min therefore

$$(v + 20) \times \frac{6}{60} = vT. \qquad \ldots(iii)$$

Solving equations (ii) and (iii), we get

$$v = 40 \text{ km/h and } T = \frac{3}{20} \text{ h.} \qquad \textbf{\textit{Ans.}}$$

Example 31. *The speed of a motor launch with respect to still water is 7 m/s and the speed of stream is $v = 3$ m/s. When the launch began travelling upstream, a float was dropped from it. The launch travelled 4.2 km upstream, turned about and caught up with the float. How long is it before the launch reaches the float ?*

Sol. The speed of the motor launch in still water = 7 m/s.
Its speed when it moves upstream
$$= 7 - 3 = 4 \text{ m/s.}$$

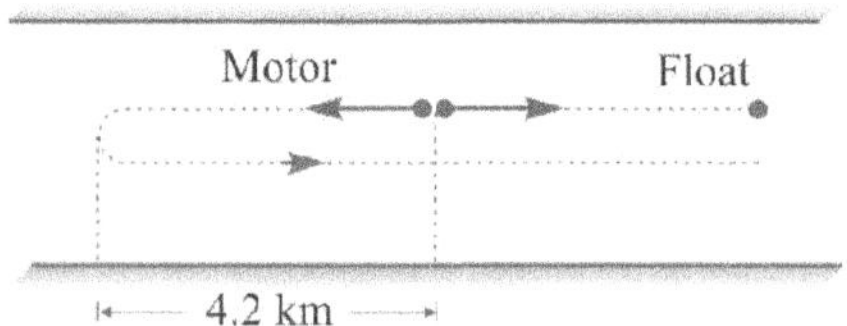

Figure. **3.40**

Distance moved $= 4200$ m

$$\text{Time taken } t_1 = \frac{4200}{4} = 1050 \ s.$$

The distance moved by float in downstream direction in this duration
$$= \text{speed} \times \text{time}$$
$$= 3 \times 1050 = 3150 \text{ m}$$
The distance to be covered by the motor launch
$$= 4200 + 3150 = 7350 \text{ m}$$
The speed of the motor launch in downstream direction with respect to the float
$$= 7 \text{ m/s.}$$

$\therefore$ $$\text{Time taken, } t_2 = \frac{7350}{7} = 1050 \ s$$

Total time taken, $$t = t_1 + t_2$$
$$= 1050 + 1050 = 2100 \text{ s} \qquad \textbf{\textit{Ans.}}$$

Example 32. *On a foggy day two drivers spot each other when they are just 80 m apart. They are travelling at 72 km/h and 60 km/h respectively. Both of them applied brakes retarding their cars at the rate of 5 m/s^2. Determine whether they avert collision or not.*

Sol. **Method-I**
Speed of the fist car, $v_1 = 72$ km/h = 20 m/s,
and speed of the second car,
$$v_2 = 60 \text{ /km/h}$$
$$= \frac{50}{3} \text{ m/s.}$$

If s_1 and s_2 are the distances moved by the cars before stop, then

$$0 = 20^2 - 2 \times 5 \times s_1$$

$\therefore$ $$s_1 = 40 \text{ m,}$$

and $$0 = \left(\frac{50}{3}\right)^2 - 2 \times 5 \times s_2$$

$\therefore$ $$s_2 = 27.78 \text{ m}$$
The distance approaches by the cars
$$s = s_1 + s_2$$
$$= 40 + 27.78$$
$$= 67.78 \text{ m.}$$

As this distance is less than the initial distance between them, so the collision will be averted.

Method-II

The initial separation between the cars
$$s = 80 \text{ m}.$$
The initial velocity of approach of the cars
$$u = u_1 + u_2 = 20 + \frac{50}{3} = \frac{110}{3} \, m/s.$$

The relative acceleration between them
$$a = a_1 + a_2 = 5 + 5 = 10 \, m/s^2$$

The final velocity of approach $v = 0$.
If s is the distance of approach before stop, then
$$0 = u^2 - 2as$$
$$0 = \left(\frac{110}{3}\right)^2 - 2 \times 10 \times s$$
$$\therefore \quad s = 67.22 \text{ m}.$$

Example 33. An elevator, in which a man is standing, is moving **upward with a constant acceleration of** $1 m/s^2$. **At some instant when speed of elevator is 10 m/s, the man drops a coin from a height of 2 m. Find the time taken by the coin to reach the floor.** ($g = 9.8$ **m/s**^{2})

Sol. Analysing the motion of coin with respect to the observer standing in the elevator. As the coin releases from rest inside elevator, its velocity with respect to ground is equal to the velocity of elevator. i.e., 10 m/s.

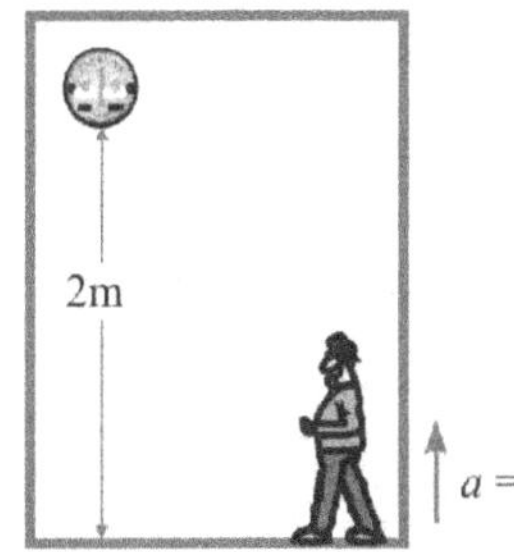

Figure. **3.41**

$$\therefore \quad [\vec{u}_{coin}]_{observer} = [\vec{u}_{coin}]_{ground} - [u_{elevator}]_{ground}$$
$$= 10 - 10 = 0$$

The acceleration of coin with respect to the observer in the elevator:
$$[\vec{a}_{coin}]_{elevator} = [\vec{a}_{coin}]_{ground} - [\vec{a}_{elevator}]_{ground}$$
$$= g - (-a) = g + a.$$

Now using second equation for relative motion
$$[s_{coin}]_{elevator} = [u_{coin}]_{elevator} t + \frac{1}{2} [a_{coin}]_{elevator} t^2$$

or
$$2 = 0 + \frac{1}{2}(g + a) t^2$$

or
$$2 = \frac{1}{2}(9.8 + 1) t^2$$

or
$$t = \sqrt{\frac{2 \times 2}{10.8}} = 0.61 \text{ s}. \qquad \textit{Ans.}$$

Example 34. A balloon is rising vertically upwards with uniform **acceleration 15.7 m/s**^{2}. **A stone is dropped from it. After 4 s another stone is dropped from it. Find the distance between the two stones 6 second after the second stone is dropped.**

Sol. Consider motion of stones with respect to the balloon. At the instant of release of stones, the initial velocity of both stones w.r.t. the balloon is zero. The acceleration of stone w.r.t. the balloon
$$[a_{stone}]_{balloon} = g - (-a) = g + a$$
where a is the acceleration of balloon which is $= 15.7$ m/s^2

Now
$$s_1 = 0 + \frac{1}{2}[a_{stone}]_{balloon} \, t_1^2$$
where
$$t_1 = (4 + 6) = 10 \text{ s}$$
$$\therefore \quad s_1 = \frac{1}{2}(g + a) \times 10^2$$
$$= \frac{1}{2}(9.8 + 15.7) \times 10^2 \text{ m}$$

and
$$s_2 = 0 + \frac{1}{2}(g + a) \, t_2^2$$
where $t_2 = 6s$
$$\therefore \quad s_2 = \frac{1}{2}(9.8 + 15.7) \times 6^2$$

The distance between s_1 and s_2 :
$$s = s_1 - s_2$$
$$= \frac{1}{2}(9.8 + 15.7)[10^2 - 6^2]$$
$$= 816 \text{ m}. \qquad \textit{Ans.}$$

In Chapter Exercise 3.3

1. A jet airplane travelling at the speed of 500kmh^{-1} ejects its products of combustion at the speed of 1500kmh^{-1} relative to the ground. What is the speed of the latter with respect to Jet plane? **[NCERT]**
   Ans. **–2000 km/h**

2. A jet plane travelling at the speed of 450 km/h ejects the burnt gases at the speed of 1200 km/h relative to the jet plane. Find the speed of the burnt gases w.r.t. a stationary observer on earth. *Ans.* **750 km/h**

3. A burglar's car had started with an acceleration of $2 \, m/s^2$. A police vigilant party came after 5 s and continued to close the burglar's car with a uniform velocity of 20 m/s. The time taken in which the police van will over take the burglar's car, in s, is **[Integer]** *Ans.* **5**

4. Two cars A and B are moving with velocities of 60 km/h and 45 km/h respectively. Calculate the relative velocity of A w.r.t. B, if

   (i) both cars are travelling eastwards and
   (ii) car A is travelling eastwards and car B is travelling westwards.
   Ans. **(i) 15 km/h eastwards (ii) 105 km/h eastwards**

5. Two buses start simultaneously towards each other from towards A and B which are 480 km apart. The first bus takes 8 hours to travel from A to B while the second bus takes 12 hours to travel from B to A. Determine when and where the buses will meet. *Ans.* **4.8 h, 288 km from A.**

6. A train is moving along a straight line with a constant acceleration 'a'. A boy standing in the train throws a ball forward with a speed of 10 m/s, at an angle of 60° to the horizontal. The boy has to move forward by 1.15 m inside the train to catch the ball back at the initial height. The acceleration of the train, in m/s^2, is **[IIT 2011]**
   [Integer] *Ans.* **5 m/s**^{2}

MISCELLANEOUS TOPICS

3.8 MOTION WITH VARIABLE ACCELERATION

If acceleration is not constant; either of the displacement, velocity or acceleration is given in terms of time or otherwise. You have to start the problem from the general equations of motion given in terms of differentiation. These are :

$$\text{acceleration,} \qquad a = \frac{dv}{dt} = v\frac{dv}{ds},$$

$$\text{and velocity,} \qquad v = \frac{ds}{dt}.$$

3.9 PROBLEMS BASED ON MAXIMA AND MINIMA

In many problems, you may be asked, the distance of closest approach, shortest distance, Minimum time or maximum time. These problems can be solved easily by using method of differentiation. Let we have to find maxima or minima of y, which is a function of x. This can be execute in following ways:

(i) For maxima, $\dfrac{dy}{dx} = 0$ and $\dfrac{d^2y}{dx^2} < 0$.

(ii) For minima, $\dfrac{dy}{dx} = 0$ and $\dfrac{d^2y}{dx^2} > 0$

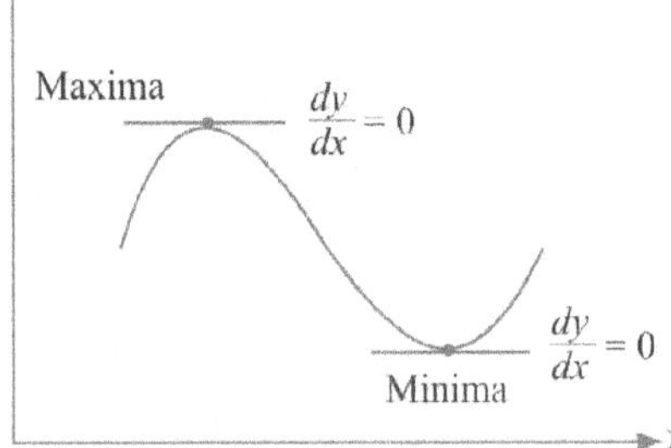

Figure. 3.42

Note:

In practice either maxima or minima occurs at a time. So there is no need to find $\dfrac{d^2y}{dx^2}$. The required result will be obtain by simply putting $\dfrac{dy}{dx} = 0$.

EXAMPLES BASED ON VARIABLE ACC. AND MAXIMA AND MINIMA

Example 35. An experiment on the take off performance of an aeroplane shows that the acceleration varies as shown in figure 3.43, and that it takes 12 s to take off from a rest position. Calculate the distance along the runway covered by the aeroplane.

Sol. From 0 to 6 second the acceleration varies linearly with time, therefore we have

$$\frac{da}{dt} = +\frac{5}{6}$$

$$\text{or} \qquad \frac{d}{dt}\left[\frac{d^2s}{dt^2}\right] = +\frac{5}{6}$$

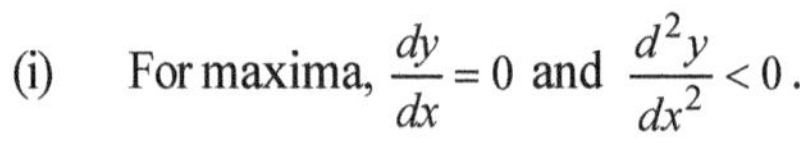

Figure. 3.43

$$\text{or} \qquad \frac{d^3s}{dt^3} = +\frac{5}{6} \qquad \qquad \text{... (i)}$$

Integrating equation (i) w.r.t. time, we get

$$\frac{d^2s}{dt^2} = \frac{5}{6}t + c_1$$

at $t = 0$, $\dfrac{d^2s}{dt^2} = 0$, $\therefore\ c_1 = 0$

$$\therefore \qquad \frac{d^2s}{dt^2} = \frac{5t}{6}.$$

Integrating again, we get

$$\frac{ds}{dt} = \frac{5t^2}{12} + c_2$$

at $t = 0$, $v = \dfrac{ds}{dt} = 0$, $\therefore\ c_2 = 0$

$$\therefore \qquad \frac{ds}{dt} = \frac{5t^2}{12} \qquad \qquad \text{...(ii)}$$

Integrating once more, we get

$$s = \frac{5t^3}{36} + c_3.$$

As $t = 0$, $s = 0$, $\therefore\ c_3 = 0$

$$s = \frac{5}{36}t^3 \qquad \qquad \text{...(iii)}$$

The distance travelled from 0 to $6s$, from equation (ii), we get

$$s_1 = \frac{5}{36} \times (6)^3 = 30\,m$$

The velocity at $t = 6\ s$,

$$v = \frac{5}{12}t^2 = \frac{5}{12} \times 6^2 = 15\ m/s$$

Now from, $6\ s$ to $12\ s$
$u = 15\ m/s,\ a = 5 m/s^2$

$$\therefore \quad s_2 = ut + \frac{1}{2}at^2 = 15 \times 6 + \frac{1}{2} \times 5 \times 6^2 = 180\ m.$$

Therefore total distance travelled on runway $= 30 + 180 = 210$ m.***Ans.***

Example 36. The velocity of a particle moving in the positive direction of the x-axis varies as $v = a\sqrt{x}$, where a is a positive constant. Assuming that at the moment $t = 0$ the particle was located at the point $x = 0$, find:
(a) the time dependence of the velocity
(b) the mean velocity of the particle averaged over the time that the particle takes to cover the first 5 metre of the path.

Sol. (a) Given, $\qquad v = a\sqrt{x}$

$$\therefore \qquad v^2 = a^2 x\ .$$

Differentiating above equation, we have

$$\frac{d}{dt}\left(v^2\right) = \frac{d(a^2 x)}{dt} \quad \text{or} \quad 2v\frac{dv}{dt} = a^2 \frac{dx}{dt}$$

Since $\qquad \dfrac{dx}{dt} = v$

$$\therefore \qquad 2\frac{dv}{dt} = a^2 \quad \text{or} \quad dv = \frac{a^2}{2}dt$$

$$\therefore \qquad \int_0^v dv = \frac{a^2}{2}\int_0^t dt$$

or $\qquad v = \dfrac{a^2 t}{2}\ .$ $\qquad\qquad$ ...(i)

(b) Let τ be the time to cover the first s meter of the path, then from equation (i), we have

$$\frac{ds}{dt} = \frac{a^2 t}{2}$$

$$\therefore \qquad \int_0^s ds = \frac{a^2}{2}\int_0^\tau t\,dt$$

or $\qquad s = \dfrac{a^2 \tau^2}{4}$

$$\therefore \qquad \tau = \frac{2\sqrt{s}}{a}$$

Now the mean velocity of the particle

$$v_{av} = \frac{\int_0^\tau v\,dt}{\int_0^\tau dt} = \frac{\dfrac{a^2\tau^2}{4}}{\tau} = \frac{a^2\tau}{4}$$

$$= \frac{a^2}{4} \times \frac{2\sqrt{s}}{a} = \frac{a}{2}\sqrt{s}\ . \qquad\qquad \textbf{\textit{Ans.}}$$

Example 37. The motion of a body is given by the equation

$$\frac{dv(t)}{dt} = 6.0 - 3v(t)$$

where $v(t)$ is the speed in m/s and t in second.
If the body was at rest at $t = 0$; then test these corrections of the following results
(a) the terminal speed is 2.0 m/s
(b) the magnitude of initial acceleration is 6.0 m/s²
(c) the speed varies with time as $v(t) = 2\,(1 - e^{-3t})$ m/s
(d) the speed is 1.0 m/s when the acceleration is half the initial value.

Sol. Given $\qquad \dfrac{dv(t)}{dt} = 6.0 - 3v(t)$

(a) The terminal speed is the constant speed when acceleration is zero. Thus

$$0 = 6.0 - 3v$$
$$\therefore \qquad v = 2\ m/s$$

(b) At $t = 0,\ v = 0$; therefore initial acceleration $a = 6.0 - 0 = 6.0$ m/s²
(c) We have,

$$\frac{dv(t)}{dt} = 6.0 - 3v(t)$$

$$\therefore \qquad dv = [6.0 - 3v(t)]\,dt$$

or $\qquad \dfrac{dv}{6.0 - 3v(t)} = dt$

Integrating both sides of above equation, we get

$$\int_0^v \frac{dv}{6.0 - 3v(t)} = \int_0^t dt$$

$$\left|\frac{\ell n(6.0 - 3v)}{-3}\right|_0^v = t$$

$$\ell n\,(6.0 - 3\,v) - \ell n\,6.0 = -3t$$

or $\qquad \ell n\left(\dfrac{6.0 - 3v}{6.0}\right) = -3t$

or $\ell n\left(1 - \dfrac{v}{2}\right) = -3t$

or $\qquad v = 2\,(1 - e^{-3t})$ m/s.

(d) Acceleration half that of initial $= \dfrac{6.0}{2} = 3.0$ m/s²

This gives $3 = 6 - 3\,v(t)$
or $\qquad v(t) = 1$ m/s
We have seen that alternatives (a), (b), (c) and (d) all are correct.

Example 38 A body of mass m is thrown straight up with velocity v_0. Find the velocity v' with which the body comes down if the air drag equals kv^2, where k is a constant and v is the velocity of the body.

Sol. The net retarding force on the body

$$m\frac{dv}{dt} = -(mg + kv^2)$$

$$\therefore \qquad \frac{dv}{dt} = -\left(g + \frac{k}{m}v^2\right) \qquad\qquad \text{...(i)}$$

We have
$$\frac{dv}{dt} = v\frac{dv}{dy}$$

$$\therefore \qquad v\frac{dv}{dy} = -\left(g+\frac{k}{m}v^2\right)$$

or
$$\frac{vdv}{\left(g+\frac{k}{m}v^2\right)} = -dy$$

Integrating both sides of above equation, we get

$$\int_{v_0}^{0}\frac{vdv}{\left(g+\frac{k}{m}v^2\right)} = -\int_{0}^{h}dy \qquad \qquad \ldots(ii)$$

On substituting $g+\dfrac{k}{m}v^2 = z$

$$\frac{d\left(g+\frac{k}{m}v^2\right)}{dv} = \frac{dz}{dv}$$

or
$$\frac{k}{m}\times 2v = \frac{dz}{dv} \qquad \text{or} \qquad vdv=\left(\frac{m}{2k}\right)dz$$

Substituting these values in equation (ii), we get

$$\frac{m}{2k}\int_{v_0}^{0}\frac{dz}{z} = -\int_{0}^{h}dy$$

or
$$\left|\ell nz\right|_{v_0}^{0} = \frac{-2k}{m}|y|_{0}^{h}$$

or
$$\left|ln\left(g+\frac{k}{m}v^2\right)\right|_{v_0}^{0} = \frac{-2k}{m}h$$

or
$$-\left[\ell ng-\ell n\left(g+\frac{kv_0^2}{m}\right)\right]=\frac{2k}{m}h$$

or
$$\ell n\frac{\left(g+\frac{kv_0^2}{m}\right)}{g} = \frac{2k}{m}h \qquad \qquad \ldots(iii)$$

or
$$h = \frac{m}{2k}\ln\left[1+\frac{k}{mg}v_0^2\right]$$

When body comes down from height h, we have

$$m\frac{dv}{dt} = (mg-kv^2)$$

$$\therefore \qquad v\frac{dv}{dy} = \left(g-\frac{kv^2}{m}\right)$$

or
$$\frac{vdv}{\left(g-\frac{kv^2}{m}\right)} = dy$$

Integrating both sides of above equation, we get

$$\int_{0}^{v'}\frac{vdv}{\left(g-\frac{kv^2}{m}\right)} = \int_{0}^{h}dy$$

or$-\ell n\left[\dfrac{g-\dfrac{kv'^2}{m}}{g}\right] = \dfrac{2kh}{m}$

or $\ell n\left[\dfrac{g-\dfrac{kv'^2}{m}}{g}\right]^{-1} = \dfrac{2kh}{m} \qquad \ldots(iv)$

From equation (iii) and (iv), we get

$$\left[\frac{g+\frac{kv_0^2}{m}}{g}\right] = \left[\frac{g-\frac{kv'^2}{m}}{g}\right]^{-1}$$

or
$$\left[\frac{g+\frac{kv_0^2}{m}}{g}\right] = \left[\frac{g}{g-\frac{kv'^2_0}{m}}\right]$$

After solving we get, $v' = \dfrac{v_0}{\sqrt{1+\dfrac{kv_0^2}{mg}}}$ *Ans.*

Example 39. **Two bodies start moving in the same straight line at the same instant of time from the same origin. The first body moves with a constant velocity of 40 m/s, and the second starts from rest with a constant acceleration of 4 m/s². Find the time that elapses before the second catches the first body. Find also the greatest distance between them prior to it and time at which this occurs.**

Sol. The distance travelled by first body in time t, $s_1 = 40\,t$.

The distance travelled by second body in time t,

$$s_2 = \frac{1}{2}\times 4\times t^2 = 2t^2.$$

The separation between them at any time t
$$s = s_1 - s_2 = 40\,t - 2t^2 \qquad \ldots(i)$$
The second body will catch the first if $s = 0$

$$\therefore \qquad 0 = 40\,t - 2t^2$$
which gives $t = 20\ s$.

For s to be greatest, $\dfrac{ds}{dt} = 0$

or $\dfrac{d}{dt}(40t-2t^2) = 0$ or $40 - 2\times 2t = 0$

or $t = 10$ s.

Thus greatest distance between them
$$s = 40\times 10 - 2\times 10^2 = 200 \text{ m.} \qquad \textit{Ans.}$$

Example 40. **Two ships are 10 km apart on a line from south to north. The one farther north is moving towards west at 40 km/h and other is moving towards north at 40 km/h. What is the distance of closest approach and how long do they take to reach it?**

Sol. In time t the distance travelled by each ship is $40\,t$. Initially ships were at A and B.

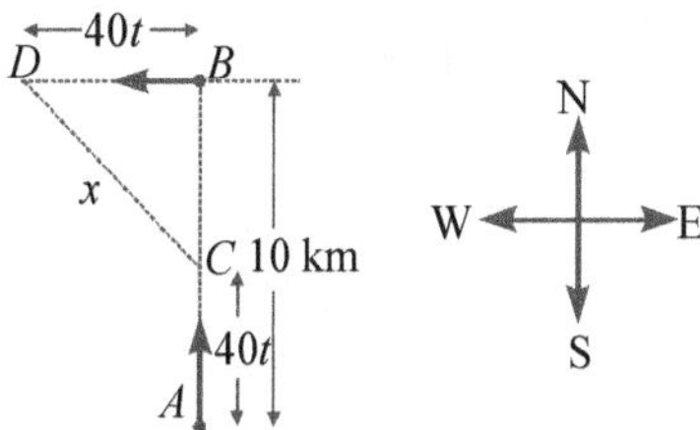

Figure. 3.44

After time t, they are at C and D, let separation between them after time t is x.

$$\therefore \qquad x^2 = (40\,t)^2 + (10 - 40t)^2 \qquad \ldots (i)$$

For x to be minimum $\dfrac{dx}{dt} = 0$.

Differentiating equation (i) with time, we get

$$2x\frac{dx}{dt} = 2 \times 40t \times 40 + 2(10 - 40t) \times (-40)$$

or $\qquad 0 = 3200\,t - 800 + 3200\,t$

which gives $\qquad t = \dfrac{1}{8}\,\text{hr}$

Now from equation (i), the closest approach

$$x_{\min} = \sqrt{\left(40 \times \frac{1}{8}\right)^2 + \left(10 - 40 \times \frac{1}{8}\right)^2}$$

$$= \sqrt{5^2 + 5^2} = 5\sqrt{2}\ \text{km.} \qquad \textit{Ans.}$$

Note: The value of closest approach does not depend on the speed of objects provided both have same speed.

Example 41. A body falling freely from a given height H hits an inclined plane in its path at a height h. As a result of this impact the direction of velocity of the body becomes horizontal. For what value of (h/H) will the body take maximum time to reach the ground?

Sol. Time taken in falling height $(H - h)$

$$(H - h) = 0 + \frac{1}{2}gt_1^2$$

or $\qquad t_1 = \sqrt{\dfrac{2(H - h)}{g}}$.

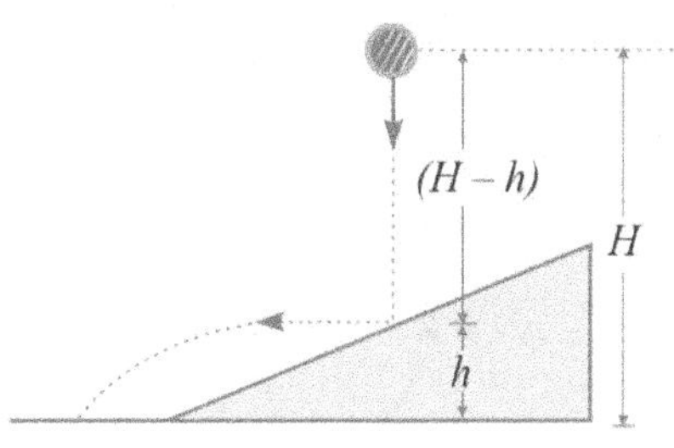

Figure. 3.45

After impact with the inclined plane the vertical component of velocity becomes zero. Let t_2 be the time taken in falling height h, then

$$h = 0 + \frac{1}{2}gt_2^2 \qquad \text{or} \qquad t_2 = \sqrt{\frac{2h}{g}}$$

The total time of motion

$$t = t_1 + t_2 = \sqrt{\frac{2(H - h)}{g}} + \sqrt{\frac{2h}{g}}.$$

For t to be minimum, $\dfrac{dt}{dh} = 0$

or $\qquad \dfrac{dt}{dh} = \dfrac{d}{dt}\left(\left(\dfrac{2}{g}\right)^{\frac{1}{2}}(H - h)^{1/2} + \left(\dfrac{2}{g}\right)^{\frac{1}{2}}(h)^{\frac{1}{2}}\right)$

or $\qquad 0 = \left(\dfrac{2}{g}\right)^{1/2} \times \dfrac{1}{2}(H - h)^{-1/2} \times (-1)$

$$+ \left(\frac{2}{g}\right)^{1/2} \times \frac{1}{2}h^{-1/2}$$

After solving, we get, $\quad h = \dfrac{H}{2}$

or $\qquad \dfrac{h}{H} = \dfrac{1}{2}.$ $\qquad\qquad$ *Ans.*

Example 42. From point A located on a highway as shown in *figure. 3.46*, one has to get by car as soon as possible to point B located in the field at a distance ℓ from the highway. It is known that car moves in the field η time slower on the highway. At what distance from point D one must turn off the highway?

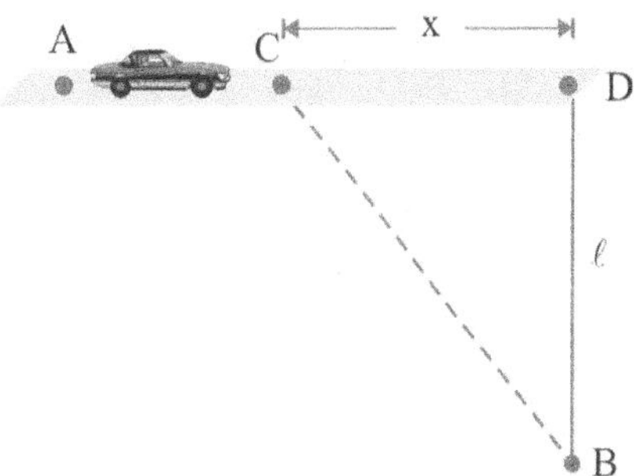

Figure. 3.46

Sol. Suppose x distance from D the car turns off the highway. Let v be the speed of car on highway, then its speed on field will be v/η. The time of motion,

$$t = \left(\frac{AD - x}{v}\right) + \frac{\sqrt{x^2 + \ell^2}}{v/\eta} \qquad \ldots(i)$$

t to be minimum, $\dfrac{dt}{dx} = 0$

or $\qquad \dfrac{dt}{dx} = \dfrac{d}{dx}\left[\dfrac{AD - x}{v} + \dfrac{\eta}{v}(x^2 + \ell^2)^{1/2}\right]$

$\qquad\qquad\qquad\qquad\qquad$ $[AD$ is constant$]$

or $\qquad 0 = -\dfrac{1}{v} + \dfrac{\eta}{v} \times \dfrac{1}{2}(x^2 + \ell^2)^{-1/2} \times 2x$

or $\qquad \eta^2 x^2 = x^2 + \ell^2$

$\therefore \qquad x = \dfrac{\ell}{\sqrt{\eta^2 - 1}}.$ $\qquad$ *Ans.*

In Chapter Exercise 3.4

1. The position of an object moving along an x axis is given by $x = t^3 - 4t^2 + 3t$, where x is in metre and t in second.

(a) What is the object's displacement between $t = 0$ and $t = 4s$?

(b) What is its average velocity for the time interval from $t = 2s$ to $t = 4s$?

Ans. **(a) + 12 m**   **(b) + 7 m/s.**

2. A point moves rectilinearly with deceleration whose modulus depends on the velocity v of the particle as

$\alpha = a\sqrt{v}$, where a is a positive constant. At the initial moment the velocity of the point is equal to v_0. What distance will it transverse before it stops? What will it take to cover that distance ?

$$\textit{Ans. } s = \left(\frac{2}{3a}\right) v_0^{3/2}, \ t = 2\,\frac{2\sqrt{v_0}}{a}$$

3. The distance between two moving particles at any time is a. If v be their relative velocity and v_1 and v_2 be the components of v along and perpendicular to a. Find the time when they are closest to each other, and the minimum distance between them.

$$\textit{Ans: } \frac{av_1}{v^2}, \ \frac{av_2}{v}$$

MISCELLANEOUS EXAMPLES FOR JEE-(MAIN AND ADVANCE)

Example 1. **A particle starts moving with constant velocity of 10 m/s. Simultaneously another particle starts with constant acceleration of 1 m/s² in the direction of first particle. Find;**
(a) **the time at which distance between them is greatest and the greatest distance between them,**
(b) **the time and distance at which second particle will cross the first particle.**

Sol.
(a) In time t;
The distance travelled by first particle $= 10\,t$.

Figure. **3.47**

The distance travelled by second particle

$$= \frac{1}{2}at^2 = \frac{1}{2} \times 1 \times t^2 = \frac{t^2}{2}.$$

Thus distance between them at any time t,

$$s = 10t - \frac{t^2}{2}.$$

The distance s to be greatest, $\dfrac{ds}{dt} = 0$,

or $\dfrac{d}{dt}\left(10t - \dfrac{t^2}{2}\right) = 0$

or $10 - t = 0$

$\therefore \qquad t = 10 \text{ s}$ *Ans.*

The greatest distance between them

$$= 10 \times 10 - \frac{10^2}{2}$$

$$= 50 \text{ m} \qquad \textit{Ans.}$$

(b) For distance between them to be zero, $s = 0$,

or $10t - \dfrac{t^2}{2} = 0$

or $t = 20 \text{ s}.$ *Ans.*

The distance at which second particle will cross the first particle

$$s = 10 \times 20 = 200\,m. \qquad \textit{Ans.}$$

Example 2. **A bird flies for 4 s with a velocity $v = (t - 2)$ m/s in a straight line, where t = time in second. Calculate the displacement and distance covered by the bird.**

Sol. The velocity-time and speed-time graphs of motion of the bird are as follows:

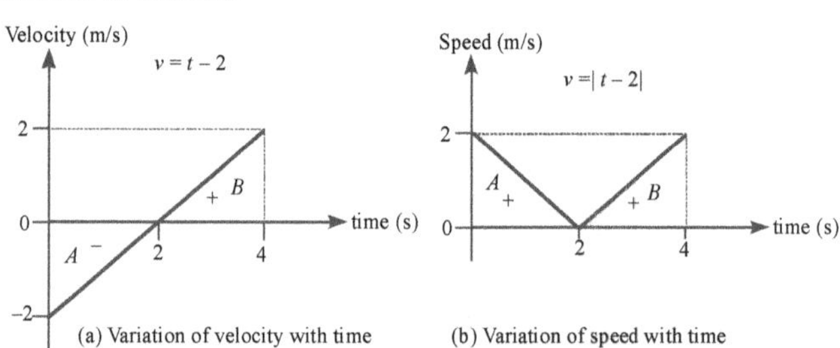

(a) Variation of velocity with time   (b) Variation of speed with time

Figure. **3.48**

From the graph, displacement $s = $ area $A - $ area $B = 0$

And distance, $\qquad s = $ Area $A + $ Area B

$$= \frac{1}{2} \times 2 \times 2 + \frac{1}{2} \times 2 \times 2 = 4\,\text{m}.$$

Example 3. **Each second a rabbit moves half the remaining distance from his nose to the head of a lettuce. Does he ever get to the lettuce? What is the limiting value of his average velocity? Draw graphs showing his velocity and position as time increases.**

Sol. Let us take x_0 is the initial distance of rabbit from the lettuce. His distance at any moment x;

At $\quad t = 0, \qquad\qquad x = x_0$

$t = 1, \qquad\qquad x = \dfrac{x_0}{2} = x_0\left(\dfrac{1}{2}\right)^1$

$t = 2, \qquad\qquad x = \dfrac{x_0}{4} = x_0\left(\dfrac{1}{2}\right)^2$

$- - - - - - - - - - - -$

$t = n, \qquad\qquad x = x_0\left(\dfrac{1}{2}\right)^n$

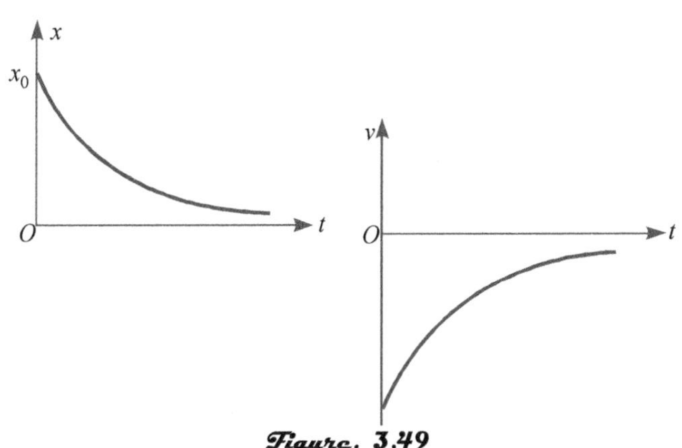

Figure. 3.49

To reach the lettuce, $x = 0$

or
$$0 = x = x_0 \left(\frac{1}{2}\right)^n$$

which gives $n = \infty$

Thus rabbit practically will never reach the lettuce.

The velocity of a body is the slope of x-t plot, that is $\frac{dx}{dt} = v$. Slope of

the plot at each instant is negative, which is drawn in the figure. Since time to reach the lettuce is infinite.

Therefore average velocity $= \dfrac{\text{displacement}}{\text{time}} = \dfrac{x_0}{\infty} = 0$ *Ans.*

Example 4. **A ball is dropped from a height of 90 m on a floor. At each collision with the floor, the ball loses one-tenth of its speed. Plot the speed-time graph of its motion between $t = 0$ to $12\ s$.**

[NCERT]

Sol. The time taken by the ball to fall a height 90 m :

(i)
$$90 = ut + \frac{1}{2} g\, t^2$$

or
$$90 = 0 + \frac{1}{2} \times 9.8 \times t^2$$

which gives $t = 4.3$ s

Now velocity just before collision with the floor
$$v = u + gt$$
$$= 0 + 9.8 \times 4.3 = 42 \text{ m/s}$$

The velocity between 0 to 4.3 s
$$v = gt = 9.8\, t.$$

In this time velocity varies linearly with time from 0 to 42 m/s during downward motion.

(ii)   After first collision with the floor, speed lost by ball
$$= \frac{1}{10} \times 42 = 4.2 \text{ m/s}$$

Thus ball rebound with a speed of $v = \dfrac{9}{10} \times 42 = 37.8$ m/s.

For upward motion, the velocity is given by the equation
$$v = u - gt$$
$$= 37.8 - 9.8 \times t$$

The speed decreases linearly and becomes zero at;
$$0 = 37.8 - 9.8\, t$$
$$\Rightarrow \qquad t = 3.9 \text{ s}$$

Thus, the ball reaches the highest point again after time t $= 4.3 + 3.9 = 8.2\ s$ from the start of the motion.

(iii)   At the highest point, the speed of ball becomes zero. It again starts falling. At any time its speed is given by $v = 0 + 9.8\ t$.

The speed increases linearly with time from 0 to 37.8 m/s in the next time interval of 3.9s. The total time of motion from start now becomes $= 4.3 + 3.9 + 3.9 = 12.1$ s.

The motion of the ball is shown by graph as in figure 3.50.

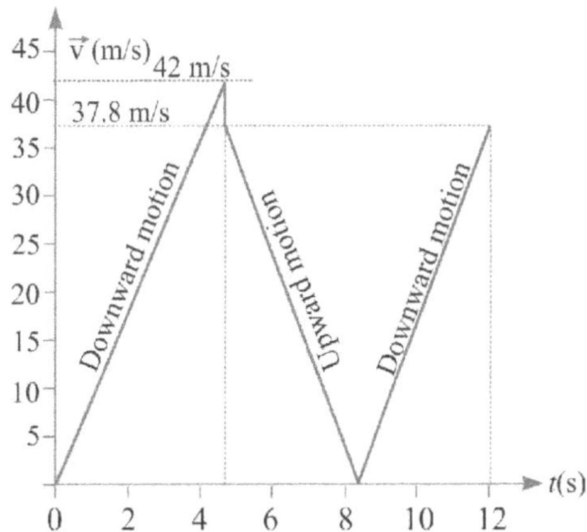

Figure. 3.50

Example 5. **Two stones are thrown up simultaneously from the edge of a cliff 200 m high with initial speeds of 15 m/s and 30 m/s. Verify that the following graph correctly represents the time variation of the relative position of the second stone with respect to the first. Neglect air resistance and assume that the stones do not rebound after hitting the ground. Take $g = 10$ m/s^2. Give equations for the linear and curved parts of the plot.**   [NCERT]

[JEE (Main) 2015]

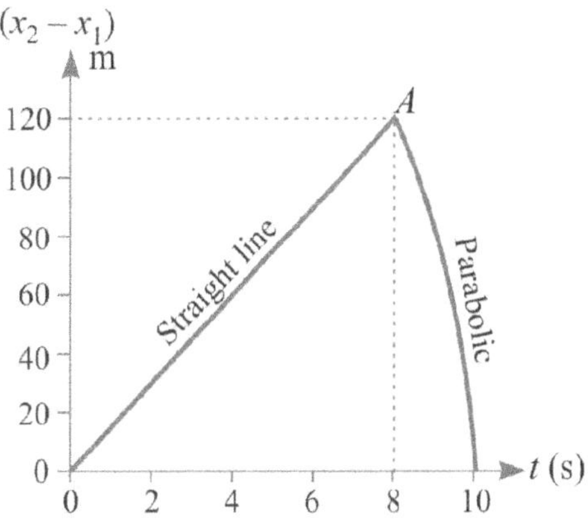

Figure. 3.51

Sol. Time to hit the ground by stones can be calculated as :

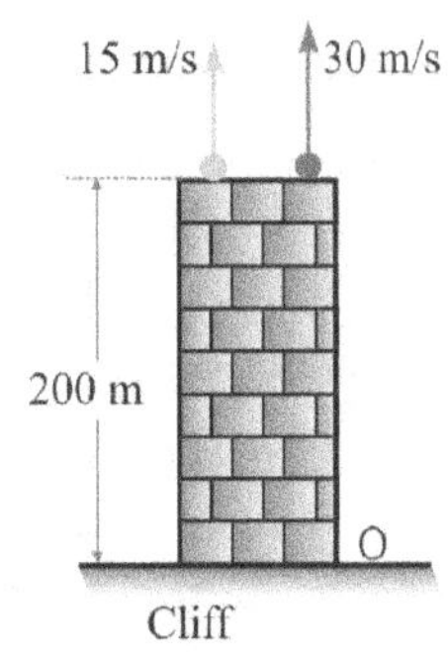

Figure. 3.52

We have
$$h = ut + \frac{1}{2} g t^2.$$

For first stone,
$$200 = -15\,t + \frac{1}{2} \times 10 \times t_1^2$$

$$\therefore \qquad t_1 = 8 \text{ s}$$

For second stone,
$$200 = -30\,t + \frac{1}{2} \times 10 \times t_2^2$$

$$\therefore \qquad t_2 = 10 \text{ s}$$

The positions of stones at anytime t, taking O as the origin are;

$$x_1 = 200 + (15\,t - \frac{1}{2} \times 10 \times t^2) \qquad \ldots(i)$$

and
$$x_2 = 200 + (30\,t - \frac{1}{2} \times 10 \times t^2) \qquad \ldots(ii)$$

(a)   The relative position of second stone w.r.t first is given by;

For $t \le 8$ s, $x_2 - x_1 = 15\,t$. $\ldots$(iii)

(b)   After 8 s when first stone stops falling, so $x_1 = 0$

$$\therefore \qquad x_2 = 200 + (30\,t - \frac{1}{2} \times 10 \times t^2)$$

and
$$x_2 - x_1 = 200 + 30\,t - 5\,t^2 \qquad \ldots(iv)$$

The equation (iii) is a straight line between $(x_2 - x_1)$ and t and equation (iv) is parabolic.

LEVEL - I (ONLY ONE OPTION CORRECT)

Average Velocity, Motion with Constant Acceleration

1. If a car covers 2/5th of the total distance with v_1 speed and 3/5th distance with v_2, then average speed is

   (a) $\dfrac{1}{2}\sqrt{v_1 v_2}$
   (b) $\dfrac{v_1 + v_2}{2}$
   (c) $\dfrac{2v_1 v_2}{v_1 + v_2}$
   (d) $\dfrac{5v_1 v_2}{3v_1 + 2v_2}$

2. A particle moving in a straight line covers half the distance with speed of 3m/s. The other half of the distance covered in two equal time intervals with speed of 4.5 m/s and 7.5 m/s respectively. The average speed of the particle during this motion is

   (a) 4.0 m/s
   (b) 5.0 m/s
   (c) 5.5 m/s
   (d) 4.8 m/s

3. Which are of the following represents uniformly accelerated motion:

   (a) $x = \sqrt{\dfrac{t-a}{b}}$
   (b) $x = \dfrac{t-a}{b}$
   (c) $t = \sqrt{\dfrac{x-a}{b}}$
   (d) $x = \sqrt{t} + a$

4. The velocity of a body depends on time according to equation $v = 20 + 0.1t^2$. The body is undergoing

   (a) uniform acceleration
   (b) uniform retardation
   (c) non uniform acceleration
   (d) zero acceleration

5. A particle experiences a constant acceleration for 20 sec after starting from rest. If it travels a distance s_1 in 10 sec and distance s_2 in the next 10 sec, then

   (a) $s_1 = s_2$
   (b) $s_1 = \dfrac{s_2}{3}$
   (c) $s_1 = \dfrac{s_2}{2}$
   (d) $s_1 = \dfrac{s_2}{4}$

6. A particle is dropped vertically from rest from a height. The time taken by it to fall through successive of 1 meter each will then be:

   (a) all equal, being equal to $\dfrac{2}{g}$ second
   (b) in the ratio of square roots of integers 1, 2, 3, ...
   (c) in the ratio of the difference in the square roots of integers i.e. $(\sqrt{1}-\sqrt{0}), (\sqrt{2}-\sqrt{1}), (\sqrt{3}-\sqrt{2}), (\sqrt{4}-\sqrt{3})$
   (d) in the ratio $\dfrac{1}{\sqrt{1}} : \dfrac{1}{\sqrt{2}} : \dfrac{1}{\sqrt{3}} : \dfrac{1}{\sqrt{4}}$

7. A point moves with uniform acceleration and v_1, v_2 and v_3 denote the average velocities in three successive intervals of time t_1, t_2 and t_3. Which of the following relations is correct

   (a) $v_1 - v_2 : v_2 - v_3 = t_1 - t_2 : t_2 + t_3$
   (b) $v_1 - v_2 : v_2 - v_3 = t_1 + t_2 : t_2 + t_3$
   (c) $v_1 - v_2 : v_2 - v_3 = t_1 - t_2 : t_1 - t_3$
   (d) $v_1 - v_2 : v_2 - v_3 = t_1 - t_2 : t_2 - t_3$

8. Speed of two identical cars are u and 4u at a specific instant. The ratio of the respective distances in which the two cars are stopped from that instant is

   (a) 1 : 1
   (b) 1 : 4
   (c) 1 : 8
   (d) 1 : 16

9. Two balls A and B of same mass are thrown from the top of the building. A thrown upward with velocity v and B, thrown down with velocity v, then

   (a) velocity A is more than B at the ground
   (b) velocity of B is more than A at the ground
   (c) both A and B strike the ground with same velocity
   (d) none of these

10. A particle displacement x of a particle moving in one dimension under constant acceleration is related to time t as $t = \sqrt{x} + 3$. The displacement of the particle when its velocity is zero is:

    (a) zero
    (b) 3 units
    (c) $\sqrt{3}$ units
    (d) 9 units

11. A particle moves a distance x in time t according to equation $x = (t+5)^{-1}$. The acceleration of the particle is proportional to :

    (a) $(\text{velocity})^{3/2}$
    (b) $(\text{distance})^2$
    (c) $(\text{distance})^{-2}$
    (d) $(\text{velocity})^{2/3}$

12. A frictionless wire AB is fixed on a sphere of radius R. A very small spherical ball slips on this wire. The time taken by this ball to slip from A to B is :

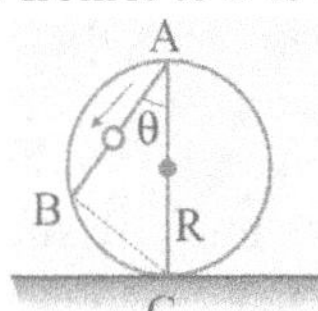

    (a) $\dfrac{2\sqrt{gR}}{g\cos\theta}$
    (b) $2\sqrt{gR}\,\dfrac{\cos\theta}{g}$
    (c) $2\sqrt{\dfrac{R}{g}}$
    (d) $\dfrac{gR}{\sqrt{g\cos\theta}}$

Answer	1	(d)	2	(a)	3	(c)	4	(c)	5	(b)	6	(c)
Key	7	(b)	8	(d)	9	(c)	10	(a)	11	(a)	12	(c)

13. A particle had a speed of 18 m/s at a certain time, and 2.4 s later its speed was 30 m/s in the opposite direction. The average acceleration of the particle in the duration is :
(a) 20 m/s^2 in the direction of initial velocity
(b) 20 m/s^2 in the direction opposite to the initial velocity
(c) 5 m/s^2 in the direction of initial velocity
(d) 5 m/s^2 in the direction opposite to the initial velocity.

14. A stone is thrown vertically upward. On its way up it passes point A with speed of v, and point B, 3 m higher than A, with speed $v/2$. The maximum height reached by stone above point B is
(a) 1 m   (b) 2 m
(c) 3 m   (d) 5 m

15. Two diamonds begin a free fall from rest from the same height, 1.0 s apart. How long after the first diamond begins to fall will the two diamonds be 10 m apart ?
(a) 1.0 s   (b) 1.5 s
(c) 2.0 s   (d) 2.5 s

16. A body is projected vertically upwards. If t_1 and t_2 be the times at which it is at height h above the projection while ascending and descending respectively, then h is
(a) $\dfrac{1}{2}gt_1t_2$ (b) gt_1t_2

(c) $2gt_1t_2$ (d) $2hg$

17. A ball is dropped from a bridge 122.5 m above a river. After the ball has been falling for two second, a second ball is thrown straight down after it. What must its initial velocity be so that both hit the water at the same time?
(a) 49 m/s   (b) 55.5 m/s
(c) 26.1 m/s   (d) 9.8 m/s

18. Two boys are standing at the ends A and B of a ground where $AB = a$. The boy at B starts running in a direction perpendicular to AB with velocity v_1. The boy at A starts running simultaneously with velocity v and catches the other boy in a time t, where t is
(a) $\dfrac{a}{\sqrt{v^2 + v_1^2}}$ (b) $\dfrac{a}{v + v_1}$

(c) $\dfrac{a}{v - v_1}$ (d) $\dfrac{a}{\sqrt{v^2 - v_1^2}}$

19. A body A starts from rest with an acceleration a_1. After 2 seconds, another body B starts from rest with an acceleration a_2. If they travel equal distances in the 5th seconds, after the start of A, then the ratio $a_1 : a_2$ is equal to
(a) 5 : 9   (b) 5 : 7
(c) 9 : 5   (d) 9 : 7

20. A body A moves with a uniform acceleration a and zero initial velocity. Another body B, starts from the same point moves in the same direction with a constant velocity v. The two bodies meet after a time t. The value of t is.
(a) $\dfrac{2v}{a}$ (b) $\dfrac{v}{a}$

(c) $\dfrac{v}{2a}$ (d) $\sqrt{\dfrac{v}{2a}}$

21. A point moves in a straight line so that its displacement x at time t is given by $x^2 = 1 + t^2$. Its acceleration at any time t is
(a) $\dfrac{1}{x^3}$ (b) $\dfrac{-t}{x^3}$

(c) $\dfrac{1}{x} - \dfrac{t^2}{x^3}$ (d) $\dfrac{1}{x} - \dfrac{1}{x^2}$

22. Two balls are dropped to the ground from different heights. One ball is dropped 2s after the other but they both strike the ground at the same time. If the first ball takes 5s to reach the ground, then the difference in initial heights is ($g = 10$ ms^{-2})
(a) 20 m   (b) 80 m
(c) 170 m   (d) 40 m

23. The time taken by a block of wood (initially at rest) to side down a smooth inclined plane 9.8 m long (angle of inclination is 30°) is

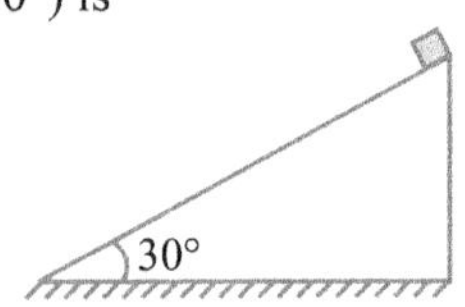

(a) $\dfrac{1}{2}$ s   (b) 2 s

(c) 4 s   (d) 1 s

24. If a ball is thrown vertically upwards with speed u, the distance covered during the last t seconds of its ascent is
(a) $\dfrac{1}{2}gt^2$ (b) $ut - \dfrac{1}{2}gt^2$

(c) $(u - gt)t$ (d) ut

25. A ball is thrown vertically upwards. It was observed at a height h twice, with a gap of time interval Δt. The initial velocity of the ball is
(a) $\sqrt{8gh + g^2(\Delta t)^2}$ (b) $\sqrt{8gh + \left(\dfrac{g\Delta t}{2}\right)^2}$

(c) $\dfrac{1}{2}\sqrt{8gh + g^2(\Delta t)^2}$ (d) $\sqrt{8gh + 4g^2(\Delta t)^2}$

26. Two bodies begin to fall freely from the same height but the second falls T second after the first. The time (after which the first body begins to fall) when the distance between the bodies equals L is

(a) $\dfrac{1}{2}T$

(b) $\dfrac{T}{2}+\dfrac{L}{gT}$

(c) $\dfrac{L}{gT}$

(d) $T+\dfrac{2L}{gT}$

27. A bus starts from rest and moves with an acceleration of $1\ m/s^2$. A boy, who is 48 m behind the bus run after with a constant speed of 10 m/s. The boy can catch the bus
    (a) only once, after 8 s form start
    (b) only once, after 12 s from start
    (c) twice after 8s and 12 s from start
    (d) never

Motion with Variable Acceleration

28. The initial velocity of particle is u and the acceleration at the time t is at, a being a constant. Then the v at the time t is given by
    (a) $v = u$
    (b) $v = u + at$
    (c) $v = u + at^2$
    (d) $v = u + \dfrac{1}{2}at^2$

29. Starting from rest, acceleration of a particle is $a = 2(t-1)$. The velocity of the particle at $t = 5s$ is
    (a) 15 m/s
    (b) 25 m/s
    (c) 5 m/s
    (d) none of these

30. The deceleration experienced by a moving motor-boat after its engine is cut off, is given by $\dfrac{dv}{dt}=-kv^3$, where k is a constant. If v_0 is the magnitude of the velocity at cut-off, the magnitude of the velocity at a time t after the cut-off is   **[AMU B.Tech. 2002]**
    (a) $\dfrac{v_0}{\sqrt{(2v_0^2kt+1)}}$
    (b) v_0e^{-kt}
    (c) $\dfrac{v_0}{2}$
    (d) v_0

31. A self-propelled vehicle of mass m whose engine delivers constant power P has an acceleration $a=\dfrac{P}{mv}$ (assume that there is no friction). In order to increase its velocity from v_1 to v_2, the distance it has to travel will be
    (a) $\dfrac{3P}{m}(v_2^2-v_1^2)$
    (b) $\dfrac{m}{3P}(v_2^3-v_1^3)$
    (c) $\dfrac{m}{3P}(v_2^2-v_1^2)$
    (d) $\dfrac{m}{3P}(v_2-v_1)$

32. The acceleration a in m/s^2 of a particle is given by $a = 3t^2 + 2t + 2$ where t is the time. If the particle starts out with a velocity $u = 2$ m/s at $t = 0$, then the velocity at the end of 2 second is

(a) 12 m/s
(b) 18 m/s
(c) 27 m/s
(d) 36 m/s

33. The displacement-time graph for two particles A and B are straight lines inclined at angles of $30°$ and $60°$ with the time axis. The ratio of velocities of $v_A : v_B$ is
    (a) $1:2$
    (b) $1:\sqrt{3}$
    (c) $\sqrt{3}:1$
    (d) $1:3$

Graphical Questions

34. The acceleration of the body travelling along a straight line changes with time as shown in the figure. What does the area under the graph measure ?

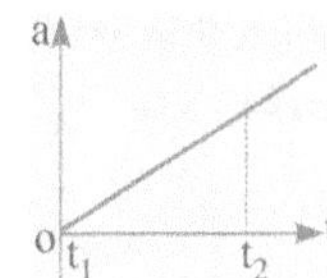

    (a) the distance travelled from time t_1 to time t_2
    (b) the average acceleration for the period under consideration
    (c) the average velocity for the period under consideration
    (d) the velocity at time t_2

35. The velocity versus time curve of a moving point is as given below. The maximum acceleration is

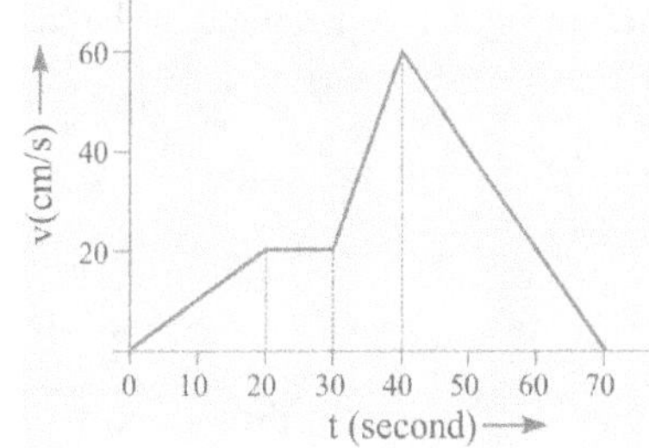

    (a) $1\ cm/s^2$
    (b) $2\ cm/s^2$
    (c) $3\ cm/s^2$
    (d) $4\ cm/s^2$

36. Displacement-time curve of a particle moving along a straight line is shown in figure. Tangents at A and B make angles $45°$ and $135°$ with positive x-axis respectively. The average acceleration of the particle during $t = 1$ to $t = 2s$

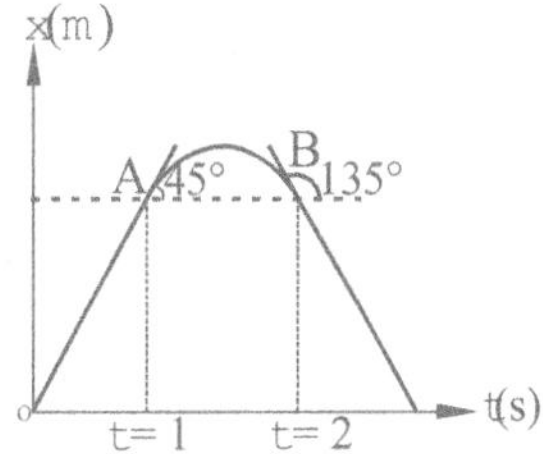

    (a) $-2\ m/s^2$
    (b) $1\ m/s^2$
    (c) $-1\ m/s^2$
    (d) zero

Answer	26	(b)	27	(c)	28	(d)	29	(a)	30	(a)	31	(b)
Key	32	(b)	33	(d)	34	(d)	35	(d)	36	(a)		

37. The position-time relation of a particle moving along the x-axis is given by $x = a - bt + ct^2$ where a, b and c are positive numbers. The velocity-time graph of the particle is

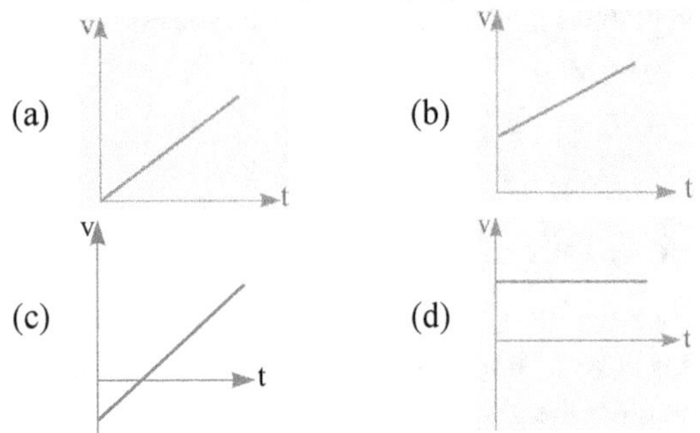

38. A particle starts from rest at $t = 0$ and moves in a straight line with an acceleration as shown below. The velocity of the particle at $t = 3$s is

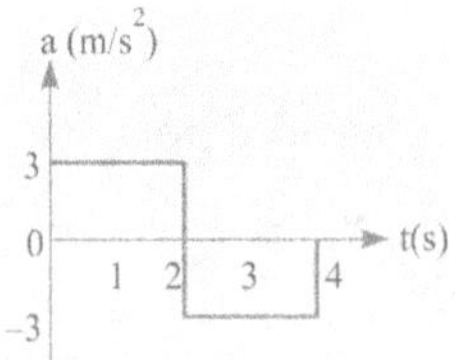

(a) 2 m/s   (b) 3 m/s

(c) 4 m/s   (d) 6 m/s

39. Acceleration-time graph of a body is shown. The corresponding velocity-time graph of the same body is:

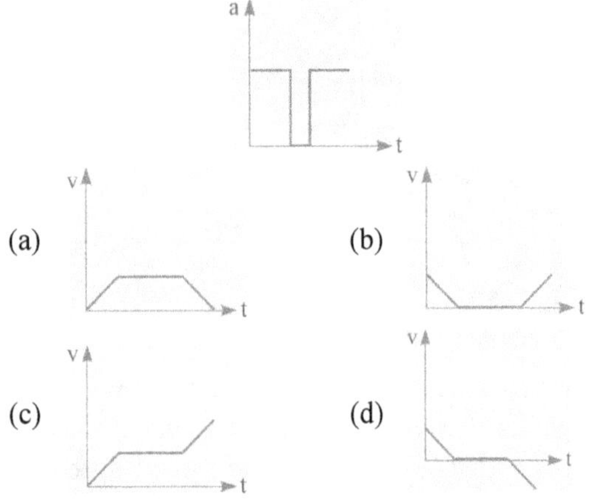

40. A batsman hits a sixer and the ball reaches out of the cricket ground. Which of the following graphs describes the variation of the cricket ball's vertical velocity v with time t_1 (the time of hitting the bat and time t_2 (the time of touching the ground)?   **[AMU B.Tech. -2007]**

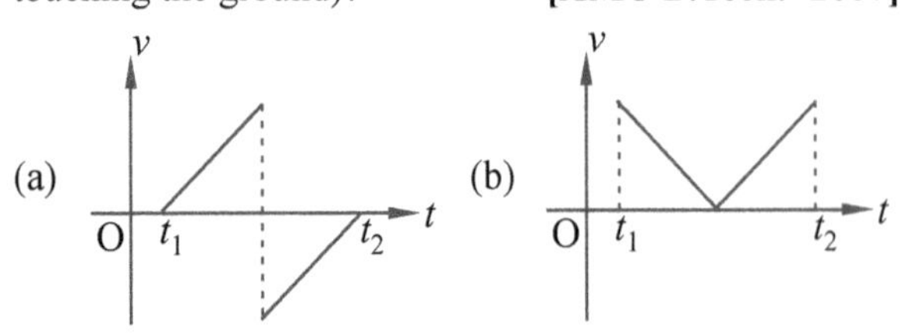

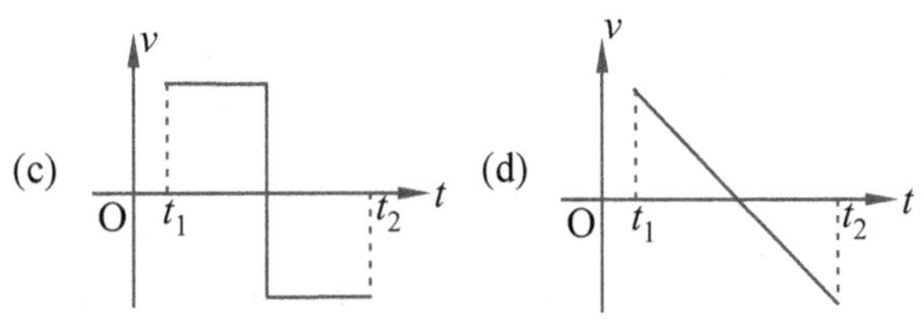

41. The graph of displacement vs time is

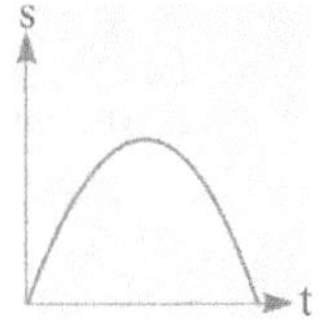

Its corresponding velocity – time graph will be

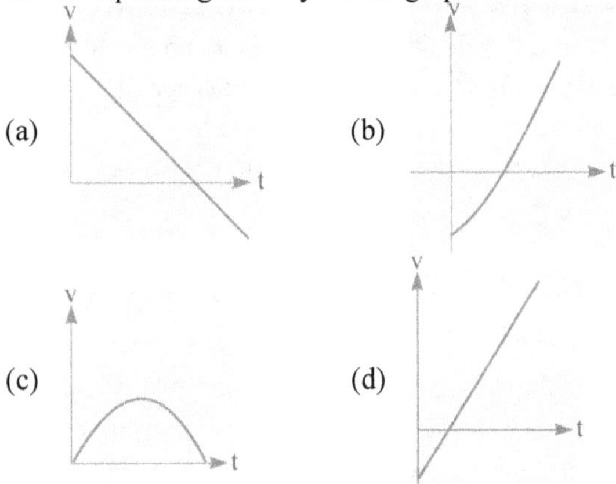

42. An object is moving with a uniform acceleration which is parallel to its instantaneous direction of motion. The displacement(s)–velocity (v) graph of this object is:

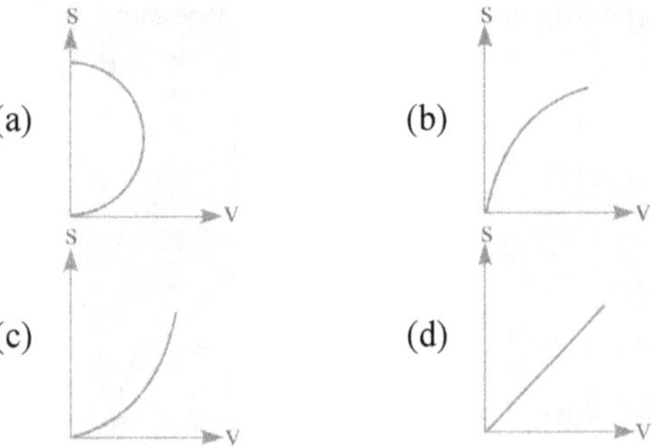

43. A graph between the square of the velocity of a particle and the distance moved is shown in the figure. The acceleration of the particle in kilometer per hour squared is

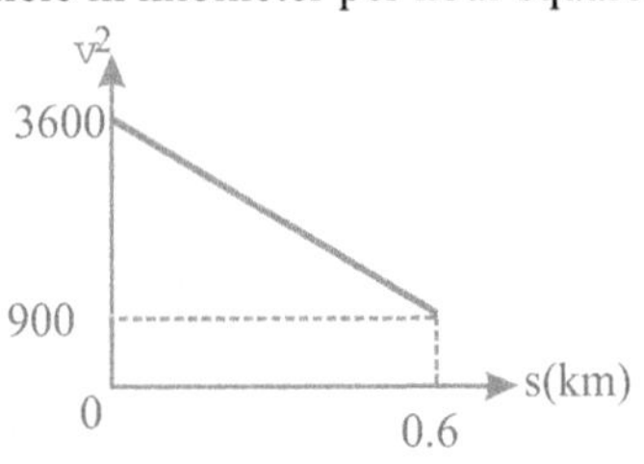

(a) 2250   (b) 22.5

(c) – 2250   (d) 225

Answer	37	(c)	38	(b)	39	(c)	40	(d)
Key	41	(b)	42	(c)	43	(c)		

44. The velocity-time graph of a body is shown in figure. The slope of the line is 'm'. The distance travels by body in time $T\,s$

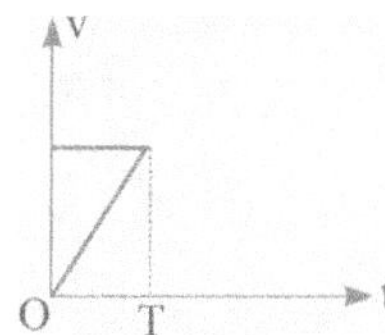

(a) $\dfrac{mv^2}{2T}$

(b) $\dfrac{v^2}{2T}$

(c) $2mv^2$

(d) $\dfrac{v^2}{2m}$

45. A particle starts from rest at $t = 0$ and undergoes an acceleration a in ms^{-2} with time t in seconds which is as shown

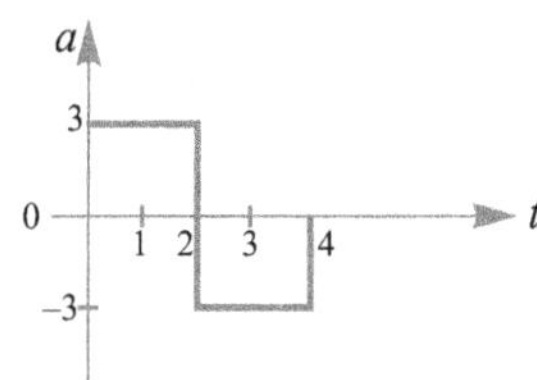

Which one of the following plot represents velocity v in ms^{-1} versus time t in seconds

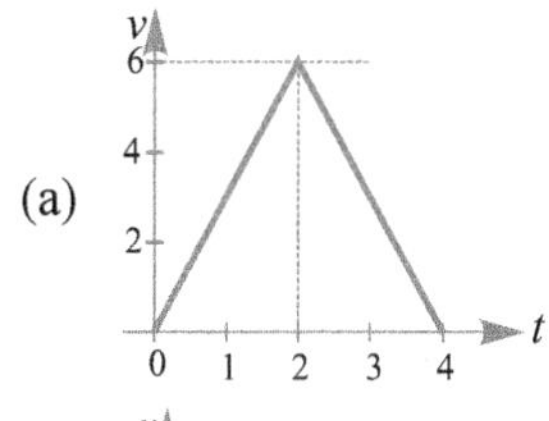

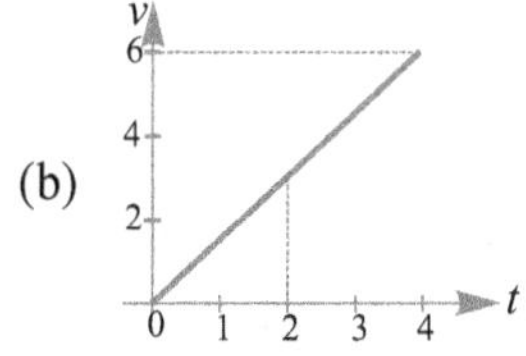

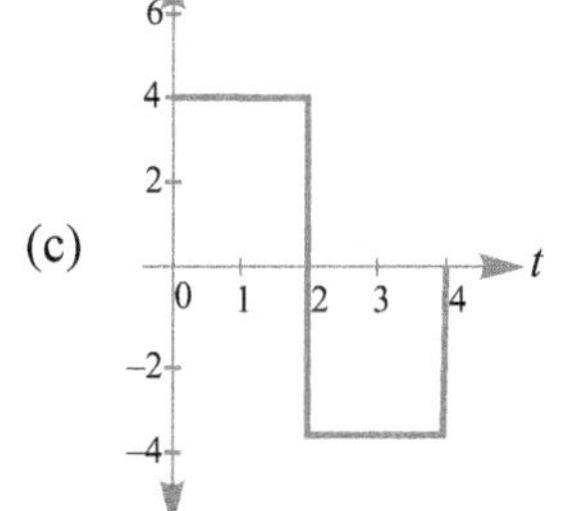

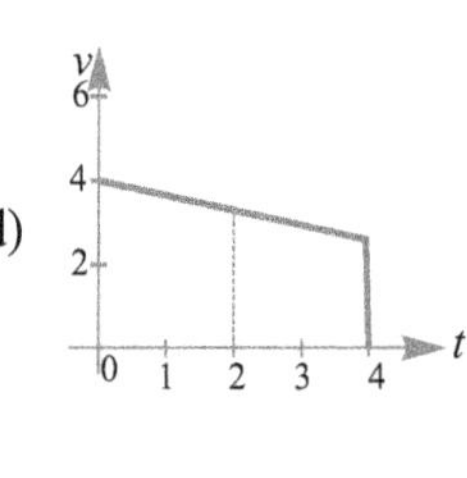

Relative Motion

46. Two trains A and B, each of length 100 m, are running on parallel tracks. One overtakes the other in 20 s and one crosses the other in 10 s. The velocity of trains are :

(a) 5 m/s, 5 m/s

(b) 10 m/s, 15 m/s

(c) 15 m/s, 5 m/s

(d) 15 m/s, 30 m/s

47. Two trains, each 50 m long are travelling in opposite direction with velocity 10 m/s and 15 m/s. The time of crossing is

(a) 2s

(b) 4s

(c) $2\sqrt{3}s$

(d) $4\sqrt{3}s$

48. A massless string of length l passes over a frictionless pulley whose axis is horizontal. Two monkeys hang from the ends of the string at the same distance $\ell/2$ from the pulley, the monkeys start climbing upward simultaneously. First monkey climbs with a speed v relative to the string and the second with a speed $2v$. Both monkeys have equal masses. Then the time taken by the first and second monkey is meeting each other are respectively

(a) $\dfrac{\ell}{3v}$ and $\dfrac{\ell}{3v}$

(b) $\dfrac{\ell}{2v}$ and $\dfrac{\ell}{4v}$

(c) $\dfrac{\ell}{4v}$ and $\dfrac{\ell}{2v}$

(d) $\dfrac{\ell}{v}$ and $\dfrac{\ell}{2v}$

49. A ball A is thrown up vertically with a speed u and at the same instant another ball B is released from a height h. At time t, the speed of A relative of B is

(a) u

(b) 2u

(c) $u - 2gt$

(d) $\sqrt{(u^2 - gt)}$

50. An elevator is moving upward with a constant speed of 10 m/s. A man standing in the elevator drops a coin from a height of 2.5 m, the coin reaches the floor of the elevator after a time $(g = 10$ m/s$^2)$:

(a) $\dfrac{1}{2}$ s

(b) $\dfrac{1}{\sqrt{2}}$ s

(c) $\sqrt{2}$ s

(d) 2s

51. Two trains A and B, each of length 400 m, are moving on two parallel tracks in the same direction (with A ahead of B) with same speed 72 km/h. The driver of B decided to overtake A and accelerates by 1 m/s^2. If after 50s, B just brushes part A, calculate the original distance between A and B : **[AMU B.Tech.-2012]**

(a) 750 m

(b) 100 m

(c) 1250 m

(d) 2250 m

Answer	44	(d)	45	(a)	46	(c)	47	(b)
Key	48	(a)	49	(c)	50	(b)	51	(c)

Average Velocity, Motion with Constant Acceleration

1. An electron moving along the x axis has a position given by $x = 20t\, e^{-t}$ m, where t is in second. How far is the electron from the origin when it momentarily stop ?

(a) 20 m

(b) $20\, e$ m

(c) $\dfrac{20}{e}$ m

(d) zero

2. A stone is dropped from a height h, simultaneously another stone is thrown up from the ground which at a height $4h$, the two stones cross each other after time

(a) $\sqrt{\dfrac{h}{2g}}$

(b) $\sqrt{\dfrac{h}{8g}}$

(c) $\sqrt{8hg}$

(d) $\sqrt{2hg}$

3. A drunkard walking in a narrow lane takes 5 steps forward and 3 steps backward, followed again by 5 steps forward and 3 steps backward, and so on. Each step is 1 m long and requires 1 s. The time when he will fall into the pit 13 m away from him is :

(a) 13 s

(b) 37 s

(c) 40 s

(d) 42 s

4. A car moves on a straight track from station A to the station B, with an acceleration $a = (b - cx)$, where b and c are constants and x is the distance from station A. The maximum velocity between the two stations is

(a) $b/\sqrt{c}$

(b) b/c

(c) $c/\sqrt{a}$

(d) $\sqrt{b}/c$

5. Balls are thrown vertically upward in such a way that the next ball is thrown when the previous one is at the maximum height. If the maximum height is 4.9 m, the number of balls thrown per minute will be :

(a) 60

(b) 40

(c) 50

(d) 120

6. Four persons K, L, M and N are initially at the corners of a square of side of length d. If every person starts moving with velocity v, such that K is always headed towards L, L towards M, M is headed directly towards N and N towards K, then the four persons will meet after :

(a) $\dfrac{d}{v}$ sec

(b) $\dfrac{\sqrt{2}d}{v}$ sec

(c) $\dfrac{d}{\sqrt{2}v}$ sec

(d) $\dfrac{d}{2v}$ sec

7. A particle moves with a velocity $(3i + 4j)$ m/s from origin. The displacement of particle along line $x = y$ after two seconds will be:

(a) 10 m

(b) $\dfrac{7}{\sqrt{2}}$

(c) $7\sqrt{2}$ m

(d) none of these

8. A target is made of two plates, one of wood and the other of iron. The thickness of the wooden plate is 4 cm and that of iron plate is 2 cm. A bullet fired goes through the wood first and then penetrates 1 cm into iron. A similar bullet fired with the same velocity from opposite direction goes through iron first and then penetrates 2 cm into wood. If a_1 and a_2 be the retardations offered to the bullet by wood and iron plates respectively, then

(a) $a_1 = 2a_2$

(b) $a_2 = 2a_1$

(c) $a_1 = a_2$

(d) data insufficient

9. A parachutist after bailing out falls 50 m without friction. When parachute opens, it decelerates at 2 m/s^2. He reaches the ground with a speed of 3 m/s. At what height, did he bail out :

(a) 111 m

(b) 293 m

(c) 182 m

(d) 91 m

Motion with Variable Acceleration

10. Starting from rest a particle moves in a straight line with acceleration $a = \{2 + |t - 2|\}$ m/s^2. Velocity of particle at the end of 4 s will be

(a) 16 m/s

(b) 20 m/s

(c) 8 m/s

(d) 12 m/s

Graphical Questions

11. An experiment on the take-off performance of an aeroplane shown that the acceleration varies as shown in the figure, and that 12 s to take-off from a rest position. The distance along the runway covered by the aeroplane is

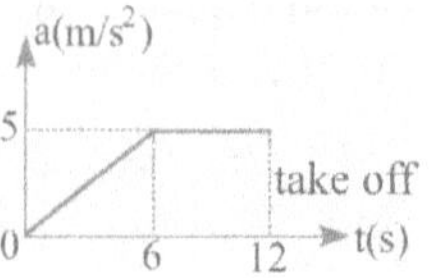

(a) 210 m

(b) 2100 m

(c) 21000 m

(d) none

Answer	1	(c)	2	(b)	3	(b)	4	(a)	5	(a)	6	(a)
Key	7	(c)	8	(b)	9	(b)	10	(d)	11	(a)		

12. The displacement of a body is given to be proportional to the cube of time elapsed. The velocity-time graph of motion of the body is:

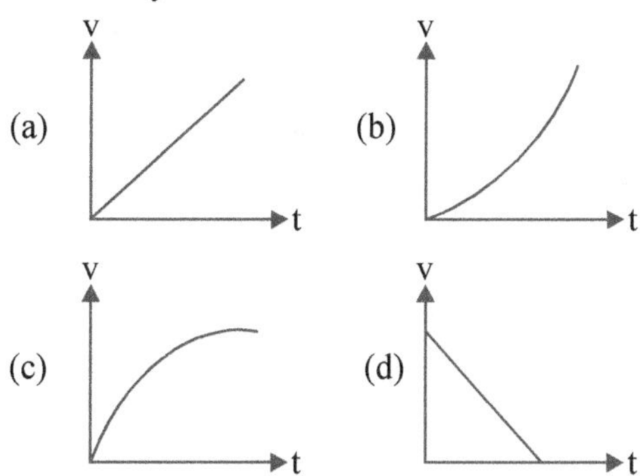

13. A ball is thrown horizontally from a height with a certain velocity at time $t = 0$. The ball bounces repeatedly from the ground with coefficient of restitution less than 1 as shown. Neglecting air resistance and taking the upward direction as positive, which figure qualitatively depits the vertical component of the balls velocity (v_y) as a function of time (t) : **[KVPY -2013]**

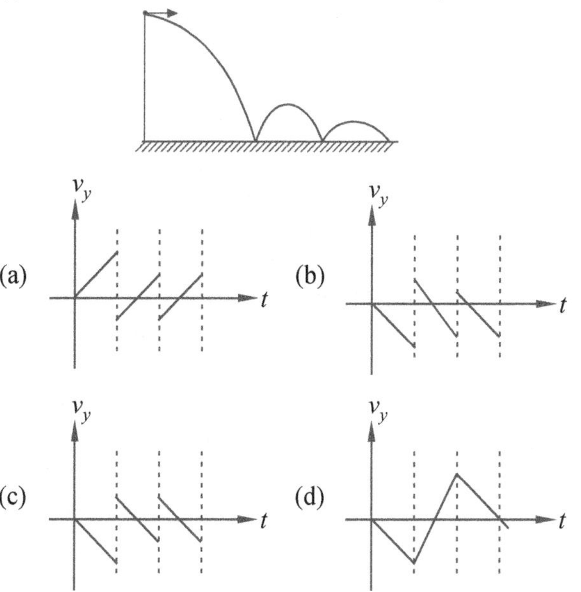

14. A ball is dropped vertically from a height d above the ground. It hits the ground and bounces up vertically to a height $d/2$. Neglecting subsequent motion and air resistance. Its velocity v varies with height h above the ground as

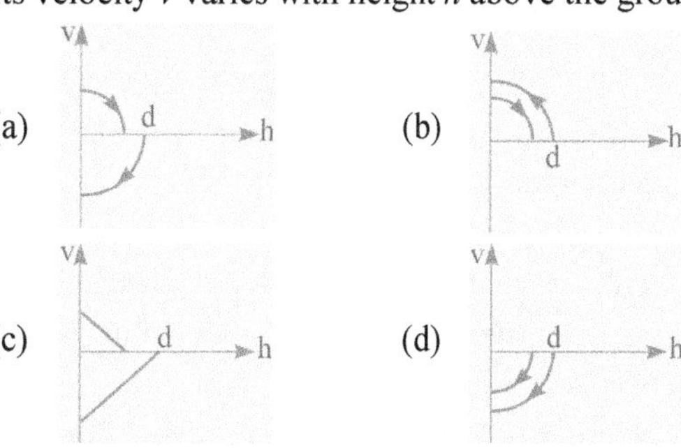

Relative Motion

15. A person walks up a stalled escalator in 90 s. When standing on the same escalator, now moving, he is carried in 60 s. The time it would take him to walk up the moving escalator will be

(a) 27 s (b) 72 s
(c) 18 s (d) 36 s

16. On a two lane road, car A is travelling with a speed of 36 km/h. Two cars B and C approach car A in opposite directions with a speed of 54 km/h each. At a certain instant, when the distance AB is equal to AC, both 1 km B decided to overtake A before C does. The minimum acceleration of car B is required to avoid an accident is

(a) 5 m/s^2 (b) 4 m/s^2
(c) 2 m/s^2 (d) 1 m/s^2

17. A car, starting from rest, accelerates at the rate f through a distance s, then continuous at constant speed for time t and then decelerates at the rate $\dfrac{f}{2}$ come to rest. If the total distance traversed is 5 s, then :

(a) $s = \dfrac{1}{4} ft^2$ (b) $s = \dfrac{1}{2} ft^2$

(c) $s = \dfrac{1}{6} ft^2$ (d) $s = ft$

Answer	12	(b)	13	(b)	14	(a)	15	(b)	16	(d)
Key	17	(b)								

| Mechanics | **MCQ Type 2** | **Exercise 3.2** |

MULTIPLE CORRECT OPTIONS

1. A particle in one-dimensional motion. Choose the correct

(a) with zero speed at an instant may have non-zero acceleration at that instant

(b) with zero speed may have non-zero velocity

(c) with constant speed must have zero acceleration

(d) with positive value of acceleration must be speeding up

2. The position-time (x–t) graphs for two children A and B returning from their school O to their homes P and Q respectively are shown in figure. Choose the correct(s) answers

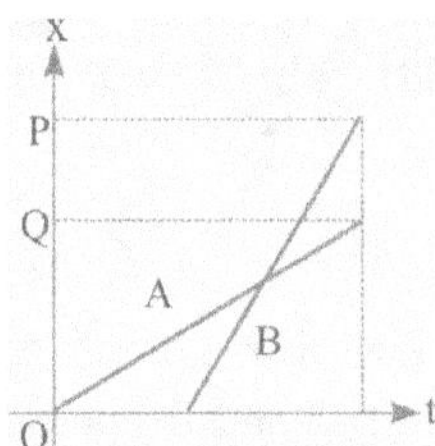

(a) A lives closer to the school than B

(b) A starts from the school at earlier than B

(c) A move faster than B

(d) A and B reach home at same time.

3. Let $\vec{v}$ and $\vec{a}$ denote the velocity and acceleration respectively of a body. Select the wrong statement(s)?

(a) $\vec{a}$ can be non zero when $\vec{v} = 0$.

(b) $\vec{a}$ must be zero when $\vec{v} = 0$.

(c) $\vec{a}$ may be zero when $\vec{v} \neq 0$

(d) the direction of $\vec{a}$ must have some correlation with the direction of $\vec{v}$.

4. Let $\vec{v}$ and $\vec{a}$ denote the velocity and acceleration respectively of a body in one-dimensional motion. Select the wrong statements?

(a) $|\vec{v}|$ must decreases when $\vec{a} < 0$

(b) speed must increase when > 0

(c) speed will increases when both $\vec{v}$ and $\vec{a}$ are < 0

(d) speed will decrease when $\vec{v} < 0$ and $\vec{a} > 0$.

5. Pick the correct statements:

(a) average speed of a particle in a given time is never less than the magnitude of the average velocity

(b) It is possible to have a situation in which $\left|\dfrac{d\vec{v}}{dt}\right| \neq 0$ but $\dfrac{d|\vec{v}|}{dt} = 0$

(c) The average velocity of a particle is zero in a time interval. It is possible that the instantaneous velocity is never zero in the interval

(d) The average velocity of a particle moving on a straight line is zero in a time interval. It is possible that the instantaneous velocity is never zero in the interval, (infinite accelerations are not allowed).

6. Consider the motion of the tip of the minute hand of a clock, in one hour:

(a) the displacement is zero

(b) the distance covered is zero

(c) the average speed is zero

(d) the average velocity is zero.

7. The motion of a body is given by the equation $\dfrac{dv(t)}{dt} = 6.0 - 3v(t)$, where $v(t)$ is speed in m/s and t in sec. If body was at rest at $t = 0$

(a) The terminal speed is 2.0 m/s

(b) The speed varies with the time as $v(t) = 2(-e^{-3t})$ m/s

(c) The speed is 0.1 m/s when the acceleration is half the initial value

(d) The magnitude of the initial acceleration is 6.0 m/s^2.

8. A particle of mass m moves on the x-axis as follows: It starts from rest at $t = 0$ from the point $x = 0$, and come to rest at $t = 1$ at the point $x = 1$. No other information is available about its motion at intermediate times $[0 \leq t \leq 1]$. If α denotes the instantaneous acceleration of the particle, then

(a) α cannot remain positive for all t in the interval 0 to 1

(b) $|\alpha|$ cannot exceed 2 at any point in its path

(c) $|\alpha|$ must be ≥ 4 at some point or points in its path

(d) α must change sign during the motion, but no other assertion can be made with the given information.

9. The figure shows the velocity (v) of a particle plotted against time (t):

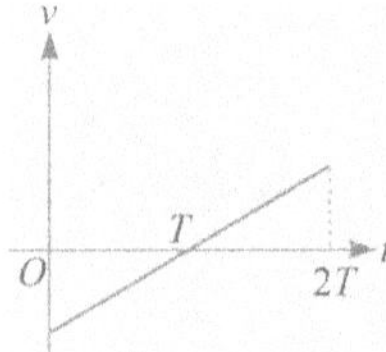

(a) The particle changes its direction of motion at some point

(b) The acceleration of the particle remains constant.

(c) The displacement of the particle is zero

(d) The initial and final speed of the particle are the same.

| Answer | 1 | (a,c, d) | 2 | (a, b, d) | 3 | (b,c,d) | 4 | (a, b, d) | 5 | (a, b) |
| Key | 6 | (a, d) | 7 | (a, b, d) | 8 | (a, c) | 9 | (a, b, c, d) | | |

10. The velocity of a particle is zero at $t = 0$
    (a) the acceleration may be zero at $= 0$
    (b) the acceleration must be zero at $= 0$
    (c) if the acceleration is zero from $t = 0$ to $t = 2s$, the speed is also zero in this interval.
    (d) if the speed is zero from $t = 0$ to $t = 2s$, the acceleration is also zero in this interval.

11. The speed versus time graph are shown in figure. Which graph(s) are possible:

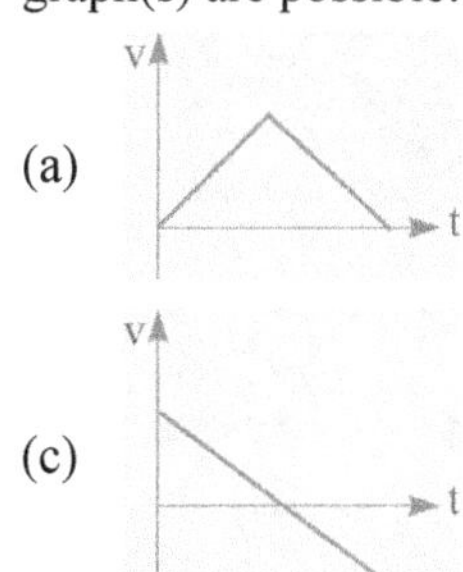

12. A body falls from some height. The velocity displacement graph is best represent in

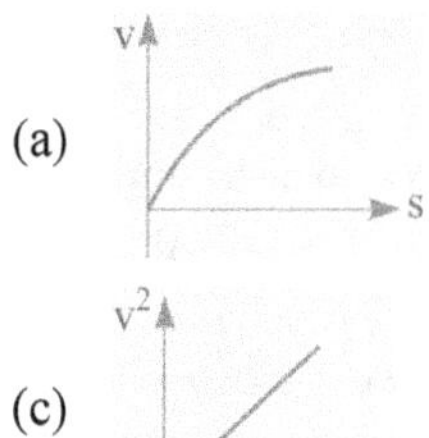
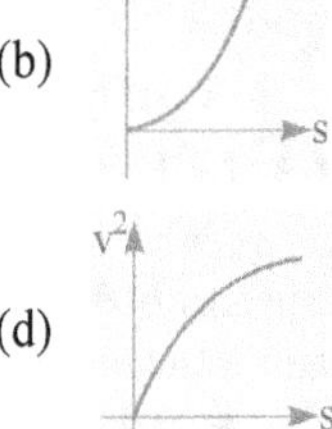

Answer Key	10	(a, c, d)	11	(a, b, d)	12	(a, c)		

Read the following questions and give your answer using the following options (a, b, c and d) :

(a) **Statement - 1** is true, **Statement - 2** is true; **Statement - 2** is correct explanation for **Statement - 1**.

(b) **Statement - 1** is true; **Statement - 2** is true; **Statement - 2** is not correct explanation for **Statement - 1**.

(c) **Statement - 1** is true, **Statement - 2** is false.

(d) **Statement - 1** is false, **Statement - 2** is true.

1. **Statement - 1**

   The average and instantaneous velocities have same value in a uniform motion.

   Statement - 2

   In uniform motion, the velocity of an object increases uniformly.

2. **Statement - 1**

   A body may be accelerated even when it is moving uniformly.

   Statement - 2

   When direction of motion of the body is changing, the body must have acceleration.

3. **Statement - 1**

   The average velocity of the object over an interval of time is either smaller than or equal to the average speed of the object over the same interval.

   Statement - 2

   Velocity is a vector quantity and speed is a scalar quantity.

4. **Statement - 1**

   A body, whatever its motion is always at rest in a frame of reference which is fixed to the body itself.

   Statement - 2

   The relative velocity of a body with respect to itself is zero.

5. **Statement - 1**

   A body can have acceleration even if its velocity is zero at a given instant of time.

   Statement - 2

   A body is momentarily at rest when it reverses its direction of motion.

6. **Statement - 1**

   For a non-uniform motion the magnitude of instantaneous velocity is equal to instantaneous speed.

   Statement - 2

   A particle in nonuniform motion may move along a curved path.

7. **Statement - 1**

   For one dimensional motion the angle between acceleration and velocity must be zero.

   Statement - 2

   One dimensional motion is always on a straight line.

8. **Statement - 1**   **[IIT-JEE-2008]**

   For an observer looking out through the window of a fast moving train, the nearby objects appear to move in the opposite direction to the train, while the distant objects appear stationary.

Statement - 2

If the observer and the object are moving at velocities $\vec{v}_1$ and $\vec{v}_2$ respectively with reference to a laboratory frame, the velocity of the object with respect to the observer is $\vec{v}_2 - \vec{v}_1$.

(a) Statement - 1 is true, Statement - 2 is true; Statement - 2 is correct explanation for Statement - 1.

(b) Statement -1 is true, Statement - 1 is true; Statement - 2 is not correct explanation for Statement - 1.

(c) Statement - 1 is true, Statement - 2 is false.

(d) Statement - 1 is false, Statement - 2 is true.

Answer	1	(c)	2	(a)	3	(a)	4	(a)
Key	5	(a)	6	(b)	7	(d)	8	(b)

Mechanics   **Passage & Matrix**   **Exercise 3.4**

Passage for Questions. 1 to 3 :

From the top of a multi-storeyed building, 39.2 m tall, a boy projects a stone vertically upwards with an initial velocity of 9.8 m/s such that it finally drops to the ground.

1. The stone reach the ground in
     (a) 1 s   (b) 4 s
     (c) 2 s   (d) 3 s

2. The stone will pass through the point of projection
     (a) 2 s   (b) 3 s
     (c) 4 s   (d) 5 s

3. The velocity before striking the ground is
   (Take $g = 10$ m/s^2)
     (a) 14.2 m/s   (b) 22.4 m/s
     (c) 29.4 m/s   (d) 34.2 m/s

Passage for Questions. 4 to 6 :

The velocity-time graph of a body moving along a straight line is given below.

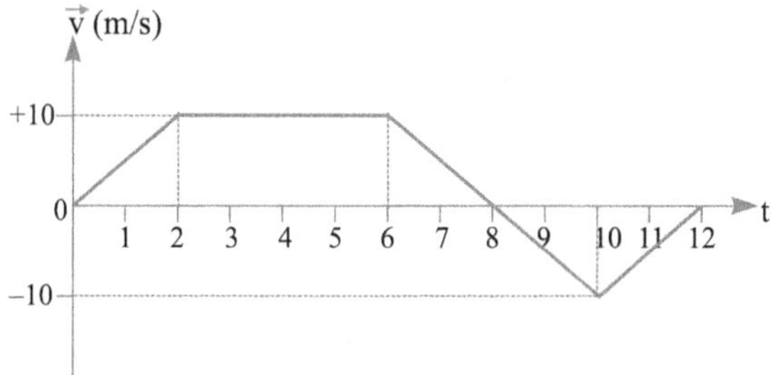

4. Average velocity in whole time of motion is
     (a) 2.22 m/s   (b) 3.33 m/s
     (c) 4.32 m/s   (d) zero

5. Average speed in whole time of motion is
     (a) 3.33 m/s   (b) 4.44 m/s
     (c) 6.67 m/s   (d) zero

6. The acceleration from 10 to 12 s is
     (a) 5 m/s^2 (b) 10 m/s^2
     (c) 12 m/s^2 (d) zero

7. $\vec{s}, \vec{v}, \vec{a}$ represent displacement, velocity and acceleration; t the time, then match the columns :

Column I	Column II
A. Zero velocity	(p)
B. Constant velocity	(q)

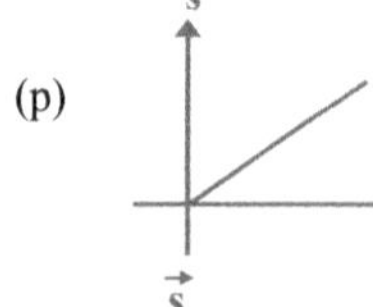

C. Constant acceleration   (r)

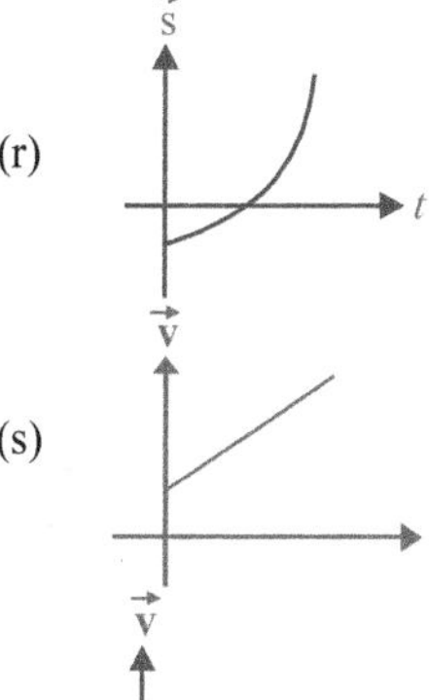

(s)

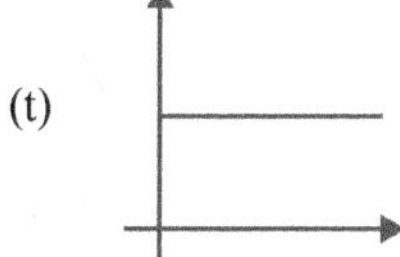

(t)

8. Column I gives a list of possible set of parameters measured in some experiments. The variations of the parameters in the form of graphs are shown in column II. Match the set of parameters given in Column I with the graphs given in Column II.

Column I		Column II
A.	Potential energy of a simple pendulum (y-axis) as a function of displacement (x-axis).	(p)

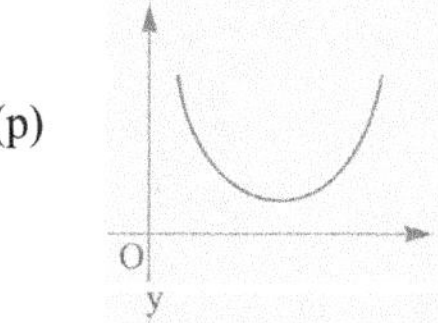

| B. | Displacement (y-axis) as a function of time (x-axis) for one dimensional motion at zero or constant acceleration when the body is moving along the positive x-direction. | (q) |

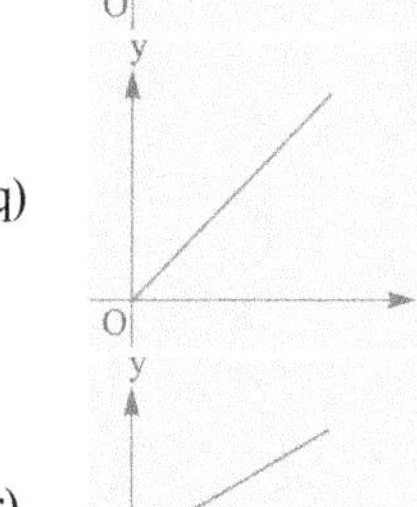

| C. | Range of a projectile (y-axis) as a function of its velocity (x-axis) when projected at a fixed angle. | (r) |

| D. | The square of the time period (y-axis) of a simple pendulum as a function of its length (x-axis) | (s) |

9. A particle is going along a straight line with constant acceleration a, having initial velocity u. Then the match the columns :

Column I		Column II
A.	$u = +$ ve and $a = +$ ve	(p)

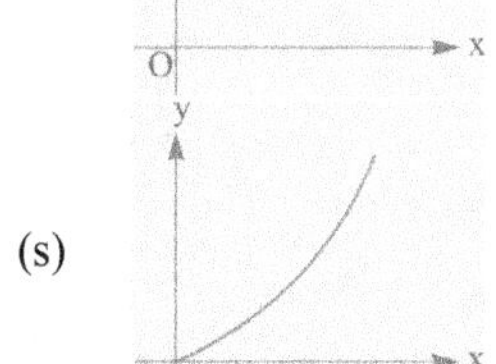

| B. | $u = -$ ve, and $a = +$ ve | (q) |

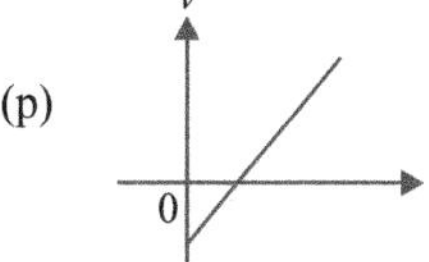

| C. | $u = +$ ve, and $a = -$ ve | (r) |

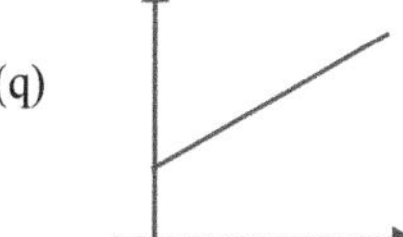

D. $u = -$ ve, and $a = -$ ve   (s)

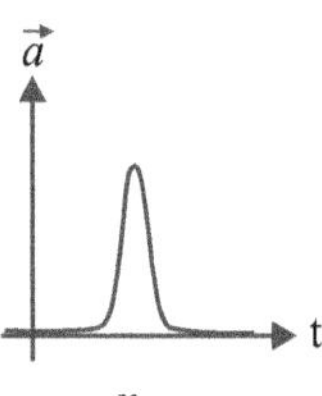

10. Column I gives some physical situation and Column II, the graphical representation. Match the columns.

Column I   **Column II**

A.   A ball hits the wall and return back and then stops. (p)

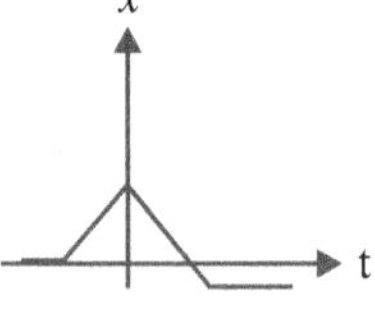

B.   A ball thrown upward and rebound again and   (q)
     again with an inelastic collision

C.   A cricket ball hits by a bat.   (r)

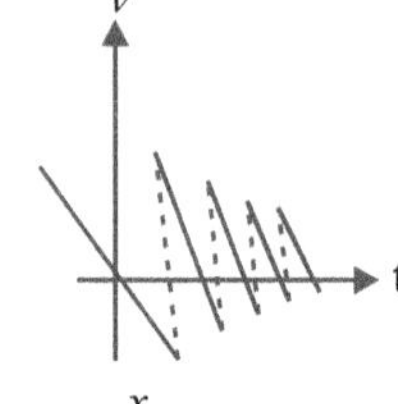

D.   A particle start moving with constant acceleration. (s)

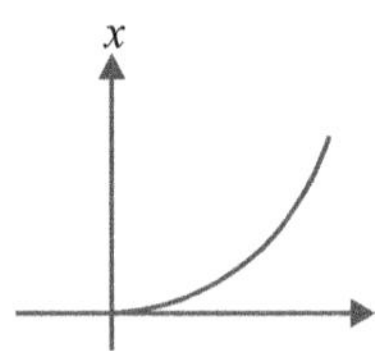

Answer Key	1	(b)	2	(a)	3	(c)	4	(b)	5	(c)	6	(a)
	7	A → q ; B → p, t ; C → r, s.					8	A → (p); B → (q, s); C → (s) ; D → (q)				
	9	A → q ; B → p ; C → s ; D → r					10	A → p ; B → r ; C → q ; D → s				

Mechanics   Best of JEE-(Main & Advanced)   Exercise 3.5

JEE- (Main)

1. A ball is thrown from a point with a speed $'v_0'$ at an elevation angle of θ. From the same point and at the same instant, a person starts running with a constant speed $\dfrac{'v_0'}{2}$ to catch the ball. Will the person be able to catch the ball? If yes, what should be the angle of projection θ ?

[AIEEE 2004]

(a) No   (b) Yes, 30°
(c) Yes, 60°   (d) Yes, 45°

2. A body is released from the top of a tower of height h. It takes t sec to reach the ground. Where will be the ball after time $t/2$ sec   [AIEEE -2004]

(a) at $h/2$ from the ground
(b) at h/4 from the ground
(c) depends upon mass and volume of the body
(d) at 3h/4 from the ground

3. The relation between time t and distance x is $t = \alpha x^2 + \beta x$ where α and β are constants. The retardation

[AIEEE -2005]

(a) $2 \alpha v^3$ (b) $2 \beta v^3$
(c) $2 \alpha\beta v^3$ (d) $2 \beta^3 v^3$

where v is the velocity

4. The velocity of a particle is $v = v_0 + gt + ft^2$. If its position is $x = 0$ at $t = 0$, then its displacement after unit time ($t = 1$) is **[AIEEE 2007]**

(a) $v_0 + g/2 + f$ (b) $v_0 + 2g + 3f$

(c) $v_0 + g/2 + f/3$ (d) $v_0 + g + f$

5. A body is at rest at $x = 0$. At $t = 0$, it starts moving in the positive x-direction with a constant acceleration. At the same instant another body passes through $x = 0$ moving in the positive x-direction with a constant speed. The position of the first body is given by $x_1(t)$ after time t and that of the second body $x_2(t)$ after the same time interval. Which of the following graphs correctly describes $(x_1 - x_2)$ as a function of time t? **[AIEEE -2008]**

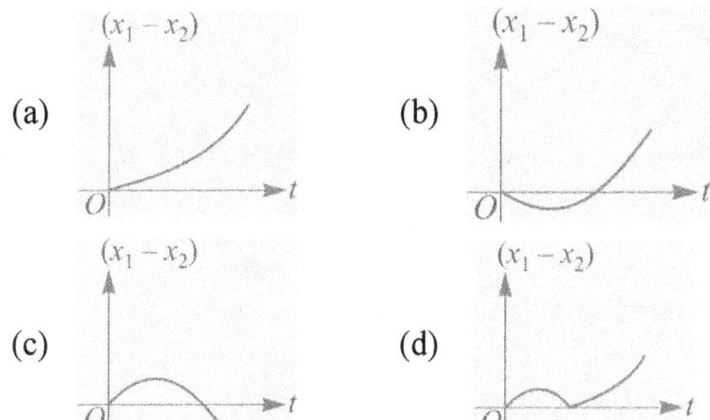

6. Consider a rubber ball freely falling from a height $h = 4.9$ m onto a horizontal elastic plate. Assume that the duration of collision is negligible and the collision with the plate is totally elastic. Then the velocity as a function of time and the height as a function of time will be : **[AIEEE 2009]**

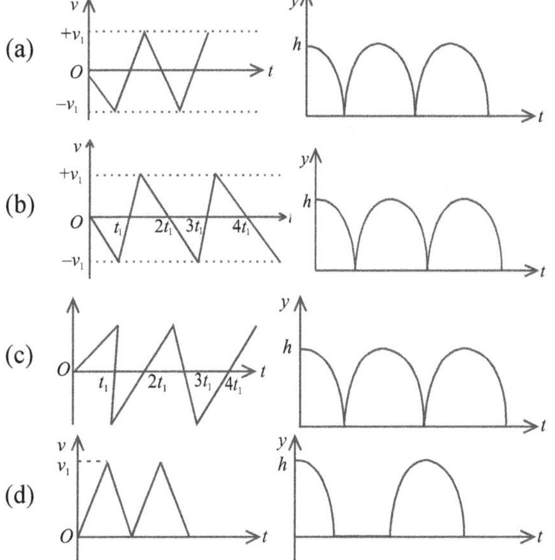

JEE- (Advanced)

7. The given graph shows the variation of velocity with displacement. Which one of the graph given below correctly represents the variation of acceleration with displacement. **[IIT-JEE 2005]**

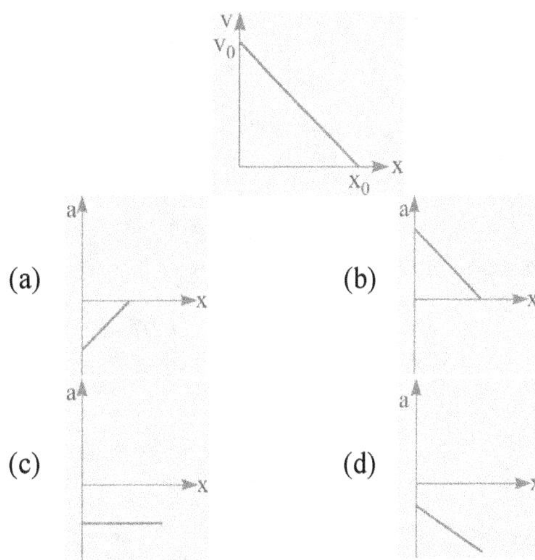

8. Two identical discs of same radius R are rotating about their axes in opposite directions with the same constant angular speed ω. The discs are in the same horizontal plane. At time $t = 0$, the points P and Q are facing each other as shown in the figure. The relative speed between the two points P and Q is v_r. In one time period (T) of rotation of the discs, v_r as a function of time is best represented by

[IIT-JEE 2012]

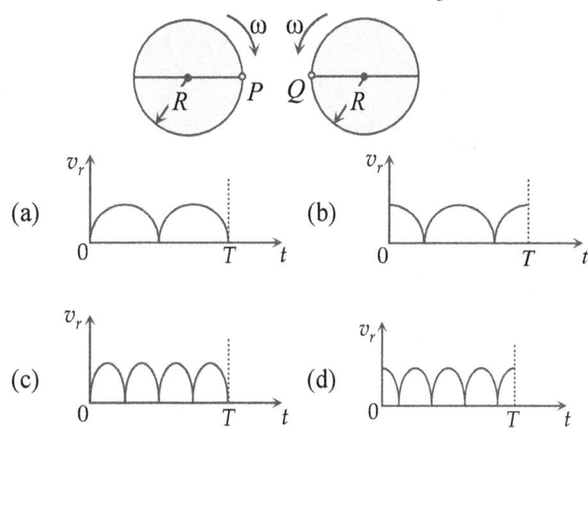

Answer	1	(c)	2	(d)	3	(a)	4	(c)
Key	5	(b)	6	(b)	7	(a)	8	(a)

Hints & Solutions

In Chapter Exercise -3.1

1. Given,
$$t = \sqrt{\frac{x - 50t}{10}}$$

or
$$x = 50t + 10t^2$$

Instantaneous velocity,
$$v = \frac{dx}{dt} = 50 + 20t$$

The average velocity,

$$\bar{v} = \frac{\int_0^3 v\,dt}{3} = \frac{\int_0^3 (50 + 20t)\,dt}{3}$$

$$= \frac{1}{3}\left| 50t + \frac{20t^2}{2} \right|_0^3$$

$$= 80 \text{ m/s} \qquad \textbf{\textit{Ans.}}$$

2. Starting from $t = 0$ the change in velocity in the duration $(t_1 + t_2)$ is equal to $a_1t_1 + a_2t_2$.

Thus average acceleration $= \left[\dfrac{a_1t_1 + a_2t_2}{t_1 + t_2} \right]$ **_Ans._**

3. Given,
$$200 = u \times 2 + \frac{1}{2} a \times 2^2$$

and
$$(200 + 200) = u \times (2 + 4) + \frac{1}{2} a (2 + 4)^2$$

After solving above equations, we get
$$u = 115 \text{ cm/s}, \ a = -15 \text{ cm/s}^2$$
$$\therefore \qquad v = u + at = 115 - 15 \times 7 = 10 \text{ cm/s}$$
$$\textbf{\textit{Ans.}}$$

4. If a_1 is the retardation, then
$$15^2 = 30^2 - 2a_1 \times 1$$
$$\Rightarrow \qquad a_1 = \frac{675}{2} \text{ km/h}^2$$

If a_2 is the acceleration, then
$$30^2 = 15^2 + 2a_2 \times 0.5$$
$$\Rightarrow \qquad a_2 = 675 \text{ km/h}^2$$

Time taken
$$t_1 = \frac{v - u}{a_1} = \frac{15}{675/2} = \frac{30}{675} \text{ h}$$

and
$$t_2 = \frac{v - u}{a_2} = \frac{15}{675} \text{ h}$$

Total time taken in the journey
$$= t_1 + t_2 = \left(\frac{30 + 15}{675} \right) \times 60 = 4 \text{ min.}$$

Time to be taken in the journey
$$t = \frac{1.5}{30} \times 60 = 3 \text{ min}$$

$$\therefore \qquad \text{Time lost} = 4 - 3 = 1 \text{ min} \qquad \textbf{\textit{Ans.}}$$

5. Suppose body falls from height h from upper point. If t is the time taken to fall h height, then

$$h = \frac{1}{2} gt^2 \qquad \text{...(i)}$$

and $h + 30 = \dfrac{1}{2} g(t + 1)^2$ ...(ii)

After solving equations, we get
$$t = 2.56 \text{ s}, \ h = 32.1 \text{ m} \ \textbf{\textit{Ans.}}$$

6. The situation is shown in figure. If a is the acceleration, then

$$x = \frac{1}{2} at^2 \qquad \text{...(i)}$$

and
$$(x + 60) = \frac{1}{2} a(t + 6)^2 \qquad \text{...(ii)}$$
$$u_A = at, \qquad \text{...(iii)}$$
$$15 = a(t + 6) \qquad \text{...(iv)}$$

After solving above equations, we get
$$u_A = 5 \text{ m/s}, \ a = 1.67 \text{ m/s}^2,$$
$$x = 7.50 \text{ m} \qquad \textbf{\textit{Ans.}}$$

7. It t is the time of motion of first body, then time of motion for second body will be $(t - \tau)$. For meeting of the bodies, their displacement must be equal, so

$$H = v_0 t - \frac{1}{2} gt^2$$

$$= v_0(t - \tau) - \frac{1}{2} g(t - \tau)^2$$

After simplifying, we get, $t = \dfrac{v_0}{g} + \dfrac{\tau}{2}$ **_Ans._**

In Chapter Exercise -3.2

1. Acceleration, $\qquad a = \dfrac{\Delta v}{\Delta t} = \dfrac{-7}{11} = 0.64 \text{ m/s}$

We can write $\qquad \dfrac{dv}{dt} = -0.64$

or $\qquad dv = -0.64 \, dt$

After integrating, we have

$$\int_7^v dv = -0.64 \int_0^t dt$$

$$v - 7 = -0.64 \, t$$

or $\qquad v = 7 - 0.64 \, t \qquad \text{...(i)}$

As $\qquad v = \dfrac{ds}{dt},$

$$\therefore \qquad \frac{ds}{dt} = 7 - 0.64t$$

After integration, we get
$$s = 7t - 0.32t^2 \qquad \text{...(ii)'}]\textbf{\textit{Ans.}}$$

2. Distance $= \dfrac{1}{2} \times 6 \times 20 + \dfrac{1}{2} \times 2 \times 20 + 2 \times 10$

$$= 60 + 20 + 20 = 100 \text{ m}$$

$$\text{Displacement} \;=\; \frac{1}{2}\times 6\times 20 - \frac{1}{2}\times 2\times 20 + 2\times 10$$

$$=\; 60 \text{ m} \qquad \textit{Ans.}$$

3. (i) $\quad$ Distance $=$ area of speed-time graph

$$=\; \frac{1}{2}\times 10\times 12 = 60 \text{ m}$$

(ii) $\quad$ Average speed $=\; \dfrac{\text{distance}}{\text{time}} = \dfrac{60}{10} = 6 \text{ m/s}$

(iii) Clearly 0 and 10 s.

(iv) Clearly 5s.

4. (i) Slope of x–t curve of car C is greatest and so its speed is highest. The speed of car A is lowest one.

(ii) There is no position at which x–t of all the cars intersect.

(iii) When A passes C, car B is 6 km from the origin.

(v) & (vi) $v_A = \dfrac{8}{1.6} = 5$ km/h;

$$v_B = \frac{14}{1.4} = 10 \text{ km/h}; \quad v_C = \frac{12}{1} = 12 \text{ km/h}$$

$$v_{CA} = 12 - 5 = 7 \text{ km/h} \;\text{ and }\; v_{BC} = 10 - 12 = -2 \text{ km/h}.$$

In Chapter Exercise -3.3

1.
$$[v_{\text{gas}}]_{\text{rocket}} \;=\; v_{\text{gas}} - v_{\text{rocket}}$$
$$=\; -1500 - 500 = 2000 \text{ km/h}$$

2.

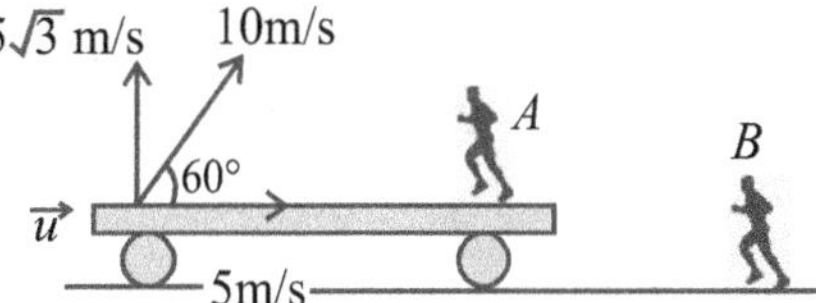

$$\left[\vec{\mathbf{v}}_{\text{gas}}\right]_{\text{jet}} \;=\; \left[\vec{\mathbf{v}}_{\text{gas}}\right]_{g} - \left[\vec{\mathbf{v}}_{\text{jet}}\right]_{g}$$

$$\therefore \qquad \left[\vec{\mathbf{v}}_{\text{gas}}\right]_{g} \;=\; \left[\vec{\mathbf{v}}_{\text{gas}}\right]_{\text{jet}} + \left[\vec{\mathbf{v}}_{\text{jet}}\right]_{g}$$

$$=\; -1200 + 450$$

$$=\; 750 \text{ km/h} \qquad \textit{Ans.}$$

3. If t is the time taken, then

$$\frac{1}{2}\times 2\left(t+5\right)^2 \;=\; 20\,t$$

After solving, $\quad t = 5$ s $\qquad$ *Ans.*

4. (i) $\quad$ Relative speed $=\; \vec{\mathbf{v}}_A - \vec{\mathbf{v}}_B$

$$=\; 60\hat{\mathbf{i}} - 45\hat{\mathbf{i}} = 15\hat{\mathbf{i}} \text{ km/h}$$

(ii) $\quad$ Relative speed $=\; v_A - v_B$

$$=\; 60\hat{\mathbf{i}} - 45\hat{\mathbf{i}} = 15\hat{\mathbf{i}} \text{ km/h}$$

5. The speed of bush A, $\; v_A = \dfrac{480}{8} = 60$ km/h

The speed of bush B, $\; v_B = \dfrac{480}{12} = 40$ km/h

If t is the time of meeting, then

$$v_A t + v_B t \;=\; 480$$

or $\qquad 60t + 40t \;=\; 480$

$$\therefore \qquad t \;=\; 4.8 \text{ h.}$$

The distance travelled by car A in this duration,

$$x_A \;=\; v_A t = 60 \times 4.8$$

$$=\; 288 \text{ km} \qquad \textit{Ans.}$$

6. **5** From the perspective of observer A, considering verti-

cal motion of the ball from the point of throw till it reaches back at the initial height.

$$u_y = +\, 5\sqrt{3} \text{ m/s}, \; s_y = 0$$
$$a_y = -\, 10\text{m/s}^2, \; t = ?$$

Applying $\qquad s \;=\; ut + \dfrac{1}{2}\,at^2$

$$0 \;=\; 5\sqrt{3}\,t - 5t^2$$

$$\therefore \qquad t \;=\; \sqrt{3} \text{ sec}$$

Considering horizontal motion from the perspective of observer B. Let u be the speed of train at the time of throw.

The horizontal distance travelled by the ball
$$=\; (u + 5)\,\sqrt{3}\,.$$

The horizontal distance travelled by the boy

$$=\; \left[u\sqrt{3} + \frac{1}{2}a(\sqrt{3})^2\right] + 1.15$$

As the boy catches the ball therefore

$$(u+5)\sqrt{3} \;=\; u\sqrt{3} + \frac{3}{2}a + 1.15$$

$$\therefore \; 5\sqrt{3} \;=\; 1.5a + 1.15 \quad \therefore \; 7.51 = 1.5a$$

$$\therefore \; a \approx 5 \text{ m/s}^2$$

In Chapter Exercise -3.4

1. Given, $\qquad x \;=\; t^3 - 4t^2 + 3t$

(a) At $\qquad t \;=\; 0, \; x_i = 0$

$t = 4,$ $\qquad x_f = 4^3 - 4\times 4^2 + 3\times 4 = 12$ m

$\therefore$ Displacement $= x_f - x_i = 12$ m

(b) At $\qquad t \;=\; 2\text{s}, \; x_i = 2^3 - 4\times 2^2 + 3\times 2 = -2$

$\qquad\qquad t \;=\; 4\text{s}, \; x_f = 4^3 - 4\times 4^2 + 3\times 4 = 12$

Displacement, $\; s \;=\; x_f - x_i = 12 - (-2) = 14$

Average velocity $\;=\; \dfrac{\text{Displacement}}{\text{time interval}}$

$$=\; \frac{14}{4-2} = 7 \text{ m/s}$$

2. Given $\qquad -\dfrac{dv}{dt} \;=\; a\sqrt{v}$

or $\qquad \dfrac{dv}{\sqrt{v}} \;=\; a\,dt$

or $\qquad \displaystyle\int_{v_0}^{v} v^{-1/2}\,dv \;=\; \int_{0}^{t} (-a)\,dt$

$$\left.\frac{v^{1/2}}{1/2}\right|_{v_0}^{v} \;=\; -\,at$$

$$\sqrt{v} - \sqrt{v_0} \;=\; \frac{-at}{2}$$

$\therefore \qquad \sqrt{v} = \sqrt{v_0} - \dfrac{at}{2} \qquad \text{...(i)}$

For stop, v to be zero i.e.,

$$0 = \sqrt{v_0} - \dfrac{at}{2}$$

$\therefore \qquad t = \dfrac{2\sqrt{v_0}}{a} \qquad$ ***Ans.***

Again from equation (i), we have

$$\dfrac{ds}{dt} = \left(\sqrt{v_0} - \dfrac{at}{2}\right)^2$$

or $\qquad ds = \left(\sqrt{v_0} - \dfrac{at}{2}\right)^2 dt$

On integrating, we get

$$s = \dfrac{\left(\sqrt{v_0} - \dfrac{at}{2}\right)^3}{3 \times \left(\dfrac{-a}{2}\right)} = -\dfrac{2}{3a}\left(\sqrt{v_0} - \dfrac{at}{2}\right)^3$$

At $\qquad t = \dfrac{2\sqrt{v_0}}{a},$

$$s = \dfrac{-2}{3a}\left(\sqrt{v_0} - \dfrac{a2\sqrt{v_0}}{a}\right)^3$$

$$= \left(\dfrac{2}{3a}\right)v_0^{3/2} \qquad \text{***Ans.***}$$

3.   Suppose particles are moving mutually perpendicular, so that

$$\vec{v}_{21} = \vec{v}_2 - \vec{v}_1$$

$$v_{21} = \sqrt{v_1^2 + v_2^2} = v \qquad \text{...(i)}$$

The distance between them at any instant

$$x^2 = (a - v_1 t)^2 + (v_2 t)^2 \qquad \text{...(ii)}$$

After differentiation, we get

$$2x\dfrac{dx}{dt} = 2(a - v_1 t) \times (-v_1) + 2v_2 t \times v_2$$

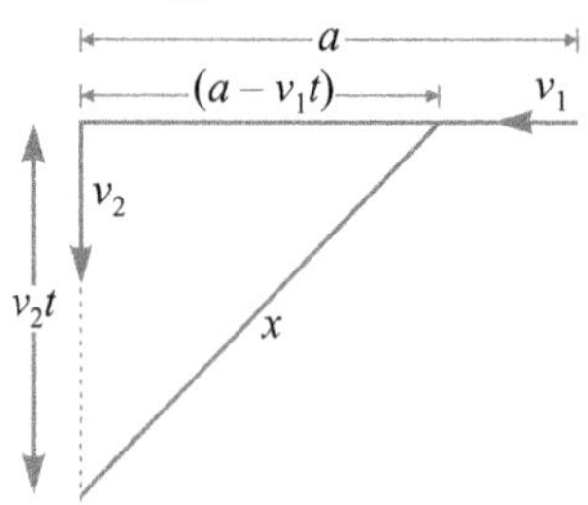

For x to be minimum, $\dfrac{dx}{dt} = 0$,

or $\qquad 0 = 2(a - v_1 t) \times (-v_1) + 2tv_2^2$

$\therefore \qquad t = \dfrac{av_1}{v_1^2 + v_2^2} = \dfrac{av_1}{v} \qquad$ ***Ans.***

After substituting this values in eq. (i), we get

$$x = \dfrac{av_2}{v} \qquad \text{***Ans.***}$$

1. (d) The average speed $= \dfrac{\dfrac{2x}{5} + \dfrac{3x}{5}}{\dfrac{2x/5}{v_1} + \dfrac{3x/5}{v_2}} = \dfrac{5v_1 v_2}{3v_1 + 2v_2}.$

2. (a) Average speed is given by

$$v_{av} = \dfrac{2v_0(v_1 + v_2)}{2v_0 + v_1 + v_2}$$

$$= \dfrac{2 \times 3(4.5 + 7.5)}{(2 \times 3) + 4.5 + 7.5} = 4 \text{ m/s}$$

3. (c) For uniformly accelerated motion, the s must be quadratic in t. So,

$$t^2 = \dfrac{x - a}{b}$$

or $\qquad x = a + bt^2$

4. (c) $\qquad v = 20 + 0.1\, t^2$

$\therefore \qquad a = \dfrac{dv}{dt} = 0.1 \times 2t = 0.2t.$

Here acceleration depends on time.

5. (b) $\qquad s_1 = \dfrac{1}{2}a(10)^2$

and $\qquad s = \dfrac{1}{2}a(20)^2 = 4s_1$

$\therefore\ s_2 = s - s_1 = 3s_1.$

6. (c) For first 1m of fall,

$$1 = \dfrac{1}{2}gt_1^2, \qquad \therefore t_1 = \sqrt{\dfrac{2}{g}}$$

For 2m of fall, $\quad 2 = \dfrac{1}{2}gt^2, \qquad \therefore t = \sqrt{\dfrac{4}{g}},$

$$\therefore\ t_2 = t - t_1 = \sqrt{\dfrac{4}{g}} - \sqrt{\dfrac{2}{g}} = (\sqrt{2} - 1)\sqrt{\dfrac{2}{g}}$$

For 3 m of fall,

$$3 = \dfrac{1}{2}gt^2, \quad \therefore t = \sqrt{3}\sqrt{\dfrac{2}{g}}.$$

$$\therefore\qquad t_3 = t - t_2 = (\sqrt{3} - \sqrt{2})\sqrt{\dfrac{2}{g}}.$$

7. (b)

Velocity changes from v_1 to v_2 in time $t_1 + t_2$, so

$$a = \dfrac{v_2 - v_1}{t_1 + t_2}.$$

Similarly $\qquad a = \dfrac{v_3 - v_2}{t_2 + t_3}$

Thus $\qquad \left(\dfrac{v_2 - v_1}{t_1 + t_2}\right) = \left(\dfrac{v_3 - v_2}{t_2 + t_3}\right).$

8. (d) $$0 = u^2 - 2as \Rightarrow s = \frac{u^2}{2a}$$

   $\therefore$ $$\frac{s_1}{s_2} = \frac{u_1^2}{u_2^2} = \frac{u^2}{(4u)^2} = \frac{1}{16}$$

9. (c) If h is the height of the building, then
   $$v_A^2 = v^2 + gh$$
   and $$v_B^2 = (-v)^2 + 2gh.$$
   Clearly $v_A = v_B.$

10. (a) Given $t = \sqrt{x} + 3$
    or $x = (t-3)^2.$
    Velocity $v = \frac{dx}{dt} = 2(t-3)$
    or $0 = 2(t-3)$
    $\therefore$ $t = 3\,s$
    Thus $x = (3-3)^2 = 0.$

11. (a) $v = \frac{dx}{dt} = \frac{d}{dt}(t+5)^{-1} = -1(t+5)^{-2}$
    and $a = (-1) \times (-2)(t+5)^{-3}$
    or $a^2 = 4(t+5)^{-6} = Cv^3$
    $\therefore a \propto v^{3/2}$

12. (c) The displacement, $s = 2R\cos\theta$,
    and acceleration, $a = g\cos\theta$.
    $\therefore$ $s = \frac{1}{2}at^2$
    or $2R\cos\theta = \frac{1}{2}(g\cos\theta)t^2$
    $\therefore$ $t = 2\sqrt{\dfrac{R}{g}}.$

13. (b) $-30 = 18 + a \times 2.4$
    $\therefore$ $a = -20 \text{ m/s}^2.$

14. (a) $\left(\dfrac{v}{2}\right)^2 = v^2 - 2g \times 3$

    $\therefore$ $v = \sqrt{8g}.$
    If h is the further height, then
    $$0 = \left(\frac{v}{2}\right)^2 - 2gh$$
    $\therefore$ $h = \dfrac{v^2}{8g} = \dfrac{8g}{8g} = 1 \text{ m}.$

15. (b) $s_1 = \dfrac{1}{2}gt^2$ and $s_2 = \dfrac{1}{2}g(t-1)^2$
    $\therefore$ $s_1 - s_2 = 10 = \dfrac{1}{2}g\,[t^2 - (t-1)^2]$
    $\therefore$ $t = 1.5\,s.$

16. (a) $h = ut_1 - \dfrac{1}{2}gt_1^2$

Also $h = ut_2 - \dfrac{1}{2}gt_2^2$
After simplify above equations, we get
$$h = \frac{1}{2}gt_1t_2.$$

17. (c) If t is the time taken by the first ball to hit the water,
    then $122.5 = \dfrac{1}{2} \times 9.8 \times t^2$
    $\therefore$ $t = 5s.$
    The time of motion for second ball is 3s. So
    $$122.5 = u \times 3 + \frac{1}{2} \times 9.8 \times 3^2$$
    $\therefore$ $u = 26.1 \text{ m/s}.$

18. (d) From the geometry, we have
    $$a^2 + (v_1 t)^2 = (v\,t)^2$$
    $\therefore$ $t = \dfrac{a}{\sqrt{v^2 - v_1^2}}$

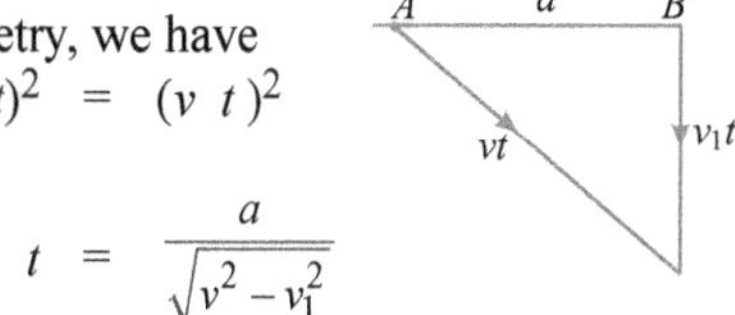

19. (a) $0 + \dfrac{a_1}{2}(2 \times 5 - 1) = 0 + \dfrac{a_2}{2}[2 \cdot 3 - 1]$
    $\therefore$ $\dfrac{a_1}{a_2} = \dfrac{5}{9}.$

20. (a) $vt = \dfrac{1}{2}at^2$
    $\therefore$ $t = \dfrac{2v}{a}.$

21. (c) $\dfrac{dx}{dt} = \dfrac{1}{2}(1+t^2)^{-1/2} \times 2t = t(1+t^2)^{-1/2}$
    $$a = \frac{d^2x}{dt^2} = (1+t^2)^{-1/2} + t\left(-\frac{1}{2}\right)(1+t^2)^{-3/2} = \frac{1}{x} - \frac{t^2}{x^3}.$$

22. (b) $h_1 = \dfrac{1}{2} \times 10 \times 5^2 = 125 \text{ m}$
    $h_2 = \dfrac{1}{2} \times 10 \times 5^2 = 125 \text{ m}$
    $\therefore$ $h = h_1 - h_2 = 80 \text{ m}.$

23. (b) $\ell = 9.8$ $a = g\sin 30° = \dfrac{1}{2} \times 10 \times 5^2 = 125 \text{ m}$
    Using $\ell = \dfrac{1}{2}at^2$
    or $9.8 = \dfrac{1}{2} \times \dfrac{g}{2} \times t^2$
    $\Rightarrow$ $t = 2\,s.$

24. (a) The time taken by the ball to reach the highest point
    $$0 = u - gn \Rightarrow n = \frac{u}{g}.$$
    $$S_n = un - \frac{1}{2}gn^2$$
    and $$S_{(n-t)} = u(n-t) - \frac{1}{2}g(n-t)^2$$

$\therefore \qquad s = S_n - S(n-t) = \dfrac{1}{2}gt^2.$

25. (c) $h = ut - \dfrac{1}{2}gt^2$ also $h = u(t + \Delta t) - \dfrac{1}{2}g(t + \Delta t)^2.$

After simplifying above equations, we get

$$u = \dfrac{1}{2}\sqrt{8gh + g^2(\Delta t)^2}\,.$$

26. (b) $\qquad L = \dfrac{1}{2}gt^2 - \dfrac{1}{2}g(t - T)^2$

$\Rightarrow \qquad t = \dfrac{T}{2} + \dfrac{L}{gt}.$

27. (c) $\qquad 48 + \dfrac{1}{2} \times 1 \times t^2 = 10t$

$\therefore \qquad t = 8\ s$ and $12\ s.$

28. (d) $\qquad \dfrac{dv}{dt} = at$

or $\qquad \displaystyle\int_u^v dv = \int_0^t (at)\,dt$

$\therefore \qquad v = u + \dfrac{at^2}{2}$

29. (a) $\qquad \dfrac{dv}{dt} = 2(t - 1)$

or $\qquad \displaystyle\int_0^v dv = \int_0^5 2(t - 1)\,dt$

or $v = 2\left|\left(\dfrac{t^2}{2} - t\right)\right|_0^5 = 2\left(\dfrac{5^2}{2} - 5\right) = 15$ m/s.

30. (a) $\qquad \dfrac{dv}{dt} = -kv^3$

or $\qquad \displaystyle\int_{v_0}^v \dfrac{dv}{v^3} = -k\int_0^t dt$

$\therefore \qquad v = \dfrac{v_0}{\sqrt{2v_0^2 kt + 1}}$

31. (b) $\qquad \dfrac{dv}{dt} = \dfrac{P}{mv}$

or $\qquad v\dfrac{dv}{ds} = \dfrac{P}{mv}$

or $\qquad \displaystyle\int_0^s ds = \dfrac{m}{P}\int_{v_1}^{v_2} v^2\,dv$

$\therefore \qquad s = \dfrac{m}{3P}(v_2^3 - v_1^3).$

32. (b) $\qquad \dfrac{dv}{dt} = 3t^2 + 2t + 2$

or $\qquad \displaystyle\int_2^v dv = \int_0^2 (3t^2 + 2t + 2)\,dt$

$v - 2 = \left|3\dfrac{t^3}{3} + 2\dfrac{t^2}{2} + 2t\right|_0^2$

$\therefore \qquad v = 18$ m/s.

33. (d) $\qquad \dfrac{v_A}{v_B} = \dfrac{\tan 30°}{\tan 60°} = \dfrac{1/\sqrt 3}{\sqrt 3} = \dfrac{1}{3}.$

34. (d) $\qquad a = \dfrac{\Delta v}{\Delta t} = \dfrac{v_2 - v_1}{t_2 - t_1}$

$\therefore \qquad v_2 = v_1 + a(t_2 - t_1)$

Here $v_1 = 0$, $\therefore v_2 = $ area of $\vec a - t$ between t_1 and t_2.

35. (d) The maximum acceleration will occur in the duration 30 s to 40s. So

$$a = \dfrac{v_2 - v_1}{t_2 - t_1} = \dfrac{60 - 20}{40 - 30} = 4\ \text{m/s}^2.$$

36. (a) $a = \dfrac{v_2 - v_1}{\Delta t}$

$= \dfrac{\tan 135° - \tan 45°}{1} = -2\ \text{m/s}^2$

37. (c) $\qquad x = a - bt + ct^2$

$\therefore \qquad v = \dfrac{dx}{dt} = -b + 2c\,t.$

It represents a straight line with negative intercept on y-axis.

38. (b) $\qquad v = $ area of $a - t$ upto $3s.$

$\qquad = 3 \times 2 - 3 \times 1 = 3$ m/s

39. (c) According to the acceleration time graph, first velocity increases, then becomes constant and thereafter it will increase.

40. (d)

41. (a) It is the $\vec s - t$ graph of a body projected upward. It has uniform acceleration downward.

42. (c) $\qquad v^2 = 2as.$

It represents a parabola about s-axis.

43. (c) We have $\qquad v^2 = u^2 + 2a\,s$

or $\qquad 900 = 3600 + 2a \times 0.6$

$\therefore \qquad a = -2250.$

44. (d) The distance, $s = \dfrac{vT}{2}$

Also, $m = \dfrac{v}{T}$, $\therefore T = \dfrac{v}{m}.$

Now $\qquad s = \dfrac{v^2}{2m}.$

45. (a) From $0 - 2\ s$: $\quad v = 0 + at = 3 \times 2 = 6$ m/s

From $2 - 4\ s$: $\quad v = 6 - at = 6 - 3 \times 2 = 0.$

46. (c) If v_1 and v_2 are the velocities, then

$(v_1 - v_2) \times 20 = (100 + 100)$ ...(i)

and $(v_1 + v_2) \times 10 = (100 + 100)$ ...(ii)

After solving above equations, we get

$v_1 = 15$ m/s and $v_2 = 5$ m/s.

47. (b) If t is the time of crossing, then

$100 = (10 + 15)\,t$

$\therefore \qquad t = 4$ s.

48. (a) The speed of approach, $= v - (-2v) = 3\,v.$

$\therefore \qquad t = \dfrac{\ell}{3v}$, each one have same time.

49. (c) $v_A = u - gt$ and $v_B = gt$.

$v_A - v_B = (u - gt) - gt = u - 2gt.$

50. (b) For the elevator going with constant velocity, we have

$$h = \frac{1}{2}gt^2$$

or $\qquad 2.5 = \dfrac{1}{2} \times 10 \times t^2$

$\therefore \qquad t = \dfrac{1}{\sqrt{2}}\, s.$

51. (c) $x_0 = \dfrac{1}{2} \times 1 \times 50^2 = 1250\, m$

1. (c) $\qquad x = 20\, t\, e^{-t}$

$\therefore \qquad v = \dfrac{dx}{dt} = 20\left(t\dfrac{de^{-t}}{dt} + e^{-t} \times 1 \right)$

or $\qquad 0 = 20\,[t\, e^{-t} \times (-1) + e^{-t}]$

$\therefore \qquad t = 1$

Thus $\qquad x = 20 \times 1 \times e^{-1} = \dfrac{20}{e}.$

2. (b) If u is the velocity of projection, then

$$0 = u^2 - 2g\,(4h)$$

$\therefore \qquad u = \sqrt{8gh}$

Now $\qquad y = -gt \qquad ...(i)$

and $\qquad h - y = ut - \dfrac{1}{2}gt^2 \qquad ...(ii)$

From above equations, we have

$$t = \frac{h}{u} = \frac{h}{\sqrt{8gh}} = \sqrt{\frac{h}{8g}}$$

3. (b) The time taken to move net 2 steps is 8s, and so for 8 steps he takes 32 s. In last 5 steps he will take 5s and fall into the pit.

4. (a) For maximum velocity, $a = 0$ and so, $0 = b - cx$ or $x = b/c$.

Now, $v\dfrac{dv}{dx} = b - cx$

$$\int_0^v v\, dv = \int_0^x (b - cx)\, dx$$

$$\frac{v^2}{2} = bx - \frac{cx^2}{2}$$

$$= b \times \frac{b}{c} - \frac{c(b/c)^2}{2}$$

or $\qquad v = \dfrac{b}{\sqrt{c}}$

5. (a) The time taken by ball to reach maximum height

$$4.9 = 0 + \frac{1}{2} \times g \times t^2$$

$\therefore \qquad t = 1\, s.$

So number of balls thrown per minute will be 60.

6. (a) $\qquad s = \dfrac{d/2}{\cos 45^\circ} = \dfrac{d}{\sqrt{2}}$

$v_{\text{effective}} = v \cos 45^\circ = \dfrac{v}{\sqrt{2}}.$

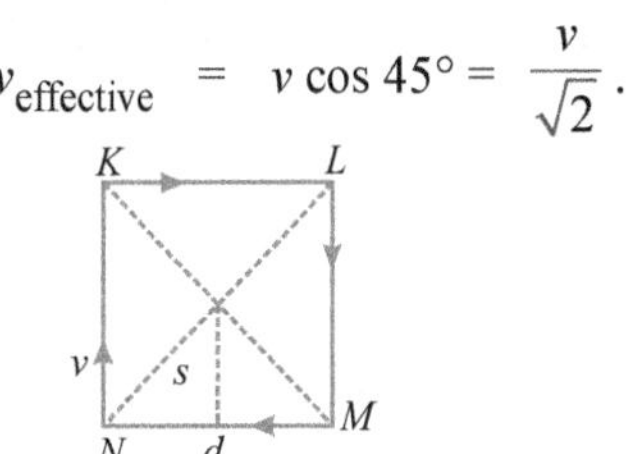

Time, $\qquad t = \dfrac{s}{v_{\text{effective}}} = \dfrac{d/\sqrt{2}}{v/\sqrt{2}} = \dfrac{d}{v}.$

7. (c) If $\vec{A}$ is the displacement along the velocity vector, then

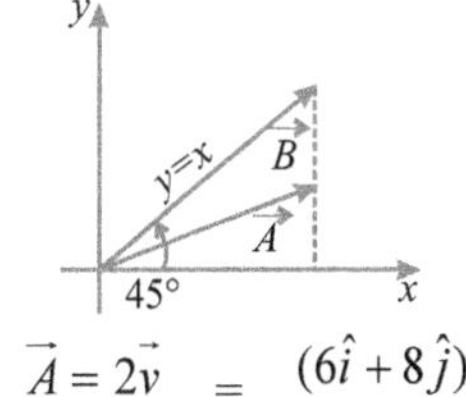

$\vec{A} = 2\vec{v} = (6\hat{i} + 8\hat{j}).$

unit vector along line $y = x$,

$$\vec{B} = \cos 45^\circ \hat{i} + \sin 45^\circ \hat{j}$$

$$= \left(\frac{\hat{i}}{\sqrt{2}} + \frac{\hat{j}}{\sqrt{2}} \right).$$

Thus the displacement along $\vec{B}$

$$A \cos \theta = \frac{AB \cos \theta}{B} = \frac{\vec{A}.\vec{B}}{B}$$

$$= \frac{(6\hat{i} + 8\hat{j}).(\dfrac{\hat{i}}{\sqrt{2}} + \dfrac{\hat{j}}{\sqrt{2}})}{1}$$

$$= 7\sqrt{2} \ \text{m.}$$

8. (b) Let a_1 and a_2 be the retardations offered to the bullet by wood and iron respectively.

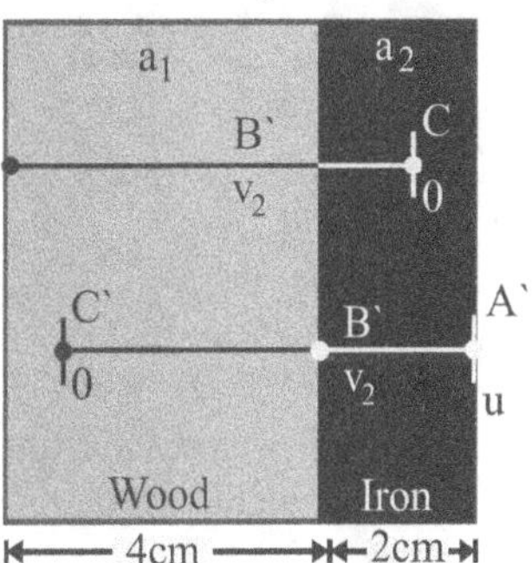

For $A \to B \to C$, $\quad v_1^2 - u^2 = 2a_1 \qquad (4),$

and $\qquad 0^2 - v_1^2 = 2a_2 \qquad \ldots(1)$

Adding, we get $-u^2 = 2(4a_1 + a_2)$

For $A' \to B' \to C'$, $v_2^2 - u^2 = 2a_2 \qquad \ldots(2)$,

and $\qquad 0^2 - v_2^2 = 2a_1 \qquad \ldots(3)$

Adding , we get, $-u^2 = 2(2a_1 + 2a_2)$

Equating (1) and (2) and solving , we get

$4a_1 + a_2 = 2a_1 + 2a_2 \Rightarrow a_2 = 2a_1$

9. **(b)** Velocity of the parachute after falling 50 m

$$u = \sqrt{2g \times 50} = 10\sqrt{g} \text{ m/s}$$

Thus $\qquad 3^2 = u^2 - 2 \times 2 \times h$

or $\qquad 3^2 = 100\,g - 4\,h$

$\therefore \qquad h = 243 \text{ m}.$

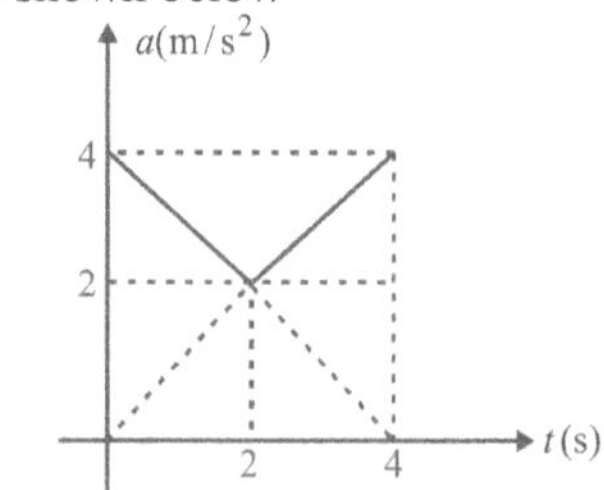

The height at which parachute bails out

$$= 243 + 50 = 293 \text{ m}.$$

10. **(d)** Acceleration can be written as $a = 2 + 2 - t$ or $a = 4 - t$ for $t \le 2s$ and $a = 2 + t - 2$ or $a = t$ for $t \ge 2\,s$ Therefore, acceleration time graph of the particle will be as shown below

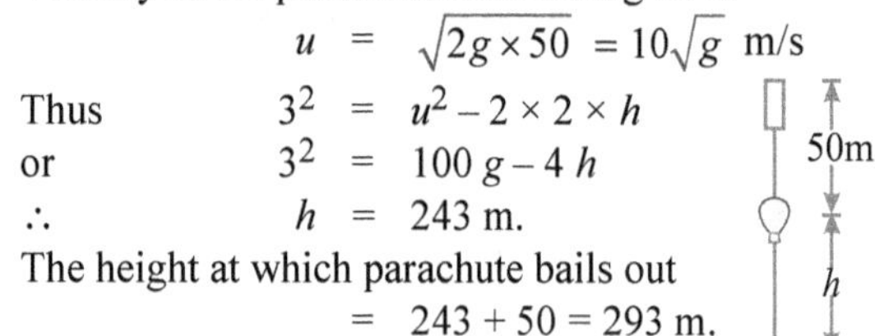

Now since, $\qquad dv = a\,dt$

$v_f - v_i = $ area under $(a\text{-}t)$ graph

or $\qquad v_f - 0 = (4 \times 4) - \dfrac{1}{2}(4)(2)$

$$= 12 \text{ m/s}$$

or velocity of particle at the end of $4s$ is 12 m/s.

11. **(a)** See examples

12. **(b)** Given $\qquad s = k\,t^3$

$\therefore \qquad v = \dfrac{ds}{dt} = 3\,k\,t^2.$

It represents a parabola between v and t.

13. **(b)**

14. **(a)** At a height y, the velocity of the ball

$$v^2 = 0 + 2g\,(d-y)$$

or $\qquad v = \sqrt{2g(d-y)}$

It represents a parabola between v and d.

At $\qquad y = d, \qquad v = 0$

$\qquad\qquad y = 0, \qquad v = \sqrt{2gd}$

Just after collision, the speed of the ball

$$v = \sqrt{2g\,d/2} = \sqrt{gd}$$

Taking downward velocity negative, one find graph of option (a) is correct.

15. **(d)** If u and v are the speeds of the person and of the escalator, then

$$\dfrac{\ell}{u} = 90, \qquad \therefore \ u = \dfrac{\ell}{90}$$

and $\qquad \dfrac{\ell}{v} = 60, \qquad \therefore \ v = \dfrac{\ell}{60}$

If t is the required time, then

$$t = \dfrac{\ell}{u+v} = \dfrac{\ell}{\dfrac{\ell}{90} + \dfrac{\ell}{60}} = 36s.$$

16. **(d)** See examples

17. **(b)**

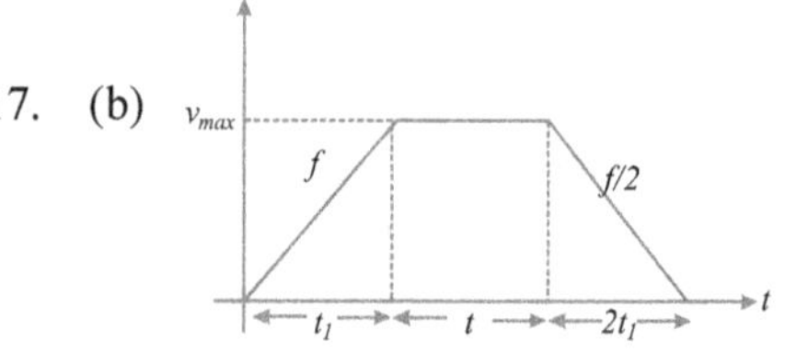

$$s = \dfrac{1}{2}ft_1^2 \; ; \; \therefore \ t_1 = \sqrt{\dfrac{2s}{f}}$$

$$v_{max} = ft_1 = f\sqrt{\dfrac{2s}{f}} = \sqrt{2fs} \ .$$

Thus $\qquad 5s = \dfrac{1}{2}\big[[t + 3t_1) + t\big] \times v_{max}.$

or $\qquad 5s = \dfrac{1}{2}\big(2t + 3t_1\big) \times v_{max}$

or $\qquad 5s = \dfrac{1}{2}\left(2t + 3\sqrt{\dfrac{2s}{f}}\right) \times \sqrt{2fs}$

$\therefore \qquad s = \dfrac{1}{2}ft^2 \ .$

1. **(a,c,d)**
   - (a) At the highest point of the projected body.
   - (c) Constant speed will have no change in velocity, so acceleration will be zero.
   - (d) $\qquad v = u + at.$

2. **(a, b, d)**

   On position axis, P is closer to O than Q.

   From time axis, it can be said that A starts earlier than B.

3. **(b, c, d)**

At the highest point of the projected body, $a = g$, so option (a) is correct only.

4. **(a,b,d)**

   Only option (c) is correct . According to it

   $$v = -u - at = -(u + at)$$

   or $\qquad |v| = u + at.$

5. **(a, b)**

   (a) $\qquad \left|\dfrac{\text{av velocity}}{\text{av speed}}\right| \le 1$

(b) In circular motion speed is constant $\left(\dfrac{d|\vec{v}|}{dt}\right)$ is constant but there is centripetal acceleration.

6. (a, d) Self explanatory.

7. (a,b,d) For constant velocity, $\dfrac{dv}{dt} = 0$

$\therefore \quad 0 = 6.0 - 3v \Rightarrow v = 6/3 = 2\,\text{m/s}$

At $\qquad t = 0, v = 0$

$\therefore \qquad a = 6 - 3 \times 0 = 6\,\text{m/s}^2.$

Again $\qquad \dfrac{dv}{dt} = 6 - 3v$

or $\qquad \displaystyle\int_0^v \dfrac{dv}{(6 - 3v)} = \int_0^t dt$

$\qquad \left.\dfrac{ln(6-3v)}{(-3)}\right|_0^v = |t|_0^t$

or $\qquad v = 2(1 - e^{-3t}).$

8. (a, c) For the data, $\vec{v} - t$ graph can be drawn as shown in figure.

The displacement in time t,

$$x = \frac{1}{2}\left(\frac{\alpha\beta}{\alpha+\beta}\right)t^2$$

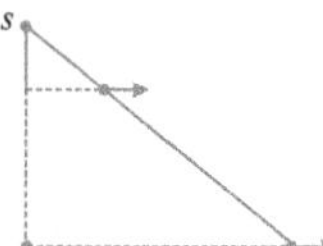

Putting $\qquad x = 1, t = 1\,s,$

if $\qquad \alpha = \beta,$

then $\qquad \alpha = 4,$

or If $\alpha > \beta$, then $\alpha > 4\,\text{m/s}^2.$

9. (a,b,c,d) From $0 - T$, the velocity is negative and from T to $2T$, the velocity is position. The area of $\vec{v} - t$ graph will be zero, so displacement will be zero. The slope of $v - t$ is same throughout, so acceleration is constant.

10. (a,c,d) If velocity is zero, the acceleration need not be zero. If initial velocity is zero and acceleration is also zero in interval $0 - 2s$, then speed must be zero in this interval.

11. (a,b,d) Speed can never be zero and so option (c) is not possible.

12. (a,c) When body falls, its velocity $v^2 = 2gs$, it represents a parabola b/w v and s and straight line $between$ v^2 and s.

Exercise 3.3

1. (c) In uniform motion the speed is same at each instant of motion.

2. (a) In uniform circular motion, there is acceleration of constant magnitude.

3. (a) Because displacement $\leq$ distance and so average velocity $\leq$ average speed.

4. (a) $\left[\vec{v}_{body}\right]_{frame} = \vec{v}_{body} - \vec{v}_{frame} = \vec{v} - \vec{v} = 0$

5. (a) At the highest point of the projected body, its acceleration is not zero.

6. (b) Instantaneous velocity is always equal to instantaneous speed.

7. (d) One dimensional motion is always along straight line. But acceleration may be opposite of velocity and so angle between them will be $180°$.

8. (b) $\qquad \vec{v}_{21} = \vec{v}_2 - \vec{v}_1$

As angular velocity is same for two points, so v_{21} is very small

Exercise 3.4

Passage for Questions 1 to 3

1. (b) 2. (a) 3. (c)

The time taken by stone to reach the highest point

$\qquad 0 = 9.8 - gt_1$

$\therefore \qquad t_1 = \dfrac{9.8}{g} = 1\,s$

The time taken to pass through the point of projection = 2s. If t is the time to reach the ground, then

$\qquad 39.2 = -9.8t + \dfrac{1}{2}gt^2$

After solving, we get, $t = 4s.$

Velocity before striking the ground,

$\qquad v^2 = u^2 + 2gh$

$\qquad = (-9.8)^2 + 2 \times 9.8 \times 39.2$

$\qquad v = 29.4\,\text{m/s}$ $\qquad$ $Ans.$

Passage for Questions 4 to 6

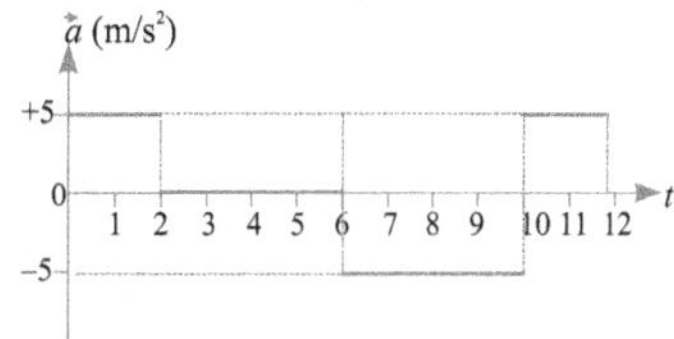

4. (b) Area of graph above time axis

$$A = \frac{1}{2} \times (8+4) \times 10 = 60m$$

Area of graph below time axis

$$B = \frac{1}{2} \times 4 \times 10 = 20\ \text{m}$$

Average velocity in whole time of motion

$$\vec{v} = \frac{\text{displacement}}{\text{total time}}$$

$$= \frac{\text{area } A - \text{area } B}{\text{total time}}$$

$$= \frac{60 - 20}{12} = 3.33\ \text{m/s}\,. \qquad Ans.$$

5. (c) Average speed in whole time of motion

$$v_{av} = \frac{\text{total distance}}{\text{total time}} = \frac{\text{area } A + \text{area } B}{\text{total time}}$$

$$= \frac{60 + 20}{12} = 6.67 \, \text{m/s} .$$ **Ans.**

6. (a) Acceleration:

From 0 to 2 s; $\quad a = \dfrac{v_2 - v_1}{t_2 - t_1} = \dfrac{10 - 0}{2 - 0} = 5 \, \text{m/s}^2$

From 2 to 6 s; $\quad a = \dfrac{v_2 - v_1}{t_2 - t_1} = \dfrac{10 - 10}{6 - 2} = 0$

From 6 to 10 s; $\quad a = \dfrac{v_2 - v_1}{t_2 - t_1} = \dfrac{-10 - 10}{10 - 6} = -5 \, \text{m/s}^2$

From 10 to 12 s; $a = \dfrac{v_2 - v_1}{t_2 - t_1} = \dfrac{0 - (-10)}{12 - 10} = 5 \, \text{m/s}^2$

Acceleration vs time graph is drawn in figure (b).

7. to 10. have been explained in the theory of the chapter.

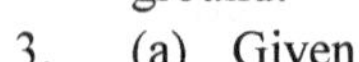

EXERCISE 3.5

1. (c) Yes, the person can catch the ball when horizontal velocity is equal to the horizontal component of ball's velocity, the motion of ball will be only in vertical direction with respect to person for that,

$$\frac{v_o}{2} = v_o \cos\theta \quad \text{or} \quad \theta = 60°$$

2. (d) $\qquad h = \dfrac{2v}{a}$

and $\qquad y = \dfrac{1}{2} g(t/2)^2 = \dfrac{h}{4}$

The ball is at a height $= h - \dfrac{h}{4} = \dfrac{3h}{4}$ from ground.

3. (a) Given $\quad t = \alpha x^2 + \beta x$

Differentiating above equation w.r.t. time, we get

$$1 = \alpha \times 2x \frac{dx}{dt} + \beta \frac{dx}{dt}$$

or $\qquad 1 = 2\alpha x v + \beta v,$

$\therefore \qquad \dfrac{1}{v} = 2\alpha x + \beta \qquad \text{...(i)}$

Differentiating again, we get

$$0 = 2\alpha \left(x\frac{dv}{dt} + v\frac{dx}{dt} \right) + \beta \frac{dv}{dt}$$

or $\qquad 0 = 2\alpha(x a + v^2) + \beta a \quad \text{...(ii)}$

From above equations, we get

$$a = -2\alpha v^3.$$

4. (c) We know that, $v = \dfrac{dx}{dt} \Rightarrow dx = v \, dt$

Integrating, $\displaystyle\int_0^x dx = \int_0^t v \, dt$

or $\quad x = \displaystyle\int_0^t (v_0 + gt + ft^2) \, dt = \left[v_0 t + \frac{gt^2}{2} + \frac{ft^3}{3} \right]_0^t$

or, $\quad x = v_0 t + \dfrac{gt^2}{2} + \dfrac{ft^3}{3}$

At $t = 1$, $\quad x = v_0 + \dfrac{g}{2} + \dfrac{f}{3}$.

5. (b) $\qquad x_1 - x_2 = ut - \dfrac{1}{2} at^2$

It represents a parabola like in option (b).

6. (b) For downward motion $v = -gt$

The velocity of the rubber ball increases in downward direction and we get a straight line between v and t with a negative slope.

Also applying $y - y_0 = ut + \dfrac{1}{2} at^2$

We get $y - h = -\dfrac{1}{2} gt^2 \Rightarrow y = h - \dfrac{1}{2} gt^2$

The graph between y and t is a parabola with $y = h$ at $t = 0$. As time increases y decreases.

For upward motion.

The ball suffer elastic collision with the horizontal elastic plate therefore the direction of velocity is reversed and the magnitude remains the same.

Here $v = u - gt$ where u is the velocity just after collision.

As t increases, v decreases. We get a straight line between v and t with negative slope.

Also $y = ut - \dfrac{1}{2} gt^2$

All these characteristics are represented by graph (b).

7. (a) From the geometry of the figure,

we have,

$$\frac{v}{x_0 - x} = \frac{v_0}{x_0}$$

$\therefore \qquad v = \left(\dfrac{x_0 - x}{x_0} \right) v_0 = \left(1 - \dfrac{x}{x_0} \right) v_0$

Also $\quad \dfrac{dv}{dx} = -\dfrac{v_0}{x_0}$

Thus acceleration,

$$a = v\frac{dv}{dx} = \left(1 - \frac{x}{x_0} \right) v_0 \times \left(-\frac{v_0}{x_0} \right) = \frac{v_0^2}{x_0^2} x - \frac{v_0^2}{x_0}$$

It represents a straight line between a and x with negative intersect.

8. (a) At $t = 0$, the relative velocity will be zero.

At $t = \dfrac{T}{4}$, the relative velocity will be maximum in magnitude.

At $t = \dfrac{T}{2}$, the relative velocity will be zero.

At $t = \dfrac{3T}{4}$, the relative velocity will be maximum in magnitude

At $t = T$, the relative velocity again becomes zero.

Motion in a Plane

(147 - 202)

Chapter contents

Joseph-Louis Lagrange

Joseph-Louis Lagrang (1736-1813) was a Mathematician and astronomer, who was burn in Turin, Piedmont, lived part of his life in Prussia and part in France, making significant contributions to all fields of analysis, to number theory, and to classical and celestial mechanics. Lagrange's treatise on analytical mechanics offered the most comprehensive treatment of classical mechanics since Newton and formed a basis for the development of mathematical physics in the nineteenth century. ....

Definitions, Explanations and Derivations

4.1 INTRODUCTION

In the previous chapter we defined kinematic parameters like position, displacement, velocity and acceleration for objects moving along a straight line. The directional aspect of these parameters could be taken by using $(+)$ and $(-)$ signs but this is not possible for objects moving in a plane and in a three dimensions. To understand motion of such objects we have to use the knowledge of vectors.

4.2 POSITION VECTOR AND DISPLACEMENT

The position vector $\vec{r}$ of a particle P located in a plane with reference to the origin of an xy-coordinate system is given by

$$\vec{r} = x\hat{i} + y\hat{j} \qquad ....(i)$$

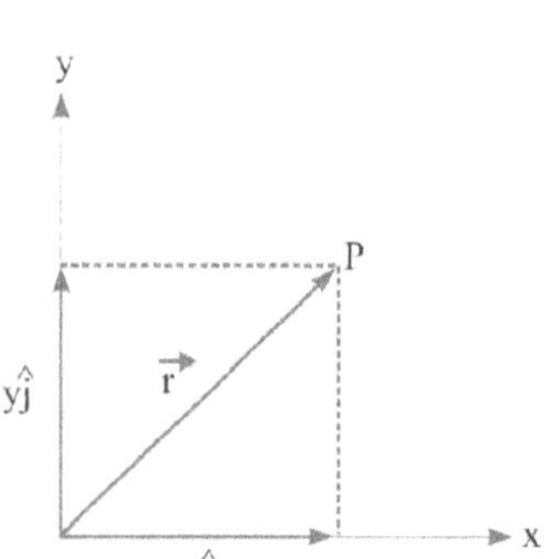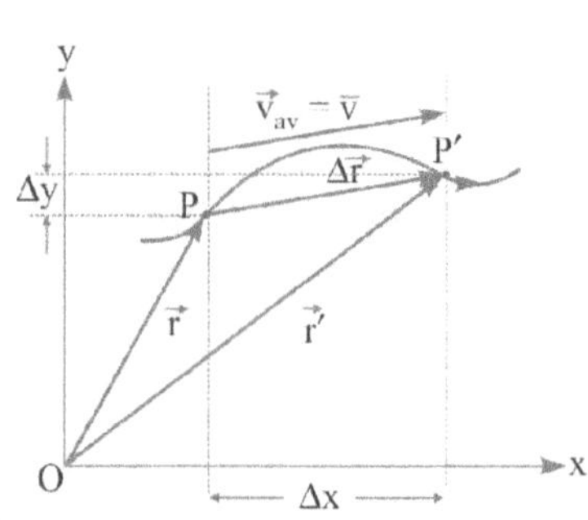

(a) Position vector $\vec{r}$

(b) Displacement $\overrightarrow{\Delta r}$ & average velocity $\vec{v}$ of a particle

Figure. 4.1

Suppose a particle moves along the path shown in fig. 4.1. The particle is at P at time t and at P' at time t', then the displacement is given by

$$\overrightarrow{\Delta r} = \vec{r'} - \vec{r}$$

$$= (x'\hat{i} + y'\hat{j}) - (x\hat{i} + y\hat{j})$$

$$= (x'-x)\hat{i} + (y'-y)\hat{j}$$

or
$$\overrightarrow{\Delta r} = \Delta x\hat{i} + \Delta y\hat{j}. \qquad ...(ii)$$

4.3 AVERAGE VELOCITY

The average velocity $\overline{v}$ of an object can be obtained by dividing displacement $\overrightarrow{\Delta r}$ by the corresponding time interval Δt. Thus average velocity

$$\vec{v}_{av} = \overline{v} = \frac{\overrightarrow{\Delta r}}{\Delta t}$$

$$= \frac{\Delta x\hat{i} + \Delta y\hat{j}}{\Delta t} = \frac{\Delta x}{\Delta t}\hat{i} + \frac{\Delta y}{\Delta t}\hat{j}$$

or
$$\overline{v} = \overline{v}_x\hat{i} + \overline{v}_y\hat{j}.$$

Since $\overline{v} = \dfrac{\overrightarrow{\Delta r}}{\Delta t}$, so the direction of the average velocity is the same as that of $\overrightarrow{\Delta r}$, see *fig.* 4.2.

Instantaneous velocity

The instantaneous velocity is given by the limiting value of the average velocity as the time interval approaches zero. Thus instantaneous velocity

$$\vec{\mathbf{v}} = \lim_{\Delta t \to 0} \frac{\Delta \vec{\mathbf{r}}}{\Delta t} = \frac{d\vec{\mathbf{r}}}{dt}$$

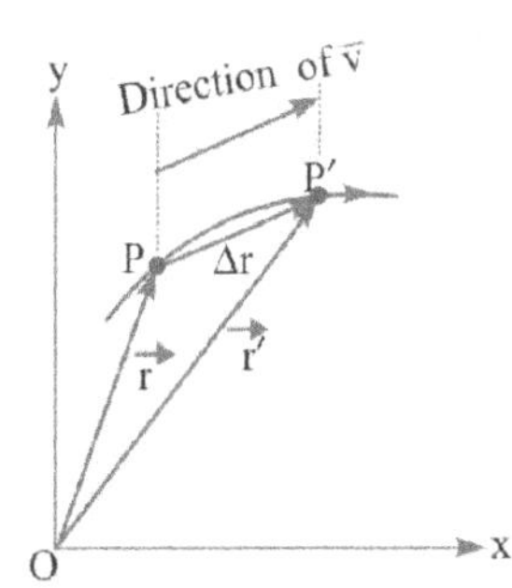

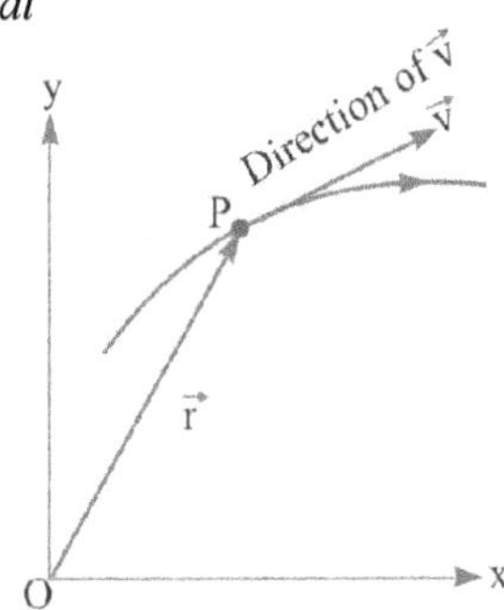

(a) Direction of average velocity   (b) Direction of instantaneous velocity

Figure. 4.2

The velocity $\vec{\mathbf{v}}$ can be expressed in component form as:

$$\vec{\mathbf{v}} = \frac{d\vec{\mathbf{r}}}{dt}$$

$$= \lim_{\Delta t \to 0} \left(\frac{\Delta x}{\Delta t}\hat{\mathbf{i}} + \frac{\Delta y}{\Delta t}\hat{\mathbf{j}} \right)$$

$$= \left(\lim_{\Delta t \to 0} \frac{\Delta x}{\Delta t} \right)\hat{\mathbf{i}} + \left(\lim_{\Delta t \to 0} \frac{\Delta y}{\Delta t} \right)\hat{\mathbf{j}}$$

or

$$\vec{\mathbf{v}} = \frac{dx}{dt}\hat{\mathbf{i}} + \frac{dy}{dt}\hat{\mathbf{j}}$$

$$\vec{\mathbf{v}} = v_x\hat{\mathbf{i}} + v_y\hat{\mathbf{j}}. \qquad \dots(i)$$

The magnitude of $\vec{\mathbf{v}}$ is

$$v = \sqrt{v_x^2 + v_y^2} \qquad \dots(ii)$$

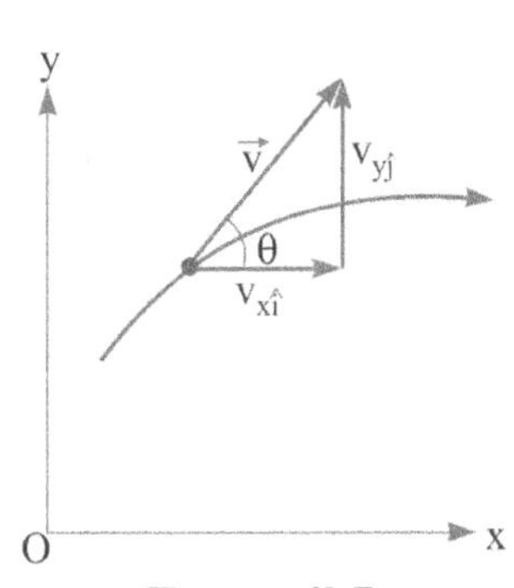

Figure. 4.3

and the direction of $\vec{\mathbf{v}}$ is given by the angle θ

$$\tan\theta = \frac{v_y}{v_x}$$

or

$$\theta = \tan^{-1}\left(\frac{v_y}{v_x} \right).$$

4.4 AVERAGE ACCELERATION

The average acceleration $\vec{\mathbf{a}}$ of an object for any time interval Δt moving in xy plane is the change in velocity divided by the time interval Δt. Thus average acceleration

$$\vec{\mathbf{a}}_{av} = \vec{\mathbf{a}} = \frac{\Delta \vec{v}}{\Delta t} = \frac{\Delta(v_x\hat{\mathbf{i}} + v_y\hat{\mathbf{j}})}{\Delta t}$$

$$= \frac{\Delta v_x}{\Delta t}\hat{\mathbf{i}} + \frac{\Delta v_y}{\Delta t}\hat{\mathbf{j}}$$

or

$$\vec{\mathbf{a}} = a_x\hat{\mathbf{i}} + a_y\hat{\mathbf{j}}.$$

Instantaneous acceleration

It is the limiting value of the average acceleration as the time interval approaches zero: Thus instantaneous acceleration

$$\vec{\mathbf{a}} \;=\; \lim_{\Delta t \to 0} \frac{\Delta \vec{\mathbf{v}}}{\Delta t} = \lim_{\Delta t \to 0}\left(\frac{\Delta v_x \hat{\mathbf{i}}}{\Delta t} + \frac{\Delta v_y \hat{\mathbf{j}}}{\Delta t}\right)$$

$$=\; \left(\lim_{\Delta t \to 0} \frac{\Delta v_x}{\Delta t}\right)\hat{\mathbf{i}} + \left(\lim_{\Delta t \to 0} \frac{\Delta v_y}{\Delta t}\right)\hat{\mathbf{j}}$$

or

$$\vec{\mathbf{a}} \;=\; a_x \hat{\mathbf{i}} + a_y \hat{\mathbf{j}}.$$

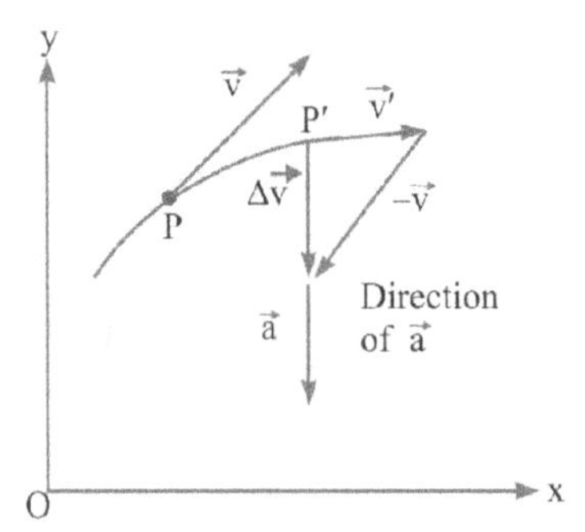

(a) Direction of average acceleration.
It is along the direction of $\Delta \vec{v}$.

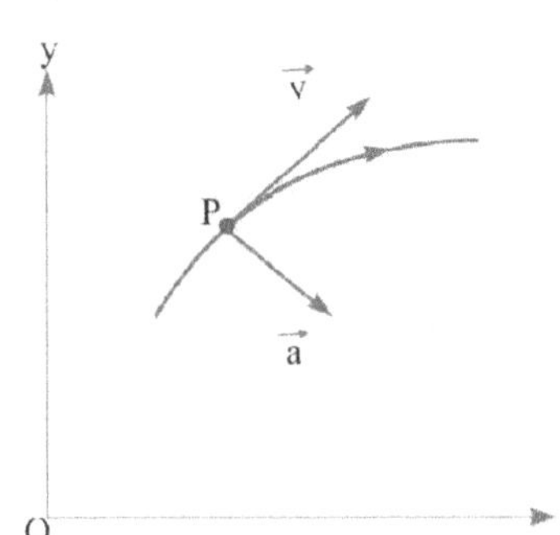

(b) Direction of instantaneous acceleration.
When $\Delta t \to 0$, $P' \to P$.

Figure. 4.4

4.5 MOTION IN A PLANE WITH CONSTANT ACCELERATION

Suppose an object is moving in xy- plane and its acceleration $\vec{\mathbf{a}}$ is constant. Let initial velocity of the object is $\vec{\mathbf{u}}$, then velocity at any time

$$\vec{\mathbf{v}} \;=\; \vec{\mathbf{u}} + \vec{\mathbf{a}}t.$$

In terms of components, we can write :

$$v_x \;=\; u_x + a_x t \qquad\qquad …(1)$$

and

$$v_y \;=\; u_y + a_y t$$

Similarly displacement at any time t is given by;

$$\vec{\mathbf{r}} \;=\; \vec{\mathbf{r}_0} + \vec{\mathbf{u}}t + \frac{1}{2}\vec{\mathbf{a}}t^2$$

In components form we can write :

$$x \;=\; x_0 + u_x t + \frac{1}{2} a_x t^2$$

and

$$y \;=\; y_0 + u_y t + \frac{1}{2} a_y t^2.$$

If x_0 and y_0 are zero, then

$$x \;=\; u_x t + \frac{1}{2} a_x t^2$$

$$y \;=\; u_y t + \frac{1}{2} a_y t^2 \qquad\qquad …(2)$$

From equations (1) and (2), we also have

$$\vec{\mathbf{v}}.\vec{\mathbf{v}} \;=\; (\vec{\mathbf{u}} + \vec{\mathbf{a}}t).(\vec{\mathbf{u}} + \vec{\mathbf{a}}t)$$

$$=\; \vec{\mathbf{u}}.\vec{\mathbf{u}} + \vec{\mathbf{a}}.\vec{\mathbf{u}}t + \vec{\mathbf{u}}.\vec{\mathbf{a}} + \vec{\mathbf{a}}.\vec{\mathbf{a}}t^2$$

$$=\; \vec{\mathbf{u}}.\vec{\mathbf{u}} + 2\vec{\mathbf{a}}.\left(\vec{\mathbf{u}}t + \frac{1}{2}\vec{\mathbf{a}}t^2\right)$$

or

$$\vec{\mathbf{v}}.\vec{\mathbf{v}} \;=\; \vec{\mathbf{u}}.\vec{\mathbf{u}} + 2\vec{\mathbf{a}}.(\vec{\mathbf{r}} - \vec{\mathbf{r}}_0)$$

In component form we can write :

$$v_x^2 = u_x^2 + 2a_x x$$

$$v_y^2 = u_y^2 + 2a_y y \qquad ...(3)$$

4.6 RELATIVE VELOCITY IN TWO DIMENSIONS

The concept of relative velocity introduced in previous chapter can be easily extended to motion in a plane. Suppose that two objects A and B are moving with velocities $\vec{v}_A$ and $\vec{v}_B$ with respect to stationary observer (ground). Then velocity of A relative to that of B is :

$$\vec{v}_{AB} = \vec{v}_A - \vec{v}_B . \qquad ...(i)$$

Similarly, the velocity of B relative to that of A is:

$$\vec{v}_{BA} = \vec{v}_B - \vec{v}_A . \qquad ...(ii)$$

Rain and man

Let us consider rain is falling and a man is running on the horizontal road. The man experiences the velocity of rain relative to himself. To prevent himself from the rain, the man should hold his umbrella in the direction of the relative velocity of rain w.r.t. man.

Suppose the velocity of rain is $\vec{v}_R$ directed vertically downward and man is moving along north with a velocity $\vec{v}_M$. Thus velocity of rain relative to man $\vec{v}_{RM} = \vec{v}_R - \vec{v}_M$. *Fig.* 4.5 shows the velocity of rain w.r.t. man.

Let $\vec{v}_{RM}$ makes angle θ with the vertical, then $\tan\theta = \dfrac{v_R}{v_M}$ south of vertical.

Thus the man should hold his umbrella at an angle θ with the vertical towards north (In the direction of his motion) to protect himself from rain. The velocity with which rain strikes the umbrella $v_{RM} = \sqrt{v_R^2 + v_M^2}$.

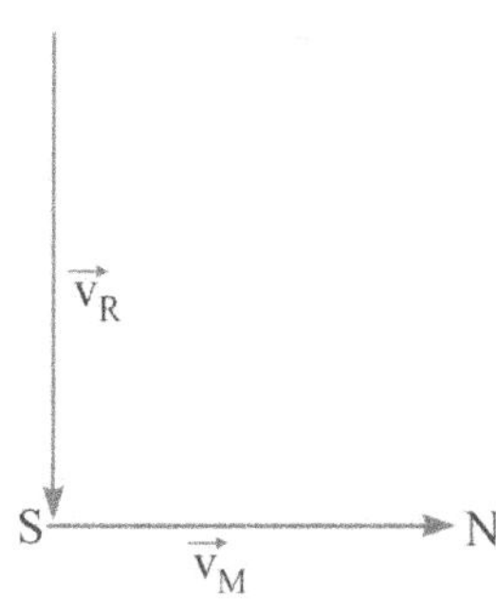
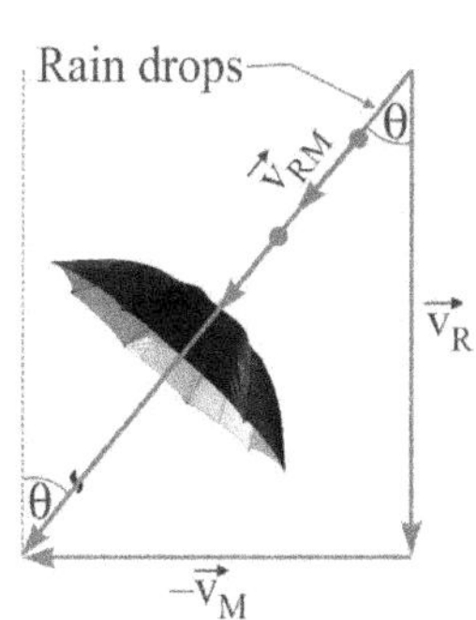

Figure. 4.5

River- boat

A river of width b is flowing with velocity $\vec{v}_r$ and a boatman can steer his boat with a velocity $\vec{v}_{br}$ with respect to river. The velocity of boatman with respect to ground

$$\left[\vec{v}_b\right]_{ground} = \left[\vec{v}_b\right]_{river} + \left[\vec{v}_{river}\right]_{ground}$$

$$\vec{v}_b = \vec{v}_{br} + \vec{v}_r .$$

(a)   The velocity of boatman when steers the boat along upstream direction (against flow)

$$\left[\vec{v}_b\right]_{up} = \vec{v}_{br} - \vec{v}_r$$

or $$\left[v_b\right]_{up} = v_{br} - v_r$$

Thus the time to travel a distance x against the flow

$$t = \frac{x}{\left(v_{br} - v_r\right)} .$$

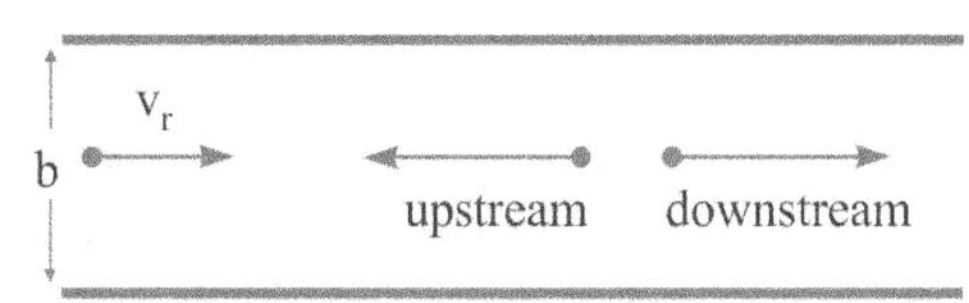

Figure. 4.6

(b)   When he steers the boat along downstream direction the velocity of boatman

$$[v_b]_{\text{down}} = v_{br} + v_r.$$

Thus the time to travel a distance x in the direction of flow

$$t = \frac{x}{(v_{br} + v_r)}.$$

Time to cross the river

Suppose the boatman steers the boat at an angle θ with the line $A\,B$ all the time of his motion. The velocity of the boatman along the line AB

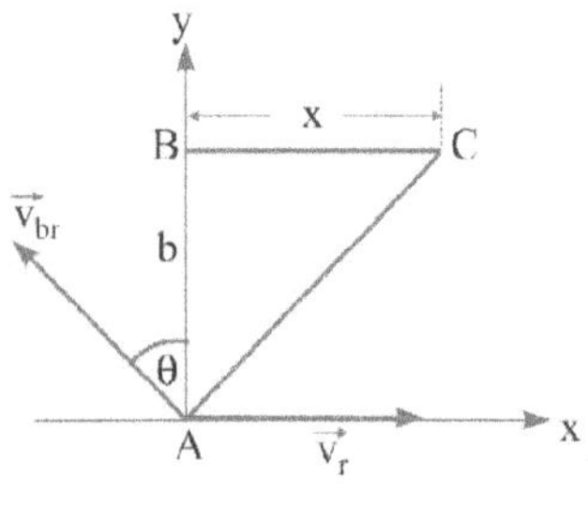

Figure. 4.7

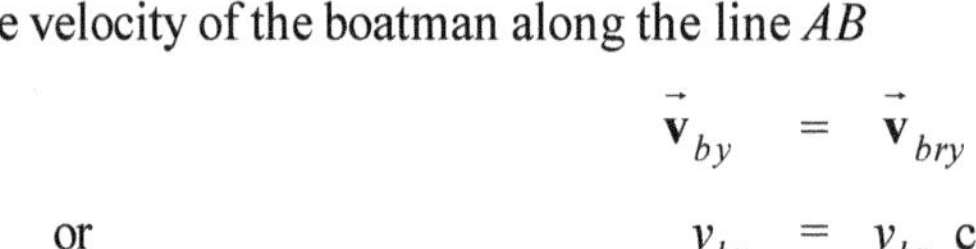

$$\vec{\mathbf{v}}_{by} = \vec{\mathbf{v}}_{bry} + \vec{\mathbf{v}}_{ry}$$

or

$$v_{by} = v_{br} \cos\theta + 0$$

$$= v_{br} \cos\theta$$

And his velocity along the flow

$$\vec{\mathbf{v}}_{bx} = \vec{\mathbf{v}}_{brx} + \vec{\mathbf{v}}_{rx}$$

or

$$v_{bx} = -v_{br} \sin\theta + v_r$$

$$= v_r - v_{br} \sin\theta$$

Thus time to cross the river

$$t = \frac{\text{displacement}}{\text{velocity along the displacement}}$$

or

$$t = \frac{b}{v_{br} \cos\theta} \qquad \ldots(i)$$

The displacement along the flow (x- axis) when he reaches on the other bank

$$x = \text{velocity of boatman along flow} \times \text{time to cross the river}$$

$$= v_{bx} \times t$$

$$= (v_r - v_{br} \sin\theta) \times \frac{b}{v_{br} \cos\theta}$$

or

$$x = b\left(\frac{v_r - v_{br} \sin\theta}{v_{br} \cos\theta}\right) \qquad \ldots(ii)$$

Let he arrive at a point C on the other bank of the river, then his net displacement

$$s = \sqrt{x^2 + y^2}$$

$$= \sqrt{x^2 + b^2} \qquad \ldots(iii)$$

The velocity of boatman with respect to ground

$$v_b = \sqrt{v_{bx}^2 + v_{by}^2}$$

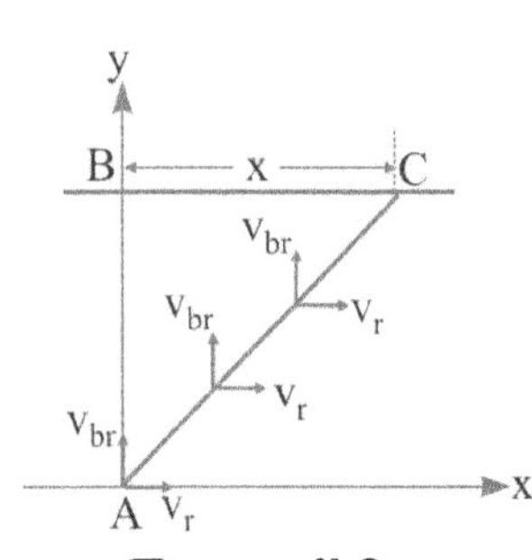

Figure. 4.8

(a)   **To cross the river in minimum time:**

From equation (i), we can see that time to cross the river is minimum when $\cos\theta = +1$, or $\theta = 0°$:

That is, the boatman steers his boat always at right angles to the direction of flow.

$$\therefore \qquad t_{\min} = \frac{b}{v_{br}} \qquad \ldots(iv)$$

His displacement along the flow (drift):

$$x = v_x \times \frac{b}{v_{br}} = b\left(\frac{v_r}{v_{br}}\right) \qquad \ldots(v)$$

(b) **To cross the river along shortest path:**
It is clear that the shortest path is from A to B.
For the drift, $x = 0$

or $\quad (v_r - v_{br}\sin\theta) \times \dfrac{b}{v_{br}\cos\theta} = 0$

or $\quad\quad\quad\quad \sin\theta = \dfrac{v_r}{v_{br}} \qquad \ldots(i)$

Hence, to reach at point B just opposite to A, boatman

should steer his boat at an angle $\theta = \sin^{-1}\left(\dfrac{v_r}{v_{br}}\right)$.

As $\sin\theta \not> 1$, so for $v_r \geq v_{br}$, the boatman can never reach the opposite bank at B. For $\sin\theta = 1; \theta = 90°$, it is impossible to reach the opposite bank, as it is clear from the following *fig.* 4.10.

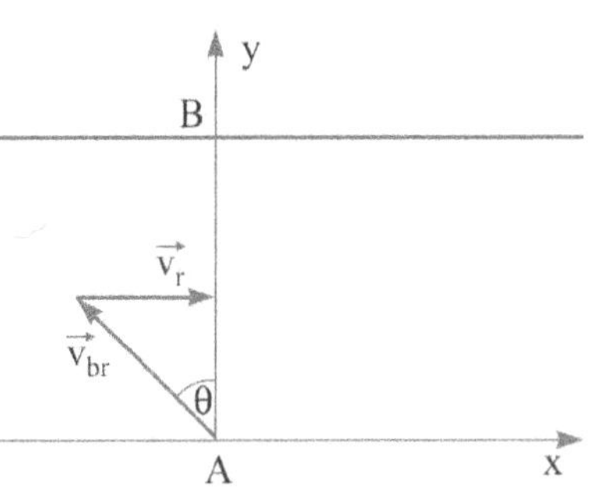

Figure. **4.9**

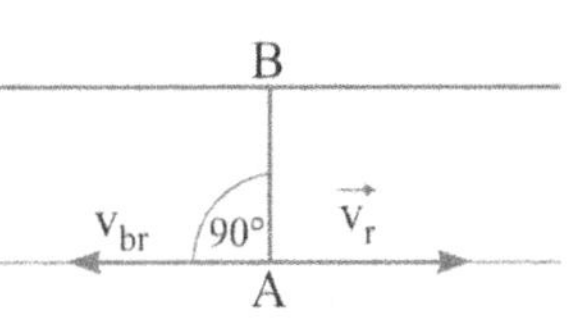

Figure. **4.10**

Note:

For $v_r \geq v_{br}$, does not mean that boatman will not reach the other bank. It means he can not reach the point opposite to starting point. Time to cross the river

$$t = \frac{b}{v_{br}\cos\theta} = \frac{b}{\sqrt{v_{br}^2 - v_r^2}}$$

Since $\cos\theta < 1$ for the possible angle θ, the time to cross the river in this case is greater than $\dfrac{b}{v_{br}}$.

FORMULAE USED

1. The velocity of rain relative to man, $\vec{v}_{RM} = \vec{v}_R - \vec{v}_M$

   If θ is the angle made by $\vec{v}_{RM}$ from vertical, then $\tan\theta = \dfrac{v_R}{v_m}$

2. The velocity with which rain strikes the umbrella $v_{RM} = \sqrt{v_R^2 + v_M^2}$

3. **River-boat :**
   (i) A boatman can cross the river in minimum time, if he always sail the boat right across the flow,

   $$t_{min} = \frac{b}{u}. \qquad \left[\begin{array}{l}\text{Here } v_r \to v \\ \text{and } v_{br} \to u\end{array}\right]$$

   Drift, $BC = v \times \dfrac{b}{u}$.

   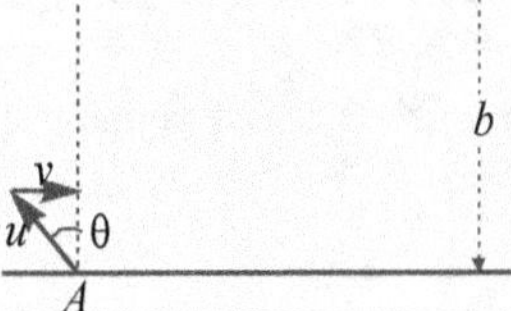

   (ii) If boatman wants to reach the opposite bank just in front of starting point, then he should sail the boat at angle θ, where

   $$\sin\theta = \frac{v}{u},$$

   and time to cross the river, $t = \dfrac{b}{u\cos\theta}$.

EXAMPLES BASED ON RAIN AND MAN & RIVER-BOAT PROBLEMS

Example 1. A particle starts from the origin at $t = 0$ s with a velocity of $10.0\ \hat{j}$ m/s and moves in the xy- plane with a constant acceleration of $(8.0\hat{i} + 2.0\hat{j})$ m/s^2. The y-coordinate of the particle when x-coordinate is 16: **[NCERT]**

Sol. Given that :
$$u_x = 0;\ u_y = 10\ \text{m/s}$$
and
$$a_x = 8.0\ \text{m/s}^2;\ a_y = 2.0\ \text{m/s}^2$$

Let at time t the x-coordinate is 16 m. We have
$$x = u_x + \frac{1}{2}a_x t^2$$
or
$$16 = 0 + \frac{1}{2} \times 8 \times t^2$$

After simplifying,
$$t = 2s$$

The y coordinate at
$$t = 2\ s\ \text{is}$$
$$y = u_y t + \frac{1}{2} a_y t^2$$
$$= 10 \times 2 + \frac{1}{2} \times 2 \times 2^2 = 24\ \text{m} \qquad \textbf{\textit{Ans.}}$$

Example 2. Rain is falling vertically with a speed of 30 ms^{-1}. A woman rides a bicycle with a speed of 10 ms^{-1} in the north to south direction. What is the direction in which she should hold her umbrella ? **[NCERT]**

Sol.

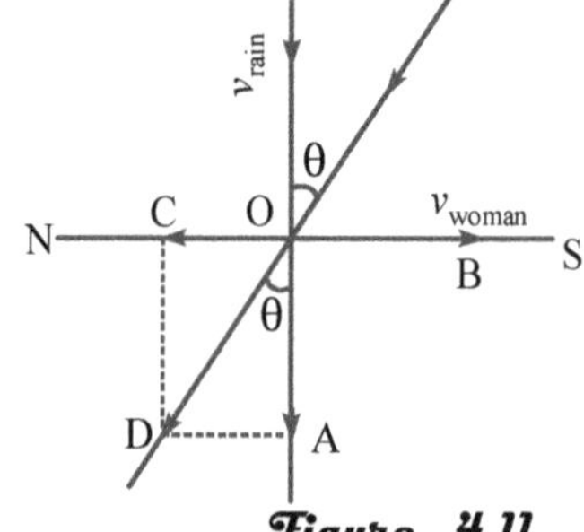

Figure. 4.11

The rain is falling along OA with speed 30 ms^{-1} and woman rider is moving along OS with 10 ms^{-1}. i.e. $OA = 30$ ms^{-1} and $OB = 10$ ms^{-1}. The woman rider can protect herself from the rain if she holds her umbrella in the direction of relative velocity of rain w.r.t. woman. To do so apply equal and opposite velocity of woman on the rain i.e. impress the velocity 10 ms^{-1} due north on rain which is represented by OC. Now the relative velocity of rain w.r.t. woman will be $(\vec{v}_{rain} - \vec{v}_{woman})$, represented by diagonal OD of parallelogram $OADC$.
If $\angle AOD = \theta$, then in ΔOAD, $\tan\theta = AD/OA = OC/OA = 10/30 = 0.33$
$= \tan 18°\ 26'$
B $= 18°26'$ north of vertical.

Example 3. A man can swim with a speed of 4.0 km/h in still water. How long does he take to cross a river 1.0 km wide if the river flows steadily at 3.0 km/h and he makes his strokes normal to the river current? How far down the river does he go when he reaches the other bank?

Sol. Time to cross the river, t = width of river/ speed of man
$$= \frac{1}{4}\ \text{h} = 15\ \text{m}.$$

Distance moved along the river in time
$$t = v_r \times t = 3\ \text{km/h} \times \frac{1}{4}\ \text{h} = 750\ \text{m} \qquad \textit{Ans.}$$

Example 4. A man running along a straight road with uniform velocity $\vec{u} = u\hat{i}$ feels that the rain is falling vertically down along $-\hat{j}$. If he doubles his speed, he finds that the rain is coming at an angle θ with the vertical. Find the actual direction and speed of the rain with respect to the ground.

Sol. Suppose velocity of rain
$$\vec{v}_R = v_x\hat{i} - v_y\hat{j}$$

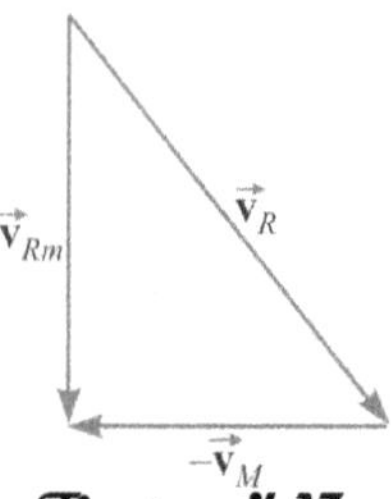

Figure. 4.12

and the velocity of the man
$$\vec{v}_m = u\hat{i}$$

$\therefore$ Velocity of rain relative to man
$$\vec{v}_{Rm} = \vec{v}_R - \vec{v}_m = (v_x - u)\hat{i} - v_y\hat{j}$$

According to given condition that rain appears to fall vertically, so $(v_x - u)$ must be zero.

$\therefore \qquad v_x - u = 0$
or $\qquad v_x = u$

When he doubles his speed, $\vec{v}'_m = 2u\hat{i}$

Now
$$\vec{v}_{Rm} = \vec{v}_R - \vec{v}'_m$$
$$= (v_x\hat{i} - v_y\hat{j}) - (2u\hat{i})$$
$$= (v_x - 2u)\hat{i} - v_y\hat{j}$$

Figure. 4.13

The $\vec{v}_{Rm}$ makes an angle θ with the vertical
$$\tan\theta = \frac{x - \text{component of } \vec{v}_{Rm}}{y - \text{component of } \vec{v}_{Rm}}$$

$$= \frac{(v_x - 2u)}{-v_y}$$

$$= \frac{u - 2u}{-v_y}$$

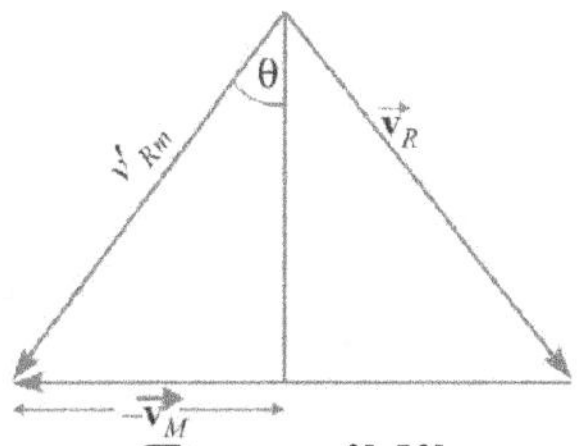

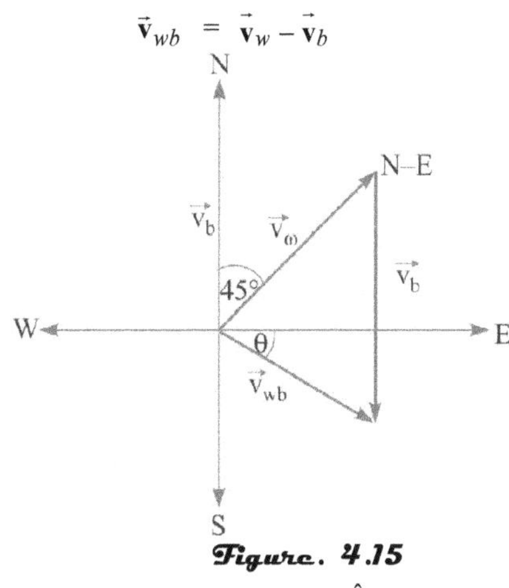

Figure. 4.14

which gives

$$v_y = \frac{u}{\tan\theta}$$

Thus the velocity of rain

$$\vec{\mathbf{v}}_R = v_x\hat{\mathbf{i}} - v_y\hat{\mathbf{i}}$$

$$= u\hat{\mathbf{i}} - \frac{u}{\tan\theta}\hat{\mathbf{j}}. \; \textit{Ans.}$$

Example 5. In a harbour, wind is blowing at the speed of 72 km / h and the flag on the mast of a boat anchored in the harbour flutters along the N- E direction. If the boat starts moving at a speed of 51 km /h to the north, what is the direction of the flag on the mast of the boat? **[NCERT]**

Sol. The speed of the wind is 72 km /h and its direction is along the direction in which flag flutters, i.e., along N -E. When boat starts moving the flag flutters in the relative direction of motion of wind with respect to boat. We have, velocity of wind

$$\vec{\mathbf{v}} = (72\sin45°\hat{\mathbf{i}} + 72\cos45°\hat{\mathbf{j}}) \text{ km /h}$$

and velocity of boat $\vec{\mathbf{v}}_b = 51\hat{\mathbf{j}}$ km/h.

The velocity of wind with respect to boat

$$\vec{\mathbf{v}}_{wb} = \vec{\mathbf{v}}_w - \vec{\mathbf{v}}_b$$

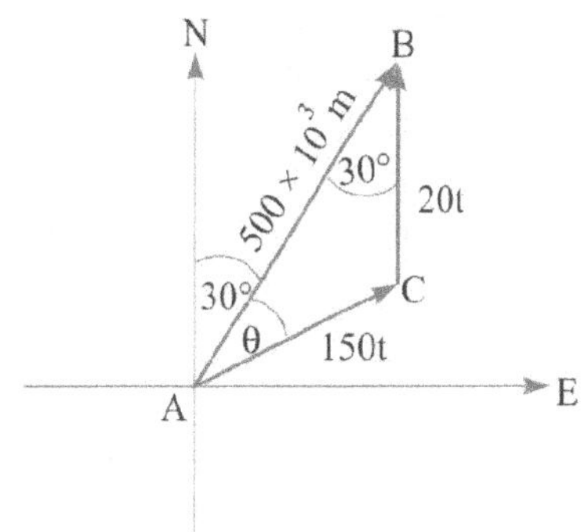

Figure. 4.15

$$= (72\sin45°\,\hat{\mathbf{i}} + 72\cos45°\,\hat{\mathbf{j}}) - (51\,\hat{\mathbf{j}}) \text{ km/h}$$

$$= (72\sin45°)\,\hat{\mathbf{i}} + (72\cos45° - 51)\,\hat{\mathbf{j}} \text{ km/h}.$$

Let $\vec{\mathbf{v}}_{wb}$ makes an angle θ with east then

$$\tan\theta = \frac{72\cos45° - 51}{72\sin45°} = \frac{0.081}{50.92} = -0.0016$$

which gives $\theta \simeq -0.01°$

Hence the flag will flutter almost along east direction

Example 6. An aeroplane has to go from a point A to another point B, 500 km away due 30°east of north. A wind is blowing due north at a speed of 20 m/s. The air -speed of the plane is 150 m/s.

(a) Find the direction in which the pilot should head the plane to reach the point B

(b) Find the time taken by plane to go from A to B.

Sol. The given points are shown in the *fig.* 4.10. The motion of aeroplane is along the resultant of air- speed of aeroplane and wind velocity. Let aeroplane should head at an angle θ with the line joining A and B, and it takes time t to reach the point B.

$$AC = \text{speed of aeroplane} \times \text{time of motion}$$
$$= 150\,t \text{ m}$$
and
$$CB = \text{speed of wind} \times \text{time}$$
$$= 20\,t \text{ m}$$

(a) By sine formula, we have

Figure. 4.16

$$\frac{AC}{\sin30°} = \frac{CB}{\sin\theta}$$

or $$\frac{150t}{\sin30°} = \frac{20t}{\sin\theta}$$

$$\therefore \quad \sin\theta = \frac{1}{15}$$

or $$\theta = \sin^{-1}\left(\frac{1}{15}\right) \text{ east of the line } AB.$$

(b) Again by sine formula we have,

$$\frac{AC}{\sin30°} = \frac{AB}{\sin[180° - (30° + \theta)]}$$

$$\left\{ \begin{aligned} \sin(30° + \theta) &= \sin30°\cos\theta + \cos30°\sin\theta \\ &= \frac{1}{2} \times 0.99 + \frac{\sqrt{3}}{2} \times \frac{1}{15} \\ &= 0.495 + 0.058 \\ &= 0.5527 \end{aligned} \right.$$

or $$\frac{150t}{\sin30°} = \frac{500 \times 10^3}{\sin(30° + \theta)}$$

or $$\frac{150t}{(1/2)} = \frac{500 \times 10^3}{0.5527}$$

$$\therefore \quad t = \frac{500 \times 10^3}{0.5527 \times 2 \times 150}$$

$$= 3015.5 \text{ s} = 50.3 \text{ min } \textit{Ans.}$$

Example 7. A river is flowing due east with a speed 3 m/s. A swimmer can swim in still water at a speed of 4 m/s shown in given figure. **[NCERT Exemplar]**

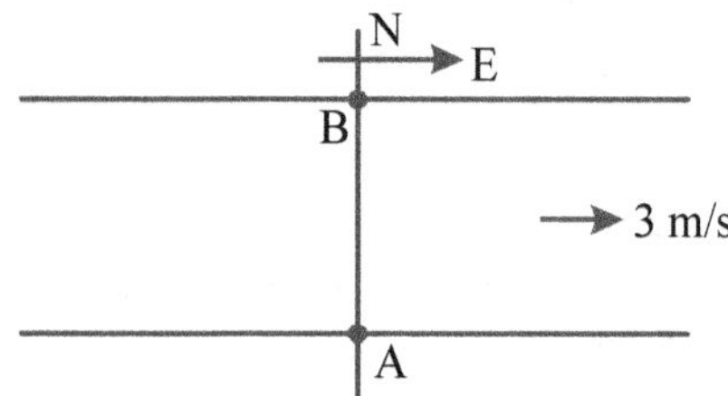

Figure. 4.17

(a) If swimmer starts swimming due north, what will be his resultant velocity (magnitude and direction)?

(b) If he wants to start from point A on south bank and reach opposite point B on north bank, then
   (i) which direction should he swim?
   (ii) what will be his resultant speed?

(c) From two different cases as mentioned in (a) and (b) above, in which case will he reach opposite bank in shorter time?

Sol. Speed of the river (v_r) = 3 m/s (east)
Speed of swimmer (v_s) = 4 m/s (north)

(a) When swimmer starts swimming due north then his resultant velocity

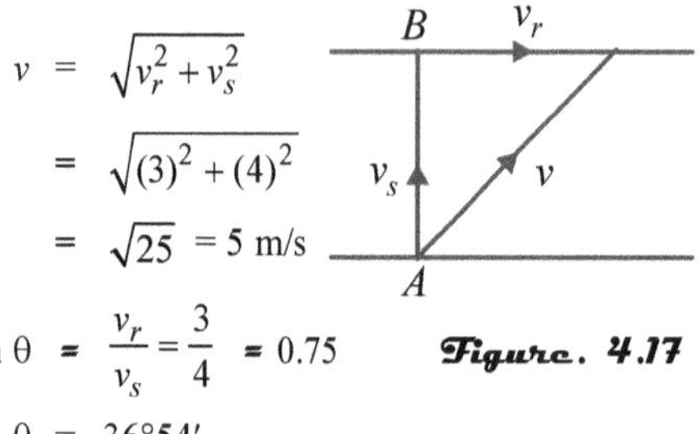

$$v = \sqrt{v_r^2 + v_s^2}$$

$$= \sqrt{(3)^2 + (4)^2}$$

$$= \sqrt{25} = 5 \text{ m/s}$$

$$\tan \theta = \frac{v_r}{v_s} = \frac{3}{4} = 0.75 \qquad \text{Figure. 4.17}$$

or $\theta = 36°54'$

(b) To reach opposite points B, the swimmer should swim at an angle θ of north.

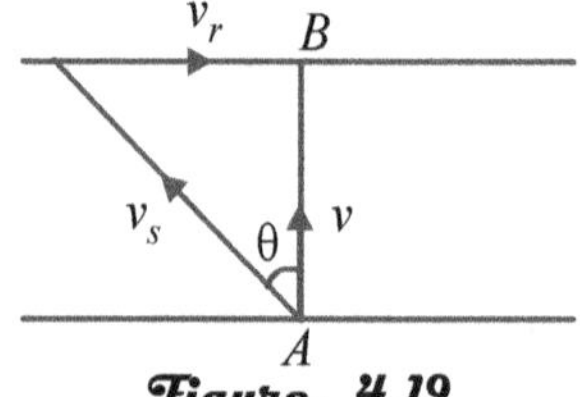

Figure. 4.19

Resultant speed of the swimmer

$$v = \sqrt{v_s^2 - v_r^2}$$

$$= \sqrt{(4)^2 - (3)^2}$$

$$= \sqrt{16 - 9} = \sqrt{7} \text{ m/s}$$

$$\tan \theta = \frac{v_r}{v} = \frac{3}{\sqrt{7}}$$

or $\theta = \tan^{-1}\left(\dfrac{3}{\sqrt{7}}\right)$ of north

(c) In case (a),
Time taken by the swimmer to cross the river

$$t_2 = \frac{b}{v_s} = \frac{b}{4} \text{s}$$

In case (b),
Time taken by the swimmer to cross the river

$$t_2 = \frac{b}{\sqrt{7}}$$

Clearly, $t_1 < t_2$.
Hence, the swimmer will cross the river in shorter time in case (a).

Example 8. Two swimmers leave point A on one bank of the river to reach point B lying right across on the other bank. One of them crosses the river along the straight line AB while the other swims at right angles to the stream and then walks the distance that he has been carried away by the stream to get the point B. What was the velocity u of his walking if both swimmers reached the destination simultaneously? The stream velocity $v_0 = 2.0$ km/h and the velocity v' of each swimmer with respect to water equal 2.5 km/h.

Sol.

Suppose width of the river is b. The time taken by swimmer to cross the river along the line AB

$$t_1 = \frac{b}{\sqrt{v'^2 - v_0^2}} \qquad \text{...(i)}$$

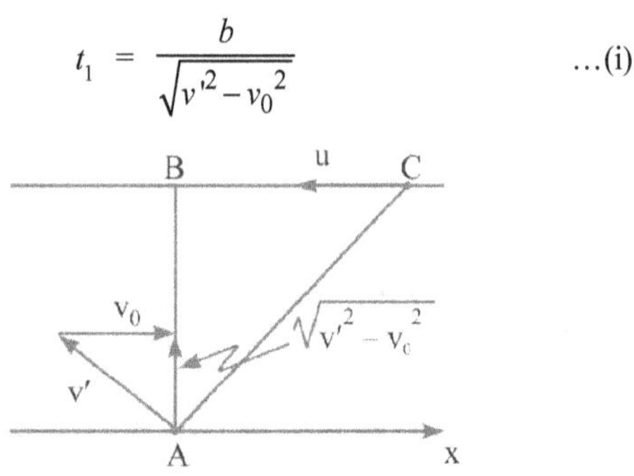

Figure. 4.20

For the other swimmer, which swims at right angle to the stream, the time to cross the river

$$t = \frac{b}{v'}$$

The second swimmer reaches at point C.
Then he walks the distance CB with velocity u. The time taken to travel the distance

$$t = \frac{BC}{u}$$

where BC = river velocity × time to cross the river

$$= v_0 \times \frac{b}{v'}$$

Thus, total time of the second swimmer takes to reach the point B on the opposite bank

$$= \frac{b}{v'} + \frac{(v_0 b / v')}{u} \qquad \text{...(ii)}$$

These two times are equal therefore from equations (i) and (ii), we have

$$\frac{b}{\sqrt{v'^2 - v_0^2}} = \frac{b}{v'} + \frac{v_0 b}{v' u}$$

or $$\frac{1}{\sqrt{v'^2 - v_0^2}} = \frac{1}{v'} + \frac{v_0}{v' u}$$

Substituting the values of v_0 and v', we have

$$\frac{1}{\sqrt{2.5^2 - 2.0^2}} = \frac{1}{2.5} + \frac{2}{2.5 u}$$

After solving, we get $u = 3$ km/h. *Ans.*

In Chapter Exercise 4.1

1. The position of a particle is given by

   $\vec{r} = 3.0t\,\hat{i} + 2.0\,t^2\,\hat{j} + 5.0\,\hat{k}$, where t is in seconds and the coefficients have the proper units for $\vec{r}$ to be in metre.

   (a) Find v(t) and a(t) of the particle.
   (b) Find the magnitude and direction of v(t) at t = 3.0 s.

   Ans. (a) $\vec{v}(t) = 3.0\,\hat{i} + 4.0t\,\hat{j},\ \vec{a}(t) = 4.0\,\hat{j}$

   (b) **12.4 m/s, 76° with x-axis.**

2. A train is moving with a velocity of 30 km/h due east and a car is moving with a velocity of 40 km/h due north. What is the velocity of car as appears to a passenger in the train ?

   Ans. **50 km/h, 36° 52' west of north.**

3. Rain is falling vertically with a speed of 24 m/s. A woman rides a bicycle with a speed of 12 m/s in east to west direction. What is the direction in which she should hold her umbrella ?

Ans. **At an angle** $\tan^{-1}\left(\dfrac{1}{2}\right)$ **with the vertical towards the east.**

4. A man in a row boat must get from point A to point B on the opposite bank of the river (see figure). The distance BC = a. The width of the river AC = b. At what minimum speed u relative to the still water should the boat travel to reach the point B? The velocity of flow of the river is v_0.

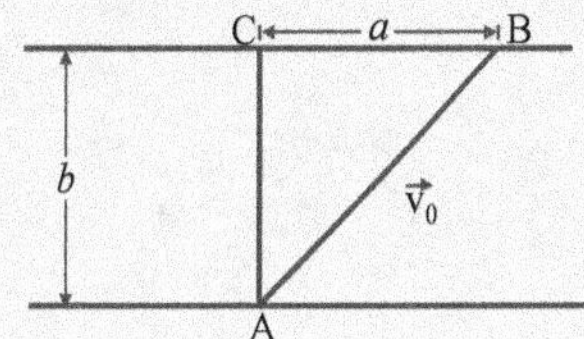

Ans. $\dfrac{v_0 b}{\sqrt{a^2 + b^2}}$

4.7 PROJECTILE MOTION

When a particle is projected obliquely near the earth surface, it moves simultaneously in horizontal and vertical directions. Motion of such a particle is called projectile motion. Since there is no force acting in horizontal direction, the velocity remains constant in this direction. In vertical direction gravitational pull of earth produces the acceleration.

Assumptions used in projectile motion

(i) Neglecting the effect of air resistance on the projectile.

(ii) Assuming the acceleration due to gravity is constant at each point of projectile.

(iii) Neglecting the effect of curvature of earth.

We will discuss the following types of projections in details :

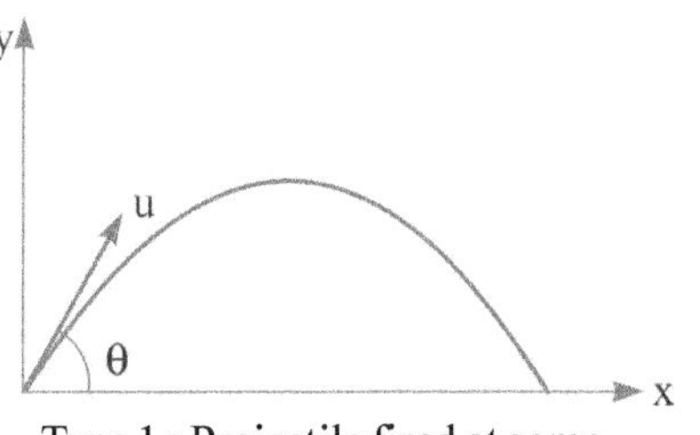

Type 1 : Projectile fired at some angle with the horizontal.

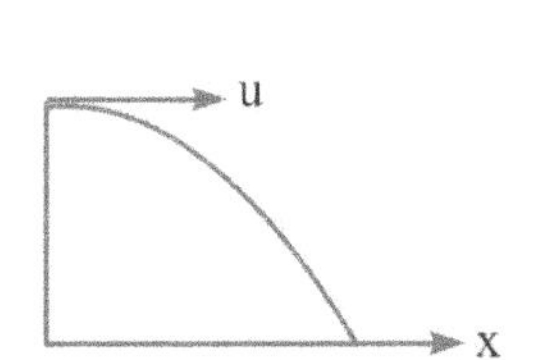

Type 2 : Horizontal projection

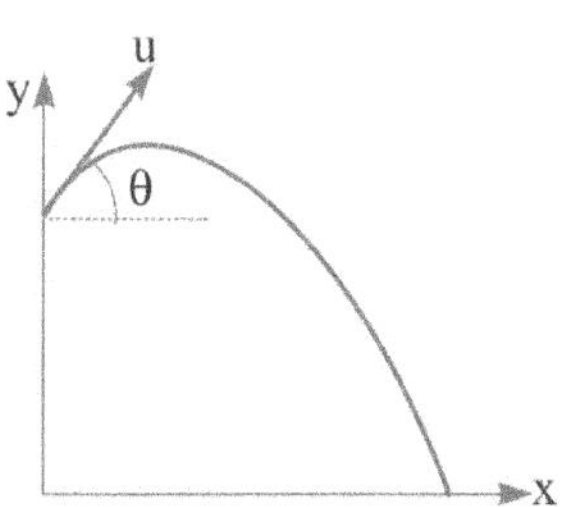

Type 3 : Projectile fired from some height

Type 4 : Projection on an inclined plane

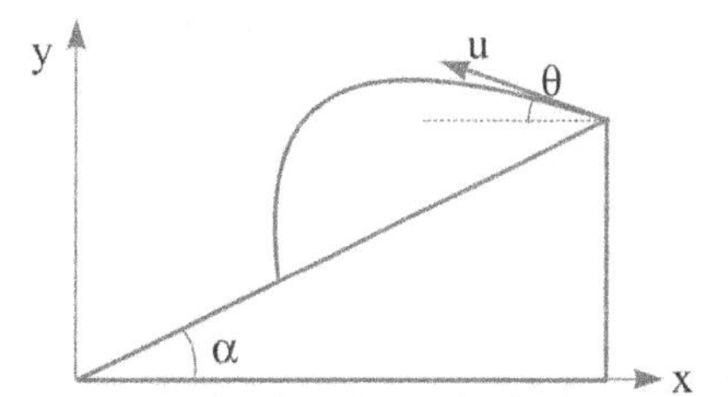

Type 5 : Projection down the inclined plane

Figure. 4.21

ANALYSIS OF PROJECTILE OF TYPE 1

Let us consider a particle is projected with initial velocity u at an angle θ with the horizontal (called angle of projection). The velocity u has two rectangular components:

(i)   The horizontal component $u\cos\theta$, which remains constant throughout the motion of particle.

(ii)   The vertical component $u\sin\theta$, which changes with time due to effect of gravity. Thus we have initial velocity

$$\vec{\mathbf{u}} = u_x\hat{\mathbf{i}} + u_y\hat{\mathbf{j}}$$

or

$$\vec{\mathbf{u}} = u\cos\theta\,\hat{\mathbf{i}} + u\sin\theta\,\hat{\mathbf{j}}$$

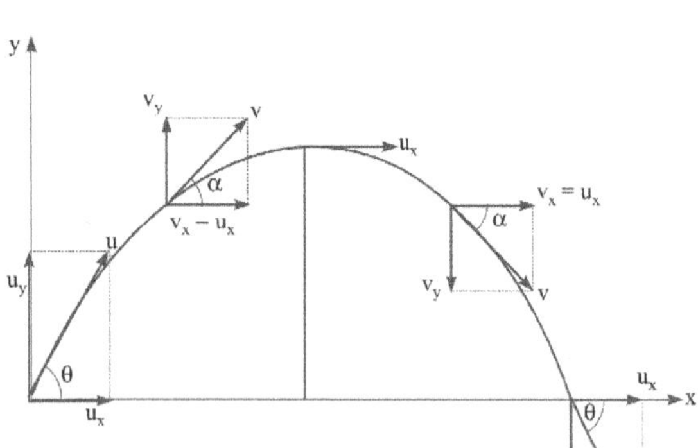

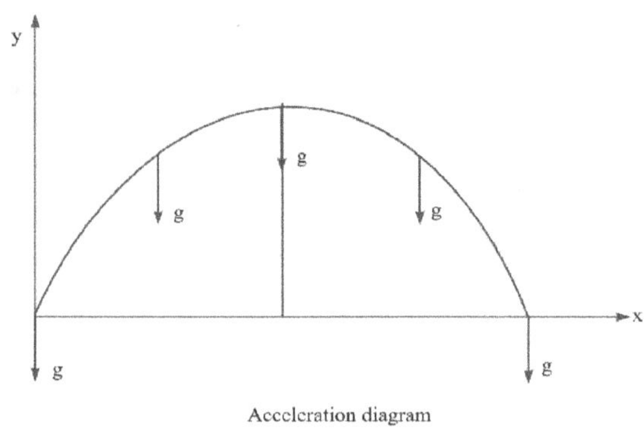

Figure. 4.22

Velocity at any time t : Using first equation of motion in vertical direction, we have

$$v_y = u_y - gt$$
$$= u\sin\theta - gt$$

$\therefore$ Velocity at any time t, $\vec{\mathbf{v}} = v_x\hat{\mathbf{i}} + \mathbf{v}_y\hat{\mathbf{j}}$

or

$$\vec{\mathbf{v}} = u\cos\theta\,\hat{\mathbf{i}} + (u\sin\theta - gt)\hat{\mathbf{j}}.$$

Velocity at any height : At any height h

$$v_x = u_x = u\cos\theta \qquad \ldots(i)$$

and

$$v_y^2 = u_y^2 - 2gh$$
$$= (u\sin\theta)^2 - 2gh \qquad \ldots(ii)$$

Squaring (i) and adding with equation (ii), we get

$$v = \sqrt{u^2 - 2gh}.$$

Position at any time t

Position of particle at any time t, is given by

$$\vec{\mathbf{r}} = x\hat{\mathbf{i}} + y\hat{\mathbf{j}}$$

where

$$x = u\cos\theta\, t \qquad \ldots(1)$$

and

$$y = u\sin\theta\, t - \frac{1}{2}gt^2$$

$\therefore$

$$\vec{\mathbf{r}} = u\cos\theta\, t\,\hat{\mathbf{i}} + \left(u\sin\theta\, t - \frac{1}{2}gt^2\right)\hat{\mathbf{j}}$$

or

$$r = \sqrt{(u\cos\theta\, t)^2 + \left(u\sin\theta\, t - \frac{1}{2}gt^2\right)^2}$$

$$= ut\sqrt{1 + \left(\frac{gt}{2u}\right)^2 - \frac{gt\sin\theta}{u}}$$

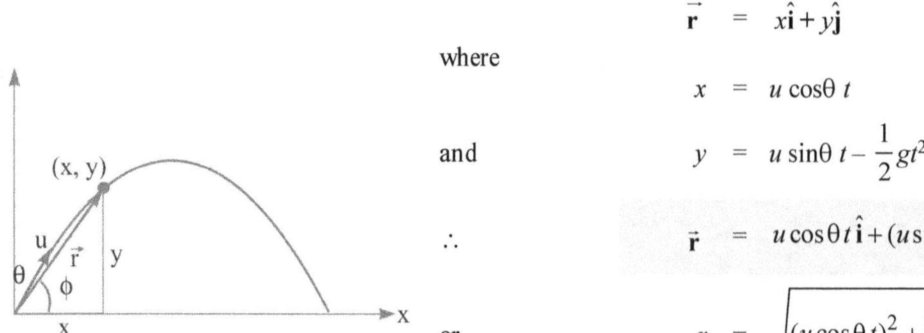

and
$$\tan\phi = \frac{y}{x}$$

or
$$\phi = \tan^{-1}\left[\frac{u\sin\theta\, t - \frac{1}{2}gt^2}{ut\cos\theta}\right]$$

$$= \tan^{-1}\left[\frac{2u\sin\theta - gt}{2u\cos\theta}\right].$$

The angle of elevation ϕ of the highest point of the projectile;

$$t = \frac{u\sin\theta}{g}$$

$$\therefore \qquad \tan\phi = \frac{2u\sin\theta - g\times\dfrac{u\sin\theta}{g}}{2u\cos\theta}$$

or
$$\tan\phi = \frac{\tan\theta}{2}$$

Equation of trajectory

We have,
$$x = u\cos\theta\, t$$

or
$$t = \left(\frac{x}{u\cos\theta}\right)$$

and
$$y = u\sin\theta\, t - \frac{1}{2}gt^2$$

$$= u\sin\theta\left(\frac{x}{u\cos\theta}\right) - \frac{1}{2}g\left(\frac{x}{u\cos\theta}\right)^2$$

$$y = x\tan\theta - \frac{gx^2}{2u^2\cos^2\theta}.$$

On comparing this equation with general equation of parabola, $y = ax \pm bx^2$, we find that path of projectile is *parabolic* in nature.

Time of flight (T) : Total time of motion of particle in air is called *time of flight*.
The displacement in vertical direction (y-axis) becomes zero in whole time of motion. So we have

$$y = u_y t - \frac{1}{2}a_y t^2$$

or
$$0 = u_y T - \frac{1}{2}g T^2$$

which gives
$$T = \frac{2u_y}{g} = \frac{2u\sin\theta}{g}.$$

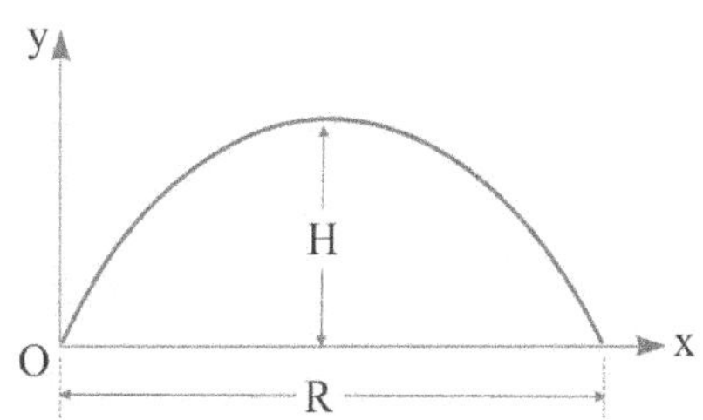

Figure. **4.25**

Maximum height attained (H): The maximum vertical distance achieved by particle is called *maximum height*.

At the highest point of projection $v_y = 0$, so we have,

$$v_y^2 = u_y^2 - 2gh$$

or
$$0 = u_y^2 - 2gH$$

which gives
$$H = \frac{u_y^2}{2g} = \frac{u^2 \sin^2\theta}{2g}.$$

Horizontal range (R) : The horizontal distance moved by particle in total time of flight is called *horizontal range*.

Horizontal range,
$$R = u_x \times T = u_x \times \frac{2u_y}{g}$$

$$= \frac{2u_x u_y}{g} = \frac{2u\cos\theta\, u\sin\theta}{g}$$

or
$$R = \frac{u^2 \sin 2\theta}{g}.$$

For maximum range,
$$\sin 2\theta = 1 \ \text{ or } \ 2\theta = 90° \ \text{ or } \ \theta = 45°.$$

Thus
$$R_{max} = \frac{u^2}{g}.$$

Corresponding,
$$H = \frac{u^2 \sin^2 45°}{2g} = \frac{u^2}{4g}.$$

There are two angles of projection for same range:

Replacing θ by $(90° - \theta)$ in the formula of range, we get

$$R = \frac{u^2 \sin 2(90° - \theta)}{g}$$

$$= \frac{u^2 \sin(180° - 2\theta)}{g}$$

$$= \frac{u^2 \sin 2\theta}{g} = R.$$

Thus, for a given velocity of projection, a projectile has the same range for angle of projection θ and $(90° - \theta)$.

Time of flight for angle of projection θ,
$$T_1 = \frac{2u\sin\theta}{g}$$

and time of flight for angle of projection $(90° - \theta)$,

$$T_2 = \frac{2u\sin(90° - \theta)}{g}$$

$$= \frac{2u\cos\theta}{g}.$$

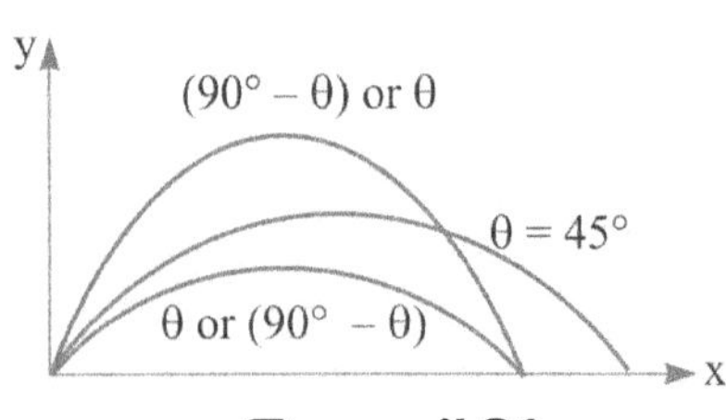

Figure. 4.26

Multiplying T_1 and T_2, we get

$$\therefore \quad T_1 T_2 = \frac{2u\sin\theta}{g} \times \frac{2u\cos\theta}{g}$$

or
$$T_1 T_2 = \frac{2}{g}\left(\frac{u^2 \sin 2\theta}{g}\right)$$

or
$$T_1 T_2 = \frac{2R}{g}.$$

More about projectile motion

1. If t_1 is the time taken by projectile to reach a point P at height h and t_2 is the time taken from point P to ground level, then

$$t_1 + t_2 = T = \frac{2u\sin\theta}{g}$$

or

$$u\sin\theta = \frac{g(t_1 + t_2)}{2}.$$

The height of point P,

$$h = u\sin\theta\, t_1 - \frac{1}{2}gt_1^2$$

$$= \frac{g(t_1+t_2)}{2}t_1 - \frac{1}{2}gt_1^2$$

or

$$h = \frac{1}{2}g\,t_1\,t_2.$$

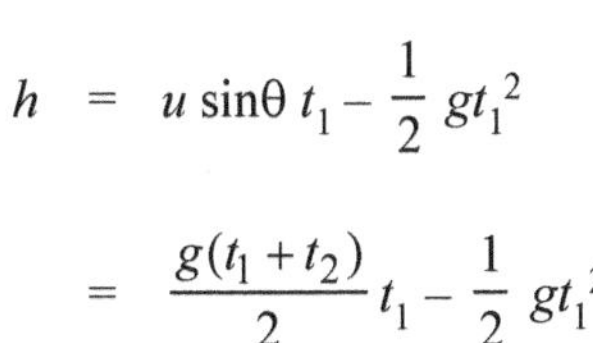

Figure. 4.27

2. **Change in momentum :** Change in momentum between two positions of projectile is given by

$$\Delta\vec{P} = \vec{P}_f - \vec{P}_i = m(\vec{v}_f - \vec{v}_i).$$

(a) Between point of projection and highest point

$$\vec{v}_i = u\cos\theta\,\hat{i} + u\sin\theta\,\hat{j}$$

and

$$\vec{v}_f = u\cos\theta\,\hat{i}$$

$\therefore$

$$\Delta\vec{P} = m[(u\cos\theta\,\hat{i}) - (u\cos\theta\,\hat{i} + u\sin\theta\,\hat{j})]$$

or

$$\Delta P = mu\sin\theta$$

(b) For the complete projectile motion

$$\vec{v}_i = u\cos\theta\,\hat{i} + u\sin\theta\,\hat{j}$$

$$\vec{v}_f = u\cos\theta\,\hat{i} - u\sin\theta\,\hat{j}$$

$\therefore$

$$\Delta\vec{P} = m[(u\cos\theta\,\hat{i} - u\sin\theta\,\hat{j}) - (u\cos\theta\,\hat{i} + u\sin\theta\,\hat{j})]$$

or

$$\Delta P = 2mu\sin\theta$$

ANALYSIS OF PROJECTILE OF TYPE 2 : HORIZONTAL PROJECTION

Let a particle be projected horizontally with initial velocity u from height h.

Velocity at any time t

We have,

$$v_x = u$$

and

$$v_y = u_y + gt$$

or

$$= 0 + gt$$

$\therefore$

$$\vec{v} = u\hat{i} - gt\hat{j}$$

and

$$v = \sqrt{u^2 + (gt)^2}$$

Also

$$\tan\alpha = \frac{gt}{u}.$$

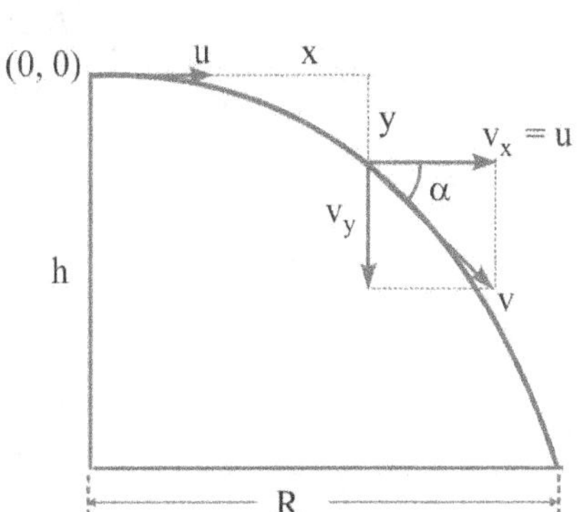

Figure. 4.28

Position at any time t

Taking point of projection as the origin, the position vector at any time t

$$\vec{r} = x\hat{\mathbf{i}} - y\hat{\mathbf{j}}.$$

where

$$x = ut$$

and

$$y = \frac{1}{2}gt^2$$

$\therefore$

$$\vec{r} = ut\hat{\mathbf{i}} - \frac{1}{2}gt^2\,\hat{\mathbf{j}}$$

Displacement

$$s = r = \sqrt{(ut)^2 + \left(\frac{1}{2}gt^2\right)^2}$$

Equation of trajectory

We have,

$$x = ut \quad \text{or} \quad t = \frac{x}{u}$$

and

$$y = -\frac{1}{2}gt^2$$

$$= -\frac{1}{2}g\left(\frac{x}{u}\right)^2$$

or

$$y = -\frac{1}{2}g\frac{x^2}{u^2}$$

Time of flight (T)

We have,

$$h = u_y t + \frac{1}{2}a_y t^2$$

or

$$h = 0 + \frac{1}{2}gT^2$$

which gives

$$T = \sqrt{\frac{2h}{g}}\,.$$

Horizontal range (R)

$$R = u_x \times T$$

$$= u\sqrt{\frac{2h}{g}}\,.$$

The average acceleration in total time of flight is g downward.

ANALYSIS OF PROJECTILE OF TYPE 3

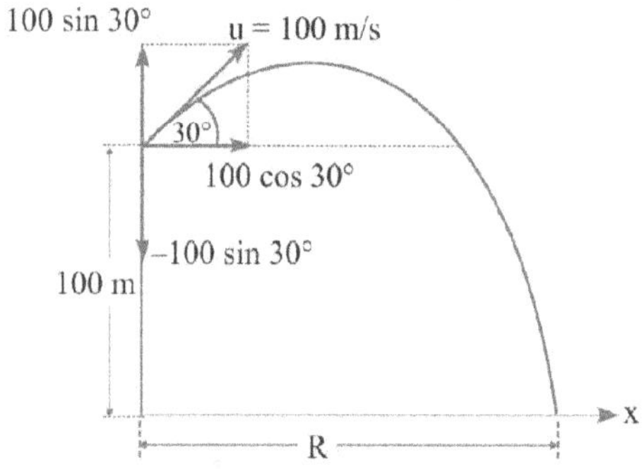

Method - I :

Let us consider a particle is projected with initial velocity 100 m/s at an angle 30° with the horizontal. The height of projection is 100 m.

Time of flight (T)

We have

$$y = u_y t + \frac{1}{2}gt^2$$

or

$$100 = -100\sin 30°\, T + \frac{1}{2} \times 10 \times T^2$$

or

$$T^2 - 10T - 20 = 0$$

Figure. 4.29

which gives $\qquad T = \dfrac{10 \pm \sqrt{(-10)^2 - 4 \times 1 \times (-20)}}{2}$

$\qquad\qquad = 11.71\,\text{s}$

$\qquad\qquad$ (consider only positive value)

The horizontal range (R)

$$R = u_x \times T = 100 \cos 30° \times 11.71$$

$$= 100 \times \dfrac{\sqrt{3}}{2} \times 11.71$$

$$= 1014\,\text{m}.$$

Method - II :

Taking point of projection as the origin, the coordinates of point of strike are $(R, -100\,\text{m})$.
We have,

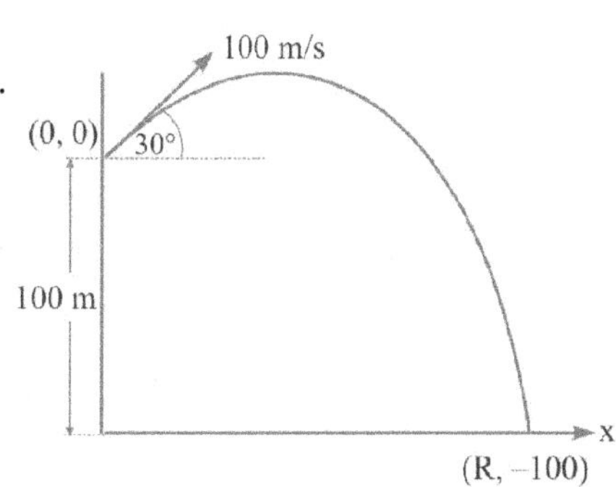

Figure. 4.30

$$y = x\tan\theta - \dfrac{gx^2}{2u^2\cos^2\theta}$$

Here $\qquad\qquad y = -100\,\text{m} \quad\text{and}\quad x = R$

$\therefore \qquad\qquad -100 = R\tan 30° - \dfrac{10R^2}{2(100)^2\cos^2 30°}$

or $\qquad R^2 - 866\,R - 150000 = 0$

which gives, $\qquad R = \dfrac{866 \pm \sqrt{(866)^2 + 4 \times 150000}}{2}$

$\qquad\qquad = 1014\,\text{m}$ (consider only positive value)

Time of flight, $\qquad T = \dfrac{R}{u\cos\theta} = 11.71\,\text{s}.$

FORMULAE USED

Projectile Type 1

1. $u_x = u\cos\theta,\; u_y = u\sin\theta$

   $a_x = 0,\; a_y = -g.$

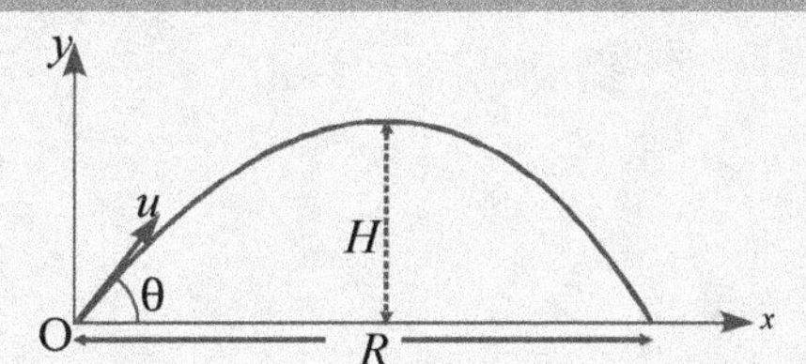

2. Position after time t

   $x = u\cos\theta\, t, \quad y = u\sin\theta\, t - \dfrac{1}{2}gt^2$

3. Equation of trajectory

   $y = x\tan\theta - \dfrac{gx^2}{2u^2\cos^2\theta}.$

4. Time of flight, $T = \dfrac{2u\sin\theta}{g}.$

5. Maximum height, $H = \dfrac{u^2\sin^2\theta}{2g}.$

6.   Horizontal range, $R = \dfrac{u^2 \sin 2\theta}{g}$

7.   Maximum range, $R_{max} = \dfrac{u^2}{g}$, for $\theta = 45°$

Projectile Type 2

1.   Position after time t

$$x = ut, \quad y = \frac{1}{2}gt^2$$

2.   Equation of trajectory, $y = \dfrac{gx^2}{2u^2}$.

3.   Velocity after time t, $v = \sqrt{u^2 + (gt)^2}$

4.   Time to hit the ground, $T = \sqrt{\dfrac{2h}{g}}$

5.   Horizontal range, $R = uT = u\sqrt{\dfrac{2h}{g}}$.

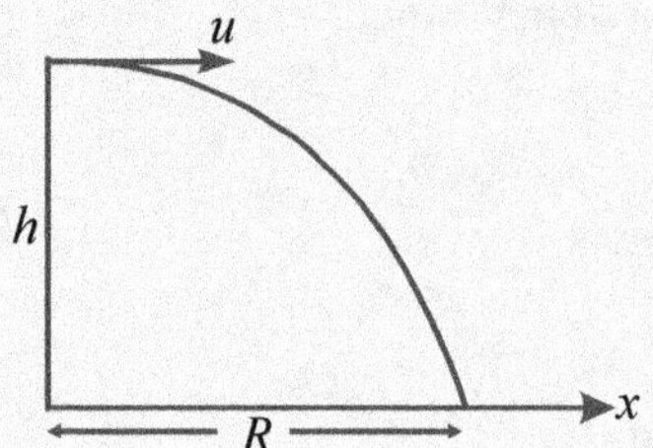

EXAMPLES BASED ON PROJECTILE TYPE 1, TYPE 2 AND TYPE 3

Example 9. A bullet fired at an angle of 30° with the horizontal hits the ground 3.0 km away. By adjusting its angle of projection, can one hope to hit a target 5.0 km away? Assume the muzzle speed to be fixed, and neglect air resistance. **[NCERT]**

Sol. Here $R = 3$ km $= 3000$ m, $\theta = 30°$, $g = 9.8$ m s^{-2}

As $R = \dfrac{u^2 \sin 2\theta}{g}$

$\Rightarrow \quad 3000 = \dfrac{u^2 \sin 2 \times 30°}{9.8} = \dfrac{u^2 \sin 60}{9.8}$

$\Rightarrow \quad u^2 = \dfrac{3000 \times 9.8}{\dfrac{\sqrt{3}}{2}} = 3464 \times 9.8$

Also, $R' = \dfrac{u^2 \sin 2\theta'}{g}$

$\Rightarrow 5000 = \dfrac{3464 \times 9.8 \times \sin 2\theta}{9.8}$

i.e. $\sin 2\theta' = \dfrac{5000}{3464} = 1.44$

which is impossible because sine of an angle cannot be more than 1. Thus this target cannot be hoped to be hit.

Example 10. A fighter plane flying horizontally at an altitude of 1.5 km with speed 720 km/h passes directly overhead an anti-aircraft gun. At what angle from the vertical should the gun be fired for the shell with muzzle speed 600 ms^{-1} to hit the plane? At what minimum altitude should the pilot fly the plane to avoid being hit? (Take $g = 10$ ms^{-2}) **[NCERT]**

Sol. Velocity of plane,

$$v = 720 \times \frac{5}{18} \text{ ms}^{-1} = 200 \text{ ms}^{-1}$$

Velocity of shell $= 600$ ms^{-1};

$$\sin \theta = \frac{200}{600} = \frac{1}{3}$$

or $\theta = \sin^{-1}\left(\dfrac{1}{3}\right) = 19.47°$

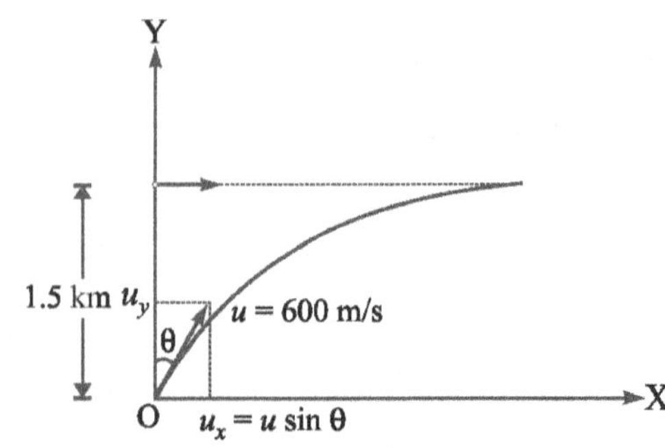

Figure. 4.31

Let h be the required minimum height. Using equation

$v^2 - u^2 = 2a\,s$, we get
$$(0)^2 - (600\cos\theta)^2 = -2 \times 10 \times h$$

or, $h = \dfrac{600 \times 600(1 - \sin^2\theta)}{20}$

$$= 30 \times 600\left(1 - \frac{1}{9}\right) = \frac{8}{9} \times 30 \times 600 \text{ m} = 16 \text{ km}.$$

Example 11. The ceiling of a long hall is 25 m high. What is the maximum horizontal distance that a ball thrown with a speed of 40 m/s can go without hitting the ceiling of the hall ?

Sol.

Given $H = 25$ m, $u = 40$ m/s.

If the ball is thrown at an angle θ with the horizontal, then maximum height of flight is given by

$$H = \frac{u^2 \sin^2\theta}{2g}$$

or
$$25 = \frac{40^2 \sin^2\theta}{2 \times 9.8}$$

which on solving gives
$$\sin\theta = 0.554 \text{ and}$$
$$\cos\theta = 0.833.$$

The maximum horizontal distance is given by

$$R = \frac{u^2 \sin 2\theta}{g} = \frac{2u^2 \sin\theta\cos\theta}{g}$$

$$= \frac{2 \times 40^2 \times 0.554 \times 0.833}{9.8}$$

$$= 150.7 \text{ m} \qquad \text{Ans.}$$

Example 12. A boy stands at 39.2 m from a building and throws a ball which just passes through a window 19.6 m above the ground. Calculate the velocity of projection of the ball.

Sol. Given $\qquad H = 19.6$ m

and $\qquad R = 39.2 + 39.2 = 78.4$ m

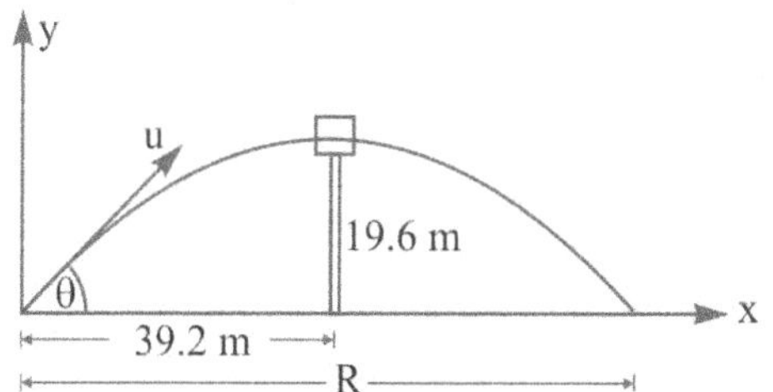

Figure. 4.32

We know that $\qquad H = \dfrac{u^2 \sin^2\theta}{2g}$ ...(i)

and $\qquad R = \dfrac{2u^2 \sin\theta\cos\theta}{g}$ ...(ii)

$\therefore \qquad \dfrac{H}{R} = \dfrac{\tan\theta}{4}$

or $\qquad \tan\theta = \dfrac{4H}{R} = \dfrac{4 \times 19.6}{78.4} = 1$

or $\qquad \theta = 45°$

From equation (ii), we have
$$R = 78.4$$

$$= \frac{u^2 \sin(2 \times 45°)}{9.8}$$

On solving, we get $\qquad u = 27.72$ m/s. $\qquad$ *Ans.*

Example 13. If R is the horizontal range for θ inclination and h is the maximum height reached by the projectile, show that the maximum range in given by $\dfrac{R^2}{8h} + 2h$.

Sol. We know that horizontal range,

$$R = \frac{u^2 \sin 2\theta}{g}$$

and maximum height, $\quad h = \dfrac{u^2 \sin^2\theta}{2g}$

$\therefore \quad \dfrac{R^2}{8h} + 2h = \dfrac{\left[\dfrac{u^2\sin 2\theta}{g}\right]^2}{8\left[\dfrac{u^2\sin^2\theta}{2g}\right]} + 2\left[\dfrac{u^2\sin^2\theta}{2g}\right]$

$$= \frac{u^4(2\sin\theta\cos\theta)^2}{g^2 \times 8\dfrac{u^2\sin^2\theta}{2g}} + \frac{u^2\sin^2\theta}{g}$$

$$= \frac{u^2}{g}(\cos^2\theta + \sin^2\theta)$$

$$= \frac{u^2}{g} = R_{\text{max}}.$$

Example 14. A hunter aims his gun and fires a bullet directly at a monkey on a tree. At the instant the bullet leaves the barrel of the gun, the monkey drops. Will the bullet hit the monkey ?

Sol. Suppose the gun situated at O directed towards the monkey at position M. Let bullet leaves the barrel of the gun with velocity u at an angle θ with the horizontal. Let bullet crosses the vertical line MB at A after time t. Horizontal distance travelled

$$OB = x = u\cos\theta\, t$$

or $\qquad t = \dfrac{x}{u\cos\theta}$

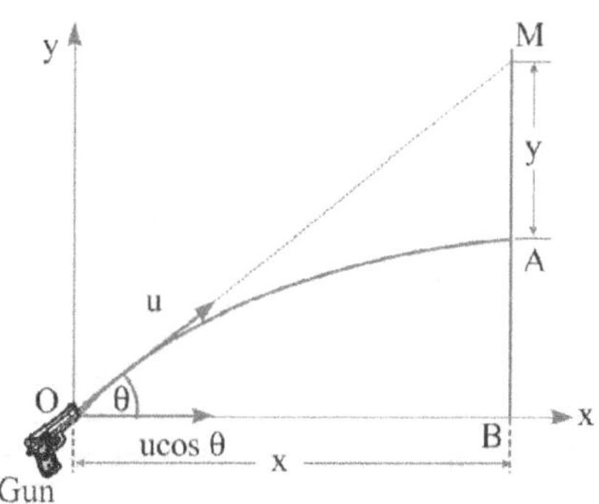

Figure. 4.33

For motion of bullet from O to B, the vertical

height $\qquad AB = u \sin\theta\, t - \dfrac{1}{2} g\, t^2$

$$= u \sin\theta \left(\dfrac{x}{u \cos\theta} \right) - \dfrac{1}{2} g\, t^2$$

$$= x \tan\theta - \dfrac{g\, t^2}{2} \qquad\qquad \text{...(i)}$$

Also $\qquad\qquad MB = x \tan\theta$

Now $\qquad\qquad y = MA = MB - AB$

$$= x \tan\theta - \left(x \tan\theta - \dfrac{g\, t^2}{2} \right)$$

$$= \dfrac{1}{2} g\, t^2$$

Thus, in time t the bullet passes through A a vertical distance $\dfrac{1}{2} g\, t^2$

below M.

The vertical distance through which the monkey fall in time t,

$$s = \dfrac{1}{2} g\, t^2.$$

Thus, the bullet and the monkey will always reach at point A at the same time.

Example 15. **A hill is 500 m high. Supplies are to be sent across the hill using a canon that can hurl packets at a speed of 125 m/s over the hill. The canon is located at a distance of 800 m from the foot of hill and can be moved on the ground at a speed of 2 m/s, so that its distance from the hill can be adjusted. What is the shortest time in which a packet can reach on the ground across the hill? Take g = 10 m/s².** **[NCERT Exemplar]**

Sol. Given, height of the hill $(h) = 500$ m

$\qquad\qquad u = 125$ m/s

To croos the hill, the vertical component of the velocity should be sufficient to cross such height.

$\therefore \qquad\qquad u_y \geq \sqrt{2gh}$

$$\geq \sqrt{2 \times 10 \times 500}$$

$$\geq 100 \text{ m/s}$$

But $\qquad\qquad u^2 = u_x^2 + u_y^2$

$\therefore \qquad$ Horizontal component of initial velcoity

$$u_x = \sqrt{u^2 - u_y^2}$$

$$= \sqrt{(125)^2 - (100)^2} = 75 \text{ m/s}$$

Time taken to reach the top of the hill

$$t = \sqrt{\dfrac{2h}{g}} = \sqrt{\dfrac{2 \times 500}{10}} = 10\text{s}$$

Time taken to reach the ground from the top of the hill $t' = t = 10$ s

Horizontal distance travelled in 10 s

$$x = u_x \times t$$

$$= 75 \times 10 = 750 \text{ m}$$

$\therefore \qquad$ Distance through which canon has to be moved

$$= 800 - 750 = 50 \text{ m}$$

Speed with which canon can move $= 2$ m/s

$\therefore \qquad$ Time taken by canon $= \dfrac{50}{2}$

$$t = 25 \text{ s}$$

$\therefore \qquad$ Total time takne by a packet to reach on the ground

$$= t'' + t + t'$$

$$= 25 + 10 + 10 = 45 \text{ s}$$

Example 16. **A gun can fire shells with maximum speed v_0 and the maximum horizontal range that can be acheived is**

$$R = \dfrac{v_0^2}{g}.$$

If a target farther away by distance Δx (beyond R) has to be hit with the same gun as shown in the figure. Show that it could be achieved by raising the gun to a height at least

$$h = \Delta x \left(1 + \dfrac{\Delta x}{R} \right). \qquad \text{[NCERT Exemplar]}$$

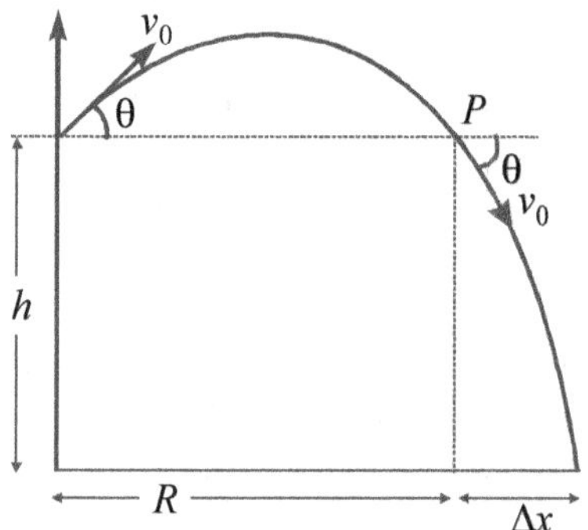

Figure. 4.34

Sol. Maximum horizontal range

$$R = \dfrac{v_0^2}{g} \qquad\qquad \text{...(i)}$$

Let the gun be raised through a height h from the ground so that it can hit the target.

Horizontal component of initial velocity $= v_0 \cos\theta$

Vertical component of initial velocity $= -v_0 \sin\theta$

Taking motion in vertical direction,

$$h = (-v_0 \sin\theta)t + \dfrac{1}{2} g t^2 \qquad\qquad \text{...(ii)}$$

Taking motion in horizontal direction

$$(R + \Delta x) = v_0 \cos\theta \times t$$

or $\qquad\qquad t = \dfrac{(R + \Delta x)}{v_0 \cos\theta} \qquad\qquad \text{...(iii)}$

Substituting value of t in Eq. (ii), we get

$$h = (-v_0 \sin\theta) \times \left(\frac{R+\Delta x}{v_0 \cos\theta}\right) + \frac{1}{2} g \left(\frac{R+\Delta x}{v_0 \cos\theta}\right)^2$$

$$h = -(R+\Delta x)\tan\theta + \frac{1}{2} g \frac{(R+\Delta x)^2}{v_0^2 \cos^2\theta}$$

As angle of projection is $\theta = 45°$ therefore,

$$h = -(R+\Delta x) \times \tan 45° + \frac{1}{2} g \frac{(R+\Delta x)^2}{v_0^2 \cos^2 45°}$$

$$h = -(R+\Delta x) \times 1 + \frac{1}{2} g \frac{(R+\Delta x)^2}{v_0^2 (1/2)}$$

$$h = -(R+\Delta x) + \frac{(R+\Delta x)^2}{R} \qquad \text{[using Eq. (i), } R = v_0^2/g]$$

$$= -(R+\Delta x) + \frac{1}{R}(R^2 + \Delta x^2 + 2R\Delta x)$$

$$= R - \Delta x + \left(R + \frac{\Delta x^2}{R} + 2\Delta x\right)$$

$$= \Delta x + \frac{\Delta x^2}{R}$$

$$\text{or} \quad h = \Delta x\left(1 + \frac{\Delta x}{R}\right).$$

Example 17. A ball rolls off the top of a stairway with a constant horizontal velocity u. If the steps are h metre high and w metre wide, show that the ball will just hit the edge of nth step if

$$n = \frac{2hu^2}{gw^2}.$$

Sol.

For n^{th} step,
Horizontal displacement ; $x = nw$ and vertical displacement, $y = nh$ if t is the time of motion then

$$x = ut \qquad\qquad \text{...(i)}$$
$$\text{or} \quad nw = ut$$
$$\therefore \quad t = \frac{nw}{u}$$

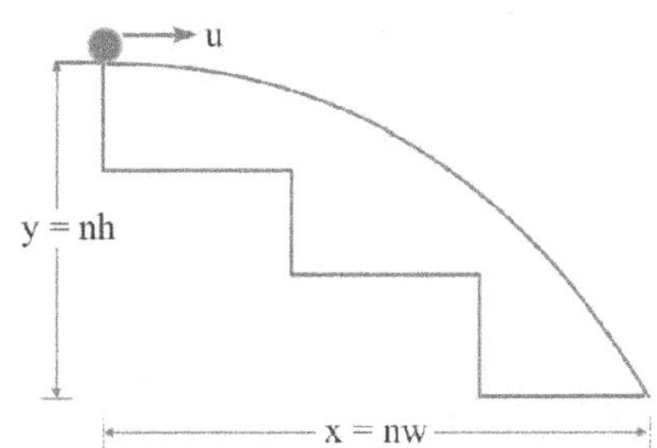

Figure. 4.35

and vertical displacement

$$y = 0 + \frac{1}{2} g t^2$$

$$\text{or} \quad n h = \frac{1}{2} g \left(\frac{nw}{u}\right)^2$$

$$= \frac{1}{2} g \frac{n^2 w^2}{u^2}$$

$$\text{or} \quad n = \frac{2hu^2}{gw^2}. \qquad\qquad\qquad \textbf{\textit{Ans.}}$$

Example 18. A shot is fired with a velocity u at a vertical wall whose distance from the point of projection is x. Prove the greatest height above the level of the point of projection at which the bullet can hit the wall is $\dfrac{u^4 - g^2 x^2}{2gu^2}$.

Sol. Let θ be the angle of projection. Suppose y is the height at which bullet hit the wall, then

$$y = x\tan\theta - \frac{gx^2}{2u^2 \cos^2\theta}$$

$$= x\tan\theta - \frac{gx^2 \sec^2\theta}{2u^2} \qquad \text{...(i)}$$

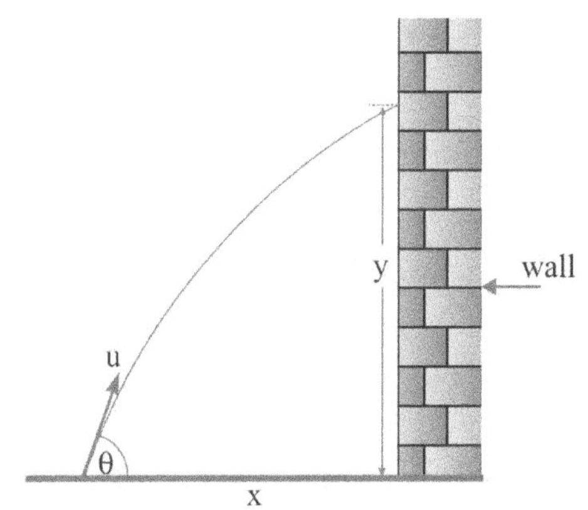

Figure. 4.36

$$\therefore \quad \frac{dy}{d\theta} = x\sec^2\theta - \frac{gx^2}{2u^2} 2\sec\theta\,(\sec\theta\tan\theta)$$

$$= x\sec^2\theta - \frac{gx^2}{u^2} \sec^2\theta \tan\theta$$

$$= x\sec^2\theta\left[1 - \frac{xg\tan\theta}{u^2}\right]$$

For y to be maximum,

$$\frac{dy}{d\theta} = 0$$

$$\therefore \quad x\sec^2\theta\left[1 - \frac{xg\tan\theta}{u^2}\right] = 0$$

$$\text{or} \quad \left[1 - \frac{xg\tan\theta}{u^2}\right] = 0$$

$$\text{or} \quad \tan\theta = \frac{u^2}{gx}$$

Substituting this value in equation (i), we get

$$y_{max} = x\frac{u^2}{gx} - \frac{1}{2}\frac{gx^2}{u^2}\left[1 + \frac{u^4}{x^2 g^2}\right]$$

$$= \frac{u^2}{g} - \frac{gx^2}{2u^2} - \frac{u^2}{2g} = \frac{2u^4 - g^2 x^2 - u^4}{2u^2 g}$$

or $$y_{max} = \frac{u^4 - g^2 x^2}{2gu^2}. \qquad \textbf{\textit{Proved}}$$

Example 19. **An aeroplane flies horizontally at a height h at a speed v. An anti-air craft gun fires a shell at the plane when it is vertically above the gun. Show that the minimum muzzle velocity required to hit the plane is $\sqrt{v^2 + 2gh}$ at an angle $\tan^{-1}\left(\dfrac{\sqrt{2gh}}{v}\right)$.**

Sol.

Suppose the muzzle velocity of the shell is u and it is fired at an angle θ with the horizontal. To hit the plane, the displacement of bullet along the motion of plane in time t is equal to the displacement of the plane. Thus we have

$$u\cos\theta\, t = vt \Rightarrow v = u\cos\theta \qquad ....(i)$$

and $$h = u\sin\theta\, t - \frac{1}{2}g\, t^2$$

or $$\frac{g\, t^2}{2} - u\sin\theta\, t + h = 0$$

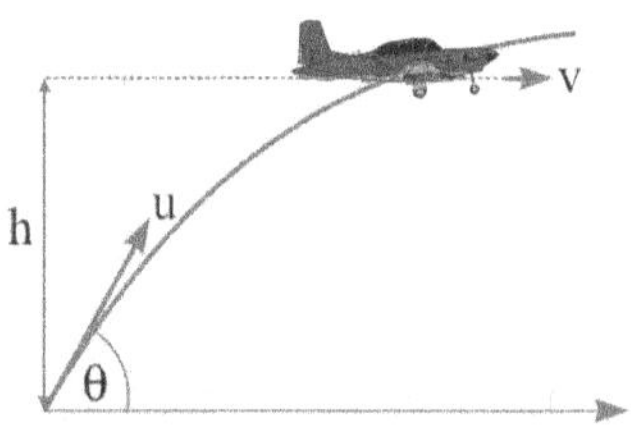

Figure. 4.37

Solving above quadratic equation for t, we have

$$t = \frac{u\sin\theta \pm \sqrt{u^2\sin^2\theta - 4\times\dfrac{g}{2}\times h}}{2\times\dfrac{g}{2}}$$

or $$t = \frac{u\sin\theta \pm \sqrt{u^2\sin^2\theta - 2gh}}{g}$$

t to be real $(u^2\sin^2\theta - 2gh) \geq 0$

or $$u^2\sin^2\theta \geq 2gh$$

or $$u^2(1 - \cos^2\theta) \geq 2gh \qquad \ldots (ii)$$

From equation (i),

$$v = u\cos\theta,$$

$$\therefore \qquad \cos\theta = \frac{v}{u} \qquad \ldots(iii)$$

Now from equation (ii), we have

$$\therefore \qquad u^2\left(1 - \frac{v^2}{u^2}\right) \geq 2gh$$

or $$u^2 - v^2 \geq 2gh$$

or $$u_{min} = \sqrt{v^2 + 2gh}$$

Substituting this value in equation (ii), we get

$$\cos\theta = \frac{v}{u_{min}} = \frac{v}{\sqrt{v^2 + 2gh}}$$

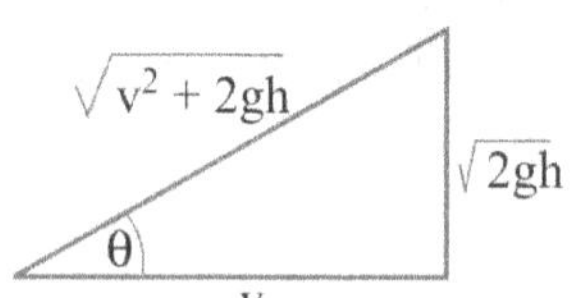

Figure. 4.38

and $$\tan\theta = \frac{\sqrt{2gh}}{v}.$$

In Chapter Exercise 4.2

1. A cricketer can throw a ball to maximum horizontal distance of 160 m. Calculate the maximum vertical height to which he can throw the ball ? Given g = 10 m/s². **[Integer]** *Ans.* **80 m.**

2. A person observes a birds on a tree 39.6 m high and at a distance of 35.2 m. With what velocity the person should throw an arrow at an angle of 45° so that it may hit the bird ? *Ans.* **41.86 m/s.**

3. A particle moves in the x y-plane with constant acceleration $\vec{a}$ directed along the negative y-axis. The equation of path of the particle has the form $y = bx - cx^2$, where b and c are positive constants. Find the velocity of the particle at the origin of coordinates. $Ans.\ v_0 = \sqrt{\dfrac{a}{2c}(1 + b^2)}$

4. A cannon fires successively two shells with velocity $v_0 = 250$ m/s, the first at an angle $\theta_1 = 60°$ and the second at an angle $\theta_2 = 45°$ to the horizontal, the azimuth being the same. Neglecting the air drag, find the time interval between firings leading to the collision of the shells.

[Integer] *Ans.* **11 s**

TOPICS FOR JEE-(MAIN & ADVANCED)

4.8 PROJECTION UP ON AN INCLINED PLANE

Let us consider a particle is projected with velocity u at an angle θ with the horizontal on an inclined plane of inclination α. In this case take x and y-axes along inclined plane and perpendicular to it.

We have,
$$u_x = u\cos(\theta - \alpha),\ a_x = -g\sin\alpha$$
and
$$u_y = u\sin(\theta - \alpha),\ a_y = -g\cos\alpha.$$

Time of flight (T)

The displacement along y-direction becomes zero in total time of flight T. Thus we have,

$$y = u_y T + \frac{1}{2}a_y T^2$$

or
$$0 = u\sin(\theta - \alpha) - \frac{1}{2}(g\cos\alpha)T^2$$

which gives,
$$T = 0 \quad \text{and} \quad T = \frac{2u\sin(\theta - \alpha)}{g\cos\alpha}$$

$T = 0$ corresponds to O. Therefore time of flight

$$T = \frac{2u\sin(\theta - \alpha)}{g\cos\alpha}. \qquad \ldots(i)$$

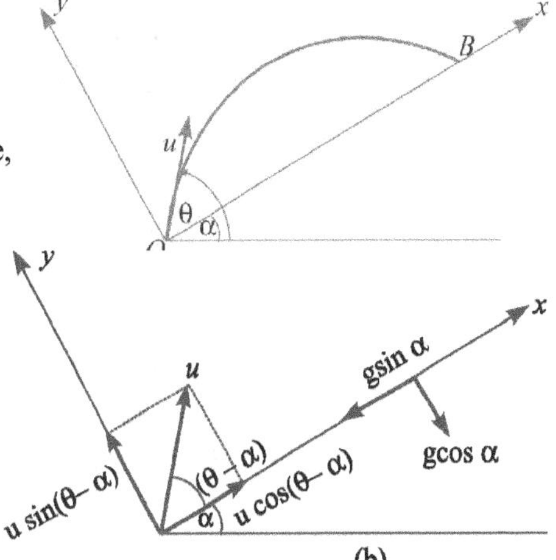

Figure. 4.39

Range along inclined plane (R)

Using second equation of motion along x-axis, we have

$$R = u_x T + \frac{1}{2}a_x T^2$$

$$= u\cos(\theta - \alpha)\times\left[\frac{2u\sin(\theta - \alpha)}{g\cos\alpha}\right] - \frac{1}{2}(g\sin\alpha)\left[\frac{2u\sin(\theta - \alpha)}{g\cos\alpha}\right]^2$$

After simplifying, we get

$$R = \frac{u^2}{g\cos^2\alpha}[\sin(2\theta - \alpha) - \sin\alpha] \qquad \ldots(ii)$$

For maximum range, $\quad \sin(2\theta - \alpha) = 1$

or $\quad\quad\quad\quad\quad 2\theta - \alpha = 90°$

or $\quad\quad\quad\quad\quad\quad \theta = 45° + \dfrac{\alpha}{2}$

$\therefore\quad\quad R_{\text{max}} = \dfrac{u^2}{g\cos^2\alpha}(1 - \sin\alpha) = \dfrac{u^2(1 - \sin\alpha)}{g(1 - \sin^2\alpha)}$

or $\quad\quad R_{\text{max}} = \dfrac{u^2}{g(1 + \sin\alpha)}.$

Time taken by projectile to become $v_y = 0$:

Using first equation of motion, we have

$$v_y = u_y + a_y t$$

or
$$0 = u\sin(\theta - \alpha) - g\cos\alpha\, t_A$$

or
$$t_A = \frac{u\sin(\theta - \alpha)}{g\cos\alpha} = \frac{T}{2}.$$

Mechanics

Let it happens at a distance x from O along the inclined plane, then

$$x = u_x t_A + \frac{1}{2} a_x t_A^2$$

$$= u \cos(\theta - \alpha) \left(\frac{T}{2}\right) - \frac{1}{2}(g \sin\alpha)\left(\frac{T}{2}\right)^2 > \frac{R}{2}.$$

Height of A from inclined plane :
By third equation of motion, we have

$$0 = u_y^2 + 2 a_y y$$

or

$$0 = [u \sin(\theta - \alpha)]^2 - 2(g \cos\alpha) y$$

or

$$y = \frac{u^2 \sin^2(\theta - \alpha)}{2g \cos\alpha}.$$

4.9 PROJECTION DOWN THE INCLINED PLANE

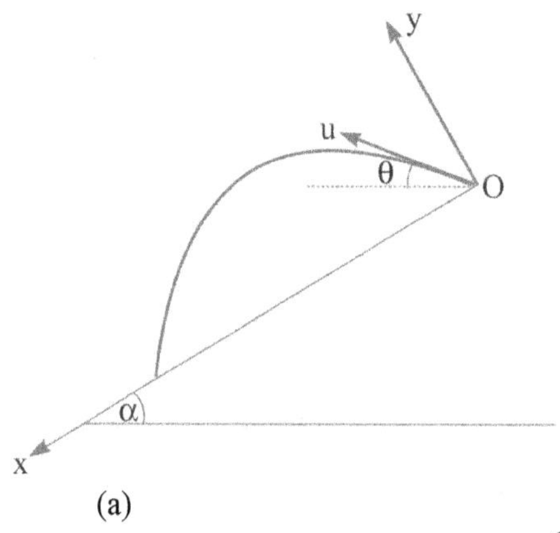

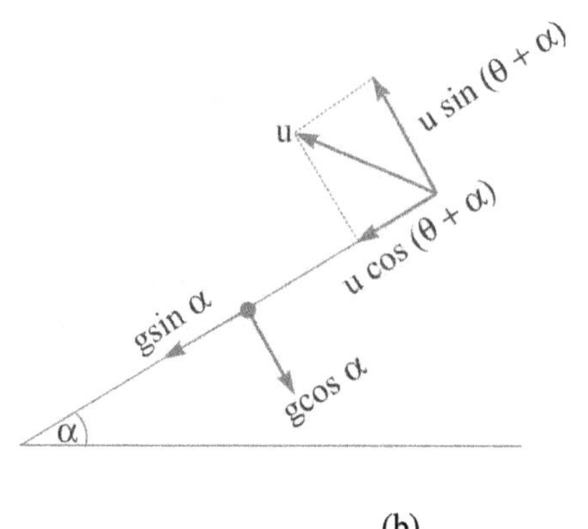

Figure. 4.40

Here we have,

$$u_x = u \cos(\theta + \alpha), \qquad a_x = g \sin\alpha$$
$$u_y = u \sin(\theta + \alpha), \quad a_y = -g \cos\alpha.$$

Time of flight
As displacement becomes zero along y-direction in time T,

$$\therefore \quad 0 = u_y T + \frac{1}{2} a_y T^2$$

or

$$0 = u \sin(\theta + \alpha) T - \frac{1}{2}(g \cos\alpha) T^2$$

which gives

$$T = 0$$

or

$$T = \frac{2u \sin(\theta - \alpha)}{g \cos\alpha}$$

$T = 0$ corresponds to O, therefore time of flight

$$T = \frac{2u \sin(\theta + \alpha)}{g \cos\alpha} \qquad \ldots(i)$$

Range along inclined plane (R) :

$$R = u_x T + \frac{1}{2} a_x T^2$$

$$= u \cos(\theta + \alpha) \left[\frac{2u \sin(\theta + \alpha)}{g \cos\alpha}\right] + \frac{1}{2} g \sin\alpha \left[\frac{2u \sin(\theta + \alpha)}{g \cos\alpha}\right]^2$$

After simplifying, we get

$$R = \frac{u^2}{g \cos^2 \alpha}[\sin(2\theta + \alpha) + \sin \alpha] \qquad ...(ii)$$

For maximum range, $\sin(2\theta + \alpha) = +1$

or $\qquad (2\theta + \alpha) = 90° \text{ or } \theta = 45° - \dfrac{\alpha}{2}$

$\therefore \qquad R_{max} = \dfrac{u^2(1 + \sin \alpha)}{g \cos^2 \alpha} = \dfrac{u^2(1 + \sin \alpha)}{g(1 - \sin^2 \alpha)}$

or $\qquad R_{max} = \dfrac{u^2}{g(1 - \sin \alpha)}.$

4.10 MOTION ALONG A CURVED PATH

For a paticle moving along a curved path, the velocity changes due to change in the direciton of motion of particle, due to which there is an acceleration called normal acceleration. Its magnitude is $\dfrac{v^2}{R}$, where v is the instantaneous speed. R is the radius of curvature at the point under consideration. If particle is moving with variable speed, it also has tangential acceleration. Its magnitude is $\dfrac{dv}{dt}$. Thus total acceleration at any point

$$a = \sqrt{a_n^2 + a_t^2}$$

where $\qquad a_n = \dfrac{v^2}{R} \text{ and } a_t = \dfrac{dv}{dt}.$

Figure. 4.41

Finding radius of curvature

The radius of curvature at any point of a curve can be obtained by following two ways :

(i) If equation of curve is known : The radius of curvature in such cases can be calculated as :

$$\frac{1}{R} = \frac{\left|\dfrac{d^2 y}{dx^2}\right|}{\left[1 + \left(\dfrac{dy}{dx}\right)^2\right]^{3/2}},$$

where $\dfrac{dy}{dx}$ is the slope of curve at the point under consideration.

(ii) If normal acceleration is known : We know that;

$$a_n = \frac{v^2}{R}$$

$\therefore \qquad R = \dfrac{v^2}{a_n}$

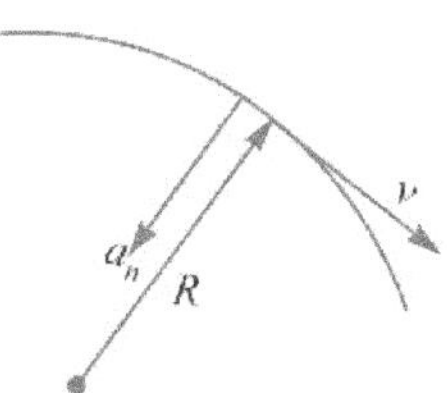

Figure. 4.42

By substituting the value of a_n, we can get radius of curvature at particular point.

Radius of curvature of projectile

(i) At point of projection :

From the figure it is clear that

$$a_n = g\cos\theta.$$

As we know,

$$a_n = \frac{v^2}{R}$$

$$\therefore \qquad R = \frac{v^2}{a_n} = \frac{u^2}{g\cos\theta}.$$

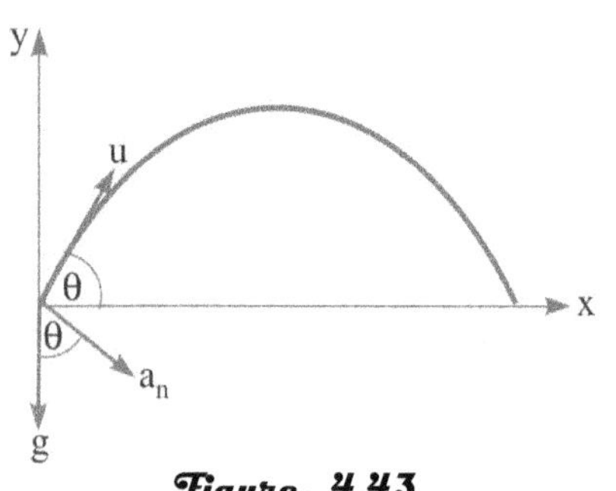

Figure. 4.43

(ii) At the highest point of projectile :

$$v = u\cos\theta$$

$$\therefore \qquad R = \frac{v^2}{a_n} = \frac{(u\cos\theta)^2}{g}$$

or

$$R = \frac{u^2\cos^2\theta}{g}.$$

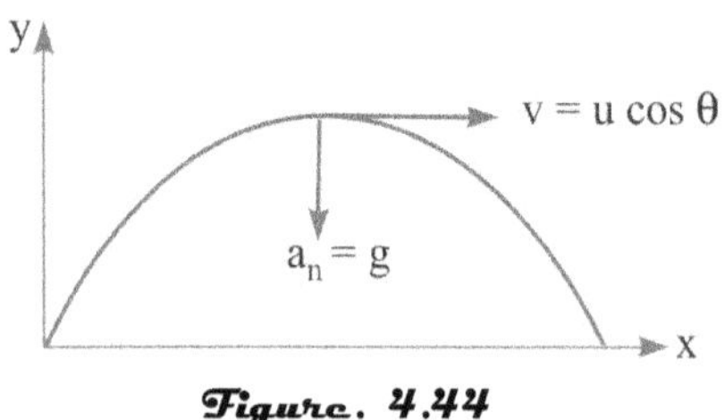

Figure. 4.44

MISCELLANEOUS EXAMPLES FOR JEE-MAIN AND ADVANCED

<u>Example</u> 1. A particle is projected over a triangle from one end of a horizontal base and grazing the vertex falls on the other end of the base. If α and β be the base angles and θ the angle of projection, prove that $\tan\theta = \tan\alpha + \tan\beta$.

Sol. Given data are shown in the *fig.* 4.45. For any point $P(x, y)$, we have

$$y = x\tan\theta - \frac{gx^2}{2u^2\cos^2\theta}$$

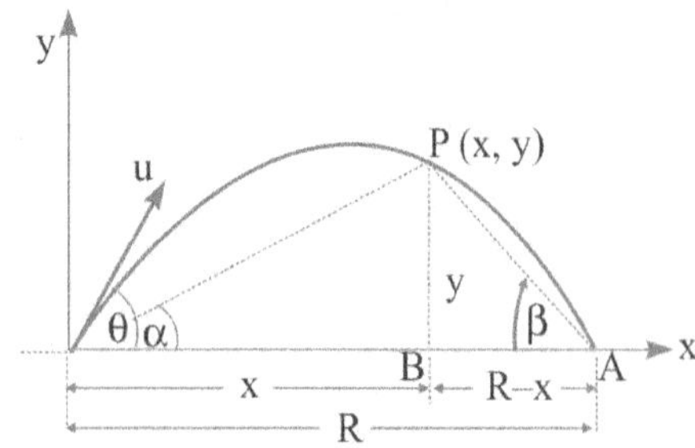

Figure. 4.45

$$= x\tan\theta\left[1 - \frac{gx}{2u^2\cos^2\theta\tan\theta}\right]$$

$$= x\tan\theta\left[1 - \frac{gx}{u^2(2\sin\theta\cos\theta)}\right]$$

$$= x\tan\theta\left[1 - \frac{x}{R}\right]$$

$$= x\tan\theta\left[\frac{R-x}{R}\right]$$

or

$$\tan\theta = \frac{yR}{x(R-x)} \qquad \text{...(i)}$$

From figure;

$$\tan\alpha + \tan\beta = \frac{y}{x} + \frac{y}{R-x}$$

$$= \frac{y(R-x)+xy}{x(R-x)}$$

$$= \frac{yR}{x(R-x)} \qquad \text{...(ii)}$$

Now from equations (i) and (ii), we get

$$\tan\theta = \tan\alpha + \tan\beta \qquad \textbf{Proved}$$

<u>Example</u> 2. A particle is projected horizontally with a speed u from the top of a plane inclined at an angle θ with the horizontal. How far from the point of projection will the particle strike the plane?

Sol. Consider the motion of the particle along the direction (x-axis) and perpendicular direction of OB (y-axis). The initial velocities and accelerations along these directions are shown in the figure. The displacement along y-axis in time T becomes zero.

By using second equation of motion along y-axis, we have

$$y = u_y t - \frac{1}{2}a_y t^2$$

or

$$0 = u\sin\theta\, T - \frac{1}{2}(g\cos\theta)\,T^2$$

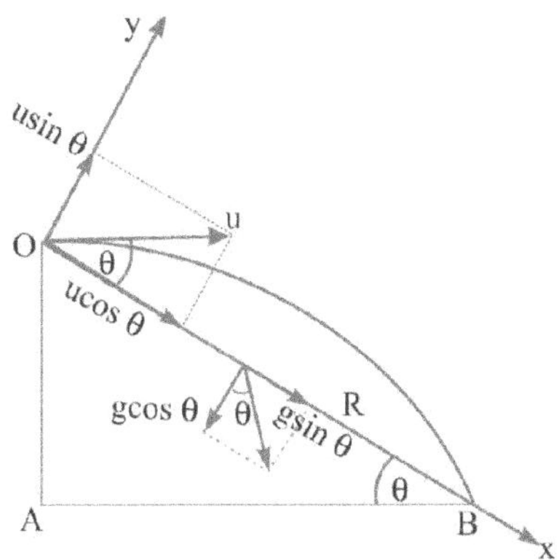

Figure. 4.46

which gives,
$$T = \frac{2u\sin\theta}{g\cos\theta}$$

$$= \frac{2u\tan\theta}{g}$$

In this duration the displacement along x-axis

$$R = u_x T + \frac{1}{2} a_x T^2$$

$$= u\cos\theta\,\frac{2u\tan\theta}{g} + \frac{1}{2}(g\sin\theta)\left(\frac{2u\tan\theta}{g}\right)^2$$

$$= \frac{2u^2\tan\theta}{g}[\cos\theta + 2\tan\theta\sin\theta]$$

$$= \frac{2u^2\tan\theta}{g}\left[\cos\theta + \frac{\sin^2\theta}{\cos\theta}\right]$$

$$= \frac{2u^2\tan\theta}{g}\left[\frac{\cos^2\theta + \sin^2\theta}{\cos\theta}\right]$$

$$= \frac{2u^2\tan\theta\sec\theta}{g}. \qquad \textbf{Ans.}$$

Example 3. Two particles move in a uniform gravitational field with an acceleration g. At the initial moment the particles were located at one point and moved with velocities $u_1 = 3.0$ m/s and $u_2 = 4.0$ m/s horizontally in opposite directions. Find the distance between the particles at the moment when their velocity vectors become mutually perpendicular.

Sol.

Supposing point of projection as the origin, the velocities of particles at time t after the projection

$$\vec{v_1} = 3.0\,\hat{i} - gt\,\hat{j} \qquad ....(i)$$

and
$$\vec{v_2} = -4.0\,\hat{i} - gt\,\hat{j} \qquad ....(ii)$$

As $\vec{v_1}$ and $\vec{v_2}$ are mutually perpendicular, so $\vec{v_1}\cdot\vec{v_2} = 0$

or $(3.0\,\hat{i} - gt\,\hat{j})\cdot(-4.0\,\hat{i} - gt\,\hat{j}) = 0$

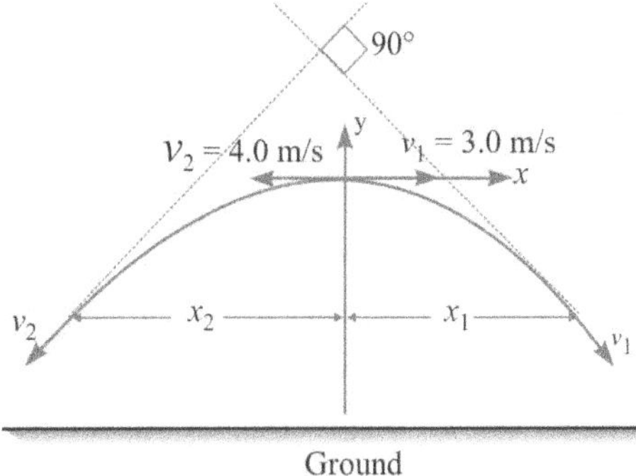

Figure. 4.47

or $\qquad 3.0 \times 4.0 - g^2 t^2 = 0$

or $\qquad t = \dfrac{\sqrt{12}}{g}.$

Both the particles have zero initial velocity in vertical direction. Therefore they fall equal vertical distances. They lie on same horizontal line. Therefore we have

$$x_1 = 3.0\,t \quad \text{and} \quad x_2 = 4.0\,t$$

$$\therefore \qquad x = x_1 + x_2 = 3.0\,t + 4.0\,t$$

$$= 7.0\,t = \frac{7.0\sqrt{12.0}}{g} \simeq 2.5 \text{ m}. \qquad \textbf{Ans.}$$

Example 4. A ball starts falling with zero initial velocity on a smooth inclined plane forming an angle θ with the horizontal. Having fallen the distance h, the ball rebounds elastically off the inclined plane. At what distance from impact point will be ball rebound for the second time ?

Sol.

The velocity of the ball just before hitting the plane is $u = \sqrt{2gh}$. Since collision is elastic, so the ball will rebound with the same speed. The velocity component along the plane, $u_x = u\sin\alpha$ and perpendicular to it $v_y = u\cos\alpha$. Using second equation of motion along y-axis

$$y = u_y t - \frac{1}{2} a_y t^2.$$

Let T is the time of flight then in total time T, y becomes zero.

$$\therefore \qquad 0 = u\cos\alpha\, T - \frac{1}{2}(g\cos\alpha)\,T^2$$

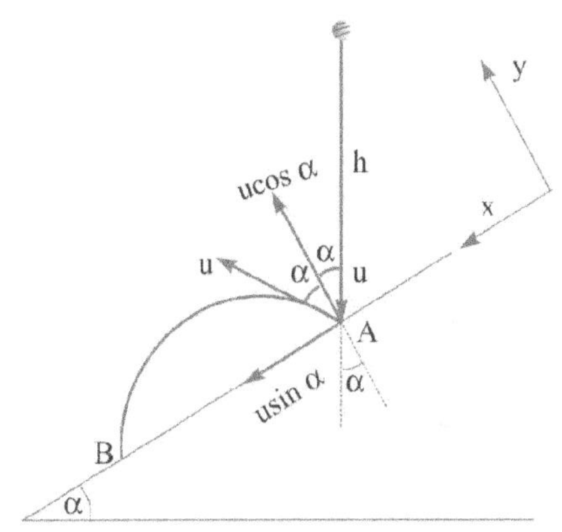

Figure. 4.48

$$\Rightarrow \qquad T = \frac{2u}{g}$$

Now, along the plane

$$AB = u_x\, T + \frac{1}{2}\, a_x\, T^2$$

$$= u\sin\alpha\left(\frac{2u}{g}\right) + \frac{1}{2}\,(g\sin\alpha)\left(\frac{2u}{g}\right)^2$$

$$= \frac{4u^2\sin\alpha}{g}$$

We have $\qquad u = \sqrt{2gh}$

$$\therefore \qquad AB = \frac{4(\sqrt{2gh})^2\sin\alpha}{g} = 8\,h\,\sin\alpha. \qquad \textbf{\textit{Ans.}}$$

<u>Example</u> 5. Two towers AB and CD are situated a distance d apart as shown in *fig.* 4.49. AB is 20 m high and CD is 30 m high from the ground. An object of mass m is thrown from the top of AB horizontally with a velocity of 10 m/s towards CD. Simultaneously another object of mass 2 m is thrown from the top of CD at an angle of 60° to the horizontal towards AB with the same magnitude of initial velocity as that of the first object. The two objects move in the same vertical plane, collide in mid-air and stick to each other.
(i)   Calculate the distance d between the towers.
(ii)   Find the position where the objects hit the ground. (g = 9.8 m/s²)

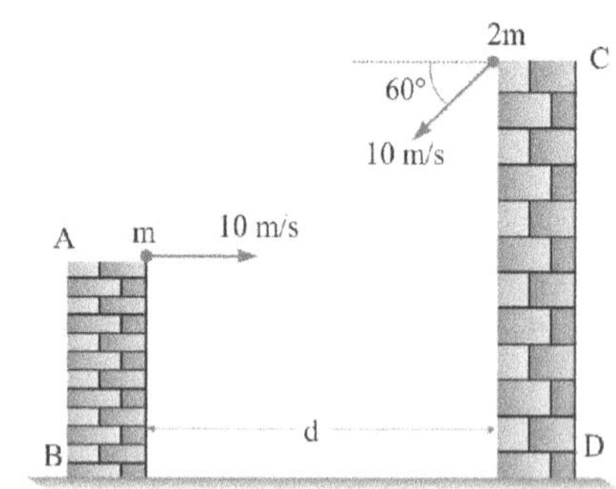

Figure. 4.49

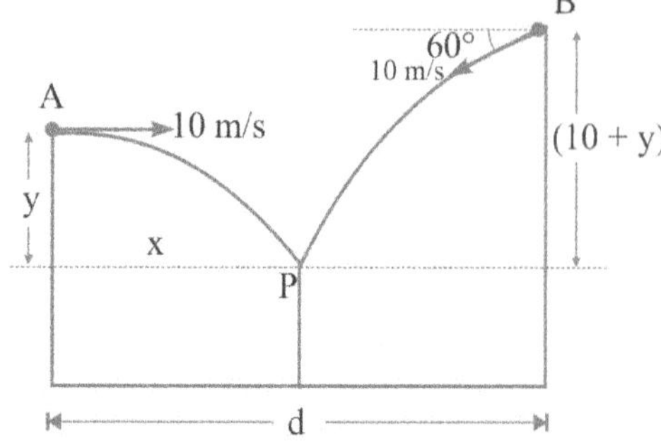

Figure. 4.50

Sol.
(i)   Let the objects collide after time t. Suppose they collide at a horizontal distance x from tower AB, then at time t

$$x = 10\, t \qquad \qquad \dots(i)$$

and $\qquad d - x = 10\cos 60° \times t$
$$= 5\, t \qquad\qquad \dots \text{(ii)}$$

Adding equations (i) and (ii), we have
$$d = 15\, t \qquad\qquad \dots \text{(iii)}$$

Let y is the vertical displacement of point of collision from A, then

$$y = 0 + \frac{1}{2}\, g\, t^2 \qquad\qquad \dots\text{(iv)}$$

and $\qquad (10 + y) = 10\sin 60°\, t + \frac{1}{2}\, g\, t^2 \qquad \dots\text{(v)}$

Subtracting (iv) from (v), we get
$$10\sin 60°\, t = 10$$

or $\qquad t = \dfrac{2}{\sqrt{3}}$ s

(ii)   The resultant momentum of the objects in horizontal direction just before collision,
$$= m \times 10 - 2\, m \times 10\cos 60° = 0$$

$\therefore$ Velocity of combined object by conservation of momentum,
$$3m \times v_x = 0 \Rightarrow v_x = 0$$

Thus the combined object falls vertically at a distance x from tower AB,

where $\qquad x = 10\, t = 10 \times \dfrac{2}{\sqrt{3}} = \dfrac{20}{\sqrt{3}}\ m \qquad \textbf{\textit{Ans.}}$

<u>Example</u> 6. Particles P and Q of mass 20 g and 40 g respectively are simultaneously projected from points A and B on the ground. The initial velocities of P and Q make 45° and 135° angles respectively with the horizontal AB as shown in *fig.* 4.51. Each particle has an initial speed of 49 m/s. The separation AB is 245 m. Both particles travel in the same vertical plane and undergo a collision. After collision P retraces its path. Determine the position of Q when it hits the ground. How much time after the collision does the particle Q take to reach the ground?   (Take $g = 9.8$ m/s²)

Sol.

As both the particles have same velocity components in horizontal and vertical directions, so they travel the equal distances in respective directions. The particle will collide at the middle of AB, i.e., $\dfrac{245}{2} = 122.5$ m from A towards B.

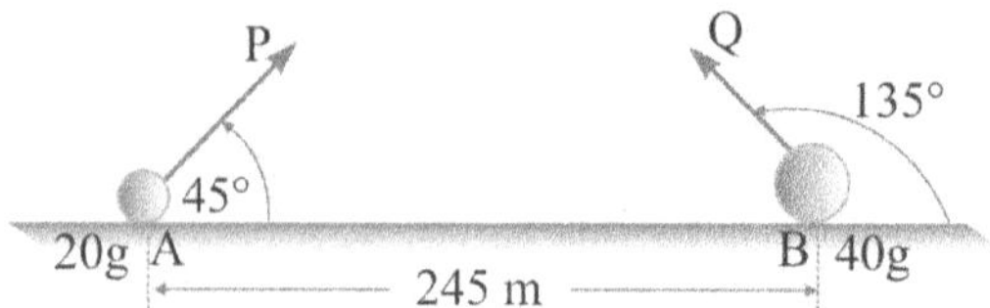

Figure. 4.51

The height at which they collide is the highest position of their path, which is

$$H = \frac{u^2\sin^2\theta}{2g}$$

$$= \frac{(49)^2\sin^2 45°}{2 \times 9.8}$$

$$= 61.25\ \text{m}$$

At the highest point each will have velocity $v_x = 49 \cos 45° = \dfrac{49}{\sqrt{2}}$ m/s

along horizontal direction. Using principle of conservation of momentum along horizontal direction, we have

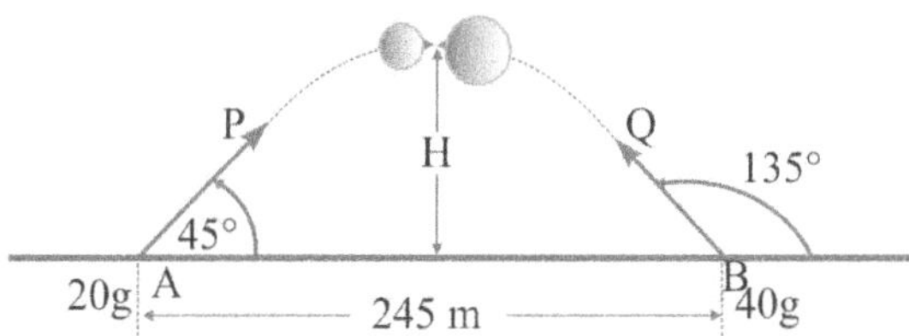

Figure. 4.52

$$20 \times 10^{-3} \times \frac{49}{\sqrt{2}} - 40 \times 10^{-3} \times \frac{49}{\sqrt{2}}$$

$$= -20 \times 10^{-3} \times \frac{49}{\sqrt{2}} + 40 \times 10^{-3} \times v_Q$$

which gives $v_Q = 0$, i.e., after collision the velocity of Q at the highest point becomes zero. So, Q will fall freely under gravity and will hit the ground at the middle of AB, i.e., 122.5 m from A.

Time taken by Q to reach the ground :

$$H = 0 + \frac{1}{2} g\, t^2$$

or

$$t = \sqrt{\frac{2H}{g}}$$

$$= \sqrt{\frac{2 \times 61.25}{9.8}}$$

$$= 3.54 \text{ s.} \qquad \qquad \textit{Ans.}$$

Example 7. A stone must be projected horizontally from a point P, which is h metre above the foot of a plane inclined at an angle θ with horizontal as shown in figure 4.53. Calculate the velocity v of the stone so that it may hit the inclined plane perpendicularly.

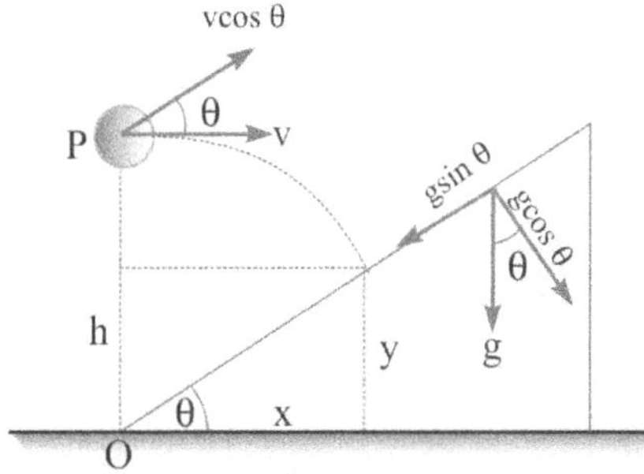

Figure. 4.53

Sol. Take O as the origin and coordinates of point at which stone hits the plane are (x, y). The velocity component along the plane $v\cos\theta$ and perpendicular to it is $v\sin\theta$. As stone hit the plane perpendicularly, its velocity component $v\cos\theta$ becomes zero. Let t is the time in which it becomes zero, then

$$0 = v\cos\theta - g\sin\theta\, t$$

which gives,

$$t = \frac{v\cos\theta}{g\sin\theta} = \frac{v}{g}\cot\theta \qquad \qquad ...(i)$$

The vertical distance falls by stone in this time t

$$h - y = 0 + \frac{1}{2} g\, t^2 \qquad \qquad ...(ii)$$

and

$$x = v\, t \qquad \qquad ...(iii)$$

Also

$$\frac{y}{x} = \tan\theta$$

or

$$y = x\tan\theta$$
$$= v\, t\tan\theta \qquad \qquad ...(iv)$$

Substituting values of t and y in equation (ii), we get

$$h - v\, t\tan\theta = \frac{1}{2} g\, t^2$$

or $$h - v\left(\frac{v}{g}\cot\theta\right)\tan\theta = \frac{1}{2} g\left(\frac{v}{g}\cot\theta\right)^2$$

or

$$h - \frac{v^2}{g} = \frac{v^2}{2g}\cot^2\theta$$

or

$$2gh - 2v^2 = v^2\cot^2\theta$$

or

$$v = \sqrt{\frac{2gh}{2 + \cot^2\theta}}. \qquad \qquad \textit{Ans.}$$

Example 8. A large heavy box is sliding without friction down a smooth plane of inclination θ. From a point P on the bottom of the box, a particle is projected inside the box. The initial speed of the particle with respect to the box is u and the direction of projection makes an angle α with the bottom as shown in *fig. 4.54.*

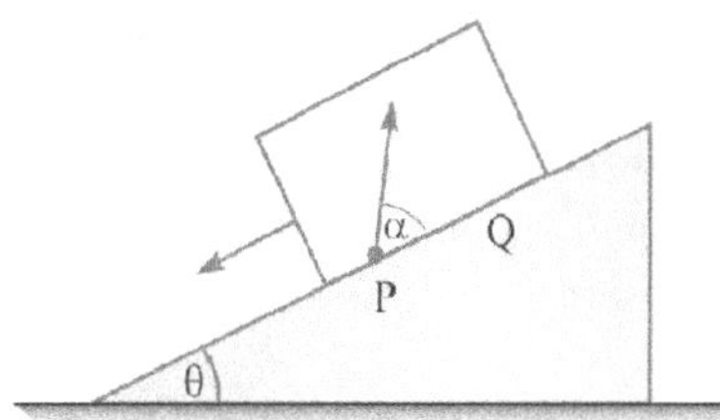

Figure. 4.54

(a) Find the distance along the bottom of the box between the point of projection P and the point Q where the particle lands (assume that the particle does not hit any other surface of the box. Neglect air resistance).

(b) If the horizontal displacement of the particle as seen by an observer on the ground is zero, find the speed of the box with respect to the ground at the instant when the particle was projected.

Sol.

(a) Consider the motion of the particle along the x and y-axes as shown in *figure. 4.55.*

With respect to box, we have

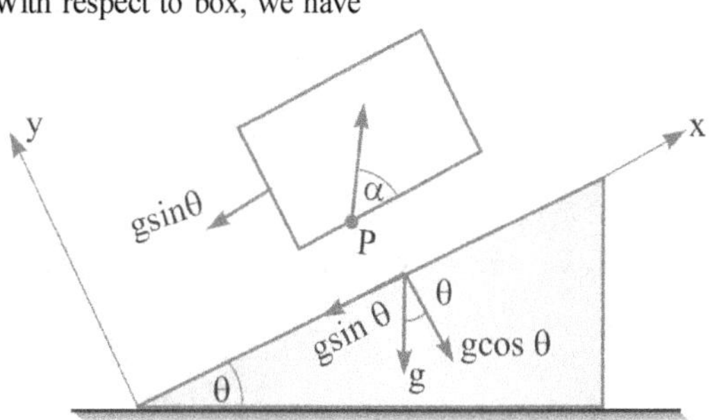

Figure. 4.55

$$\vec{u}_x = [\vec{u}_{particle}]_x - [\vec{u}_{box}]_x$$

$$= u\cos\alpha - 0 = u\cos\alpha$$

and

$$\vec{a}_x = [\vec{a}_{particle}]_x - [\vec{a}_{box}]_x$$

or $\qquad a_x = g\sin\theta - g\sin\theta = 0$

and $\qquad u_y = u\sin\alpha$

$\qquad\qquad a_y = -g\cos\theta$

(a) Particle will hit the box after time t, then we have

$$y = u_y t + \frac{1}{2}a_y t^2$$

or $\qquad 0 = u\sin\alpha - \frac{1}{2}(g\cos\theta)\,t^2$

which gives $\qquad t = 0$

or $\qquad t = \dfrac{2u\sin\alpha}{g\cos\theta}$ *Ans.*

Thus distance travelled in time t inside the box

$$PQ = u\cos\theta \times t$$

$$= u\cos\alpha \times \frac{2u\sin\alpha}{g\cos\theta}$$

$$= \frac{u^2\,2\sin\alpha\cos\alpha}{g\cos\theta} = \frac{u^2\sin 2\alpha}{g\cos\theta}. \quad \textit{Ans.}$$

(b) Let v is the velocity component of box along horizontal direction. The horizontal displacement as seen by the observer on the ground v to be zero, we have

$v - u\cos(\theta + \alpha) = 0$ or $v = u\cos(\theta + \alpha)$.

If velocity of box along the plane is v_x, then $v_x\cos\theta = v$

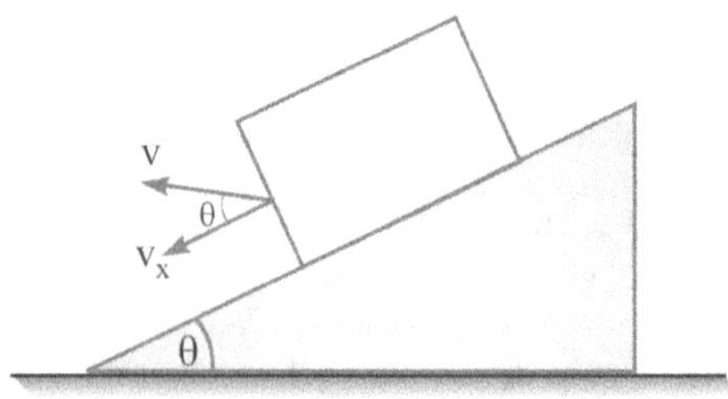

Figure. 4.56

$\therefore \qquad v_x = \dfrac{v}{\cos\theta} = \dfrac{u\cos(\theta+\alpha)}{\cos\theta}$ *Ans.*

Example 9.
A boat moves relative to water with a velocity which is $\eta = 2.0$ times less than the river flow velocity. At what angle to the stream direction must the boat move to minimise drifting?

Sol.

Suppose velocity of river flow $v_r = v$, then velocity of boat relative to

water $v_{br} = \dfrac{v}{2}$. Let boat moves at an angle θ with the direction of

stream, then time to cross the stream $t = \dfrac{b}{v_{br}\sin\theta}$

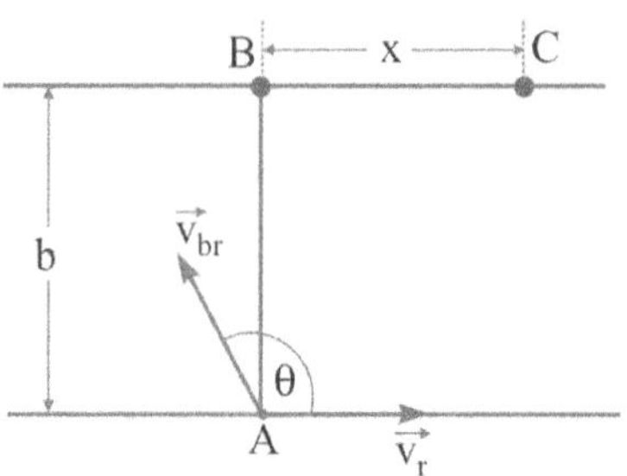

Figure. 4.57

where $v_{br}\sin\theta$ is the velocity of boat along AB.

The velocity of boat along the direction of flow,

$$v_{bx} = (v_r + v_{br}\cos\theta)$$

and drift in the direction of flow,

$$x = v_{bx} \times t$$

$$= (v_r + v_{br}\cos\theta) \times \frac{b}{v_{br}\sin\theta}$$

$$= \left(v + \frac{v}{2}\cos\theta\right) \times \left(\frac{b}{\frac{v}{2}\sin\theta}\right)$$

$$= b\left(\frac{2+\cos\theta}{\sin\theta}\right)$$

where b is the width of the river. For the drift to be minimum,

$$\frac{dx}{d\theta} = 0$$

or $\qquad \dfrac{d}{d\theta}\left[b\left(\dfrac{2+\cos\theta}{\sin\theta}\right)\right] = 0$

or $\qquad \sin\theta \times (-\sin\theta) - (2+\cos\theta) \times (\cos\theta) = 0$

or $\qquad \sin^2\theta + 2\cos\theta + \cos^2\theta = 0$

or $\qquad 2\cos\theta = -(\sin^2\theta + \cos^2\theta)$

or $\qquad 2\cos\theta = -1$

$\therefore \qquad \cos\theta = -\dfrac{1}{2}$

or $\qquad\qquad \theta = 120°$

Hence to minimise drifting boat should move at an angle $120°$ with the direction of stream.

Thus $\qquad x_{min} = b\left(\dfrac{2+\cos 120°}{\sin 120°}\right)$

$$= b\left(\frac{2-1/2}{\sqrt{3}/2}\right) = \sqrt{3}\,b. \qquad \textit{Ans.}$$

Example 10.
Two boats A and B, move away from a buoy anchored at the middle of a river along the mutually perpendicular straight lines : the boat A along the river and the boat B across the river. Having moved off an equal distance from the buoy the boat returned.

Find the ratio of times of motion of boats $\dfrac{\tau_A}{\tau_B}$, if the velocity of each boat with respect to water is $\eta = 1.2$ times greater than the stream velocity.

Sol.

Suppose the stream velocity is $v_s = v$, then the velocity of each boat with respect to water is $v_b = 1.2\,v$. Let each boat travel a distance ℓ. Then for boat A, time of motion

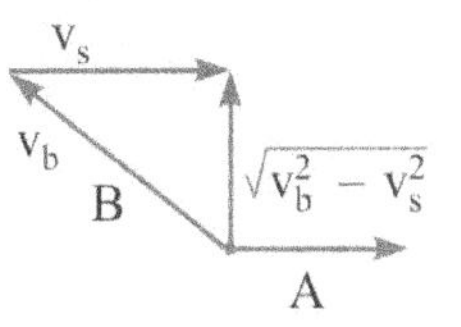

Figure. 4.58

$$\tau_A = \frac{\ell}{v_b + v_s} + \frac{\ell}{v_b - v_s}$$

$$= \left[\frac{\ell}{1.2v + v} + \frac{\ell}{1.2v - v}\right] = \frac{60\ell}{11v} \quad ....(i)$$

For the boat B, time of motion

$$\tau_B = \frac{\ell}{\sqrt{v_b^2 - v_s^2}} + \frac{\ell}{\sqrt{v_b^2 - v_s^2}}$$

$$= \frac{2\ell}{\sqrt{v_b^2 - v_s^2}} \quad ....(ii)$$

$$= \frac{2\ell}{\sqrt{(1.2v)^2 - v^2}} = \frac{3.01\ell}{v}$$

The ratio $\quad \dfrac{\tau_A}{\tau_B} = \dfrac{(60\ell/11v)}{(3.01\ell/v)} \approx 1.8.$ **Ans.**

Example 11. The current velocity of a river grows in proportional to the distance from the bank and reaches its maximum v_0 in the middle. Near the banks, the velocity is zero. A boat is moving along the river in such a manner that it is always perpendicular to the current and the speed of the boat in still water is u. Find the distance through which the boat crossing the river will be carried away by the current if the width is b. Also determine the trajectory of the path of the boat.

Sol.

Suppose v_x is the velocity of the river flow at a distance y from the bank. Thus according to given condition $v_x = ky$, where k is a constant.

Also when $y = \dfrac{b}{2}, v = v_0$

$$\therefore \quad v_0 = k\frac{b}{2}$$

$$\Rightarrow \quad k = \frac{2v_0}{b}$$

Now, $\quad v_x = \dfrac{2v_0}{b}y \qquad ...(i)$

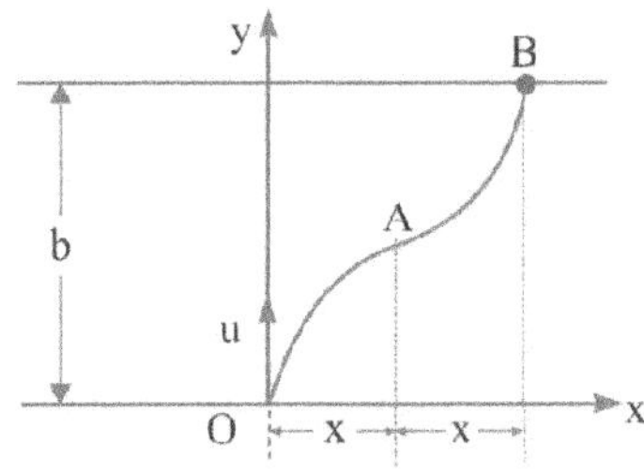

Figure. 4.59

Along y-axis the displacement in time t, $y = ut$

$$\therefore \quad v_x = \left(\frac{2v_0}{b}\right)ut \qquad ...(ii)$$

The rate of change of velocity along x-axis

$$a_x = \frac{dv_x}{dt} = \frac{2v_0 u}{b} \text{ (constant)} \qquad ...(iii)$$

The distance x travelled is given by second equation of motion

$$x = u_x t + \frac{1}{2}a_x t^2$$

$$= 0 + \frac{1}{2}\left(\frac{2v_0 u}{b}\right)t^2$$

From $y = ut, t = \dfrac{y}{u}$

$$\therefore \quad x = \frac{1}{2}\left(\frac{2v_0 u}{b}\right)\left(\frac{y}{u}\right)^2$$

$$= \frac{v_0 y^2}{ub}$$

or $\quad y^2 = \dfrac{ubx}{v_0} \qquad ...(iv)$

Equation (iv) is an equation of a parabola, so, the trajectory of the boat is a parabola OA upto the mid stream. The other half of the trajectory is of same nature.

When boat is at the middle of the river, $y = \dfrac{b}{2}$

$$x = \frac{v_0}{ub}\left(\frac{b}{2}\right)^2 = \frac{v_0 b}{4u} \qquad ...(v)$$

Above equation gives the drift along x-axis for first half. During second half of motion, it is also x. Thus, total drift along the direction of river flow = $2x$

$$= 2\left(\frac{v_0 b}{4u}\right) = \frac{v_0 b}{2u}. \qquad \textbf{Ans.}$$

Example 12. A balloon starts rising from the surface of the earth. The ascension rate is constant and equal to v_0. Due to the wind the balloon gathered the horizontal velocity component $v_x = ay$, where a is a constant and y is the height of ascent. Find how the following quantities depend on the height of ascent :

(a) the horizontal drift of the balloon x (y);

(b) the total, tangential, and the normal accelerations of the balloon.

Sol.

(a) It is given that the ascension rate,

$$v_y = \frac{dy}{dt} = v_0 \text{ or } \frac{dv_y}{dt} = v_0$$

$$\therefore \quad dy = v_0 \, dt$$

or $\quad y = \displaystyle\int_0^t v_0 dt = v_0 t. \qquad ...(i)$

Also
$$v_x = \frac{dx}{dt} = ay$$
$$= a v_0 t$$
$$\therefore \quad dx = a v_0 t \, dt$$

or
$$x = \int_0^t a v_0 t \, dt$$
$$= \frac{a v_0 t^2}{2} \qquad \text{...(ii)}$$

From equation (i), we have $t = \dfrac{y}{v_0}$. Substituting this value in equation (ii), we get

$$x = \frac{a v_0}{2}\left(\frac{y}{v_0}\right)^2$$

or
$$x = \frac{a y^2}{2 v_0} \qquad \text{...(iii)}$$

(b) Since velocity in vertical direction is constant,

$$\therefore \quad a_y = \frac{dv_y}{dt} = 0$$

The acceleration in horizontal direction,

$$a_x = \frac{dv_x}{dt} = \frac{d(a v_0 t)}{dt} = a v_0$$

Thus total acceleration,

$$a = \sqrt{a_x^2 + a_y^2}$$
$$= \sqrt{(a v_0)^2 + 0} = a v_0$$

The total acceleration is $a v_0$ and directed along horizontal direction.
Let θ is the angle that the resultant velocity makes with horizontal, then Normal acceleration $a_n = a\sin\theta$ and tangential acceleration $a_t = a\cos\theta$, we have

$$x = \frac{a y^2}{2 v_0}$$

Figure. 4.60

or
$$y = \sqrt{\frac{2 x v_0}{a}}$$

Differentiating both sides of equation (iii) w.r.t. x, we get

$$1 = \frac{a}{2 v_0} \times 2y \times \frac{dy}{dx}$$

or
$$\frac{dy}{dx} = \frac{v_0}{ay} = \tan\theta$$

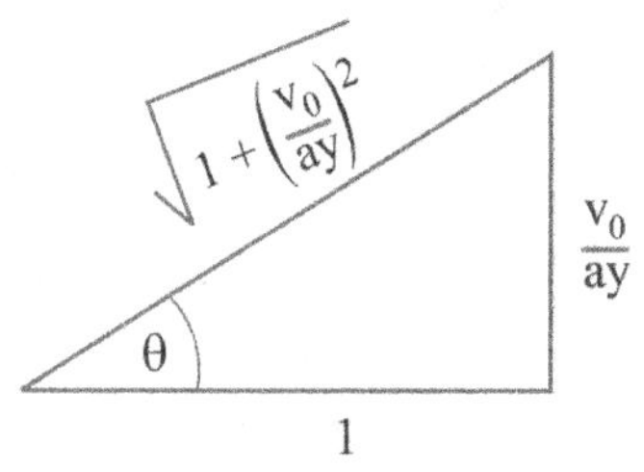

Figure. 4.61

Now
$$a_x = a\sin\theta$$
$$= a v_0 \times \frac{(v_0/ay)}{\sqrt{1+\left(\dfrac{v_0}{ay}\right)^2}}$$
$$= \frac{a v_0^2}{\sqrt{(ay)^2 + v_0^2}} = \frac{a v_0^2}{v_0\sqrt{1+\left(\dfrac{ay}{v_0}\right)^2}}$$
$$= \frac{a v_0}{\sqrt{1+\left(\dfrac{ay}{v_0}\right)^2}}$$

and $a_t = a\cos\theta$

$$= a v_0 \times \frac{1}{\sqrt{1+\left(\dfrac{v_0}{ay}\right)^2}} = a v_0 \frac{ay}{\sqrt{(ay)^2 + v_0^2}}$$
$$= \frac{a^2 v_0 y}{v_0\sqrt{1+\left(\dfrac{ay}{v_0}\right)^2}} = \frac{a^2 y}{\sqrt{1+\left(\dfrac{ay}{v_0}\right)^2}} \quad \textit{Ans.}$$

Example 13. **Consider a collection of a large number of particles each with speed v. The direction of velocity is randomly distributed in the collection. Show that the magnitude of the relative velocity between a pair of particles averaged over all the pairs in the collection is greater than v.**   **[NCERT]**

Sol.

Let $\vec{v}_1$ and $\vec{v}_2$ are the velocities of any two particles and θ is the angle between them. As each particle has same speed, so
$$v_1 = v_2 = v$$
The relative velocity of particle 2 w.r.t. 1 is given by
$$\vec{v}_{21} = \vec{v}_2 - \vec{v}_1$$

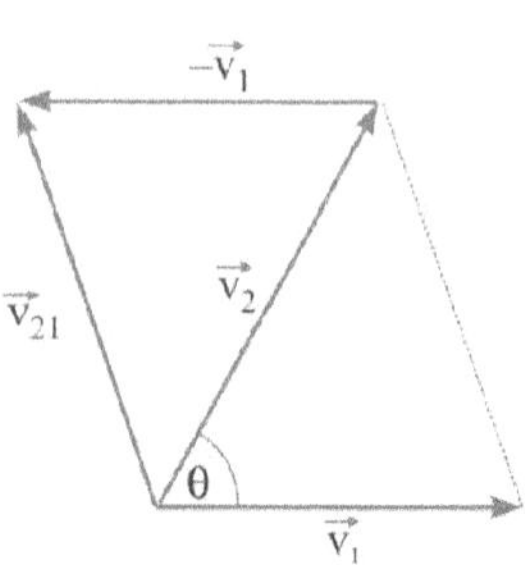

Figure. 4.62

or
$$v_{21} = \sqrt{v^2 + v^2 - 2vv\cos\theta}$$
$$= \sqrt{2v^2(1-\cos\theta)}$$
$$= \sqrt{2v^2 \times 2\sin^2\theta/2}$$
$$= 2v\sin\frac{\theta}{2}.$$

As the velocities of the particles are randomly distributed, so θ varies from 0 to 2π. The magnitude of average velocity when averaged over all such pairs. Thus

$$v_{21} = \frac{\int_0^{2\pi} v_{21} d\theta}{\int_0^{2\pi} d\theta}$$

$$= \frac{\int_0^{2\pi}\left(2v\sin\frac{\theta}{2}\right)d\theta}{\int_0^{2\pi} d\theta}$$

$$= \frac{2v\left[\dfrac{-\cos\theta/2}{(1/2)}\right]_0^{2\pi}}{[\theta]_0^{2\pi}}$$

$$= \frac{-4v\left[\cos(\theta/2)\right]_0^{2\pi}}{(2\pi - 0)}$$

$$= -\frac{2v}{\pi}\left[\cos\pi - \cos 0\right]$$

$$= \frac{4v}{\pi} = 1.273\,v$$

$$> v. \qquad\qquad \textbf{Proved}$$

4.11 CONSTRAINT RELATIONS

In some devices of mechanics, the connected objects do not have same velocity or acceleration. The relation between their velocities or accelerations is known as constraint relation. In the shown device, the velocity of ring and block are not same. Here $v_{\text{ring}} = \dfrac{v_{\text{block}}}{\cos\theta}$.

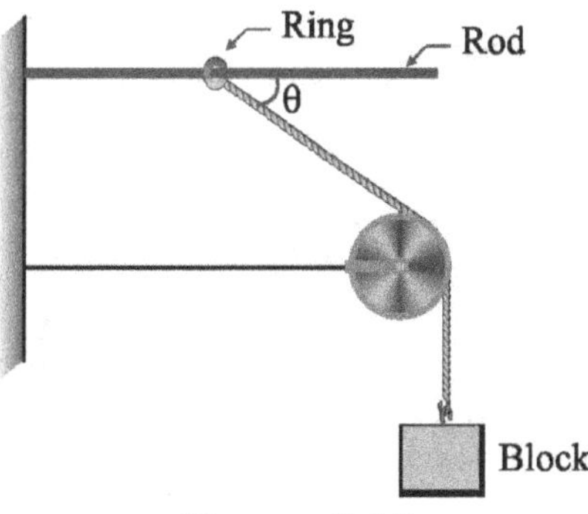

Figure. 4.63

Steps to find constraint relations :

Step 1 : Trace the directions of motion of bodies, which are connected together.

Step 2 : Make geometric relationship between their linear variables or between linear and angular variables.

Step 3 : Differentiate the obtained relations w.r.t. time, to get relationship between their velocities or accelerations etc.

CONSTRAINT RELATIONS EXAMPLES

E
w... ion shown in figure 4.64. Now the system is released. If $M_1 > M_2$ find $\dfrac{v_1}{v_2}$, ...d by the distance h.

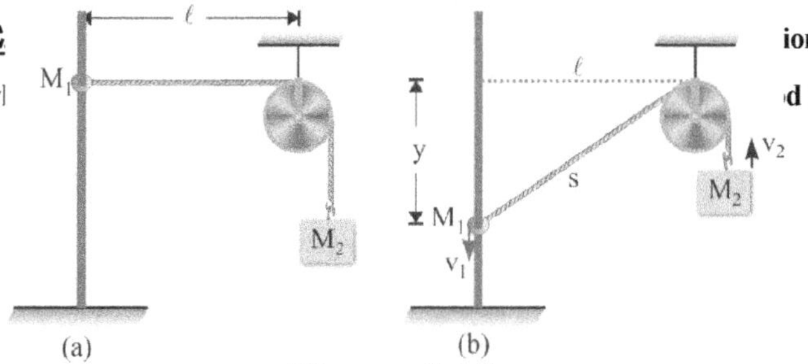

Figure. 4.64

Sol.

Let ring has moved down a distance y. From figure (*b*), we have

$$y^2 + \ell^2 = s^2 \qquad ....(i)$$

Here ℓ is the length of string which is constant.
Differentiating equation (i) w.r.t. time, we get

$$2y\frac{dy}{dt} + 0 = 2s\frac{ds}{dt} \qquad ....(ii)$$

or
$$\frac{dy}{dt} = \frac{s}{y} \cdot \frac{ds}{dt}$$

Here
$$\frac{dy}{dt} = v_1 \text{ and } \frac{ds}{dt} = v_2$$

For
$$y = h,\ s = \sqrt{h^2 + \ell^2}$$

$\therefore$ Equation (ii) takes the form

$$v_1 = \frac{\sqrt{h^2 + \ell^2}}{h} \cdot v_2$$

or
$$\frac{v_1}{v_2} = \frac{\sqrt{h^2 + \ell^2}}{h} \qquad\qquad \textit{Ans.}$$

Example 15. In the arrangement shown in *fig.* 4.65, the ends P and Q of an inextensible string move downwards with uniform speed u and v respectively. Pulley A and B are fixed. Find the velocity of mass M at the instant shown in the figure 4.65.

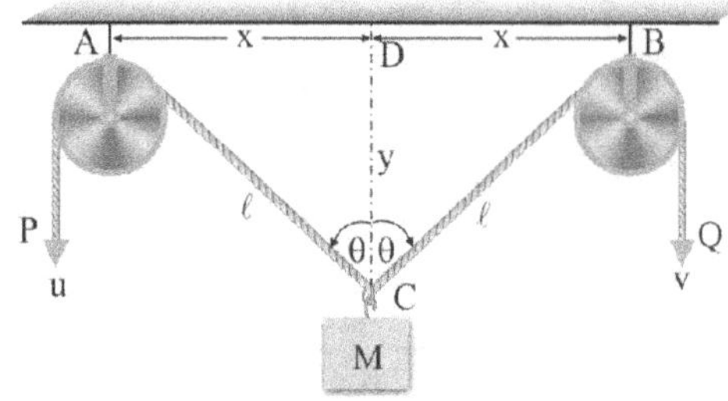

Figure. 4.65

Sol.

Let at any instant the block is at a distance y from line AB and length of string between A and C is ℓ. In ΔACD, we have

$$x^2 + y^2 = \ell^2 \qquad \text{.... (i)}$$

Here x remain constants while $\dfrac{d\ell}{dt}$, the rate of change of length of string, which is equal to the rate at which it pulls i.e. u. Differentiating equation (i) w.r.t. time, we get

$$\frac{d}{dt}(x^2 + y^2) = \frac{d}{dt}(\ell^2).$$

$$2y\frac{dy}{dt} = 2\ell\frac{d\ell}{dt}$$

or $$\frac{dy}{dt} = \frac{\ell}{y}\frac{d\ell}{dt} = \frac{u}{\cos\theta} \qquad \text{.... (ii)}$$

Similar relation can be obtained from ΔBCD. That is

$$\frac{dy}{dt} = \frac{v}{\cos\theta} \qquad \text{....(iii)}$$

Adding equations (ii) and (iii), we get

$$\frac{dy}{dt} = \frac{(u+v)}{2\cos\theta}$$

Thus velocity of block, $\dfrac{dy}{dt}$ in upward direction is $\dfrac{(u+v)}{2\cos\theta}$. ***Ans.***

Example 16. A block is dragged on a smooth plane with the help of a rope which is pulled with velocity v as shown in figure 4.66. Find the horizontal velocity of the block.

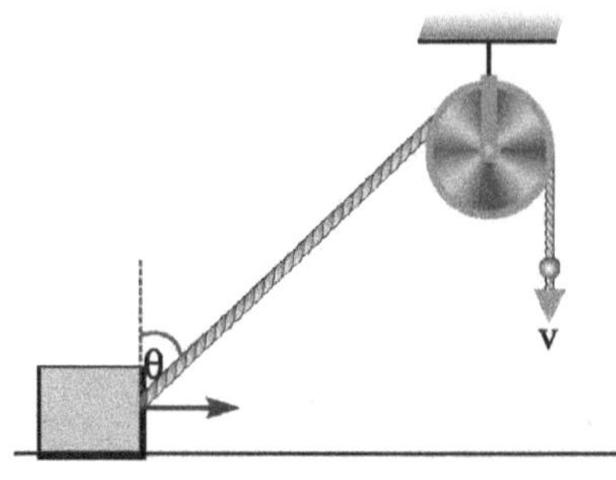

Figure. 4.66

Sol. Short-cut method

Let velocity of block along horizontal direction is v_x, then its component along the rope will be $v_x \sin\theta$. Since each point on the rope will move with same velocity v

$$\therefore \qquad v_x \sin\theta = v$$

or $$v_x = \frac{v}{\sin\theta}. \qquad \text{***Ans.***}$$

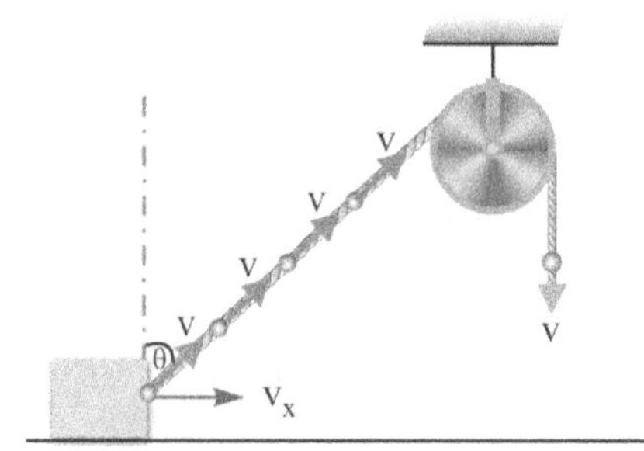

Figure. 4.67

Example 17. A rod of length ℓ is inclined at an angle θ with the floor against a smooth vertical wall. If the end A moves instantaneously with velocity v_1, what is the velocity of end B at the instant when rod makes θ angle with the horizontal.

Sol.

Let at any instant, ends B and A are at a distance x and y respectively from the point O.

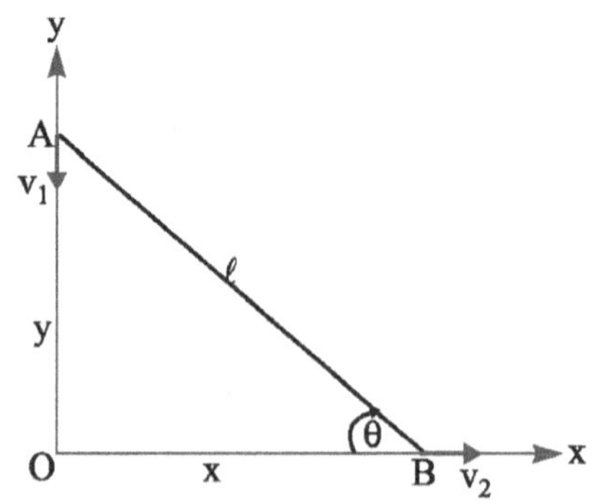

Figure. 4.68

Thus we have

$$x^2 + y^2 = \ell^2 \qquad \text{.... (i)}$$

Here ℓ is the length of the rod, which is constant. Differentiating equation (i) with respect to time, we get

$$\frac{d}{dt}(x^2 + y^2) = \frac{d(\ell)^2}{dt} \quad \text{or} \quad 2x\frac{dx}{dt} + 2y\frac{dy}{dt} = 0 \quad \text{.... (ii)}$$

where $$\frac{dx}{dt} = v_2, \text{ and } \frac{dy}{dt} = -v_1$$

Now from equation (ii), we have

$$x(v_2) + y(-v_1) = 0$$

or $$v_2 = \frac{y}{x}v_1 = v_1\tan\theta. \qquad \text{***Ans.***}$$

Example 18. A point A moves uniformly with a velocity v in such a way that the direction of its velocity continually points at another point B, which in turn, moves along a straight line with a uniform velocity u ($u < v$). **At the initial moment u and v are right angles and the points are separated by a distance ℓ. How soon will the points meet ?**

Sol.

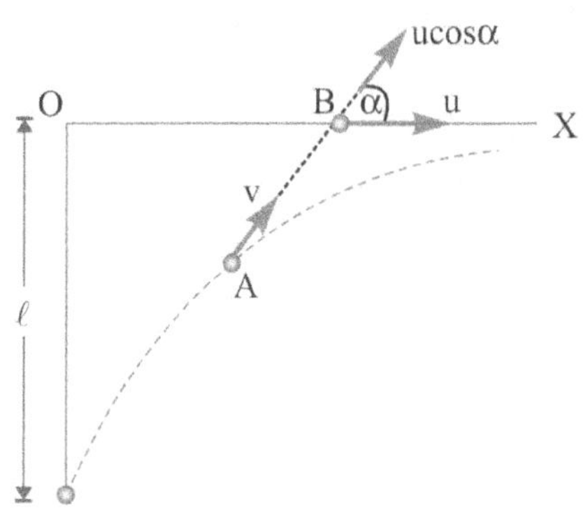

Figure. 4.69

Let at any instant points A and B are at the positions shown in figure 4.89. The point A moves towards B with velocity v. At the same time B move away from A with the speed $u\cos\alpha$ where α is the inclination of the line AB with x-axis. The distance between them decreases at the rate of $(v - u\cos\alpha)$. The initial moment the separation between them is ℓ. This separation reduced to zero when A and B meet.

Suppose A and B meet after time T, then

$$\int_0^T (v - u\cos\alpha)\,dt = \ell$$

or $\qquad \int_0^T v\,dt - \int_0^T u\cos\alpha\,dt = \ell$

or $\qquad vT - u\int_0^T \cos\alpha\,dt = \ell \quad$ .... (i) $\qquad$ [Here α is not constant]

Along x-axis, the distance described by B in time T is uT. The velocity of A parallel to x-axis is $v\cos\alpha$. Therefore, distance describes by A in time T is $\int_0^T v\cos\alpha\,dt$.

When point A and B meet

$$\int_0^T v\cos\alpha\,dt = uT \qquad .... \text{(ii)}$$

From equation (ii), we have

$$v\int_0^T \cos\alpha\,dt = uT$$

or $\qquad \int_0^T \cos\alpha\,dt = \dfrac{uT}{v} \qquad .... \text{(iii)}$

Substituting the value in equation (i), we get

$$vT - u\left(\frac{uT}{v}\right) = \ell$$

or $\qquad \dfrac{(v^2 - u^2)}{v}T = \ell$

or $\qquad T = \dfrac{v\ell}{v^2 - u^2}. \qquad$ **Ans.**

Example 19. Three points are located at the vertices of an equilateral triangle whose side equal to a. They all start moving simultaneously with velocity v constant in modulus, with first point heading continually for the second, the second for the third, and the third for the first. How soon will the points converge?

Sol.

The motions of the points are sketched in the figure. As they start moving simultaneously symmetrically, they will meet at the centroid of the triangle.

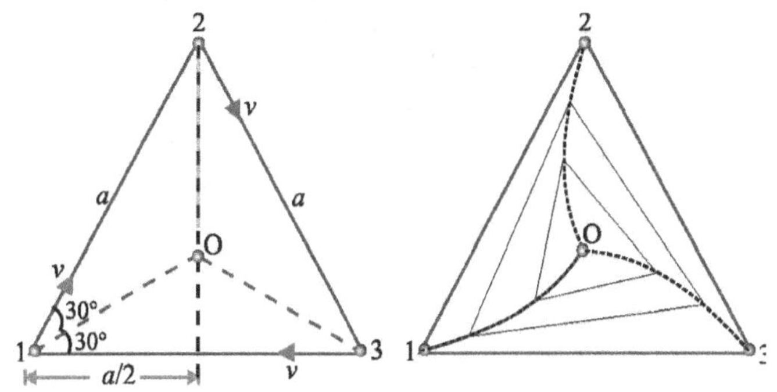

Figure. 4.70

The velocity of any point towards centroid of triangle O

$$= v\cos 30° = \frac{\sqrt{3}v}{2}.$$

And its displacement $\qquad = \dfrac{a/2}{\cos 30°} = \dfrac{a}{\sqrt{3}}.$

The time taken to converge the points

$$= \frac{\text{displacement}}{\text{velocity}} = \frac{a/\sqrt{3}}{\sqrt{3}v/2} = \frac{2a}{3v}. \ \textbf{\textit{Ans.}}$$

In Chapter Exercise 4.3

1. A boy stands $\ell = 4$ m away from a vertical wall and throws a ball. The ball leaves the boy's hand at $h = 2$ m above the ground with initial velocity $v_0 = 10\sqrt{2}$ m/s at an angle of 45° from the horizontal. After striking the wall elastically the ball rebounds. Where does the ball hit the ground ?

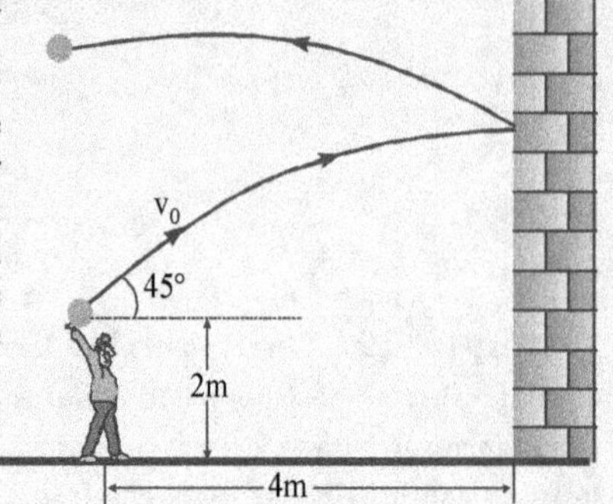

Ans. **18 m from the wall**

2. A ball falls freely from a height h onto an inclined plane forming an angle α with the horizon. Find the ratio of the successive ranges of the ball along the plane. Consider the impacts between the ball and the plane to be absolutely elastic.

Ans. $R_1 : R_2 : R_3 : \ldots\ldots = 1 : 2 : 3\ldots\ldots$

3. Two guns are projected at each other, one upward at an angle of 30° and the other at the same angle of depression, the muzzles being 30 m apart as shown in the figure. If the guns are shot with velocities of 350 m/s upward and 300 m/s downward respectively. Find when and where the bullets may meet.

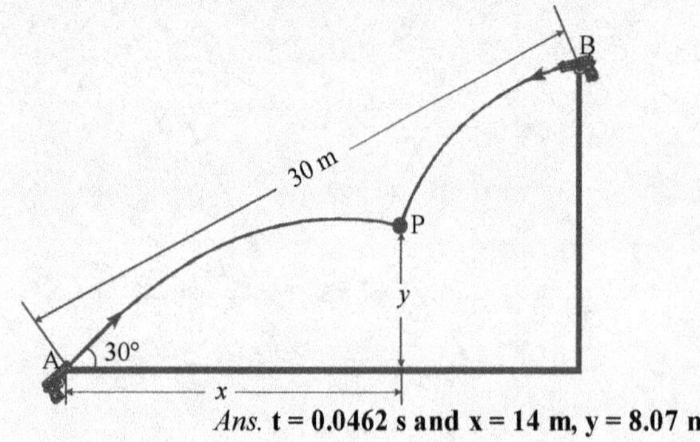

Ans. **t = 0.0462 s and x = 14 m, y = 8.07 m**

4. A boat is approaching the shore with a speed of $5\sqrt{3}$ m/s. At the instant when it is at a distance of $30\sqrt{3}$ m from the shore, a stone is to be projected at an elevation of 30° for it to just reach the shore. What should be the speed of the stone relative to the boat ?

Ans. **19.77 m/s**

5. A rocket is fired vertically and tracked by the radar R as shown in the figure. At a particular position $\theta = 60°$, measured parameters are r = 9km and $\dfrac{d\theta}{dt} = 0.02\,rad/s$. Find the velocity of rocket at this position.

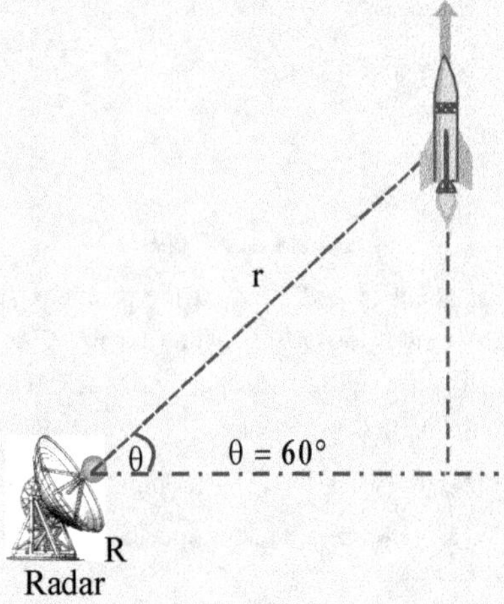

Ans : **360 m/s**

6. Six particles situated at the corners of a regular hexagon of side a move at a constant speed v. Each particle maintain a direction towards the particle at the next corner. Calculate the time the particles will take to meet each other.

Ans : $\dfrac{2a}{v}$

Mechanics | **MCQ Type 1** | Exercise 4.1

Motion in 2D, River-boat, Rain-umbrella

1. An ion's position vector is initially $\vec{r}_i = 5\hat{i} - 6\hat{j} + 2\hat{k}$ and 10 s later it is $\vec{r}_f = -2\hat{i} + 8\hat{j} - 2\hat{k}$, all in metre. The average velocity during 10 s is :

(a) $\left(-0.7\hat{i} + 1.4\hat{j} - 0.4\hat{k}\right)$ m/s

(b) $\left(0.7\hat{i} + 0.8\hat{j} - 0.4\hat{k}\right)$ m/s

(c) $\left(1.4\hat{j} - 0.7\hat{j} + 0.8\hat{k}\right)$ m/s

(d) $\left(\hat{i} - 1.4\hat{j} + 2\hat{k}\right)$ m/s

2. A particle has initial velocity $\left(3\hat{i} + 4\hat{j}\right)$ and has acceleration $\left(0.4\hat{i} + 0.3\hat{j}\right)$. Its speed after 10 s is :

(a) 7 unit   (b) $7\sqrt{2}$ unit

(c) 8.5 unit   (d) 10 unit

3. A smooth square platform $ABCD$ is moving towards right with a uniform speed v. At what angle θ must a particle be projected from A with speed u so that it strikes the point B

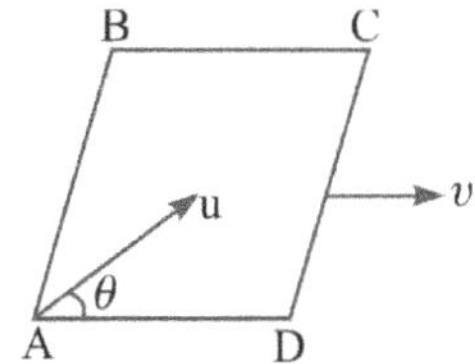

(a) $\sin^{-1}\left(\dfrac{u}{v}\right)$ (b) $\cos^{-1}\left(\dfrac{v}{u}\right)$

(c) $\cos^{-1}\left(\dfrac{u}{v}\right)$ (d) $\sin^{-1}\left(\dfrac{v}{u}\right)$

4. The height y and the distance x along the horizontal plane of a projectile on a certain planet [with no surrounding atmosphere] are given by $y = [5t - 8t^2]$ metre and $x = 12t$ metre where t is the time in second. The velocity with which the projectile is projected, is:

(a) 5 m/s   (b) 12 m/s

(c) 13 m/s   (d) not obtainable from the data

5. A particle moves in x-y plane according to law $x = a \sin \omega t$ and $y = b \cos \omega t$ where a and b are constants. Then the particle follows:

(a) a parabolic path

(b) a circular path

(c) a straight line path equally to x and y-axis

(d) an elliptical path

6. A body starts from rest from the origin with an acceleration of 6 m/s^2 along the x-axis and 8 m/s^2 along the y-axis. Its distance from the origin after 4 seconds will be

(a) 56 m   (b) 64 m

(c) 80 m   (d) 128 m

7. A particle moves along the parabolic path $y = ax^2$ in such a way that the x-component of the velocity remains constant, say c. The acceleration of the particle is:

(a) $ac\hat{k}$ (b) $2ac^2\hat{j}$

(c) $2ac^2\hat{k}$ (d) $a^2c\hat{j}$

8. Two particles A and B are separated by a horizontal distance x. They are projected at the same instant towards each other with speeds $u\sqrt{3}$ and u at angle of projections $30°$ and $60°$ respectively figure. The time after which the horizontal distance between them becomes zero is :

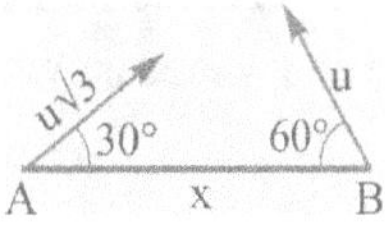

(a) $\dfrac{x}{u}$ (b) $\dfrac{x}{2u}$

(c) $\dfrac{2x}{u}$ (d) $\dfrac{4x}{u}$

9. A swimmer crosses a 200 m wide channel with straight bank and return in 10 minute at a point 300 m below the starting point (downstream). The velocity of the swimmer relative to the bank if he heads towards the bank to the channel all the time at right angles is.

(a) 2 km/h   (b) 3 km/h

(c) 4 km/h   (d) 5 km/h

10. A boat which has a speed of 5 km/h, in still water crosses a river of width 1 km along the shortest possible path in 15 minute. The velocity of the river water in km/h is

(a) 1   (b) 3

(c) 4   (d) $\sqrt{41}$

Answer	1	(a)	2	(b)	3	(b)	4	(c)	5	(d)
Key	6	(c)	7	(b)	8	(a)	9	(b)	10	(b)

11. A man crosses a 320 m wide river perpendicular to the current in 4 minute. If in still water he can swim with a speed $\frac{5}{3}$ times that of the current, then the speed of the current, in m/min is:

(a) 30 (b) 40
(c) 50 (d) 60

12. A river is flowing from west to east at a speed of 5m/min. A man on the south bank of the river capable of swimming at 10 m/min in still water wants to swim across the river

(a) due north to reach in shortest time

(b) at an angle 30° west of north to reach in minimum time

(c) at an angle 60° west of north to reach along shortest path

(d) at angle 45° west of north to reach along shortest path

Projectile Motion

13. A stone is just released from the window of a train moving along a horizontal straight track. The stone will hit the ground following

(a) straight path (b) circular path
(c) parabolic path (d) hyperbolic path

14. When air resistance is taken into account while dealing with the motion of the projectile. Of the following properties of the projectile, the one which shows an increase, is:

(a) range

(b) maximum height

(c) speed at which it strikes the ground

(d) the angle of which the projectile strikes the ground

15. At the top of the trajectory of a projectile, the acceleration is

(a) maximum (b) minimum
(c) zero (d) g

16. It was calculated that a shell when fired from a gun with a certain velocity and at an angle of elevation $\frac{5\pi}{36}$ radian should strike a given target. In actual practice it was found that a hill just prevented in the trajectory. At what angle of elevation should the gun be fired to hit the target:

(a) $\frac{5\pi}{36}$ (b) $\frac{11\pi}{36}$
(c) $\frac{7\pi}{36}$ (d) $\frac{13\pi}{36}$

17. The angle of projection, for which the horizontal range and the maximum height of a projectile are equal, is:

(a) 45° (b) $\theta = \tan^{-1}4$
(c) $\theta = \tan^{-1}(0.25)$ (d) none of these.

18. The range of a projectile which is launched at an angle of 15° with the horizontal is 1.5 km. What is the range of the projectile if it is projected of an angle 45° to the horizontal?

(AMU B.Tech.-2003)

(a) 1.5 km (b) 3 km
(c) 6 km (d) 0.75 km

19. An aeroplane is flying horizontally with a velocity of 600 km/h at a height of 1960 m. When it is vertically at a point A on the ground, a bomb is released from it. The bomb strikes the ground at point B. The distance AB is

(a) 1200 m (b) 0.33 km
(c) 3.33 km (d) 33 km

20. A body is projected with velocity v_1 from point A. At the same time another body is projected vertically upwards with velocity v_2. The point B lies vertically below the highest point. For both the bodies to collide $\dfrac{v_2}{v_1}$ should be:

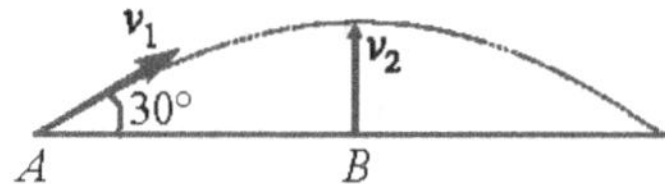

(a) 2 (b) $\dfrac{\sqrt{3}}{2}$
(c) 0.5 (d) 1

21. A boy throws a ball with a velocity u at an angle θ with the horizontal. At the same instant he starts running with uniform velocity to catch the ball before it hits the ground. To achieve this he should run with a velocity of:

(a) $u \cos \theta$ (b) $u \sin \theta$
(c) $u \tan \theta$ (d) $\sqrt{u^2 \tan \theta}$

22. A cricketer can throw a ball to a maximum horizontal distance of d. How high above the ground can the cricketer throw the same ball ?

(a) d/2 (b) d
(c) 2d (d) 5d/2

23. A particle is projected from the ground with a velocity of 25 m/s. After 2 second, it just clears a wall 5 m height. Then the angle of projection of particle is [$g = 10$ m/s^2]:

Answer	11	(d)	12	(a)	13	(c)	14	(d)	15	(d)	16	(d)
Key	17	(b)	18	(b)	19	(c)	20	(c)	21	(a)	22	(a)

(a) 30°   (b) 45°
(c) 60°   (d) 75°

24. The horizontal and vertical components of the velocity of a projectile are 10 m/s and 20 m/s, respectively. The horizontal range of the projectile will be [$g = 10$ m/s^2]

(a) 5 m   (b) 10 m
(c) 20 m   (d) 40 m

25. A cart is moving horizontally along a straight line with constant speed 30 m/s. A projectile is to be fired from the moving cart in such a way that it will return to the cart after the cart has moved 80 m. At what speed (relative to the cart) must the projectile be fired   (Take $g = 10$ m/s^2)

(a) 10 m/s   (b) $10\sqrt{8}$ m/s
(c) $\dfrac{40}{3}$ m/s   (d) none of these

26. For an object thrown at 45° to horizontal, the maximum height (H) and horizontal range (R) are related as

(a) $R = 16\,H$ (b) $R = 8\,H$
(c) $R = 4\,H\bullet$ (d) $R = 2H$

27. A ball is thrown up at an angle 45° with the horizontal. Then the total change of momentum by the instant it returns to ground is

(a) zero   (b) $2\,mv$
(c) $\sqrt{2}\,mv$ (d) $\dfrac{mv}{\sqrt{2}}$

28. A stone projected with a velocity u at an angle θ with the horizontal reaches maximum height H_1. When it is projected with velocity u at an angle $\left(\dfrac{\pi}{2} - \theta\right)$ with the horizontal, it reaches maximum height H_2. The relation between the horizontal range R of the projectile, H_1 and H_2 is

(a) $R = 4\sqrt{H_1 H_2}$ (b) $R = 4\left(H_1 - H_2\right)$
(c) $R = 4\left(H_1 + H_2\right)$ (d) $R = \dfrac{H_1^2}{H_2^2}$

Constraint Relation

29. The end A of a rod slides down a smooth wall and its end B slides on a smooth floor. When AB makes an angle α with the horizontal. A has speed v. The speed of end B will be

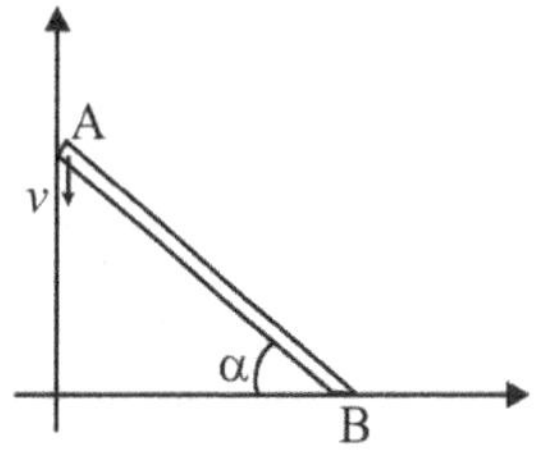

(a) $\dfrac{v}{\tan\alpha}$ (b) $v \tan\alpha$
(c) $\dfrac{v}{\cos\alpha}$ (d) $v \sin\alpha$

30. A block is dragged on a smooth plane with the help of a rope which is pulled by velocity v as shown in figure. The horizontal velocity of the block is:

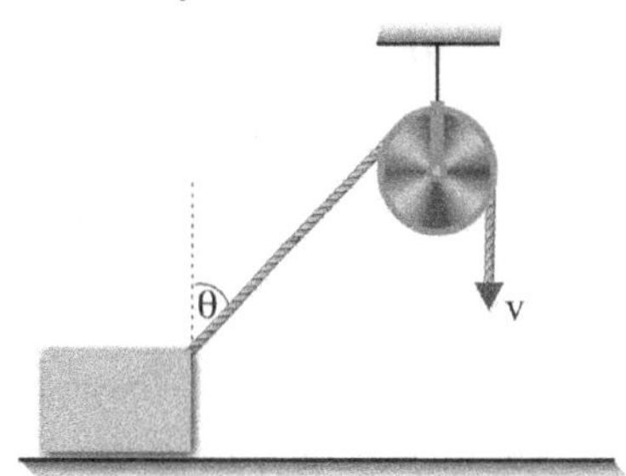

(a) v (b) $v/\sin\theta$
(c) $v \sin\theta$ (d) $v/\cos\theta$

Answer	23	(a)	24	(d)	25	(c)	26	(c)
Key	27	(c)	28	(a)	29	(b)	30	(b)

Motion in 2D, River-boat, Rain-umbrella

1. A particle starts from the origin at t = 0 s with a velocity of 10.0 $\hat{j}$ m/s and moves in the xy- plane with a constant acceleration of $(8.0\hat{i} + 2.0\hat{j})$ m/s^2 . The y-coordinate of the particle when x-coordinate is 16:

(a) 2 m   (b) 24 m
(c) 8 m   (d) 16 m

2. The distance between two moving particles at any time t is 'a'. If v be their relative velocity and v_1 and v_2 be the components of v along and perpendicular to 'a', then the time when they are closest to each other:

(a) a/v_1 (b) a/v_2
(c) $\dfrac{av_1}{v^2}$ (d) $\dfrac{av_2}{v^2}$

3. Two particles start simultaneously from the same point and move along two straight lines, one with uniform velocity v and other with a uniform acceleration a. If α is the angle between the lines of motion of two particles then the least value of relative velocity will be at time given by

(a) $\dfrac{v}{a}\sin\alpha$ (b) $\dfrac{v}{a}\cos\alpha$
(c) $\dfrac{v}{a}\tan\alpha$ (d) $\dfrac{v}{a}\cot\alpha$

4. Passengers in the jet transport A flying east at a speed of 800 kmh^{-1} observe a second jet plane B that passes under the transport in horizontal flight. Although the nose of B is pointed in the $45°$ north east direction, plane B appears to the passengers in A to be moving away from the transport at the $60°$ angle as shown. The true velocity of B is

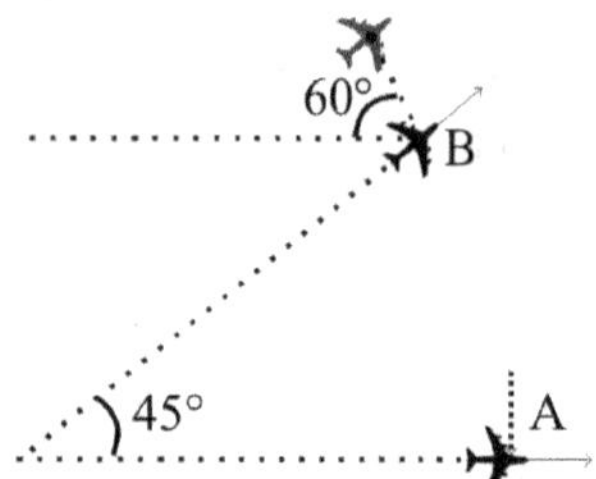

(a) 586 kmh^{-1}
(b) $400\sqrt{2}$ kmh^{-1}
(c) 717 kmh^{-1}
(d) 400 kmh^{-1}

5. A river is flowing with a velocity of 1 m/s towards east directions. When the boat runs with a velocity of 3 m/s relative to the river is the direction of the river flow, the flag on the boat flutter in north direction. If the boat runs with the same speed but in north direction relative to river, the flag flutters towards north-east direction. The actual velocity of the wind should be : ($\hat{i} \rightarrow$ east direction and $\hat{j} \rightarrow$ north direction).

(a) $4\hat{i} + 6\hat{j}$
(b) $6\hat{i} + 4\hat{j}$
(c) $4\hat{i} - 6\hat{j}$
(d) $6\hat{i} - 4\hat{j}$

Projectile Motion

6. You throw a ball with a launch velocity of $\vec{v} = \left(3\hat{i} + 4\hat{j}\right)$ m/s towards a wall, where it hits at height h_1. Suppose that the launch velocity were, instead, $\vec{v} = \left(5\hat{i} + 4\hat{j}\right)$ m/s. If h_2 is height, then

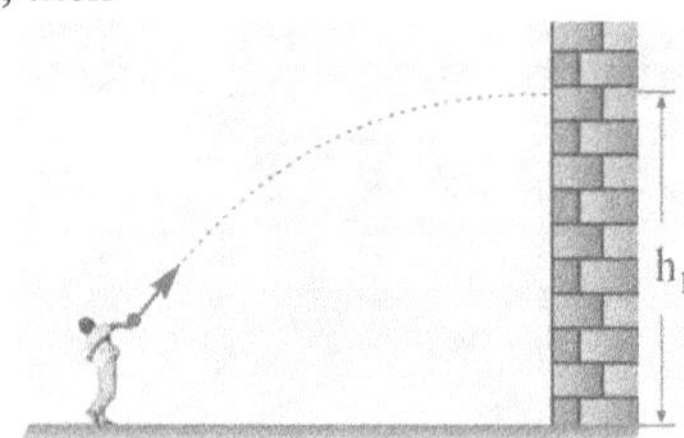

(a) $h_2 = h_1$
(b) $h_2 < h_1$
(c) $h_2 > h_1$
(d) unanswerable

7. A ball is shot from the ground into the air. At a height of 9.1 m, its velocity is observed to be $\vec{v} = 7.6\hat{i} + 6.1\hat{j}$ in m/s. The maximum height the ball will rise is :

(a) 10 m
(b) 11 m
(c) 12.5 m
(d) 15 m

8. The equation of trajectory of a particle is given by the equation $y = ax - bx^2$, where a and b are constant. The horizontal range is:

(a) a
(b) b
(c) ab
(d) a/b

9. Two balls are projected simultaneously in the same vertical plane from the same point with velocities v_1 and v_2 with angle θ_1 and θ_2 respectively with the horizontal. If $v_1 \cos \theta_1 = v_2 \cos \theta_2$, the path of one ball as seen from the position of other ball is :

(a) parabola
(b) horizontal straight line
(c) vertical straight line
(d) straight line making $45°$ with the vertical

10. A projectile moves from the ground such that its horizontal displacement is $x = Kt$ and verticle displacement is $y = Kt(1 - \alpha t)$, where K and α are constants and t is time. Find out total time of flight (T) and maximum height attained (Y_{max}) its

(a) $T = \alpha, Y_{max} = \dfrac{K}{2\alpha}$
(b) $T = \dfrac{1}{\alpha}, Y_{max} = \dfrac{2K}{\alpha}$
(c) $T = \dfrac{1}{\alpha}, Y_{max} = \dfrac{K}{6\alpha}$
(d) $T = \dfrac{1}{\alpha}, Y_{max} = \dfrac{K}{4\alpha}$

11. An object is projected with a velocity of 20 m/s making an angle of $45°$ with horizontal. The equation for the trajectory is $h = Ax - Bx^2$ where h is height, x is horizontal distance, A and B are constants. The ratio A : B is ($g = 10$ ms^{-2})

(a) $1 : 5$
(b) $5 : 1$
(c) $1 : 40$
(d) $40 : 1$

12. If retardation produced by air resistance of projectile is one-tenth of acceleration due to gravity, the time to reach maximum height

(a) decreases by 11 percent
(b) increases by 11 percent
(c) decreases by 9 percent
(d) increases by 9 percent

13. An aircraft moving with a speed of 250 m/s is at a height of 6000 m, just overhead of an anti aircraft gun. If the muzzle velocity is 500 m/s, the firing angle θ should be:

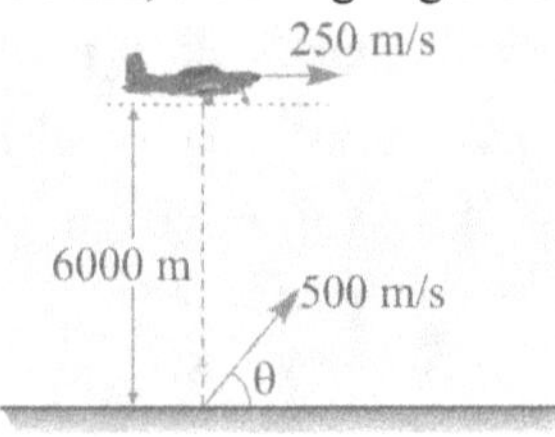

(a) $30°$
(b) $45°$
(c) $60°$
(d) none of these.

Answer	1	(b)	2	(c)	3	(b)	4	(c)	5	(a)	6	(b)	7	(b)
Key	8	(d)	9	(c)	10	(d)	11	(d)	12	(c)	13	(c)		

14. A particle is ejected from the tube at A with a velocity v at an angle $30°$ with the vertical y-axis. A strong horizontal wind gives the particle a constant horizontal acceleration a in the x- direction. If the particle strikes the ground at a point directly under its released position and the downward y -acceleration is taken as g then

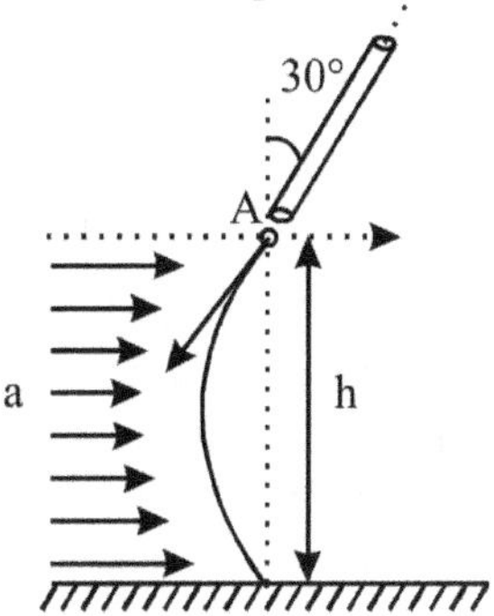

(a) $h = \dfrac{\sqrt{3}v^2}{2a}$

(b) $h = \dfrac{\sqrt{3}v^2}{2g}$

(c) $h = \dfrac{v^2}{g}\left(\dfrac{\sqrt{3}}{2} + \dfrac{a}{2g}\right)$

(d) $h = \dfrac{v^2}{a}\left(\dfrac{\sqrt{3}}{2} + \dfrac{g}{2a}\right)$

15. A particle P is projected from a point on the surface of long smooth inclined plane and Q starts moving down the plane from the same position. P and Q collide after 4 second. The speed of projection of P is : $(g = 10 \text{ m/s}^2)$

(a) 5 m/s

(b) 10 m/s

(c) 15 m/s

(d) 20 m/s

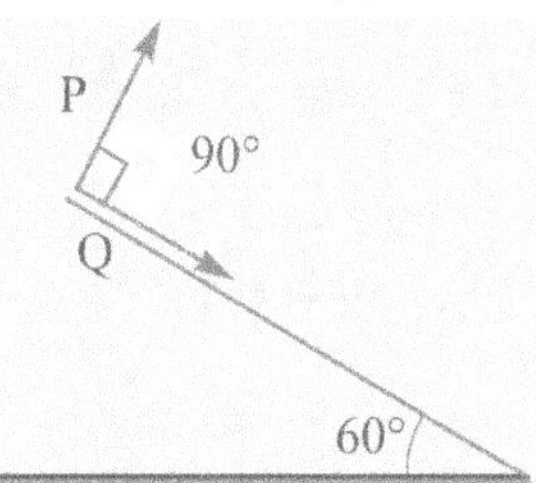

16. Which of the following plots correctly represents the variation of the magnitude of radial acceleration $\left|a_R\right|$ with time t for a particle projected at $t = 0$ with speed v_0 at an angle θ above the horizontal?

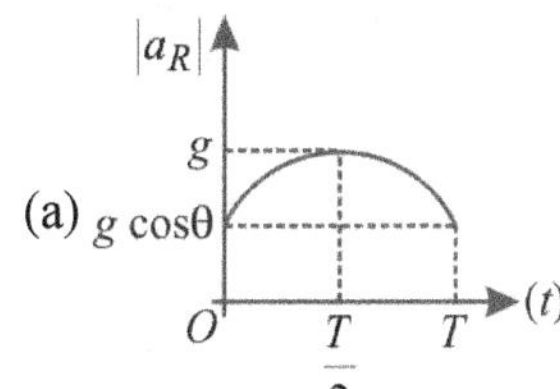

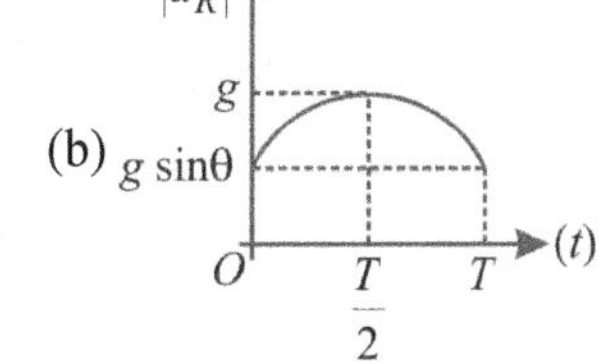

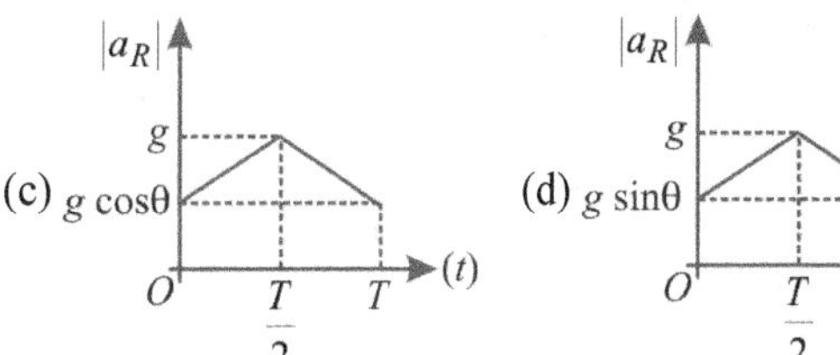

17. A boy throws a ball upward with velocity $v_0 = 20$ m/s making an angle θ with the vertical. The wind imparts a horizontal acceleration of 4 m/s^2 to the left. The angle at which the ball must be thrown so that the ball returns to the boy's hand is $(g = 10 \text{ m/s}^2)$

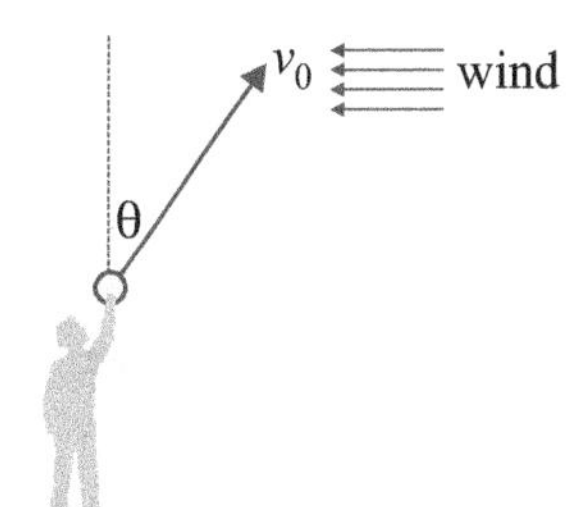

(a) $\tan^{-1}(1.2)$

(b) $\tan^{-1}(0.2)$

(c) $\tan^{-1}(2)$

(d) $\tan^{-1}(0.4)$

18. In figure the angle of inclination of the inclined plane is $30°$. The horizontal velocity V_0 so that the particle hits the inclined plane perpendicularly is

(a) $V_0 = \sqrt{\dfrac{2gH}{5}}$

(b) $V_0 = \sqrt{\dfrac{2gH}{7}}$

(c) $V_0 = \sqrt{\dfrac{gH}{5}}$

(d) $V_0 = \sqrt{\dfrac{gH}{7}}$

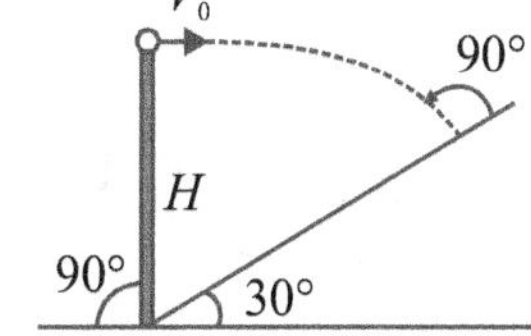

19. A stone is projected from a horizontal plane. It attains maximum height H and strikes a stationary smooth wall and falls on the ground vertically below the maximum height. Assuming the collision to be elastic, the height of the point on the wall where ball will strike is:

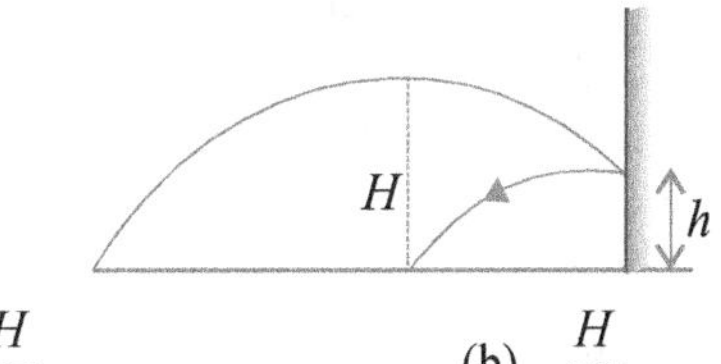

(a) $\dfrac{H}{4}$

(b) $\dfrac{H}{2}$

(c) $\dfrac{3H}{4}$

(d) $\dfrac{7H}{8}$

Answer	14	(d)	15	(b)	16	(c)
Key	17	(d)	18	(a)	19	(a)

Constraint Relations

20. A racing car travelling along a track at a constant speed of 40 m/s. A television cameraman is recording the event from a distance 40 m directly away from the track as shown in figure. In order to keep the car under view, with what angular velocity the camera should be rotated when $\theta = 45°$?

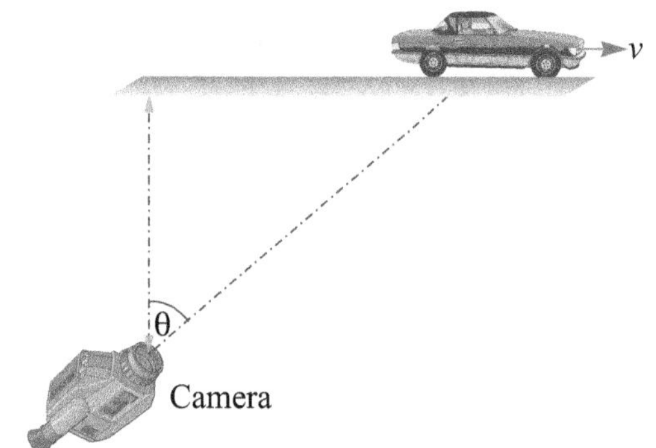

(a)   5/2 rad/s   (b)   2 rad/s

(c)   3/2 rad/s   (d)   1/2 rad/s

21. A jet plane flying at a constant velocity v at a height $h = 8$ km, is being tracked by a radar R located at O directly below the line of flight, if the angle θ is decreasing at the rate of 0.025 rad/s, the velocity of the plane when $\theta = 60°$ is :

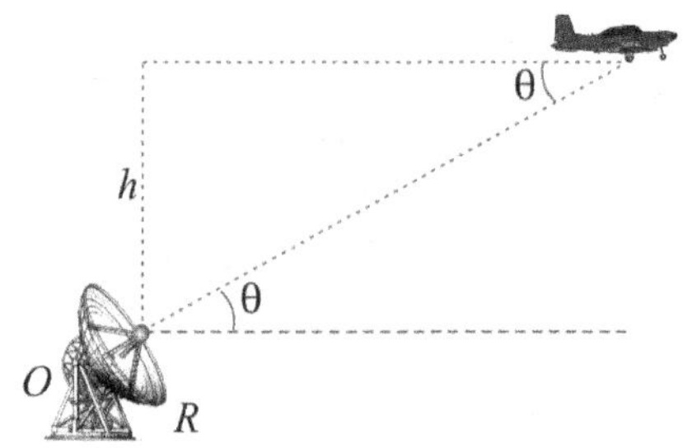

(a)   1440 km/h   (b)   960 km/h

(c)   1920 km/h   (d)   480 km/h

22. In the arrangement shown in the figure the block B starts from rest and moves towards right with a constant acceleration. After time t the velocity of A with respect to B become v. The acceleration of A is

(a) $\dfrac{v}{t}$ (b) $\dfrac{2v}{t}$

(c) $\dfrac{3v}{t}$ (d) $\dfrac{4v}{t}$

Answer	20	(d)	21	(b)	22	(c)					
Key											

Mechanics   # MCQ Type 2   Exercise 4.2

MULTIPLE OPTIONS CORRECT

1. River is flowing with a velocity $\vec{v}_R = 4\hat{i}$ m/s. A boat is moving with a velocity of $\vec{v}_{BR} = \left(-2\hat{i} + 4\hat{j}\right)$ m/s relative to river. The width of the river is 100 m along y-direction. Choose the correct alternative(s).

(a)   The boatman will cross the river in 25 s

(b)   Absolute velocity of boatman is $2\sqrt{5}$ m/s

(c)   Drift of the boatman along the river current is 50 m

(d)   The boatman can never cross the river.

2. A plane is to fly due north. The speed of the plane relative to the air is 200 km/h, and the wind is blowing from west to east at 90 km/h.

(a)   The plane should head in a direction given by $\theta = \sin^{-1}(0.65)$

(b)   The plane should head in a direction given by $\theta = \sin^{-1}(0.45)$

(c)   The velocity of plane relative to the ground is 179 km/h.

(d)   The velocity of plane relative to the ground is 159 km/h.

3. A ball is released from the window of a train moving along a horizontal straight track with constant velocity. The path as observed:

(a)   from ground, will be parabolic

(b)   from ground, will be vertical straight line

(c)   from train, will be parabolic

(d)   from train, will be vertical straight line

4. Three balls are projected with same speed as shown in figure. First and third balls are projected from same height h and second ball is projected is ground. In these three cases, times of flights are T_1, T_2 and T_3 respectively, then choose correct relations :

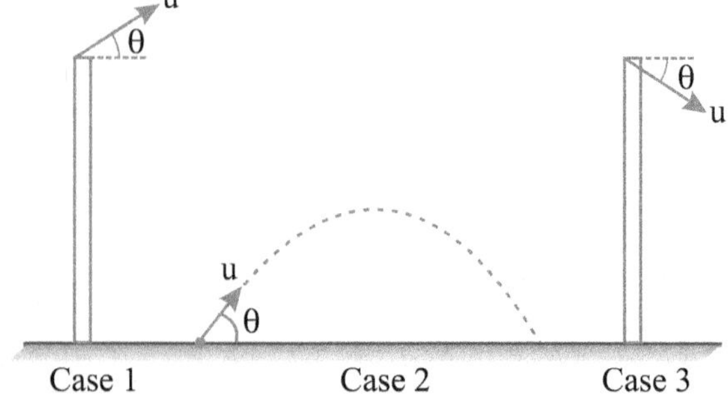

(a) $T_1 = T_2 + T_3$

(b) $T_2 = T_1 + T_3$

(c) $T_1 > T_2$

(d) $T_1 > T_3$

5. A body is projected with certain angle from the ground. The motion of the body is described by the equations $x = 2t$, $y = 3t - 4t^2$. Then:

(a) equation of trajectory is $y = \dfrac{3x}{2} - x^2$

(b) angle of projection is $45°$

(c) the velocity of projection is $\sqrt{13}$ m/s

(d) the acceleration due to gravity is 10 m/s^2

6. Two second after projection, a projectile is moving at $30°$ above the horizontal; after one more second it is moving horizontally. Then:

(a) angle of projection is $30°$

(b) velocity of projection is $20\sqrt{3}$ m/s

(c) velocity at any time will be 40 m/s

(d) maximum horizontal range attained $= 60\sqrt{3}$ m

7. The velocity of a particle moving in a positive direction of the x-axis varies as $v = \alpha\sqrt{x}$, where α is a positive constant. Assuming that at the moment $t = 0$, the particle was located at the point $x = 0$:

(a) in the motion, the acceleration is constant

(b) velocity at any time will be α/t

(c) velocity at any time will be $\dfrac{\alpha^2 t}{2}$

(d) mean velocity of particle averaged over the time that the particle takes to cover first s meter is $\dfrac{\alpha\sqrt{s}}{2}$

8. Two particles are projected from ground with same initial velocities at angles $30°$ and $60°$ (with horizontal). Let R_1 and R_2 be their horizontal ranges, H_1 and H_2 their maximum heights and T_1 and T_2 are the time of flights. Then :

(a) $\dfrac{H_1}{R_1} > \dfrac{H_2}{R_2}$

(b) $\dfrac{H_1}{R_1} < \dfrac{H_2}{R_2}$

(c) $\dfrac{H_1}{T_1} > \dfrac{H_2}{T_2}$

(d) $\dfrac{H_1}{T_1} < \dfrac{H_2}{T_2}$

9. A particle is projected from a point P with a velocity v at an angle θ with horizontal. At a certain point Q it moves at right angles to its initial direction. Then:

(a) velocity of particle at Q is $v \sin\theta$

(b) velocity of particle at Q is $v \cot\theta$

(c) time of flight from P to Q is $(v/g)\,\text{cosec}\,\theta$

(d) time of flight from P to Q is $(v/g)\sec\theta$

10. Trajectories are shown in figure are for three kicked footballs, ignoring the effect of the air on the footballs. If T_1, T_2 and T_3 are their respective time of flights then:

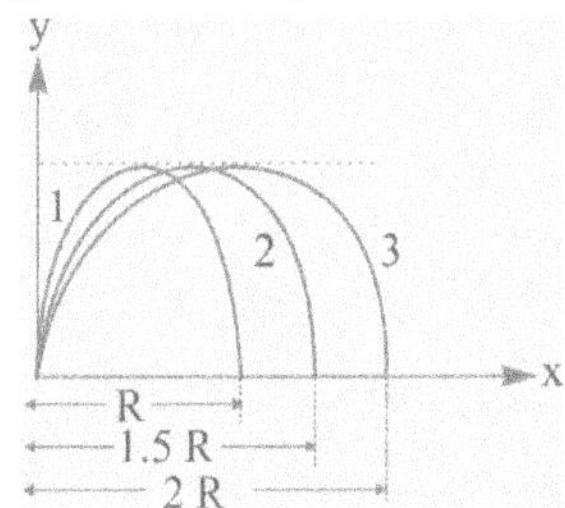

(a) $T_1 > T_3$

(b) $T_1 < T_3$

(c) $T_2 = \dfrac{T_1 + T_3}{2}$

(d) $T_1 = T_2 = T_3$

Answer	1	(a, b, d)	2	(b, c, a)	3	(a, d)	4	(a, c, d)
Key	5	(a, c)	6	(b, d)	7	(a, c, d)	8	(a, c)

Mechanics   # Reasoning Type Questions   Exercise 4.3

Read the two statements carefully to mark the correct option out of the options given below:

(a) **Statement - 1** is true, **Statement - 2** is true; **Statement - 2** is correct explanation for **Statement - 1**.

(b) **Statement -1** is true, **Statement - 2** is true; **Statement - 2** is not correct explanation for **Statement - 1**.

(c) **Statement - 1** is true, **Statement - 2** is false.

(d) **Statement - 1** is false, **Statement - 2** is true

1. **Statement - 1** When a body is dropped or thrown horizontally from the same height, it would reach the ground at the same time.

Statement - 2

There is no acceleration in horizontal direction.

2. **Statement - 1**

If there were no gravitational force, the path of the projected body always be a straight line.

Statement - 2

Gravitational force makes the path of projected body always parabolic.

3. **Statement - 1**

The maximum possible height attained by the projected body is $\dfrac{u^2}{2g}$, where u is the velocity of projection.

Statement - 2

To attain the maximum height, body is thrown vertically upwards.

4.   Statement - 1

When the range of projectile is maximum, the time of flight is the largest.

Statement - 2

Range is maximum when angle of projection is 45°.

5.   Statement - 1

A shell fired from a gun is moving along the parabolic path. If it explodes at the top of the trajectory, then no part of the shell can fly vertically.

Statement - 2

The vertical momentum of the shell at the top of the trajectory is zero.

6.   Statement - 1

A projectile, launched from ground, collides with a smooth vertical wall and returns to the ground. The total time of flight is the same had there been no collision.

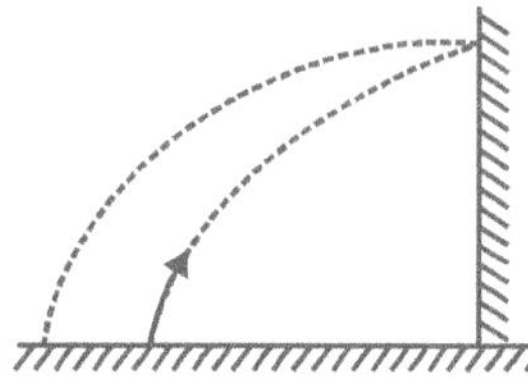

Statement - 2

The collision changes only the horizontal component of velocity.

7.   Statement - 1

A body is thrown with a velocity u inclined to the horizontal at some angle. It moves along a parabolic path and falls to the ground. Linear momentum of the body, during its motion, will remain conserve.

Statement - 2

Throughout the motion of the body, a constant force acts on it.

8.   Statement - 1

Two projectiles having same range must have the same time of flight.

Statement - 2

Horizontal component of velocity is constant in projectile motion under gravity.

9.   Statement - 1

A man projects a stone with speed u at some angle. He again projects a stone with same speed such that time of flight now is different. The horizontal ranges in both the cases may be same. (Neglect air friction)

Statement - 2

The horizontal range is same for two projectiles projected with same speed if one is projected at an angle θ with the horizontal and other is projected at an angle $(90° - \theta)$ with the horizontal. (Neglect air friction)

Answer	1	(b)	2	(c)	3	(a)	4	(d)	5	(d)
Key	6	(a)	7	(d)	8	(d)	9	(a)		

 Mechanics   **Passage & Matrix**   **Exercise 4.4**

Passage for (Q. 1 - 2) :

A particle is projected at an angle θ with the horizontal such that it just able to clear a vertical wall of height h at a distance h from point of projection as shown in figure.

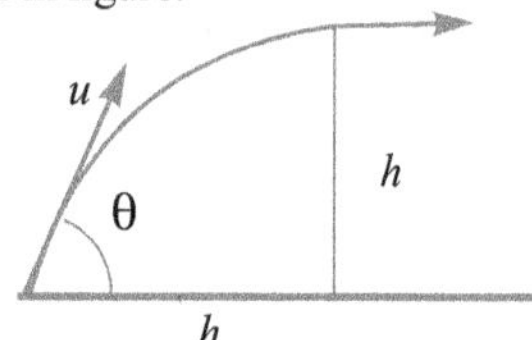

1.   The angle of projection θ is :

(a) $\tan^{-1}(2)$ (b) $\tan^{-1}\sqrt{3}$

(c) $\tan^{-1}(\sqrt{2}/3)$ (d) $\tan^{-1}(\sqrt{3}/2)$

2.   The velocity of projection u is :

(a) $\sqrt{2gh}$ (b) $\sqrt{gh}$

(c) $\sqrt{5gh}$ (d) $\sqrt{\dfrac{5}{2}gh}$

Passage for (Questions 3 to 5) :

Consider the case of the collision of a ball with a wall. In this case the problem of collision can be simplified by considering the case of elastic collision only. When a ball collides with a wall we can divide its velocity into two components, one perpendicular to the wall and other parallel to the wall. If the collision is elastic then the perpendicular component of velocity of the ball gets reversed with the same magnitude.

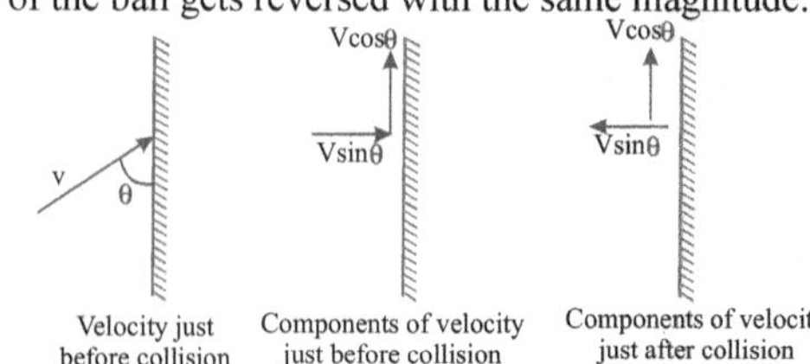

The other parallel component of velocity will remain constant if wall is given smooth.

Now let us take a problem. Three balls A and B & C are projected from ground with same speed at same angle with the horizontal. The balls A, B and C collide with the wall during their flight in air and all three collide perpendicularly with the wall as shown in figure.

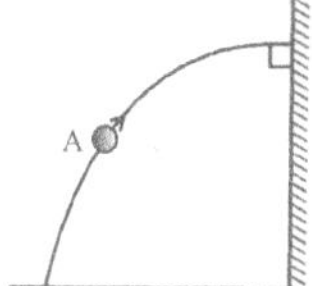 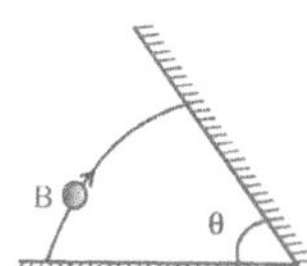 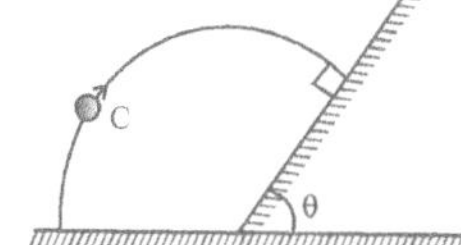

3. Which of the following relation about the maximum height H of the three balls from the ground during their motion in air is correct:
   (a) $H_A = H_C > H_B$ (b) $H_A > H_B = H_C$
   (c) $H_A > H_C > H_B$ (d) $H_A = H_B = H_C$

4. If the time taken by the ball A to fall back on ground is 4 seconds and that by ball B is 2 seconds. Then the time taken by the ball C to reach the inclined plane after projection will be –
   (a) 6 sec.   (b) 4 sec.
   (c) 3 sec.   (d) 5 sec.

5. The maximum height attained by ball A from the ground is–
   (a) 10m   (b) 15 m
   (c) 20 m   (d) Insufficient information

6. The equation of trajectory of a particle projected from the surface of the planet is given by the equation $y = x - x^2$.
   Then match the columns :(suppose, $g = 2$ m/s^2)

	Column - I	**Column - II** (magnitude only)
A.	angle of projection, $\tan \theta$	(p) ¼
B.	time of flight, T	(q) 1
C.	maximum height attained, H	(r) 2
D.	horizontal range, R	(s) 4

7. A particle is projected with some angle from the surface of the planet. The motion of the particle is described by the equation; $x = t$, $y = t - t^2$.
   Then match the following columns :

	Column - I (quantity)	**Column - II** (magnitude only)
A.	velocity of projection	(p) 1
B.	acceleration	(q) $\sqrt{2}$
C.	time of flight	(r) 2
D.	maximum height attained	(s) 3
		(t) $\dfrac{1}{4}$

Answer	1	(a)	2	(d)	3	(a)	4	(c)	5	(c)
Key	6	$A \to q$; $B \to r$; $C \to p$; $D \to q$			7	$A \to q$; $B \to r$; $C \to p$; $D \to t$				

JEE- (Main)

1. A projectile can have the same range R for two angles of projection. If t_1 and t_2 are the times of flight in the two cases, then the product of two times of flight is: **[AIEEE 2004]**
   (a) $\dfrac{R^2}{g}$ (b) $\dfrac{2R}{g}$
   (c) $\dfrac{R}{2g}$ (d) $\dfrac{4R^2}{g}$

2. A ball is thrown from a point with a speed v_0 at an angle of projection θ. From the same point and at the same instant a person starts running with a constant speed $v_0/2$ to catch the ball. Will the person be able to catch the ball ? If yes, what should be the angle of projection **[AIEEE 2004]**
   (a) yes, 60°   (b) yes, 30°
   (c) no   (d) yes, 45°

3. A particle is moving with velocity $\vec{v} = k(y\hat{i} + x\hat{j})$, where k is a constant. The general equation of its path is **[AIEEE 2010]**
   (a) $y^2 = x^2 +$ constant   (b) $y = x^2 +$ constant
   (c) $y^2 = x +$ constant   (d) $xy =$ constant

4. A large number of bullets are fired in all directions with same speed v. What is the maximum area on the ground on which these bullets will spread **[AIEEE 2011]**
   (a) $\pi \dfrac{v^2}{g}$ (b) $\pi \dfrac{v^4}{g^2}$
   (c) $\pi^2 \dfrac{v^4}{g^2}$ (d) $\pi^2 \dfrac{v^2}{g^2}$

Answer Key	1	(b)	2	(a)	3	(a)	4	(b)

Hints & Solutions

In Chapter Exercise -4.1

1. Given, $\vec{r} = 3.0t\hat{i} + 2.0t^2\hat{j} + 5.0\hat{k}$

   (a) $\vec{v} = \dfrac{d\vec{r}}{dt} = 3.0\hat{i} + 4.0t\hat{j} + 0 = (3.0\hat{i} + 4.0\hat{j})\,\text{m/s}$

   $\vec{a} = \dfrac{d^2\vec{r}}{dt^2} = 0 + 4.0\hat{j} = 4.0\hat{j}\,\text{m/s}^2$

   (b) At, $t = 3.0\ s$, $\vec{v} = 3.0\hat{i} + 4.0 \times 3\hat{j} = 3.0\hat{i} + 12.0\hat{j}$

   $\therefore \qquad v = \sqrt{3.0^2 + 12.0^2} = 12.4\ \text{m/s}$

   and $\tan\theta = \dfrac{12.0}{3.0} = 4, \quad \therefore \theta = 76°$ **Ans.**

2. Given $\vec{v}_{\text{train}} = 30\hat{i}$

   and $\vec{v}_{\text{car}} = 40\hat{j}$

   $[\vec{v}_{\text{car}}]_{\text{train}} = [\vec{v}_{\text{car}}] - [\vec{v}]_{\text{train}}$

   $= 40\hat{j} - 30\hat{i}$

   or $v_{car} = \sqrt{40^2 + (-30)^2} = 50\ \text{km/h}$

   $\tan\theta = \dfrac{30}{40}$

   $\therefore \qquad \theta = 36° \, 52'$ **Ans.**

3. Given, $\vec{v}_{\text{rain}} = 24\hat{j}\,\text{m}/s$

   and $\vec{v}_{\text{woman}} = 12(-\hat{i})\,\text{m/s}$

   $[\vec{v}_{\text{rain}}]_{\text{woman}} = \vec{v}_{\text{rain}} - \vec{v}_{\text{woman}}$

   $= 24\hat{j} - (-12\hat{i})$

   $= 24\hat{j} + 12\hat{i}$

   $\tan\theta = \dfrac{12}{24} = \dfrac{1}{2}$

   Ans.

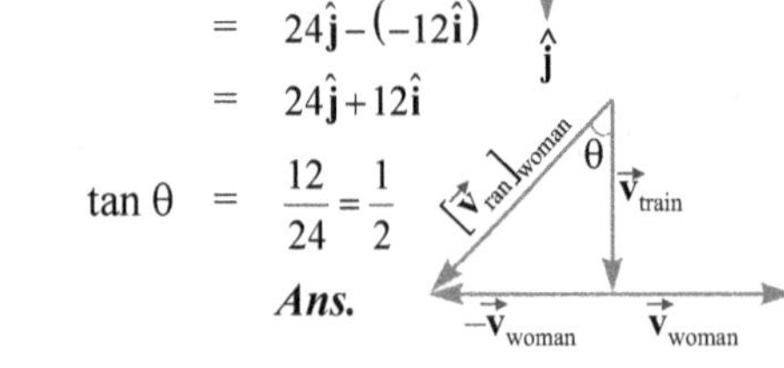

4. Suppose u is the speed of the boat relative to water, then velocity of the flow (w.r.t. bank)

   $v_x = (u\cos\theta + v_0),$

   and perpendicular to flow will be

   $v_y = u\sin\theta$

   Time to cross the river $t = \dfrac{b}{u\sin\theta}$.

   In this time the distance travelled by the boat in the direction of flow

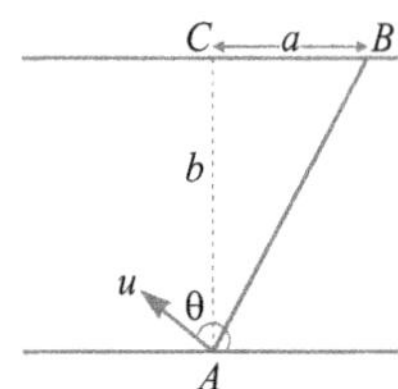

$a = v_x t = (u\cos\theta + v_0)\,\dfrac{b}{u\sin\theta}$

or $au\sin\theta = ub\cos\theta + v_0 b$

$\therefore \qquad u = \dfrac{v_0 b}{(a\sin\theta - b\cos\theta)}$ ...(i)

u to be minimum, $du/d\theta = 0$

or $\dfrac{d}{d\theta}\left[\dfrac{v_0 b}{a\sin\theta - b\cos\theta}\right] = 0$

$(a\sin\theta - b\cos\theta) \times 0 - (a\cos\theta + b\sin\theta) = 0$

or $\tan\theta = -\dfrac{a}{b}$

$\therefore \qquad \cos\theta = \dfrac{b}{\sqrt{a^2 + b^2}}$

On substituting these values in equation (i), we get

$u_{\min} = \dfrac{v_0 b}{\sqrt{a^2 + b^2}}$ **Ans.**

In Chapter Exercise -4.2

1. $R_{\max} = \dfrac{u^2}{g} = 160\ \text{m}$

   $H_{\max} = \dfrac{u^2}{2g} = \dfrac{R_{\max}}{2} = \dfrac{160}{2} = 80\ \text{m}$

2. If u is the velocity of arrow, then

   $u_x = u\cos 45° = \dfrac{u}{\sqrt{2}}$

   and $u_y = u\sin 45° = \dfrac{u}{\sqrt{2}}$

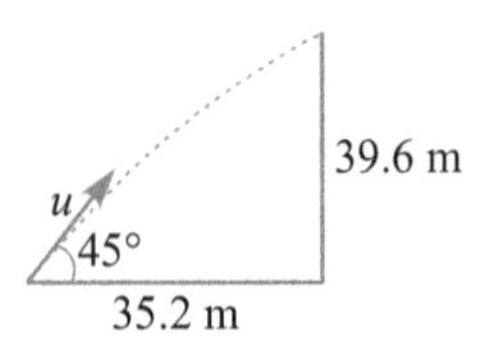

If t is the time taken to reach the bird, then

$35.2 = u_x t$

or $35.2 = \dfrac{u}{\sqrt{2}}t$ ...(i)

and $39.6 = u_y t - \dfrac{1}{2}gt^2$

$= \dfrac{u}{\sqrt{2}}t - \dfrac{1}{2}gt^2$ ...(ii)

After solving, we get, $u = 41.86\ \text{m/s}$.

3. Given, $y = bx - cx^2$

$\therefore \qquad \dfrac{dy}{dt} = b\dfrac{dx}{dt} - 2cx\dfrac{dx}{dt}$ ...(i)

and
$$\frac{d^2y}{dt^2} = b\frac{d^2x}{dt^2} - 2c\left[x\frac{d^2x}{dt^2} + \frac{dx}{dt}\cdot\frac{dx}{dt}\right]$$

At $t = 0$, $x = 0$; Also $\dfrac{d^2y}{dt^2} = -a$ and $\dfrac{d^2x}{dt^2} = 0$,

$\therefore$
$$-a = -2c\,v_x^2$$

or
$$v_x^2 = \frac{a}{2c}$$

From equation (i), $\quad v_y = b\sqrt{\frac{a}{2c}} - 0 = b\sqrt{\frac{a}{2c}}$

$$v_0 = \sqrt{v_x^2 + v_y^2}$$

$$= \sqrt{\frac{a}{2c} + b^2 \times \frac{a}{2c}}$$

$$= \sqrt{\frac{a}{2c}\left[1 + b^2\right]} \qquad \textbf{Ans.}$$

4. For the collision $x = v_0\cos 60° \, t_1 = v_0\cos 45° \, t_2 \quad$ ...(i)

and $\quad y = v_0\sin 60° t - \dfrac{1}{2}gt_1^2 = v_0\sin 45° \, t_2 - \dfrac{1}{2}gt_2^2 \quad$ ...(ii)

After solving equations (i) and (ii), we get
$$\Delta t = t_1 - t_2 = 11\,\text{s} \qquad \textbf{Ans.}$$

In Chapter Exercise -4.3

1. The velocity components at the point of projection are
$$u_x = 10\sqrt{2}\,\cos 45° = 10\,\text{m/s}$$
$$u_y = 10\sqrt{2}\,\sin 45° = 10\,\text{m/s}$$
Time taken to cover horizontal distance 4 m,
$$t = \frac{4}{10} = 0.4\,\text{s}$$
At the instant of collision with the wall, the velocity components are
$$v_x = 10\,\text{m/s}$$
$$v_y = 10 - g \times 0.4 = 6.1\,\text{m/s}$$

The height attained by the ball above point of projection
$$h = 10 \times (0.4) - \frac{1}{2}g(0.4)^2$$
$$= 3.2\,\text{m}$$
The total height of the ball from the ground
$$H = 2 + 3.2 = 5.2\,\text{m}$$
The time taken by ball to hit the ground
$$5.2 = -6.1T + \frac{1}{2}gT^2$$
or $\quad 4.9\,T^2 - 6.1T - 5.2 = 0$

$\therefore \qquad\qquad T = 1.8\,\text{s}$

The horizontal distance travelled by the ball in this time
$$x = v_x\,T = 10 \times 1.8 = 18\,\text{m} \quad \textbf{Ans.}$$

2. If u is the velocity of ball before collision with the inclined plane, then after impact, its two components of velocity along and perpendicular to plane are;
$$u_x = u\sin\theta$$
and $\qquad u_y = u\cos\theta$
If T_1 is the time between first and second impact, then
$$0 = u\cos\theta\, T_1 - \frac{1}{2}(g\cos\theta)T_1^2$$

$\therefore \qquad\qquad T_1 = \dfrac{2u}{g}. \text{ (constant)}$

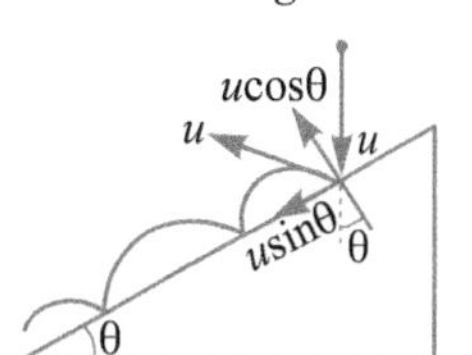

The range along the inclined plane
$$R_1 = u\sin\theta\, T_1 + \frac{1}{2}(g\sin\theta)T_1^2$$
$$= u\sin\theta \times \frac{2u}{g} + \frac{1}{2}g\sin\theta\left(\frac{2u}{g}\right)^2$$
$$= \frac{2u^2\sin\theta}{g} + \frac{2u^2\sin\theta}{g}$$
$$= \frac{4u^2\sin\theta}{g}$$

The velocity after second impact,
$$v = u\sin\theta + g\sin\theta t$$
$$= u\sin\theta + g\sin\theta \times \frac{2u}{g} = 3u\sin\theta$$

Range $\qquad R_2 = (3u\sin\theta)T_1 + \dfrac{1}{2}(g\sin\theta)T_1^2$

$$= 3u\sin\theta \times \frac{2u}{g} + \frac{1}{2}g\sin\theta\left(\frac{2u}{g}\right)^2$$
$$= \frac{8\,u^2\sin\theta}{g}$$

So $\quad R_1 : R_2 : R_3 \ldots\ldots = 1 : 2 : 3 \ldots\ldots \quad \textbf{Ans.}$

3.
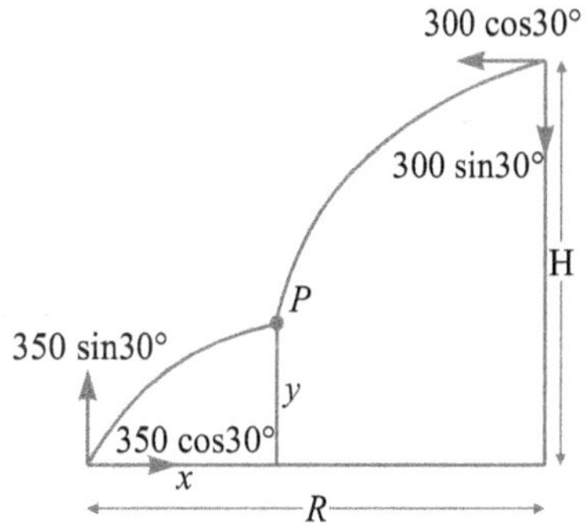

The situation is shown in figure.
$$R^2 + H^2 = 30^2 \qquad\qquad \text{...(i)}$$

If t is the time when bullets meet, then
$$x = 350 \cos 30° \, t, \qquad ...(ii)$$
$$R - x = 300 \cos 30° t, \qquad ...(iii)$$

Also
$$y = 350 \sin 30° t - \frac{1}{2} g t^2, \quad ...(iv)$$

and
$$H - y = 300 \sin 30° t + \frac{1}{2} g t^2 \quad ...(v)$$

After solving above equations, we get $t = 0.0462$ s,
$$x = 14 \text{ m and } y = 8.07 \text{ m}$$

4. Suppose u is the speed of the stone relative to boat. The components of speed of stone relative to ground
$$u_x = u \cos 30° + 5\sqrt{3} \text{ m/s}$$
$$= \left(\frac{\sqrt{3}u}{2} + 5\sqrt{3} \right) \text{m/s}$$

and
$$u_y = u \sin 30°$$
$$= \frac{u}{2} \text{ m/s}$$

If T is the time of motion of stone, then for vertical displacement to be zero,
$$0 = u_y T - \frac{1}{2} g T^2$$
$$\therefore \qquad T = \frac{2u_y}{g} = \frac{u}{g}$$

For horizontal motion, we have
$$30\sqrt{3} = u_x T$$
$$= \left(\frac{\sqrt{3}u}{2} + 5\sqrt{3} \right) \times \frac{u}{g}$$

After solving, we get $u = 19.77$ m/s   ***Ans.***

5. If y is the height of the rocket at any instant, then
$$y = x \tan \theta$$
Differentiating above equation w.r.t. time, we get
$$\frac{dy}{dt} = x \sec^2 \theta \frac{d\theta}{dt}$$

or
$$v = (r \cos \theta) \sec^2 \theta \left(\frac{d\theta}{dt} \right)$$
$$= \left(9 \times 10^3 \right) \times \left(\frac{1}{\cos 60°} \right) \times (0.02)$$
$$= 360 \text{ m/s} \qquad \textbf{\textit{Ans.}}$$

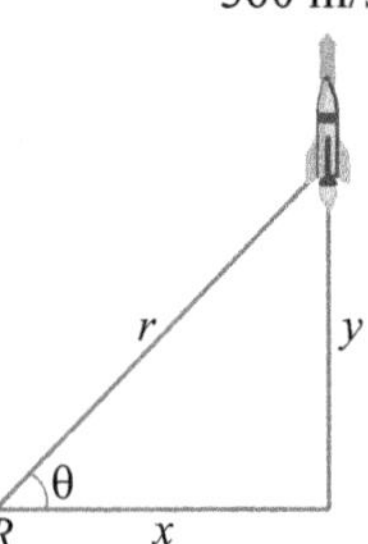

6. The particles will meet at the centre of the hexagon. The displacement of any particle from its initial position
$$s = \frac{l/2}{\sin 30°}$$

The effective velocity $v_e = v \cos 60° = \dfrac{v}{2}$.

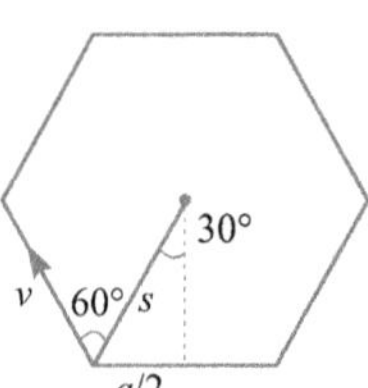

$$\therefore \qquad \text{Time taken} = \frac{s}{v_e} = \frac{2a}{v} \qquad \textbf{\textit{Ans.}}$$

1. (a) The average velocity,
$$\vec{v}_{av} = \frac{\vec{r}_f - \vec{r}_i}{\Delta t} = \frac{(-2\hat{i} + 8\hat{j} - 2\hat{k}) - (5\hat{i} - 6\hat{j} + 2\hat{k})}{10}$$
$$= (-0.7\hat{i} + 1.4\hat{j} + 0.4\hat{k}) \text{ m/s}.$$

2.
$$\vec{v} = \vec{u} + \vec{a}t = \left(3\hat{i} + 4\hat{j} \right) + (0.4\hat{i} + 0.3\hat{j}) \times 10$$
$$= 7\hat{i} + 7\hat{j}$$

or $v = \sqrt{7^2 + 7^2} = 7\sqrt{2}$ unit

3. (b) Particle will strike the point B if velocity of particle with respect to platform is along AB or component of its relative velocity along AD is zero, i.e. $u \cos \theta = v$

or $\theta = \cos^{-1}\left(\dfrac{v}{u} \right)$

4. (c)
$$v_x = \frac{dx}{dt} = \frac{d(12t)}{dt} = 12$$

and
$$v_y = \frac{dy}{dt} = \frac{d(5t - 8t^2)}{dt} = 5 - 16t.$$
$$\therefore \qquad v_{t=0} = \sqrt{v_x^2 + v_y^2} = \sqrt{12^2 + 5^2} = 13 \text{ m/s}$$

5. (d)
$$x = a \sin \omega t,$$
$$\therefore \qquad \sin \omega t = x/a$$
and
$$y = b \cos \omega t,$$
$$\therefore \qquad \cos \omega t = y/b.$$
$$\therefore \qquad \frac{x^2}{a^2} + \frac{y^2}{b^2} = 1. \text{ It represents an ellipse.}$$

6. (c)
$$x = \frac{1}{2} \times 6 \times 4^2 = 48 \text{ m}$$
and
$$y = \frac{1}{2} \times 8 \times 4^2 = 64 \text{ m}$$
$$\therefore \qquad s = \sqrt{x^2 + y^2} = \sqrt{48^2 + 64^2} = 80 \text{ m}.$$

7. (b)
$$y = ax^2$$
$$\therefore \quad v_y = \frac{dy}{dt} = a \times 2x \frac{dx}{dt}$$
$$= 2ax\, v_x = 2\,a\,c\,x$$

Now, $\quad a_y = \dfrac{dv_y}{dt} = 2\,ac\left(\dfrac{dx}{dt}\right) = 2\,ac^2.$

8. (b) Their velocity of approach is
$$v = u\sqrt{3}\cos 30° + u\cos 60°.$$
$$= 2u.$$
$$\therefore \quad t = \frac{x}{v} = \frac{x}{2u}.$$

9. (b) Time to cross the river = 5 min.
The displacement perpendicular to flow = 200 m.

$\therefore$ Velocity of swimmer
$$v_{sy} = \frac{200}{5 \times 60} = \frac{2}{3}\,m/s$$

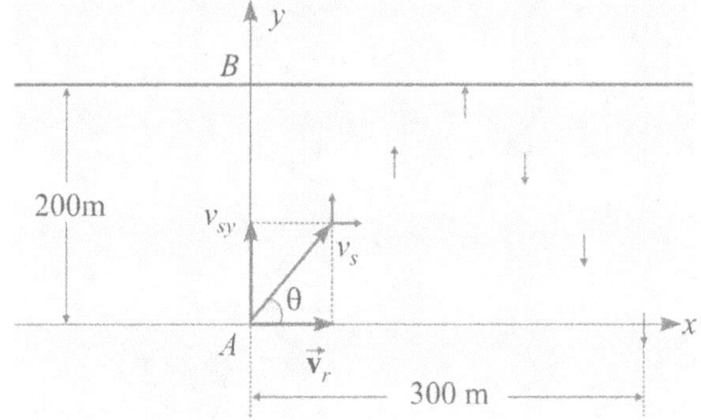

The displacement covered in the direction of flow = 300 m in 10 min.

$\therefore$ The velocity of river flow
$$v_r = \frac{300}{10 \times 60} = \frac{1}{2}\,\text{m/s}$$

The velocity of swimmer in the direction of flow
$$\vec{v}_{sx} = \vec{v}_r + \vec{v}_s$$

or $\quad v_{sx} = \dfrac{1}{2} + 0 = \dfrac{1}{2}\,\text{m/s}$

His velocity with respect to bank
$$v_s = \sqrt{v_{sx}^2 + v_{sy}^2} = \sqrt{\left(\frac{2}{3}\right)^2 + \left(\frac{1}{2}\right)^2}$$
$$= \frac{5}{6}\,m/s$$
$$= 3\,\text{km/h}$$

The velocity $\vec{v}_s$ makes an angle θ with the bank, then
$$\tan\theta = \frac{v_{sy}}{v_{sx}} = \frac{2/3}{1/2}$$
$$= \frac{4}{3}$$

or $\quad \theta = \tan^{-1}(4/3)$ *Ans.*

10. (b)
$$u = \frac{1}{1/4} = 4\,\text{km/h}$$

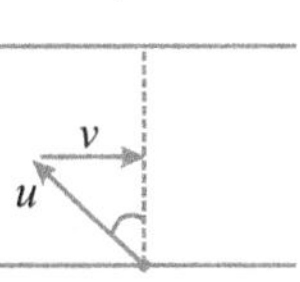

$\therefore \quad v = \sqrt{5^2 - 4^2} = 3\,\text{km/h}.$

11. (d)
$$\sqrt{u^2 - v^2} = \frac{320}{4} = 80$$

$$\sqrt{\left(\frac{5}{3}v\right)^2 - v^2} = 80$$

$\therefore \quad v = 60\,\text{m/min}$

12. (a) The man can cross the river in minimum time when he swim across perpendicular to flow direction.

13. (c) The resultant path of constant velocity and acceleration will be parabolic.

14. (d) Because of the constriction of the path, the angle of strike becomes greater than angle of projection.

15. (d) At the highest point of trajectory, the acceleration is equal to g.

16. (d) $\theta = \dfrac{5\pi}{36}$; the other possible angle to get the same range is,
$$\frac{\pi}{2} - \theta = \frac{\pi}{2} - \frac{5\pi}{36} = \frac{13\pi}{36}.$$

17. (b)
$$\frac{u^2 \sin 2\theta}{g} = \frac{u^2 \sin^2\theta}{2g}$$
$\therefore \quad \tan\theta = 4.$

18. (b)
$$R_1 = \frac{u^2 \sin(2 \times 15°)}{g} = \frac{u^2}{2g}.$$
and $\quad R_2 = \dfrac{u^2 \sin(2 \times 45°)}{g} = \dfrac{u^2}{g}$
$\therefore \quad R_2 = 2R_1 = 2 \times 1.5 = 3\,\text{km}.$

19. (c)
$$1960 = \frac{1}{2} \times 9.8 \times t^2$$
$\therefore \quad t = 20\,s$

Now $\quad AB = ut = \left(600 \times \dfrac{5}{18}\right) \times 20$
$$= 3333\,\text{m}.$$

20. (c) The vertical components of the velocities must be equal so.
$$v_1 \sin 30° = v_2$$

or $\qquad \dfrac{v_2}{v_1} = \dfrac{1}{2}$.

21. (a) The boy velocity = horizontal velocity of the ball
$$= u\cos\theta.$$

22. (a) Let u is the velocity of projection, then
$$R_{\max} = \dfrac{u^2}{g} = d$$

or $\qquad u = \sqrt{gd}$

Let h is the height upto which ball rise, then
$$0 = u^2 - 2gh$$

or $\qquad h = \dfrac{u^2}{2g} = \dfrac{gd}{2g}$

$$= \dfrac{d}{2}$$

23. (a) $\qquad u_y = u\sin\theta.$

$$y = u_y\, t - \dfrac{1}{2}gt^2$$

or $\qquad 5 = 25\sin\theta - \dfrac{1}{2}\times 10 \times 2^2.$

$\therefore \qquad \sin\theta = \dfrac{1}{2},$

or $\qquad \theta = 30°.$

24. (d) $\qquad R = \dfrac{2u_x u_y}{g} = \dfrac{2\times 10 \times 20}{10} = 40$ m.

25. (c) Time of motion,
$$t = \dfrac{x}{u_x} = \dfrac{80}{30} = \dfrac{8}{3}s.$$

Thus, $\qquad 0 = u\sin\theta\, t - \dfrac{1}{2}gt^2$

$\Rightarrow \qquad u\sin\theta = \dfrac{40}{3}$

$\therefore \qquad u_y = 40/3$ m/s.

26. (c) $\qquad H = \dfrac{u^2\sin 45°}{2g} = \dfrac{u^2}{4g}$

$$R = \dfrac{u^2}{g} = = 4\,H.$$

27. (c) $\qquad \Delta P = 2\,mu\sin\theta$

$$= (mg)\times \dfrac{2u\sin\theta}{g}$$

$$= \text{weight} \times \text{time of flight.}$$

28. (a) $\qquad H_1 = \dfrac{u^2\sin^2\theta}{2g}$

and $\qquad H_2 = \dfrac{u^2\sin^2(\pi/2-\theta)}{2g} = \dfrac{u^2\cos^2\theta}{2g}$

$$H_1 H_2 = \dfrac{u^2\sin^2\theta}{2g} \times \dfrac{u^2\cos^2\theta}{2g}$$

$$= \dfrac{(u^2\,2\sin\theta\cos\theta)^2}{16g^2} = \dfrac{R^2}{16}$$

$\therefore \qquad R = 4\sqrt{H_1 H_2}\;.$

29. (b)

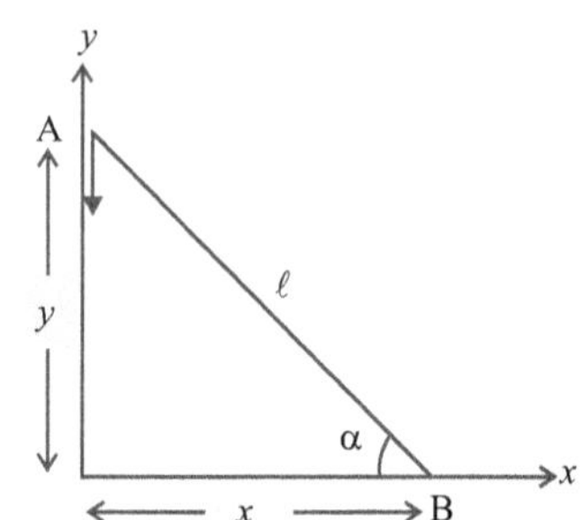

At any instant,

$$x^2 + y^2 = \ell \text{ (constant)}$$

or $\quad 2x\dfrac{dx}{dt} + 2y\dfrac{dy}{dt} = 0$

or $\quad 2x\,v_B + 2y\,v_A = 0$

or $\quad v_B = -\dfrac{y}{x}v_A$

or $\quad |v_B| = v\tan\alpha$

30. (b) If u is the horizontal velocity of the block, then
$$u\sin\theta = v,$$

$\therefore \qquad u = \dfrac{v}{\sin\theta}$

1. (b) Given that :
$$u_x = 0; \quad u_y = 10 \text{ m/s}$$
and $\qquad a_x = 8.0 \text{ m/s}^2; \quad a_y = 2.0 \text{ m/s}^2$

Let at time t the x-coordinate is 16 m. We have
$$x = u_x + \dfrac{1}{2}a_x t^2$$

or $\qquad 16 = 0 + \dfrac{1}{2}\times 8 \times t^2$

After simplifying,
$$t = 2s$$
The y coordinate at
$$t = 2\,s \text{ is}$$

$$y = u_y t + \dfrac{1}{2}a_y\, t^2$$

$$= 10\times 2 + \dfrac{1}{2}\times 2 \times 2^2 = 24 \text{ m} \quad \textbf{\textit{Ans.}}$$

2. (c)

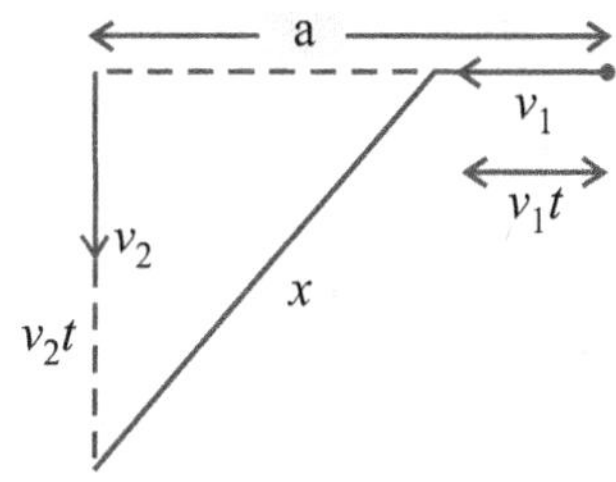

At any time 't'

$$x^2 = \left(a - v_1 t\right)^2 + \left(v_2 t\right)^2$$

For minimum value of x, $\dfrac{dx}{dt} = 0$

So $2x\dfrac{dx}{dt} = 2\left(a - v_1 t\right)\times\left(-v_1\right) + v_2^2 \times 2t$

or $0 = -2av_1 + 2t\left(v_1^2 + v_2^2\right)$

$\therefore\ t = \dfrac{av_1}{v_1^2 + v_2^2} = \dfrac{av_1}{v^2}$

3. (b)

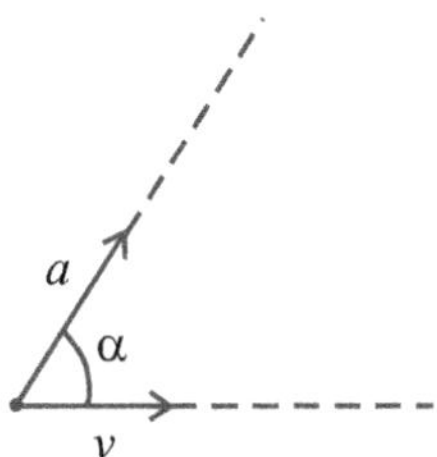

The velocity of first particle, $v_1 = v$

The velocity of second particle, $v_2 = at$

Relative velocity, $\vec{v}_{12} = \vec{v}_1 - \vec{v}_2$

or $v_{12}^2 = v^2 + \left(at\right)^2 - 2v\left(at\cos\alpha\right)$

For least value of relative velocity, $\dfrac{dv_{12}}{dt} = 0$

or $\dfrac{d}{dt}\left[v^2 + a^2 t^2 - 2vat\cos\alpha\right] = 0$

or $0 + a^2 \times 2t - 2va\cos\alpha = 0$

or $t = \dfrac{v\cos\alpha}{a}$

4. (c) According to law of sines or Lami's Theorem

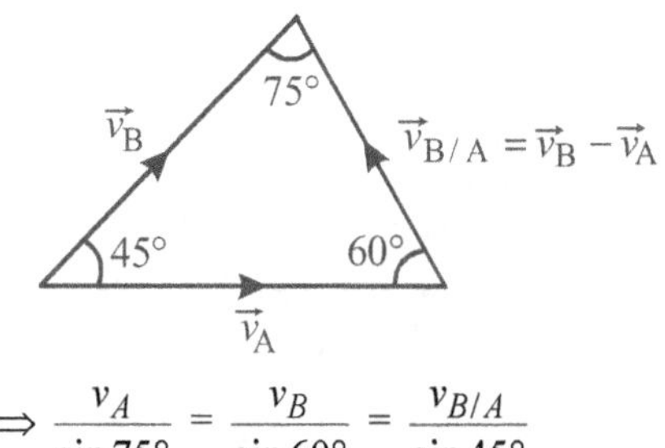

$\Rightarrow\ \dfrac{v_A}{\sin 75°} = \dfrac{v_B}{\sin 60°} = \dfrac{v_{B/A}}{\sin 45°}$

$\Rightarrow\ v_B = 717\ \text{kmh}^{-1}$

5. The velocity of wind, $= \vec{v} = v_x\,\hat{i} + v_y\,\hat{j}$

Velocity of boat w.r.t. bank $v_b = 3 + 1 = 4$ m/s

Now $\left[\vec{v}_w\right]_b = \vec{v}_w - \vec{v}_b = (v_x - 4)\,\hat{i} + v_y\,\hat{j}$

Given; $v_x - 4 = 0 \Rightarrow v_x = 4$ m/s.

And $\left[\vec{v}_w\right]_h^0 = \vec{v}_w - \vec{v}_b = \left(v_x\hat{i} + v_y\hat{j}\right) - 3\hat{j}$

$\qquad\qquad = v_x\hat{i} + \left(v_y - 3\right)\hat{j}$

Given $\tan 45° = \dfrac{v_y - 3}{v_x} \Rightarrow v_y = v_x + 3 = 3 + 3 = 6$ m/s

6. (b) $\qquad x = 3t_1 = 5t_2 \ \Rightarrow t_1 = x/3$ and $t_2 = x/5$

Now $\qquad h_1 = 4t_1 - \dfrac{1}{2}gt_1^2$

$\qquad\qquad = 4\,(x/3) - \dfrac{1}{2}g(x/3)^2 = \dfrac{4}{3}x - \dfrac{gx^2}{18}$.

and $\qquad h_2 = 4t_2 - \dfrac{1}{2}gt_2^2$

$\qquad\qquad = 4(x/5) - \dfrac{1}{2}g\,(x/5)^2 = \dfrac{4x}{5} - \dfrac{gx^2}{10}$

Clearly, $\quad h_2 < h_1$.

7. (b) $\qquad v_y = 6.1$ m/s.

Thus $\qquad v_y^2 = u_y^2 - 2gh$

$\qquad\qquad 6.1^2 = u_y^2 - 2 \times 9.8 \times 9.1$

or $\qquad\qquad u_y = 14.68$ m/s

$\therefore\qquad h = \dfrac{u_y^2}{2g} = \dfrac{14.68^2}{2\times 9.8} = 11$ m.

8. (d) $\qquad y = ax - bx^2$

or $\qquad 0 = aR - bR^2$

$\therefore\qquad R = a/b$

9. (c) If u_1, u_2 and θ_1, θ_2 are the velocities and angles of projections then $x_1 = u_1\cos\theta_1\,t$ and $x_2 = u_2\cos\theta_2\,t$

$\therefore\ x_2 - x_1 = (u_2\cos\theta_2 - u_1\cos\theta_1)t$

and $y_1 = u_1\sin\theta_1\,t - \frac{1}{2}gt^2$ and $y_2 = u_2\sin\theta_2 - \frac{1}{2}gt^2$

$\therefore\ y_2 - y_1 = (u_2\sin\theta_2 - u_1\sin\theta_1)t$

Now $\dfrac{y_2 - y_1}{x_2 - x_1} = \left(\dfrac{u_2\sin\theta_2 - u_1\sin\theta_1}{u_2\cos\theta_2 - u_1\cos\theta_1}\right)$

It represent vertical straight line for $u_1\cos\theta_1 = u_2\cos\theta_2$

10. (d) If t is the time of height, then,

$$y = 0 = Kt\,(1 - \alpha t)$$

$\therefore\qquad t = \dfrac{1}{\alpha}$.

Maximum height
will occur at $t/2$, and so

$$Y_{max} = K\left(\frac{1}{2\alpha}\right)\left(1 - \alpha\frac{1}{2\alpha}\right)$$

$$= \frac{K}{4\alpha}.$$

11. **(d)** Given $h = Ax - Bx^2$, on comparing with

$$y = x\tan\theta - \frac{gx^2}{2u^2\cos^2\theta}, \text{ we get}$$

$$A = \tan\theta = \tan 45° = 1,$$

and $B = \dfrac{g}{2u^2\cos^2\theta} = \dfrac{10}{2\times 20^2\times\cos^2 45°} = \dfrac{1}{40}$

$$\therefore \qquad \frac{A}{B} = 40.$$

12. **(c)** The time to reach the maximum height without air resistance

$$t_1 = \frac{u}{g} = \frac{u}{10},$$

and

with air resistance,

$$t_2 = \frac{u}{10+1} = \frac{u}{11}$$

Thus, $\dfrac{\Delta t}{t_1}\times 100 = \dfrac{t_1 - t_2}{t_1}\times 100 = \left[\dfrac{\dfrac{u}{10} - \dfrac{u}{11}}{\dfrac{u}{10}}\right]\times 100$

$$= 9\ \%\ \text{(decreases)}$$

13. **(c)** $\quad 500\cos\theta = 250 \Rightarrow \cos\theta = \dfrac{1}{2}$
    or $\qquad \theta = 60°.$

14. **(d)** Since $0 = (v\sin\theta)t + \dfrac{1}{2}(-a)t^2 \Rightarrow t = \dfrac{2v\sin\theta}{a}$

Also, $h = (v\cos\theta)t + \dfrac{1}{2}g t^2$

$$\Rightarrow h = \frac{2v^2}{a}\sin\theta\left(\cos\theta + \frac{g}{a}\sin\theta\right)$$

15. Particle will collide when P hits the inclined plane. So time of flight of P,

$$0 = ut - \frac{1}{2}(g\cos 60°)\,T^2$$

or $\qquad T = \dfrac{2u}{g\cos 60°}$

or $\qquad 4 = \dfrac{2u}{g\times\dfrac{1}{2}} \Rightarrow u = g.$

16. **(a)** $\qquad a_R = g\cos\theta.$

The value of θ lies between:

$$\theta = 0,$$

at highest point and $< 90°$ at the
point of projection, and so

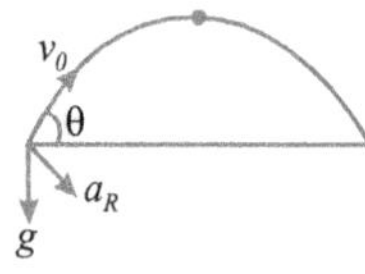

$$|a_R|_{max} = g\cos 0° = g.$$

17. **(d)** $v_0\cos\theta$

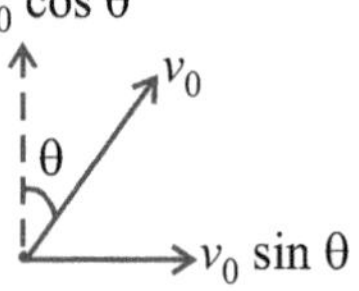

If t is the time taken by ball to return the boy's hand, then

$$0 = v_0\cos\theta\, t - \frac{1}{2}g t^2$$

or $\qquad t = \dfrac{2v_0\cos\theta}{g}$

Now, $v_0\sin\theta\, t = \dfrac{1}{2}at^2$

or $\quad v_0\sin\theta = \dfrac{1}{2}a\left[\dfrac{2v_0\cos\theta}{g}\right]^2$

$$\therefore \qquad \tan\theta = \frac{a}{g}$$

$$= \frac{4}{10} = 0.4$$

18. **(a)**

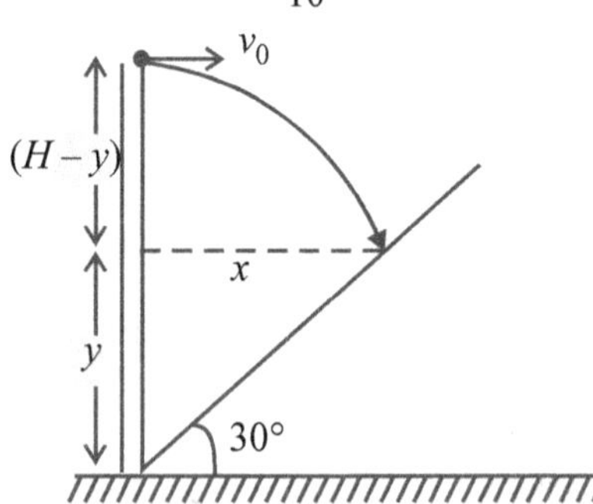

If t is the time to hit the inclined, then

$$x = v_0 t \qquad\qquad ...(i)$$

and $\qquad H - y = \dfrac{1}{2}g t^2, \qquad ...(ii)$

$$0 = v_0\cos 30° - g\sin 30°\, t \qquad ...(iii)$$

Also $\dfrac{y}{x} = \tan 30° \qquad\qquad ...(iv)$

After solving above equations, we get

$$v_0 = \sqrt{\frac{2gH}{5}}$$

19. **(a)** $R = \dfrac{u^2\sin 2\theta}{g}$ and $\dfrac{R}{4} = u\cos\theta\times\sqrt{\dfrac{2b}{g}}$

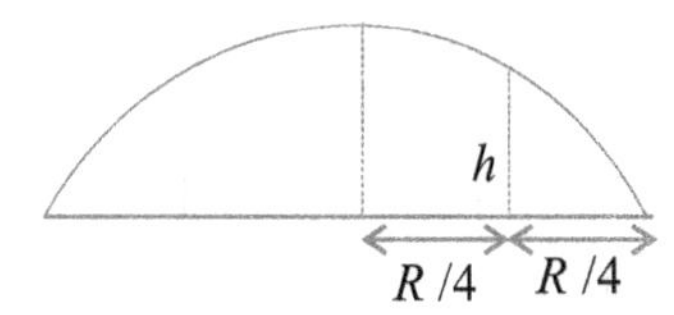

Also, $H = \dfrac{u^2 \sin^2 \theta}{2g}$; solving above equations

We get $\dfrac{H}{4} = h$.

20. (d) Let the car is at a distance x from A.

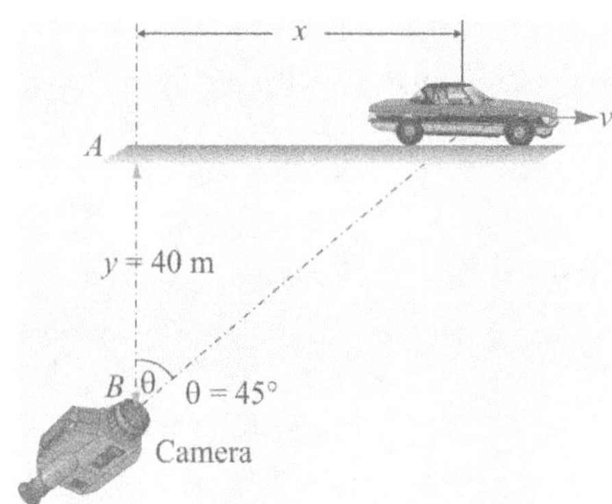

The line of sight with car makes an angle θ with AB, then we have

$$x = y \tan \theta. \qquad .... (i)$$

Here y remain constant.

Differentiating equation (i) w.r.t. time, we get

$$\frac{dx}{dt} = \frac{d}{dt}[y \tan \theta]$$

or $$\frac{dx}{dt} = y \sec^2 \theta \left(\frac{d\theta}{dt} \right)$$

$\therefore$ $$v = y \sec^2 \theta \left(\frac{d\theta}{dt} \right)$$

or $$\frac{d\theta}{dt} = \frac{v}{y \sec^2 \theta} = \frac{40}{40 \sec^2 45°}$$

$$= \frac{1}{2} \text{rad} / s .$$

21. (b) $$x = h \cot \theta$$

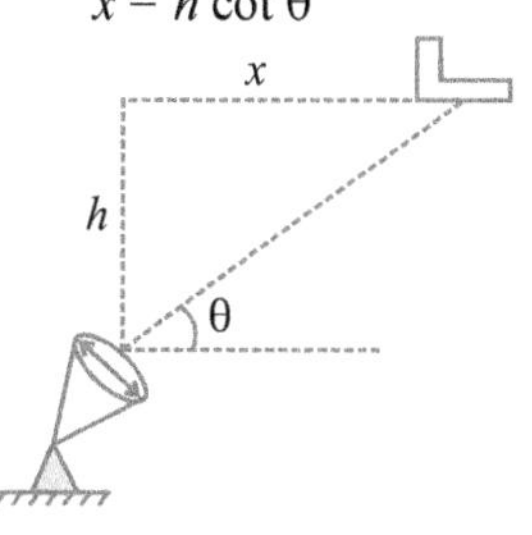

$\therefore$ $$\frac{dx}{dt} = h \frac{d(\cot \theta)}{dt}$$

$$= h (-\text{cosec}^2 \theta) \frac{d\theta}{dt}$$

or $$v = h \, \text{cosec}^2 \theta \left(\frac{-d\theta}{dt} \right)$$

$$= (8 \times 10^3) \, \text{cosec}^2 60° \times 0.025$$
$$= 266.67 \text{ m/s}$$
$$= 960 \text{ km/h}$$

22. (c)

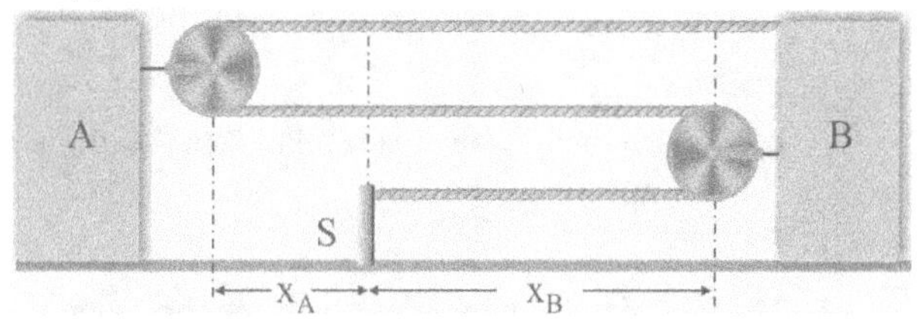

Taking reference line through support S, let x_A and x_B are the distances of blocks A and B respectively from S. The total length of the string, $\ell = 2x_A + 3x_B + c$,

where c is the some part of string which is over pulley and somewhere else which remain constant.

Differentiating above relation w.r.t. time, we get

$$\frac{d\ell}{dt} = \frac{d}{dt}(2x_A + 3x_B + c)$$

or $$0 = 2 \frac{dx_A}{dt} + 3 \frac{dx_B}{dt}$$

or $$\frac{dx_A}{dt} = \frac{3}{2} \frac{dx_B}{dt}$$

or $$v_A = \frac{3}{2} v_B \qquad .... (i)$$

Also $$a_A = \frac{3}{2} a_B \qquad .... (ii)$$

We have $$\vec{v}_{AB} = \vec{v}_A - \vec{v}_B$$
or $$v_B = v_A - v_{AB}$$

or $$v_B = \frac{3}{2} v_B - v_{AB}$$

or $$v_B = 2 v_{AB} \qquad [\text{Given } v_{AB} = v\,]$$
$$= 2v$$

The acceleration of block B ;

$$aB = \frac{\Delta v}{\Delta t} = \frac{2v - 0}{t} = \frac{2v}{t}$$

The acceleration of block A

$$= \frac{3}{2} a_B = \frac{3}{2} \times \left(\frac{2v}{t} \right) = \frac{3v}{t}.$$

1. (a, b, d)
   Absolute velocity of boatman is
   $$\vec{v}_B = \vec{v}_{BR} + \vec{v}_R$$
   $$= \left(-2\hat{i} + 4\hat{j} \right) + \left(4\hat{i} \right)$$
   $$= 2\hat{i} + 4\hat{j}$$

Time $t = \dfrac{100}{4} = 25\, s$

Drift $x = (2)(25) = 50$ m

$$|\vec{v}_B| = \sqrt{(4)^2 + (2)^2} = 2\sqrt{5} \text{ m} / s$$

2. **(b, c, a)**

Since the wind is blowing toward the east, the plane must head west of north as shown in figure. The velocity of the plane relative to the ground $\vec{v}_{pg}$ will be the sum of the velocity of the plane relative to the air $\vec{v}_{pa}$ and the velocity of the air relative to the ground $\vec{v}_{ag}$.

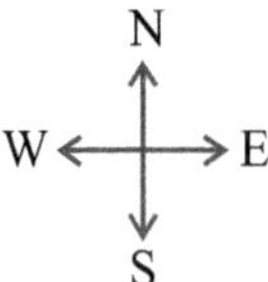
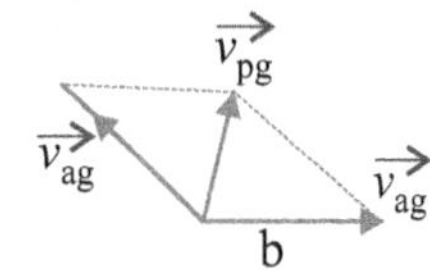

(b) **1.** The velocity of the plane relative to the ground is given by equation :
$$\vec{v}_{pg} = \vec{v}_{pa} + \vec{v}_{ag}$$

2. The sine of the angle θ between the velocity of the plane and north equals the ratio of v_{ag} and v_{pa}.

$$\sin \theta = \frac{v_{ag}}{v_{pa}} = \frac{90\,\text{km/m}}{200\,\text{km/h}} = 0.45$$

(c) Since v_{ag} and v_{pg} are perpendicular, we can use the Pythagorean theorem to find the magnitude of $\vec{v}\,pg$.

$$v^2_{pa} = v^2_{ag} + v^2_{pg}$$

$$v_{pg} = \sqrt{v^2_{pa} - v^2_{ag}}$$

$$= \sqrt{\left(200\,\text{km/h}\right)^2 - \left(90\,\text{km/h}\right)^2}$$

$$= 179 \text{ km/h}.$$

3. **(a,d)**

For the ground observer,
$$x = ut \text{ and } y = \frac{1}{2}gt^2,$$

$$\therefore \qquad y = \frac{1}{2}g\frac{x^2}{u^2}, \text{ it represents a parabola.}$$

For observer inside train,
$$x = 0, \text{ and so ball apears to fall vertically.}$$

4. **(a, c, d)** The path of case 1 is (see figure)

Thus $T_1 = T_2 + T_3$.

5. **(a,c)**
$$x = 2t,$$

$$\therefore \qquad t = \frac{x}{2}$$

and
$$y = 3\left(\frac{x}{2}\right) - 4\left(\frac{x}{2}\right)^2 = \frac{3}{2}x - x^2.$$

$$ux = \frac{dx}{dt} = 2$$

and
$$u_y = \frac{dy}{dt} = 3 - 8t$$

$$\therefore \qquad u = \sqrt{u_x^2 + y_y^2} = \sqrt{2^2 + (3 - 8t)^2}$$

$$= \sqrt{2^2 + 3^2} = \sqrt{13} \text{ m/s.}$$

6. **(b,d)**
$$u \cos \theta = v \cos 30°$$

and
$$0 = u \sin \theta - g \times 3,$$

$$\therefore \qquad u \sin \theta = 30 \text{ m/s.}$$

Also
$$0 = v \sin 30° - g \times 1,$$

$$\therefore \qquad v = 20 \text{ m/s.}$$

Now
$$u \cos \theta = 20 \cos 30° = 10\sqrt{3} \text{ m/s.}$$

$$\therefore \qquad u = \sqrt{30^2 + (10\sqrt{3})^2} = 20\sqrt{3} \text{ m/s.}$$

$$R = \frac{2(u \cos \theta)(u \sin \theta)}{g} = \frac{2 \times 10\sqrt{3} \times 30}{10}$$

$$= 60\sqrt{3} \text{ m.}$$

7. **(a,c,d)**
$$v = \alpha \sqrt{x}$$

$$\frac{dv}{dx} = \alpha \frac{1}{2}x^{-1/2} = \frac{\alpha}{2\sqrt{x}}.$$

Thus acceleration,

$$a = v\frac{dv}{dx} = \alpha\sqrt{x} \times \frac{\alpha}{2\sqrt{x}} = \frac{\alpha^2}{2}.$$

Also
$$\frac{dv}{dt} = \frac{\alpha^2}{2}$$

or
$$v = \int_0^t \frac{\alpha^2}{2} dt = \frac{\alpha^2 t}{2}.$$

Mean velocity,

$$\bar{v} = \frac{\int_0^t \frac{\alpha^2 t}{2} dt}{t} = \frac{\alpha^2 t^2}{4t} = \frac{\alpha^2 t}{4}$$

$$s = \frac{1}{2}at^2 = \frac{1}{2}\left(\frac{\alpha^2}{2}\right)t^2$$

$$\therefore \qquad t = 2\frac{\sqrt{s}}{\alpha}$$

Now
$$\bar{v} = \frac{\alpha^2 \times \frac{2\sqrt{s}}{\alpha}}{4} = \frac{\alpha\sqrt{s}}{2}.$$

8. **(a,c)**

At 30° and 60°, $R_1 = R_2$

Further, $H \propto \sin^2 \theta$ and $T \propto \sin \theta$

$$\therefore \qquad \frac{H}{R} \propto \sin^2 \theta$$

and
$$\frac{H}{T} \propto \sin \theta$$

$\sin 60° > \sin 30°$

$\therefore \dfrac{H_1}{R_1} > \dfrac{H_2}{R_2}$ and $\dfrac{H_1}{T_1} > \dfrac{H_2}{T_2}$

9. (b, c)
Initial velocity of particle in vector form can be written as

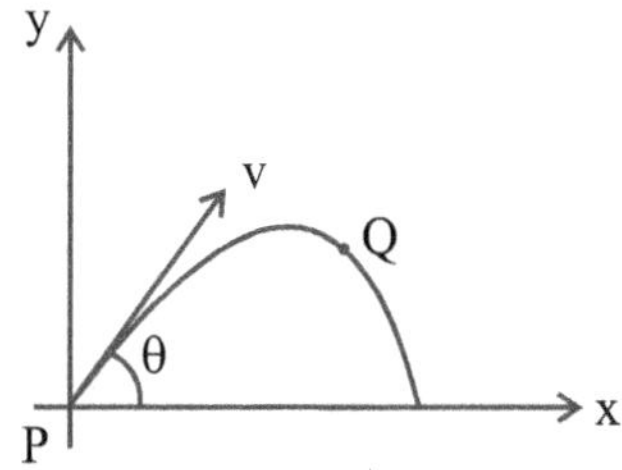

$\overrightarrow{v_P} = v\cos\theta\,\hat{i} + v\sin\theta\,\hat{j}$ ...(1)

Velocity of particle at any time t will be:

$\overrightarrow{v_Q} = v\cos\theta\,\hat{i} + (v\sin\theta - gt)\,\hat{j}$ ...(2)

Given that $\overrightarrow{v_P} \perp \overrightarrow{v_Q}$

$\therefore \quad \overrightarrow{v_P}\cdot\overrightarrow{v_Q} = 0$

or $v^2\cos^2\theta + v^2\sin^2\theta - v\sin\theta\,gt = 0$

or $v^2 = v\sin\theta\,gt$ or $t = \dfrac{v}{g}\cosec\theta$

Substituting this value of t in Eq. (2), we get

$\overrightarrow{v_Q} = v\cos\theta\,\hat{i} + \left(v\sin\theta - \dfrac{v}{\sin\theta}\right)\hat{j}$

or $\left|\overrightarrow{v_Q}\right| = \sqrt{v^2\cos^2\theta + v^2\sin^2\theta + \dfrac{v^2}{\sin^2\theta} - 2v^2}$

$= v\cot\theta$

10. (c,d)
As maximum height attained by each one is same, so u_y is also same. As

$$T = \dfrac{2u_y}{g},$$

So $\qquad T_1 = T_2 = T_3.$

1. (b) The initial velocity along vertical direction is same ($u_y = 0$) for both the bodies, and so

$$h = 0 + \dfrac{1}{2}gt^2,$$

or $\qquad t = \sqrt{\dfrac{2h}{g}}.$

2. (c) If gravitational force is zero, then $a_y = 0$.
So, $\qquad x = u\cos\theta\,t$ and $y = u\sin\theta\,t$
$\therefore \qquad y = x\tan\theta$. It represent straight line.
The resultant path of the body depends on initial velocities and acceleration.

3. (a) For maximum height $\theta = 90°$, or body must be projected straight upwards. Then

$$0 = u^2 - 2gh,$$

$\therefore \qquad h = \dfrac{u^2}{2g}.$

4. (d) $T = \dfrac{2u\sin\theta}{g}$, it will maximum, when $\theta = 0°$.

$$R_{\max} = \dfrac{u^2}{g}, \text{ for } \theta = 45°.$$

5. (d) At the highest point of the trajectory,
$\qquad v_y = 0$, and
so, $\qquad \vec{P}_y = 0.$
For the two pieces, it is
$$\vec{P}_{1y} + \vec{P}_{2y} = 0.$$

6. (a) The time of flight depends only on the vertical component of velocity which remains unchanged in collision with a vertical wall.

7. (d) Linear momentum during parabolic path changes continuously.

8. (d) Statement-1 is false because angles of projection θ and $(90° - \theta)$ give same range but time of flight will be different. Statement-2 is true because in horizontal direction acceleration is zero.

9. (a) In statement-2, if speed of both projectiles are same, horizontal ranges will be same. Hence statement-2 is correct explanation of statement-1.

Passage for (Questions 1 & 2)

1. (a) Given, $h = \dfrac{u^2\sin^2\theta}{2g}$ and $2R = \dfrac{u^2\sin 2\theta}{g}$

After simplifying, we get
$\qquad \tan\theta = 2.$

2. (d) $\qquad \sin\theta = \dfrac{2}{\sqrt{5}}$

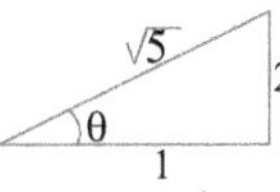

On substituting the value of $\sin\theta$ in above equation, we get

$$u = \sqrt{\dfrac{5}{2}gh}$$

Passage for (Questions 3 to 5) :

3. (a) $H_A = H_C > H_B$
Obviously A just reaches its maximum height and C has crossed its maximum height which is equal to A as u and θ are same. But B is unable to reach its maximum height.

4. (c)

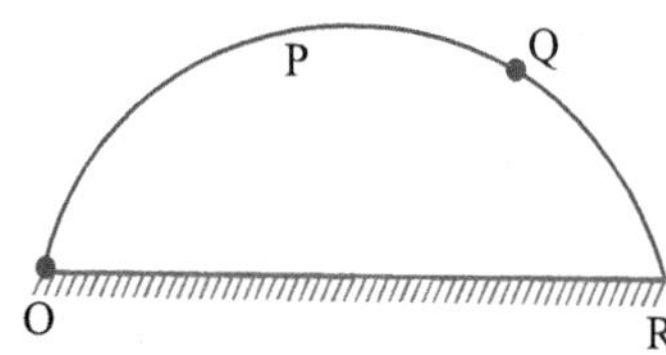

Time of flight of A is 4 seconds which is same as the time of flight if wall was not there.

Time taken by B to reach the inclined roof is 1 sec.

$$T_{OR} = 4$$
$$T_{QR} = 1$$
$$\therefore \quad T_{OQ} = T_{OR} - T_{QR} = 3 \text{ sec.}$$

5. (c) From above $\quad T = \dfrac{2u\sin\theta}{g} = 4s$

$\therefore u\sin\theta = 20\text{m/s} \Rightarrow$ vertical component is 20 m/s

for maximum height

$v^2 = u^2 + 2as \Rightarrow 0^2 = 20^2 - 2 \times 10 \times s \Rightarrow s = 20\text{m}$

6. $\mathbf{A \rightarrow q ; B \rightarrow r ; C \rightarrow p ; D \rightarrow q}$

7. $\mathbf{A \rightarrow q ; B \rightarrow r ; C \rightarrow p ; D \rightarrow t}$

(A) $\qquad U_x = \dfrac{dx}{dt} = 1$

and $\qquad U_y = \dfrac{dx}{dt} = 1 - 2t$

$\therefore U_{t=0} = \sqrt{u_x^2 + y_y^2} = \sqrt{1^2 + 1^2} = \sqrt{2}$ m/s.

(B) $\qquad a_x = \dfrac{d^2x}{dt^2} = 0$

$\qquad d_y = \dfrac{d^2y}{dt^2} = -2$

(C) For time of flight,

$$y = 0$$
or $\qquad 0 = t - t^2$
$\therefore \qquad t = 1s.$

(D) For maximum height,

$$t = \dfrac{1}{2}\, s.$$

$\therefore \qquad H = t - t^2 = \dfrac{1}{2} - \left(\dfrac{1}{2}\right)^2 = \dfrac{1}{4}$ m.

1. (b) $\qquad t_1 = \dfrac{2u\cos\theta}{g}$

and $\qquad t_2 = \dfrac{2u\cos(90° - \theta)}{g} = \dfrac{2u\sin\theta}{g}$

$\therefore \qquad t_1 t_2 = \dfrac{4u^2\sin\theta\cos\theta}{g^2} = \dfrac{2R}{g}.$

2. (a) $\qquad v_0\cos\theta = v_0/2$

$\therefore \qquad \cos\theta = \dfrac{1}{2},$
or $\qquad \theta = 60°.$

3. (a) On comparing with, $\vec{v} = v_x\hat{i} + v_y\hat{j}$, we get

$$v_x = \dfrac{dx}{dt} = ky \qquad \text{...(i)}$$

and $\qquad v_y = \dfrac{dy}{dt} = kx \qquad \text{...(ii)}$

Dividing equation (ii) by (i), we get
$$y\,dy = x\,dx$$

Now $\displaystyle\int_0^y y\,dy = \int_0^x x\,dx$

or $\dfrac{y^2}{2} = \dfrac{x^2}{2} + k$

or $y^2 = x^2 + \text{constant}$

4. (b) Maximum area,
$$A = \pi R^2$$
$$= \pi\left[\dfrac{v^2}{g}\right]^2 = \pi\dfrac{v^4}{g^2}.$$